The Saddlers

Express & Star

The Saddlers

The Complete Record of Walsall Football Club

by Tony Matthews
with Geoff Allman, Brian Tabner and
Mervyn Sargeant

**The Breedon Books
Publishing Company
Derby**

First published in Great Britain by
The Breedon Books Publishing Company Limited
Breedon House, 44 Friar Gate, Derby, DE1 1DA.
1999

© Tony Matthews, Geoff Allman, Brian Tabner and Mervyn Sargeant, 1999

All Rights Reserved. No part of this publication may be reproduced, stored in a retrieval system, or transmitted in any form, or by any means, electronic, mechanical, photocopying, recording or otherwise without the prior permission in writing of the copyright holders, nor be otherwise circulated in any form or binding or cover other than in which it is published and without a similar condition being imposed on the subsequent publisher.

ISBN 1 85983 156 7

Printed and bound by Butler & Tanner Ltd., Selwood Printing Works,
Caxton Road, Frome, Somerset.

Colour separations and jacket printing by Green Shires Ltd, Leicester.

Contents

Introduction

IN 1992 this first in-depth history of Walsall Football Club was published. Indeed, it was one of the most comprehensive books ever compiled on a League club currently based in the lower Divisions. Now the book has been updated to take into account the last years of the 20th century and in particular the 1998-99 season when Walsall FC enjoyed quite a renaissance in their fortunes.

There are many thousands of statistics as well as hundreds of facts and figures, plus scores of photographs, contained in this publication, which originally took well over two and a half years to compile. And, despite their mammoth task, I can assure you that the compilers certainly enjoyed their work.

Statistics can be a real nightmare for those who choose to study them, and consequently the seasonal grids covering the period from 1892 to 1901, which give all the relevant match facts with dates, results, scorers, attendances and line-ups, proved the biggest headache. But we have achieved our goal and each and every season (from 1888 to 1999) has been completed right down to the last detail. Errors which inevitably crept into the first edition have now been corrected.

During the compilation of this book, all the vital statistics which are recorded have been diligently researched and checked, using every available source, including a variety of local newspapers with the *Express & Star, Sporting Star, Sports Argus, Free Press, Weekly News, Birmingham Daily Gazette, Evening Mail, The Saturday Night, Birmingham Post, The Athletic News* and *Walsall Observer* being the main ones which we have meticulously thumbed through, checking match reports by the hundred, detail by detail.

We have also read through hundreds of old programmes, many soccer magazines, periodicals and football annuals, as well as scanning through many other club histories, in our efforts to clarify or substantiate certain facts and figures.

Obviously mistakes will still creep through – but one has to accept this with so many entries being made covering more than 100 years of soccer action involving the Saddlers. Thus, our apologies in advance if you come across some, but if you do find any, we would appreciate it if you could let us know immediately.

Some of these mistakes, made in previous references to Walsall Football Club have subsequently been passed down through the years as further stories on the Saddlers have been written and duly printed in various annuals and other publications, errors I might add, which have been a constant thorn in my side ever since I first decided to become a soccer statistician in 1964.

These, I hope, have now all been rectified – thanks to my hardworking colleagues who, in truth, have all done marvellously well sorting out discrepancies from as far back as 1888, including all the attendances which were so often given in round figures especially in the early years (i.e. 2,500, 5,000 etc.)

I, personally, have made frequent visits to public libraries, and I have called on quite a few former Walsall players and old-time supporters of the club during the time this book was being put together, and I have come across some very interesting facts indeed, all of which are entered in the pages that follow.

Geoff, Brian, Mervyn and myself have endeavoured to cover the history of Walsall Football Club in depth and I would like to stress to everyone that all the views expressed, comments passed and choice of famous stars in this publication are those of myself and my colleagues and not necessarily those of Walsall FC.

Tony Matthews
July 1999

Acknowledgements

This book could not have been put together without the considerable help of the following: Geoff Allman, Charles Archer, Mr P. Bayliss, Rob Bishop, Mike Bondy, David Bowler, Jack Bridgett, Mrs Carlisle, Steve Carr, Mr A. F. Cooper, Jim Creasy, Mike Davage, Mrs P. Duncan, Micky Evans, Mr Franks, James Greenway, Mr R. Hateley, John Hendley, Eddie Holding, Jack Huskinson, Ron Jukes, Chris Latimer, Mr Loynes, Les Mason, Adrian Millench, Mervyn Sergeant, M. O'Shea, Mr Pass, Willie Penman, Simon Penn, Mrs Pritchard, Steve Richards, Charles Riley, Mr C. Shildow, Don Stanton, Brian Tabner, Mr M. J. Thomas, Simon Thompson, Geoff Tonks, John Woodward. I would like to give special thanks to my wife, Margaret, for her help, patience and understanding.

The Story of Walsall Football Club

FOOTBALL rivalry invariably runs deep in any town or city boasting more than one club and although that may not seem appropriate in modern-day Walsall, it was certainly the case towards the end of the 19th century. Thankfully, the two teams in question decided to put aside their differences and join forces – and their amalgamation, on 6 April 1888, marked the beginning of Walsall Football Club.

The first evidence of organised football in Walsall was way back in 1873 when a team calling themselves Victoria Swifts played on a ground known as the Lammasland, where the Midland Road Railway Goods Yard stands today.

This stretch of land had, in medieval days, been an area where Walsall people could graze their sheep for six months from Lammastide (1 August) onwards.

The Swifts then switched to a bigger and better pitch in nearby Follyhouse Lane. And in the summer of 1875, after becoming founder members of the newly-formed Birmingham & District Football Association, they moved to a new ground on the main Birmingham Road near to where the Crest Motel now stands.

In 1877, they changed to yet another ground – in Follyhouse Lane, Highgate – and by this time funds were being raised by sending a collecting box amongst the supporters.

Around 1873 there were several other clubs already playing in the Walsall area, including Walsall Albion, Walsall Alma, Bott Lane Mission, Rycroft White Star, Ryecroft Unity, Caldmore Rovers and St Matthews Church Institute. But there is little or no newspaper coverage of how many of the matches ended, or indeed how many were played.

Meanwhile, some 12 months later, at a meeting at the Dragon Hotel in High Street on 17 September 1874, it was agreed, unanimously, that a Walsall Town Football Club should be formed.

By this time neighbouring Rushall had a team that was playing fairly regularly, and the opening game for the newly-formed Walsall team was in fact, against Rushall at a ground called The Chuckery on 3 October 1874.

So many players turned up that it was decided to field 15-a-side with the surplus Walsall men being 'loaned' out to make up the Rushall team.

Rushall, with that extra slice of experience, won 3-1, although some argue that the game should have finished 2-2 as one of the Rushall goals was scored by a Walsall player.

By the end of the 1874-75 season both the Town (the 'toffs" club) and Swifts (very much the working men's club) were playing regularly, and a typical Town line-up (fielding 15 players) looked like this: A .C. Greatrex, I. T. Cottam, I .Russell, W. Addenbrooke, T. I. Addenbrooke, F. Wood, H. Anderson, A. Thacker, W. Thacker, I. F. Ashworth, H. C. Powell, R. Leighton, C. Lindon, J. Dorricott and H .M. Blackburn.

The Swifts meanwhile used 12 players in their matches and they were: I. Robinson, I. Hawley, W .Hawley, W. Dyoss, C. Harrison, I. I. Carter, A. Stanton, L. Cooper, A. Aulton, R. Mason, D. Pearce and C. H. Jones.

The Town tried to maintain their reputation as the top team in Walsall by taking on a side comprised of players from three other Walsall-based clubs, the Swifts, the Albion and White Star, in a game played on Easter Monday 1880. They won the 'showdown' 3-2. It appears, however, that the Town v Swifts rivalry did not really get under way until season 1880-81 when the Swifts put the Town out of the Staffordshire Cup in a replay.

The Swifts also put the Town out of the Birmingham Cup the following January, and therefore at that time they could justifiably claim to have been the top team in Walsall.

Four years later, in 1881, the Swifts moved to The Chuckery, playing on a pitch parallel with that of the Town team, and both sets of players used the same place to change, the Royal Exchange in nearby Ablewell Street.

Admission to watch a game at The Chuckery was three old pence (or sixpence for a spot on 'reserved' ground) and season tickets cost three shillings each (15p in today's money).

In season 1881-82 the Swifts met the Town on four separate occasions, twice in the Staffordshire Cup Final which the Town won 4-0 in a replay at Stoke.

The Swifts also won the Walsall Cup that season and lost to Aston Villa in the Birmingham Cup Final.

At this time both clubs were attracting crowds of between 2,500 and 3,500 to their home matches when the population of Walsall itself was only a fraction higher than it was in the early 1990s when only one club attracted that number.

As early as 1882 both the Swifts and Town sides played in the English Cup (the original label for the FA Cup). Town put out Staveley and Stafford Road, both by the same score of 4-1, before going out 2-1 to Aston Villa who had already beaten the Swifts in the first round.

There was no form of League competition in those days and teams played a series of friendly matches in addition to taking part in the various Cup tournaments. But in 1883-84, a Dr Hubbard (surely one of the first-ever football statisticians) worked out that the Swifts were the tenth most successful club in the country.

There were some amazing scorelines in those early days. In 1884-85, for instance, Town beat Willenhall 17-0 and Burton Strollers 10-1 in the space of eight days, and on the very same afternoon as Town's win over Burton, the Swifts hammered luckless Nettle-

The Swifts line-up of 1881-82, before the amalgamation with the Town club.

folds Athletic 19-0. Thus, on the two adjacent pitches on The Chuckery ground a total of 36 goals were scored in one day.

In that same season a grandstand designed to hold between 300 and 400 spectators was erected at The Chuckery. It cost £46 and other interesting statistics of that term were that the Swifts' income of £503 exceeded their expenditure by just £2.

A notable feat near the end of the 1885-86 season was that of Walsall Swifts taking West Bromwich Albion to a replay in the Birmingham Cup Final. Although they ultimately lost the contest 1-0, this was a tremendous achievement against a side who had reached the FA Cup Final that same season.

Several times in the 1880s, the Town and the Swifts contested the Final of the Walsall Cup (now the Walsall Senior Cup) while the Swifts won the Birmingham Cup in 1880-81, and the Town won the Staffordshire Cup in both 1881-82 and 1884-85.

In fact, the last Town v Swifts game was in the semi-final of the Walsall Cup in March 1888, the Swifts winning 1-0 after a replay.

Oddly enough the Swifts then lost the Final to West Bromwich Albion a few days after the combined Town-Swifts team had played their first-ever game against Aston Villa in April 1888 following the amalgamation of the two clubs.

One can only quote from the report of that Town v Swifts game in the *Walsall Observer*. It read: 'This ends the battle of the giants and henceforth let all dissensions cease.'

The venue of that 1888 Final (played on 9 April) was Villa's old ground in Perry Barr, and around 500 Walsall supporters travelled to Birmingham to witness the game.

Walsall Swifts, incidentally, had played the Villa in three previous Birmingham Cup Finals, those of 1882, 1883 and 1885.

They lost the first two by scores of 4-1 and 8-0, but in the third clash they held their redoubtable opponents to two drawn games before the committee decided that each club should hold the trophy for six months.

Now was the time for Walsall to win the star prize outright and their line-up featured five players from the Town and six from the Swifts, the full team being: goalkeeper Jack Tracey (Swifts); the former Town full-back pairing of Alf Jones and 'Sammy' Reynolds (real first name Thomson, who in fact, appeared in Walsall Town's first-ever FA Cup-tie v Staveley in October 1882); half-backs Jack Morely (Swifts), Billy Lee (Town) and George Morris (Swifts), and the forwards David Wykes (soon to join Wolves), George 'Barney' Cope (Town), Tommy Athersmith (Swifts – and brother of the more famous Charlie Athersmith of Aston Villa and England), Charlie 'Shiner' Shaw (Town) and George Tapper (Swifts). The brothers Holmes, Charlie and Sammy (both from the Swifts), were also in the party. Sammy was to go on to give the club tremendous service, along with Jones, Morely and Shaw.

The Villa put out their full strength side except that 'Rich' Davies, later to play for Walsall, took the place of the great Archie Hunter.

The attendance topped 12,000 and Villa, who had beaten many of the leading clubs in England and Scotland that season, were red hot favourites to lift the prize.

Walsall Town, circa 1884., around the time they were running up some amazing scorelines.

Walsall, though, had other ideas and put up a sterling performance, matching their more illustrious opponents kick for kick. At the end of 90 minutes the teams were deadlocked at 0-0. That scoreline remained the same ten minutes into extra-time before bad light caused the game to be abandoned.

It was reported in the local press that this was 'one of the hottest games played on the Villa ground this season, and from start to finish most exciting'.

There was, however, an unfortunate sequel to the Final. The Birmingham Association ordered the replay to take place at either Perry Barr or Small Heath, but Walsall, considering that they were entitled to have a second chance on their own ground, declined to visit either of those two venues and withdrew from the competition, the trophy accordingly being awarded to the Villa.

Walsall may not have won the cup, but a moral victory was theirs at least.

After this the next step was a meeting of members and friends of the newly-formed Walsall club at the town's Dragon Hotel, High Street on 8 August 1888, with Councillor J. Noake, presiding over a large assembly.

He expressed the belief that the club had players as good as any in the district and said if the supporters continued to rally round them to ensure good 'gates' at all home games, then Walsall would have no cause to fear any rival.

It was decided that the club should continue to utilise The Chuckery as its home ground; the club's colours should be red and white vertical striped shirts; and the following 20 players were signed for the start of the 1888-89 campaign: full-back Arthur Aldridge, forward Athersmith, wing-half Jack Beech, centre-half Joe Brettle, inside-left George Cope, winger Richmond Davies (ex-Aston Villa who was enticed out of retirement), Wally Davis, goalkeeper George Edge, winger Frank Gray, Sammy Holmes, Frank Horton, Charlie Jenkins, England full-back Alf Jones, goalkeeper Seymour Lewis, Jack Morely, George Morris (who was elected captain), outside-left Bill Paddock, George Tapper, Frank Rich, Charlie 'Shiner' Shaw, Jack Tonks, and goal-keeper George Wood. Quite a few more were to join the ranks as the season progressed including inside-left Arthur Brown, goalkeepers Joe Wilson and George Reynolds (no relation to 'Sammy') and utility forward Wilbert Hicklin.

As the Football League came into operation for the first time in 1888-89, the new Walsall club (which was not to gain election to the League until 1892) entered all the local Cup competitions and also took part in the Midland Association (with seven other clubs).

Following a home friendly against Derby St Luke's, on Saturday, 8 September, when 1,200 fans saw Sammy Holmes score four goals, including the first for the newly-formed Walsall Town Swifts club, the strong Lancashire team, Burnley – one of the 12 founder members of the new Football League – came to The Chuckery on the Monday afternoon and were beaten 1-0. The goal this time came from George Cope.

It was stated that: 'The enthusiasm displayed in these two matches bodes well for the future of the club and fully justified the action of the committee in their scheme of amalgamation. With judicious and careful management, together with unity of action amongst the committee and players, football in Walsall should attain a far higher standard that it has up to the present obtained.'

The question was raised whether there had ever been seen on The Chuckery ground a better contested game than that against Burnley.

On 22 September 1888, Crewe Alexandra, 10-1 victors over Blackpool South Shore earlier in the month, came to Walsall and forced a 2-2 draw.

The next home game was against the FA Cup holders, West Bromwich Albion, and this also ended in a 2-2 draw. There were 7,000 fans present for this encounter.

Then the Swifts won their first away game, beating Derby Junction 2-1 on the last Saturday of the month, Sammy Holmes claiming both goals.

Interest was growing and there followed another 2-2 home draw, this time against Small Heath (today Birmingham City) in mid-October, the visitors scoring twice in the last eight minutes.

A couple of home defeats, at the hands of Long Eaton Rangers and Notts Rangers (4-0), disrupted progress somewhat, although for the latter game Walsall were without four key players – Aldridge, Morely, Morris and 'Shiner' Shaw – who were all representing the Birmingham Association.

Later in the season Aldridge, Morely and Shaw were selected to play for Staffordshire against Lancashire, while Brettle was named as reserve. Aldridge, who had been re-signed from West Bromwich Albion, was subsequently honoured by being chosen to play for England against Ireland on the Everton ground in March 1889, and thus became the 'new' club's first international, although not the first in the town.

A few years earlier, full-back Alf Jones had served England in three internationals, lining up against Wales and Scotland (twice) in the 12 months up to March 1883.

Three wins produced 14 goals around Christmas, Walsall overcoming Long Eaton Rangers (4-3), Notts Olympic (6-4 in the Birmingham Cup) and Blackpool South Shore (4-2), Frank Gray hitting a treble in the latter.

Before the FA Cup competition got under way, Walsall beat West Manchester, Derby Junction, Birmingham St George's and Notts Rangers in a little over three weeks and they were in tip-top form to take on Sheffield Heeley in the FA Cup.

The game was played at The Chuckery on 2 February 1889, and the Swifts went to town, whipping their Yorkshire challengers 5-1, this being the biggest victory in any of the ties played that day. A crowd of 1,600 saw the contest in which Holmes scored twice for the Swifts.

Sadly, in the next round, a trip to Wolverhampton ended in a 6-1 defeat at the hands of the Wanderers, who fielded five Walsall-born players in their side. Gray gave the Saddlers an early lead, but a series of injuries didn't help matters and in the end the Wolves ran out convincing winners in front of a 4,000 crowd.

In the second round of the Birmingham Cup, Walsall again met Aston Villa, but this time, after another cracking encounter, victory went to the

Villains by 3-1, watched by a crowd of 5,000 at The Chuckery.

In the Staffordshire Cup, Walsall reached the semi-final stage after a 3-0 win over Stoke, but alas, at the neutral Wood Green Oval, challengers West Bromwich Albion proved far too good on the day and ran out comfortable 5-0 winners.

In another competition – the Walsall Senior Cup – the Swifts accounted for Oldbury Town (5-0), Great Bridge Unity (2-0) and Wednesbury Old Athletic in the semi-final (3-0) and were scheduled to meet Small Heath in the Final.

But this was never played, as the Heathens had other commitments in another Cup competition and failed to arrive at the ground on the day of the Final. Consequently, in accordance with the custom of the times, Walsall duly went out on to the pitch, put the ball between the posts, claimed the match and at a meeting of the Walsall Association at the end of the season, the trophy was presented to them.

Walsall ended their first season with a useful record. Of the 36 games played by the seniors, 22 had been won, ten lost and four drawn, with eight of those victories coming in the Midland Association (out of their 14 fixtures). They had the third-best record of the eight teams in this competition.

They scored 88 goals and conceded 64. The reserves, too, made a good start, winning 18 and losing nine of their 29 matches, claiming 63 goals against 47.

Unfortunately the financial position of the club was not so good, and at the annual meeting a deficit of about £21 was reported. Income totalled £714 while the expenditure was £735. It was stated that a raffle was expected to yield about £30, but on the other hand there were outstanding debts amounting to £118.

Mr J. Noake was re-elected president of the club, and other appointments saw Mr T. E. Cooke made honorary treasurer. Messrs C. Bates and W. Smallman became honorary secretaries, while the committee comprised Messrs E. Brown, T. Burton, A. Cash, C. Cox, F. Horton, W. Patten, O. Smallwood, J. Stone and A. Toon.

Alf Jones was elected captain of the team for the 1889-90 season with Morris his vice-captain. And a major annoucement came when it was stated that Walsall would play in the Football Alliance, a stepping stone to the Football League itself.

At the meeting of the Football Association in the summer of 1889, an application from Walsall for exemption from the qualifying rounds of the FA Cup was refused and therefore the club had to face the arduous task of playing through the preliminary stages of the competition in 1889-90, despite putting up good performances against Sheffield Heeley and Wolves in the previous tournament.

Over 3,000 fans attended the first home game of the 1889-90 season when Walsall lost 3-1 to Nottingham Forest, fielding this team: George Edge; Alf Jones, Charlie Holmes, Morris, Bert Jones, Morely, Doug Sheldon, Shaw, Sammy Holmes, Cope and Josiah Millington.

In their first away Football Alliance game of the campaign, however, a 3-2 victory was achieved at Crewe Alexandra.

The Invincibles of Preston North End – the 1888-89 Football League championship and FA Cup double winners – visited The Chuckery on 21 September 1889, and a bumper 4,500 crowd turned out to see the Lilywhites, as they were also known, putting out their strongest side, win comfortably by 4-0.

Indeed, the 1889-90 season turned out to be one of mixed fortunes for Walsall. They registered some quite excellent victories (including Cup triumphs), yet also suffered a handful of humiliating defeats – 6-2 at Sunderland Albion, 4-0 at Sheffield Wednesday, 6-3 at Darwen and 4-0 at Grimsby to name just four.

But they were perhaps unlucky on many other occasions when misfortune, poor refereeing and injuries caused them to lose matches which they might otherwise have won.

Wellington Town were beaten 3-0 at home in one friendly game which finished prematurely after a heavy rain and a hail storm drove the players off the pitch; Burton Wanderers were also defeated 3-0 when another four goals were disallowed, and Newton Heath (today's Manchester United) were easily beaten 4-0 in the League, while revenge was gained over Darwen (5-3).

In other friendly encounters, Nottingham Forest were pipped 1-0 at Trent Bridge and a convincing 5-0 victory was recorded away to West Manchester, while at home Stoke were beaten 5-2, and Kidderminster Olympic were also defeated 5-2 in the Birmingham Cup, although in the semi-final of this same competition a strong West Bromwich Albion side ousted understrength Walsall by 2-1.

An emphatic 8-0 win over Burton Wanderers set Walsall on their way to winning the Walsall Cup where they beat Hednesford Town 7-1 in the Final. And they proudly claimed a magnificent 3-2 triumph over Football League neighbours West Brom in the semi-final of the Staffordshire Cup, only to lose in the Final to Birmingham St George's by 5-3, when their defence surprisingly caved in.

One interesting point is that from the end of October until 18 January, apart from two home friendly matches against the South Staffordshire Regiment side over the Christmas period, Walsall had to play all their other games away from The Chuckery.

At the club's annual meeting it was announced that receipts were £820, including £520 in gate money. Some £138 had come in from away matches and £55 in subscriptions, indicating a loss of £17 on the season, partly because some old accounts had to be paid. Players' wages amounted to £352; travelling expenses came to £103; training costs were £41; refreshments £57 and visiting clubs' share of gate takings £94.

It was stated that everyone had 'pulled together manfully' and there was no doubt that generally the first two seasons had been quite satisfactory.

Cllr J. Noake was once again re-elected as president, although he had hoped that someone would take office after he had succeeded in raising the club to a reasonable force in Midlands football.

Walsall opened their 1890-91 programme in style by beating Small Heath 5-2 at home in an Alliance match on 6 September, when around 5,000 fans saw this team take the field: Edge; Sid Withington, Reynolds, Jack Tonks, Morely, Alf Stokes, Shaw, S.Holmes, Tipper, Jerry Wilson (ex-Kidderminster Olympic) and Gray.

Three weeks later, in the first qualifying round of the FA Cup, Walsall travelled to Warmley (Bristol) and came away 12-0 winners, the scorers being ex-Nantwich player Ernie Whittick (with four goals), Frank Gray, 'Shiner' Shaw and Sammy Holmes (two apiece), Jack Morely and Jerry Wilson. This still remains as Walsall's best-ever victory at senior level.

Thereafter results fluctuated and on 3 November, Derby County came to The Chuckery for a friendly and inflicted upon Walsall their heaviest home defeat since the amalgamation took place, winning 7-1, with Irish international Archie Goodall scoring four of the visitors' goals. Another up-and-coming team, Liverpool, made their first visit to Walsall and returned to Merseyside with a 6-1 win under their belts.

'Proud' and mighty Preston North End were held to a 0-0 draw at The Chuckery in front of a 5,000-plus crowd (which included many women) and a similar audience witnessed the game against Aston Villa which ended in a 2-1 defeat for the Saddlers.

In their last Alliance game of the season, at Darwen, Walsall were hammered 9-0, but they did have an excuse, albeit a small one, as they were forced to play through the entire 90 minutes with only ten men on the field, Bill Hunter (ex-Kidderminster Olympic) having failed to meet the team bus prior to its departure to Lancashire. Earlier in the season, against Crewe Alexandra, only ten men lined up and Walsall crashed 6-1.

But realistically the 1890-91 season on the whole, was a chequered one. Walsall were frequently brought into prominence, but mostly it was undesirable exposure. They finished their Alliance programme with this record: P22, W9, L3, D10, For 34, Against 61 – finishing seventh, a shade better than the previous season's ninth place.

An impressive Stoke side were declared the champions.

There was a dispute with the Birmingham Association following an unsavoury incident in a Cup-tie against Warwick County, then the club was involved in a transfer row concerning two Wolves players, Harry Wood and David Wykes (formerly of Walsall), which led to several Football League teams threatening not to play any games against Walsall.

Another spot of bother came when Walsall took on Stoke at The Chuckery. A few minutes before full-time, Withington was injured when 'charging' a Stoke player, who had to be carried off with a damaged ankle. A spectator then raced on to the pitch and remonstrated with another Stoke player after an early incident involving the Walsall forward, 'Shiner' Shaw.

The Stoke player retaliated by punching the spectator twice in the face and there followed a scene of considerable confusion, the game being abandoned with Stoke 4-3 ahead.

A local newspaper reported: 'Whilst the visitors certainly incensed the spectators by their play, this is no excuse for the unwarrantable conduct of the latter, and some steps will have to be taken to prevent a recurrence of such thing or Walsall will find itself with a very bad reputation.'

Eventually things were sorted out, but these were not happy times at Walsall.

The only worthwhile performances of a rather poor season came when the Walsall Cup was lifted at the expense of Wednesbury Old Athletic who were beaten 3-0 in the Final, and non-Leaguers Warmley, were hammered 12-0 in an FA Cup-tie in early October – Walsall's record victory in this competition.

The 1891-92 campaign was marked by two important changes to the Laws of the Game.

Season 1890-91 had seen the introduction of goal nets, but there were other major innovations for 1891-92: linesmen took over from umpires (they used to stand near the uprights to indicate whether the ball had or had not passed between them.) and the penalty-kick was introduced.

On the playing side Walsall had Harry Wood (ex-Wolves) back in their camp along with Great Bridge Unity's goalkeeper Tom Hawkins, who in later years turned out in both full-back positions for the club, and Tom Pangbourn (from Warwick County) and Billy Loynes from Brierley Hill. The latter, however, was not available for selection until October, due to a back injury.

The likes of Charlie and Sammy Holmes, Stokes, Withington and Edge were still around.

An important change as far as the administration of the club was concerned was the formation of a limited liability company and a thorough reorganisation of the constitution.

Walsall began 1891-92 with a home Alliance game against Birmingham St George's and they lined up: Hawkins; Tommy Proffitt, Withington, Tonks, Stokes, Alf Pinches, Holmes, Shaw, Wood, Norman Forsyth (a highly-rated new recruit) and Wilson. Some 5,000 fans saw the game which ended in a 3-1 win for the visitors.

It was not the greatest of starts – and worse was to follow when Nottingham Forest ran up a 5-1 victory by the River Trent, although in this game injury reduced Walsall to nine men, Shaw having three front teeth kicked out.

Another heavy defeat – 6-1 in the return fixture with St George's – was quickly followed by a home lapse against Wednesbury Old Athletic in a friendly, meaning four successive defeats.

Fortunately that dismal run came to an end – when least expected – as Sheffield Wednesday, fielding a strong team, were nudged out 2-1.

Encouraged at having 'broken their duck' Walsall then duly thumped Wednesbury Old Athletic 7-1 in the FA Cup, only to collapse yet again when losing another friendly 2-1 to Middlesbrough Ironopolis, 4-1 versus Small Heath in the Alliance and, surprisingly, 4-2 at home to Burton Swifts in the FA Cup.

Walsall's form was certainly dismal for the rest of the season. They lost 6-0 to Ardwick (now Manchester City), went down 3-2 to the touring Canadians in a rough and tumble friendly at The Chuckery (a game they should have won hands down), crashed 4-0 away to both Sheffield Wednesday and Burton Swifts, nose-dived to a humiliating 4-1 home reverse against Newton Heath and lost 3-2 at home to Burton Swifts, a game which was held up for 15 minutes after two players had been sent-off but later called back into the action.

The best, of only a handful of wins achieved by Walsall was recorded on Christmas Day morning against Bootle, 7-0 in the Alliance, when the opposition was far from impressive. On the final day of a quite disastrous season, Walsall again fielded only ten men for an Alliance game, losing 2-0 at Grimsby Town, and had to apply for re-election to the Football Alliance, having finished next to bottom of the table with 15 points out of a possible 44, winning only six of their 22 games, losing 13 and drawing three while scoring 33 goals and conceding 59.

During the course of the 1891-92 campaign the following announcement was made: 'Walsall football as represented by Walsall Town Swifts is fast dwindling into little more than a burlesque of the game with no signs of any decided improvement. The collapse of the team cannot altogether be laid at the door either of 'luck' or 'accident' and has to be attributed to some degree to other and more preventable causes. For instance, the incessant and unnecessary shifting of the players from one position to another without any thought as to their fitness for the new positions, is one of the causes of failure. Another cause is the want of regular and systematic training, without which no club can expect to go through their Alliance matches with success.'

But that statement was not necessary because during the summer of 1892, Walsall became one of the founder-members of the newly-formed Football League Division Two – and thus began the second important period in the club's history. But it opened, it must be confessed, very inauspiciously as Walsall lost their opening five matches – three at home.

The Football Alliance effectively became the new Division Two and Walsall's first-ever Football League game was against Darwen, a Lancashire cotton town club, at home, on 3 September 1892, when this team took the field: Hawkins; Withington, Pinches, Forsyth, Whittick, Henry Robinson (ex-Wednesbury Old Athletic), Fred Marshall (from Birmingham St George's), Sammy Holmes, Joe Turner, Pangbourn and Frank Gray.

Some 4,000 fans turned up, but they went away disappointed as Walsall lost 2-1, the winning goal coming in the very last minute. Left-winger Frank Gray had the honour of scoring Walsall's first-ever Football League goal – the equaliser after 43 minutes.

The Saddlers lost their first five League games and their first League win was not recorded until 8 October, 2-1 over Lincoln City at The Chuckery, Pangbourne and new signing Tom Shaw scoring late goals after the visitors had dominated the opening two-thirds of the game.

Brief progress was made in the FA Cup, Stourbridge being whipped 7-0 in the second qualifying round, before Burton Swifts ended Walsall's hopes at the next hurdle.

Walsall 7 Stourbridge 0
FA Cup Second Qualifying Round, 29 October 1892

AFTER beating Lincoln City 2-1 and Grimsby Town 3-1 in Second Division League games, the Saddlers were in good form when they met Stourbridge from the Birmingham League in the second qualifying round of the FA Cup at their Chuckery ground

Kicking with the wind behind them in the first half the Saddlers – who gave a debut to right-back Bill Siddons – scored after barely a minute's play. Inside-left Tom Marlow dashed clear and his well struck shot slipped through the hands of 'keeper Dick Partridge.

Tom Hawkins then saved twice within a matter of five minutes as Stourbridge counter-attacked.

The Saddlers then forced a series of corners in an attempt to press home their advantage – but it was the visitors who came nearest to scoring when Tommy Wain had an effort ruled out for offside.

In the 30th minute Joe Turner made it 2-0, lashing in a shot from Fred Marshall's pass.

The Saddlers began the second-half in terrific style, scoring three times in double-quick time to seal victory.

Marlow raced through to make it 3-0 with a powerful drive on 49 minutes and then Norman Forsyth grabbed two goals in the 51st and 52nd minutes after some intricate forward play involving three players.

At 5-0 Walsall were coasting and midway through the half Sammy Holmes drew the 'keeper to score a sixth and soon afterwards he had the confidence to dribble past two defenders to claim his side's seventh.

Only twice in the second period was the Walsall 'keeper Hawkins called into action and near the end Forsyth had his hat-trick 'goal' ruled out for offside.

Walsall: Hawkins; Siddons, Pinches, Robinson, A. Withington, Whitehouse, Marshall, Holmes, Turner, Marlow, Forsyth.

Stourbridge: Partridge; Roberts, Hanes, Heath, Thorpe, Jones, G. Whitehouse, Bond, Bowen, Wain, Crabtree.

Walsall's first away win in the League came at Crewe Alexandra, where they took the points with a 6-5 triumph in a thrilling, crackerjack contest on, what was appropriately, 5 November.

The Saddlers were 6-2 ahead with ten minutes remaining, but the Alex scored three goals in double-quick time and right at the death the Walsall goalkeeper, Tom Hawkins, saved two more goal-bound efforts, both with his feet.

Halfway through November, Walsall's financial secretary, Mr Allso, tendered his resignation 'owing to the apathy and indifference displayed by the general body of committee men'.

Things continued to go from bad to worse, and despite an 8-2 Walsall Cup win over Coalville when the ageing Charlie 'Shiner' Shaw lined up at full-back to give him the distinction of appearing in all 11 positions for the club, the Saddlers' League form deteriorated even more. Against Small Heath, on 17 December, Walsall crashed 12-0 (a scoreline which was to be repeated three years later when only eight Town Swifts players turned up for a game at Darwen) and after leading 4-2 at home against Bootle on Christmas Eve, the team relaxed and allowed the visitors to draw level with two late goals.

Only 500 spectators bothered to turn out for this match against Bootle (which incidentally was played in heavy snow) and it prompted one writer to ask: 'Are there no gentlemen of sufficient public spirit to come forward and give a helping hand (with money and advice) to keep an old and useful organisation in going order?'

At the turn of the year Walsall found themselves at the bottom of the League table where they stayed until the season ended, finishing with only 13 points out of a possible 44, registering only five wins (four at home) and scoring 37 goals while conceding 75.

Early on in 1893 Walsall had received notice to quit their Chuckery ground and this bombshell of course, brought about another crisis in the affairs of the club. Initially they were asked to give up their headquarters in March and that arrangements would be made for them to play the rest of their home matches elsewhere.

A meeting of those interested in the future of the club was held at the Stork Hotel on 21 March and it was then explained that Mr Alfred Potter, agent to Lord Bradford, had informed the committee that he had received repeated complaints from residents in the neighbourhood of Sutton Road and under no conditions could he allow the field (The Chuckery) to be used for football matches after 25 March.

A financial statement was presented at the same meeting and according to this the income for the season had amounted to a mere £645 10s 10d and the expenditure to £646 14s 7d. The gate receipts of only £477 were described as 'scandalous'.

It was therefore decided to make a general appeal to the public and one suggestion which was put forward was that a limited liability company should be formed with a capital of 1,000 shares at £1 each, to be paid for in instalments of five shillings (25p).

Later, however, the club received permission to remain at the ground until the end of the season, and a few more matches were played there, the last fixture being the final League game, against Sheffield United who needed to beat Walsall to pip Small Heath for the title. The result was a 1-1 draw as the Saddlers put on one of their best displays of the season in front of a 2,000 crowd, and thus United had to settle for the runners-up slot behind the Blues.

For the start of the 1893-94 season, Walsall had hoped their new ground on West Bromwich Road, would be ready for use, but it wasn't – and therefore they had to utilise the Wood Green Oval for the first month of the campaign.

Everybody was looking forward to better things and over 5,000 witnessed the opening Second Division match against Small Heath. But sadly the visitors won 3-1 and immediately eyes began to twitch and heads began to shake.

More defeats followed, including a 4-0 hiding at Woolwich Arsenal, and as new players, namely Joey Lee (from Walsall Unity), Bethel McDonald and Archie Taylor (both from Burnley), goalkeeper Jack McLachnan, and Walter McWhinnie were brought into the team, so one writer in the *Birmingham Gazette* found space and time to say: 'I'm afraid the Walsall executive in their desire to do great things have made the mistake of overlooking promising juniors in the Saddlery town in order to bring men with a past reputation from a distance. In many cases these men have little or no interest in the success or otherwise of the club, being merely content that their weekly wage is regularly forthcoming.'

Walsall apparently took heed of the hint and soon Harry Gee of Willenhall Pickwick and Levi Mann of Bloxwich Strollers had been signed.

Walsall, 1893-94. Back row (players only): Baillie, Hawkins, Smellie. Middle row: Davies, Cook, Forsyth. Front row: Holmes, S. McWhinnie, Copeland, Cox, O'Brien.

A 5-1 triumph over Crewe – Walsall's first win of the season – triggered off something of a run and occasionally some fine victories were forthcoming, as well as some high-scoring encounters, including a 13-goal thriller at Burton when the Saddlers lost 8-5 to the Swifts.

When the campaign closed, the Saddlers had done a shade better than in their initial League season, finishing a respectable tenth with 23 points (out of 56), although they had been knocked out of the FA Cup, at home, by non-League Brierley Hill Alliance. Yet they won the prestigious Walsall Cup, beating Ironbridge 3-1 at Wellington in the Final.

One of the better League wins came against Lincoln as this report indicates:

Walsall 5 Lincoln City 2
Division Two, 26 March 1894

AFTER beating fifth-placed Grimsby Town 5-0 on the Easter Saturday, Walsall met mid-table Lincoln in a Second Division game at West Bromwich Road just 48 hours later. Some 2,000 fans attended in the hope of another goal feast and they were not disappointed. The weather was excellent, although having lost the toss Walsall had the sun in their eyes as they kicked-off.

How the crowd roared when the Saddlers raced away to score in the very first minute with a splendid shot from little 'Mac' McWhinnie. Lincoln then had a spell of attacking towards what was known as the 'top' goal and Tom Hawkins saved a fierce shot from Raby while Cook did well to get in the way of a fierce toe-poke from Graham. Then O'Brien, who on his day was a great crowd pleaser, had the home supporters roaring as he went past man after man before Stothart hammered the ball into touch. O'Brien then set up new signing Harley, but the latter drove wide.

Soon afterwards, however, Walsall went two up when, after what was described at the time as a 'rush on goal' Gee hammered the ball home. By half-time it was 3-0 when Harley made up for his earlier lapse by slotting the ball home following a corner.

After the break Gee headed a fourth and then when Lincoln pressed Hawkins was twice loudly applauded for punching clear from amidst a welter of attackers. The visitors stuck at it and following a corner Bill Lees, who had got two hat-tricks earlier that season, reduced the arrears. Then Leatherbarrow got the goal of the game for Walsall after a spectacular run from midfield and finally Lees pulled back a further consolation goal with a snap shot to make the final score 5-2.

Walsall: Hawkins; Cook, Pinches, Holmes, Brettle, Forsyth, Harley, Gee, Leatherbarrow, McWhinnie, O'Brien.
Lincoln City: Gresham; Stothart, Neale, Shaw, Mettan, Wiltshire, Chadband, Raby, Lees, Flewitt, Graham.

The 1894-95 season, Walsall's third in the Football League, was perhaps one of the most critical the club had faced so far in its history.

Despite a reported loss of £502 on the previous year, one or two new players were introduced, including Len Benwell, a goalkeeper from Aston Villa, who played twice at inside-left in January 1895 when injuries seriously affected the squad, and Norman Brettle from the local Unity club (no relation to Joe from earlier years), and for the opening game of the League programme against Burslem Port Vale, Walsall fielded: Benwell; Henry Robertson, Pinches, Holmes (who had now been converted into a wing-half), Brettle, Forsyth, Claude Hartley, Charlie Leatherbarrow, David Copeland, McWhinnie and Joe O'Brien. Vale won the match 1-0. Holmes missed a penalty for Walsall and the majority of the 3,000 spectators went home happy.

Around the start of this season, Walsall were awarded quite a few penalties – they had six spot-kicks in six games – and Leatherbarrow (the fourth different player to try his luck) was given the job against Grimsby Town on 8 September 1894. He, too, failed to score, although it didn't affect the result, Walsall winning 4-3.

Will Devey, signed from Aston Villa on 5 May 1894 (later to be sold to Bolton in 1895, then re-signed by Walsall from Notts County in 1897) and Archie Roberts, both came into the side as results continued to favour Walsall and after three more wins and a draw the Saddlers found themselves in fourth spot and going for promotion.

But shocks were in store – and they were not long coming.

A 6-1 hammering at Manchester City was followed by an FA Cup defeat against Burton Wanderers, a team made up of entirely local players – 'no high-priced Scotsmen' as one local reporter stated. And the decline quickly set in.

A critic wrote: 'It is no good mincing matters, it is absolutely necessary if the team is going to play at all that several good men should be obtained, and the sooner the powers-that-be realise this the sooner they will be on the way to getting out of their present position.'

Only 1,500 spectators saw the home game with Bury at the end of October and then, Arthur 'Artful' Taylor, who only ever made one League appearance for Walsall, suffered a broken leg during a friendly against Burslem Port Vale.

A 4-1 win over Arsenal bucked up morale – but only temporarily – for soon after Walsall crashed 6-1 at Rotherham. Leatherbarrow, so disgusted, then left the club, joining Small Heath.

December was a complete disaster as Walsall lost five successive League games – against Darwen (a) 2-0, Leicester Fosse (h) 3-1, Newcastle United (a) 7-2, Notts County (a) 5-0 and Newton Heath (h) 2-1. The return game with Newcastle was abandoned 12 minutes from time owing to a blizzard, and in a friendly Walsall were clipped at home 5-1 by West Brom.

These results had very serious consequences.

A meeting of the club's shareholders was called and it was also stated that several players had been dismissed. Also, it was made known that Newcastle United had covered Walsall's travelling expenses to the North-East by paying out the sum of £12 10s on condition that the money would be refunded out of the takings of the return game at Walsall. The players, however, refused to accept this and said that they would not turn out against Newcastle unless they had an agreement in writing from the directors that they would be paid the gross 'gate' and they actually had every penny taken at that subsequently abandoned match and all the cash taken from the Newton Heath fixture on

Boxing Day. The total receipts for both games amounted to just £39.

Some of the players remained loyal to the club and agreed nominal terms but the results were disastrous as Walsall lost 9-1 at Leicester, 7-0 at Burton (when Adrian Capes scored six) and 6-2 at West Bromwich Albion in the Birmingham Cup.

On 16 January 1895, at a meeting of the club's shareholders (at the Stork Hotel) it was stated that the balance sheet showed a deficiency of £631, for which the laying of the track around the West Bromwich Road ground was said to be largely responsible; that each of the directors had found at least £100; and that the players had been offered five shillings (25p) a match, plus the same amount for a win.

It was further announced that an application for the voluntary winding up of the company was to be made, and that was afterwards granted in the County Court.

Notwithstanding the terms on which the players were turning out, it was written of them: 'Whatever weakness there may be in the team, every man is now playing for all he is worth and is doing his level best for the old club.'

And to prove it, on 26 January, Crewe Alexandra, who were at the foot of the Second Division, were beaten 4-0 in a home match.

At this time the weather was atrocious and after snow had been cleared from the pitch Walsall won a home Staffordshire Cup-tie against Burton in front of just 23 spectators – an attendance described as 'a disgrace to the football fraternity of Walsall'. Burton complained about the state of the ground and the tie was replayed.

In consequence of the difficulties which had arisen, a Town's Meeting was held on the 22 February, Councillor Peter Bull presiding over an extra large audience to consider the position and what steps could be taken to improve it.

It was stated that for sums advanced to enable the team to travel to fulfil away fixtures, £12 9s was owing to Newcastle United, £10 to Burton Wanderers, £5 to Leicester Fosse and £4 to Burton Swifts, and there were other liabilities amounting to £10 which had been defrayed in the next 12 days or the club would be suspended by the Football League. Mr J. Zeller had promised to let the club have the use of the ground to the end of May and to give a donation of £5 5s if another £50 was raised.

"One thing the club has suffered from is that it has always had more critics than supporters," the chairman remarked.

After considerable discussion it was agreed that the club should carry on until the end of the season, although only £1 11s 2d was collected from those in attendance while another £25 was guaranteed to be placed in the club's account.

Around this time the weather was still quite awful and only 800 fans bothered to turn out for a benefit match held for 'Art' Taylor. Soon afterwards, on 9 March, arriving at Newton Heath's ground for a League game, Walsall found the pitch in a sorry state and refused to play, asking that the fixture should be in the context of a friendly. This was agreed and Walsall lost 14-0 – and 11 of the goals came in the second-half.

When the League match was played (in early April), the Saddlers didn't fare much better – they crashed 9-0.

Results, in general, picked up a shade, although not enough points were gathered to save Walsall from figuring in the re-election zone, and when the season ended the Saddlers lay in 14th place with Port Vale and Crewe below them in the table.

On 20 May, at the annual meeting of the Football League, a big shock was forthcoming when it was learned that the club's application for re-election had been unsuccessful, Loughborough Town being admitted instead.

The blame for this was placed entirely on the club's officials. They had done little or no canvassing of the other clubs and had failed to send a representative to the League meeting. It was a deplorable state of affairs mainly due to their own mismanagement.

Having lost their place in the Football League after only three seasons, Walsall subsequently joined the Midland League, which at the time was thought to provide a better opportunity of regaining Football League status than would the Birmingham League.

As it happened Walsall failed to win the Midland League, finishing third with 40 points, five behind the champions Kettering with Gainsborough Trinity in second spot, and they made only limited progress in the FA Cup. Yet on the credit side the club did lift the Birmingham Charity Cup, defeating First Division champions Aston Villa and Sheffield United on the way, while impressive Midland League wins were recorded against Matlock (7-1 and 5-0), Barnsley St Peter's (5-0), Wellingborough (6-1) and Doncaster Rovers (9-1). In fact, Walsall scored in all but one game (at Long Eaton) and they netted a total of 92 goals in their 28 Midland League matches, of which 17 were won and six drawn.

Happily, though, a well-presented case for re-election to the Football League proved successful and Walsall got back into the 'big time' with Blackpool and Gainsborough Trinity, while Crewe Alexandra, Port Vale and Rotherham all dropped out.

At this time the club decided on a change of colours and out went the old claret and blue stripes, which were replaced by white shirts and blue shorts.

There were also problems over the lease of the West Bromwich Road ground, and as a result the move was made to Hillary Street, which was later to be renamed Fellows Park (1930) in honour of long-serving director, Mr H. L. Fellows, a prominent local businessman, who was chairman of the club from 1938 to 1944, having been a director since 1921. The stand and banking at Hillary Street was not quite ready for occupation at the start of the 1896-97 season, but the pitch was – and the first game there was a friendly against Glossop North End on 1 September 1896, which Walsall won 4-1; Jack Aston (two), David Copeland and ex-Wolves star Alf Griffin were the scorers in front of a crowd of just over 1,000.

The first-ever Football League game at Hillary Street was played four days later, Walsall beating Burton Wanderers 2-0 before 2,500 enthusiastic spectators.

Despite very wet conditions the pitch itself looked in perfect condition and the turnout was big enough to make it desirable for pre-set plans to be put in motion to make an additional exit at the

Hillary Street end of the ground as there was something of a crush on the way out into Wallows Lane. The main stand was still not complete, but the adjacent dressing rooms and the referee's changing quarters were utilised.

The first Football League goal scored at Hillary Street came from the lethal right boot of Jack Aston after only four minutes play. Alf Griffin knocked in a second soon afterwards and although Burton's centre-forward Will Devey (later to rejoin Walsall) struck the crossbar at the Laundry End, there was no more scoring in the first-half.

The visitors pressed hard after the break, but Walsall's defence held on and in the end they deserved their victory. George Lewis, at right-back, had an outstanding game for the Saddlers.

The Walsall team was: Hawkins; George Lewis, Pinches, Charlie Aston, centre-half Bill Taylor (from Halesowen), former West Brom left-half Jack Taggart, Doug Horobin (ex-Walsall Wood Athletic), 'Soldier' Aston, Griffin, Copeland and the exciting left-winger Tommy Johnson (secured from Wrockwardine Wood)

Around this time there were allegations made in the newspapers that betting had taken place within the club, and that a turnstile had been tampered with in order to defraud visiting teams. An FA Commission looked into these allegations and thankfully the club was cleared of any wrong-doing.

There was another embarrassing event on Boxing Day 1896, when Walsall played against Darwen in a League game at Darley Bank.

That afternoon only eight players took the field for the Saddlers, including goalkeeper Charlie Bunyan's older brother, George, who was a committee member and whose registration was rushed through just in time for him to take the field at right-back – his only game for the club. Perhaps the four missing players had celebrated too much after drawing 3-3 with Small Heath 24 hours earlier.

Against Darwen, Walsall won the toss and, with the aid of a strong wind and the clever disposition of players, managed to work the offside trap well, holding Darwen at bay for 15 minutes. But then a slip by Jack Taggart resulted in the first goal going in and after that the Saddlers had no answer to the home attack and crashed to a 12-0 defeat.

A week after this demolition job in Lancashire, Walsall returned to the same county and this time, having to play 35-year-old goalkeeper Tom Hawkins at left-back due to the absence of Charlie Aston who failed to turn up at the railway station on the morning of the match, the Saddlers were hammered 5-0 by Manchester City.

The 1896-97 season ended on a high, however. The last two League games, both at home, were won in style: 5-0 v Lincoln City and 4-0 v Darwen, the latter some revenge for that hammering earlier in the campaign.

The Birmingham Senior Cup was carried off after remarkable wins over First Division Derby County and Wolves, and soon afterwards the Lord Mayor of Birmingham's Charity Cup was won, Walsall beating Aston Villa in the Final at the newly-opened Villa Park. This last victory was a tremendous triumph, considering that Villa had just achieved the Football League and FA Cup double.

It was a pity that Walsall could not show the same sort of form in the League as they produced in Cup competitions – they finished 12th of 16 teams in Division Two – and their best win of the season came when they crushed Dresden United 11-0 in the third qualifying round of the FA Cup – Walsall's second best win in this competition (they had beaten Warmley 12-0 in 1890). The clash with Dresden was quite remarkable.

At the time Dresden were fighting it out with Kettering Town at the top of the Midland League and things didn't seem to be going too well for the Saddlers when it was found that neither of the two registered goalkeepers, Charlie Bunyan (who conceded 26 goals playing for Hyde against Preston in an FA Cup tie in 1887) and Jack Winkles, were eligible to play and consequently the ageing Tom Hawkins was brought out of retirement to fill the gap.

Walsall attacked the Laundry End in the first period and visiting 'keeper Hull was unlucky when a shot from Tommy Johnson was brilliantly saved only for the same player to follow up and force the rebound over the line. Then Hull punched away a goal-bound effort from Griffin only to see the ball loop up in the air, allowing George Johnson to dart forward to head home from close range. Griffin made it 3-0 before the interval.

In the second-half it was all Walsall and the goals rained thick and fast – from Tommy Johnson who added another three to finish up with a four, two more from George Johnson who thus completed his hat-trick, another two fine efforts from Griffin, who also registered a treble and one from 'Soldier' Aston, a toe-poke from fully 30 yards.

The 1897-98 season began with a great deal of uncertainty, and after a

Walsall in 1897. Back row (left to right): Mountford (trainer), Hodson, Loynes, Jenkyns, C. Bunyan, Peers, G. Johnson, Taggart, Ashwell (trainer). Front row: Horobin, Aston, S. Holmes, Wilkes, Copeland, Griffin.

series of disappointing results, on 8 December a crisis meeting was held at the Stork Hotel, Walsall, to discuss ways and means of surviving financially. At the time Walsall were again deep in debt, gate receipts were alarmingly low, players wages were high and general expenses were continually rising.

Mr Zeller, in the chair, stated, however, that a 'friend' of his had agreed to cover the losses – for the time being – but the meeting closed with the statement that all season-ticket holders would have to pay admission to the next three matches.

Prior to this meeting Walsall had included in their team as captain, the Welsh international centre-half, Caesar Jenkyns, the ex-Small Heath hardman, and Will Devey (for his second spell with the club), and the players had also been promised a £5 incentive bonus if they could stay clear of the bottom three places in the League.

This made no difference at first, Walsall suffering a 6-0 defeat against Jenkyns' former club, Small Heath. But gradually his presence made the rest of the players 'pull up their socks' and following a 6-0 win over Blackpool, an 11-0 slaughter of Wrockwardine Wood in the Birmingham Cup and a 5-0 thrashing of in-form Luton Town, Walsall eventually finished in tenth place (29 points), well clear of the danger zone.

During the summer of 1898 three players – full-back Charlie Aston, inside-left George Johnson and defender Albert Wilkes, who actually played one game in goal against Notts County in November 1896 – were all transferred to Aston Villa – and there was a great deal of hostility aimed at the Walsall committee for allowing this to happen.

In addition goalkeeper Charlie Bunyan (who later became manager of the Tivoli Concert Hall in Walsall High Street), Copeland, Devey and Horobin had severed their connections with the club through various reasons, and consequently there were an unusual number of vacancies in the team. Fortunately the financial position was by now considerably better than it had been for quite some time and therefore a few new faces were recruited, at a cost of £500, to bolster up the playing strength.

Among those signed were Billy Tennant, a weighty goalkeeper from Wolves, Tommy Vail, the Chatham and former Dundee centre-forward, Jack Martin from Blackpool, Henry Davies, a hard-tackling Scottish-born full-back from Cambuslang who had represented Scotland in a Junior international, Frank Greatwich, a winger, also from Wolves, the Cannock defender Alf Wedge, who had played two games on trial the previous season, George Shaw and George Smith from Huddersfield Town, inside-left Harry Peers from Wednesfield and 18-year-old David Lunn from Smethwick.

Walsall, thus, started off the 1898-99 League campaign with this line-up: Tennant; Ernie Peers, Davies, Martin, Caeser Jenkyns, Jack Taggart, Greatwich, 'Soldier' Aston, Vail, Harry Peers (no relation to the full-back) and Alf Griffin.

The early results were exceptionally good (7-0 v Loughborough, 4-1 v Grimsby and 4-1 v Arsenal) and indeed Walsall were a shade unlucky in the Final of the Birmingham Charity Cup, when high-flying Aston Villa pipped them 1-0 at the Lower Grounds before a 9,000 crowd (receipts £189).

A poor display against the Welsh club, Druids, saw Walsall knocked out of the FA Cup but in the League, their form held and they ran up some magnificent victories including a 6-1 thrashing (with ten men) of Gainsborough Trinity, a 6-0 hiding of Blackpool and a 10-0 hammering of Darwen, sweet revenge (again) for that 12-goal drubbing Walsall had received from the Lancashire side back in December 1896.

March 1899 saw Walsall in fifth spot in Division Two but with no real chance of winning promotion, Manchester City and Glossop being well set at the top.

Walsall finally took sixth place in the table, registering 42 points from 15 wins and 12 draws from their 34 fixtures, and remaining unbeaten at home. They were the Second Division's top scorers with 75 goals, and only Port Vale and the champions Manchester City had fewer scored against them.

During the course of the summer, various improvements were made at the ground, which had by now been purchased by Mr Joseph Zeller, the president of the club, and let to the committee at a rent of £30 a year. Another change was that the club introduced a reserve team, which gained entry to the Birmingham & District League.

On the playing side the chief changes were that 'Soldier' Aston, both the Peers and Vail all departed and the newcomers, some from beyond the border, including two from Dundee Wanderers, Jock Lyons and Hugh Dailly (the latter once of Wolves), Willie McAuley from Glasgow Celtic, Jim Moffatt, a Scottish Junior International from Bo'ness, inside-forward Joe Connor from West Bromwich Albion, who later won three caps for Ireland, winger Jimmy McLean from Worcester City, Harry Pointer from nearby Small Heath and Walter Bunch (another ex-Wolves player) from Eastville Rovers.

A new trainer was appointed, too – ex-sergeant instructor Richard Dillon, late of the Royal Scots Fusiliers.

Notwithstanding a 3-2 defeat in the opening match of the 1899-1900 campaign, at Small Heath, the team's display was, on the whole, regarded as encouraging, but an inconsistent spell soon set in and the club's affairs quickly took a turn for the worse.

One vitally important reason for the decline was the behaviour of two or three players which earned the rest of the team an unenviable reputation for roughness. A local critic went so far as to comment on their 'brutal tactics' and in what was supposed to be a 'friendly' away game with the London Casuals, a Walsall player (Henry Davies) was sent-off.

In striking contrast to the previous season, when several of the local clergy and other prominent townsfolk, to say nothing of the influx of quite a few women, were attracted to Walsall's home matches, attendances were now so seriously affected by the disgusting language and abominable behaviour inside the ground, that before the season was halfway through, Mr Joe Zeller, the president, and the committee had another financial crisis on their hands – lack of income through the turnstiles.

It was probably the worst that had

ever arisen, and at one time it was touch and go whether the club would be able to carry on.

But carry on they did – and at the end of a rather disappointing season Walsall found themselves in 12th place, due mainly to a good home record (ten wins and five draws), with a 6-3 victory over Chesterfield and a 7-3 win against Luton Town the high spots.

In the FA Cup, Walsall were paired at home with neighbours West Bromwich Albion in the first round, and a bumper crowd of 9,106 (paying over £328) packed into Hillary Street to see the contest, which ended 1-1, Scotsman Dailly equalising for the Saddlers after Dick Roberts had edged the Baggies in front with a disputed goal. The replay, though, was a complete disaster for Walsall who crashed 6-1.

There now came one of the most important seasons in the history of Walsall Football Club, 1900-01, which was to mark the end of Football League membership for a period of 20 years, until the formation of the Third Division in 1921.

The previous campaign had closed with a loss of more than £1,000, on top of deficiency of £255 on the previous season – and it was debateable whether the club would continue in League Football. But they did – for just nine more months.

As the 19th century drew to its close, amazingly the prospects of Walsall Football Club looked much brighter, but alas, the improvement was not maintained for long, and almost immediately the tide governing the club's affairs began to turn. It was never to change and at the end of the season Walsall lost their Second Division place again.

In 1900-01 Walsall were in trouble, first due to a misunderstanding about the playing of League games on the Saturday following the death of Queen Victoria, when they failed to fulfil a fixture at Middlesbrough, and soon afterwards they ran into more trouble over a fee of £120 for the transfer of Alfred Dean to Nottingham Forest, which was finally settled in their favour after West Bromwich Albion had said that the money should go to them after they had allowed Dean to join Walsall for nothing.

Dean had been in sparkling form this season, scoring 11 League goals and six more in the FA Cup, including a five-timer against Wellington Town. But he wanted to move on and Walsall refused to hold up his progress.

There then followed a claim by Messrs Zeller, the president, and Louis Ford, the secretary, who had ironically arrived in the Walsall camp from West Bromwich Albion, on the grounds that they were entitled to be reimbursed towards the £1,000 they had provided to keep the Walsall club going during the previous season.

There was not much money available... and one or two players struggled to get their wages paid.

So much so that performances on the field suffered and right at the death it all depended on the last match of the season – Walsall at home to Middlesbrough.

To avoid having to seek re-election for the second time Walsall had to win. They didn't, drawing 0-0, and thus missed out by 0.06 of a goal.

At the League's annual meeting, whilst Stockport County and Burton Swifts, who had worse records, were both re-elected, Walsall received a mere seven votes and consequently lost their place in the League, choosing to play in the Midland League in 1901-02.

The Midland League was, of course, a big drop from competing in the Second Division, but what Walsall lost on the Football League roundabout, they more than made up for in the FA Cup, reaching the second round proper after beating, in turn, Brierley Hill Alliance (h) 2-1 (in a replay), Berwick Rangers from Worcester (h) 2-1, Burslem Port Vale (a) 2-1, New Brompton (h) 2-0 and Second Division Burnley (h) 1-0. In round two, Bury ended Walsall's hopes with a convincing 5-0 win on a snow-covered pitch at West Bromwich Road, and many said that it might well have been a totally different scoreline had the Walsall players been as suitably shod as were the Shakers. (Not the least remarkable feature of that illustrious Cup run was the fact that there was a 'B' starting part of the name of each of the six clubs that Walsall met in that season's competition.)

In the Midland League programme of 1901-02, Walsall lost five of their first six matches, including an 8-1 hammering away to Sheffield United Reserves.

They showed a vast improvement from November onwards, however, and in mid-January whipped Coalville Town 7-0 at home with the promising youngster Alf Green claiming a hat-trick. Green, in fact, top-scored with 14 goals in League and Cup.

The best League attendance this season was 4,000, for the visit of Burton United Reserves on Boxing Day, while in the Cup 9,045 fans watched the Burnley tie and 9,551 saw the clash with Bury.

Nothing outstanding was achieved in the League the following season, and Walsall also made an early exit from the FA Cup, beaten 2-0 at home by Brierley Hill Alliance in the second qualifying round.

In the two seasons Walsall spent in the Midland League, 1901-03, they finished fifth and eighth respectively, collecting 35 points (from 14 wins and seven draws) in the first and two points fewer in 1902-03.

In this latter season official printed match cards (indicating the team line-ups) were issued for the first time at home games.

By June 1903 it had become clear to everyone associated with the club that Midland League football was unlikely to be a financial success, (not once in 1902-03 did Walsall's home crowd top 2,500) and the club's committee therefore decided to seek admission to the Birmingham & District League.

Walsall were duly accepted, joining up in readiness for the 1903-04 season with the reserve teams of Aston Villa, Small Heath (now Birmingham City), West Bromwich Albion and Wolves. Another distinct advantage in addition to having several local derbies, was that the shorter distances to away games would make a considerable saving in travelling expenses. And another bonus was that Hillary Street would again be available for home matches.

Walsall were to stay in the Birmingham & District League for the next 14 competitive seasons, with a break of four seasons because of World War One.

Generally speaking the competition was dominated by the four reserve teams mentioned, of whom Aston Villa were usually the favourites for the championship.

The rest (including Walsall) were never really in with a shout – that is until Mr Harry Keys, a director of West Bromwich Albion, introduced the Keys Cup, a trophy to be played for by members of the Birmingham & District League.

Walsall became the holders of this prize in 1915 – their only success over a number of years.

From 1903 to 1909, Walsall somehow struggled along – basically on low support (many times they drew attendances of under 1,000 for their home games) – but there were some good turnouts from time to time, and although income was in short supply, a new stand, costing £130, was eventually erected at the ground, and a stretch of wire-netting put up at the Laundry End to save the ball from repeatedly disappearing over the wall.

The club's colours were changed – to amber and navy-blue – while several players came and went during these six rather sad and very disappointing years.

Things began to pick up a shade from 1909 and attendances certainly improved (two crowds of 8,000 were recorded before the war, while in 1920-21, there was a turnout of 11,500 for the Boxing Day home encounter with Willenhall). Yet the club – and indeed, the diehard supporters – desperately wanted to regain their Football League status. But that was not going to be for some considerable time yet.

Going back a few years, to 5 September 1903, for the first game 'back' at Hillary Street against Brierley Hill, the Walsall team comprised the following: Harry Jones (ex-West Bromwich Albion); Jack Waters, Jamie Ore (formerly with Britannia Victoria), Tommy Nicholls, George Pickering, Richard Pee, Billy Griffiths (once of Bilston United), Reg Bastock, George Beale and Laurie Pember (the latter two both ex-Aston Villa) and Billy Law (late of Rushall Olympic).

The game finished 2-2, both Walsall's goals came from Pember, with Gil Brookes netting twice for the visitors, and there were 1,500 spectators present.

More new faces arrived in the course of the season – men like Stan Bywater (from Selly Oak), Fred 'Ike' Burden and Theodore Leadbetter, but after the last fixture was played in 1903-04, Walsall ended their first season in the Birmingham League in 13th place with 29 points out of 68, having chalked up just 11 wins, including a 1-0 home success over Kidderminster Harriers when they fielded only ten men.

After that campaign, the following comments appeared in the *Walsall Observer*: 'The football season has now come to an end and for Walsall the ending is hardly a pleasant one. At the beginning of the season great hopes were held out that the Walsall club with the large number of promising players it had secured, would occupy a place worthy of the town, and for a long time these hopes were justified, the team maintaining its position well up amongst the leaders of the League.

Later on, however, the players began to fall off in form and in spite of numerous changes in personnel of the team, match after match was lost.'

The next season (1904-05) Walsall finished a place lower, losing 17 of their 34 matches, while averaging home crowds of just under 2,000.

They suffered three crushing defeats, all away, to Aston Villa Reserves 8-0, Small Heath Reserves 7-1 and Shrewsbury Town 6-2.

Among the new men signed were centre-forward Tommy Sawyer from Kidderminster Harriers, 'Gus' Adams from Willenhall Pickwick, Charlie Cole and Archie Owen, goalkeeping-policeman Bill Sheldon (from Salford), Duncan Thomas (ex-Shrewsbury Town) and Richard Wright (from Blackpool).

Many changes were made during the course of the campaign with the following most prominent – Tommy Thorpe, Adams, Pickering; Nicholls, Joe Flavell, Burden, Pearson, Bert Franks, Ted Burton, Jimmy Ellard, Tommy Sawyer, Jack Archer and Oscar Clarkson.

And more changes were to follow as the committee set about improving the playing staff all down the line.

For the opening fixture of 1905-06, Walsall fielded this strong looking team against a useful Wellington Townside at home: Jack Reddall; Adams, George Hewitt, Burden, Pearson, Franks, Arthur Owen, Bywater, Tommy Holt, Sid Managhan and Clarkson. Victory was gained to the tune of 4-1, but five days later almost the same band of players were crushed 9-2 by West Bromwich Albion Reserves at The Hawthorns and no-one was at all happy about what had gone on out on the park.

Results hardly improved and after two seven-goal defeats, at Wolves and Small Heath, plus three five-goal reverses, Walsall eventually came 16th in the final League table of 1905-06, having lost 21 games (eight on the trot from mid-October to early December) and the defence conceded a staggering 90 goals.

During these last two seasons a total of 80 players were utilised – and things were not improving one iota out on the pitch.

The committee, disgusted at what was going on, called for a vast improvement, but alas, it never materialised and the disenchanted Saddlers, despite putting everything they had into the games, had to settle for 13th place in 1906-07. They again suffered some heavy defeats – the worst coming at Stoke early in January when they nose-dived 10-3 in front of a 2,000 crowd. Their best victory was at home over Burslem Port Vale, who they beat 6-1 in mid-March. Alfred Hunt was leading scorer.

Amazingly, the 1907-08 campaign, from one point of view, opened most auspiciously, for there was a balance in the black of £100.

Moreover, improvements had been effected on the ground, including provision for seating in the main stand in addition to extra banking on the popular end.

As far as the team was concerned, a useful nucleus of experienced players had been retained including Seymour Urmson, Adams, Burden, Jack Bird, who was to give the club superb service for a number of years, Eric Wright, Hunt, Pickering and Jimmy Hirons, while among the new recruits were full-back Tommy Moreton (from Crewe Alexandra), local man Dick Williams, inside-right Gilbert Bytheway (from

Wrexham), centre-forward Frankie Pope (ex-Notts County), and a new left-wing pairing of Charlie 'Nudger' Newton (Bloxwich Strollers) and Ted Newman (from Erdington).

Later on, Tommy Rogers (from King's Royal Rifles), George Garrattly (from Chapel End United), later to play 232 games at full-back for Wolves, and Jack Wilson (Rood End Wesley), who sadly broke his leg and was forced to quit whilst in his early 20s, were all secured.

But alas, although Walsall's overall form-rate picked up a shade on previous seasons, they still finished tenth with only 33 points from 34 games.

They lost 8-2 at Stoke (again), 6-0 at Aston Villa and 4-0 at Crewe, whilst at home they were beaten 4-1 by Worcester City and 4-2 by West Bromwich Albion. Bytheway weighed in with 17 goals this term with Hunt netting 12.

At the annual meeting in July 1908 it was revealed that the financial position of the club was good.

There was a bank balance in hand of £89, the assets were valued at £213 and there were no liabilities.

Mr Robert A. Cooper, a Unionist Candidate for the Borough, was elected president in place of Mr W. J. Lee and Mr J. Shutt was re-elected as the club secretary.

One or two of the older players left: 'Ike' Burden moved to Stockport County, Garrattly to Wolves, Robinson to Lincoln City, and both Bytheway and Moreton to Darlaston, while Hunt, Pickering and Hirons also departed.

Into the camp came Dickey Bourne (ex-West Bromwich Albion), who was engaged as player-trainer, with Sid Scholey as his assistant (he became Walsall's manager in 1929), full-back Harry Smith (from Stoke), defender Jack Jones (Wolves), Bill Rochelle (Stafford Rangers), Sid Davies (Burton), Frank Davis (Darlaston), Harry Cook (Hurst Hill), Benny Chance (from Wednesbury), who after spending a season in the reserves went on to make over 150 appearances for the Saddlers in the Birmingham League, Tommy Richards (Wolves), who also became a grand servant to the club going on to amass in excess of 200 first-team appearances, Albert Walker (Ettingshall), Sid Francis (Worcester City), Teddy Bailey (Burton United) and Dennis Sheldon (Stafford Rangers).

On the field of play, however, all these new faces failed to brighten up the scene, and poor old Walsall again failed to impress, finishing a disappointing 15th, some 26 points behind the champions Aston Villa (54-28). The team did, however, win the prestigious Walsall Cup, beating Bilston United 1-0 in the Final.

At the close of the 1908-09 season the club's balance sheet revealed a deficit of £103 8s. All looked rather depressing and perhaps most alarming was the fact that out of the town's population of 101,400, only 35 people had registered as club members. A sorry state of affairs – and it clearly indicated how much the general public thought of Walsall Football Club.

Mr Cooper unwillingly was re-elected as president and before the 1909-10 season began many more new players arrived at the club: full-backs Wally Cook (Sheffield Amateurs), Jack Wilden (Handsworth); half-backs Jack Hinett (Bournbrook), Joe Dickenson (Kettlebrook), Eddie Bateman (Stafford Rangers) and Ernie Watts (Moseley); forwards John Sidwell (Handsworth), Gregory Peters (Wednesbury Corinthians), Tom Price (Edgbaston), and Stan Sheppard and David Sadler (both from Wilnecote United), many of whom never got a chance in the first team.

The start of the season was almost as unpromising as it could be. Even in their opening home match in the Birmingham League, Walsall fared badly, losing to Kidderminster Harriers 2-0. They beat a weak Stourbridge side 4-2 but then crumbled to a 5-1 defeat at Stoke – their bogey team.

And when Cannock Town, who were members of the Birmingham Combination, came over the 'Chase' and knocked the Saddlers out of the FA Cup, the outlook became very bleak indeed.

Fortunately, however, the team's affairs almost immediately took a turn for the better – so much so that it was not until early December that the Saddlers suffered another defeat, losing narrowly to a strong Wolves outfit, and by that time they had risen to second place in the League table.

Walsall held their form reasonably well until the end of the season, beating

Walsall players, directors and staff pictured in 1909-10, the season in which they finished fifth in the Birmingham League, their highest-ever position in the competition to that time.

Halesowen 7-0 on the way, and they finished up in their highest-ever Birmingham League position (fifth) with only the strong Aston Villa Reserves side, Crewe Alexandra, Wolves Reserves and Brierley Hill Alliance above them.

The regulars in 1909-10 were goalkeeper Harry Cooch (ex-Aston Villa), who, incidentally, lost part of a finger early in his career, Benny Chance, Jack Bird, Tom Richards, former West Brom left-winger Tommy Dilly, Billy Walker, Harry Davies, George Walker and the two top-scorers, Billy Caddick (19 goals) and Jack Crump (17).

Steps were taken to improve the team for the 1910-11 campaign, and one new recruit was the amateur centre-forward, Hubert Parsonage. Several local players were also recruited as the club decided to place a team in the Second Division of the Southern League.

In the end it was, surprisingly, a series of poor home results which contributed most to Walsall not winning the Birmingham League championship. They lost four and drew five of their 17 games at Hillary Street and eventually had to settle for third spot in the table.

Their best win came against second-placed Wolves Reserves, who were beaten 7-3 in December (the Saddlers doubled up later in the season, winning 2-0 at Molineux), but there were only 500 present to witness that marvellous ten-goal encounter when a further four 'goals' were disallowed.

In contrast, there were some harsh words spoken after the Saddlers were hammered 6-0 at Wellington in mid-January. There were also some exceptionally close games, full of excitement, three in particular coming when the Saddlers won 4-3 at Stoke, who were destined to be the champions, shared the spoils 3-3 at Wrexham on April Fool's Day when two penalties were missed, and lost 4-2 at home to Stourbridge, when another spot-kick went astray.

Against the Potters, Walsall scored three goals in six minutes near the end to snatch an incredible victory, but against the Glassblowers from Stourbridge, the boot was on the other foot, as Walsall's defence conceded three goals in four minutes to lose a six-goal thriller.

In the end the Saddlers chalked up 44 points, recording 20 wins and scoring 60 goals against 44.

Their average home attendance for the season was around 2,900, boosted somewhat by the 8,000-plus turnout on Easter Monday for the visit of Aston Villa Reserves.

The experiment of running a reserve team in Division Two of the Southern League proved unsuccessful. Crowds were very low – the average home attendance was a mere 741 – and Walsall finished in ninth place, accumulating only 18 points out of a possible 44. Their lowest gate was just 150 for the visit of Kettering on a cold Saturday in February.

Having had one of their most successful seasons for some considerable time – a £100 debt had been wiped out and there was a bank balance of £90 – Walsall started 1911-12 with a great deal of confidence.

Most of the players had been retained; George Rampton, however, had left for Grimsby and Parsonage had moved to London, and despite a poorish record in the Southern League, the club had decided to give it another go in that competition, which meant extra midweek matches for a number of first-team members.

The Saddlers also broke new ground by entering another reserve side in the newly-formed Central League.

Two new men now in the ranks were Edwin Humphries (from Halesowen) and Billy Stanton (from Hednesford Town) and both were included in the first team for the opening game of the season against Wellington Town.

Over 4,000 fans saw the contest which ended in a 1-1 draw, Walsall fielding these 11 players: Jack Moult (once of Aston Villa and Coventry), Cook, Chance, Richards, Bird, Humphries, Davies, Rogers, Stanton, Nicholls, Price.

The season, on the whole, was a good one in terms of performances and Walsall took fourth place in the Birmingham League, their best win coming late on when Stourbridge were beaten 7-2 at home, Billy Izon netting a fine hat-trick.

In the FA Cup, after 2-1 home victories over both Stoke and Accrington Stanley in the qualifying rounds, the Saddlers succumbed to Aston Villa in the first round proper, being thrashed 6-0 in front of an 18,000 crowd at Villa Park.

The Saddlers didn't do too well in the Southern League either (only 14 wins and 11 defeats from 26 matches) and attendances were appallingly low – only 70 watched the last home game of the season against Pontypridd. Not once did the attendance at Hillary Street top the 600 mark and as a result; the club pulled out of this competition for the 1912-13 campaign, obviously wanting no more episodes similar to the one at Pontypridd on 18 December.

It cost the club £15 to travel down to South Wales and from the 'gate' Walsall received a mere £1 8s 0d – ending up £13 12s 0d out of pocket.

Come that 1912-13 season and at first things looked promising (how often has that been said) but sadly the results deteriorated and the campaign soon developed along disappointing lines and ended as a failure financially as well as in other respects.

Walsall, with new signing Amos Baddeley from Stoke in their attack, did well in their first five matches, winning three and drawing one. Stoke Reserves were trounced 7-0 (Harry Davies scoring four), but the rot set in around October, and coupled with a period of inclement weather which caused attendances to slump, the performances of the team simply fell away, and at the death Walsall had to be content with seventh place in the table. As a consolation, however, they did win the Walsall Senior Cup (beating Willenhall Pickwick in the Final), but lost in the Final of the Staffordshire Cup (to Stoke). Halifax Town knocked the Saddlers out of the FA Cup after a replay.

The 1913-14 season turned out to be rather mediocre as well. Thirteen League games were won and 13 lost, including heavy defeats at Stoke (7-1), Shrewsbury Town (6-0), West Bromwich Albion (6-1) and Worcester City (5-0). It was not until the very last day of the season (25 April) that the Saddlers sparked into top form – beating Wolves 6-1 at home.

The fans were bitterly disappointed

with the team's performances, and they were particularly angry after Worcester City hammered the Saddlers out of the FA Cup, slamming them 7-0 in the first qualifying round. This incidentally is still Walsall's heaviest defeat in this competition.

In mid-November barely 500 supporters bothered to turn up for the home game against Coventry City Reserves and just on 900 watched the next home game, against Brierley Hill Alliance.

During the course of this season Walsall fielded an Egyptian, Alfafi Lebeta, on the left-wing, and they also gave a debuts to former Welsh international George Williams (ex-West Brom) who played only once before being injured, and to young Arthur Campey, a rough and ready Yorkshire-man from Leeds. Arthur started off at right-back; he was then moved into the right-half berth late in the season, and finished up at centre-forward, a position he made his own for the next term.

The 1914-15 campaign, was, of course, overshadowed by war, which broke out a few weeks before the opening matches were due to take place.

The authorities decided, however, that in view of its importance in providing relaxation for the troops in training and for those working long hours on munitions, football should continue as far as possible, and the Birmingham League carried on very much as usual. And for the first and last time in the competition, Walsall carried off a couple of honours by winning the non-reserve championship and the Keys Cup.

Such success was certainly not foreshadowed by the team's early success, but the usual experience of starting off in promising style and then falling away was this time instantly reversed.

Only one point was gained from the first four matches, but then came the turning point when, on 17 October, Wolves Reserves were beaten 3-1 and from then until 23 January, the Saddlers dropped only one point (against Willenhall Swifts). They took third place in the end, piling up 47 points, six behind champions Birmingham Reserves, who they beat 3-1 at home to achieve perhaps their best win of the season, although in the return fixture at St Andrew's, the Blues redressed the balance by winning 6-0.

After six victories in the qualifying rounds of the FA Cup (over Willenhall Pickwick, Cannock, Hednesford, Cradley Heath St Luke's, Stoke and Wrexham), Walsall were finally knocked out by Shrewsbury Town, 2-1, to squash all hopes the Saddlers had of reaching the first round proper.

Arthur Campey had a marvellous season, rattling in 20 Birmingham League goals and another 11 in the FA Cup, including all five in the demolition job on Cradley Heath. Charlie Wootton, Tommy Pointon and David Walker (ex-West Brom) each weighed in with 11.

As football gave way to fighting many of the players went to war, among them most of those who had served the Saddlers in that last peacetime season of 1914-15, including goalkeeper George Rushton, classy defenders Wally Corbett, Joey Wilcox, Ted Bradburn, Tom Richards and Sid Wilkes, and forwards Enos Burnett, Charlie Wootton, Herbert Bates, Arthur Campey, who had been converted from right-back, Wally Freeman, the speedy Tommy Pointon and the Walker brothers William and David.

Thereafter there was very little football played during World War One with Walsall not even fielding a team for the last two of the four seasons.

In 1915-16 they participated in the local Walsall & District League and finished fifth.

Welsh international goalkeeper Teddy Peers guested for the Saddlers during this campaign, as did the Wolves full-back Ted Collins, who scored a hat-trick in one game (v Cannock) after being played at centre-forward.

However, when the Birmingham League programme resumed in 1919-20, the Saddlers fared badly, finishing third from bottom in the Birmingham League with just 28 points out of a possible 68 after losing nine of their remaining ten matches, four at home.

Regulars in the team – and indeed at the club – in the first full season after the hostilities included goalkeeper Jack Merrick, full-backs Corbett and Frank Smith, half-backs Harry Johnson and Eddie Wilkins, centre-forward Jack Radford, inside-left Harry Parsonage (no relation to the former player of the same surname), left-winger Billy Bird and utility star George Benton, who occupied five different positions, including four in the front-line.

Dublin-born Bill Renneville, a Northern Ireland international, was also secured from Aston Villa, having earlier announced his retirement through injury in 1912. In fact, Renneville took the Villa to court over a contract (he lost).

Season 1920-21 brought a welcome upturn in overall performances, and with a total of 42 points, the Saddlers climbed up into fifth place in the now very competitive Birmingham League.

Welshman Albert Groves, a centre-half or right-back, had been recruited from Wolverhampton Wanderers in May 1920, after making over 220 appearances during his 11 years at Molineux, and initially he looked after team affairs as player-manager, although the latter position was only a temporary post. He later stepped aside, allowing secretary Joe Birchell to take charge of running the team so that he could concentrate on playing rather than organising.

Unfortunately a serious knee injury ended Albert's career in 1924, but not before he had created a club record (which lasted a little over ten years, up to 1936, when goalkeeper Harry Wait beat it) in being the oldest player to appear for Walsall's first team up to that time (aged 38 years, 4 months).

In 1920-21 attendances at home games were better than they had been for quite a while with 10,000 or more being topped on four separate occasions.

On 29 January a record crowd for a Birmingham League game, 20,122, saw the Birmingham v Walsall fixture at St Andrew's.

New signing Ernie Edwards, a swashbuckling centre-forward from West Bromwich Albion, who had recovered from a broken leg, scored 21 League goals and was ably assisted up front by the enterprising Tommy Bowyer, who struck home 13.

The year 1920 had seen the formation of the new Third Division, which consisted largely of former members of the Southern League, and in 1921 an additional Northern Section was introduced, of which Walsall became founder-members, and thus regained their Football League status under chairman Mr Alfred Medlam, the licensee of the Spring Cottage Hotel in The Paddock.

Walsall had by now appointed club secretary Joe Burchell as team manager-secretary on a full-time basis, and they kicked off in their first Football League game for 20 years fielding this team for an away game against Lincoln City, which ended in a 1-0 defeat: Merrick, Timmins, Joe Mackenzie, Groves, Len Wall, Christie, Bowyer, Tommy Butler, 'Paddy' Reid, Terry Barber and David Spence.

The return fixture a week later resulted in a 3-0 win, Reid getting two of the goals.

Reid went on to net 24 League and Cup goals that season, finishing up on a high note with a hat-trick in both the home and away games against Accrington Stanley in the space of eight days.

Walsall took eighth place in the final table that season, claiming 32 points at home (15 wins and two draws) with only promoted Stockport County winning at Hillary Street. Sadly, though, it was Walsall's away record which let them down – only seven points gained out of a possible 36.

In the FA Cup, following fine wins over Shrewsbury Town, Chesterfield and Mansfield, Walsall succumbed 4-0 in a muddy replay at First Division Bradford City after holding the Yorkshire club to a 3-3 draw before a record 15,340 crowd at Hillary Street.

Indeed, the Saddlers, who fought back magnificently to lead 3-2 after going in 2-0 down at half-time, might have gone through. Only a slip by full-back Albert Jackson in the last few minutes ruined their hopes.

Walsall in 1922-23 when they won the Walsall Senior Cup and lost in the Staffordshire Cup Final.

Walsall 3 Bradford City 3
FA Cup First Round, 7 January 1922

WALSALL had already battled through three qualifying rounds of the FA Cup, beating Shrewsbury Town, Chesterfield and Mansfield Town, to earn this 'plum' tie against Bradford City, who were then in Division One and had won the FA Cup as recently as 1911. This was Walsall's first season in the new Division Three North and the fact that they were unbeaten at home up to then added extra interest to the game.

There was a record attendance at Hillary Street with 15,340 packed inside and in an entertaining first half the visitors moved into a two-goal lead – one of the goals looking yards offside. The Saddlers refused to let their heads drop, however, and by half-time they were level. Tommy Butler reduced the arrears with an opportunist effort and then Albert Groves calmy slotted home a penalty to equalise.

Early in the second half Walsall's winger Spence raced away from what again looked an offside position and crossed superbly for 'Paddy' Reid to head home. Pandemonium broke out and when the game resumed the kicking was rather wild on both sides. In one incident City's Tommy Robb was caught retaliating and ordered off and Walsall's hopes of going through were high at that point. City stuck to their task, however, and a moment's hesitation by Walsall right-back Jackson gave their ace striker Bill Hibbert the chance to bang home a tremendous shot that gave Merrick no chance.

The game ended 3-3 and in a mudbath at Valley Parade Walsall lost the replay 4-0 the following Wednesday.

Walsall: Merrick; Jackson, Timmins, Wilson, Groves, Christie, Bowyer, Bowen, Reid, Butler, Spence.
Bradford City: Wilkinson; Cheetham, Watson, Robb, Pratt, Duckett, Bond, Logan, Hibbert, Howson, Rigby.

The 1921-22 season was the first time the Saddlers had reached the first round proper of the FA Cup in 20 years and on the local scene, Walsall retained the Wednesbury Charity Cup and reached the Final of the Staffordshire Cup for the second successive season before being beaten by Wolves Reserves.

In contrast to that excellent FA Cup run of 1921-22, a little under 10,000 fans saw Walsall knocked out at home by Wigan Borough in 1922-23 – a season when, after a poorish start, they rallied to take third place in the League table after having been in with a great chance of winning promotion around Easter... all this after a rather disappointing start when only one win was recorded in the first ten matches, which included a 6-0 hiding at Chesterfield, and notwithstanding that two of the club's best players were transferred halfway through the campaign: David Spence to Oldham Athletic for £400 and 'Paddy' Reid to Cardiff City for £1,500.

A draw at Crewe on Good Friday was followed by successive defeats at Southport and at home to Accrington, which left Walsall, at the end, five points behind promoted Nelson and one adrift of Bradford (Park Avenue).

Teddy Groves took over from Reid in attack and ended the season as leading scorer with 13 goals.

Thus Walsall had bounced back well and had clearly launched themselves back on the road of League football with some significance after such a long exile in the soccer wilderness.

After just missing out on promotion, the players were full of confidence as the 1923-24 campaign got under way and they started well by beating Rotherham County 2-0 at home in front of an 11,000 crowd. But then results became inconsistent, and consequently the home attendances began to drop.

On 3 November 1923, the die-hard Walsall supporters witnessed one of the most controversial incidents ever to have occurred at Hillary Street.

It happened in the game with Chesterfield. Close to half-time a scramble near the Walsall goal ended with Harry Wait gathering the ball and clearing downfield. To everyone's amazement the referee awarded a goal, although Harry maintained until his dying day that the ball never crossed the line. Both Harry and a section of the 4,336 crowd expressed heated opinions to the referee as he left the field at the interval and as a result Harry was suspended and the Hillary Street ground was closed for a fortnight.

And to make matters worse, Chesterfield won the game 1-0.

With the ground closed, Walsall had to play their 'home' FA Cup-tie against Aberdare in Wales where they crashed out of the competition, beaten by a debatable 88th-minute penalty.

The 1923-24 season did, however, have its moments. Wolves, also based in Division Three North, were carrying all before them, but Walsall went to Molineux and forced a goalless draw shortly before Christmas, and in the return fixture on an unforgettable April evening, they beat the Wanderers 2-1 at Hillary Street in front of a then record crowd for a League game on the ground. It is said that there were 14,000 present, as the gates at the popular end were forced open, although the official figure was recorded as 12,281.

Walsall 2 Wolverhampton Wanderers 1
Division Three North, 7 April 1924

THIS was the first season that neighbours Wolves had ever played in the Third Division and they had made the running for most of the time while Walsall languished in mid-table, although the Saddlers had enjoyed a moment of glory in December when they became the first team to avoid defeat at Molineux that season, forcing a goalless draw.

Before the game started unprecedented scenes had occurred outside Hillary Street with thousands of fans milling about well over an hour before the kick-off. Motor vehicles (then in their relatively early years) arrived from all directions, trams deposited jam-packed loads and many made their way on foot to join the throngs.

Twenty minutes before kick-off some wooden fencing in Hillary Street gave way and hundreds of fans surged in before police formed a human barrier to keep them out.

While the official attendance was given as 12,281, hundreds more saw the game without paying, and the total number present was probably not too far short of the ground record of 15,340, set for the Bradford Cup-tie 15 months earlier. At any event it was certainly far and away the biggest ever attendance for a Walsall home League game at that time.

Wolves were without four regulars - Watson, Getgood, Kay and Harrington - after a bruising game at Barrow the previous Saturday, and the lively ball didn't help either side nor did the considerable gusts of wind, which took players unexpectedly when seeking possession. The visitors, however, caused Walsall goalkeeper Harry Wait one or two anxious moments as they attacked the Laundry End goal in the opening minutes, but then the Saddlers broke well for Teddy Groves to send Lewis Bedford away down the wing and he eluded Baugh to put the ball into the path of Archer, who whipped it smartly past Noel George to put the Saddlers one up.

Then the over-worked Wait dealt well with fierce long shots from Fazackerley and Baugh but Walsall hung on and were still ahead at half-time.

Ten minutes into the second half, the industrious Archer crossed inch-perfect for Harper to make a lunge which landed both himself and the ball in the net to give the Saddlers a 2-0 lead.

Four minutes later Wolves got a goal back in rather bizarre circumstances with Edwards taking advantage of Webster's slip as he went for the ball to send in a cross-shot that Wait seemed to have covered until it bobbled on the bumpy ground and went in off a post. Walsall were under some pressure after that, but they managed to hold on for a memorable victory. Wolves generously allowed the Saddlers to keep their 20 per cent share of the gate and went on to gain promotion at the end of the season.

Walsall: Wait; Webster, Marshall, Walton, Binks, Leedham, Birch, Harper, E.Groves, Archer, Bedford.
Wolves: George; Baugh, Shaw, Crew, Caddick, Bradford, McMillan, Fazackerley, Phillipson, Marson, Edwards.

Walsall's link with Wolves was strengthened by the transfer of two leading players, defender Ben Timmins and winger Tommy Bowen, to Molineux for a combined fee of £1,300, while Eddie Cameron moved to Nelson. The money received from these deals reduced Walsall's loss on the season to £57. There was a dramatic drop of £1,794 in gate receipts compared with the previous season.

The team ended 1923-24 in 17th position, scoring only 44 goals, of which 11 went to hot-shot Teddy Groves, Archer netted eight and Bowen seven.

Albert Groves, no relation to Teddy, played his last game for the Saddlers that season. He was forced to retire following a crippling knee injury and was well into his 38th year when he kicked a ball for the last time for the Saddlers in the match against Southport on 16 February.

In 1924-25 one more point was picked up but Walsall slipped a further two places down the table, and as always players were continually either arriving or leaving the club.

On the credit side, former England international Sid Bowser was secured from West Bromwich Albion, Jack Pendleton, formerly of Aston Villa, arrived from Wigan Borough, while full-back George Smith (a former Chelsea reserve) was bought from Gillingham, ex-Bolton star Tommy Hill came down from Bradford City, and Jack Sibbald arrived from Southport.

Fred Burrill, who had been a member of Wolves' 1921 FA Cup Final side, was obtained from Charlton Athletic, Albert Duggins from Preston, Archie Tetlow from Nottingham Forest and Fred Walters from Shrewsbury Town.

Burrill top-scored in 1924-25 with 14 League goals, but the season had few bright spots.

Only three times did the attendance figure at Hillary Street pass the 7,000 mark in League games, yet close on 9,800 saw the FA Cup-tie against Coventry City, when Walsall lost 2-1 to their Second Division opponents.

Some £808 was lost on the season and the offer from a local man, Bob Parsons, to promote an open-air boxing tournament at the Walsall ground at Whitsuntide to help the club's finances, was gratefully accepted.

In consequence of a loss of around £800 on the preceding season, a more economical policy was decided upon for the 1925-26 campaign and accordingly the team was drastically changed to begin with. Of the old players, only Harry Wait, Teddy Groves (who had now switched to full-back), George Smith and Lewis Bedford were retained, and only three newcomers, with experience of senior football were engaged, these being Sid Gibbins and Jack Pitt (both from Wolves) and Bill Thatcher, who returned to the club via Hednesford Town and Wrexham.

The side was completed mainly with local players and it soon became apparent that the experiment was anything but a success.

It was not long before Fred Binks was signed again, and the transfer was obtained from Accrington Stanley of centre-forward Harry Crockford who had served with Chesterfield, Port Vale and Exeter City.

Later in the season there was another important development in the engagement of David Ashworth as the club's first full-time manager, Joe Burchell having up to then combined his duties of that position with those of secretary. Ashworth possessed a wide knowledge of the game and it was thought that he was the man to get the team ticking again.

His appointment was followed shortly afterwards by the acquisition of utility forward Bert White, who had seen service with Fulham, Blackpool and Arsenal, and Jimmy Torrance, a centre-half from Fulham, as well as Alex Mutch of Aberdeen, Accrington Stanley and Lincoln City fame.

Before these changes were made, however, so much ground had been lost that, although they effected such an improvement that near the end of the season ten points were gained from eight matches, Walsall eventually finished next to the bottom of the Northern Section, and consequently, for the first time, had to seek re-election. Of their 21 home games, only nine were won, whilst just one away victory was recorded (at Wrexham). Walsall's defence conceded 107 League goals – which created a new record for the Third Division North, the previous highest being 88, scored against Rotherham United the previous season. But that massive total was partly accounted for by the change in the offside rule which came into operation for the first time. Walsall used a record 31 players in 1925-26, with only goalkeeper Harry Wait and full-back George Smith appearing in every match. Harry Crockford top-scored with 17 goals while Harry Alcock netted ten.

Almost inevitably, of course, it followed, too, that the season was a failure financially, especially as Walsall were knocked out of the FA Cup in the first round, beaten 1-0 by Grimsby Town at Hillary Street in front of 4,982 fans.

The highest League attendance of the campaign was 5,608 (v Wigan Borough in March) and the lowest was just 1,047 for the January midweek fixture against Halifax. The position in this respect was eased slightly, however, by the receipts from a match for the benefit of the club arranged by Billy Walker, the Aston Villa forward, later manager of Sheffield Wednesday and Nottingham Forest, which attracted a crowd of 7,205.

In season 1926-27 Walsall did a certain amount of experimenting with the centre-forward position, using nine different players to lead the attack, with Bert White claiming the position in nearly half of the League games.

Having succeeded in the application for re-election, several new faces were introduced to the team, among them Bill Bradford (from Brighton), Ted Parry, a former Welsh international full-back, and Archie Rawlings from Liverpool, Harry Beck (Burton), Jack Walker (Stoke), centre-forwards George Pumford and Jimmy Bancroft from Derby and Rugby respectively, George Robson (New Delaval) and Bobby Scholes, an outside-left from Oldham who had previously assisted Glossop. With Harry Wait, Teddy Groves, Jimmy Torrance (who was soon to be appointed player-manager, in February 1927), Bert White, Fred Binks, Fred Walters, Tommy Holt and Lewis Bedford retained on the staff, it seemed as though Walsall had the makings of a useful side, perhaps the strongest the club had put out in the Third Division. Unfortunately those high expectations soon took a nose-dive.

After a 2-2 draw in the opening game at Doncaster, Walsall then disappointed a 9,670 crowd by losing to Stoke City in the first home match, and soon afterwards suffered two further defeats. Strangely enough, for a time the team fared almost as well on opponents' grounds, where in nine contests, two wins were recorded with five draws while from ten homes fixtures, only ten points were forthcoming. Walsall were never in danger of finishing in the bottom two places, but neither were they ever serious challengers for a spot in the leading group. In the second half of the season attendances slumped alarmingly and only one of over 4,000 was seen with several others hovering below the 2,000 mark. Consequently, it was not surprising that when offers for certain players came in, they were duly accepted, and Rawlings left for Bradford (February 1927), while White and Bedford moved on to Nelson the following month.

Walsall finished in 14th place, but they did break two club scoring records – netting 68 goals in all, and 33 in away games, these being the highest totals obtained whilst playing in the Third Division.

Wait, for the third season running, starred in every game and he took his tally to 131 consecutive League and FA Cup appearances for the club. White was top marksman with 24 goals, Walters netted 11.

There was a black moment, however, when the famous amateur club, Corinthians, dumped Walsall out of the FA Cup, winning a third-round tie 4-0 at Hillary Street watched by a record crowd of 16,607.

Walsall 0 Corinthians 4
FA Cup Round Three, 8 January 1927

IF CERTAIN games rival each other as the most famous Walsall victories, this one surely ranks as the most famous defeat.

At the time of this Cup-tie the Saddlers were in mid-table in Division Three North and had reached this stage of the competition by beating Bradford (Park Avenue) and Mansfield Town at home.

Walsall played some excellent football in the first half, twice hitting the woodwork as Bedford ran the amateurs a merry dance down the left wing despite the presence there of A. G. Bower, who had won three full England caps. Before half-time, however, the visitors went ahead with a rather fortunate goal, Walsall 'keeper Harry Wait slipping as he went for a simple shot from Norman Creek and the ball bouncing over him into the net.

This seemed to take the steam out of the Saddlers who came under heavy pressure for the remainder of the half. Corinthians came out for the second period looking far more relaxed and played some quite splendid flowing football. Soon Hegan and Hartley were combining to set-up Claude Ashton who netted off a post. On 68 minutes it was clear that Walsall were not going to get back into the game and fans and players seemed to stand equally bemused as first Hegan raced through from the left wing and hammered the ball into the roof of the net as Wait came off his line, and then Ashton went clean through the centre of the Saddlers defence and slipped the ball almost casually past Wait as he came out again in vain.

For pace and skill Walsall's fans had rarely seen anything like that display by the amateurs in the second half. Corinthains went on to lose 3-1 at home to Newcastle United in round four.

Walsall: Wait, Groves, Parry, Holt, Torrance, Beck, Rawlings, Sarvis, White, Walters, Bedford.

Corinthians: B. Baker; A. G. Bower, A. E. Knight; J. R. Moulsdale, A. H. Chadder, F. H. Ewer; R. J. Jenkins, F. N. S. Creek, C. T. Ashton, F. Hartley, K. E. Hegan.

After five seasons in Division Three North, Walsall found themselves on the move in the summer of 1927. They were asked to try their luck in the Third Division South since the two teams relegated from the Second Division at the end of the previous campaign were Bradford City and Darlington, and consequently Walsall's geographical location made them obvious candidates for a move.

But before the action could begin, new player-manager Jimmy Torrance made what transpired to be some exceptionally good signings when he snapped up former Birmingham and Derby County striker Moses Lane from Worcester City, who incidentally had been with the club for a short time in 1920-21, and two full-backs, Adam Plunkett from Bury and David Fairhurst from New Delavel. He also added to his staff Bill Caesar, the amateur international centre-half from Dulwich Hamlet, half-back Harry Staley who had played three seasons with Birmingham, Henry Hughes from Torquay United, George Springell from Reading and Bill Davies from Merthyr Town.

During the course of the season two young forwards were also recruited, these being David Walker, a member of the well-known footballing family, and Billy Lake, the son of club director, Harry Lake, and right on the transfer deadline, when the team was again faced with the possibility of having to seek re-election, the experienced figure of centre-half Alec McClure, once of Aston Villa, Birmingham and Stoke, was signed from Coventry City. Alec had earlier played almost 200 games for the Blues, helping them win the Second Division title in 1921. He later returned to St Andrew's as assistant manager (1928-32).

The 1927-28 League programme began disappointingly when the Saddlers crashed 5-2 away to Bristol Rovers, but two successive home wins – 2-0 v Watford and 2-1 over Plymouth, a game which attracted over 13,000 fans – boosted morale, only for a decline in fortunes to set in almost immediately. Indeed, before the turn of the year, the Saddlers had nose-dived to the bottom end of the table after a dismal run which saw them lose 11 League matches out of 17, including heavy reverses at Northampton Town (10-0 on Guy Fawkes' Day), Millwall (7-1) and Swindon Town (5-0). Exit from the FA Cup was suffered against Bristol Rovers at Eastville and crowds at homes matches dropped alarmingly – only 3,180 turned up when Bournemouth were the visitors in November and when Torquay came to the Midlands in December the figure was even worse – 2,832.

Happily, though, things improved slightly in the New Year – especially after winger Lewis Bedford had returned to the club from Nelson. Coventry City were slammed 7-0 in mid-February – but in the end Walsall had to be content with 18th place, just clear of the re-election zone, after amassing a mere 33 points from their 42 games, registering 12 victories and conceding for the first time ever over 100 League goals. Moses Lane top-scored with 35 League goals – and on many occasions Walsall were mighty thankful he was in the side. He was pipped at the post by Morris of Swindon Town for the distinction of being leading scorer in the Southern Section that season.

An important change for season 1928-29, Walsall's second in the Southern Section of the Third Division, was the appointment in May of Jimmy Kerr (formerly of Coventry City) as manager, in succession to Jimmy Torrance, and the signing of Mick O'Brien, the talented Irish international, who had been with several English clubs and had also had a brief spell in America. Other players were also recruited, including classy left-half Duggie Lochhead from St Johnstone, full-back Charlie Houldey and wing-half Bill Hunter both from Coventry City, the Torquay United duo of full-back Frank Wragg and winger David Thompson, Roy John, a hard-tackling full-back from South Wales who was later to represent his country as a goalkeeper, left-half Bill Narrowmore from Reading, forwards Norman

Walsall in 1928-29, the season in which they finished third in Division Three South.

Thompson and Arthur Gough from Brighton, Hugh Moffatt, an outside-right from Oldham Athletic and formerly of Everton, Luton Town and Arsenal, and two left-wingers, 'Cockney' Billy Bell from Millwall and Vic Murphy from Bournemouth.

On the retained list from the previous season were Harry Wait, David Fairhurst, Teddy Groves, Bill Bradford, George Robson, Moses Lane, David Walker, Fred Walters and Billy Lake, and during the course of 1928-29 Eric Hague and Jack Johnson arrived from West Ham United as well as former Army sergeant Duggie Attwood.

Eventually, after a certain amount of experimenting, manager Kerr finally agreed on his line-up, which read (when all players were fit and available): Wait, Houldey, Fairhurst, Lochhead, O'Brien, Groves, Hunter, Moffatt, N. Thompson, Lane and Attwood, with Robson, Bradford, Arthur Gough and Murphy the other regular squad members.

After a disappointing start, Walsall's form suddenly picked up and as the season progressed their performances at home were almost good enough to win promotion (11 wins and seven draws from 21 starts), but in the end the team had to be content with 14th place, an improvement of four places on the previous season.

In the final League game of the programme Charlton Athletic came to Hillary Street requiring both points to make certain of promotion – and they got them with a 2-0 victory in front of a 6,000 crowd, half of them from London.

Walsall 7 Exeter City 2
League Division Three (South),
1 December 1928

WHEN the Grecians visited Fellows Park on this cold winter's afternoon they were lying perilously close to the relegation zone while the Saddlers were occupying tenth position.

The Saddlers got off to a fine start, going ahead after only six minutes when Bill Bradford fired home after some smart work by Arthur Gough.

After a few close shaves at either end Exeter equalised on 35 minutes when Arthur Doncaster punished a mistake by the Saddlers' scorer Bradford to net from ten yards.

Seconds before half-time George Purcell crossed for Harry Houghton to head the visitors into the lead.

With a minute of the resumption, however, it was all-square again when Norman Thompson chased a long ball and collided with the Exeter goalkeeper Tom Holland. With both players on the ground, Thompson reacted quickest to force the ball into the unguarded net ahead of the onrushing Bradford.

Unfortunately Holland had to leave the field allowing future Wolves skipper Wilf Lowton to takeover in goal.

From that moment on it was all Walsall and in the 48th minute Doug Attwood scored following a left-wing corner. Then Lowton, after failing to reach Hugh Moffatt's cross, could only look on in anguish as the limping Teddy Groves tapped in number four.

And in the 52nd minute it was 5-2 when Thompson took Mick O'Brien's pass in his stride to fire in off an upright.

Lowton saved well from both Thompson and Groves but with time running out Thompson got on the end of another pin-point cross from Gough to complete his hat-trick on 77 minutes and cracked home Walsall's seventh goal two minutes later.

Walsall: Wait; Houldey, Hunter, Groves, O'Brien, Lochhead, Moffatt, Thompson, Attwood, Bradford, Gough.

Exeter City: Holland; Lowton,

Miller, Clarke, Pool, Dennington, Purcell, McDevitt, Doncaster, Houghton, Death.

In the FA Cup competition Walsall reached round three after knocking over Worcester City (3-1) and Sittingbourne (2-1). But after holding Middlesbrough to a 1-1 draw at Hillary Street when the attendance was almost 15,000, the replay was rather one-sided as 'Boro stormed through 5-1 at Ayresome Park.

Goalkeeper Harry Wait was forced to miss the replay because of a boil on his leg and thus ended a run of exactly 200 consecutive appearances in the first team in League and FA Cup (207 in all competitive matches).

Without a reserve 'keeper available, his place was taken by full-back Charlie Houldey, who in the cicumstances could hardly be blamed for conceding five goals.

Many more changes took effect before the 1929-30 season got under way, following the appointment of a new manager in the April, Sid Scholey, who was promoted from the rank of trainer to succeed Jimmy Kerr who had left for Norwich City where he was eventually joined by three classy players – O'Brien, Lochhead and Norman Thompson.

Other departures saw Moffatt go to QPR, Gough to Merthyr Town, Walker to Brighton, and Lane and Smith to Birmingham League clubs. Into the club came goalkeeper Fred Biddlestone (from Bloxwich Strollers), Sid Helliwell and Irish international Tommy Muldoon (both from Spurs) who were formerly with Reading and Aston Villa respectively, Johnny Eyres from Stoke City, Albert Walters and Tommy Roe from Luton, Billy Lanyon from Portsmouth and speed merchant Jackie Barnes from Coventry City.

The season, on the whole, turned out to be a disappointing one, certainly in the League, although the Saddlers put up a battling display in an epic FA Cup-tie against Aston Villa.

Although the Saddlers were drawn at home in this fourth-round tie, the Walsall directors had little choice but to change the venue to Villa Park. A massive 74,626 crowd turned up, which was over 1,000 more than the previous ground record. There were some 5,000 unfortunate supporters, many of them from Walsall, locked outside, and gate receipts totalled £4,867, Walsall's share being a healthy £1,959. Walsall's home ground could have housed only around 20,000 for this same fixture.

After knocking out Exeter City 1-0 (thanks to a late effort from Tommy Roe), Newport County 3-2 in Wales (the highlight being a cracking hat-trick from Walters) and Swansea Town 2-0 at home, the Saddlers travelled to Birmingham full of confidence for that epic showdown against the might of Aston Villa.

It was a real 'David v Goliath' confrontation. The Saddlers fought every inch of the way and although beaten 3-1, they were certainly not disgraced.

They were unfortunate to be without Jack Barnes and went a goal down after only four minutes when England's Billy Walker scored. The same player made it 2-0 after Albert Walters had been unlucky not to have equalised when his shot struck a post.

Johnston reduced the arrears shortly before half-time, but another international forward, George Brown, made it 3-1 ten minutes from time to send the Villains through. Biddlestone played a blinder in goal for Walsall that day and shortly after this tie he was transferred to Villa Park. He later became a regular in the first team, going on to amass more than 150 appearances and helping the Villa win the Second Division championship in 1937-38.

Referring back to the League action, after 25 matches had been completed, Walsall had collected only 23 points from nine wins and five draws. The best performances at home included victories of 4-0 over QPR and Swindon Town, 6-0 over Methyr Town, 7-0 versus Torquay United (when Fyres grabbed a superb hat-trick) and 5-2 v Exeter City, but in the end the team had to settle for 17th place with 34 points, only four clear of relegation.

Albert Walters top-scored with 25 League goals (29 in all); Eyres netted 17 and along with Bradford played in every match.

Defender Roy John was tried out in goal for the first time on 1 March 1930, as Biddlestone's replacement against Watford at home. He was a revelation and went on to win 14 caps for Wales in that position after being transferred to Stoke and then to Arsenal.

During the summer of 1930, Walsall's home ground – Hillary Street – was renamed Fellows Park. And the outstanding feature of Walsall's performances there in 1930-31 was their FA Cup replay against Blackburn Rovers when a record 18,819 crowd packed in, this comfortably beating the previous highest of 16,607 for the visit of the Corinthians four years earlier. Unfortunately Rovers won that contest, but more about that later.

In the League, the Saddlers again finished 17th, gaining 37 points out of a possible 84, nine clear of relegated Newport County, but 22 fewer than the runaway champions Notts County who walloped Walsall 6-1 at Meadow Lane.

Several changes to the playing staff had been made, with old boys Tommy Roe and Teddy Groves moving to Coventry City and Shrewsbury Town respectively, and Len Capewell to Wellington Town. On the credit side, Walsall signed Tommy Gretton from Queen's Park Rangers, full-backs Bernard Bradford (a six-footer from Hull City) and Joe Wilson (from Gillingham), half-backs Tommy Godfrey (Stoke) and West Bromwich-born Jack Gardner (Norwich City, who previously assisted Coventry) and forwards Jimmy Parle (ex-Birmingham and Chesterfield), Joe Bartley and Howard King (ex-Wolves), Jim Cooper (Birmingham) and Gilbert Shaw (a centre-forward from Bristol Rovers who had earlier been with Grimsby Town). Later, ace marksman Billy Mays arrived from Burnley and he claimed nine goals in his first seven outings for the club, including a treble in a 5-2 win at Exeter.

Cooper also scored a hat-trick – on his debut v Clapton Orient – and he smashed in another treble in a 7-0 win over Norwich City, but he was soon struck down by injury and was unable to maintain his form, hence the arrival of striker Mays.

The team also hit a bad patch around mid-season and suffered eight successive defeats, including a 4-0 home reverse against Torquay United and a 6-3

Walsall fans packed in the Witton End of Villa Park for the fourth-round FA Cup tie between the two West Midlands rivals in January 1930 when a record 74,626 saw Villa win 3-1.

hammering at Crystal Palace when the turnout was 16,000.

With all this going on, yet another new face appeared in the manager's office, Peter O'Rourke from Bradford taking the position in October 1930 following the surprise resignation of Sid Scholey.

By coincidence, the results took a turn for the better when O'Rourke joined the club, and eight League games and three Cup-ties passed without defeat, Thames being crushed 6-0 (revenge for a 4-1 defeat suffered earlier in the season) and Clapton Orient 5-2 in League action.

As mentioned earlier, Blackburn eventually sent Walsall tumbling out of the FA Cup, but not until the Saddlers had once more put on a sterling performance against First Division opposition.

On a treacherous surface and watched by a near-19,000 crowd at Ewood Park, Walsall forced a 1-1 draw, equalising through Eyres after Rovers had taken the lead only two minutes into the game through Bruton.

The replay attracted a record crowd, and after a rapid thaw, the pitch resembled a quagmire. This sort of surface suited Rovers down to a tee, their hefty defenders and strong running forwards relishing the conditions.

They won the replay convincingly by 3-0 – but Walsall made them fight every inch of the way.

It was after this game that Roy John began to attract the attention of several leading clubs and he was duly capped by Wales against Ireland at Wrexham after a string of superb performances between the posts.

In May 1931 the crowd's favourite, Johnny Eyres, left the club for Brighton (soon after playing a blinder at the Goldstone Ground in a League game) but a more profitable transaction was made with Everton for Jackie Archer, a young left-half from Wednesbury who appeared in 25 games in 1930-31 including 22 of the last 23 but who was eventually sold to the Merseysiders for £750. And on top of that sum, over £800 was banked from the two Cup-ties with Blackburn Rovers.

In August 1931, after the club had announced a loss in excess of £4,000 and had been switched from the Southern Section into the Northern Section of the Third Division to accommodate Reading and Cardiff City, Walsall boss Paddy O'Rourke signed a player who was to become one of the greatest goalscorers ever to pull on the club's colours.

His name was Gilbert Alsop who was secured from Coventry City. He cracked in a terrific goal on his debut (v Doncaster Rovers on 17 October 1931) and he got another against Crewe a fortnight later. He continued to hit the back of the net for many years to come, and when he finally called it a day, after his second spell at Fellows Park came to an end in May 1947, he had amassed a terrific record with Walsall: 169 goals in a total of 222 senior appearances, plus a few more during wartime..

Gilbert was top-scorer in 1931-32 with 16 goals in 29 League and Cup games. Turner also netted 15, while one opposing player – Tommy Jays of Chester – netted all his side's goals in their emphatic 5-1 win over the Saddlers in January.

Around the same time as Alsop was recruited, Walsall also obtained the services of Chris Ball (from Bristol City) and Johnny Reed (from Wolves), and surprisingly, a total of 25 players were utilised by the club during the course of the 1931-32 campaign, when Walsall took 16th spot, well clear of both the promotion and re-election places.

It was, however, a bad season generally, with only 35 points coming from 40 games. Only four away victories were recorded and in all some 20 players left Fellows Park during the course of the campaign, among them: Barnes (to Watford), Mays (Halifax), Joe Partridge (Swindon Town), Cooper (Torquay), Murphy (Notts County), Parle (New Brighton), Albert Walters (Shrewsbury Town) Roy John (Stoke City) and Houldey (back to Coventry).

Signed on were Ben Olney, an international goalkeeper once of Aston Villa and Derby County, who had arrived at Fellows Park in April 1932, Archie Hunter (Bradford Park Avenue), Scotsman Billy Watson (Bradford City, who had earlier been with Airdrie), Charlie Henry and ex-West Brom man Billy Bushell (both from Leicester City), experienced centre-forward Tom Phillipson (Sheffield United, ex-Wolves), Billy Rotton (also ex-Wolves and also West Brom), Jimmy Pointon (Torquay), Jack Scott (from Norwich City, who had earlier played Rugby League for Featherstone Rovers), Tommy Cooper (Burton Town), Dennis Prentice (Plymouth Argyle) and Jack Vaughan (Shrewsbury Town).

After a poor first half to the season, attendances dropped to just under the 3,000 mark (2,840 watched the game with the club's Cup conquerors Darlington in mid-February) and although Walsall did everything possible to stop the rot, they simply couldn't find the right blend.

Even after a plucky display at The Feethams, a 73rd minute goal sealed Walsall's fate in the FA Cup-tie against Darlington.

But with Bill Slade now in charge of the team – he took over as manager from O'Rourke in February 1932 – the 1932-33 season was to be a real humdinger in terms of success for the Saddlers, although in all fairness there was certainly little in the prospects to indicate that such triumphs were in store after what had gone in the immediate past few years.

Indeed, as the new League programme started there wasn't much for the diehard supporters to gloat over.

On the previous season there had been a loss of £2,267, notwithstanding that 'rigid economies' had been exercised, and the directors in their annual report had stated: 'If the attendances do not show a very substantial increase during the season it will be impossible to carry on the club.'

The financial problem, of course, complicated the problem of building up a team, of which unfortunately only the nucleus was left.

Added to the squad, which, of course, still comprised Alsop, Ball, Reed and Turner, were the duo of Joey Cunningham and Billy Coward from QPR, Sid Bird from Fulham, Alf Langford and George Leslie from Charlton Athletic, Nottingham-born full-back Jack Bennett from Blackburn Rovers (who earlier served with Birmingham), Harry Salt from Brentford, Freddie Lee from Coventry City, Sam Taylor from Wrexham and Archie Chappell from Guildford.

After a certain amount of experimenting, the side finally settled down and eventually it selected itself after Bill Shepherd had been signed from Coventry to team up once more with Alsop and Lee.

Walsall's League form was in and out although only one defeat was suffered at home (3-2 v Wrexham).

It was in the FA Cup where it all happened – and what a great tournament Walsall had in 1932-33.

In the opening round Mansfield Town were bowled out 4-1 in front of a near 10,000 crowd at Fellows Park; Hartlepools United were then defeated 2-1 at the next hurdle when Ball headed the winner with time fast running out at the end of a scrappy game ruined by a gale-force wind; and in round three the draw paired Walsall with the mighty Gunners, Arsenal, the tie to be played at Fellows Park.

Arsenal, perhaps the greatest club side in the world at that time, had won the trophy in 1930, been runners-up at Wembley in 1932, and they had also lifted the First Division championship in between times as well as taking second spot the previous year.

When they were due to play at Fellows Park they were in line to carry off the Double. But Walsall soon put a stop to that.

But the first thing Walsall had to decide when the draw was known was where should the tie be played. Apart from the question whether their ground would hold all who wanted to attend the game, there was the obvious temptation to transfer it to Highbury and make sure of a substantial cheque from a bumper 60,000 crowd.

In the end it was decided to stay at home and the game was made all-ticket with a limit of 22,000.

It was anticipated that everyone in Walsall would want to see the game, but surprisingly only 11,149 tickets were sold, with receipts totalling a record £1,487 13s 6d which held firm until £1,586 was banked from the visit of Liverpool in the FA Cup in January 1947.

But any disappointment there might have been from the financial point of view was, of course, amply compensated for by the final result – Walsall 2 Arsenal 0 – a scoreline which stunned the nation, never mind the Arsenal players and their supporters.

One newspaper became almost lyrical about the differences between the teams: 'Arsenal, the Rich, the Confident, the League leaders, the £30,000 aristocrats, against little Midland Third Division team that cost £69 all-in. Arsenal train on ozone, brine-baths, champagne, golf and electrical massage in an atmosphere of prima donna preciousness. They own £87 worth of football boots. Walsall men eat fish and chips and drink beer, and the entire running expenses of the club this season have been £75.'

When England left-back Eddie Hapgood was ruled out by injury, Arsenal boss, the great Herbert Chapman, was not at all worried. He was more concerned when 'flu struck the club and claimed left-half Bob John, a Welsh international, and two of his main goalscorers, Jack Lambert and Tim Coleman. At least one of the 'flu victims could have played, with a push, but Chapman decided not to rush anyone back into action. Nor did he recall England winger Joe Hulme, who had been dropped because of loss of form, and whose experience would have been invaluable.

After all, Chapman reasoned Arsenal had the assurance of a First Division club and even with reserves the quality of their game should see them through.

So he confidently promoted four relatively 'unknowns' with only one - Norman Sidley – having played in the senior side before. But the other seven members of the team were all internationals, including the elegant David Jack, the first player ever to cost over £10,000 on the transfer market and the scorer of the first-ever goal at Wembley (in the 1923 FA Cup Final for Bolton); Scottish-born inside-forward Alex James, he of the long baggy shorts; left-winger Cliff Bastin, known as the 'ice cool executioner of goals' who in fact had won all the game's honours by the time he was 21; goalkeeper Frank Moss; England full-back George Male and 'stopper' centre-half Herbie 'The Policeman' Roberts, who turned out to be one of the finest pivots of his era.

Walsall 2 Arsenal 0

FA Cup Round Three, 14 January 1933

WALSALL began the match with a 'rush' – as was expected – but when their enthusiasm waned they refused to allow Arsenal to settle down and dictate the play. Some of the tackling was very stern and on two occasions an Arsenal player ended up over the wall surrounding the pitch.

Action from the most famous game in Walsall's history, the FA Cup tie against Arsenal at Fellows Park in January 1933, when goals from Gilbert Alsop and Bill Sheppard gave the Saddlers a sensational 2-0 victory over the mighty Gunners. Walsall are wearing the striped shirts.

Walsall's players went to meet the ball, whereas the Gunners' waited for it.

Walsall's full-backs Bennett and Bird and big centre-half Leslie were magnificent as Arsenal strove forward in search of the opening goal.

Walsall's confidence increased and when the half-time whistle sounded, the Londoners had managed only one shot at the Saddlers goal.

After the break, and attacking the Hillary Street end, Walsall continued to run the show, and on the hour Gilbert Alsop's brave header from Lee's floated corner-kick broke the deadlock, sending the Saddlers fans wild, with hundreds of hats and programmes flying into the air.

Arsenal supremo, Herbert Chapman, immediately went to the touchline to order a reshuffle, telling Jack to lead the attack.

Yet five minutes after the first goal, Walsall grabbed a second, and again Alsop was deeply involved. The bustling centre-forward darted into the Arsenal area following a long punt downfield by Leslie. The ball ended up in the hands of goalkeeper Marks but unfortunately for the visitors, their young full-back, Tommy Black, aimed a reckless kick at Alsop, who fell to the ground. Chris Ball charged at Black and there was a general free-for-all before calm was restored, and able referee Mr Arthur Taylor from Wigan pointed to the spot, awarding Walsall a penalty. Bill Sheppard duly stepped up to smash the ball into the net, past a groping Frank Moss, thus scoring his first goal in Walsall's colours.

This certainly put the skids under Arsenal, who never recovered from the double body blow, although Cunningham in the Walsall goal saved well from both Bastin and Black, who was eager to make amends for his misdemeanour at the other end of the field.

So, one of the biggest shocks in football had been recorded.

Walsall: Cunningham; Bennett, Bird, Reed, Leslie, Salt, Coward, Ball, Alsop, Sheppard, Lee.

Arsenal: Moss; Male, Black, Hill, Roberts, Sidley, Warnes, Jack, Walsh, James, Bastin.

Five days after their magnificent triumph over the Gunners, confident Walsall slammed luckless Mansfield Town 8-1 to chalk up their highest ever victory in a home League game, yet amazingly after the heroics against Arsenal, there were only 3,000 fans present to see the slaughter of the Stags.

Walsall 8 Mansfield Town 1
Division Three South, 19 January 1933

THIS could so easily have been an anticlimax after all the celebrations of the Arsenal victory. Schoolchildren were given half a day's holiday and granted free admission as guests of the Walsall directors at a time when floodlights were

The most famous team in Walsall's history? Here are the men who beat Arsenal. Back row (left to right): Bird, Read, Bennett, Wait (trainer), Cunningham, J. G. Wilson (assistant secretary), Leslie, Salt, Sheppard. Middle row: W. G. Slade (secretary-manager), E. Jackson, H. L. Fellows (chairman), Mayoress (Mrs W. Dean) Mayor (Councillor W. Dean), H. Lake (director), A. J. Eyre (director). Front row: Coward, Ball, Alsop, Lee.

unheard of and mid-week games in winter had to be played in the afternoon (this one kicked-off at 2pm).

Both teams were in mid-table in Division Three North and this was reflected in the fairly even play in the opening minutes. Then Freddy Lee put the Saddlers ahead with the visitors' eyes all on Gilbert Alsop, to whom they expected the winger to play the ball. Then visiting centre-forward George Bowater hit the bar before Alsop made it 2-0 with a terrific shot after Freddy Lee had crossed accurately. Then the in-form Alsop made it 3-0, this time netting superbly from a Bill Sheppard cross. Bowater then scored and quickly hit the bar again as both goals came under fire, but by half-time it was 4-1 to Walsall as a splendid bout of interpassing put ace marksman Alsop clear of the defence to complete his hat-trick.

Soon after the break another telling cross from Lee was turned over the line by Billy Coward and with the pitch cutting up badly, Alsop raced in and made it 6-1 from a Coward cross. Sheppard and Lee then worked a brilliant one-two 20 yards from goal which resulted in the latter making it 7-1, and with the crowd counting and calling for more, Billy Coward burst through to hammer the ball into the roof of his net and so make the final score 8-1.

Walsall: Cunningham, Bennett, Bird, Reed, Leslie, Salt, Coward, Ball, Alsop, Sheppard, Lee.

Mansfield Town: Wilson, Anthony, England, Readman, Robinson, Slack, Prior, Broom, Johnson, Wannacott, Bowater.

Although they slipped out of the Cup in the next round, beaten by Manchester City in front of a bumper 52,000-plus crowd at Maine Road, the Saddlers lost only three of their remaining League games in 1932-33, finishing a creditable fifth in the table with 48 points.

Attendances improved after those Cup epics and 8,722 attended the home game against Wrexham on 8 February, the best attendance at Fellows Park for a League game since October 1930, when 12,000 turned out for the Coventry City game.

When the season ended it was revealed that the average turnout at Fellows Park had topped 5,000. Things seemed to be looking up. Or were they? The club received £2,719 from that excellent run in the FA Cup and banked over £2,000 in extra gate receipts, but when the balance sheets were drawn up, it was revealed that a loss of £358 had been made on the season, which, whilst it was substantially less than the adverse balances on the two previous seasons, was certainly disappointing after the team had done so well.

However, things were at long last, looking up on the playing front, and there was talk in the camp of an all-out effort being made to try to gain promotion in 1933-34.

After being eliminated from the FA Cup by Clapton Orient in a replay, Walsall were able to pin their efforts solely on trying to get into the Second Division – a place they hadn't visited since 1901. But sadly they missed out again, having to settle for fourth place.

There can be little doubt that Walsall would have been well in the running if they had not unaccountably failed to find their best form when playing away from home. They lost 6-2 at Wrexham and 4-0 at Doncaster, as well as going down to struggling teams like Accrington and Gateshead and drawing with the bottom two, Rotherham and Rochdale. There was one ding-dong contest with Barrow in January which finished level at 5-5, Lee scoring a hat-trick for the Saddlers.

At Fellows Park they were almost invincible – so much so that in the whole of the Football League only Barnsley (who pipped Chesterfield at the post for the Northern Section title after the Derbyshire team had once held a nine-point lead) and Stockport County had better home records.

In the end Walsall finished up eight points adrift of Barnsley after losing 11 and drawing five of their 21 away games.

They did create a handful of records – the highest number of points (53), most home wins in a season (18), the biggest goals for total (96) and last but by no means least, the best individual scoring performance which Gilbert Alsop achieved with his haul of 39 goals (40 in all).

In season 1933-34 there was a strong element of ex-Coventry players at the club, as well as one or two exciting newcomers in the reserve team, one being ace-striker Harry Wiles who claimed a total of 64 goals – three when on first-team duty and the rest while playing in the Birmingham Combination, Midland Midweek League and various minor Cup-ties. This tally is surely one of the biggest ever obtained by one player for the club he was with for any one season.

Walsall called up 20 players for first-team duty in 1933-34, with only Ben Woolhouse appearing in all 42 League matches.

They collected one trophy – the Worcestershire Senior Cup – after beating Worcester City 4-0 in the Final at Fellows Park, in front of a near 4,000 crowd.

The average attendance at Third Division North home games was just on 6,000, but that early dismissal from the FA Cup made an inevitable difference to the club's financial position and there was a loss on the season of £681, which was disappointing in view of the splendid displays that the supporters had enjoyed for the second campaign running.

Walsall 5 Tranmere Rovers 3
Division Three North, 10 March 1934

THIS entertaining game was played towards the end of one of Walsall's most successful seasons in Division Three North and the Saddlers maintained their excellent record of having dropped only three points at home up to that time.

It took just 11 minutes for Walsall to open the scoring with Johnny Reed going past two men before crossing for Freddy Lee to shoot high into the net. Rovers levelled things up five minutes later when Pennington added the finishing touch after the ball had bobbled about in the goalmouth. Back came the Saddlers and after several narrow escapes, Ben Woolhouse crossed for Bill Sheppard to make it 2-1.

This was the score at half-time and soon after the break George Wiles crossed from near the corner flag and the ball swirled out of Roper's reach and into the net off the far post. Woodward pulled one back for the visitors soon afterwards, but the energetic Chris Ball and powerhouse Bill Sheppard both netted, only for their goals to be ruled offside. Sheppard also hit the bar before Gilbert Alsop carved out an opening for Woolhouse who gleefully skated past two defenders to make it 4-2.

Defences were in control for some time after this flurry of scoring before a late burst saw Alsop skilfully lob the ball into the net following a cross from Bennett (5-2) and after hesitation between George Leslie and Johnny Reed the visitors got clear and Woodward made the final score 5-3.

The crowd of 5,530 went home feeling they had got value for money, this being the fifth time in the season that Walsall had scored five goals in a home game.

Walsall: McSevich; Bennett, Bird, Reed, Leslie, Wiles, Woolhouse, Ball, Alsop, Sheppard, Lee.

Tranmere Rovers: Roper; Platt, Dawson, Meacock, Watson, Spencer, Pearson, Woodward, Bell, Pennington, Urmson.

The Walsall public was by now becoming restless and indeed so too were the club's directors as well as one or two players. And in truth there wasn't much to look forward to as the 1934-35 season loomed. Yet, lo and behold, the Saddlers started off like chumps and finished like champs.

Most of the senior players had been retained with the notable exception of Bill Sheppard, who had moved to Chester.

Former Coventry City star, Peter McSevich, was regarded as first-choice 'keeper, while Bird, Bennett, Reed, George and Harry Wiles, Leslie, Bradford, Ben Woolhouse, Ball, Alsop and Lee, were joined by experienced left-back Arthur Tilford from Fulham who had earlier been with Nottingham Forest, Blackpool, Coventry City and Southampton, defender Lew Morgan and goalkeeper Frank Higgs (from Aldershot) the latter having previously served with Chelsea, Linfield, Barnsley and Manchester City, winning several medals with the Irish club (1930-32), centre-half Tommy Grice (from Torquay United, who had earlier served with Birmingham and Mansfield Town), Arthur Haddleton (from Swindon Town), Dick Griffiths (from Southport) and two youngsters from the Chase Terrace district, Jack Shelton (who had been with Wolves as an amateur) and centre or inside-forward Bill Evans.

Bird, Leslie and Lee had all suffered injuries towards the end of the previous season and whilst it was hoped that they had all made, or would make, satisfactory recoveries, not one of them was found to be match-fit when put to the test. Lee managed only one game and was then out of the side until well into the season when he made seven more appearances, but was obviously not fully fit even then. Bird struggled on at left-back but was then rested and, in fact, that proved to be the end of his career. Leslie did not become available until the 14th match, and it was soon apparent that the knee which had given him some problems since Easter (at Rotherham) continued to cause him trouble and altogether he played in only 11 games during the season.

To lose the regular services of three of the club's best players, for all of whom Walsall had received good offers before they met with their misfortunes,was a big blow, and as one or two of the new men did not come up to expectations, it was not altogether surprising that a certain amount of experimenting had to be resorted to before anything like a settled side evolved.

That, to some extent, accounted for the disastrous opening spell when only one win was registered in the first 16 matches.

There was also a change in managership around this time with the famous Scotsman Andy Wilson, succeeding Bill Slade, and former favourite Bill Sheppard returning to the club from Chester. He marked his homecoming by scoring five goals in as many matches.

By the time an improvement had taken effect, the attendances at Fellows Park had dropped considerably – for the opening fixture the turnout was 9,031, and a few weeks later it was down to 3,980.

A run in the FA Cup boosted spirits and Walsall reached the third round where they met Southampton. A crowd of 14,475 (receipts £826) turned up at Fellows Park but the Saddlers went down 2-1 after putting up a gallant fight. Fishlock scored twice for the Saints, his second effort being a fly-kick from fully 25 yards, the ball finding its way through a posse of bodies into the net.

To complete the story of Walsall's Cup exploits in 1934-35, in the Northern Section Cup they beat Lincoln City (in a replay), Chesterfield (also at the second attempt) and Crewe Alexandra before losing 2-0 in the Final against Stockport County at Maine Road, Manchester, where the turnout was a disappointing 4,035.

A strong finish, especially in home matches, saw the Saddlers take 14th position in the League table (36 points) and if they had only improved on their travels, then promotion might well have been on the cards.

Also, hot-shot Gilbert Alsop weighed in with a total of 48 goals in all games – 39 in the Third Division North, including ten in the last five games of the campaign.

Transfers out in 1934-35 resulted in £5,045 coming into the Walsall kitty plus an increase of £1,200 from gate receipts, and therefore when the club's accounts were made public they showed a balance on the right side of £4,587 compared with a previous best of £875 in 1928-29 – and another ten years were to elapse before that figure was beaten.

As usual, changes were made in the playing staff at Fellows Park during the summer of 1935 and into the camp came Billy Bryan, a goalkeeper from Sunderland, full-back Kilburn Wilmot from Coventry City (who was also a county cricketer with Warwickshire), Billy Richmond, a Scottish-born half-back from Bournemouth, and four forwards – Jack Stevenson and Jimmy Collins from Stockport County, Jerry Poxton from Watford and George Cunningham from Cambuslang in Scotland.

One daily newspaper carried an article stating that Walsall were 'tipped for promotion', so altogether the directors and manager Wilson were in a fairly optimistic mood as the Saddlers entered their 15th season in the Third Division, notwithstanding that the club's financial position had been aggravated by a loss of £2,576 on the previous campaign.

For the initial matches the team selection was: McSevich; Bennett, Wiles, Reed, Morgan, Richmond, Woolhouse, Collins, Alsop, Stevenson and Poxton.

There was a crowd of over 10,000 for the first home fixture against Gateshead, when Walsall donned a new strip given to them by the Supporters' Club, and not since 1927 had such a big crowd assembled for an opening Saturday game at Fellows Park.

Gilbert Alsop scored in that opener against Gateshead (won 2-0 by Walsall) and he quickly followed up with a smart hat-trick v Darlington (won 4-1), but then he was sidelined through illness and his place at centre-forward was filled by left-winger Bill Evans, who, in his first game as leader of the attack rammed in five goals as Walsall whipped Mansfield Town 7-0 at Fellows Park. Evans went on and scored a few more important goals before returning to the wing when Alsop was fit enough to resume his duties up front.

As it happened Alsop's days with Walsall were numbered (for the time being) and eventually he went off to join West Bromwich Albion, signing for the Baggies in May 1937. Thus it came about that Evans took over the centre-forward berth more or less permanently until well on into the season when Dunderdale appeared there for seven matches.

In the League programme of 1935-36, Walsall did well at home (15 wins) but they struggled yet again on their travels (only one victory recorded – at Stockport) and tenth place was where they finished, 19 points behind champions Chesterfield.

They did, however, record some excellent home wins, 6-0 v York City being one of their best when Jimmy Collins netted four times. Collins was later sold to Liverpool for £2,000 plus another £500 after he had played six games for the Merseyside club. When he left Walsall he had netted 14 goals in 22 League outings.

Newcastle United eliminated Walsall from the FA Cup in round three, after a crowd of 11,707 (543 more than had witnessed the Arsenal Cup-tie of a few years earlier) had seen the Saddlers knock out Lincoln City in the opening game and then account for Chesterfield (in a replay) in round two.

An interesting feature was that in 1935-36 veteran Harry Wait (aged 44) was recalled to keep goal after Peter McSevich had been injured. Harry had not performed for six years and his five

Walsall, 1935-36, when they finished tenth in Division Three North and Harry Wait came out of retirement to play again. Back row (left to right): J. Bewick, J. Bradford, L. Morgan, J. Shelton, J. Wait (trainer), J. Leckie, J. Bennett, N. Smith, J. Reed, G. Wiles. Middle row: L. Dunderdale, T. Jones, I. Harwood, Andy Wilson (manager), E. Wilson (secretary), R. Woolhouse, C. Bulger, J. Landells. Front row: G. Cunningham, J. Green, K. Harper, H. Dover, W. Evans, J. Bell, W. Richmond.

appearances this term took his overall total to an impressive 275 (264 League and 11 in the FA Cup). He also set a new club record (which still holds good today) that of being the oldest footballer ever to appear in a competitive game for the Saddlers (44 years 2 months) thus taking over the honour from Albert Groves.

At the League's annual meeting in the summer of 1936 Walsall were transferred from the Third Division North to the Third Division South and they aimed to make a go of it by recruiting more players to the ranks. Among the newcomers were goalkeeper Ken Tewkesbury, a former England amateur international, who had served with both Aston Villa and Birmingham as well as Bradford Park Avenue, another 'keeper in Irishman Jack Leckie, once of Raith Rovers, Port Vale and Stockport County who arrived from the Welsh club Cardiff City, Joe Bewick, a strapping centre-half from Port Vale, Jack Landells who had helped Millwall back into the Second Division before going north to Carlisle, Yorkshireman Irvine Harwood, who after leaving Bradford City and Wolves had appeared for Bristol Rovers in 51 matches in two seasons, Charlie Bulger, signed on a free transfer from Lincoln City and Jackie Bell, late of Middlesbrough and West Ham United.

Added to the list in November when things were not going too well, was Joe Carter, the former West Bromwich Albion and England inside-right who had started the season with Tranmere Rovers.

A crowd of 10,029 witnessed the first home game against Cardiff City when a debut goal by Harwood gave the Saddlers a 1-0 victory.

A few mediocre displays followed, mainly at home, but occasionally things started to look up and after Carter had been introduced into the side in good time for the FA Cup-tie against Scunthorpe, he saw Bill Evans play a blinder that day, scoring a hat-trick in a 3-0 win to send the Saddlers into the next round where they met non-Leaguers Yeovil & Petters.

It proved to be a tough battle with Yeovil, and after being held to a draw at home, Walsall travelled south and won 1-0 on their famous slope thanks to a late goal from Charlie Bulger.

Barnsley were next on the agenda. They were managed by Brough Fletcher, later to take charge at Fellows Park, and in front of a 13,339 crowd, Evans hit two more crackerjacks to see the Saddlers through 3-1.

So it was into the fourth round for only the second time of asking – and on this occasion Walsall had to travel away to Grimsby Town.

The match was staged on an ice-bound pitch and the bitter cold kept the gate down to just over 10,600. Walsall were beaten 4-1.

After all the Cup action, Walsall, having changed managers yet again – Tommy Lowes coming south from Barrow to succeed Andy Wilson in April – eventually settled for 17th place in the League table.

Evans top-scored with 15 goals and the average League attendance at Fellows Park was a rather disappointing 5,346.

Walsall started the 1937-38 season in circumstances which, in some respects, were more calculated to cause anxiety rather than to arouse enthusiasm.

A loss of £3,159 on the previous campaign had made the financial position so difficult that manager Tom Lowes had been seriously handicapped in his efforts to strengthen the team, there being little or no money available to delve into the transfer market, and consequently he was only able to secure the services of cast-off players.

He did sign four forwards – the large frame of coal miner Ronnie Dodd (from Doncaster Rovers), Doug Redwood (from Cardiff City), Harry Knott (from Brentford) plus the Northampton Town duo of Tommy Robinson (once of Birmingham, Blackpool, Chesterfield and Lincoln City) and wing-half Bill Simpson, who had earlier assisted Aston Villa.

Also on the books was a goalkeeper, Bert Williams, who, after moving to Wolves, went on to win 24 full England international caps and appeared in the 1950 World Cup finals.

The line-up for the first League game at Torquay United read: Tewkesbury; Shelton, Wiles, Richmond, Morgan, Simpson, Woolhouse, Knott, Dodd, Robinson and Bulger, who thankfully had recovered from a cartilage operation.

A 1-0 defeat was not too bad a start, but it was the first of eight in succession and of 17 altogether in away matches, of which only one was won and three drawn – Walsall's worst record since season 1925-26 when they only registered two victories on opponents' grounds.

The beginning of their home

programme, too, was very inauspicious, although this was not due to any shortcomings on the part of the players.

A severe thunderstorm caused the abandonment, after 31 minutes play, of the first home League game of the campaign, against Mansfield Town.

But afterwards results did improve although the attendances at Fellows Park suffered considerably, and a meagre crowd of 1,708 diehard supporters bothered to turn out for the game against Reading.

The team rose to the occasion in the FA Cup, beating Gateshead at home 4-0 in the opening round, a tie watched by a crowd of over 7,800.

But in round two, with the youthful figure of Bert Williams in goal, Watford took the glory with a convincing 3-0 victory.

After this Cup exit the Saddlers' League form slumped dramatically and they crashed 8-2 at home against Bristol City, a scoreline which still stands as the heaviest defeat suffered on home territory by a Walsall side.

The Bristol club certainly had the run of the ball although the Saddlers did miss one or two chances. In the end victory was well deserved by City.

Walsall 2 Bristol City 8
Division Three South, 26 February 1938

ALTHOUGH Walsall were next to the bottom of Division Three South at the time of this game and Bristol City were third in the table, this was a quite an amazing result and still stands as the Saddlers' heaviest home defeat. A week earlier Walsall had beaten Cardiff City at home by a goal to nil and were hoping for at least a draw though the visitors had won two and drawn one of their previous three games.

Walsall opened well enough and Ben Woolhouse almost backheeled the ball home in one sustained attack, but then midway through the half City landed three goals in as many minutes in the laundry net.

Fred Peters, Alec Rowles and Jim Brain all beat the young Bert Williams and though Billy Evans got an opportunist goal for Walsall soon afterwards, it was 4-1 by half-time as Rowles hammered another high shot into the net.

Soon after the break Bob Brook scored direct from a free-kick to make it 5-1, and then the former Coventry City star, Clarrie Bourton, weighed in with number six for the visitors. Still the goals went in and on 80 and 82 minutes Peters and Rowles got further goals to rub salt into Walsall's aching wounds.

In a stray Walsall attack midget winger Jimmy Prew had a powerful shot pushed out and Billy Evans nipped in to make the final score 8-2.

Yet despite this traumatic experience 'keeper Bert Williams went on to become one of the greatest goalkeepers the game has known.

Walsall: Williams; Shelton, Bennett, Askew, Morgan, Payne, Prew, Woolhouse, Evans, Robinson, Redwood.
Bristol City: Dawson; Brook, Turner, Morgan, Pearce, Armstrong, Peters, Bourton, Rowles, Brain, Dryden.

At the end of a rather disappointing 1937-38 season, the Saddlers were forced to apply for re-election for the second time, having failed to overhaul Torquay near the foot of the table.

The 1938-39 season opened on a sad note. Within six weeks of it getting under way, club chairman and benefactor, Mr H. L. Fellows, died after a lengthy illness.

It turned out to be a rather interesting season although Walsall, who had ex-Halifax Town winger E. (Charlie) Davies on the right-flank early on, never showed the skill in the League that they produced in the FA Cup.

For the first ten weeks of the campaign not a single win was recorded, and it was not until after Gilbert Alsop had returned to the club in October that two points were picked up on one day, Northampton Town being the victims on 12 November in their 14th match. It was not all dull stuff, however. Walsall played some good football at times and the fans enjoyed what they saw.

This was emphasised clearly when Ipswich, newly-elected to the League, came to town. A record League crowd of 13,728 packed into Fellows Park only for the visitors to take the points with a hard-earned 1-0 win.

Halfway through this last full season before World War Two, Walsall were languishing at the bottom of the Southern Section of the Football League. But in the FA Cup they seemed to spark into life and reached round five before losing to the 1938 beaten Finalists Huddersfield Town.

If only they could have produced the same sort of form in the League as they showed in knockout Cup football.

Walsall fielded the same 11 players in four of their six Cup-ties in 1938-39 – Ken Tewkesbury, George Beeson (ex-Aston Villa), Norman Male, Leslie Woodward, Fred Walker (later sold to Sheffield Wednesday), Les Payne (ex-Doncaster Rovers), star of the future Johnny Hancocks, Gilbert Alsop, former Irish international Joe Bambrick (signed from Chelsea), Bill Simpson and Charlie Bulger.

On two occasions, the injured Beeson was replaced at full-back by Yorkshireman Ken Harper, a former junior international.

They ousted Carlisle United 4-1 at home in the opening round, Bambrick netting a hat-trick; mopped up Clapton Orient by 4-2 (watched by 13,570 fans – 2,500 more than had been present at the previous Cup-tie) in the next round; took care of Newport County 2-0 in round three (when 'keeper Ken Tewkesbury saved a vital penalty) and then saw off Notts County in a fourth-round replay after 34,462 fans had watched the draw at Meadow Lane.

Walsall 4 Notts County 0
FA Cup fourth round replay, 26 January 1939

HAVING forced a goalless draw at Notts County in front of more than 34,000 fans at Meadow Lane on the previous Saturday, bottom-of-the-table Walsall had a great chance of reaching the fifth round of the FA Cup for the first time ever when they took on the Magpies at Fellows Park in the replay.

However, there were fears that the game would be called off as the pitch had snow near the touchline and mud right down the middle even before the start, but referee E. W. Baker of Manchester was just as adamant that the game should go on as many referees are adamant that games should be called off.

Walsall's tactics were the right ones from the start, using the firmer parts of the pitch down the wings in order to develop attacks and early in the game Simpson hit the bar with a header. It was half an hour before the Saddlers scored, but when the goal arrived, it was a classic one with Johnny Hancocks getting away down the right flank and crossing for Gilbert Alsop to turn the ball into the Laundry End goal. Then Irish international Joe Bambrick raced clear of the defence only to hit a post when it seemed easier to find the net. Walsall went close again before half-time when Alsop shot wide from ten yards.

Taylor, County's eager-beaver outside-right, fully tested Ken Tewksbury in the Saddlers' goal early in the second half before Alsop made it 2-0 from a Charlie Bulger cross. Taylor was doing his best for County and another effort of his was cleared off the line by George Beeson, the former Villa full-back. But Walsall remained on top, although defender Morgan was twice laid out by heavy knocks. He bravely resumed and then with 15 minutes to go helped set up Alsop for his hat-trick goal, the final pass coming in from the impressive Bulger. Alsop was again on target for the Saddlers soon after, firing in Bulger's centre and thus becoming the first Walsall player to get four goals in an FA Cup-tie for the first time since 1915 when Arthur Campey had done so in a preliminary round.

In the very last minute Alsop almost got another when his right-foot shot hit a post and came out. The 9,563 supporters who somehow missed work in order to see the game on that wintry Thursday afternoon went away happy and looking forward to the fifth-round tie at Huddersfield.

Walsall: Tewkesbury; Beeson, Male, Woodward, Morgan, Payne, Hancocks, Alsop, Bambrick, Simpson, Bulger.
Notts County: Flower; Mills, Blood, Hindmarsh, Moulson, Read, Taylor, Clayton, Martin, Hatton, Cooper.

Unfortunately Walsall succumbed 3-0 to the 1938 Finalists, Huddersfield Town, at Leeds Road in the next round of the Cup before a 33,500-plus gate, and two weeks later the Saddlers were rocked in a game at Crystal Palace when they found themselves 3-0 down after only three minutes play.

The young, inexperienced Bert Williams was standing between the posts that day, making his first League appearance of the season, and the first three times he touched the ball was to pick it out of the net. The final score was 4-0.

Manager Tommy Lowes made bold efforts to sign new players but his efforts were all in vain and in spite of some enterprising performances late on, including a last-match 6-3 win over Cardiff City when future England winger and Wolves star, Johnny Hancocks scored two, Walsall failed to pull clear of the bottom two and had to apply for re-election yet again.

The total attendances at home matches in 1938-39 established a new record for the club since it had been in the Third Division. No fewer than 146,870 spectators paid to watch the team, an average of around 7,000 per match. The average for the three home Cup-ties was over 11,000, in spite of atrocious weather for that replay against Notts County.

Alsop, with 23 goals, topped the League scoring list and in April scored four, two, three, three and four times in consecutive games; Bambrick, who was the perfect partner for Alsop, netted 15 and Hancocks nipped in with nine (including five penalties). And here we must give a mention to that pint-sized winger, Johnny Hancocks, who was signed from Oakengates Town in August 1938. He made such progress during the season that several leading clubs, including Arsenal, Manchester United and Everton, sought his transfer. He eventually moved to Wolves where he became an England international and big favourite with the Molineux fans.

When the players reported back for training on 1 August 1939 there were several new faces in the group. Goalkeeper Jim Strong, ex-Hartlepool, Chesterfield and Portsmouth, arrived from Gillingham – being signed as cover for Williams following Tewksbury's decision to retire to go into the jewellery business in Birmingham; Tommy Jones came down from Tranmere Rovers to join George Beeson, Norman Male (ex-West Brom) and Harper in the full-back category; former boxer Bill Thayne, ex-Northampton Town and once of Crystal Palace, Hartlepools United and Luton Town, entered the half-back sector and the forwards included Tommy Taylor (from Notts County) and Les Talbot (the former Hednesford Town and Blackburn Rovers inside-forward from Cardiff City). Inside-right George Walton arrived ten days before the first game, also from Cardiff City.

But perhaps the most significant signing was that of Dai Richards from Birmingham, whose papers were not finalised until 24 hours after that initial pre-season training session had been completed.

A Welsh international wing-half, he had served with Wolves and Brentford, and Walsall won the fight for his signature in the face of determined efforts from at least four First and Second Division clubs.

After only three games had been played at the start of the ill-fated 1939-40 season, World War Two broke out and competitive football (on a League basis) was suspended for the duration, resuming in full in August 1946, after an enforced break of seven years.

Consequently, during the 1939-46 period Walsall, along with all the other League clubs, played in selected regional zones and all-told they fulfilled close on 250 matches, while performing in the Regional League (Midland Division) and League Cup: 1939-40, Regional League (South) and Midland Cup: 1940-41; Football League South and League Cup 1941-42; Football League North: 1942-43, 1943-44 and 1944-45; and Football League Division Three South (North), League Cup and FA Cup: 1945-46.

Walsall chose to wear claret and blue hoops in their wartime matches.

Full-back Jack Shelton appeared in most matches (194), followed by defensive partner Norman Male (184) and goalkeeper Bert Williams (114). Gilbert Alsop obtained a total of 58 goals and thus headed the scoring charts, with Jack Vinall (53) and Wally Brown (49) pushing him hard.

Several guest players turned out for

Walsall team in the wartime season of 1940-41. Back row (left to right): Richards, Thayne, Jones, Morgan, Rowley. Front: Hancocks, Wood, Male, Vinall, Starling, Godfrey. Guest players include Jack Rowley and Ronnie Starling.

the club including that talented Irish international Peter Doherty (Manchester City), Manchester United's Jack Rowley, Jack Vinall from Luton Town, former Walsall 'keeper Fred Biddlestone, Ronnie Starling and George Edwards (all from Aston Villa), Harry Ashley, Ike Clarke, George Dudley (brother of Jimmy, later to play for the Saddlers), Alun Evans, Charlie Evans, Sammy Heaselgrave, Harry Lowery, Scottish international wing-half Sandy McNab, Bobby Newsome, Jack Sankey and hotshot centre-forward 'W. G.' Richardson (all of West Brom) and Jack Screen (Wrexham) plus a few others.

Walsall's best season during the hostilities was in 1940-41 when they won 15 and drew seven of their 34 matches, scoring 104 goals, of which Vinall claimed a creditable 27 and Rowley 23, including four four-timers. Alsop himself top-scored in 1939-40 with 28 goals.

Walsall's best win in wartime football was 11-4 v Notts County (h) in November 1940 when Rowley and Vinall each netted four goals. In that same season West Brom were hammered 10-3 in May and Rowley again hit four.

Unfortunately Walsall finished bottom of the Midland Regional League in 1939-40, picking up only 19 points out of a possible 56.

The following season they finished higher in the table than rivals Birmingham, West Brom, Leicester, Nottingham Forest and Stoke, and had only Coventry ahead of them at the finish. Walsall also reached the Midland Cup Final that season only to lose to Leicester City 2-0, with the Wolves pair of Billy Wright and Jimmy Mullen guesting for City.

In October 1943 Walsall pulled off one of the great recovery acts in the club's history. They were 4-0 down at half-time against Aston Villa in an away Regional League game yet rallied superbly after the break to force a 4-4 draw – and then with barely 30 seconds remaining on the watch, Alsop almost gave the Saddlers a memorable 5-4 win, when his shot scraped an upright with the 'keeper stranded.

In the transitional season of 1945-46, under the management of Harry Hibbs, the former Birmingham and England

Walsall, 1945-46. Back row (left to right): Harry Wait (trainer), R. Crutchley, I. Methley, J. Lewis, W. Skidmore, A. Newman, D. Wilshaw. Front row: G. Alsop, W. Brown, A. Mullard, Harry Hibbs (manager), D. Darby, K. Davies, R. Foulkes.

goalkeeper who had been appointed manager in 1944, Walsall, rebuilding their team like all the other clubs up and down the country (they sold Bert Williams to Wolves for starters), contested the League South Cup Final with Bournemouth, only to lose a closely-fought contest by the odd goal watched by a crowd of 19,715 (including some 3,000 fans from Walsall) at Stamford Bridge, Chelsea.

Walsall put out this team for that game: Jack Lewis in goal who went on to serve the Saddlers right up until 1952 making more than 270 League appearances; full-backs Irvine Methley and Jack Shelton who had played regularly through the war; local man Ron Crutchley, later to join Shrewsbury Town, centre-half Reg Foulkes, who had been an amateur with Manchester United, Albert 'Nutty' Newman signed from West Bromwich Albion; tiny winger Johnny Hancocks, ex-Cardiff City inside-forward Les Talbot, Walsall-born striker Albert Mullard, Dennis Wilshaw who was on loan from Wolverhampton Wanderers and ace-marksman of the 1930s, Gilbert Alsop.

Unfortunately Walsall couldn't hold on to winger Hancocks who left the club in the summer of 1946, teaming up with Wolves. He later became the star winger at Molineux and went on to represent England.

When normal League football began again in August 1946 the fixtures scheduled for the 1939-40 campaign were re-issued, and Walsall started off on a poor note, losing their opening three games.

They didn't register their first win until match number seven (4-2 v Ipswich Town), but with that victory safely under their belts, Walsall quickly climbed into the top half of the table.

As a highlight the Saddlers became the first team that season to win at Ashton Gate, beating Bristol City 2-1 in November, and they also hammered Northampton Town 8-0 at the County Ground on Easter Tuesday afternoon to achieve their best-ever away win in the Football League. There were hat-tricks here for Mullard and Wilshaw, Doug Lishman, later to serve Arsenal so well, scored the other two.

In the end Walsall had to be satisfied with sixth place in the table with 46 points – 20 behind the runaway winners Cardiff City. Wilshaw, with a total of 21 goals, finished up as top-scorer, while Methley and Newman played in every game.

In the 1946-47 FA Cup competition Walsall got off to a flier, slamming non-League Leytonstone 6-1 away. They next beat Ipswich Town 1-0 in a replay at Portman Road, Lishman knocking in the winner, before Liverpool came to Fellows Park for a third-round tussle and won 5-2 with Scotsman Billy Liddell having an excellent game for the Reds in front of a bumper 18,360 crowd.

Fred Kelly shot Walsall into a fourth minute lead; Wilshaw, who had been injured early on, then put the Saddlers 2-1 ahead after the Merseysiders had equalised – and at that stage all looked rosy for the Saddlers. Fortune, however, did not favour the brave, and with far greater experience in their ranks, Liverpool ran out convincing winners at the end of a truly enthralling contest which was appreciated by the crowd.

In 1947-48, with Hibbs still in charge, Walsall enjoyed one of their most successful seasons ever when they finished third in Division Three South and reached the third round of the FA Cup, before losing to Coventry City (2-1).

Everyone within the club felt that the team was good enough to challenge for promotion – and it was looking good until February and March arrived. But in those two months only a couple of wins were recorded and that ruined any hopes Walsall had of regaining their Second Division place, although they did finish the season on a high, winning six of their remaining eight fixtures.

The Saddlers started off the proceedings in really cracking form with ex-Blues striker Dave Massart grabbing a hat-trick in each of the first three home games when Exeter City (4-0), Leyton Orient (3-1) and Southend United (6-0) were swept aside by a free-running Walsall outfit, inspired by right-half Henry Walters (ex-Wolves), right-winger Jackie Maund, late of Aston Villa, and the strike-force of Massart, Wilshaw and Lishman.

A few hiccups came and went before the turn of the year and luckless Brighton were hammered 4-0 at Hove in November when Massart netted all four goals. Then, after Walsall had been knocked out of the FA Cup, a record crowd of 20,383 packed into Fellows Park to see Notts County (Tommy Lawton included) beaten 2-1 on the last day of January.

By now injuries had begun to hit the team hard, Irvine Methley suffering one particularly nasty knock against Notts County which sidelined him for the rest of the season. Massart, despite scoring a goal every other game, left for Bury in March.

And towards the end of the campaign Charlie Humphries, signed from Paget Rangers and Methley's replacement, twisted his knee and was never fit again for the rigours of League football. QPR took the title in 1948, finishing four points ahead of Bournemouth (61-57) and ten in front of Walsall.

Walsall 2 Notts County 1
Division Three South, 31 January 1948

THIS was a game that really captured the public's imagination. At the time Walsall were still in with a great chance of gaining promotion to the Second Division, being just six points behind the leaders QPR (remember this was when only one club went up from each section of Division Three). Notts County included England's star centre-forward Tommy Lawton, who had amazed the football world earlier that season by leaving First Division Chelsea to move into the Third Division, joining a County side managed by a future Walsall director Eric Houghton and with a future Walsall manager Bill Moore as trainer.

Walsall kicked-off towards the Hillary Street end and had most of the play in the first half. Prolific marksman Dave Massart missed a couple of chances – the kind that he had been putting away confidently earlier in the season – while Johnny Devlin hit the angle of the bar and upright. Massart did get the ball into the net, but the referee had already whistled for an infringement. At the other end centre-half Reg Foulkes had kept a close watch on Tommy Lawton, while full-back Norman Male had given him every assistance and on the two occasions that

Lawton did get half chances, 'keeper Jack Lewis handled his efforts confidently. Early in the second half Walsall took the lead. Devlin's adept pass sent Massart darting into the penalty area where he was brought crashing down. Up stepped Devlin to bang the spot-kick past Harry Brown. Then Irvine Methley was hurt in a tackle and was forced to hobble on the right wing, with Ken McGowan, moving inside. And it was McGowan who made it 2-0 for the Saddlers with a neat shot inside a post after Dennis Wilshaw's free-kick had been partially cleared.

Soon afterwards the limping Methley almost scored again when Walsall were well on top. Then in the 86th minute the raven-haired Lawton scored a spectacular goal for County. As the ball dropped inside the penalty area, he swivelled on a 'sixpence' and hammered it home in one movement. Fortunately he didn't get another chance and Walsall's fans went home happy in that they had witnessed a convincing victory while at the same time they had also seen a class striker in Tommy Lawton.

Walsall: Lewis, Methley, Male, Crutchley, Foulkes, Newman, McGowan, Devlin, Massart, Lishman, Wilshaw.

Notts County: Brown, Southwell, Howe, Cannon, Corkshill, Baxter, Freeman, Sewell, Lawton, Marsh, Parkes.

The Walsall team which beat Newport County 3-1 at Fellows Park in a Third Division South game at Fellows Park in September 1948. Back row (left to right): Devlin, Walters, Jones, Lewis, Ross, Morgan. Front row: Condie, Newman, Foulkes, McCloughlin, Tinkler.

Having finished fifth and third respectively in the previous two seasons the Saddlers were hoping to chalk up similar performances in 1948-49. But it was not to be and they had a rather dismal campaign, which saw them end up in 14th position with a mere 38 points.

In the 1948 close season they had sold Lishman to Arsenal and with Wolves keen to recall Dennis Wilshaw who had been on loan from Molineux since 1945 (he eventually went back in early September), it clearly meant that the Saddlers would soon lose their left-wing pairing, which they would surely find hard to replace. And this proved so.

The line-up at the start of the 1948-49 League programme against Norwich City away (lost 2-0) was: 'Mr Consistent' Jack Lewis in goal; right-back Syd Jones, signed from Arsenal to ease the problems caused by injuries; left-back Norman Male, who was still going strong having made his senior debut back in 1938; hard-working right-half Henry Walters; classy centre-half Reg Foulkes; and rock-like left-half Albert Newman; outside-right Jimmy Condie who had been transferred from Kilsyth Rangers in December 1947; inside-right Johnny Devlin, who was to become a great goalmaker as well as goalscorer for the club; centre-forward Albert Mullard; inside-left Stan Morgan, another ex-Arsenal man who went on to score 40 goals in 156 League games for Millwall (1948-53) and 26 in 96 for Leyton Orient (up to 1956); and outside-left Luke Tinkler, once of West Brom, who was recruited from Plymouth Argyle.

Highlights were few and far between as the season progressed and perhaps the only bright spot was the form of a young lad from Chase Terrace, Phil Chapman, who managed to score 28 League and Cup goals in his first season of League football. There was certainly one good game at Fellows Park when Millwall won 6-5 in mid-November, a game which saw full-back Norman Male score twice from the left-wing after getting injured.

Sadly, Norman Male failed to recover from the injury he suffered against Millwall and indeed he never played competitive football again. He did, however, remain at Fellows Park, acting as trainer to the reserve side for many years.

Following that disastrous 1948-49 campaign which ended with seven defeats in nine games, many steps were taken during the close season to try and avoid further trouble in the new term.

Four new players arrived – Gordon Medd from Worcester City, Eric Betts from Nuneaton Borough and the West Brom duo of Jimmy Whitehouse and Gordon 'Johnny' Morris. And in the September defender Billy Green arrived from Wolves. He proved to be a great asset to the team and appeared in almost 200 competitive games before transferring to Wrexham in June 1954.

The biggest change though was the adoption of red and white as the club colours, replacing the old claret and blue hooped shirts. The matchday programme also showed signs of inflation, rising 50 per-cent from twopence to threepence (in old money).

All these changes, however, did very little to improve the side on the field, for although Walsall registered a 7-1 evening win over Torquay United when Johnny Devlin rapped in five goals, a 4-2 victory against Brighton (two goals here for Whitehouse), and a 5-1 triumph over Ipswich Town (two goals apiece for Ron Hewitt and Chapman) things in general continued to go badly. This was not helped when new man Morris broke a leg playing against Southend in October – an injury which ruined his career.

Four successive 1-1 draws were quickly followed by four straight wins, but then a 13-match run without a victory sent the Saddlers sliding down the table and out of the FA Cup (beaten 4-1 at Mansfield).

Only two victories were recorded in their last 12 matches and in fact the Saddlers were left requiring two points from their final game against Crystal Palace to avoid seeking re-election. They beat the Londoners thanks mainly to the skill of Don Dearson, the former Birmingham and Welsh international, signed on the transfer deadline, who rose to the occasion and netted two smart goals in a nail-biting 3-1 victory to make the position safe. Incidently, keeping goal for Palace in that game was Dick Graham, later to become manager at Fellows Park.

Walsall 5 Millwall 6

Division Three South, 13 November 1948

AS SO often happened, a rain-soaked pitch at Fellows Park helped to produce a memorable match with thrills, spills and goals throughout the 90 minutes. Nothing much was at stake at the time with both sides making a reasonable but not remarkable start to the season. Millwall were just above mid-table with Walsall a place behind them on goal average.

The ball started to play tricks right from the start and after 16 minutes Walsall 'keeper Jack Lewis misjudged a cross as he came out and Mansfield's shot flew into the net off Reg Foulkes. Then Malcolm Finlayson, later to play for Wolves, was injured in a collision with Johnny Devlin, and Jimmy Constantine went into goal while Finlayson went to hospital. Walsall took full advantage of playing against ten men and an emergency 'keeper, and duly moved into the lead shortly before half-time with two goals in quick time, the first a shot from Jimmy Condie and the second from Phil Chapman's head. Before the break Walsall's reliable full-back Norman Male had also been injured and he resumed, limping on the right wing.

Yet it was Male who made it 3-1 for the Saddlers on 48 minutes, netting with a screamer of a shot. There was drama outside Fellows Park at this stage as Finlayson had returned from hospital with a Millwall director, but neither could get back inside the ground. The director somehow managed to climb in at the Wallows Lane End, the door was unlocked for Finlayson and the goalkeeper returned with his head bandaged to a great cheer from both sets of fans.

This inspired the visitors and three goals quickly flew into Walsall's net, two from Jack Short and one from Jimmy Hurrell. Back came the Saddlers and the limping Norman Male quickly squared things up at 4-4. Then with just seven minutes to go, Tommy Brolly floated in a free kick to edge the Lions back in front, but immediately Phil Chapman raced through at the other end to make it 5-5. Great stuff – what excitement. And still the action flowed. Then, with four minutes remaining, Short charged through the Walsall back division again and tried his luck with a pot shot from 25 yards, the ball flew into the net past a startled Lewis and thus the Millwall striker recorded his hat-trick as well as claiming the match-winner for the Londoners.

Walsall: Lewis, Methley, Male, Walters, Foulkes, Newman, Aldred, Mullard, Chapman, Devlin, Condie.

Millwall: Finlayson, Fisher, G. Tyler, Reeves, Simmonds, Brolly, Johnson, Short, Constantine, Hurrell, Mansfield.

After this narrow escape, the 1950-51 season again looked very bleak with only two points and five goals coming from the first nine games.

There were plenty of new faces around the place including utility forward Fred Morris, who came down from Oswestry, striker Fred Sutcliffe who was snapped up from Millwall, the former Blyth Spartans duo of Bobby Millard and Jack Allison who both arrived from Reading, Harry Knowles, a Wolverhampton-born winger, and forward George Dean, ex-Hillary Street Old Boys. To complete the set, 'Toddy' Bowen, whose father had played for Walsall 20 years earlier, joined the staff from Newport County. He quickly settled in on the left-wing and gave the fans something to cheer about at last.

Midway through the term Walsall were sharing last place with Crystal Palace – and in mid-January two more players were snapped up: centre-forward Jack Winter from Sheffield United and Billy O'Neill from Burnley.

Winter immediately made his presence felt, scoring twice on his debut. Walsall then went on to lose only five more games before the season ended, and from a perilous position rose in the table to finish well clear of bottom spot, after collecting 24 points from their last 22 games. Winter and Dearson finished up as joint top-scorers.

Unfortunately there was no rally the next season as Walsall finished in bottom spot, having topped the table after the opening two fixtures. New signing Hugh Evans grabbed the match winner in both of those early games (v Brighton and Aldershot). He then hit a hat-trick in a 4-0 win over Norwich City in match number five.

Full-back Bill Green played in every game, even turning out in goal at Southend on Boxing Day. Young goalkeeper Peter Atkinson was beaten eight times at Norwich on 29 December – and with veteran custodian Jack Lewis nearing the end of a fine career, teenager Gordon Chilvers (signed from Fordhouses) came into the side and gave several excellent performances between the posts. A total of 27 players were used in 1951-52 – a clear indication of how difficult it had been for the manager to field a settled side.

These dismal early 1950s saw Walsall applying for re-election at the end of three successive seasons 1951-52, 1952-53 and 1953-54, after they had finished bottom of the Third Division South twice and next-to- bottom once, mustering a total of only 81 points out of a possible 276.

On the surface, that three-year period had been a disaster, but there was certainly no lack of interest, particularly during Major Frank Buckley's spell as manager.

Several heavy, and embarrassing defeats were suffered in each of these three seasons.

In 1951-52 three teams put five past the Saddlers (Plymouth Argyle, Brighton and Bristol Rovers) while Norwich City's striker Roy Hollis grabbed

Walsall in 1951-52. Back row (left to right): J. Nelson (trainer), H. Walters, R. Russon, J. Lewis, W. Green, G. Dean, Tony McPhee (manager). Middle row: T. Bowen, L. O'Neill, J. Winters, J. Hughes, J. Barber. Front row: J. Devlin, S. Jones.

five in that one-sided contest shortly after Christmas.

In 1952-53 the Saddlers conceded 118 League goals (76 away from home) and among their 29 losses were those of 5-3 v Bristol Rovers and 5-1 v Northampton, both at at Fellows Park. On their travels they suffered humiliating defeats at Bristol City, Colchester and Exeter (all by 6-1), 5-0 at Ipswich and 5-1 at Bournemouth. A 4-4 draw against Shrewsbury on 15 January was perhaps the most enjoyable and certainly the most entertaining fixture at Fellows Park during this disappointing campaign.

Having said that, there were a few bright spots this term in respect of the players, especially the form of Phil Giles, an England Youth International, who had turned professional at Fellows Park in May 1948. He struck ten goals in 1952-53 to finish second top-scorer behind Jack Bridgett.

Another 29 defeats came in 1953-54, including 19 away, the two heaviest being those of 5-1 at Northampton and 5-3 at Brighton. Indeed, the Saddlers lost seven of their opening nine games and eight out of nine leading up to Christmas.

The introduction, on Boxing Day, of Don Colombo, a left-winger, failed to arrest the dismal form of the team and in his first six outings a further four defeats were suffered.

The remarkable total of 41 players appeared in the first team in 1953-54, including tough-tackling full-back, Jack Flavell, who later opened the bowling for England at Test cricket against the Australians, goalkeeper Doug Flack (ex-Fulham), Scotsman Jock Finlay who had served with New Brighton and Leeds United, Birmingham-born wing-half Frankie Slynn, formerly with Sheffield Wednesday and Bury, amateur centre-forward Bob Burgess from Third Lanark, Welshman Gwyn Jones who had previously been on the books of both Leeds and York City without breaking into League action, Kenny Lewis from Bangor City and another goalkeeper, Harry Baldwin, who assisted West Brom before the war and had made 164 League appearances for Brighton between 1946 and 1951. Surprisingly, home attendances actually rose this season and the average was over 9,000. There were 16,536 spectators at Fellows Park for a Thursday afternoon FA Cup replay against Lincoln City in January, and in the second replay at Nottingham Forest's ground on the following Monday, Walsall came agonisingly close to knocking out their Division Two opponents, losing 2-1 in a ding-dong battle in front of a 12,000-plus crowd.

Manager Buckley's tendency towards shock team selections almost achieved a major surprise in those games when defender Jack Flavell gave a whole-hearted display in his first-ever game up front. Forgotten inside-forward John Finlay, an ex-Leeds man, came back into the side to score in the first and third clashes and winger Alan Grubb fitted in well in midfield.

Unfortunately the tremendous fighting spirit against Lincoln did not carry over into the League programme and there was only the occasional relief in the series of defeats. Yet occasionally Walsall gave a display worthy of a team well up the table as when they beat Leyton Orient 4-2 in March with Fred Morris and Don Colombo stretching the visitors' defence down the flanks. 'Fearless Fred' was equal top-scorer with George Dean at the end of the season, but like Bill McIntosh a year earlier, and Hugh Evans and Bill O'Neill 12 months before that, Walsall's leading marksman was transferred during the summer.

When the 1954-55 campaign started it was hard to feel optimistic about Walsall's chances of doing anything special after such a series of catastrophic performances.

The first away game at Reading yielded a point – only a late goal robbed the Saddlers of two – but this proved to be only a spark of hope as the team failed to score or pick up another point in their next five matches. Walsall, in fact, lost 12 of their first 16 games and slumped to the foot of the table.

Despite many changes being made, it was not until 2 October that the first victory was gained (2-0 at Brentford) and then it took a further month before the first home win was chalked up (3-1 v Colchester). In the next game at Fellows Park, Bournemouth were slammed 6-1.

Yet, despite their lowly League position, attendances averaged around the 12,000 mark and when Walsall lost 2-0 to Chelsea in the third round of the FA Cup at Stamford Bridge early in January, the turnout was over 40,000.

For a struggling Third Division outfit, the Saddlers put up a great fight against the team that would lift the Football League championship that season, and it was hoped that things would improve in the bread and butter of Walsall's League programme thereafter. But alas, as so often happens, this brought about a period of anticlimax and it took until the beginning of April before the next win was registered – a 6-0 drubbing of Northampton Town.

The Saddlers lost only three of their remaining 12 games, but a 4-1 home defeat by Leyton Orient on the last day of the campaign (when over 17,500 fans turned out) finally sealed their fate and destined them to another fight for re-election.

Despite this, the season had certainly been an improvement upon recent times with a total of 75 goals being scored and attendances averaging 11,000, almost double what they had been when Major Frank Buckley arrived as manager. So although the success had not yet come on the field, the bleak days seemed to be coming to an end elsewhere.

These thoughts were further encouraged by the fact that Walsall had now discovered a prolific scorer in Tony Richards (he netted 22 goals in 1954-55), who had been released by Birmingham City, whilst centre-half Albert McPherson, signed from Stalybridge Celtic, had given a great deal of stability in the heart of the defence that had been sadly lacking in recent years.

However, there had been yet another fair turnover in players in 1954-55 and it is interesting to recall the comparatively large number who appeared only once in the days when Major Buckley was in charge.

Going back to 1953-54 for a minute, there were six who made just one League appearance – striker Alf Bailey (from Darwen), two amateurs in outside-left Alf Smith and centre-forward George Smith (not related), winger Jack Haddington (from Quarry Bank), goalkeeper Frank Pidcock and inside-left Barry O'Shaughnessy (later to give good service to Hednesford Town).

Scotsman Bob Burgess played in only two games, but he did manage to score in one of them.

In the 1954-55 season another six players figured in just one game each, including the portly figure of Billy Knott in attack. There was left-winger Brian Taylor (who was later to establish himself in the side), full-back Darrol Pritchett from Hull City, and Johnny Maher who came to the Midlands following trials with Manchester City. The Saddlers also gave debuts this term to Dudley-born wing-half Ron Hall and to young right-back Ronnie Beddow who had been an amateur with the club for two years.

Towards the end of the campaign centre-forward Bob Webb was signed from Leeds United. He scored three times in seven games, including a brace in a 6-1 win over Northampton Town, but he couldn't settle down in the Midlands, and in July was sold to Bradford City for whom he hit 59 goals in 209 League outings before switching to Torquay United in 1962.

At this point, Jack Love was taking a more active roll in matters as Major Buckley's assistant and he was soon to take over from the great man.

Thankfully re-election was gained once again, and astonishingly a crowd of 7,125 turned out at Fellows Park to watch the pre-season public practice match in early August 1955 – showing just how much the fans appreciated having a Football League team in Walsall.

Oddly enough, the Saddlers kicked off the new campaign against the side against whom they had ended the previous season – Leyton Orient – but even with 18,786 cheering them on, and several new players in the line-up, including Dave Walsh, the former West Brom and Aston Villa Irish international centre-forward, Scottish inside-left Johnny Davidson from Alloa Athletic, the former Derby County and Nottingham Forest winger Hugh McLaren, and defender Bill Gallier, also from The Hawthorns, Walsall just couldn't do a thing right and lost 2-0.

It was not until mid-September (after Love had been appointed manager) that the first win was recorded – 2-1 at Swindon when Walsh netted twice – and on 1 October, Aldershot were beaten 4-2 at Fellows Park, Walsall's initial home win of the campaign, at their sixth attempt.

A good run was put together, however, when most needed (February-April) when only three games were lost out of 14 and in the end there were four teams below the Saddlers at the foot of the table. Consequently after four successive re-election applications it was a welcome relief to finish out of the danger zone.

In the FA Cup this season, the Saddlers went out to Port Vale in round three (beaten 1-0 at home in front of a 21,811 attendance) this after ousting non-League Margate 6-1 in a replay (a hat-trick here for Walsh) and fellow Third Divion club Southampton 2-1, both at Fellows Park.

In season 1956-57 Walsall finished 15th in Division Three South – their highest placing since 1950-51 when they had taken the same spot.

There was a fine unbeaten run of 11 games strung together (from mid-November to the end of January) including a 7-0 hammering of Brentford when both Sammy Moore and Tony Richards hit hat-tricks, a 7-1 thrashing of Millwall Athletic when Don Dorman claimed a treble, and a 6-3 triumph over Norwich City, a game watched by the best League crowd of the season at Fellows Park – 16,169.

Don Dorman proved an inspiring

Walsall, 1957-58. Back row (left to right): Guttridge, Brownlee, Jones, Billingham, Southam, Chilvers, Perkins, Brown, Tarrant. Middle row: Jack Love (manager), Stewart, Rawlings, McPherson, Hodgkisson, W. Davies, Jack Maund (trainer). Front row: Price, Moore, Richards, Jarman, Taylor, Haddington.

skipper, while two more new signings from West Bromwich Albion, Eric Perkins and Tim Rawlings, both fitted in splendidly at full-back and wing-half respectively.

John Jarman, a former Barnsley player who had also been on Wolves' books, and young Scottish inside-forward Clem Johnson did well, too, in opportunities limited by injury, while in the course of that unbeaten run, the former Ipswich inside-forward Tommy Brown and ex-Wolves winger Sammy Moore added sparkle up front. The former Nottingham Forest and Notts County inside-forward Ronnie Leverton and schemer Kenny Hodgkisson, who had also arrived from neighbouring West Brom the previous season, also played their part.

Walsall kicked off the 1957-58 season without Don Dorman, who had been at the top of his form throughout the previous campaign. He was tempted by the security of the chief scout's job at Birmingham City, which he was to fill with distinction for many years, taking many fine players to St Andrew's.

Two new Scottish faces in the Walsall camp were the former St Mirren and Luton Town inside-forward, Willie Davie, from Huddersfield Town and Jackie Stewart from East Fife. But it was Albert McPherson, promoted to captain, who scored the Saddlers' first goal of the season, a penalty in the opening day win over Northampton Town.

Unfortunately Walsall could not maintain their momentum as they had wished and they burst into life in fits and starts, eventually having to settle for 20th place in the table.

In December, Walsall went out of the FA Cup at the first hurdle but during this same month Fellows Park saw floodlights installed, and to celebrate them being switched on, young Scot Tommy Brownlee scored a hat-trick in a 5-1 win over the Scottish club, Falkirk.

Early in the new year it looked as if the team was slipping towards the re-election zone, but the acquisition of two former Manchester City players, giant goalkeeper John Savage, who possessed an enormous goal-kick, and striker Roy Faulkner, boosted the rest of the side and the danger was averted.

The 1958-59 campaign (Bill Moore's first full season in command – he was appointed manager on 30 December 1957) saw the old Third Division South and North sections replaced by Divisions Three and Four, with Walsall playing in the Fourth.

Manager Moore was confident of success after a pretty good first half to the proceedings but an injury to former Port Vale winger Colin Askey (playing against his former club in January) disrupted his plans. Although an exceptionally fine run was put together over Easter when only one point was dropped in seven games with six clean sheets being kept in the process, defeats at Bradford PA and Shrewsbury Town left Walsall in sixth place at the end.

Tony Richards top-scored with 27 goals, and Colin Taylor, who had replaced his namesake, Brian Taylor, on the left-wing, weighed in with a creditable tally of 11 in his first full season in the side.

Things were beginning to buzz – and they really hotted up in 1959-60 when at long last the dedicated supporters at Fellows Park had something to cheer about when the Saddlers carried off the Fourth Division title in magnificent style.

It was that lethal scoring trio of Tony Richards, Roy Faulkner and Colin Taylor who spearheaded Walsall's success.

Of Walsall's tally of 102 League goals, Richards grabbed 24, and both Faulkner and Taylor weighed in with 21 apiece. There were also very welcome – and decisive – contributions made by Kenny

Walsall, Fourth Division champions in 1959-60. Back row (left to right): Jones, Sharples, Billingham, V. Potts (trainer), Davies, Richards, Rawlings. Middle row: Faulkner, Askey, Taylor, Christie, Gregg, Hodgkisson, Dudley. Front row: Bill Moore (manager), Mr E. Wood (director), Guttridge, Mr E. Thomas (chairman), McPherson, Mr W. L. Aston (director), Mr E. Wilson (secretary).

Hodgkisson (another ex-West Brom man) and the big, strong-running John Davies, known for his flying headers, who both claimed 12 – thus for the first time in the club's history, five men had reached double figures in the goalscoring stakes.

Sixty-five points were gained – five more than runners-up Notts County – and 28 wins were registered, 14 both at home and away.

Southport were hammered 8-0 at Fellows Park, while on their travels Walsall demolished Crewe Alexandra 5-1 – these being their best two wins out of the 28 recorded. The Saddlers clinched promotion on 12 April with a 4-2 victory at Oldham in front of a 21,000-plus crowd, 5,000 of them from Walsall.

Hot-shot Colin Taylor was outstanding and cracked in two 'specials' that night.

Perhaps the only disappointment was defeat by Midland League Peterborough United in the FA Cup, Posh winning a second round tie 3-2 at Fellows Park in front of a 20,585 crowd.

It was fortunate, in some respects, that manager Moore was able to field a settled side for most of the campaign, his team usually reading: John Christie; Harry Haddington and Bill Guttridge; Peter Billingham then Jimmy Dudley, Albert McPherson, Tim Rawlings; and that terrific forward-line of Davies, Faulkner, Richards, Hodgkisson and Taylor. Haddington and Richards were ever-presents, while Colin Taylor missed only one game, Ken Hodgkisson two and Christie three.

Walsall's average home League attendance for the season was 12,045 and altogether more than 279,000 fans passed through the Fellows Park turnstiles.

The 1960-61 season was one which exceeded everything that had happened in the previous campaign, for even though the Saddlers topped Division Four in 1959-60 few dared hope that they would end up in one of the top two places in Division Three.

Yet that was just what they did by remaining unbeaten at home and producing a run of ten wins in 11 games when the crunch came in March and April. This terrific spell included some memorable victories: 4-0 v Bristol City and 4-0 at Colchester, after Bradford City had been beaten by the same score in February, a month which began with triumphs over Watford (5-2) and Tranmere 4-1 at Prenton Park.

Though skipper Harry Haddington broke a leg in the game against Tranmere Rovers in September, Walsall rallied to win that game with ten men (there were no substitutes in those days) and an FA Cup defeat at Fellows Park by Southern League Yeovil Town proved only to be the spur for the thrilling

Christmas programme in which the double was achieved over promotions rivals and eventual champions Bury, this after Port Vale had just been whipped 6-2.

No one who was there will ever forget that Wednesday evening in April 1961 in front of a record crowd of 18,917 at Gay Meadow.

QPR lost on that same night and thus the door leading to the Second Division opened up for the Saddlers to step right through.

Shrewsbury Town 1 Walsall 2
Division Three, 26 April 1961

IT WAS Walsall who dictated play in the early stages putting the Shrews under considerable pressure. Colin Taylor had the first shot which went wide and then Tony Richards saw his effort kicked clear by Skeech.

It was Taylor then who sent the Saddlers fans wild when he whipped in one of his left-foot specials on four minutes to give Walsall the lead.

In the next attack Taylor almost made it two with another powerhouse effort which shaved an upright.

Shrewsbury's player-manager Arthur Rowley counter-attacked with two cracking shots, both saved by John Christie, one rebounding off the 'keeper's body as he dived.

In fact, Shrewsbury held the upper hand during the 20 minutes leading up to half-time and 60 seconds before the interval they drew level with a disputed penalty. Jimmy Dudley, late of West Brom, was adjudged to have handled inside the box and Rowley stepped up to smash the ball home, thus claiming his 379th League goal to equal the record held at the time by Dixie Dean.

Rowley went on to net 434 League goals – a record which still stands today.

After the break Walsall, backed by 10,000 travelling supporters, surged at the Shrewsbury goal and their efforts were rewarded in the 56th minute when right-winger Colin Askey met Kenny Hodgkisson's deep cross superbly to head the ball wide of the diving Gibson in the home goal.

Richards should have put the result beyond all doubt on the hour but he screwed his 12-yard shot inches wide. Then Taylor and Hodgkisson both went close before Christie had to save magnificently from Rowley and Baker. Walsall's defence, with Albert McPherson in terrific form, held on and as the final whistle sounded, hundreds of delighted Saddlers fans raced across the pitch to carry off their heroes. It was a good five minutes before the last player, Richards, found his way to the dressing-room where he joined his colleagues in a glass of champagne.

Shrewsbury Town: Gibson; Walker, Skeech, Wallace, Pountney, Harley, Jones, Starkey, Baker, Rowley, McLaughlin.
Walsall: Christie; Palin, Sharples, Hill, McPherson, Dudley, Askey, Hodgkisson, Wilson, Richards, Taylor.

Reaching Division Two was essentially a team effort, but one must still pay tribute to the solidity of John Christie in goal; the reliability and drive of the two former West Brom wing-halves Jimmy Dudley and Tim Rawlings; Albert McPherson's marvellous control in the centre of the defence; the 36 goals notched by ace striker Tony Richards (second only to Gilbert Alsop for a season's tally) which sent him to the top of the all-time scoring charts for the Saddlers; and Colin Taylor's haul of 33 goals – the highest-ever seasonal total registered by a Walsall winger.

During the course of this 1960-61 campaign Walsall played their first-ever League Cup-tie, losing 3-1 to Everton at Goodison Park where John Davies scored for the Saddlers in this new competition which took time to take off, most leading clubs refusing to participate during its early years.

Unfortunately in the FA Cup competition, the Saddlers again succumbed to non-League opposition, losing at the first hurdle at home by 1-0 to Yeovil Town.

So the scene was set for Second Division football to return to Walsall for the first time in 60 years – but the question being asked was simple: 'Could the magic last?'

An all-ticket gate of over 18,400 saw Tony Richards get a hat-trick in a pulsating opening game against Sunderland which Walsall won 4-3.

Walsall 4 Sunderland 3
Division Two, 19 August 1961

THIS was a game that had just about everything – only the second all-ticket game ever to be staged at Fellows Park, although not all 22,000 tickets were sold, Brian Clough's debut for Sunderland, Walsall's first game in Division Two for just over 60 years – and seven goals.

Clough had just moved from Middlesbrough for a £45,000 fee, but it was the Saddlers' own star striker Tony Richards who made his mark early on, banging home a 13th-minute penalty after Colin Askey had been brought down. Sunderland hit back quickly and were level within minutes – and it was Clough who got the goal, being in just the right place to turn a George Herd cross past the stranded John Christie.

After 32 minutes Sunderland went ahead when centre-half Charlie Hurley moved up to head a Harry Hooper corner into the path of George Herd, who nodded home completely unchallenged from ten yards. Walsall, however, pulled back just before the interval, when Tommy Wilson forced the ball home after a Colin Taylor shot had been partially cleared.

It was all Walsall at this stage, but Sunderland moved swiftly out of defence and with the home defence struggling, John Sharples handled to prevent a Clough pass reaching Hooper. The former Wolves winger took the spot-kick himself and slid the ball home to put Walsall behind yet again.

The Saddlers were not finished, though, and on 66 minutes the perseverance of Tommy Wilson skilfully put Richards through for the equaliser. Still Walsall pressed and in the 74th minute came a replica of that third goal, Wilson again drawing the defence off Tony Richards who gratefully accepted the through ball to make the score 4-3.

Although Sunderland came again at the death, Walsall's defence was in command and the Saddlers ran out narrow winners after a pulsating contest.

Such was Walsall's supreme fitness that they played the game at full pace throughout and what magnificent support the crowd gave to the lads on the field with an almost continuous roar throughout the 90 minutes.

Walsall: Christie; Palin, Sharples, Hill, McPherson, Dudley; Askey, Hodgkisson, Wilson, Richards, Taylor.
Sunderland: Wakeham; Nelson, Ashurst, Anderson, Hurley, McNab, Hooper, Herd, Clough, Fogarty, Overfield.
Attendance: 18,420.

And then a narrow defeat in the hands of Newcastle United was followed by a deserved 3-1 win at Derby's Baseball Ground when Bill Younger scored on his debut.

The fourth League match was the eagerly awaited return fixture with Newcastle United which was played on 29 August 1961, and attracted a record crowd (which stood forever) of 25,453 to Fellows Park. This time Walsall gained revenge for that reverse at St James's Park by winning 1-0, Younger again on target.

Walsall 1 Newcastle United 0
Division Two, 29 August 1961

THIS was the night a record gate of 25,453 packed into Fellows Park, with no crowd trouble whatsoever despite many being locked out and many who were in the ground having difficulty in seeing.

Several fans watched (or attempted to watch) the action from the Wallows Lane railway bridge and from the area originally designated for a new ground, but they missed most of the early first half action at the Hillary Street end when Tommy Wilson's 15-yard shot was fumbled by 'keeper Dave Hollins and then Tommy Younger, playing against a side from his native Tyneside, fired over the top.

Younger went close again on 18 minutes before the same player broke the deadlock when he whipped in a remarkable swerving shot from fully 30 yards after 28 minutes.

Soon afterwards George Meek bent the crossbar with a piledriver and although the little winger was injured a couple of minutes later, taking the brunt of a heavy tackle, he bravely stayed on the field – remember these were pre-substitute days. The great Welsh international schemer Ivor Allchurch began to come more and more into the game at this point and Walsall's defence were under the cosh for long spells.

It was Newcastle who held the upper hand in the early exchanges of the second half but Walsall stood firm and managed a few attacks themselves, Younger, Wilson and Taylor all going close. Newcastle came strong again towards the end, but the Saddlers hung on to register another famous victory.

Walsall: Christie; Palin, Sharples, Hill, McPherson, Dudley, Meek, Hodgkisson, Wilson, Younger, Taylor.
Newcastle United: Hollins; Keith, McMichael, Neale, Thompson, Dalton; White, Wright, Leek, Allchurch, Scanlon.

After crashing 5-1 at Orient on the Saturday following the win over Newcastle, Walsall were never quite the same team again. They did, however, still manage to pull off one or two excellent victories, such as a 5-0 drubbing of Rotherham in October. They also suffered a few heavy defeats, including a 6-1 hiding at Liverpool.

Alan Boswell made his debut in goal and he did well, holding his place in the side and putting on a terrific show against Fulham in the FA Cup.

The fractured collar-bone suffered before Christmas by Tommy Wilson, who had scored for Nottingham Forest in their 1959 FA Cup Final win over Luton, cost Walsall dear in the end, and although Richards struck home 20 goals and four players appeared in every League game, Walsall had to be content with 14th position with 39 points, 23 fewer than the champions Liverpool but only six more than relegated Bristol Rovers.

The average home League crowd at Fellows Park this term was 12,704.

Walsall's youngsters this season did themselves proud by completing the Midland Intermediate League and Cup double. They pipped Aston Villa by a point to carry off the title and then accounted for Port Vale (4-2 on aggregate) in the Cup Final.

The 1962-63 season turned out to be one of the saddest, and perhaps unluckiest, in Walsall's history, for it brought the end of an all too brief stay in Division Two. Yet at one stage the Saddlers seemed to be well on the way to a comfortable mid-table position.

They got over a humiliating 6-0 home defeat in the hands of Newcastle in late September, after having completed the double over Middlesbrough (1-0 and 3-2), and things were looking good. The rot, though, really set in with a 5-3 home defeat against Portsmouth in mid-December, a game which Walsall could have so easily won after two well-taken goals by debutant Jimmy O'Neill. It was two and a half months before the atrocious weather of that winter relented enough for football to take place again and when it did, Walsall continued a losing sequence which stretched to eight matches (League and Cup).

At this stage Tony Richards moved to Port Vale, having missed a penalty against Derby County in what proved to be his last outing for Walsall.

He was missed up front and although the Saddlers rallied bravely in the last few weeks of the season with wins over Chelsea (1-0 at Stamford Bridge), Cardiff, Rotherham, Newcastle and Norwich City, everything depended on the very last game against Charlton who, like the Saddlers, were fighting against the drop.

The initial match was abandoned at half-time with the scores level, but when the re-arranged match took place on 24 May, Walsall were crippled with injuries to Graham Newton and goalkeeper Alan Boswell. A draw against the Londoners would have been sufficient to keep Walsall up, but alas, they crashed to a 2-1 defeat and went down with Luton Town. A crowd of 16,761 saw that crucial game with Charlton, and the average home attendance for the season was 9,821, down by almost 3,000 on the previous year.

Following the transfer of Tony Richards to Port Vale in March 1963, the summer break saw the departure from Fellows Park of such giants as Tim Rawlings, who was released after 200 games in Walsall's colours, Ken Hill who moved to Norwich, and Colin Taylor who left for Newcastle.

In addition Alan Boswell signed for Shrewsbury Town after a quarrel with the chairman, Ernie Thomas, and it was a dispirited group of players and fans that saw in the 1963-64 campaign.

New signings Jimmy Fell (from

Walsall, 1962. Back row (left to right): Roper, Hodgkisson, Partridge, Palin, Ball, Christie, Boswell, Sharples, Foster, Younger, Rawlings. Middle row: Wilson, Richards, Guttridge, Meek, V. Potts (trainer), Askey, Eden, Taylor, Dudley. Seated: Bill Moore (manager), Mr W. L. Aston (director), Mr W. Longmore (vice-chairman), McPherson, Mr E. Thomas (chairman), Hill, Mr E. Wood (director), Mr V. McBride, Mr E. Wilson (secretary). On ground: Rowe, Allen, Bennett, Smith, Gregg.

Lincoln City) and Graham Matthews combined to score within a minute of the start of the first home game against Colchester, but it took Walsall until the seventh game (at Reading) to chalk up their first win. Though they gained a thrilling League Cup victory over Ipswich, it was not until mid-October that the Saddlers recorded their first home League win in Division Three (against Crewe). Then came one of the team's bravest performances in winning at Peterborough, who had Derek Dougan in their line-up. Fell was injured in the first-half, Ron Howells cracked an ankle bone in the second half, and at one stage Walsall had only nine men on the park. Even so they held on to win and just five days later collected another two points when Graham Matthews notched a last-minute winner at Notts County.

Soon, however, things began to change – and first of all manager Bill Moore departed, to be replaced as caretaker boss by ex-Coventry City goalkeeper Alf Wood, who was promoted from reserve-team trainer. He was later given the position on a full-time basis (February 1964) but was to resign before the turn of the year. All five games were lost in November, including an FA Cup disaster at Southport, and it was a hard long winter, but thankfully relegation was avoided after Peterborough United had been beaten in the last game. The average home attendance was a shade over 7,300 – well down yet again, on the 1962-63 figure.

One or two promising youngsters came forward, including goalkeeper Dave Tennant and flying winger Roger Smith, while Graham Matthews weighed in with 15 goals.

At youth team level Walsall beat Wolves 5-3 on aggregate to lift the Midland Intermediate League Cup for the second time in three years.

Early results in 1964-65 were disastrous with five defeats coming in the first six games, and by early November another seven had been suffered. At this juncture manager Alf Wood was replaced by Ray Shaw.

Immediately there was a change in form when Brentford (third in the table) were beaten 4-3 by next-to-bottom Walsall at Fellows Park, Colin Taylor netting a hat-trick. The team, however, struggled to get into any sort of rhythm into their play, with new centre-half John Leedham no substitute for Albert McPherson, who had been released the previous summer.

Something had to be done. Bill Harrison was made chairman, while manager Shaw quickly brought a host of new players into the camp. Things picked up a little but after another perilously hard campaign Walsall finally settled for 19th place, the same as in the previous season.

By this time Allan Clarke had emerged as a major striker and netted 23 goals. Stan Bennett was settling in at centre-half and Nick Atthey was now manning midfield.

Colin Harrison was another young starlet, while men like John Harris (an excellent skipper) and Graham Sissons (ex-Blues) did well in defence. Inside-forward Jimmy McMorran was a fine back-up to the forwards, with wingers Ken Satchwell, and Colin Taylor (back from St James' Park for a third stint at Fellows Park) giving cause for optimism as the 1965-66 season loomed.

After that quite traumatic transformation of 1964-65, when home crowds averaged 6,750, the new season was eagerly awaited, particularly as much-travelled striker George Kirby had been signed during the summer to add strike power up front.

An Allan Clarke winner at Bournemouth on a Saturday night got the Saddlers off to a good start and indeed, Walsall went on to make one of the best-ever starts to a season, being unbeaten in their first eight League and Cup matches. This run included a remarkable recovery in the first round League Cup replay against Queen's Park Rangers when they pulled back a two-goal deficit in the last 20 minutes with Clarke netting a last-ditch winner from the penalty spot.

This victory earned the Saddlers a lucrative, mouth-watering clash with West Bromwich Albion at The Hawthorns, where a bumper crowd of 41,188 turned up to see Walsall put on a great performance before going down 3-1. Tony Brown gave the Baggies the lead but when the scoreline stood at 1-1, after Colin Taylor had equalised, Walsall's Nick Atthey had a goal ruled out for offside (by another player) and Stan Bennett conceded an own-goal. In the end Albion's experience took them

Walsall staff pictured before the start of the 1966-67 season. Back row (left to right): Clive Ford, Colin Harrison, Ken Satchwell, Roger Smith, Philip Saunders, Paul Colton, Roy Cross, Harry Middleton, Milton Wright. Second row: Roger Jones, Mick Evans, Trevor Meath, Terry Carling, Stan Bennett, Keith Ball, John Harris, Derek Pace, Gerry Summers. Seated: Ray Shaw, Gerry Harris, Graham Sissons, Frank Gregg, Colin Taylor, Howard Riley, Nick Atthey, Jimmy McMorran, Arthur Cox. On ground: George Kirby, Geoff Morris, Derek Clarke, Frank Carsley, Bobby Gough, Brian Horton, Martin Bristow, Alan Baker.

through – and they went on to win the trophy that year.

Bennett was the hero of a terrific FA Cup run by Walsall a few months later when Swansea were whipped 6-3 (Kirby scoring twice against his former club), Aldershot were knocked out 2-0 and First Division Stoke were dismissed at the Victoria Ground. The score stood at 0-0 when Walsall's midfielder Jimmy McMorran was put out of the game by a cruel tackle that went unpunished except for a free-kick. From that kick, however, the ball rebounded to Howard Riley who cracked home a superb goal and incredibly Walsall were 2-0 up by half-time thanks to another Allan Clarke penalty. Somehow the battling ten men from Fellows Park held out in the second half with Kirby, a tower of strength in defence having moved back there to help contain the threat of the City centre-half Maurice Setters who had been pushed up front.

After this quite memorable win luck was against Walsall in the next round and after twice taking the lead they went out of the competition, beaten 3-2 by Norwich City.

Shortly after this Cup exit, Allan Clarke left for Fulham, being replaced by Shrewsbury's Harry Middleton, who was soon among the goals, grabbing four in a game against Gillingham on Easter Saturday. He ended up with 14 in 18 outings as the season closed with Walsall in ninth place.

During the campaign, a prestigious friendly was played against the great Moscow Dynamo side from Russia, but Walsall were whipped 5-0 before a 10,697 crowd. In the September, a 16-year-old newcomer, Geoff Morris, was introduced to League action for the first time. Geoff had to wait quite a while, though, before gaining a regular place in the side, owing to the form and consistency of one ginger-haired, cannonball-shooting, outside-left by the name of Colin Taylor.

Taylor's form was perhaps the only bright spot as Walsall suffered several set-backs early in 1966-67, the worst being a serious knee injury to skipper John Harris in the opening game against Mansfield. Sadly, Harris, although he reappeared briefly until November 1968 making ten more appearances, was never again fully fit for first-team duty and his calm and generalship were sorely missed. Gradually, however, the young Mike Evans made the number-three spot his own and Walsall enjoyed a marvellous run in the League Cup, winning at Port Vale, beating Stoke City 2-1 at Fellows Park and getting the better of Exeter City at St James's Park. Alan Baker, ex-Aston Villa, notched one of the finest goals ever seen on that ground when he went past at least five men before netting with an unstoppable shot.

Eventually the Saddlers fell to Sheffield United (2-1) at Bramall Lane, while in the FA Cup any hopes of progress ended in round three when they lost to Bury. Walsall's League action, meanwhile, was rather inconsistent. Whilst recording a few excellent wins, they also suffered some pretty heavy defeats: 6-2 at Oldham, 5-1 at Colchester, 5-2 at Torquay and 4-0 at Workington, and finally settled for 12th place in the table. The average home attendance was a fraction over 8,500 – well up on the previous season's average of 7,731.

With former Wolves centre-forward Jimmy Murray moving in from Manchester City to replace George Kirby, who was surprisingly released in the summer, Walsall made an excellent start to the 1967-68 campaign.

They lost only two of their first 13 games and although crashing out of the League Cup, going down 5-1 to West Ham, the Saddlers were right on course to gain promotion as Christmas arrived.

However, a Boxing Day defeat at Stockport started a winless spell that lasted eight games, although during this barren period a notable 2-1 win at Crystal Palace in an FA Cup replay helped ease the pain.

Over 21,000 witnessed a home fourth round FA Cup-tie against Liverpool, Walsall putting up a spirited performance to draw 0-0. But in the replay at fog-bound Anfield, the Reds proved far too strong and ran out convincing winners by 5-2.

After that, Walsall's season virtually collapsed. A five-point lead at the top of the Division quickly eroded away and after home defeats against promotion rivals Shrewsbury and Oxford, promotion was nothing but a dream and seventh place was the team's final position. So near, yet so far, but for the die-hard supporters it had been a much better campaign, emphasised by a substantial increase in the average home attendance which rose to over 9,000.

One of Walsall's best wins in 1967-68 came at home against Tranmere in October when they registered a 5-1 victory.

Walsall 5, Tranmere Rovers 1
Division Three, 3 October 1967

WALSALL surged to victory against Tranmere with an exciting, if unsophisticated, five-goal romp.

Yet really the scoreline fails to do justice to the Tranmere attack. But for some cruel luck in the second half the Merseysiders may well have forced a cliff-hanging finale.

And it was typical of their refreshing enthusiasm that even when they were 4-1 down with ten minutes to go they played as if there was still a chance of a miracle.

At one stage the match took on the flavour of an old Hollywood western.

On one side there was the fastest shot in the Third Division – Walsall winger Colin 'Thunderbolt' Taylor, and to face him Tranmere had the League's new top-scorer, George 'Hotshot' Yardley.

All that was missing was the high noon kick-off. But at the end of the match old hand Taylor had out-gunned the Tranmere pretender. Taylor netted twice to Yardley's once.

Taylor's first goal was a gem, the barrel-chested red-head blasting in a typical 25-yarder to give his side the lead in 13 minutes. At the other end Yardley had a good effort blocked on the line.

In between this private duel, Walsall's new boy, Tommy Watson nipped in for his first goal for the club and, just before half-time, schemer Alan Baker rounded off a cleverly taken free-kick by Jim McMorran by tapping into an unguarded net from six yards.

Yardley finally got his sights adjusted midway through the second half when he rose beautifully to a Hill cross to pull one back for Tranmere.

But it was Taylor who broke Tranmere's heart and proved himself the better man on the night by lashing in a free-kick deflected off Alan King.

And a minute from the end Jimmy Murray collected a fifth as the Tranmere defenders wearily fell back.

A crowd of 7,250 saw these teams in action:

Walsall: Ball; Gregg, Evans, Simpson, Bennett, Atthey, Watson, Baker, Murray, McMorran, Taylor.

Tranmere Rovers: Cumbes; Storton, Robertson, Pritchard, Martin, King, Hill, Sinclair, Yardley, Beamish, Williams.

After the collapse from a strong promotion position in the second half of 1967-68, Walsall received another blow during the close season with the death of chairman, Bill Harrison, who had done so much in the three years that he was in office after taking his seat during 1964-65.

His son, Ron, became chairman and former Gillingham defender and Newcastle United and Everton coach, Ron Lewin, was appointed manager in succession to Dick Graham who had been in charge of the team for the latter part of the 1967-68 campaign. Former boss Ray Shaw moved up the ladder to become general manager. On the playing side, Walsall's favourite son, Colin Taylor, was transferred to Crystal Palace.

Four draws came in the opening five League games of 1968-69, but then Walsall began to slip down the table, and flagging spirits were only slightly raised by a gallant third-round FA Cup display against Tottenham Hotspur in January, this after hard fought wins over non-Leaguers Leytonstone (1-0) and St Albans City (3-1 in a replay).

A crowd of 18,779 saw that tie at Fellows Park, decided by a Jimmy Greaves goal on 75 minutes, but most of the fans still don't know how the Spurs defender, Joe Kinnear managed to make a dramatic goal-line clearance from Dave Wilson.

At the end of the next month, Bill Moore, who was manager during Walsall's Third and Fourth Division promotion seasons of 1959-60-61, came back to take charge of the team – and immediately he got a response from the players with four wins coming on the trot.

But the momentum faded again and perhaps the only bright spot before the season ended was the fine form shown in goal by young Phil Parkes, later to become a star in the First Division with both QPR and West Ham as well as

Walsall, 1969-70. Back row (left to right): Colin Harrison, Trevor Meath, Stan Jones, Mick Evans, Derek Trevis. Second row: Jimmy MacEwan (trainer), Stan Bennett, Roy Cross, Bob Wesson, Phil Parkes, John Woodward, Frank Gregg, John Harris (reserve-team manager). Third row: Tommy Watson, Geoff Morris, Nick Atthey, Bill Moore (manager), Allan Baker, Ken Stephens, Dave Wilson. Front row: Terry Mighalls, Steve Williams, Chris Ainge, Gary Fleet, Keith Gough, Ray Train.

winning England honours. The average turnout for a League match at Fellows Park in 1968-69 was under 5,900 – the lowest for some considerable time.

Could manager Bill Moore achieve the sort of success that he had done during his first spell at the helm? That was the question being asked by the supporters as the 1969-70 season dawned. Sadly he couldn't, although there was no lack of effort on his part.

The first full season after his return saw the Saddlers finish in mid-table yet again with the highlights coming in the FA Cup when victory was achieved at promotion-chasing Orient, and a four-match marathon against Brighton before Crystal Palace ended the run.

Colin Taylor, was in good form after having returned (from Palace for his third spell at Fellows Park), and goalkeeper Phil Parkes was in great form in all of those Cup-ties and in many League matches too.

It was obvious that Walsall had discovered another 'keeper, fit to rank with the best in the game – and in future years he proved that beyond all doubt.

In the early close season of 1970, Walsall played three games in the Sudan – only the club's second major tour abroad (they had earlier played two games in West Germany in June 1966 against Wuppertal and Opel Russelheim, winning the first, losing the second). It was certainly an experience for a lot of the players and indeed the staff, who made the long trip into the desert where the temperature regularly topped 90 degrees.

Of the three games played (the first in Khartoum) two were lost and the

Colin Taylor thumps home his penalty in the Saddlers' 3-0 win over Aston Villa in a Third Division game at Fellows Park in January 1971. Over 19,000 saw the game.

other drawn, and the Saddlers in fact, failed to score a goal on the tour.

By the start of the following season, Parkes had moved to QPR and ironically his replacement, Bob Wesson, who won back his place between the sticks, was voted the Supporters' Player of the Season.

But on the whole 1970-71 was another poor campaign for the Saddlers. Little progress was made in either Cup competition, and perhaps the best two performances from the team came at home and away against Aston Villa.

In January, Walsall won 3-0 at Fellows Park, with Geoff Morris scoring twice before a 19,203 attendance (producing record receipts at that time of £5,945), and in March they forced a 0-0 draw at Villa Park when the turn-out was 37,642.

Villa Park certainly proved to be a lucky ground, because on the last day of the season Reading lost 2-1 there and so went down to Division Four instead of Walsall.

After narrowly avoiding relegation at the end of the previous season, Walsall kicked off the 1971-72 campaign with a Scottish tour which saw them win at Hamilton and East Stirling and draw at Arbroath. But, alas, the League programme brought little joy in the first three months, despite the inclusion of two new men in the front-line, John Smith and John Manning.

But then came an exciting FA Cup run in which Bernie Wright and Mark Wallington (who played in one Cup game) emerged as major discoveries and in due course both helped the club on to a firmer financial basis by their transfers to Everton (Walsall's Cup conquerors this term) and Leicester City respectively. Nor did their moves affect the results as the Saddlers achieved a remarkable 16-game unbeaten run that carried them from 19th position at the beginning of March to a final placing of ninth. During that spell Bobby Shinton (signed from Lye) showed his talent as a goalscorer and the versatile Colin Harrison made an outstanding contribution in midfield to win the Supporters' Player of the Season award.

One player who left the club was midfielder Ray Train, who joined Carlisle United in December 1971. He later served with Sunderland, Bolton Wanderers, Watford, Oxford United, Bournemouth, Northampton Town and Tranmere Rovers before returning to Walsall in 1986.

Walsall's hopes were set high for season 1972-73 with the introduction of some exciting new players, but early exits from both the League Cup (beaten 4-1 at Southport) and the FA Cup (eliminated by Charlton Athletic in round two) put a dent in the proceedings. And they struggled to find a 'settled' goalkeeper during the second half of the campaign when they utilised no fewer than seven: Bob Wesson, John Osborne (on loan, West Brom), Ian Turner (on loan, Grimsby Town; later to return in 1979), Keith Ball (who had been with the club during the 1960s), Glen Johnson (on loan, Doncaster Rovers), Dennis Peacock (on loan, Nottingham Forest) and young amateur Jimmy Inger from Derbyshire side Long Eaton United, who played in the last two League matches, conceding a goal in each.

Despite winning nine of his first 13 League games, manager Moore resigned his post after a defeat at Brentford in October, being succeeded by John Smith, who moved up from the position as player-coach. While the team were by then in the midst of a dreadful run of seven games with only one point gained, Ron Harrison quit as chairman and with the club threatened with oblivion, Ken Wheldon stepped in to take over the chair. Around this time secretary Ernest Wilson, who had been with Walsall for almost 40 years, died in hospital after a four-month illness, but somehow the club survived.

Although he found it (as he himself put it) 'wrapped in waste paper and tied up with string', Ken Wheldon worked tirelessly to satisfy creditors and inspire better results.

The new set-up also saw former Birmingham County FA secretary, John Westmancoat, move up to take Ernie Wilson's secretarial seat (he had previously been assistant secretary).

Bernie Wright returned from Goodison Park to get the winning goal in a ding-dong contest against Bristol Rovers when Walsall pulled back from 3-2 down to win 4-3 in injury time and the season ended with the Saddlers two points clear of relegation after a nail-biting last month.

That clash with the Pirates was certainly one of the best matches of the season.

Walsall 4 Bristol Rovers 3
Division Three, 19 March 1973

THIS was a truly incredible game that lasted close on two hours including the interval despite the fact that there was no official extra-time. For a start it began five minutes late because of a bomb scare in the stand. Few people left their seats and they were rewarded with a game that they will not have forgotten.

Walsall began well and after nine minutes, following some good work by Nick Atthey and Frank Gregg, the bearded Bobby Shinton volleyed the Saddlers into the lead. Soon afterwards visiting defenders Phil Roberts and Stuart Taylor were booked and although a lot of pressure was put on the Rovers goal, Walsall couldn't add to their tally before half-time.

The Saddlers resumed after the break with 16-year-old Alan Birch making his debut, having come on as substitute for Bobby Shinton, who injured a shoulder in the first half and before Birch had touched the ball, Walsall suffered a further blow when Stan Bennett broke his nose in a heavy collision.

Gallantly he stayed on the field and continually headed high balls in the face of the twin threat of Alan Warboys and Bruce Bannister.

Rovers seemed to have turned the game their way when Bannister headed an equaliser and Warboys swept them into the lead with two goals inside four minutes, but halfway through the second period Chris Jones pounced to equalise, hooking the ball home following a John Saunders corner. Soon afterwards it was 3-2 to Rovers as Warboys took full advantage of hesitancy by goalkeeper Dennis Peacock.

The game was well into injury time and Rovers still led when Chris Jones chased a long through ball from Nick Atthey and made it 3-3. Rovers were wasting time whenever they could at this stage, but with Alan Birch buzzing in midfield and referee Jim Whalley of Cheshire ready to blow his whistle, the Saddlers won a free-kick. John Saunders took it and Bernie Wright, still battling for everything, headed home.

It was almost 9.30pm. and some supporters had left almost half an hour earlier thinking the Saddlers could not come back from the 3-2 deficit. What a memorable night for those who stayed.

Walsall: Peacock; Gregg, Harrison, Penman, Bennett, Atthey, Saunders, Shinton(Birch), Wright, Jones, Dainty.
Bristol Rovers: Eadie; Roberts, Parsons, Aitken, Taylor, Stanton, Stephens, B. Jones, Warboys, Bannister, Rudge.

Before the start of the 1973-74 season, Ronnie Allen, one-time England international with West Bromwich Albion, was appointed manager, with Davey Burnside (also ex-West Brom) as his assistant.

But after three memorable League Cup matches against Wembley-bound Manchester City, success was limited and both Allen and Burnside departed in December to let in another ex-Albion man, Doug Fraser, an unlikely choice. Fraser's playing career by this time was slowly coming to an end, his lack of pace on the field being something of an embarrassment at times.

Happily Alan Buckley, who had arrived in the camp from Nottingham Forest during Allen's reign as manager, was scoring goals regularly and Walsall enjoyed a splendid run of five successive wins at the turn of the year. They eventually finished in 15th place, with Buckley grabbing 21 of the 51 League goals scored. He also netted a marvellous hat-trick in a 6-1 League Cup win over Shrewsbury in August.

In September 1973, Bernie Wright scored one of the fastest-ever goals (from the start of a game) by a Walsall player, netting after just 17 seconds of the home match against Bournemouth. And during this season Alan Buckley grabbed Walsall's first-ever Sunday goal, against Wrexham at Fellows Park on 20 January 1974 when over 9,000 fans turned out.

Alan Birch was now emerging as a great little midfielder and he was to play a prominent part in 1974-75 when Walsall enjoyed perhaps the greatest FA Cup run in the club's history.

It began in modest fashion with a 3-1 win at non-League Ashford. But then it gathered momentum and a similar scoreline was achieved at Newport County.

After this came a superb display, a goalless draw at Old Trafford in round three when the turnout was 43,353. The replay attracted a crowd of 18,105 to Fellows Park and Walsall roared through in terrific style with a 3-2 win in front of the TV cameras. Alan Buckley missed a number of penalties in his time, but he cracked home a vital one that night against Manchester United to steer the Saddlers through to the next round where they beat Newcastle United in front of a home crowd of 19,998.

Walsall 3 Manchester United 2
FA Cup Third Round Replay,
7 January 1975

IT HAS been said that lightning never strikes in the same place twice, but this game was the climax of two tremendous displays in the space of four days when Walsall not only outplayed Second Division Manchester United at Old Trafford on the Saturday (although having to be satisfied with a goalless draw) but beat them at Fellows Park after extra-time on the Tuesday.

The Saddlers made a tremendous start in the replay with Bernie Wright challenging for everything and keeping the United defenders on tenterhooks as the home side surged forward again and again. It was fitting that after Brian Taylor had raced 50 yards down the right wing and had wrong-footed the United defence with his cross, Wright was the man on the spot to hammer the ball home with his left foot.

It seemed disaster had struck when, before half-time, referee Peter Willis awarded a penalty to United after the ball had struck Stan Bennett on the arm. Irishman Gerry Daly netted from the spot, but his manager Tommy Docherty admitted that it was a penalty that should never have been.

Therefore at the interval it was all square at 1-1.

Walsall, to their credit, were not put off by this incident, however, and they certainly had the better of the second period, coming perilously close to scoring when Alan Buckley miscued a header from a Brian Taylor corner when it seemed easier to score.

The game went into extra-time and twice the Saddlers were denied penalty claims. Then United had an appeal turned down, but as the second period of extra-time began Walsall at last got the goal they deserved, Alex Stepney dropping a John Saunders cross only for Alan Buckley to whip the ball home from close range. Soon it was 3-1 as George Andrews was upended and this time a penalty was awarded. Stepney got his hands to Buckley's spot-kick, but couldn't prevent the ball from flying high into the top of the net.

Two minutes later Sammy McIlroy made it 3-2, but Walsall were never in serious danger of losing their lead – and the celebrations went on long into the night with Tommy Docherty's words ringing in the Walsall players' ears: "They played well and good luck to them."

Walsall: Kearns; Saunders, Harrison, Robinson, Bennett, Atthey, Taylor, Andrews, Wright, Buckley, Birch.
Manchester United: Stepney; Young, Houston, Greenhoff, Sidebottom, Buchan, McCalliog, McIlroy, Pearson, Macari, Daly(Davies).

Walsall 1 Newcastle United 0
FA Cup Fourth Round,
25 January 1975

ONCE again Walsall delivered the goods on a Fellows Park pitch that hardly looked fit to start the game much less finish it. Happily referee David Wallace of Crewe ruled that the contest could go on – and despite Stan Bennett, the star of the win over Manchester United in the previous round, having to drop out with 'flu, the side was reshuffled in a way that was to prove vital.

John Saunders moved from the right flank to replace Bennett in the centre, and Colin Harrison switched from left to right to accommodate Roger Fry. And it was Fry who, after 34 minutes of mainly Walsall pressure, floated over a free-kick (awarded for a foul on Bernie Wright) for George Andrews to move in smoothly and head past Ian McFaul into the 'Laundry' goal.

Soon afterwards Alan Buckley was robbed in his last stride by a timely tackle from Alan Kennedy, and before half-time Andrews went close with another header. Newcastle's only threat came from a tame shot by John Tudor and a weak header from Malcolm Macdonald, who was closely shackled by Saunders.

After the break Tudor, Macdonald and Geoff Nulty all had reasonable chances for United while Buckley, Wright, Birch and Nick Atthey all went close for the Saddlers and then Macdonald was set up by Nulty but somehow he turned the ball wide from eight yards.

Walsall held out and as one critic put it afterwards: 'On a pitch where the ball wouldn't run, the players had to – and Walsall won the race'.

Walsall: Kearns: Harrison, Fry, Robinson, Saunders, Atthey, Taylor, Andrews, Wright, Buckley, Birch.
Newcastle United: McFaul; Nattrass, Kennedy, Smith(Gibb), Keeley, Howard, Burns, Nulty, Macdonald, Tudor, Craig.

Marvellous stuff that Cup run, but it all came to an end at St Andrew's in round five when over 43,800 fans saw Birmingham City beat Walsall 2-1 in another tremendous contest.

Anything else that season was bound to be an anticlimax and Walsall ended up in eighth place in Division Three.

Season 1975-76 saw Walsall improve steadily after a slow start, and with Alan Buckley, achieving his best-ever tally of goals – 35 – the Saddlers were right in amongst the promotion challengers at the end of March.

Sadly they managed to win only one of their remaining six League games and slipped down to seventh place.

The regular front line comprised Bernie Wright and George Andrews alongside Buckley and Miah Dennehy, the Irish winger who supplied the crosses. Indeed this was one of the finest attacks the Saddlers had fielded for quite some time. And they were pretty solid at the back, too, with the hefty Scot, Roger Hynd, signed in December, and the ever-present 'keeper Mick Kearns performing majestically.

In fact Walsall missed promotion by a mere six points, but this counted for nothing as the 1976-77 season was generally a rather undistinguished one, although Walsall did reach the third round of the FA Cup again and for the second time in three years were drawn against Manchester United at Old Trafford.

Unfortunately this time, unlike 1975, the result went against the Saddlers, United winning 1-0 after a closely-fought encounter.

Fraser's two-year reign as manager came to an end in March following three successive defeats, against Wrexham, Northampton Town and Mansfield Town, although only a month earlier he had seen Reading slammed 6-1, with Buckley scoring his 100th League goal of his career.

Fraser's last transfer deal was to sell Bernie Wright to Bradford City in February – and this did not go down too well with the fans.

Fortunately the presence of new boss Dave Mackay, the former Scottish international of Hearts, Spurs and Derby County, had an immediate effect on the team and results picked up considerably with only two of the last 15 games being lost.

Relegation was clearly avoided and there was a great deal of optimism within the club as another new season approached, especially when it was announced that Alf Wood, the Shrewsbury Town striker, had been signed to fill the vacancy left after the release of the popular George Andrews.

All these high hopes, however, quickly faded and Walsall met with limited success in 1977-78. They did manage to put together a useful FA Cup run with Dagenham, Port Vale, Swansea and Leicester all biting the dust to earn a money-spinning clash with Arsenal at Highbury.

Although they went out 4-1 to the Gunners, Walsall's fans had plenty to cheer and left London still wondering what might have happened if Colin Harrison's magnificent run in the opening minutes had ended in a goal.

Walsall took sixth place in the table this term, thanks to a late run. But in 1978-79 they again started off badly and this time there was no recovery plan.

Alan Buckley was transferred to Birmingham City in October and Mackay's successor as manager, Alan Ashman, who had guided West Bromwich Albion to FA Cup glory in 1968, enjoyed little success at Fellows Park.

Ashman's replacement, Frank Sibley, fared even worse – and from a their last 12 games Walsall collected only four points and so ended a 16-season spell in Division Three.

Once again, however, the Saddlers rose from the ashes of adversity and with Buckley returning as player-manager they took the Fourth Division by storm to clinch promotion at the first attempt, ensuring Third Division status for the next season with a

Walsall, 1976-77. Back row (left to right): Colin Harrison, Bernie Wright, Vince O'Keefe, Roger Hynd, Dave Serella, Roger Fry. Middle row: Doug Fraser (manager), Brian Taylor, Alan Buckley, Dave Robinson, George Andrews, Alun Evans, Mick Bates. Front row: Miah Dennehy, Kelvin Clarke, Gary Shelton, Ian Brittain, Alan Birch.

Jimmy Kelly scores Walsall's second goal against Stockport County in August 1979. The Saddlers won 2-1.

convincing 2-0 home win over Tranmere Rovers on Easter Monday, Kenny Mower and Dave Serella scoring in front of a near 6,000 crowd.

Not a single game was lost until the 14th fixture (against Halifax Town) and in that time a point was earned with nine men at Lincoln after Ian Paul and Roy McDonough had both been sent-off.

Although Buckley was not quite as prolific in his scoring as before, he formed a fine partnership with Don Penn, who cracked in 26 goals (in League and Cup). Kenny Mower came to power in defence, Ron Green performed exceedingly well in goal and Ian Paul looked promising in midfield.

At one stage in 1979-80, Walsall played through a record 21 League games without defeat and only five matches were lost all season, two of these coming right at the death against Wigan and Newport, which cost the Saddlers the championship, Huddersfield Town pipping Walsall at the post

Walsall's first season back in the Third Division began uncertainly and ended sensationally.

Newcomers included defender Steve Baines (from Bradford City) and former Huddersfield Town captain, Peter Hart, who began in midfield and then moved to a defensive role. Meanwhile, loyal servant Colin Harrison was coming to the end of his time at Fellows Park. In 1980-81 he made 18 full appearances and one as sub. He added one more League outing to his tally in 1981-82 (at Chesterfield in September) to finish with a new club appearance record of 529 in major competition, including 473 in the Football League alone.

Compared with the previous season, Don Penn found it harder to score goals, and illness cruelly ended the career of midfielder Ian Paul at the age of 20.

The Saddlers played some stirring games, however, beating both Carlisle United and Chesterfield at home by 4-3 margins and sharing in an eight-goal thriller at Fellows Park with Sheffield United in December.

In the earlier away match with the Spireites both Ian Paul (again) and Steve Waddington were dismissed, but Walsall still managed to win with nine men. Sadly, Paul had to retire from football soon afterwards.

With only two games remaining, Walsall were almost certain to go down to Division Four, being three points behind fellow strugglers, Sheffield United.

But surprise, surprise. The Saddlers won their penultimate fixture 2-1 against Swindon Town while United drew at Hull. And consequently everything depended on the very last game of the campaign – Sheffield United v Walsall at Bramall Lane. A win for the Saddlers would keep them up – any other result would mean disaster. It was tense from the start – and with barely five minutes remaining and the game goalless, right out of the blue, Don Penn calmly converted a penalty to give the Saddlers the lead. But amazingly there was more drama to come and within a matter of seconds, United were awarded a spot-kick at the other end.

In one of the tensest moments in any Walsall game over the years, brave 'keeper Ron Green dived and saved Republic of Ireland international Don Givens' kick. Walsall were safe – United went down.

And so to season 1981-82 ...and yet another close shave.

Neil Martin returned to the club as joint manager with Buckley. Neil had done a terrific job with the Reserves before going out to Kuwait, and it was thought that he was just the right man to get things ticking over again after that nerve-jangling end to 1980-81.

After a mediocre start to 1981-82, two convincing wins, over Portsmouth and Swindon Town, in the space of four days in October, quickly raised the Saddlers' hopes. Things looked even better after a terrific 4-1 win at Gillingham in December with promotion a distinct possibility at this juncture.

But then came a spell of severe weather, and for a period of six weeks, the only game Walsall played was a second-round FA Cup-tie at Peterborough which they lost 2-1.

Particularly disappointing was the postponement of the Boxing Day game against Huddersfield Town after an army of volunteers had cleared the Fellows Park pitch of snow during the morning.

Walsall's season simply fell apart following that winter snap. They won only four of their last 28 matches (including an excellent victory over Newport when Richard O'Kelly netted a fine hat-trick, the first by a Walsall player since Alan Birch at Peterborough in May 1977) and morale was at a very low ebb in April when on the day that the story of a possible ground-sharing scheme with Wolves leaked out, the Saddlers lost 3-0 at home to Preston.

Barrie Blower, then an avid terrace

fan, organised a protest movement in response to this, and a march was arranged before the last game against Doncaster Rovers.

This brought a slight improvement to the attendance which, at 3,799, was the highest for seven matches. But the game finished goalless and it was only the fact that Swindon lost their last game, at Newport, that kept the Saddlers up.

The 1982-83 season was a far better one for the Saddlers despite them losing their first two matches by the same score of 3-0, and being bottom of the table at Christmas.

A useful run in the FA Cup saw non-Leaguers Kettering Town and North Shields both beaten 3-0 and almost 13,000 turned up at Fellows Park to see the Saddlers earn a goalless draw in round three against Birmingham City. It could have been much better had not Buckley fluffed an early penalty by hitting the crossbar. The replay went to extra-time, and it ended in a 1-0 win for Blues with, ironically, the deciding goal coming from Kevin Summerfield, who was on loan to Walsall from St Andrew's before and after that Cup-tie.

By this time, however, Walsall had run into form and they won 14 and drew six of their last 26 matches to finish a creditable tenth in Division Three.

Over 22,000 fans saw the penultimate fixture of the season, at Fratton Park where the champions, Portsmouth, won a tight contest 1-0.

The 1983-84 season was an outstanding campaign and to kick-off proceedings Walsall fielded the following team for their opening Third Division match away to Exeter City: Mick Kearns; Phil Hawker (signed from Birmingham City), Kenny Mower, Craig Shakespeare, Lee Sinnott, Peter Hart, Mark Rees, Ally Brown, Kevin Summerfield, David Preece and former Birmingham City and Wolves man Colin Brazier, who was signed on a free transfer from Lincoln City. Player-manager Alan Buckley was on the subs' bench.

Walsall won the game 1-0 thanks to a Peter Hart goal – but their next three League fixtures were all lost, including an 8-1 walloping away at Bolton, the Saddlers heaviest for some considerable time. Tony Caldwell scored five times for the Wanderers that afternoon.

But soon after that humiliation at Burnden Park, and a 6-3 defeat at Oxford, things started to pick up.

Experienced defender Brian Caswell came back into the side along with midfielder Gary Childs (secured from West Brom) and a fit-again striker Richard O'Kelly, while goalkeeper Tony Godden was taken on loan from West Brom.

Results improved dramatically, and after stringing together a 12-match unbeaten run in the League, the Saddlers suddenly found themselves in fourth place a week before Christmas.

Confidence within the club was sky high, and although the team struggled to beat Blackpool in the opening round of the League Cup, they played superbly to oust Barnsley over two legs in round two. A last-minute strike Gary Childs accounted for Shrewsbury Town in the next round, and there is no doubt that a magnificent 2-1 victory at First Division Arsenal at the fourth hurdle boosted morale tremendously.

The goals at Highbury were scored by Mark Rees and Ally Brown, and at the time everyone was certainly talking about that other famous Walsall win over the Gunners back in 1933.

Early in the new year, midfielder Ian

Walsall, 1983-84. Back row (left to right): Garry Pendrey, Mark Rees, Kevin Summerfield, Ollie Kearns, Lee Sinnott, Ron Green, Peter Hart, Colin Brazier, Kenny Mower. Front: Brian Caswell, Vince O'Kelly, Philip Hawker, Alan Buckley, David Preece, Craig Shakespeare, Mick Bates. The Saddlers finished sixth in Division Three and reached the League Cup semi-finals.

Handysides, signed for £17,000 from Birmingham City, came into the side, and Walsall continued to flourish, in both the League and the League Cup.

On 14 January, the Saddlers went to the top of the Third Division after slamming Exeter City 4-1 at Fellows Park – and four days later, with the dashing Rees in scintillating form, they won 4-2 at Rotherham in the League Cup to progress to the semi-finals, and a clash with mighty Liverpool, the holders of the trophy.

The whole town of Walsall was now buzzing – and good results continued to be achieved.

Ron Green had now taken over in goal, and at this point manager Buckley was fielding this team: Green; Caswell, Mower, Shakespeare, Brazier, Hart, Handysides, Brown, O'Kelly, Summerfield and/or Preece or Childs.

The first leg of the semi-final with Liverpool took place at Anfield and a crowd of over 31,000, including 7,000 travelling Walsall supporters, saw the Saddlers fight back to earn a splendid 2-2 draw, Mark Rees having another outstanding game. His searching runs at the Liverpool defence will forever linger with Saddlers' fans who made that trip to Merseyside.

The performance of Buckley's men was quite outstanding and it duly received high praise from the national press.

An all-ticket crowd of 19,591 packed into Fellows Park for the return leg and although Walsall battled well, the experience of the Merseysiders told in the end and they went through 2-0 (4-2 on aggregate).

Soon after this epic battle, Walsall's League form began to lose its momentum – and with promotion looking a realistic possibility by mid-March, when they lay third, the run-in was rather disappointing, with only five wins coming in 13 matches.

In the end, Walsall's fine team – one of the best assembled for quite a while – had to settle for sixth place and everyone reflected on what might have been in a season when the football served up was methodical, enterprising and generally exciting. It was a pity that there wasn't more support at home games – the average for the season was only 4,814.

However, there were now plenty of naturally talented players within the club and the basis was there for a good side with future prospects looking extremely healthy.

David Kelly, who made his debut in the Associate Members' Cup match against Northampton Town and then went on to score in three successive League games, was perhaps the pick of the bunch, and he turned out to be a really fine player for his clubs and country.

Chairman Ken Wheldon and his board of directors, along with manager Buckley, and indeed the players, were all confident that season 1984-85 would be another exciting one for Walsall FC, but sadly, only on rare occasions did the team manage to reproduce the form of the previous campaign, and in truth, their best performances were yet again reserved for the League Cup, the highlight being a splendid 3-0 win at Coventry in the second round, the Saddlers having lost the home leg 2-1.

The third round saw Chelsea visit Fellows Park and at this stage hopes were high of another Cup shock. However, watched by a crowd of more than 11,000, a disallowed goal and an equaliser six minutes from time robbed the Saddlers of another giant-killing victory.

In the replay Chelsea grabbed an early lead and although the Saddlers fought back gallantly (having a goal ruled out) the Stamford Bridge side eventually won 3-0 and dreams of another League Cup run were over.

Such was the disappointment during the last third of the season, that chairman Wheldon issued a 'pull your finger out' warning to the management, and promised money for new players.

However, with the entire senior squad being retained for another season, it was difficult to foresee many new arrivals coming into the camp.

So to 1985-86 – and once again it was inconsistency that let Walsall down in their promotion challenge.

With two new faces in the camp, striker Nicky Cross bought from neighbours West Bromwich Albion for £48,000 and ex-Wolves man Steve Daley in midfield, it was generally thought that performances would improve and indeed, at home the Saddlers won 15 and drew seven of their 23 matches, but their away form was rather disappointing with 14 matches lost.

The season started well enough with seven of the first nine League games won. Progress was made in the League Cup after Wolves were beaten 2-1 on aggregate, but shortly after a superb 0-0 draw at Leeds in round two, a 2-0 reverse at Wigan started the decline which saw the Saddlers register only one more win in their next seven games.

A 6-3 League win over Cardiff (with Elliott scoring a hat-trick) and a 7-3 hammering of Preston in the FA Cup (a treble here for Naughton) boosted hopes momentarily, as did a thrilling 6-0 hammering of top-of-the-table Reading. But there were far too many terrible away performances for the Saddlers to maintain a position in the top four and they were always just off the pace, eventually having to settle for sixth position.

Scoring from the penalty spot was also letting them down – and they fluffed vital spot-kicks at home to Brentford and Derby and two away to Cardiff.

The Saddlers failed in all the Cup competitions, but surprisingly the home attendances remained steady (slightly up on the previous season) and those who watched at Fellows Park certainly got good value for money with a total of 107 goals being scored in the 29 matches staged there.

Summing up, 1985-86 was a thoroughly entertaining season – but at times a very frustrating one, especially away from home. But there were rumblings in the background and talk was that Walsall could be moving from their beloved Fellows Park headquarters.

Supporters were uneasy and demanded an explanation.

Then chairman Ken Wheldon and wealthy businessman Jack Harris had a plan to sell Fellows Park to developers and move Walsall FC to share St Andrew's with Birmingham City. They saw it as financial commonsense at a time when soccer generally was going through a difficult period.

But Saddlers fans saw it differently. It was a sell-out, they argued, and felt it would mean an early death for the club if supporters refused to travel to Birmingham for home fixtures.

How could this be prevented? One man had the vision to take on Messrs Wheldon and Harris against all the odds – Barrie Blower, director of Caldmore Area Housing Association.

With the willing help of Tom Hargreaves and a number of other key figures in the Supporters' Club, he recruited an 'army' for a fight to the finish and packed the Town Hall at public meetings to draw up battle plans.

Those indeed were emotional nights, with the massed ranks chanting "We love you Walsall, we do," and "We won't go to Birmingham". Even one avid Blues fan travelled to Walsall to support the campaign to keep the two clubs running separately.

It was a long, hard campaign, but it received its first boost when the Football League, having been swamped by mail and telephone calls from angry Walsall people, kicked out the application to ground-share.

But that was still not the end of the road. Everything depended on a new buyer being found – a man, or company, who was prepared to invest a great deal of cash in the Saddlers.

Barrie Blower got to work. He managed to talk self-confessed London multi-millionaire racehorse owner, Terry Ramsden, into tackling the job of lifting Walsall from the Third to the First Division because that was definitely the target for a man who only liked to back winners.

After several last-minute snags were overcome, 'Our Tel' bought the club for £400,000 on the first of August 1986. He did so in a blaze of publicity, arriving in Walsall in style – his helicopter landing on playing fields near to Fellows Park.

He immediately sacked manager Alan Buckley and coach Garry Pendrey because he wanted his own men to run the show. He was also determined to remove all links with the old regime.

Mr Ramsden announced free admission for senior citizens and he agreed to give them free turkeys at Christmas, but all the euphoria was shattered for a time when the team made a disastrous start to the campaign.

New boss Tommy Coakley, unknown to many people, and his coach Gerry Sweeney, kept their heads, however, and the team gradually climbed from the bottom of the table to eighth position where, for a time, they certainly looked capable of challenging strongly for a promotion Play-off spot.

The poor start, though, had left the Saddlers with an awful lot to do and they eventually had to settle for that moderate position.

It had been quite a memorable season – in more ways than one. The team had been involved in a terrific run in the FA Cup with early victories over Chesterfield (2-0) and Port Vale (5-0) before an even bigger scalp at First Division Charlton Athletic (2-1 in London). Then came a moment to savour for the freedom fighters, who had successfully prevented that ridiculous merger with Birmingham City. The fourth round draw paired Walsall with, yes, you've guessed it, Blues.

On an icy pitch in January, the Saddlers gained the revenge they wanted with a 1-0 win in front of a near 15,000 crowd. It was magic.

If that match was full of drama and tension – which it certainly was – it had nothing on the next round when First Division Watford came to Fellows Park and scraped a 1-1 draw.

Walsall had high hopes of doing well in the replay – and in a quite unbelievable match, filmed by the TV cameras for millions to savour – the Saddlers battled every inch of the way to force an incredible 4-4 draw watched by 23,350 fans. Twice they were ahead and twice they had to fight back to earn a second replay which they narrowly lost 1-0 at Fellows Park, an unfortunate own-goal sending the Hornets through to the quarter-final, where they beat Arsenal.

No doubt some fans dreaded that the Saddlers, shattered by that Cup disappointment, would flop in the League. It had happened in the past.

But this time round they continued where they'd left off, and won their next three matches to revive promotion hopes.

Manager Coakley always insisted that his players were good enough to get out of the Third Division but on this occasion they just couldn't manage it, in spite of losing only two of their remaining 15 games, and consequently Ramsden's and Coakley's ambition of promotion at the first attempt was not fulfilled.

Nevertheless, in all the circumstances it was a highly entertaining season. The average attendances at Fellows Park topped 5,300, indicating clearly that the support was there.

The team netted over 100 goals (26 going to young David Kelly) to underline the entertainment value of the football.

Many exciting new players in the camp around this time included goalkeeper Fred Barber (a £75,000 buy from Everton), Manchester City striker Trevor Christie (once of Leicester, Notts County, Nottingham Forest and Derby County), defenders Graeme Forbes and Andy Dornan (both from Motherwell) and experienced Scottish midfielder Bobby Hutchinson (from Bristol City).

Director Alan Harkett and new secretary Roy Whalley also contributed greatly to a fine season as the club prepared for its centenary celebrations.

Sadly, the 1987-88 season began badly both on and off the field.

Many dedicated supporters were angered by the horrific price rises for admission to Fellows Park, which went up by as much as 127 per cent in some instances and the opening League game at home to Fulham ended in defeat in front of a 4,691 crowd.

However, only two of the next 24 matches were lost and neighbours West Brom were knocked out of the League Cup (3-2 on aggregate). Good form and good results kept the Saddlers in touch with the leaders in Division Three although early exits were made from each of the three Cup competitions.

Yet, overall performances out on the park began to deteriorate and were certainly not in keeping with results. But Walsall hung in there, picking up vital points with some rather undistinguished displays, both at home and away. David Kelly was often left to battle it out alone up front, and he did supremely well, but when Nicky Cross was transferred to Leicester City in January and a handful of reserve-team players were also released, the goals seemed to dry up completely.

Avid fans were now becoming frustrated with what was being served up on the field of play and only 3,920 bothered to turn out to see the home game with Bury in March. But Walsall, amazingly, were still in there with a fighting chance of winning promotion despite failing to look real promotion material.

After beating both Chester City and Mansfield Town in early April Walsall found themselves nestled in second spot, and all of a sudden promotion was there for the taking.

Over 6,600 roared the Saddlers to a vital victory over Doncaster Rovers and there were 11,913 present to see Notts County beaten 2-1 at Fellows Park. Victory in their last two matches would have meant automatic promotion but alas, Walsall slipped up at Bristol Rovers, losing 3-0, and then played out a tame goalless draw at home against Gillingham to end up in the Play-offs.

Here they were paired with Notts County and after two ding-dong battles, Walsall went through to the final 4-2 on aggregate. Bristol City were their opponents in one of the most important contests for many a day.

The first leg at Ashton Gate was seen by over 25,000 fans and Walsall won it 3-1 thanks to two late goals by David Kelly. But in the return game, watched by almost 14,000, City stormed back to win 2-0 and thus bring the scores level on aggregate. Walsall, thankfully, won the penalty shoot-out which gave them ground advantage for the replay… and they certainly made the most of it, walloping the Bristolians 4-0 in front of a delirious 13,007 crowd, ace marksman Kelly grabbing a hat-trick. Walsall were back in the Second Division for the first time in 25 years and manager Tommy Coakley and his players celebrated in style.

Walsall 4 Bristol City 0
Third Division Play-off Final Replay, 30 May 1988

FOR the first time ever Walsall found themselves playing on Spring Bank Holiday Monday and on a perfect day weatherwise they chalked up a tremendous triumph.

After a season of being there or thereabouts in the promotion race, the Saddlers had only just missed out on going up without the Play-offs, but then having disposed of Notts County in the semi-final they took a 3-1 lead in the first leg of the Final against Bristol City only to lose it in the second leg in front of their own supporters.

After ending up 3-3 on aggregate, two great saves by Fred Barber in the penalty shoot out earned Walsall ground advantage in the replay and this took place just 48 hours later.

Manager Tommy Coakley somehow talked new life into his men on the intervening Sunday and in one of the most thrilling first halves ever seen at Fellows Park the Saddlers kept landing the ball in the City goalmouth and their defence just couldn't cope. In the space of eight minutes, three goals flew into the Robins' nest. David Kelly struck twice – after 11 minutes and again on 17 – followed by a third strike from Phil Hawker soon after. City made a couple of isolated attempts to come back either side of the interval, but then superstar David Kelly settled the issue beyond all doubt with a fine run and cross-shot into the Hillary Street End goal after 64 minutes to complete a memorable hat-trick

What scenes at the end – a new era had come, Kelly grabbed the matchball and Walsall were on their way into the Second Division.

This was some game – one of the greatest events at Fellows Park since the World War Two and a match that will never be forgotten.

Walsall: Barber; Taylor, Dornan(M. Jones), Shakespeare, Forbes, Goodwin (Sanderson), Hawker, Hart, Christie, Kelly, Naughton.

Bristol City: Waugh; Llewellyn, Newman, Humphries, Pender, McClaren, Milne, Galliers, Shutt, Walsh, Jordan.

A mid-season takeover bid and yet more proposals for a new stadium occurred virtually unnoticed as promotion fever gripped the supporters who had become so accustomed to these sort of stories.

Nevertheless, all credit went to manager Coakley, for he became only the second man in the club's history to steer a Walsall side to promotion (the other was, of course, Bill Moore).

But it was common knowledge that performances on the field would have to improve ten-fold if the Saddlers were to have any chance of surviving in the higher division.

For the record, in their promotion winning season of 1987-88, Walsall's home attendances averaged almost 5,600; David Kelly top-scored with 30 goals in all competitions and Nicky Cross netted the first hat-trick of his career in a 5-2 win over Rotherham in January. Fred Barber was the only ever-present in the side, while the impressive Craig Shakespeare missed out only once.

In August 1988 star-man David Kelly was transferred to West Ham United for a Walsall club record fee of £600,000. In later years he moved to Leicester City and Newcastle United and also did well for the Republic of Ireland.

Walsall's first Second Division match for 25 years was against Plymouth Argyle, at home, on 27 August 1988 and a crowd of 6,178 turned out to witness a 2-2 draw, the Saddlers fielding: Barber; Dornan, Mark Taylor, Shakespeare, Forbes, Hart, Pritchard, Goodwin, Alex Taylor, Christie and Naughton with the subs Hawker and young Chris Marsh.

Alex Taylor, a £100,000 signing from Hamilton (to replace Kelly), scored both goals on his debut and looked a really classy player. Sadly, injury problems were to ruin his career.

Yet, after making a sound start to the campaign, occupying a secure midfield position by October, and near neighbours Birmingham City having been walloped 5-0 at Fellows Park (all the goals coming in the space of 29 minutes in the second half), the Saddlers suddenly lost confidence and form, and suffered 15 consecutive League defeats (including 7-0 at home to Chelsea), a run which left them stranded at the foot of the table by the turn of the year. And to add salt to the wound, they were knocked out of all the Cup competitions as well.

Promotion-winning manager Tommy Coakley and his assistant, Gerry Sweeney, were sacked just after Christmas, and eventually the job in the hot seat went to former Wolves boss, John Barnwell, who had been released by Notts County.

To his credit Barnwell worked hard

Defenders Graeme Forbes and Peter Skipper join a raid on the Preston goal at Fellows Park in September 1989. The Saddlers won 1-0.

to avert danger. He snapped up strikers Stuart Rimmer (from Notts County for £150,000) and Andy Saville (from Hull City for £100,000), but the task was far too great, and Walsall duly went back to the Third Division after only one season in the Second.

During the early part of 1989 work started on the construction of a brand new £3 million stadium, with a capacity of just 12,000. Situated half a mile down the road from Fellows Park, near the Bescot railway sidings, it was due to be completed in time for the start of the 1990-91 campaign. But the blow of relegation took the gloss of things and after having been in such high spirits during the summer of 1988, Walsall Football Club, its players and staff, and supporters, were all down in the dumps once again, not relishing yet another hard time in Division Three.

During the summer of 1989 manager Barnwell assessed the playing side of the club, but once the players had reported back for training and following the arrival of midfielder Steve Gritt (on a free transfer from Charlton), forward John Kelly (£35,000 from Swindon), defender Peter Skipper (from Oldham) and winger Adrian Thorpe (from Notts County for £75,000) it seemed as if he had a useful squad at his disposal.

The season started reasonably well with a 1-0 home victory over Northampton Town on the opening day and a 2-2 draw at Rotherham in their third game. Those results flattered only to deceive, for the Saddlers managed only three more League wins up to 20 March, registering only one victory in 22 starts from 17 October. They dropped quickly to the bottom of the table, landing there after crashing to a 4-0 defeat at Brentford on New Year's Day. They never got going again, remaining at the foot of the ladder until the season's end, thus falling straight through into the Fourth Division without a murmur. And they hardly troubled anyone in the three knockout competitions either, going out to Port Vale and Hereford United in the League and FA Cups respectively, although in the Leyland DAF Trophy they did flourish for a while, before succumbing to Bristol Rovers on penalties in the Southern Area semi-final.

Barnwell was dismissed in March, being replaced by Paul Taylor who assumed the role of caretaker manager.

All in all it turned out to be a disastrous last season at Fellows Park for the Saddlers whose final Football League game there was against Rotherham United on 1 May when a crowd of 5,697 watched the 1-1 draw.

Taking stock of the situation was difficult, but it all boiled down to a complete lack of confidence on behalf of the players. Scoring had been a problem, too, with only 40 goals coming in 44 League games.

So, with a lot of hard work to be done in readiness for the new campaign, at a brand new ground – Bescot Stadium -the Walsall chairman Barrie Blower and his board of directors went out and appointed the former Wolves midfielder, Kenny Hibbitt, as their new manager, asking him to refloat a sinking ship – and Walsall Football Club was, at this point in time, sinking pretty fast.

Having suffered relegation at the end of the two previous seasons, it was something of a relief for the Saddlers to finish the 1990-91 campaign in 16th place in Division Four.

For Hibbitt it was something of a baptism of fire into Football League management. He inherited a rather depleted squad of players whose confident had gone completely. But he got stuck in to the task in hand and did a major rebuilding job on limited resources.

After the formal official opening ceremony at their new ground (a friendly against Aston Villa was arranged) Walsall's first home League game drew a 5,219 crowd for the visit of Torquay United on 25 August – a game which finished 2-2. But the team did not get off to a good start and not a single victory was recorded from the first seven games.

Then an aggregate victory over Cambridge United in the League Cup earned the Saddlers a lucrative second-round clash with Chelsea. But although the Londoners ran up two convincing wins, Walsall equipped themselves well and afterwards they strung together a run of five League wins and a draw which pushed them up to ninth place in the table by Christmas. After the introduction of veteran defender Colin Methven, from Blackpool, the defence performed solidly, eventually conceding a total of 51 goals in 46 games.

It was basically in attack where Walsall failed. Even before top marksman Stuart Rimmer left for Barnsley, they had found goals hard to come by and when the season ended they had only 48 to show for their

Colin Methven celebrates his goal against League newcomers Barnet in the Saddlers' 2-0 Fourth Division victory in October 1991. Paul McCloughlin, on loan from Wolves, rushes to congratulate him.

efforts, which was why they had to settle for a place in the lower half of the table.

There were some fine performances during the course of the season, but certainly not enough to please manager Hibbitt, who, in fairness, was hampered by financial problems, which caused him to sell his prize asset, Rimmer, for a knockdown fee of £150,000.

Seven players appeared in more than 30 League games and they were veteran defender Colin Methven, full-back Chris Hutchings (ex-Huddersfield, Brighton and Chelsea), striker Rod McDonald, who was signed from Colne Dynamo, West Bromwich-born Dean Smith, the dashing Cameroon World Cup star Charlie Ntamark, hard-working Peter Skipper and the consistent Ron Green in goal. The last two named both surprisingly left the club during the summer of 1991, along with nine others including full-backs Hutchings and Kenny Mower (after many years excellent service with the club), forward Willie Naughton and promising youngster Adrian Littlejohn, who moved into the First Division with Sheffield United and reached Wembley, qualifying for the Rumbelows Sprint Challenge Final which took place prior to the League Cup Final between Manchester United and Nottingham Forest.

As usual every close season saw some new faces come into the camp, and among those recruited for the 1991-92 campaign by manager Hibbitt were the former West Brom, Southampton, Stoke and England left-back Derek Statham, who came on a free transfer from the Victoria Ground, defenders Wayne Williams (from Northampton Town) and Russell Musker (from Torquay United), goalkeeper Mark Gayle, a £15,000 buy from non-League Worcester City, and the experienced figure of Kevin MacDonald (ex-Liverpool and Coventry City) who was made team captain.

Hibbitt was also looking to several of his youngsters to do their duty out on the park, players like 18-year-old Robbie Jackson (signed in March 1991 on a free from Manchester City), and three 20-year-olds, defenders Steve O'Hara and Dean Smith and utility man Chris Marsh, plus of course Ntamark, who was voted Player of the Year by the Walsall fans.

The big question mark hung over the team's attack. Was it good enough? Hibbitt thought it was and he was pinning his hopes on Mike Cecere and Rod McDonald to do the business up front.

It was thought that Gayle, who was once on Blackpool's books, would develop into a capable 'keeper and that he would follow in the footsteps of a long line of successful Walsall goalies, many of whom were plucked from non-League clubs.

Veteran centre-half Colin Methven, whose ability in the air was so vital, would be the key man at the back, with Williams and Statham, and his experience would be invaluable to the youngsters like Smith and O'Hara. Also Anderson and Tony Grealish, the former Republic of Ireland midfielder, who would be key members of the squad.

All in all then, Hibbitt and his staff were looking for better things in 1991-92.

But the League programme didn't start too well, Walsall losing their opening away game 3-0 at Blackpool where Hibbitt fielded this team: Gayle; Williams, Statham, Methven, Musker, Smith, McDonald, Ntamark, Jackson, Cecere, MacDonald. Subs: Marsh and Lane. And to make matters worse, Statham was sent off after 38 minutes for scything down Andy Garner.

An early exit from the League Cup (beaten by Swansea City who went through 3-2 on aggregate after a blunder by 'keeper Gayle in the second leg at Bescot) cost the Saddlers at least £70,000 in revenue, because had they qualified for round two then they would have played Tottenham Hotspur over two legs.

Walsall's first League win of the season came against Scarborough (at the McCain Stadium) where they took the points with a 3-2 victory thanks to goals by Rod McDonald (2) and Mike Cecere. But a home lapse against Rochdale cancelled out that triumph by the sea, although in their next game Halifax were dumped 3-0 at Bescot as the Saddlers moved up to halfway in the Fourth Division table.

After six League games had been fulfilled, Walsall had mustered just seven points and had scored only eight goals. This lack of strike-power was causing manager Hibbitt some concern and he attempted to rectify the matter by introducing Paul McLoughlin (on loan from Wolves) who netted on his debut against Halifax. His presence in the side helped considerably, but unfortunately the price put on McLoughlin's head by Wolves was far beyond Walsall's means, despite the fact that the Supporters' Club handed over a cheque for £100,000.

But another new face did come in,

Colin Anderson, who was signed on a free from West Brom.

In the meantime Chairman Barrie Blower resigned and was replaced by Jeff Bonser, while performances out on the park were showing a slight improvement.

As October gave way to November, the Saddlers lay eighth in the table (23 points from 14 games), seven behind the leaders Mansfield.

The team at this point was: Ronnie Sinclair (signed on loan from Bristol City to replace the out-of-form Gayle); Williams, Statham, Methven, Walsh, O'Hara, McDonald, Grealish, McLoughlin, Marsh, MacDonald. Subs: Cecere and Lane.

In their respective group in the Autoglass Trophy, Walsall were joined by Stoke City and Birmingham City. They were beaten at home by Stoke (2-0) and then later caused a major upset by beating Blues 1-0 at St Andrew's to qualify for the next round. They duly disposed of Hereford United at Edgar Street before, ironically, they met Stoke again, this time at the Victoria Ground, where they lost 3-1 to the eventual winners of the competition.

The draw for the FA Cup first round paired Walsall away with the GM Vauxhall Conference side, Yeovil Town. The tie ended 1-1, Neil Tolson scoring for the Saddlers who fielded their new goalkeeper from Rotherham, Allen McKnight, who had previously served with West Ham United. He was given a contract by manager Hibbitt until the end of the season (following Sinclair's return to Ashton Gate), but long before then he was released after a bizarre incident in a game at Gillingham when he stupidly gave away a comic goal after only 40 seconds, and in front of the TV cameras. Walsall lost the game 4-0.

The replay with Yeovil on 27 November 1991 was something of an historic event, it being the first FA Cup-tie to be staged at Bescot Stadium. A crowd of 3,869 turned up but the Saddlers contingent went home bitterly disappointed after the visitors, famous giantkillers as they were, had claimed all the glory, winning 1-0.

At this stage in the season Walsall FC was losing between £7,000 and £8,000 a week, and director Mike Lloyd said: "The revenue from money coming through the turnstiles is just not good enough to keep us in profit. Bescot cannot just be used 25 times a year for football matches." In this he was right. Thus, a series of sporting events were planned by the club with a Sunday market and three pop concerts expected to raise as much as £600,000 in the coming few years.

Chairman Jeff Bonser was optimistic about it all and had lengthy talks with officials from the local authority, stating: "At the moment it's a case of balancing the books and we must generate commercial income other than from football, otherwise we shall be in deep trouble."

By the first week of December, Walsall had dropped down to 12th place in the Fourth Division. They were still struggling to score goals, and had managed only 23 from 17 games, although defensively they were far better, having conceded only four goals in seven games at Bescot.

One or two youngsters were now being fielded regularly by manager Hibbitt, among them David Edwards, who was voted Barclays Young Eagle of the Month for December, Steve Winter and Tolson.

On the opening Saturday in January 1992 Walsall crashed 3-1 at home to the bottom club in the Football League, Doncaster Rovers.

The Saddlers were woeful and were given the 'bird' by their suffering fans. It was Rovers' first win in 22 games and manager Hibbitt's comments after the match must have blistered the dressing-room paintwork.

One sad note to reach the club was the death of a fine football administrator, John Westmancoat, who had been associated with Walsall for many years, mainly as secretary of the club. He had also served in the same capacity with Birmingham City, West Brom and Port Vale.

On the brighter side, in the Queen's New Year's Honours List, long serving Walsall head checker, Fred Lloyd, aged 82, was awarded the British Empire Medal. His link with the club began back in 1924 when Joe Burchell was secretary-manager. He used to help out with ticket distribution at the turnstiles.

With the best part of the 1991-92 season over Walsall were still in 12th place in Division Four (31 points out of a possible 75). They were just about in touch with the teams chasing a Play-off slot but it was going to take an almighty effort to even claim seventh position, at the least.

Kenny Hibbitt was ringing the changes left, right and centre, but injuries to key players were causing him some concern (Statham with a fractured toe and MacDonald with a damaged knee among the casualties).

His team against leaders Burnley early in February (a game which ended in a 2-2 after the Saddlers had led 2-0 after 47 minutes) was: Gayle; Williams, Richard Brown, Methven, Anderson, O'Hara, Winter, Ntamark, Marsh, Cecere, McDonald. Subs: Edwards and Tolson.

Around this time young Neil Tolson was scoring regularly for the Reserves and Intermediates, and he was being watched by scouts from several top line clubs. In one Intermediate game against Northampton Town he cracked in four as the Saddlers won 7-0.

The seniors, in contrast, simply couldn't score at all and went 11 League games without a win before finally recording a 1-0 victory at Northampton in mid-February.

Early in March, Walsall submitted planning application to build a £300,000 floodlit all-weather pitch on part of the car-park behind the Gilbert Alsop stand at Bescot Stadium. If granted this would generate around £50,000 a year and help the club financially.F

Out on the field of play, Walsall's first team met the Swedish side FF Malmo in a friendly and won 2-1, producing some excellent football. But unfortunately they couldn't repeat this sort of form when it mattered most, in the League.

The transfer deadline of 26 March saw Neil Tolson sold to First Division Oldham Athletic for £150,000 and at the same time the club also received a bumper pay-out of £250,000 in the form of a grant from the local council.

Chairman Jeff Bonser was delighted with the cash in-take and said: "We were at the time in a critical financial position, needing a large injection of cash. And we got it."

Mark Gayle gathers the ball as Chesterfield players swarm around in April 1992. The Saddlers drew 2-2. Other Walsall players are Rod McDonald (10), Derek Statham and Steve O'Hara (right).

Manager Hibbitt commenting on the sale of young Tolson, said: "The only reason I let 'Tolly' go was because he was joining a First Division team. If any Second, Third or Fourth Division club had come in for him they would have had no chance. I am pleased for the lad."

With all this activity going on, Walsall's results in the League left a lot to be desired. They had slipped down to 17th place in the table by mid-April and for players and supporters alike, the season was by now slowly fading away. The fans certainly had given up hope, and the lowest League crowd at Bescot Stadium – just 2,045 – saw the game against Maidstone United on 30 March.

The Saddlers won only two of their remaining ten Fourth Division games and eventually finished in 15th position.

A lot of people wanted to make a lot excuses for a very disappointing season. And it was without doubt, a poor campaign for everyone associated with Walsall Football Club.

Injuries didn't help the situation one iota – nor did the financial status of the club – but Saddlers manager Kenny Hibbitt publicly admitted that he did not want to complain about any of these.

One has to grin and bear it when injuries prevent key players from lining up, and if the team is not producing the goods, then the fans will stay away from matches and consequently there is less money coming through the turnstiles.

Hibbitt confessed that there were some exceptionally good youngsters based at the club, players like Dean Smith, Chris Marsh and Steve O'Hara.

These were just kids when Hibbitt took charge, and they had matured greatly and now looked set for bright futures in the game. Indeed, Walsall's youngsters reached the Midland Youth Cup Final in 1992, only to lose a tightly fought contest 5-4 over two legs against a useful Aston Villa side.

Walsall's stadium is one of the finest outside the Premier League, compact, smart-looking with fine viewing points from all four corners of the ground. And in some respects, this is why some visiting clubs seem to raise their game when they come to play at Bescot.

As for 1991-92, far too many games were drawn – 13 in total, ten at home – yet Walsall's away results were just as good as quite a number of teams in the top half of the Division. It was their home form which let them down in the end.

One or two players subsequently were allowed to leave Bescot at the end of the campaign, among them a couple of ex-West Brom men, Colin Anderson, who joined Hereford United, and former Republic of Ireland international midfielder Tony Grealish, who linked up with Bromsgrove Rovers.

As Mervyn Sargeant wrote in the *Football Club Directory:* '...1992-93 marked the turning point in the fortunes of Walsall Football Club with the team having by far its best season since winning promotion in 1988.'

The Saddlers finished a very creditable fifth in the Third Division thus earning them qualification for the Play-offs, which unfortunately ended rather disappointingly with a 9-3 aggregate defeat at the hands of Crewe Alexandra, who, in fact, had finished a place lower than Walsall in the League.

In retrospect, it was perhaps a poor January – when they failed to register a single League victory – which prevented Walsall from gaining automatic promotion. They also went out of the Autoglass Trophy during the same month, and after that they never rose to fourth position again, slipping down to ninth at one stage before ending with a flourish – an eight-match unbeaten run which ended in five straight wins after two draws.

There were also early exits from both the League Cup (beaten 4-0 on aggregate by Chelsea) and the FA Cup (lost 4-0 at Rotherham).

The signing of Wayne Clarke from Manchester City in the summer certainly raised the supporters' hopes inasmuch that the absence of goals might be a thing of the past – and so it proved with Clarke ending up as top marksman with a haul of 24, followed closely by Mike Cecere with 18.

The Saddlers, in fact, notched a total of 85 goals in all competitions. They claimed three fours (including victory in a seven-goal thriller with Bury) and 11 threes and failed to score in only three League matches.

Walsall 4 Bury 3
Endsleigh League Division Three,
15 September 1992

THIS midweek encounter attracted a rather disappointing crowd of 3,097 to the Bescot Stadium, but those present witnessed a marvellously entertaining match which produced seven goals and hat-trick for Saddlers' striker Wayne Clarke, two of his efforts coming in the final five minutes to produce an unexpected late victory.

Referee Dermot Gallacher annoyed

the supporters in the first half with some rather dubious decisions, but he did allow two goals from Bury's Liam Robinson to stand.

Walsall never really threatened during the first 45 minutes and it was the Shakers who did most of the attacking. Only a snatched effort from Charlie Ntamark, tame shots from Clarke and Ollerenshaw and a toe-poke from Chris Marsh tested Gary Kelly in the visitors' goal. But at the other end of the field Mark Gayle was beaten in the 30th and 36th minutes by the skill and direction of Robinson's finishing.

After the break it was a completely different story. The Saddlers were fired up from the first whistle and after some near misses, quickly drew level with two goals in two minutes, first through the anticipation of Clarke on 67 and then a smartly-taken equaliser from Gary West with 50 seconds of the restart.

Bury, though, buckled down to business once more and in the 77th minute stunned the home crowd by edging back in front at 3-2 when Kevin Hulme netted from close range.

Enter substitute Mike Cecere, who replaced Derek Statham with ten minutes to go. He threatened immediately and after going close himself, he then set up Clarke for his 85th-minute equaliser. He didn't finish there and with a draw on the cards, the former Oldham and Huddersfield striker got free again and Clarke was in position to wrap up the points with a last-gasp winner.

Walsall: Gayle; Williams, Statham (Cecere), O'Hara, West, Smith, Ntamark, Clarke, Marsh, Ollerenshaw, McDonald.
Bury: Kelly; Anderson, Kearney, Daws, Valentine, Reid, Mauge, Robinson, Hulme, Kilner(Lyons), Scott.

There is no doubt that the Saddlers' defence struggled during the first half of the season, conceding 40 goals. But then team tactics and the formation was changed as manager Hibbitt introduced a five-man back-line, and it worked well, keeping the goals-against column down to a minimum.

As 1992 gave way to 1993, Walsall were well placed in third position. But then came that bleak January and it was always going to be a tough fight from February onwards for the whole team. Nevertheless, the players stuck to their task manfully and ended the campaign in excellent form, to close right up on fourth-placed York City, but were six points behind promoted Barnet in third spot.

Walsall won as many away games as they did at home (11) and in the end some cynics thought that the four League defeats suffered at Bescot (including those against the champions Cardiff City and bottom club Halifax Town) would be crucial at the death – and so it proved.

The home attendances were fractionally up on 1991-92 and that in itself was a boost for the club, indicating that those ardent supporters were ready to return if manager Hibbitt could retain his style of playing purposeful football. Losing in the Play-offs was a sad occasion, but on the other hand it was a blessing in disguise, for many folk believed that money was tight and what small amount there was in the kitty would go towards bringing in some more new faces... because the team was nowhere near strong enough to pull up too many trees in the Second Division.

Failure to succeed in 1993, was perhaps the main reason why a pre-planned music festival at the Bescot Stadium in the summer had to be cancelled. Who knows!

Unfortunately manager Hibbitt was not allowed a great deal of money to spend on replenishing his squad and as a result he lost the services of his two main strikers: Wayne Clarke (sold to Shrewsbury Town) and Mike Cecere (transferred to Exeter City).

He was forced to scour the non-League scene and brought in two players, who proved real bargains – ex-Wolves defender Stuart Watkiss (from Rushall Olympic) and full-back Wayne Evans (from Welshpool).

Both men did superbly, appearing in 49 and 46 matches respectively in their first season with the club. And they came first and second in the Player of the Year awards.

However, other experienced players failed to perform up to expectations and after going so close in the previous season, Walsall's form was mixed throughout the 1993-94 campaign and they finished in tenth position, missing the Play-offs this time round by four points.

Goalscoring was a problem – only 48 came in 46 League games – and on several occasions it was a late goal which either resulted in an unwanted defeat or a disappointing draw.

Again Walsall's away form was impressive with ten wins against the seven recorded at home, but they also lost nine times in front of their own supporters and this was a key factor at the end of the day.

Walsall 5 Lincoln City 2
Endsleigh League Division Three, 20 November 1993

THIS was a cracking match, full of exciting, all-action football which produced a hat-trick for Saddlers' former Birmingham City star Dean Peer.

In front of a 4,580 crowd, Walsall played well, especially in the first half, but Lincoln also played their part in making this great entertainment for the fans with two fine first-half goals.

The Saddlers, unchanged after their FA Cup draw at Wrexham, stormed into a three-goal lead inside the first 13 minutes of the match.

After only 54 seconds Kyle Lightbourne made a powerful run down the left to force a corner. Chris Marsh whipped over the inswinging flag-kick and there was Peer, well placed to head into the top right-hand corner of the net.

It was fast and furious stuff as both sets of strikers burst forward at every opportunity. After a near miss on their goal, Walsall went two-up in the ninth minute when Peer, taking Rod McDonald's square pass in his stride, thrashed his shot home from fully 20 yards.

Again Lincoln hit back, but it was Walsall who scored again, this time through Lightbourne in the 13th minute. It followed a splendid three-man move which ended when Lightbourne and McDonald exchanged passes allowing the former to fire his effort towards goal from the edge of the penalty-area, the ball taking a deflection before sailing over 'keeper Mike Pollitt's head.

It was too good to last and Lincoln stormed back, deservedly reducing the arrears on 16 minutes when David Hill buried a low drive from 20 yards past 'keeper Jim Walker.

After Marsh, McDonald and Peer had all gone close, the Imps cut the deficit to one when Grant Brown thundered in his side's second goal in the 31st minute following a high cross which Watkin and Ryder misjudged.

Just after this Lincoln should have been level, but Alan Johnson's centre was headed over the top by Neil Matthews when it looked easier to score.

Lincoln started the second half with all guns blazing and Dean West was only inches wide with a flashing drive.

McDonald replied with an angled drive and Wayne Evans almost deceived the 'keeper with a cross-cum-shot.

On the hour mark Walsall went 4-2 ahead when Lightbourne lunged forward to steer Ryder's low centre into the net after Lincoln had failed to clear McDonald's cunning free-kick.

A few niggling clashes crept into the game at this juncture but the Walsall players kept their heads and Peer duly completed a fine hat-trick when he planted a glorious header into the net from Marsh's magnificent cross.

Right at the end the former Wolves striker Steve Mardenborough brought the best out of Walsall's 'keeper Walker.

Walsall: Walker; Evans, Marsh, Watkins, Keister, Ryder; Ntamark, Wright, Lightbourne, Peer, McDonald(Lillis). Subs. D.Smith, Gayle.

Lincoln City: Pollitt; P. Smith, Baraclough, Hill, Brown, Schofield, West, Lormer, Matthews(Mardenborough), Johnson, Loughlin. Subs. Clarke, Dickson.

Walsall went out of all three domestic Cup tournaments early on – losing to Exeter in the League Cup, to Northampton Town and Hereford United in the Autoglass Trophy and to Scunthorpe in the second round of the FA Cup.

The highest position Walsall attained in the Third Division table was third which they held going into the New Year. But after a 4-2 home win over Wycombe they could only register six more League wins to the end of the season (from 21 matches) and slithered slowly down the ladder.

Amazingly the average attendance at the Bescot rose again to 4,233, but those hardy souls who stood firm were not too pleased at the way Walsall performed during the second half of the season.

After that rather mediocre 1993-94 season, those loyal Saddlers' fans were pleasantly surprised with the excitement and success at the club in 1994-95.

During the summer, manager Kenny Hibbitt made two crucial signings, bringing in goalkeeper Trevor Wood (from Port Vale) and the experienced Northern Ireland international and former Derby, Ipswich and Chelsea player, Kevin Wilson, who went on to win the club's Player of the Season award.

Wilson linked up superbly well with Kyle Lightbourne and, indeed, between them they scored 49 goals (more than half of the club's seasonal tally of 95 in League and Cup) with Lightbourne netting 27 goals and Wilson 22.

Yet the season started off badly with only one win gained from the first four League games. Hibbitt departed and Paul Taylor took over as caretaker boss before the former Aston Villa and Southampton centre-half Chris Nicholl moved into the Bescot Stadium hot seat.

Nicholl quickly turned things round. He got the team playing as a unit, performing with passion, commitment and a lot of skill.

The more experienced players in the camp were given a new lease of life and the up-and-coming youngsters came to the fore, with Stuart Ryder gaining an England Under-21 call-up.

Despite an early exit from the League Cup at the hands of West Ham United, who were beaten 2-1 at the Bescot Stadium in the first leg before winning the return clash at Upton Park, and elimination from the Auto Windscreen Shield (beaten by Birmingham City and Peterborough) the Saddlers powered on in the League, and by the turn of the year were lying in second place, having accounted for Fulham (5-1), Hereford United (4-3) and Barnet (4-0) on the way, all at home.

Walsall 5 Fulham 1
Endsleigh League Division Two, 17 September 1994

WALSALL, who were lying 16th, outplayed tenth-placed Fulham in this game at the Bescot Stadium – and, indeed, it was the Cottagers' heaviest defeat for five years.

The Saddlers were in command as early as the third minute when a cross from Dean Peer was turned on to the post, only for the lurking Chris Marsh to fire in the rebound from close range.

After some near misses – mainly at the Fulham end – Walsall went 2-0 up in the 25th minute when Kyle Lightbourne outjumped two defenders to head past Jim Stannard.

Walsall kept up the pressure and on the stroke of half-time, following two near misses, Marsh cracked in his own second and his side's third goal from a superb Scott Houghton pass.

On the resumption it was all Walsall, who attacked the Fulham goal incessantly and in the 50th minute another brilliant pass from man of the match Houghton allowed Lightbourne to claim his second goal to make it 4-0.

Fulham were reeling and two minutes later Houghton got on the scoresheet himself by finishing off a smart move involving four players when he glided home Marsh's clever header.

At 5-0 Fulham boss Ian Branfoot made two substitutions, to no avail, and Walsall continued to bombard Stannard's goal. Amazingly there was no more scoring until the 84th minute when Gary Brazil closed in and beat Trevor Wood in the Walsall goal with a splendid cross-shot.

Walsall: Wood; Evans, Rogers, Gibson, Marsh, Palmer, O'Connor, Lightbourne, Wilson(Ntamark), Houghton, Peer. Subs: Watkiss, Walker.

Fulham: Stannard; Morgan, Hurlock, Moore, Jupp, Brazil, Hails(Haworth), Marshall, Thomas(Blake), Herrera, Cork. Sub: Harrison.

Leeds United won a replayed third-round FA Cup-tie by 5-2 at Elland Road after a 1-1 draw, but this didn't upset the Saddlers' plan of attack, and they continued to amass the points in the League, holding third place in the table from mid-March to early May when they moved into second spot after a run of four straight wins.

Comfortably placed with games in hand throughout the second-half of the season, Walsall lost their way momentarily, but they picked up six vital points late on against fellow promotion challengers Scunthorpe United and in-form Scarborough (both by 2-1) while second-placed Chesterfield won at Darlington but lost at home to champions-elect Carlisle.

With one game to play, at Bury, the Saddlers (with a much better goal-difference) needed only a draw to gain automatic promotion. Chesterfield were at home to Colchester on the same day and they had to win just in case the Saddlers did slip up.

Some 3,000 fans (most of them with radios) made the trip to Gigg Lane and they looked on nervously as Nicholl's battlers secured a place in the Second Division by drawing 0-0.

For the record Chesterfield also drew, leaving Walsall home and dry with two points to spare.

The average home League attendance at Bescot was 4,068 – a significant rise – and a delighted chairman Jeff Bonser praised his team's loyal supporters, saying: "You've been great – now let's get into the First Division."

The start of the 1995-96 campaign was eagerly awaited by everyone associated with Walsall Football Club. Indeed, hopes were high for another successful season. Manager Nicholl was satisfied with what he had regarding his squad and just two new faces were brought in – Ray Daniel from Portsmouth and Darren Bradley from West Bromwich Albion, both on free transfers.

Unfortunately the team struggled during the early part of their League programme and were soon knocked out of the League Cup by Brentford.

The Saddlers won only three of their first 14 League games and kept only one clean sheet in the opening 16.

In October, Adrian Viveash arrived from Swindon Town and he was soon followed by the experienced Derek Mountfield.

Scoring goals was proving difficult except in the Auto Windscreen Shield and FA Cup competitions. In fact, an amazing FA Cup midweek replay against Torquay ended 8-4 in Walsall's favour after extra-time.

Viveash and Mountfield settled in quickly and Walsall's form picked up considerably. After suffering only one defeat in 11 games, the Saddlers found themselves within sight of the Play-offs, but a downturn in the weather and defeat in a several-times-postponed FA Cup-tie at Ipswich disrupted their progress considerably. By early March the team had slipped down to 19th place – and amazingly were hovering on the brink of the relegation zone.

Walsall 8 Torquay United 4
FA Cup Round Two,
12 December 1995

HAVING held the League's basement team, Torquay, to a 1-1 draw at Plainmoor ten days earlier, Walsall were confident of making progress into the next round when the replay took place at the Bescot Stadium on a chilly pre-Christmas evening.

But all credit to the visitors, who put up a terrific show and played their part in a wonderfully entertaining game of football which produced 12 goals, six of them in extra-time.

Walsall opened the scoring in the 14th minute when Martin O'Connor powered his way into the penalty area before setting up Chris Marsh who netted with a well struck left-foot shot.

United hit back and after a spell of good pressure they deservedly equalised when ex-Saddler Mark Hawthorne's 25-yard effort was deflected past 'keeper James Walker.

It was 1-1 at the break, and after some early second-half pressure Walsall suddenly found themselves behind as Lee Barrow leapt to plant his header firmly into the net from Ian Hathaway neatly flighted corner.

The Saddlers bounced back quickly and within five minutes it was 2-2 as Kevin Wilson rose smartly to head Darren Bradley's free-kick past Ashley Bayes from ten yards.

On 65 minutes Torquay edged back in front with another headed goal, this time from Ian Gore with Hathaway again the provider with a telling flag-kick.

Walsall, though, would not lie down and six minutes later it was all-square at 3-3 when Bradley, set free by Marsh, fired home from just inside the penalty area.

The excitement carried on into extra-time and with players on both sides tiring rapidly, goal chances came thick and fast.

In the 93rd minute Walsall went in front at 4-3 when the unmarked Marsh turned in a right-foot volley from two yards following Lightbourne's deft cross.

Soon afterwards Lightbourne made it 5-3 when he put away Houghton's pass from five yards and in the 97th minute Marsh worked an opening for O'Connor to score right-footed from just inside the box.

But at 6-3 down Torquay never gave in and they reduced the arrears in the 101st minute through Spaniard Jose Mateu, who netted from Richard Hancox's through ball.

Walsall, though, were much the stronger side and they added two more goals before the final whistle.

Houghton raced through on his own in the 104th minute to score a fine solo goal with a left-foot shot from 18 yards, and in the 119th minute Lightbourne bundled the ball over the line following a centre from Marsh. What a game, what a scoreline – and for the Saddlers it meant Wigan Athletic at home in the next round.

Walsall: Walker; Ntamark, Rogers, Viveash, Marsh, Mountfield(Watkiss), O'Connor, Bradley, Keister (Lightbourne), Wilson, Houghton. Sub. Wood.

Torquay United: Bayes; Gore, Barrow, Curran, Watson, Coughlin, Jack (Mateu), Hall(Bedeau), Hancox, Hawthorne, Hathaway. Sub. Monk.

The return to goalscoring form of striker Kyle Lightbourne, along with the ability to collect points when not playing all that well, averted any further worries and when the curtain came down Walsall found themselves in 11th position – just four points off the Play-offs. This came about after an encouraging end-of-season run when only three defeats were suffered in their last 15 games, and a unbeaten run of seven games right at the death. The introduction of exciting youngsters like Clive Platt and Michael Ricketts certainly made a big difference and with some cash available to spend, manager Nicholl was quietly optimistic about his team's chances for the coming season.

In the summer of 1996 influential midfielders Scott Houghton and Martin O'Connor both left Bescot for Peterborough United and with the only newcomer being Mark Blake (from Leicester City) it was no surprise that the Saddlers made a poor start to the new season.

They were on the bottom of the table after four League games and recorded only one win in their first eight, as well as being dumped out of the League Cup by Watford.

The arrival of John Hodge from Swansea City coincided with an upturn in fortunes as only three defeats were suffered in the next eight League matches. But successive defeats at Notts County and Millwall saw the Saddlers slip back into the bottom four.

At this point a none-too-pleased Chris Nicholl called for more effort from his players, and the response he got was as impressive as it was surprising. A season's best 4-0 win over Peterborough sparked off an excellent run of only three defeats in 22 competitive matches, but the team was eliminated from the FA Cup by Burnley on penalties and from the Auto Windscreen Shield by Posh.

Walsall 4 Peterborough United 0
Nationwide League Division Two,
9 November 1996

WHEN fellow strugglers Posh, with ex-Saddlers midfield stars Scott Houghton and Martin O'Connor in their line-up, visited the Bescot Stadium, Walsall were lying in 22nd position in the League table. They were completely out of touch and had already lost ten times during the first three months of the season.

But things improved ten-fold in this game as the Saddlers eased their relegation fears by recording their first victory in five matches.

In fact, it was the first time that the Saddlers had netted four goals during the season while for poor Peterborough it was their sixth defeat in eight.

Kyle Lightbourne gained the breakthrough in the 23rd minute when he took Kevin Wilson's angled pass in his stride before firing hard and low past 'keeper Mark Tyler.

Close to half-time Walsall went 2-0 up via the penalty spot. Mike Basham fouled Mark Blake inside the area and Wilson stepped forward to claim the 200th goal of his career as he sent Tyler the wrong way with his decisive spot-kick.

After some mediocre play by both teams, especially Peterborough, Walsall all but sewed up the points with a third goal in the 76th minute when Louie Donowa raced on to Lightbourne's through ball to crack a low drive into Tyler's net.

A minute later former Walsall player O'Connor was sent-off by Scunthorpe referee Neale Barry for a clumsy foul.

With Posh now a man short, Walsall picked up their game and notched a fourth goal in the 87th minute, courtesy of man of the match Kyle Lightbourne, who collected a rebound on the edge of the 18-yard box to fire the ball straight back past a startled Tyler.

Walsall: Walker; Ntamark, Daniel, Viveash, Thomas(Keister), Mountfield, Blake, Donowa, Lightbourne, Wilson(Watson), Marsh. Sub. Evans.

Peterborough United: Tyler; Heald(Ebdon), Clark, Basham, Foram, Bodley, Willis(Carter), O'Connor, Cleaver, Charlery, Houghton(Rowe).

With Kyle Lightbourne once more starting to score goals, having again struggled early on, and a change to the 'wing-back' system in January, the side now had a decidedly more solid, if unspectacular, look about it.

When Bristol City were defeated 2-0 in early March, the Saddlers had climbed to within sight of the Play-offs – and there were still 13 games to go. But a return to their indifferent early-season form severely dented any hopes Walsall had of achieving a top-six finish. They mustered only 15 points from their remaining 13 matches and losing four of the last six, they eventually settled for a disappointing 12th place.

Walsall, in fact, lost only three home games all season, but their away form was very poor (12 losses out of 23) with only one victory coming in their first 11 matches (1-0 at Bournemouth).

Chris Nicholl decided to stand down at the end of the season, allowing Jan Sorensen to take over his role and so become the first foreign manager of the club.

Sorensen took office in June 1997 and following the sale of leading scorer Kyle Lightbourne to Coventry City for £500,000, he quickly brought in two French stars – Ivory Coast-born striker Roger Boli and the former Caen and RC Strasbourg left-sided midfielder Jean-Francois Peron (both from Lens) – and he also added to his squad goalkeeper Mark Smith (from Crewe Alexandra), the experienced midfielder Gary Porter (from Watford) and striker John Williams (from Hereford United).

But Sorensen saw the Saddlers make another poor start, winning only once in their first seven League games, a sequence which saw them drop to 22nd in the Division.

All was not doom and gloom, however, for Boli and Peron were both playing well as was striker Andy Watson – and as the season wore on so performances improved. Two First Division teams – Nottingham Forest and Sheffield United – were knocked out of the League Cup and come mid-October the Saddlers had risen to halfway.

An FA Cup win over non-League Lincoln United was followed by exit from the League Cup at the hands of West Ham, but the Saddlers then ran in six straight wins, including an emphatic 7-0 victory at Macclesfield in the second round of the FA Cup (this being the Silkmen's first home defeat of the season).

As the New Year came around, Walsall were lying 16th in the table and after knocking out Peterborough, Manchester United were next on the agenda for the Saddlers in the FA Cup.

An intriguing fourth-round tie at Old Trafford attracted a 54,669 crowd, but the Premiership side proved far too strong for Sorensen's men, who lost 4-1 despite Boli's fine goal.

Back in the League, Walsall strove on as Sorensen made desperate loan signings to boost his squad, bringing in Jean-Jacques Eydelie and Didier Tholot from the Swiss club, FC Sion.

The team failed to make progress in

the League, but they continued to do well in the Auto Windscreen Shield, and a first-ever Wembley appearance looked on the cards for the Saddlers when they met Bournemouth in the two-legged semi-final.

Alas the Saddlers lost 2-0 at home and although they won at Dean Court in the return fixture, the Cherries sneaked a 4-3 aggregate win to deny Sorensen, his players and the fans their big day out.

After this bitter disappointment Walsall's League form still left a lot to be desired and after the fans had shown their disgust yet again, chairman Jeff Bonser resigned and put the club up for sale.

Out on the pitch, meanwhile, the team struggled on and mustered only three more victories from their remaining 11 Second Division matches to finish a poor 19th in the table.

The enterprising 'Jeff' Perron was undoubtedly the Saddlers' best performer overall, closely followed by Boli – and he duly collected the Player of the Year award, but he went on the transfer list and eventually moved to Portsmouth.

Boli himself top-scored with 24 goals, but he, too, was ready to move – to the Scottish club Dundee United.

Of the others, the evergreen Chris Marsh was strong at the back, young Dean Keaton looked purposeful in midfield, while goalkeeper James Walker did well between the posts, taking his appearance tally to the club to past the 150 mark.

Unfortunately manager Jan Sorensen paid the penalty for a poor season and was dismissed in May, paving the way for the former Aston Villa winger Ray Graydon to take over as team boss the following month.

Immediately Graydon set about sorting out his playing staff and when the League season kicked-off with an away game at Gillingham, the Saddlers' line-up had a much-changed look about it from the one which finished the previous campaign when losing 1-0 at home to Wycombe Wanderers. It was: James Walker; Chris Marsh, Neil Pointon, John Keister, Ian Roper, Adrian Viveash, Darren Wrack, Jason Brissett, Andy Rammell, Gary Porter and Dean Keates, with Andrew Watson, Neil Davis and Michael Ricketts on the bench.

Pointon was signed from the Scottish club Heart of Midlothian, the former Derby County reserve Darren Wrack arrived, Rammell came from Southend United, Porter was recruited from Watford and Davis was signed from Aston Villa.

The Saddlers got off to a fine start, winning their opening League game 1-0 at the Priestfield Stadium against Gillingham.

Despite an early exit from the Worthington Cup at the hands of Queen's Park Rangers, the Saddlers had a very good first seven weeks and indeed, come the end of September they were lying in sixth position having chalked up six wins, although they had been beaten twice at home – by York City and Reading.

Manager Graydon was reasonably pleased and obviously quite happy that he had been able to field a relatively settled side while at the same time adding an extra newcomer to his squad – the Swedish midfielder Bjarni Larusson from Norkopping.

Three wins and a draw from six starts during October kept the Saddlers well in contention for honours and when November closed, following three more League wins and a draw, the team lay in second place just behind the leaders Fulham.

At this time another new face arrived at the Bescot Stadium – the Argentinian Walter Otta joining the ranks from Chilean football – but December saw the Saddlers go out of the FA Cup at Preston. Yet they remained in touch with the Cottagers and as 1998 gave way to 1999 they were still in the Auto Windscreen Shield after a tense 5-4 penalty shoot-out win over Bristol Rovers.

Morale in the team was now exceedingly high; performances out on the park were both confident and professional and Graydon, highly delighted with what was taking place, boosted his squad by recruiting Darko Mavrak and Colin Cramb (from Bristol City) and he was able to call on a fit-again Andy Watson.

A fairly difficult January in terms of results plus a record crowd at the Bescot – 9,517 v Manchester City – was followed by a much better February but the Saddlers slipped out of the automatic place, allowing Preston to overtake them. At the same time, however, progress was being made in the Auto Windscreen competition with Brentford (away) and Cambridge United (home) both ousted in penalty shoot-outs with impressive goalkeeper James Walker the hero in both matches.

The Saddlers battled on and come March they were in sight of the twin towers of Wembley, only to lose out in the Auto Windscreen to Millwall in the two-legged Southern Area Final, the Lions winning 2-1 on aggregate.

Now it was all out for promotion – and having brought in experienced midfielder Nick Henry (from Sheffield United), striker Rob Steiner (from Bradford City) and the Icelandic forward Siggi Eyjolfsson, all on loan on transfer deadline day, Graydon was now in a position to go for broke – and it worked.

Walsall won four of their six League matches in April but lost a vital one at Deepdale. Thankfully their nearest challengers, Manchester City and Preston, both dropped points as well and with three games remaining the Saddlers' fate was in their own hands. They required only three points to gain automatic promotion and on 1 May 1999 they met Oldham Athletic at the Bescot knowing a win would be enough.

And that's how it was – the Latics, battling to avoid relegation, were beaten 3-1 in front of a near 9,200 crowd and Division One football returned to Walsall for the first time in a decade.

It was a day of celebrations and Ray Graydon, in his first season as a manager, was as delighted as anyone as he and the players showered each other with champagne.

Walsall 3 Oldham Athletic 1
Nationwide League Division Two,
1 May 1999

NEEDING to win this penultimate home game of the season to gain automatic promotion to the First Division after a ten-year absence, Walsall put on a sizzling first half performance against relegation-threatened Athletic in front of a near capacity crowd at the Bescot Stadium, almost 1,000 supporting the visitors.

The Saddlers cruised through the opening 45 minutes to go in at the break 2-0 up with goals by Darren Wrack and Chris Marsh. But the gallant Latics struck back 11 minutes after half-time when Lee Duxbury scored and there were undoubtedly a few uneasy moments inside the ground before substitute Siggi Eyjolfsson clinched victory and promotion 12 minutes from time to set off joyous celebrations among supporters, players and club personnel.

Manager Ray Graydon put out his strongest side, recalling Chris Marsh (after injury) and Jason Brissett (after suspension and the axe following his third sending off of the season at Preston). And none of the starting line-up cost a penny.

The Latics, defending the Gilbert Alsop end, came close to scoring in the first 30 seconds when Jimmy Walker had to tip the ball over the bar following a flick-on from Andy Holt's long throw-in.

Walsall hit back and indeed should have gone ahead on three minutes. Some neat play between Nick Henry and Brissett sent Rob Steiner racing clear from the halfway line but his shot was blocked by 'keeper Gary Kelly.

The atmosphere was electric as Brissett whipped past Steve Thom before crossing for Wrack, whose close range effort was blocked. Both Wrack and Latics' midfielder Paul Reid cracked heads and the Walsall star had to leave the pitch for five minutes to receive treatment,

On his return Wrack chased Adrian Viveash's long ball and centred for Steiner to head narrowly wide. Walsall were flying and in the 22nd minute they got the breakthrough.

Neil Pointon, playing against one of his former clubs, floated a high cross into the Latics' penalty area from out on the left. There seemed no immediate danger but Latics' 'keeper Kelly misjudged the flight of the ball and when it came down Wrack duly claimed his 14th goal of the season with a crisp right-footed drive from an acute angle.

In the 27th minute Viveash's timely challenge denied Paul Beavers and equaliser and seconds later Andy Rammell shot wide for Walsall.

It was action all the way and in the 34th minute long-serving defender Chris

Walsall's Eyjoffsson celebrates his goal against Oldham Athletic in May 1999 as the Saddlers clinch promotion to the First Division

Marsh put the Saddlers 2-0 in front. Henry began the move with a swift pass up to Steiner on the edge of the area. The on-loan striker, with his back to goal, held the ball up and then laid it off to his left right, straight into Marsh's path as he charged into the box. The chipped finish was tremendous and the fans raised the roof.

The visitors came closest to scoring before the interval when Reid's goalbound shot cannoned off Viveash's outstretched foot.

The second half began with Oldham on the offensive but first Ian Roper and then 'keeper Walker thwarted the danger.

In the 56th minute the Latics reduced the deficit and stunned Saddlers fans. John Sheridan's deep cross took a deflection and sailed on to the head of skipper Duxbury who planted the ball in the top right-hand corner of Walker's net.

The Saddlers went through a nervous five minutes before again pressing their opponents back, Wrack crossing into Kelly's hands from out on the right wing.

At the other end Marsh, with a cool back-header, eased a tight situation as the Latics sensed an equaliser.

In the 66th minute boss Graydon sent on Siggi Eyjolfsson in place of Steiner and within seconds got in a powerful shot.

With 12 minutes remaining Walsall clinched promotion with a third goal. Brissett got free down the left and from his delightful pass Eyjolfsson turned sharply to fire the ball into the corner of the net. The crowd went wild – the Saddlers had done it and the celebrations went on long into the night!

After the game, manager Ray Graydon admitted that the pressure to win promotion had been so great that he stopped having sex!

"I'm delighted for the players, the supporters and Walsall Football Club," he said.

Lowly Oldham defend a Walsall corner.

Manager Ray Graydon toasts promotion.

"Many of the players will never surpass what they have achieved this season. They have never buckled under pressure. They have been magnificent," enthused the 51-year-old former Bristol Rovers, Aston Villa and Coventry City winger who duly celebrated his first season as a manager in terrific style.

Walsall: Walker; Marsh, Pointon; Henry, Viveash, Roper; Wrack, Steiner (Eyjolfsson), Rammell(Green), Keates (Larusson), Brissett.

Oldham Athletic: Kelly; McNiven (Tipton), Holt; Garnett, Thom, Duxbury; Allott, Sheridan, Beavers (Sugdeon), Rickers, Reid..

Walsall ended the 1998-99 campaign in second place with a total of 87 points, 14 behind champions Fulham who forced a 2-2 draw at the Bescot in the penultimate game of the season when Ian Roper scored his first ever goal for the senior side. The Saddlers rounded off the campaign with a 2-0 defeat at Stoke.

Andy Rammell had an excellent season, top-scoring with 20 goals in League and Cup competitions; Darren Wrack (second top-scorer) and goalkeeper James Walker were the only ever-presents, both appearing in all of Walsall's 56 senior matches; and the average League attendance at the Bescot Stadium was 5,458 – a rise of almost 1,400 on the previous season.

So what now for the Saddlers as we approach the Millennium?

Well, we know for a fact that the 1999-2000 season will bring Midlands rivals Nottingham Forest, West Bromwich Albion and Wolverhampton Wanderers to the Bescot Stadium and there is no doubt that attendances at all these matches will be in the region of 9,500.

Manager Ray Graydon has vowed to remain at the club for the foreseeable future and so, too, have the star players.

Walsall are on the way back – and who who knows what might transpire as the 21st century approaches? Could we yet see Premiership football at the Bescot? Time will tell of course – but there is now a real buzz around the town and given the breaks the Saddlers can certainly make their mark in the First Division.

Andy Rammell joins in the fans' celebrations.

Walsall's Grounds

Since 1888 the Saddlers have played competitive home matches on six different grounds as follows:

The Chuckery

1888-1893

This multi-purpose sports ground was situated in a district near to the famous Walsall Arboretum. It comprised some 12 soccer pitches and four good-sized cricket squares, and before their amalgamation, both the Walsall Swifts and Walsall Town clubs utilised this ground regularly, especially at weekends, sometimes having home games on the same afternoon.

The first home game of the Walsall Town Swifts was staged at the Chuckery Ground on 8 September 1888 against Derby St Luke's in a friendly and the Saddlers were still playing there when the club played its first-ever Football League match, at home to Darwen on 3 September 1892.

However, after several complaints from the residents in the Sutton Road area, Walsall were forced to leave the Chuckery after just one season of Second Division football, the last game there being against Sheffield United on 15 April 1893 which finished in a 1-1 draw. The best attendance for a Football League game at the Chuckery was that of 2,500 v Small Heath (Division Two) 10 September 1892; the lowest was 500 (registered twice) v Bootle on 24 December 1892 and v Northwich Victoria on 11 February 1893.

Wood Green Oval (Wednesbury)

1893

After the Chuckery, the site of the new ground was in nearby West Bromwich Road, but because the construction workers had met with some interruptions, this was not quite ready for use by the required date, and consequently Walsall's first two home League matches of the 1893-94 season were played at the Wood Green Oval (capacity 6,000). The Saddlers lost on both occasions: 3-1 to Small Heath (Birmingham) and 5-0 to Burslem Port Vale.

The best attendance for a League game at the Wood Green Oval was 5,000 v. Small Heath (Division Two) on 2 September, 1893; the lowest 3,000 v Burslem Port Vale a week later.

West Bromwich Road

1893-1896 & 1900-01

The new ground in West Bromwich Road, which had a capacity of just over 4,500, proved to be a lucky omen for the Saddlers.

They won their opening League game there – on Saturday, 23 September 1893 – beating Crewe Alexandra 5-1.

Three years were spent at this venue, up to September 1896 when Hillary Street (Fellows Park) was officially opened. In December 1900, however, the Saddlers returned briefly to their old West Bromwich Road ground after being unable to pay the rent on their Hillary Street ground. They stayed there for the remainder of that season, playing their last Second Division game for 60 years there before dropping out of the Football League in April 1901.

Walsall's best attendance for a home League game at West Bromwich Road was 4,000 v Liverpool, 11 November 1893; the lowest was 500 v Lincoln City (Division Two), 20 April 1895.

Hillary Street/Fellows Park

1896-1900 & 1901-1990

Walsall's first game at their Hillary Street ground was played on Tuesday, 1 September 1896. It was a friendly against Glossop North End and resulted in a 4-1 victory before a crowd of just over 1,000. Four days later the first Football League game took place and again the Saddlers recorded a victory – this time 2-0 over Burton Wanderers when the turnout was 2,500.

Mr H. L. Fellows

After seven years of unrest regarding leasing, rent and general maintenance of this ground, an agreement on leasing Hillary Street was at last finalised in early September 1903. The name Hillary Street remained so until the summer of 1930 when it became known as Fellows Park (named after Mr H. L. Fellows, a club director) and surprisingly was one of only three established Football League grounds in the country to be named after an individual, the other two being those of AFC Bournemouth (Dean Court) and Cardiff City's Ninian Park. The Saddlers stayed at Fellows Park until the summer of 1990, when they switched to the new Bescot Stadium.

It took quite sometime for Hillary Street to look like a compact football stadium, especially with a brick wall seemingly resident at the Laundry End of the ground (this was finally removed in May 1965, to become an open terrace, mainly for visiting supporters). The Main Stand was eventually built on the east side of the ground and soon afterwards a roof was erected over the popular side terracing in readiness for the fans to watch the Walsall-Arsenal FA Cup-tie in January 1933. A lot of general work was carried out during the 1940s and early 1950s and the first floodlit match to take place at Fellows Park was between Walsall and Falkirk in December 1957. New dressing-rooms were installed following Walsall's return to the Second Division in 1961 (after an absence of 60 years) and on 29 August 1961, a record crowd of over 25,000 packed into the ground to watch the Saddlers play Newcastle United in a League match. Soon after this game the crowd limit was reduced to 22,600 for safety reasons.

In the summer of 1965 the Hillary Street end of Fellows Park (behind the goal) was covered and a decade later, thanks to some ready cash banked from a successful Cup run, an extension was added to the Main Stand with the dressing-rooms being switched back to this area of the ground. This extra section provided another 1,490 seats and pushed the overall capacity back up to just over 24,000. This was then reduced by half, to 12,000, in 1985 (following recent football ground tragedies) with the seating inside the ground being cut to just 844.

The last first-team game at Fellows Park was Peter Hart's testimonial against West Bromwich Albion on 11 May 1990. The final League game was Walsall v Rotherham United on 1 May when a crowd of 5,697 witnessed a 1-1 draw. Scottish-born full-back Andy Dornan had the distinction of scoring Walsall's last League goal on the ground – his only strike for the Saddlers.

The record attendance for a League game at Fellows Park is 25,453 v Newcastle United (Division Two) on 29 August 1961; the lowest was 1,047 v Halifax Town (Division Three North) on 25 January 1926.

The late 1960s saw the first pop group appear at Fellows Park – The Jaguars – who were managed by Walsall season ticket holder, Ron Hawkins.

Bescot Stadium

1990 onwards

MUCH of the credit for the creation of Bescot Stadium must be handed to the club's former chairman, Barrie Blower.

An aerial view of the Bescot Stadium in 1995.

It was due to his inspirational leadership that League football was saved in Walsall and it was through his dynamism, resilience, sheer determination and vision that countless obstacles were successfully overcome, resulting in the town of Walsall inheriting one of the most modern stadiums in the Football League in the early 1990s.

Situated less than a mile from junction 9 on the M6, Bescot Stadium is close to the Walsall ring road; it has a mainline railway station within easy walking distance and there is parking for around 1,200 vehicles.

There are 28 electronically operated turnstiles admitting spectators to the ground, and all viewing areas inside are under cover. At the press of a button all steel exit doors/gates can be opened automatically, with a manual override facility added for any emergency (power-cuts etc.).

The PA system is of British Standard specifications and there is strip-lighting in all spectator areas to ensure a safe passage to and from seats and terraces at evening matches.

The floodlights (with 360 lux value lamps) are situated on six stanchions, three on each of the Highgate Mild and H. L. Fellows Stands. The latter, which can seat 2,378 spectators all of whom enrol under the Walsall FC Membership Scheme, was named after the former director and chairman of the club (1921-38).

The main entrance to the stadium is in this same H. L. Fellows Stand which also contains 13 executive boxes, the Swifts Club Executive Lounge, the Directors' Lounge, the Stadium Restaurant, club offices and dressing-rooms.

To the right of the main stand lies the William Sharp Stand (named after a local company which supplied steel for the stadium and has since sponsored the stand) which initially catered for 3,215 visiting supporters standing on the covered terracing (this was to change in 1992).

Facing the H. L. Fellows Stand is the Highgate Mild Stand with seating for 2,296 spectators with blocks 'A' and 'B' designated a family section, and blocks 'G', 'H' and 'I' reserved for away fans.

The home terrace to the left of the H. L. Fellows Stand is named after one of the club's greatest players, Gilbert Alsop, who died in 1992.

A total of just over 3,000 fans can stand and cheer the Saddlers from this covered section. The South Staffs Pools Lottery Office is also situated at this end of the ground.

The Matchday Ticket Office and Club Shop are both based just outside the H. L. Fellows Stand.

The superb Saddlers Club is situated at the Bescot Crescent End of the ground, near to the corner of the H. L. Fellows and William Sharp Stands.

This salubrious facility has a function room able to cater for 300 people, a lounge for a further 100 supporters, plus games and family rooms. At the rear of this club you will find the programme shop which, in fact, faces on to the offices of Bescot Stadium.

It cost £4.5 million to build the Bescot Stadium – work began in June 1989 and was finished in July 1990 – but for another £150,000 cantilever roofed-stands could have been added on all four sides, removing the solid, thick pylons which certainly restrict viewing from various points. The 1991 capacity was set at 11,104. But in the summer of 1992 workmen started installing seats in the visitors' end of the ground (the William Sharp stand) at a cost of £28,000 with a 75 per cent grant coming in from the Football Trust. The capacity for the 1992-93 season was therefore cut to around 10,000.

Aston Villa were Walsall's first opponents at the Bescot Stadium, Sir Stanley Matthews officially opening the ground on 18 August 1990. That afternoon an excellent crowd of 9,551 saw the friendly encounter which the Villa won 4-0.

The opening League game (in Division Four) took place seven days later (25 August) between the Saddlers and Torquay United. The outcome was a 2-2 draw watched by a crowd of 5,219. Martin Goldsmith and Stuart Rimmer netted for the Saddlers.

The ground, now rated one of the best outside the Premiership, staged the 'B' international match between England and Switzerland on 20 May 1991 when a record crowd of 10,628 saw the Swiss beaten 2-1. There has also been a ladies match staged on the same ground, and in 1993 three Youth internationals had been pencilled in to take place at the Bescot Stadium.

The top League crowd at Bescot Stadium as yet (to end of 1998-99 season) has been 9,517 v Manchester City (Division Two) 23 January 1999; the lowest, just 2,045 v Maidstone United (Division Four) on 30 March 1992; and only 1,837 saw the Auto-Glass Trophy game v Mansfield Town on 8 December 1992.

The Hawthorns 1970

On 25 February 1970, Walsall played a 'home' Third Division League game against Brighton & Hove Albion on the ground of neighbours West Bromwich Albion because Fellows Park had been waterlogged for some weeks and the Saddlers desperately needed to ease a congested fixture list. Brighton won the match 3-0 and the crowd was 7,535.

Walsall's Managers

PRIOR to 1920, like several other League clubs, Walsall did not have an official team manager. The secretary usually looked after team affairs and he liaised with a committee, including the delegated captain, to select the first team line-up.
For season 1920-21, Walsall named defender Albert Groves, ex-Wolverhampton Wanderers, as their player-manager, but this was only a temporary measure, and when the Saddlers regained their Football League status in the summer of 1921, club secretary Joe Burchell was appointed the Saddlers' first team manager (taking the role as secretary-manager) and the list has grown ever since.

Albert Groves
May 1920-August 1921

Albert Groves had been a key figure in the Wolves team since 1909 and during his stay at Molineux he became a firm favourite with the fans, amassing in excess of 220 senior appearances, mainly as a rugged, no-nonsense defender. Born in South Wales, he started off as an out-and-out goalscorer with Aberdare Athletic but after moving to the Midlands he was successfully converted into a defender. He was given the job of looking after the team (as player-manager) when he was signed in the summer of 1920, and he did a good job, so much so that Walsall regained their place in the Football League for the following season. He was forced to retire as a player in 1924 following a serious knee injury (*see Walsall Stars*).

Joe Burchell
August 1921-February 1926

Joe Burchell was born in Walsall in April 1873 and played football for the old Walsall Unity club. After a spell as a member of the Walsall Town Swifts committee, he succeeded Hayden Price as secretary of Walsall during World War One, duly taking over as secretary-manager to become the club's first 'real' team boss. He began his double daily duties on 8 August 1921, soon after the team had been voted back into the Football League following 20 years in the wilderness. Burchell was a local man, born in Walsall in 1876. He did a reasonable job for four years, but then, as the results began to go against the team and the pressures built up around him, he resigned from his post in February 1926, handing over to Irishman David Ashworth. He continued as club secretary until 1931, when he became licensee of the Vine Inn, Rugeley, and thereafter of the Cross Keys Hotel at Hednesford, also becoming a director of Hednesford Town FC. He died following a short illness in October 1932.

Dave Ashworth
February 1926-February 1927

Dave Ashworth was Walsall's first full-time team manager, accepting the position in mid-February 1926. Ashworth possessed a wide knowledge of the game and it was thought that he was the right man to get the team back to winning ways. He quickly added some experience and steel to the side, signing centre-half Jimmy Torrance from Fulham and utility forward Bert White who had also served at Craven Cottage as well as Blackpool and Arsenal. Alas, things didn't improve a great deal and after the Saddlers had finished next to bottom of the Third Division North at the end of the 1925-26 season, they were forced (successfully) to seek re-election.
Results improved slightly in 1926-27 and the Saddlers edged up to finish 14th, but in February that season Ashworth handed over his duties to Jimmy Torrance, who became player-manager.

An Irishman, Ashworth had been a first-class referee prior to stepping out into Football League management with Oldham Athletic in 1906. He stood barely five feet tall – making him one of the smallest managers ever – and was often seen wearing a bowler hat. His waxed moustache made him look more strict and dominant than he really was. Indeed, he had a fine sense of humour and his moustache was altered in style after a match because if his team had won he would curl both ends upwards; if it had lost, then the ends would be turned down; and if a draw had materialised, then one end would be up and the other down!

In his first stint as a manager he guided Oldham Athletic from the Lancashire Combination to the First Division of the Football League within four years before leaving Boundary Park in April 1914 when he moved into Cheshire to take charge of Stockport County. He was appointed manager of Liverpool in December 1919 and after twice leading the Merseysiders into fourth place in Division One, he finally took them to the League title in 1922. He was well on his way to taking the Reds to their second League championship when the directors of Oldham Athletic enticed him back to Boundary Park for a second spell (January 1923) but he was signed up too late to save the Latics from relegation to the Second Division. He left Oldham second time round in July 1924, taking over at Manchester City where he remained until November 1925.

After a brief spell out of the game, he returned to management with Walsall. From June 1927 to May 1930 he was manager of the progressive Welsh club, Caernarvon, and managed Llanelli during the early 1930s and scouted for Blackpool from January 1938.

'Little Dave' as he was so often called, died in Blackpool on 23 March 1947, aged 79.

Jimmy Torrance
February 1927-May 1928

Jimmy Torrance took over from the man who had initially signed him as a player, David Ashworth, but he spent only one season in charge before handing over to Jimmy Kerr in May 1928.

Born in Coatbridge, Scotland, in 1889, Torrance was a utility forward, with Glasgow Ashfield and Fulham (1910-26) before joining Walsall in July 1926. He appeared in four different positions in attack for the Cottagers, making 355 senior appearances and scoring 35 goals.

Sadly 1927-28 was not the greatest of seasons, but Walsall, under Torrance, had their moments, a 7-0 win over Coventry perhaps the best. Torrance did, however, sign some useful players, including David Fairhurst, from Newcastle, and the former Birmingham and Derby County marksman, Moses Lane, who went on to net 36 goals in his first season with Walsall.

Torrance played in a total of 40 League and Cup games for Walsall, including the famous FA Cup-tie against the Corinthians in January 1928.

He dropped out of football after relinquishing the manager's job at Walsall, and for some years after worked for a telephone company. He died of cancer in July 1949, the year when Walsall beat his former club, Fulham, in the FA Cup at Craven Cottage.

Jimmy Sharp, who also came from Craven Cottage, was assistant manager to Torrance.

Jimmy Kerr
May 1928-April 1929

Jimmy Kerr was born in Scotland in November 1881 and served with the Bathgate club for many years before becoming manager of Coventry City in July 1925, a position he held until February 1928. Unfortunately his stay at Highfield Road coincided with three of the most dismal years in Coventry's history.

After three months out of the game, Kerr was given the Walsall job in May 1928 and quickly went into the transfer market, securing the services of two players from Highfield Road, full-back Charlie Houldey and wing-half Billy Hunter. He also recruited Scotsman Duggie Lochhead from St Johnstone and Roy John, a hard-tackling defender who was later to become a Welsh international goalkeeper. Sadly for Kerr, nothing went right on the pitch and like his predecessor he was quickly replaced, this time handing over team affairs to Sid Scholey who was promoted from the rank of trainer.

Kerr, who always donned a bowler hat in public, joined Norwich City as manager on 4 April 1929. He held that position for four years (to June 1933) and took with him from Walsall to Carrow Road three very useful players – Irish international Mick O'Brien, Duggie Lochhead and Norman Thompson, the former Torquay United winger. Kerr did an excellent job with Norwich, turning things round in splendid style after the Canaries had struggled for two seasons in Division Three South.

Norwich were well on course to carry off the Southern Section championship when, in January 1933, Kerr was admitted to the Norfolk and Norwich Hospital with bronchial pneumonia. Up to the previous November he had never suffered a serious illness, but this time his condition worsened and on 18 February 1933 he died, aged 51.

Sid Scholey
April 1929-October 1930

Walsall-born Sid Scholey had been trainer at Fellows Park – from 1908 to 1911 and then since April 1928 – before being asked to succeed Jimmy Kerr, becoming the fifth man to take over team affairs in eight years. Scholey never got to grips with management and he quit in October 1930, after Walsall had finished 17th in the Third Division South at the end of his first full season in charge.

He managed the team when Walsall played in front of that bumper 74,600 plus crowd at Villa Park in the fourth round of the FA Cup in January 1930.

After leaving Fellows Park, Scholey worked for some years at the Marine Hydro in Rhyl, being an expert masseur, and while there he treated many famous players.

After his first spell at Walsall, just before World War One, Scholey moved to Stockport County and then after four years' wartime service in the RAMC, he switched to Birmingham as their trainer in 1920. In his first season at St Andrew's, Blues won promotion to Division One. He then had a short spell as caretaker manager of Birmingham (during 1927-28) before rejoining Walsall. Scholey worked as a masseur for Marine Hydro at Rhyl from 1930-33. He died in 1960.

Peter O'Rourke
October 1930-February 1932

Peter ('Pat') O'Rourke, born at Newmilns in June 1873, was a solid centre-half who played for Chesterfield for quite some time before transferring to Bradford City in August 1903. He made 49 appearances for City (one goal scored) before taking over as player-manager at Valley Parade in November 1905, following a month in charge as caretaker boss after Bob Campbell's departure. He played his last game in City's colours against Darlington in the FA Cup in December 1905 and after that concentrated entirely on management. He spent 16 years in charge of the Yorkshire club, and became a very popular figure, being shrewd and deliberate in everything he did.

He completely rebuilt the Bradford team and after only five years in office had guided them into the First Division, immediately securing a five-year contract for this magnificent achievement.

The pinnacle of his success came in 1910-11 when Bradford City won the FA Cup and finished fifth in Division One – the club's highest-ever position.

After World War One, O'Rourke suffered a tragedy when his son died. This affected him deeply and he was forced to resign through ill-health in June 1921. He returned to the game as manager of Pontypridd, a position he held for five months, and after this spell in Wales he took charge of Dundee Hibernians. In April 1924 he returned to Bradford, this time as manager of Park Avenue. In his ten months there he saw another son, Peter, score twice on his League debut against Durham City. O'Rourke came out of retirement to rejoin Bradford City in May 1928 and steered the Bantams to the Third Division North title. He left Valley Parade for a second time in May 1930, unable to maintain the club's resurgence in Division Two.

Thus, in October 1930, he was installed as Walsall's new manager and results soon took a change for the better with a run of 11 games unbeaten in League and FA Cup. Things were ticking over pretty well and it was O'Rourke who signed a player who was to become one of the greatest ever to don a Walsall shirt. His name was Gilbert Alsop, whom O'Rourke signed from Coventry City in October 1931. It was a master stroke by the manager and Alsop went on to to become a terrific goalscorer, breaking many records before, during and after the war. In February 1932, Bill Slade came in to replace O'Rourke, who moved to Llanelly before finally leaving football in July 1933. He died in January 1956, aged 82.

Bill Slade
February 1932-October 1934

Bill Slade, born in Walsall in 1898, was educated at St John's School, Pleck, and played amateur football for several local teams up to the age of 24, when he became a director of Coventry City in 1922. He was appointed acting manager at Highfield Road for a while before Harry Storer took over the position in 1931. The following year Slade left Coventry and became manager of Walsall in February 1932. He maintained the strong link between Coventry and the Saddlers when he signed Bill Coward, Chris Ball, Bill Sheppard and Freddie Lee all from the Highfield Road club.

Slade was in charge of the team when Walsall caused that major shock in beating Arsenal 2-0 in the FA Cup of January 1933. In fact, the whole Walsall forward-line against the Gunners that day were all ex-Coventry players and for the occasion Walsall wore Coventry's blue and white striped shirts.

He saw the Saddlers finish fifth in the Northern Section in 1932-33 and fourth the following season, but lost his job after Walsall made a dreadful start to the 1934-35 season. He died *c.*1968.

Andy Wilson
October 1934-April 1937

Andy Wilson moved to Walsall in October 1934 and during the course of his first season at Fellows Park he saw the team recover from a terrible start to finish 14th in the Third Division North.

Born in Newmaine, Lanarkshire, in 1896, Wilson played for Cambuslang Rangers before joining Middlesbrough in 1914. During World War One his left arm was shattered but he recovered and went on to assist Heart of Midlothian and Dunfermline Athletic before returning to Middlesbrough in 1921. In his first season back at Ayresome Park he scored 31 goals in 32 games and became a regular in the Scotland team. In November 1923 he was transferred to Chelsea for £6,000 and spent eight years at Stamford Bridge prior to signing for neighbours QPR in October 1931. After leaving QPR he served with Nimes (France) for two seasons and then became manager of Clacton Town in 1934. It was from Clacton that he came to Walsall, succeeding Bill Slade.

In each of Wilson's first three seasons in charge, the Saddlers reached the third round of the FA Cup and it was he who bought future Wolves and England goalkeeper Bert Williams to the club. He also persuaded another great 'keeper, Harry Wait, to come out of retirement (1935-36) following an injury to Peter McSevich. Wilson was eventually succeeded by Tommy Lowes in April 1937, and after leaving Walsall he managed Gravesend for a short while, returning to Chelsea as coach shortly before the World War Two. After the war Wilson, who represented England at bowls, was employed by the Ministry of Works. He died in 1973, aged 77.

Tommy Lowes
April 1937-September 1939

Tommy Lowes was a Newcastle United player before World War One and he played for Coventry City, Caerphilly and Newport County immediately afterwards. He then served Yeovil Town as player-coach and later as manager in the mid-1920s before becoming manager of Barrow in 1930, leaving there for Walsall on 30 April 1937.

Unfortunately his reign at Fellows Park was short-lived, although he did sign one of the club's greatest players, Johnny Hancocks. Only at the end of the 1938-39 season did he instill any confidence in the side and he parted company soon after the outbreak of World War Two.

Under the leadership of Tommy Lowes, the Saddlers struggled and twice had to apply for re-election to the Third Division South, in the summers of 1938 and 1939.

After leaving Fellows Park, Lowes scouted for Arsenal and Norwich City, 'discovering' John Barnwell for the Gunners. He was associated with the Canaries throughout the 1960s and was still at Carrow Road when Norwich City reached the Division One for the first time in the club's history in 1972. Lowes was born in Walker, Newcastle upon Tyne, in April 1902 and died *c.*1993.

Sam Longmore
September 1939-August 1944

Sam Longmore, a local businessman and long time supporter, was elected a director of Walsall Football Club in 1934. In the summer of 1938 he took over as chairman, replacing Mr H. L. Fellows, but following the departure of Tommy Lowes shortly after the start of the ill-fated 1939-40 season, he surprisingly agreed to look after team affairs, assisted, when possible, by former goalkeeper and trainer Harry Wait. Longmore and Wait held the fort until Harry Hibbs was given the managerial job in 1944.

Sam Longmore also retired as chairman in 1944, thus ending a spell of ten years on the board at Fellows Park. Harry Barlow took over the chair.

Harry Hibbs
August 1944-June 1951

After a long and distinguished career as a goalkeeper for Birmingham and England, Harry Hibbs became Walsall's first post-war manager, being first appointed in 1944. Born in Wilnecote, near Tamworth, in May 1906, he played for Wilnecote Holy Trinity and Tamworth Castle before joining Birmingham as an amateur in April 1924, turning professional the following month.

He went on to make 389 appearances for the Blues and collected 25 full England caps as well as representing the Football League XI (three games) and touring South Africa with the FA in 1929.

He retired in May 1940 and took over as Walsall boss in August 1944, holding office until June 1951.

Hibbs signed some grand players during his time at Fellows Park, including one of the club's finest post-war defenders Reg Foulkes, ace goalkeeper Jack Lewis, and star strikers Dave Massart and Duggie Lishman.

Perhaps Walsall's best season under Hibbs came in 1945-46 when they reached the Third Division South Cup Final at Stamford Bridge before losing to Bournemouth, although in the Third Division South his team finished fifth in 1947 and third in 1948.

Hibbs's shoot-on-sight policy paid some rich dividends for the Walsall attack in the late 1940s and supporters certainly got good value for money during his reign as manager. Hibbs left the club in the summer of 1951 to be replaced by the former Reading goalscorer, Tony McPhee. He then became a permit player for de Havillands FC (February 1953-May 1954) and later managed Ware Town (1960-61) and Welwyn Garden City (1962-63). He died in Hatfield, Herts, in May 1984, four days before his 78th birthday.

Tony McPhee
July 1951-December 1951

A Scotsman, born in Edinburgh in April 1914, Tony McPhee was christened Magnus, but throughout his playing career he was always known as Tony.

He started as a goalscorer with Belfast Celtic in 1929-30 and then moved across the Irish Sea into Cumbria to assist Workington in the North Eastern League. In July 1936 he switched to Bradford Park Avenue, making an immediate impact with 17 goals in 30 games for the Yorkshire club in his first season.

In May 1937 he was transferred to Coventry City whose goalkeeper at the time was Alf Wood, destined to become Walsall's manager in the mid-1960s.

McPhee started off well enough at Highfield Road (six goals in three games) but he lost his form and in June 1938 went south to Reading, scoring on his debut for the Biscuitmen against QPR. He ended the last full peacetime season with 26 goals to his credit.

He served Reading regularly throughout the war and in the period from 1939 to 1946 he weighed in with 160 goals in 226 games being top-scorer in six out of the seven seasons.

In the first three post-war campaigns in Division Three South he claimed a further 60 League goals (in only 90 appearances) before hanging up his shooting boots in May 1949, having become one of the finest centre-forwards in Reading's history. A tall, commanding player, McPhee possessed deft footwork and could unleash a thunderous shot.

After retiring he spent two years at Elm Park as assistant manager to Ted Drake before succeeding Harry Hibbs at Walsall in July, 1951.

He had the pleasing experience of seeing the Saddlers go top of the League after they had won their first two matches under his charge.

Indeed, four of the opening six games resulted in wins but then, after the next 11 games produced only one victory, his programme notes became more and more pessimistic as he lamented that money was not available to strengthen the team. Suddenly McPhee resigned, the reason given being that he was having problems finding a house in the area.

His last game in charge was against his former club, Reading, who won 3-0 at Elm Park. After leaving football he kept the George Hotel, Basingstoke, for a time and was only 46 years of age when he died in 1960.

Brough Fletcher
March 1952-April 1953

Brough Fletcher was manager at Fellows Park for 13 months and was 56 when he took over a desperate situation from

Tony McPhee, who had resigned three months earlier.

Born in the village of Mealsgate, Cumberland, on 9 March 1893, Fletcher joined Barnsley in 1913 after playing inside-right for Chiltern Colliery. He was a regular in the Barnsley side before and after World War One, and was switched to wing-half in the early 1920s. In 1926 he was transferred to Sheffield Wednesday, but moved back to Oakwell soon after and in 1930 was appointed team manager in succession to Arthur Fairclough. Fletcher remained in charge of the Tykes until 1937, lifting them out of the Third Division North, but after they had slipped down again, he retired having spent, in all, some 24 years with the Oakwell club, scoring 73 goals in 312 games as a player.

In 1938 he became manager of Bristol Rovers, a position he held until 1949, and he teamed up with Walsall in March 1952 after the Saddlers had been without a manager for three months following the resignation of McPhee. The Saddlers successfully applied for re-election at the end of 1951-52 and in the summer Fletcher signed 11 new players, adding a few more as the season progressed. Yet all in all, the 1952-53 campaign was another poor one, Walsall finishing bottom again, and Fletcher duly resigned in the Easter, being replaced by a man even older than himself, Major Frank Buckley.

Brough Fletcher died in Bristol on 12 May 1972, aged 79.

Major Frank Buckley
April 1953-September 1955

Frank Buckley was associated with football for 53 years but he certainly won more fame as a manager than he did as a player.

One of five brothers, he was born at Urmston, Manchester, on 9 November 1882 and soon after leaving school he enlisted in the Army in 1898 and served in the Boer War. In 1903 he signed for Aston Villa as an attacking centre-half, but failed to breakthrough with the Birmingham club and in 1905 moved to Brighton.

He spent a season at Hove, did likewise with Manchester United (up to August 1907) and then played in turn for Manchester City (to July 1909), Birmingham (to August 1911 – making 56 appearances for Blues), Derby County (to May 1914) and then Bradford City, although his association with the Yorkshire club was limited due to the outbreak of World War One.

Upon the outbreak of World War One in 1914, Buckley joined the 17th Middlesex Regiment, the famous Footballers' Battalion, and rose to the rank of major. He proudly retained the title for the rest of his life.

Whilst at Derby he won a full England cap – playing against Ireland at Middlesbrough in 1914, when the Irish won 3-0 – having helped the Rams win the Second Division title two years earlier.

In March 1919 Buckley was appointed manager of Norwich City, a position he held until May 1920 when he left football for a while to become a commercial traveller, based in London.

In July 1923 he returned to the game as manager of Blackpool and spent four years at Bloomfield Road prior to moving in the same capacity to Wolves in July 1927. He had a long and successful spell at Molineux which ended in March 1944. During those 17 years Wolves won the Second Division championship (1932) and reached the FA Cup Final (1939) as well as carrying off the Wartime League Cup in 1942.

Following that marvellous career with Wolves, Buckley had a couple of years as manager of Notts County and then he took over as boss of Hull City in May 1946.

Two years later, in May 1948, he was appointed manager of Leeds United and signed the great John Charles while he was at Elland Road. In April 1953 he arrived at Fellows Park where he stayed until retiring from competitive football at the age of 72 in September 1955, handing over to Jack Love.

Buckley was a ruthless disciplinarian and it is said that youngsters, at whichever club he was associated with, were genuinely afraid of him.

That approach did little to help Walsall, however, who finished 24th and 23rd in his two full seasons with them.

He died on 22 December 1964, aged eighty-one.

Jack Love DFC
September 1955-December 1957

Jack Love, a Scotsman born in Edinburgh on 18 March 1924, was a hard inside-forward with strong shot. He had performed well for Albion Rovers before signing for Nottingham Forest in February 1949. He went on to score 21 goals in 62 League and Cup games whilst at the City Ground, helping Forest win promotion from the Third Division South in 1950-51. Four years later, following a good spell with Llanelli, he was transferred to Walsall in early March 1955 and stayed in the side for the rest of that season, scoring twice in 16 League games. The following season he scored eight goals in 24 League games, but from September he was player-manager, having taken over from Buckley who had resigned. It was Love's last season as a player as he retired through injury at the end of it.

Altogether he was Walsall's manager for only a year and a quarter – in which time Walsall finished 20th and 15th – before he in turn handed over to Bill Moore. Love moved into Wales to become manager of Wrexham (1957-58) and later served with a number of minor clubs.

His DFC was awarded when he was wounded by shrapnel during the Allies' Rhine crossing in 1944. Love served as an RAF flight-lieutenant and then as a glider pilot.

Bill Moore
December 1957-December 1963
& February 1969-October 1972

Bill Moore was a real character and the man who took Walsall into the Second

Division in 1961. Born in Washington, County Durham, in 1913, Moore played for Walker Celtic in the late 1920s and early 1930s before joining Stoke City, for whom he made a handful of senior appearances when he partnered Arthur Turner (later to play for and manage Birmingham City) in defence behind some fine forwards like Stanley Matthews, Freddie Steele and Joe Johnson.

In 1938 he moved to Mansfield Town and scored a goal against Walsall when playing in the FA Jubilee match in 1939.

After the war, Moore was appointed trainer of Notts County, who at the time were managed by the former Aston Villa and England forward Eric Houghton. Tommy Lawton and Jackie Sewell were two of the star players under Moore's supervision at Meadow Lane.

When Houghton returned to Villa Park as manager, Bill Moore went with him as his right-hand man and he played a big part in Villa's FA Cup triumph over Manchester United in 1957.

In the December following that Wembley victory, Moore was asked to take over from Jack Love as manager of Walsall who had been going through a difficult time and were deep in trouble at the foot of the Third Division South. In no time at all he rallied the players, re-election was averted, the Fourth Division title was won in 1960 and 12 months later promotion was gained to the Second Division.

After Walsall slipped back into the Third Division in 1963, in the most unfortunate of circumstances, being reduced to nine men in the final game of the season from which they needed a point (they lost 2-1 to Charlton), Moore left Fellows Park early the following season to take up a scouting position with Fulham. He returned to Fellows Park in February 1969, to succeed Ron Lewin, and over the next three years developed some superb players, such as Phil Parkes and Ray Train. But as financial problems loomed large, Moore resigned his post in March 1972 after a disagreement with coach, John Smith, over a substitution. In later years Bill Moore kept the Fox Hotel in Stafford. He died in 1982, remembered with respect as the man at the helm when Walsall FC were having their greatest period.

Alf Wood
November 1963-October 1964

Alf Wood had a splendid playing career, which spanned some 20 years. As a goalkeeper, he appeared in well over 500 competitive matches (371 in the Football League). He played for Nuneaton Borough and Sutton Town before joining Coventry City as a 20-year-old in 1935. He left Highfield Road in December 1951, joining Northampton Town for £2,100, and in his three and a half years with the Cobblers amassed 139 League appearances.

In July 1955 he started his second spell as a player with Coventry which finally ended in 1959 after he had played his last game against Plymouth in the FA Cup, while trainer-coach of the Sky Blues, a position he held until being sacked in November 1961.

He was subsequently out of football for a short time, but returned as Walsall's coach in October 1963, taking over as manager the following month. Wood left the Saddlers in October 1964 but during his short spell as manager at Fellows Park he had unearthed a fine talent in Allan Clarke. Incidently, when he was fired by Walsall, Wood became the 500th manager of a Football League club to lose his job since World War Two. He moved back to Coventry where he worked at the Massey Ferguson factory, managing their football team.

Born in Aldridge on 14 May 1915, Wood made only two League appearances for Coventry before World War Two, but he did well during the hostilities, turning out in 96 games when allowed time off from Army duties. He also guested for Northampton and represented the Army in forces football (mainly as deputy to Frank Swift). But towards the end of the war he contracted spinal meningitis and doctors told him that he would never play football again. Wood defied orders and worked his way back to full fitness, going on to make 260 consecutive appearances for Coventry (218 in the Football League) in the next six seasons (1946-52).

Ray Shaw
October 1964-March 1968

Ray Shaw was a constructive player with Birmingham City for a decade (May 1937 to May 1947) during which time he appeared in almost 130 first-team games, 111 in wartime football. After retiring he was appointed coach at St Andrew's and became manager of Walsall in October 1964, a position he held until March 1968 when he handed over to Dick Graham. Following his spell with the Saddlers, Shaw spent sometime as coach with Leicester City.

During his time at Fellows Park he guided the Saddlers to two good FA Cup runs, in 1966 and 1968, and to seventh place in Division Three in 1967-68. He signed the experienced Trevor Smith and Howard Riley in his first season but it was the youngsters at the club who did best for him. Shaw sold one of these, Allan Clarke, to Fulham for £35,000 to help balance Walsall's books.

Born in Walsall on 18 May 1913, Shaw was an amateur with the Saddlers in 1928. but then played for Streetly Works FC and Darlaston before turning professional with the Blues at the age of 24. He died in August 1980, aged 67.

Dick Graham
March-May 1968

Dick Graham, a tall, commanding man, played professionally as a goalkeeper for Northampton Town (1937) and Leicester City before World War Two, for Southport, Crewe Alexandra and Crystal Palace as a guest during the hostilities, and for Leicester and Palace afterwards, making 155 League appearances for the London club (1946-51) after recovering from letting in ten goals at Reading in September 1946.

After being forced to retire with a serious back injury he took over a pub in Croydon. He became a brewer's representative and part-time reporter and coached with the Surrey FA before, in November 1956, he was taken on by West Brom as trainer-coach under manager Vic Buckingham. He remained at The Hawthorns until November 1960 before going back to Selhurst Park as assistant manager to Arthur Rowe.

He became team manager at Palace in March 1963 and held the position for three years, during which time he took Palace to the sixth round of the FA Cup and to promotion from Division Three. Sacked in January 1966, he became manager of Leyton Orient for two years before resigning in protest against the club's decision not to buy new players.

Graham took over at Walsall the following month, when he replaced Ray Shaw, and hoped to steer the Saddlers to promotion. He did not succeed and left Fellows Park in May 1968, later having a successful spell as manager of Colchester United (from July 1968 to May 1972) during which time his side beat West Brom in the Watney Cup Final and then knocked mighty Leeds United out of the FA Cup. He resigned from Layer Road in 1972 and became chief scout for Cambridge United. In July 1973 he was appointed manager of Wimbledon but quit that post in March 1974, claiming interference by directors.

Born at Corby, Northants, on 6 May 1922, Graham played for Corby Town at the age of 14 and, like Major Frank Buckley, was a disciplinarian. His brother played centre-forward for Clapton Orient, Nottingham Forest and York City.

Ron Lewin
July 1968-February 1969

Ron Lewin spent just seven months as manager of the Saddlers from July 1968 to February 1969.

A Londoner, born at Edmonton on 21 June 1920, he played professionally as a full-back with Bradford City (from 1942 to 1944), Fulham (for four years: June 1946 to June 1950) and Gillingham, up to May 1955, totalling 310 competitive matches, including 191 in the League for the Gills and playing for Fulham in their Second Division promotion season of 1948-49.

Lewin then served the Norwegian club, Skeid of Oslo, as player-coach, Chelmsford City and Wellington Town as manager, and both Everton and Newcastle United as a coach before taking charge at Fellows Park. After leaving the Saddlers he returned to Newcastle (as coach) and later held coaching positions in Kuwait, Greece and Iceland. He returned to England and joined Bradford Park Avenue as coach just before the Yorkshire club's closure and as recently as 1986, the year of his death, he was still active in football, coaching Workington.

John Smith
October 1972-March 1973

John Smith was only 49 when he died in 1988. As a player he gained England caps at both Youth and Under-23 levels and amassed in excess of 400 senior appearances as a scheming inside-forward with West Ham (his first club), Tottenham Hotspur, Coventry City, Leyton Orient, Torquay United, Swindon Town and Walsall.

Born at Shoreditch on 4 January 1939, he joined the Upton Park staff as an amateur in the summer of 1954, turning pro for the Hammers on his 17 birthday. He left for White Hart Lane in March 1960, switched to Highfield Road in March 1964 and went back to London with Orient in October 1965. His spell with Torquay began in October 1966, he was with Swindon from June 1968 until June 1971 and then he moved to Fellows Park.

He helped the Hammers win promotion from Division Two in 1958 and Swindon to victory in both the League Cup Final at Wembley in 1969 and the Anglo-Italian Tournament in 1971. When Spurs lifted the League and FA Cup double in 1961 he managed only one game, though.

His managerial duties at Walsall lasted for just six months – from October 1972 to March 1973 inclusive – before Jimmy MacEwan took over on a caretaker basis.

Jimmy MacEwan
March 1973-June 1973

Jimmy MacEwan, although a fragile-looking winger, was a regular scorer in Scottish football during the 1950s, being Raith Rovers' leading marksman in 1956-57, '57-58 and '58-59, totalling 54 League goals in 209 outings. He played for the Scottish League and Scotland 'B' and was reserve to the full international side before signing for Aston Villa for £8,000 in July 1959.

MacEwan quickly established himself at Villa Park and helped Villa win the Second Division title and the League Cup in successive years (1960 and 1961). He missed the 1963 League Cup Final after losing his place to Alan Baker who was later to sign for Walsall. MacEwan scored 31 goals in 181 games for Villa before he moved to Fellows Park in August 1966, a month after Baker.

He struggled with injuries and was forced to retire in 1968 immediately being appointed trainer of the Saddlers, a position he held until 1975. He acted as caretaker manager following John Smith and prior to the arrival of Ronnie Allen. MacEwan then coached in South Africa, returning to Birmingham in 1977 to work first at Ansells Brewery (Aston) and then in the Social Services Department at Handsworth.

Born in Dundee on 22 March 1929, Jimmy MacEwan played with Ashdale FC before joining Arbroath, first as an amateur in 1946, turning professional in November 1947. He moved to Raith in June 1950.

Ronnie Allen
July 1973-December 1973

Ronnie Allen was another Walsall manager who had an exceptionally fine career as a player. Between 1944 and 1965 he made a total of 804 senior appearances and netted 354 goals (276 coming in 637 League outings) mainly as an outside-right or centre-forward. Born in Fenton, Stoke-on-Trent, on 15 January 1929, Allen played regularly at school and for local teams at weekends until he signed for Port Vale in 1944, turning professional in 1946. He also served in the RAF during the war.

In March 1950 he was transferred to West Bromwich Albion for a club record £20,000 and became a household name at The Hawthorns where he stayed for 11 years, up to May 1961 when he moved to Crystal Palace for £4,500.

For the Baggies he hit 208 goals (all in the First Division) which stood as a club record for 17 years (up to 1978 when Tony Brown eventually topped it). He gained an FA Cup winners' medal in 1954 (scoring two goals at Wembley in a 3-2 win over Preston) and collected five England caps as well as representing the 'B' team and the Football League.

He left Selhurst Park for Molineux in 1964, taking a position as coach before being appointed manager of the Wolves in March 1965, a position he held for three and a half years, up to November 1968 when he was dismissed. In March 1969 he took over as manager-coach of Athletic Bilbao; three years later he was made boss of the Portuguese side Sporting Lisbon (May 1972); and in July 1973, a month after leaving Lisbon, he took over as manager at Fellows Park.

Sadly Allen spent only six months in the proverbial hot seat before relinquishing the position. He was then out of football for some time before returning as scout for West Brom, moving up to scouting advisor in January 1977. In June of that year he was appointed manager at The Hawthorns, but held the job for barely six months, leaving for a lucrative job as a football advisor in Saudi Arabia. In June 1980 he took over as manager-coach of the Greek club, Panathiniakos, but again spent only six months in office. He returned as manager of West Bromwich Albion (July 1981) leading the Baggies to the semi-final of both the FA Cup and League Cup that season but was then surprisingly replaced by Ron Wylie. Ronnie Allen stayed on at the club, however, taking the job of general manager until June 1983. He applied, unsuccessfully, to get on the Albion board in 1983-84 and then offered his services as a coach at The Hawthorns, later retiring through ill health.

Ronnie Allen, incidentally, was the only player to score in each of the first 20 post-war seasons: 1945-46 to 1964-65 inclusive.

Doug Fraser
January 1974-March 1977

Doug Fraser, a craggy Scot, born in the village of Busby, near Glasgow, Lanarkshire, on 8 December 1941, played for Rolls Royce FC, Eaglesham Amateurs and Blantyre Celtic as well as having trials with Celtic and Leeds United before signing for Aberdeen in 1958, turning professional at Pittodrie Park in December 1959. As a hard tackling wing-half he had some 70 games for the Dons before transferring to West Bromwich Albion for £23,000 in September 1963. He did well at The Hawthorns, making 325 appearances (12 goals) and gaining League Cup and FA Cup winners medals in 1966 and 1968 respectively. He also played in the 1967 and 1970 League Cup Finals, skippering Albion in the latter (v Manchester City) having by then switched to right-back.

Capped twice by Scotland (v Holland and Cyprus in the mid-1960s), Fraser left Albion in January 1971, moving to Nottingham Forest for £35,000. In July 1973, after 112 League games for Forest, he was snapped up by Walsall (for £8,000) and took over from another ex-West Brom player, Ronnie Allen, as manager of the Saddlers in January 1974, holding office until March 1977. He led the Saddlers to FA Cup glory over Manchester United and Newcastle in 1975.

Fraser then pulled out of football completely and went into the prison service, working as a warder at Nottingham Gaol. He turned out in a number of charity matches between 1979 and 1982, pulling on a jersey for the Warders against the Prisoners in 1981. He resigned from the prison service in 1997.

Dave Mackay
March 1977-May 1978

Dave Mackay, born in Edinburgh on 14 November 1934, had a superb career as a player, accumulating over 800 appearances at various levels despite breaking the same leg twice. He progressed through junior football in Scotland to become one of the game's celebrities, a most inspirational wing-half, being the driving force of the great Tottenham Hotspur side of the early 1960s.

A schoolboy international at the age of 15, Mackay played for Slatefield Athletic and Newton Grange Star before turning pro with Heart of Midlothian in April 1952. He helped Hearts win the Scottish League title in 1958, the Scottish Cup in 1956, the League Cup in 1955 and 1959, gained the first of his 22 full caps (v Spain 1956), represented the Scottish League twice and appeared in four Under-23 games for his country before transferring to Spurs in March 1959 for £32,000.

Mackay quickly settled at White Hart Lane and became part of the magnificent half-back line of Blanchflower, Norman and Mackay. The medals continued to flow: the League and Cup double in 1961, two more FA Cup triumphs in 1962 and 1967 and a European Cup-winners' Cup prize in 1963 (although Mackay did not play in the Final). He made 318 appearances for

Spurs (51 goals) and skippered the side on numerous occasions.

In July 1968, after nine marvellous years in London, he moved to Derby County for £5,000 and in his first season at the Baseball Ground his experience and know-how guided the Rams to the Second Division title under Brian Clough, Mackay being voted joint FWA Player of the Year (he had earlier been voted Scottish Footballer of the Year in 1958). In May 1971 he left Derby to take over as player-manager of Swindon Town. In November 1972 he was appointed boss of Nottingham Forest and then returned as manager of Derby County in October 1973 in the wake of Clough's controversial resignation. He took Derby to their second League championship and to an FA Cup semi-final before himself leaving in controversial circumstances in November 1976. He then had four months away from football before returning to the game as manager of Walsall in March 1977. He stayed at Fellows Park for 14 months – up to May 1978 – and in August of that year became manager of the Arabic Sporting Club in Kuwait (Al-Arabi), later taking a similar position with Alba Shabab (in Dubai). Mackay did well in the Middle East but couldn't resist the offer made to him by Doncaster Rovers in 1987, returning to the Football League as manager at Belle Vue. In April 1989 he came back to the West Midlands, taking charge of struggling Birmingham City, but he couldn't get the Blues going and in January 1991 he lost his job at St Andrew's, being replaced a month later by Lou Macari.

His spell at Walsall saw the Saddlers finish sixth in Division Three and reach the fifth round of the FA Cup in 1977-78.

Alan Buckley
July 1978-August 1978, July 1979-July 1981, July 1981-January 1982 (joint) & May 1982-June 1986.

Alan Buckley had four separate spells in the manager's seat at Fellows Park, starting in 1978 and ending in 1986 when he left the Football League before returning to do so well with Grimsby Town.

A Nottinghamshire man, Buckley became a professional with his boyhood heroes, Forest, in 1968 and moved to Fellows Park for the first time in August 1973. He had ten months with Birmingham City (October 1978 to July 1979) before returning to Walsall for whom he scored 205 goals in 483 senior appearances.

He first tasted management in 1978 when he took over as caretaker boss for a few weeks (July-August) following Dave Mackay's departure and before the arrival of Alan Ashman, who sold him to Birmingham. Frank Sibley then moved into the manager's job only for Buckley to be given the post for a second time July 1979, this time holding it for two years, recently relegated Walsall finishing runners-up in Division Four in his first season in charge. He was then joined by joint-manager Neil Martin, who took over the manager's job on his own in January 1982. Four months later Buckley was back in charge and this time he held the position until July 1986 when he moved to Stourbridge, to be replaced at Fellows Park by the relatively unknown figure of Tommy Coakley. After Stourbridge Buckley assisted Tamworth and was player-manager of Kettering Town, before he found his way to Blundell Park, Grimsby in June 1988. Under his management, Kettering won the Bob Lord Trophy and finished third in the Conference. At Grimsby he steered the Mariners to successive promotions and to the fifth round of the FA Cup. In 1995 he switched from Grimsby to West Brom but after failing to achieve to win honours for the Baggies he returned to Blundell Park in 1997. In 1997-98 he twice guided the Mariners to Wembley victories, in the Second Division Play-off Final and the Auto Windscreen Shield Final. (*See Walsall Stars*)

Alan Ashman
August 1978-February 1979

Alan Ashman was the man who guided West Bromwich Albion to FA Cup glory in 1968 at the end of his first full season in charge at The Hawthorns.

A Yorkshireman, born in Rotherham on 30 May 1928, Ashman was an amateur centre-forward with Sheffield United during the war, towards the end of which he turned professional with Nottingham Forest. In June 1951, after scoring three goals in 13 League matches for the Reds, he was sold to Carlisle United and he stayed with the Cumbrian club until 1958, netting 98 goals in 207 Third Division North matches. He then worked on a poultry farm and managed Penrith in his spare time before becoming manager of Carlisle in February 1963, taking them down into the Fourth Division in his first season in charge (they were already bottom when he took over) and then, in quick succession, up to third place in Division Two.

Ashman moved to The Hawthorns in the summer of 1967 after Jimmy Hagan had left – and at once things started to happen for him at West Brom. In all he spent four years in charge of the Baggies, taking them to the European Cup-winners' Cup quarter-finals as well as to the 1968 FA and 1970 League Cup Finals.

After a disappointing season he was sacked in May 1971 (he was on holiday in Greece when a journalist told him he had lost his job) to be replaced by former player Don Howe, and immediately took up a position as manager-coach of the Greek club, Olympiakos Piraeus after turning down a scouting job with Stoke City. He took Olympiakos to runners-up in the Greek League in 1971-72, but left in the summer to return as manager of Carlisle United, signing the forms on 4 June 1972. He guided the Cumbrian club to promotion to the old First Division in 1974 but after suffering relegation immediately, he resigned in October 1975.

Two months later he went to Workington as their boss but in February 1977 he was sacked with the club sitting on the bottom of the Fourth Division. Remaining in football, he then scouted for Manchester United before Walsall named him as successor to Dave Mackay in August 1978.

Ashman spent less than one season at Fellows Park – Walsall were relegated to Division Four at the end of it – and at the age of 51 he became chief scout of Derby County in October 1979. He later became assistant manager to John Newman at the Baseball Ground, but was dismissed by the Rams in November 1982. The following March he took over as assistant manager at Hereford. Released from Edgar Street in July 1987, Ashman then scouted for Plymouth Argyle and Mansfield Town.

Former West Brom centre-half John Wile said of Alan Ashman: "He was a perfect gentleman... he was probably too easy going for his own good, and that of the team. But he couldn't change the way he was... a smashing fellow."

Frank Sibley
March 1979-April 1979

Frank Sibley, born in Uxbridge on 4 December 1947, began his career in football by signing as an apprentice for Queen's Park Rangers in June 1964. He turned professional at Loftus Road in February 1965 and made his senior debut against Aldershot in the FA Cup. After gaining England Youth honours as captain of the Under-18s in the International Tournament in Yugoslavia, he quickly established himself in Rangers' first team as a forceful wing-half and was an ever-present in the side which won promotion to Division Two and lifted the Football League Cup at Wembley in 1966-67. The following season he was a member of the England Under-23 party which toured Greece, Turkey and Bulgaria.

He skippered Rangers and remained a regular first-team player until a knee injury forced him into an early retirement in 1972 after he had amassed exactly 150 League appearances.

A natural leader, Sibley settled into his new career as a fully qualified coach, staying initially at Loftus Road under manager Gordon Jago and his assistant, Stan Anderson. In 1977-78 he was given the manager's job, taking over from Dave Sexton. Unfortunately Rangers struggled in the First Division that season, finishing 19th, and it was no surprise when Sibley was replaced by Steve Burtenshaw. In February 1979 he was appointed manager of Walsall – succeeding Alan Ashman – but after barely two months in charge at Fellows Park he was replaced by Alan Buckley, who returned to the club as player-manager following a spell at St Andrew's.

Five years later, in July 1984, Sibley returned as manager of QPR, who had qualified for the UEFA Cup, but again Rangers had a poor campaign, eventually finishing 19th in Division One. Consequently Sibley once more lost his job, being replaced by Jim Smith. He remained as coach under Smith and held the same post thereafter, under the managerships of Peter Shreeve, Trevor Francis, Don Howe, Gerry Francis and Ray Wilkins, thus continuing his long association with the Loftus Road club right through to 1996 when he moved across London to join Fulham's backroom staff. Although he had successful spells as assistant manager at QPR, Sibley was probably the least successful of all Walsall managers, his few weeks in charge producing hardly any points as the Saddlers completed the drop into Division Four.

Neil Martin
July 1981-January 1982 (joint) and January-May 1982

Neil Martin was born in Tranent, Alloa, on 20 October 1940, and as an out-and-out centre-forward he spent 18 years scoring goals, initially in his native Scotland for Alloa Athletic, Queen of the South and Hibernian and then in England, with Sunderland, Coventry City, Nottingham Forest, Brighton and Crystal Palace, before retiring to take up coaching and then management, becoming boss of Walsall in 1981, initially in partnership with Alan Buckley.

He moved south from Easter Road to Roker Park in October 1965 and struck 38 goals in 86 League games for Sunderland before transferring to Coventry in February 1968. At Highfield Road he continued to hit the target, grabbing 45 goals in his 122 League and Cup outings for the Sky Blues, helping them become established in the First Division. He left Coventry for Forest in February 1971 and joined Brighton in July 1975 after adding 28 goals to his overall tally in 119 League games for the Reds. He ended his senior career with a brief spell at Selhurst Park (March-May 1976). All told he scored 115 goals in his 337 appearances.

He was capped three times by Scotland, gained one Under-23 cap and also represented the Scottish League whilst with Hibs, for whom he scored 40 goals in 1964-65.

He was appointed as joint team manager at Fellows Park in July 1981 (with Buckley) after having coached abroad in the Middle East for five years. He was then took over complete control of the team in January, but was replaced in May 1982 by Buckley again, Walsall avoiding relegation only by goal-difference at the end of his time in sole charge. Later Martin, who served an apprenticeship as a mining engineer whilst playing for Alloa Athletic, returned to coaching in the Middle East.

Tommy Coakley
August 1986-December 1988

"Tommy who?" asked fans and journalists alike when Tommy Coakley was appointed manager following the arrival of Terry Ramsden as chairman in the summer of 1986.

Yet in his first two seasons with the Saddlers, Coakley took the club further in the FA Cup than they had ever gone before or since, and became only the

second manager ever to lead the Saddlers to promotion to Division Two.

A Scotsman, born at Belshill on 2 May 1947, Coakley played for Motherwell before joining Arsenal in May 1966 just in time to go with the Gunners on their close-season tour to Turkey.

An orthodox outside-right he made only nine First Division appearances for the Gunners (scoring one goal) before being transferred to to Detroit Cougars, moving back into Scottish football with Morton in 1969-70.

Then it was on to Chelmsford City and then Maldon Town, who he led to the Essex League championship before taking charge of Bishops Stortford, switching to Fellows Park as a surprise choice as Walsall's boss in August 1986. Coakley, though, proved himself a tremendous motivator and at the end of his first season Walsall finished eighth and then he was voted Barclays Manager of the Month for April 1988 as the Saddlers raced into the promotion Play-offs. Unfortunately the sale of David Kelly to West Ham during the following close season weakened the team for life in the Second Division and Coakley became more and more isolated after Ramsden's departure although he still remained popular with the players.

He came under particular pressure during the first half of the 1988-89 season when Walsall struggled in the higher division, and when they propped up the table, after 11 successive defeats, he was dismissed, allowing John Barnwell to move in early in 1989 after Ray Train had looked after team affairs for a short period.

After leaving Fellows Park, Coakley had a spell in charge of Blakenhall and in January 1992 he joined Telford United as coach under Gerry Daly.

Ray Train
December 1988-January 1989

Ray Train acted as caretaker manager for a month prior to the arrival of John Barnwell. Born in Nuneaton in 1951, he had 20 years in the game as a player and amassed over 600 senior appearances for nine different clubs. He had two spells at Fellows Park and in between times served with Carlisle, Sunderland, Bolton, Watford, Oxford United, Bournemouth (on loan), Northampton Town and Tranmere Rovers. He later became coach, first with Walsall and then at Middlesbrough. His brief spell in charge of Walsall did nothing to arrest the club's terrible sequence of results. (*See Walsall Stars*)

John Barnwell
January 1989-March 1990

John Barnwell took over as Walsall's team manager on 17 January 1989 just a few weeks after being sacked by Notts County, but he could not prevent their relegation from the Second Division, their situation already hopeless when he arrived. He lost the job late the following season with the Saddlers heading towards yet another relegation.

Barnwell was born in Newcastle upon Tyne on 24 December 1938, and his playing career as a wing-half or inside-forward spanned almost 20 years, during which time he served Bishop Auckland (1953), Arsenal (professional November 1956), Nottingham Forest (March 1964) and Sheffield United (April 1970). He retired through injury at the age of 33 in 1972 to become assistant manager to Colin Addison, his former playing colleague, at Hereford United, having amassed a fine record as a player, appearing in well over 400 senior games, 360 of which came in the Football League (138 with Arsenal and 182 with Forest). He also gained England caps at Youth and Under-23 levels. His time with Arsenal coincided with an unusually medicore period in that club's history but he helped Forest to become runners-up to Manchester United in 1966-67.

From Edgar Street, Barnwell moved in the same capacity to Peterborough United, working under Noel Cantwell, whom he eventually succeeded in July 1977. He resigned his position as manager of Posh after problems over money for team strengthening, and he duly took over at Wolves in November 1978, leading them to an FA Cup semi-final in 1979 and a League Cup triumph at Wembley the following year. With Wolves he was involved in two big transfers, selling Steve Daley to Manchester City for £1.5 million and then signing Andy Gray from Villa for £1.4 million. Gray repaid him by heading the winner in the 1980 League

Cup Final against Barnwell's old club, Forest.

Whilst at Molineux, Barnwell was involved in a serious car accident, suffering a fractured skull, and after a disappointing start to the 1981-82 campaign he parted company with Wolves. Barnwell then had a brief spell in charge of the Greek side, AEK Athens (he was banned after making unflattering remarks about the standard of Greek domestic football) before returning to the Football League as boss of Notts County in June 1987.

County were pipped by Walsall in the Third Division promotion Play-offs that season of 1987-88 , but within a few months he found himself in charge of the players who such a short time previously had been his chief rivals.

Things didn't work out for Barnwell at Fellows Park and following Walsall's relegation to Division Three (when they were replaced by his former club Wolves) he was dismissed in March 1990, being succeeded initially by his assistant, Paul Taylor, before Kenny Hibbitt moved into the camp for the start of the 1990-91 campaign, by which time Walsall had been relegated to Division Four. After a period out of the game Barnwell returned as a scout before becoming managerial consultant to Northampton Town in 1993. Three years later he was appointed to lead the League Managers' Association.

Paul Taylor
March 1990-May 1990

Paul Taylor had what must be the shortest reign as the 'permanent' manager of Walsall, holding the job for just over a month prior to the engagement of Kenny Hibbitt.

Born on 3 December 1949 in Sheffield, Taylor joined his boyhood heroes, Sheffield Wednesday, as an apprentice in 1969 and turned professional at Hillsborough in June 1971. A midfielder, he failed to hold down a regular place in the side and after only six League games was transferred to York City in July 1973. Again he failed to establish himself, making only four senior appearances, and after a loan spell with Hereford United (one sub appearance in January 1974) he was loaned to Colchester United in March that year. At Layer Road he was called into action only nine times and then went to Southport (July 1974) where he fared much better, going on to top 100 appearances for the Haig Avenue club (16 goals) before switching to the NASL with Tampa Bay Rowdies in July 1977. He returned to England in 1981 as assistant manager to Keith Peacock at Gillingham, and halfway through the 1987-88 season he took over at the Priestfield Stadium when Peacock departed.

When he was assistant to Peacock, the Gills reached the 1987 Third Division Play-off Final (where they lost to Swindon at Selhurst Park), but his first season in sole charge saw Gillingham flounder and after a terrible start to 1988-89, Taylor was sacked after a 5-0 defeat at Preston. They were eventually relegated.

He was then taken on as first-team coach and assistant to Barnwell early in 1989 and replaced Barnwell briefly during another relgation season before Hibbitt arrived. Taylor was promoted to general manager in 1994-95.

Kenny Hibbitt
May 1990-September 1994

Kenny Hibbitt was a fine goalscoring midfielder who amassed an excellent career record of 694 appearances for his four clubs – Bradford Park Avenue, Wolves, Coventry City and Bristol Rovers – as well as gaining one England Under-23 cap, coming on as a sub against Wales in 1970-71.

A Yorkshireman, born in Bradford on 3 January 1951, Hibbitt's early football was played in the Bradford area and he joined the Park Avenue club as an amateur in June 1966, turning professional on his 17th birthday in 1968. He played 15 League games for Bradford PA before transferring to Wolves for a bargain fee of £5,000 in November 1968.

Although homesick at first, Hibbitt soon settled down at Molineux and the fans grew to love him. Always a grand competitor, he was a key figure in the midfield engine-room for some 16 years up to 1984. He gained two League Cup winners' medals (1974 and 1980), scoring in the first Final against Manchester City. He also helped Wolves win promotion from the Second Division on two occasions (in 1977 and 1983) and lined up in the 1972 UEFA Cup Final against Spurs. Given a deserved testimonial by Wolves in 1982, he left the club two years later to join Coventry after amassing a fine set of statistics: 114 goals in 574 appearances for the Wanderers.

He spent two seasons at Highfield Road and in August 1986 went to Bristol Rovers. A broken leg, suffered against Sunderland in February 1988, ended his playing days and he became Gerry Francis's assistant at Twerton Park, seeing Rovers win the Third Division title and finish runners-up in the Leyland DAF Trophy Final at Wembley in 1989.

Hibbitt had always wanted to try his luck as a manager and when the opportunity arose to apply for the Walsall job, his ambition came true. But it wasn't all plain sailing, and Hibbitt's first two seasons (the first two at Bescot Stadium incidentally) were rather disappointing to say the least, as the Saddlers finished 16th and 15th respectively in the Fourth Division. However, he wheeled and dealed frequently in the transfer market, securing the services of some experienced professionals to blend with the up-and-coming youngsters, and from time to time there were some useful performances. However, soon after the start of the 1994-95 season, Hibbitt left, to be replaced by the former

Aston Villa and Northern Ireland defender, Chris Nicholl. He later became manager of Cardiff City and then director of football and coaching at Ninian Park.

Kenny Hibbitt's brother, Terry, played for Leeds United, Newcastle United and Birmingham City.

Chris Nicholl
September 1994-June 1997

Chris Nicholl was a natural defender, capped 51 times by Northern Ireland and who, during a long career, made 754 appearances in League and Cup football. Born in Wilmslow, Cheshire on 12 October 1946, Nicholl represented Macclesfield Schoolboys before joining Burnley as an apprentice in June 1963, turning professional at Turf Moor in April 1965. Surprisingly he failed to make the grade with the Clarets and in 1966 moved to Witton Albion, returning to the Football League with Halifax Town for £1,000 in June 1968. A little over a year later he was transferred to Luton Town for £25,000 and it was with the Hatters where his defensive qualities were first noticed.

In March 1972, Aston Villa, who were ready to climb out of the Third Division, bought Nicholl to bolster their defence, manager Vic Crowe paying £75,000 for his services, with another £15,000 to follow once Villa had got back into the top flight. Nicholl replaced veteran George Curtis (ex-Coventry City) in the centre-half position and over the next five years he scored 20 goals in 252 appearances for the Villa, helping them reach the First Division in 1975 and twice lift the League Cup, in 1975 and 1977, scoring a terrific goal in the second replay of the latter encounter at Old Trafford. He was also voted the Supporters' Player of the Year in 1975.

He left Villa Park in June 1977, signing for Southampton for a fee of £90,000. He stayed at The Dell for six seasons, playing in Saints' beaten League Cup Final side against Nottingham Forest in 1979, a year after helping them gain promotion from Division Two. In August 1983, Nicholl was appointed player-assistant manager of Grimsby Town, and stayed at Blundell Park for two years before retiring as a player in May 1985 to become boss of Southampton in place of Lawrie McMenemy. In May 1991, after guiding Saints to second place in the old First Division (their highest-ever League position) and leading them into the UEFA Cup, he departed company, handing over the reins to Ian Branfoot. After a period out of the limelight, Nicholl became Walsall's 25th post-war manager in September 1994 when he replaced Kenny Hibbitt.

His reign at Bescot Stadium lasted three years, until the summer of 1997, when the relatively unknown Dane Jan Sorensen took charge. During his term of office with the Saddlers, Nicholl did reasonably well without achieving particular success. He perhaps knew he had done what he could at Bescot and decided to call it a day at the age of 50. He is now reasident in Southampton and plays a lot of tennis in his spare time.

Jan Sorensen
June 1997-May 1998

Jan Sorensen was the man chosen by chairman Jeff Bonser to take over from Nicholl, being appointed in June 1997 at the age of 42. As a hard-working midfielder, Sorensen played for four of Europe's leading clubs – three in Holland, namely Ajax, FC Twente Enschede and Feyenoord, and FC Bruges, who won the 1977 Belgium League championship and then reached the European Cup Final the following year before losing 1-0 to Liverpool at Wembley. He also starred for Portomonense in Portugal. Capped 15 times by Denmark, he had been player-manager of Portomonense prior to his arrival at Bescot Stadium.

Sorensen had a mixed season with Walsall. He saw his team enjoy excellent runs in all three domestic Cup competitions, reaching the fourth round of both the Coca-Cola Cup and FA Cup and the semi-finals of the Auto Windscreen Shield. But he failed to produce the goods in the bread and butter of League football and after the Saddlers had struggled to finish a disappointing 19th, he handed over the duties to Ray Graydon, another former Aston Villa player, who, like Nicholl before him, had played in those two League Cup winning teams in the 1970s.

Ray Graydon
June 1998-

Ray Graydon was a League club footballer for 18 years, during which time he amassed well over 400 appearances in various competitions and scored more than 120 goals. An orthodox outside-right, Graydon was born in Frenchay, Bristol on 21 July

1947 and signed for his home town club, Bristol Rovers, as an apprentice in July 1963, turning professional at Eastville in September 1965. He gained youth and amateur honours for England early in his career and after netting 33 times in 133 outings for the Pirates, he was transferred to Aston Villa for £50,000 in July 1971, with Brian Godfrey leaving for Rovers.

A speedy winger, with good, close ball control and powerful right-foot shot, Graydon (who had future Walsall boss Chris Nicholl as his colleague) scored Villa's winning goal against Norwich City in the 1975 League Cup Final, cracking home the rebound after his penalty had been saved by ex-Villa keeper Kevin Keelan, and then played in the second replay of the 1977 Final when Everton were beaten 3-2 at Old Trafford. Graydon notched 82 goals in 231 games for Villa before joining Coventry City in July 1977. The following summer he had a spell in the NASL with Washington Diplomats, returning to England to sign for Oxford United for £35,000 in November 1978. After three years as a player at the Manor Ground, Graydon retired to become Oxford's coach, later serving in the same capacity at Watford (1988-89) and then as coach at Southampton.

Once he had settled in at the Bescot Stadium Graydon imposed a strict code of discipline on the players – no earrings, no mobile phones on the team coach, no stereos in the changing rooms, no caps! It all paid off as he saw the team do tremendously well in his first season in charge, winning promotion from the Second Division as runners-up to Fulham.

Having himself signed only one player for cash – defender Richard Green for £35,000 – Graydon's squad was made up basically of free transfers, loan stars and youngsters who had developed through the ranks, although Andy Watson had been purchased prior to his arrival for £60,000 from Blackpool.

With home attendances averaging around the 4,000 mark during the first part of the season, Graydon simply couldn't afford to go out a buy the players he wanted to strengthen his squad. Instead he stuck with those he had and blended them into a competent unit which not only matched the best in the Second Division but beat most of the other 23 teams and at the same time almost made it to Wembley in the Auto Windscreen Shield.

The 1998-99 campaign was Ray Graydon's first season as a club manager and one he will never forget – nor will his players and the Saddlers' supporters who were delighted with his efforts and more so with the news that he was to remain at the Bescot Stadium.

Walsall FC Chairmen

Walsall Football Club became a limited company in 1921 and Mr H. L. Fellows was a director from the start, although not as chairman until 1926. Consequently he has therefore been the second longest-serving chairman of the board of directors of Walsall FC (12 years), behind Ken Wheldon.

Here is a detailed list of the respective chairmen of Walsall FC 1926 to date:

H. L. Fellows	1926-38
S. Longmore	1938-44
H. J. Barlow	1944-47
N. Longmore	1947-58
E. Thomas	1958-64
W. H .L. Harrison	1964-68
R. Harrison	1968-72
K. F. Wheldon	1972-85
J. A. Harris	1985-86
T. Ramsden	1986-89
B. S. Blower	1989-91
J. W. Bonser	1991-97

(no chairman since 1997)

Ken Wheldon, chairman for 13 years.

Walsall's Longest-serving directors

(since 1921)

N. Longmore	1944-64
J. A. Harris	1968-86
H. L. Fellows	1921-38
E. Jackson	1930-47
H. S .Hawley	1954-69
Sir A. G. B. Owen	1954-69
K. E. Wheldon	1972-85
H. J. Barlow	1934-47
S. Bowler	1973-85
R. Homden	1973-85
F. J. H. Wood	1960-71
H. Fullwood	1945-55
S. Longmore	1934-44
W. H. L. Harrison	1955-60 & 1964-68
R. Harrison	1964-72

The duo of Ken Wheldon, Dick Homden and Jack Harris, who were joined later by Steve Bowler (1973), have been the longest-ever serving three/four directors in the club's history, that have actually stayed together on the board.

Walsall FC Secretaries

Mr Ernest Wilson was secretary of Walsall FC for almost 40 years (up to 1972). Prior to his appointment the club had been well served in this department by a number of people including Louis Ford (from the turn of the century), Jack Shutt (before World War One) and Joe Burchell (1920s, who also acted as team manager for a time). The late John Westmancoat, followed by his wife, Mrs Betty Westmancoat, and then Roy Whalley, who took office at the old Fellows Park ground in 1986, have been secretaries since 1972.

A-Z of Walsall Stars

GILBERT ALSOP

Centre-forward; 222 apps, 169 goals.

Born: Frampton Cotterill, Bristol, 10 September 1908. Died: Walsall, 16 April 1992.

Undoubtedly one of the greatest centre-forwards of his era, certainly of pre-war times, Walsall's champion goalscorer, Gilbert Alsop, was a hard, robust, never-say-die striker. After leaving school in Bristol, he played for

Latterbridge FC, then Bath City (from August 1923) and Coventry City (joining them in the summer of 1929) prior to teaming up with Walsall in September 1931. Alsop had two separate spells with the Saddlers, the first one ending in 1935 and his second running from 1938 to 1947.

In his professional career he appeared in a total of 448 competitive matches and scored 308 goals, 167 of which came in 220 Third Division South games, broken down as follows: four in 16 outings for Coventry; 151 in 195 starts for Walsall; and two in nine appearances for Ipswich Town. He also hit 56 goals in over 100 wartime matches for the Saddlers and guested for a number of other clubs during the hostilities including Leicester City, and three 'Towns', Luton, Mansfield and Northampton. He headed the opening goal when Walsall dumped mighty Arsenal out of the FA Cup in 1933 and registered four goals in a game for the Saddlers on five separate occasions.

Alsop surprisingly left Walsall for West Bromwich Albion (as cover for W. G. Richardson) for £3,000 in November 1935 this after representing the Football League in a game against the Baggies. Alas, he had a disappointing time at The Hawthorns, making only one first-team appearance. He a much better spell with Ipswich Town (May 1937 to October 1938) during which he netted 30 goals in 39 games at first-team level (which included a season in the Southern League), before returning to Fellows Park where he saw out his career, retiring as a player in May 1948, although he played his last senior game the previous year. He spent his last full season as player-coach to Walsall's third team.

Alsop worked behind the scenes at Fellows Park for a further 20 years or so and later became groundsman of the playing fields adjoining Walsall Arboretum. He was still attending home games at the Bescot Stadium right up to his death in April 1992 at the age of 83.

GEORGE ANDREWS

Centre-forward; 173+4 apps, 40 goals.

Born: Dudley, 23 April 1942.

A Black Country man who joined Luton Town as a professional in January 1960, Andrews failed to break through at Kenilworth Road and returned to the Dudley area to play for Lower Gornal Athletic in the West Midlands League, before transferring to Cardiff City in October 1965. He signed for Southport in a £6,000 deal in February 1967, switched to Shrewsbury Town in November 1969 and then rounded off his senior career at Walsall (January 1973 to May 1977). He

was an opportunist whose goal return was consistent wherever he played. A fine marksman, who thrived on hard work, he scored exactly 150 goals in 443 League appearances as a professional, 21 in 43 games for Cardiff, 41 in 117 whilst at Haig Avenue, another 50 in 124 outings for the Shrews and 38 in 159 matches for the Saddlers including the match-winner against Newcastle in a fourth-round FA Cup-tie in January 1975. He continued to play local non-League football until he was 40 and turned out in charity matches at the age of 50.

COLIN ASKEY

Outside-right; 88 apps, 12 goals.

Born: Milton, Stoke, 3 October 1932.

An 'old-fashioned' winger, Askey scored 23 goals in exactly 200 League games for his first club, Port Vale, who took him on the groundstaff as a 15-year-old after he had started work as a storekeeper with a local firm, playing at weekends for a factory team. He signed professional forms for Vale in October 1949 and went on to gain a Third Division North championship winners' medal with the Valiants in 1953-54, also playing against West Brom in that season's FA Cup semi-final.

He joined Walsall on a free transfer in July 1958 (to replace Sammy Moore who himself had taken over from Scotsman Jackie Stewart) and performed well on the right flank for the Saddlers. When Walsall won the Fourth Division title in 1960-61 he scored twice in 12 appearances and when they were Third Division runners-up the following season he played in 38 games, scoring four times. After four seasons at Fellows Park, Askey moved to Mansfield Town (June 1962), staying in League football until May 1963 by which time he had topped 300 appearances in the competition and scoring 37 goals. Following a cartilage operation, from which he never recovered full fitness, he went on to play for Wellington Town and later Stafford Rangers, and then he became an insurance agent. He still lives in the Potteries.

CHARLIE ASTON

Full-back; 70 apps, 1 goal.

Born: Wolverhampton, March 1870. Died: Birmingham 1941.

A very efficient right-back who was an expert at floating passes either directly down the touchline or across centre-field rather than giving the ball a hefty kick, Aston played for Walsall from August 1895 to April 1898 when he joined Aston Villa. He moved to QPR in August 1901 and two years later teamed up with Burton United and went to Watford in the summer of 1906 before rounding off his career with Leyton from September 1908 to May 1910.

JACK ('SOLDIER') ASTON

Forward; 108 apps, 52 goals.

Born: Walsall, June 1877. Died: West Bromwich.

Jack Aston was a natural footballer and one of Walsall's earliest scoring heroes with 38 goals in 88 League games in the late 1890s. He was certainly a vital member of the Saddlers' front line, giving nothing but 100 per cent effort every game. A powerful, forcing player, he teamed up well with David Copeland and Alf Griffin for season 1896-97, scoring ten goals in 28 League games. The following term he was joint top scorer in the League with George Johnson and in 1898-99 he shared top spot with Vail. He was then transferred to Woolwich Arsenal (May 1898), being replaced in the Saddlers front line by the Irish international Joe Connor.

He began his career with Walsall White Star in 1892, played next for Fullbrook Saints, then Willenhall Pickwick, Bloxwich Strollers and Wednesfield before signing for Walsall in July 1896. After one game he was arrested by the Military Police, but soon afterwards Walsall bought him out of the Army to prevent any futher embarrassment. After spending two years with Arsenal he moved back to the Midlands to join Birmingham in 1900 and scored 24 goals in 61 games for Blues before transferring to Doncaster Rovers (July 1902). After reverting to his native Midlands, he played for Bilston, Blakenhall St Luke's and Walsall Wood before retiring in 1906.

NICK ATTHEY

Defender/midfield; 492+10 apps, 18 goals.

Born: Tantobie, Newcastle, 8 May 1946.

Nick Athey was a dedicated club man who made more than 500 appearances for the Saddlers over a period of 14 seasons at Fellows Park. As an eight-year-old he was a regular member of the East Stanley Junior School and when his parents moved to Coventry he played for Foxford School (in all age groups) and helped Coventry Boys win the Birmingham and District Shield. He was also selected for the county team and skippered the side in his last schoolboy match

before joining Walsall as an amateur in June 1961. He turned professional under manager Bill Moore on 5 July 1963, and made his League debut at Queen's Park Rangers in his first season as a full-time player, gaining a permanent spot in the side in 1964-65. Athey was an honest footballer, whose heart and soul were always in the game. He retired from League football in the summer of 1977 and later played for Rushall Olympic. His wife is the daughter of the former Football League referee, Arthur Rowbotham.

STEVE BAINES

Central defender; 49+1 apps, 5 goals.

Born: Newark, 23 June 1954.

Steve Baines' playing career was ended by arthritis in the neck in the summer of 1986, but he remained in the game and qualified as a referee. He was voted Referee of the Year in Chesterfield in 1988-89 and he progressed through non-League football to take charge of matches in the Nationwide Football League by 1995. Said Steve: "For some time the PFA had been itching to get more ex-pros into the refereeing business, but one or two people from the hierarchy didn't believe a former footballer would have the right credentials or pedigree to control top matches. I was aiming to prove everyone wrong and lead a revolution."

As a player, Baines joined Nottingham Forest as an apprentice in June 1970 and turned pro at the City Ground on his 18th

birthday two years later. He made only two League appearances for Forest before transferring to Huddersfield Town in July 1975, for whom he went on to appear in 132 League and Cup matches up to March 1978 when he switched to Bradford City. Two. After a further 111 senior outings, he left Valley Parade for Walsall and made exactly 50 first-team appearances for the Saddlers before leaving the Midlands to join Scunthorpe United in August 1982, having been on loan to Bury, making seven appearances in December 1981).

After one season and nearly 40 League games with the Iron, Baines moved again, this time to Chesterfield, where he stayed, adding another 133 League and 21 Cup appearances to his tally until being forced into retirement at the age of 32. He ended his career with a creditable total of 494 senior appearances for his seven major clubs (441 in the Football League) and he scored 46 goals.

ALAN BAKER

Midfield; 155+9 apps, 36 goals.

Born: Tipton, Staffs, 22 June 1944.

After developing his skills playing for

Willingsworth School Tipton, Alan Baker starred for Brierley Hill, Tipton and Sedgley Boys, and Staffordshire and Birmingham County Boys and won England honours at both Schoolboy (at Wembley) and Youth team levels, scoring a penalty in one international against West Germany. He joined Aston Villa as an amateur in July 1959, turning professional in July 1961. A clever ball player, Baker made his League debut at Fulham in April 1961, while still an amateur, and gained a League Cup runners-up medal two years later when Villa beat their arch rivals Birmingham City 3-1 in the two-legged Final.

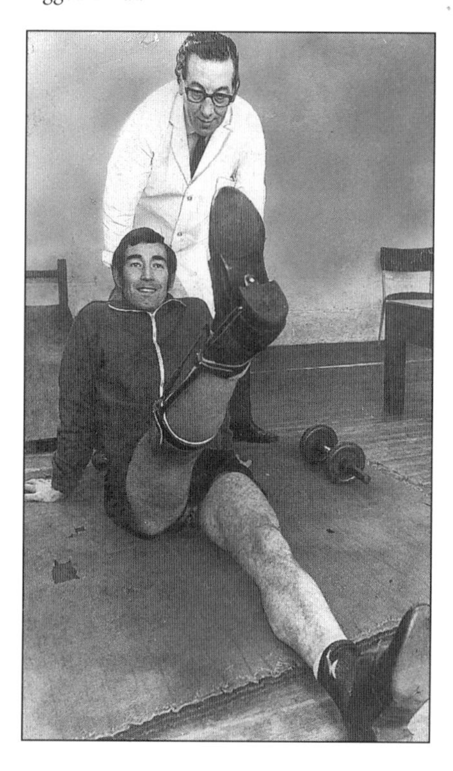

He broke his collar-bone in a reserve-team game at Hillsborough in October 1963, but recovered to score 17 goals in 109 games for Villa before transferring to Fellows Park for £10,000 in July 1966. He went on to give the Saddlers five years' excellent service after an impressive debut against Mansfield Town. He netted some important goals during his spell at Walsall, including a superb 30-yard lob over the head of the Oxford 'keeper Jim Barron in November 1966. Forced to retire through injury in 1971 Baker later became a leather cutter in Walsall.

HARRY BALDWIN

Goalkeeper; 40 apps.

Born: Erdington, Birmingham, 17 July 1920.

A reliable goalkeeper, Harry Baldwin played for Sutton Town before becoming an amateur with West Brom in January 1937, turning pro at The Hawthorns the following year. He made only five appearances for the Baggies who transferred him to Brighton &

Hove Albion in July 1939. Baldwin stayed at Hove until July 1952, making 164 League appearances and saving 11 out of 15 penalties in two seasons including five in a row. He then had a season and a half with Kettering Town, signing for Walsall on 29 December 1953 (initially on trial, becoming a full-timer in January 1954). He played in 37 League games for the Saddlers before drifting into non-League football in 1955 with Wellington Town. Baldwin retired in 1957 and later became a director of an engineering firm at Kenilworth, Warwicks. A fine all-round sportsman who enjoyed golf, cricket and tennis, he guested for Northampton Town and Nottingham Forest during World War Two.

CHRIS BALL

Inside-forward; 123 apps, 23 goals.

Born: Leek, Staffs, 31 October 1906. Died: JGreat Barr, Birmingham, 1 February 1987.

Chris Ball was a deep lying inside-forward,

rather on the small side at 5ft 8ins and weighing 11st 2lbs, but a player who was fully committed. Indeed, occasionally he was perhaps too committed and was sent-off twice in corresponding matches against Crewe Alexandra in March 1932 and March 1933, each time by the same referee, Mr Bert Mee from Mansfield. Ball played for Leek St Luke's in the Staffordshire Junior League before turning pro at the age of 18 with Coventry City. He played with Colwyn Bay from July 1929, Bristol Rovers (then in Division Three South) from August 1930, making 15 appearances, and Bristol City (August 1931, three appearances) prior to trying his luck at Fellows Park. He signed for Saddlers in February 1932. After making only 16 appearances for Bristol Rovers he suffered a serious knee injury which threatened to end his career, but he bounced back and became one of the 11 legends who played for Walsall when they beat mighty Arsenal 2-0 in the FA Cup in 1933. After leaving Walsall, Ball played briefly for Cradley Heath and Brierley Hill Alliance, and then returned to Colwyn Bay, retiring during World War Two.

KEITH BALL

Goalkeeper; 51 apps.

Born: Walsall, 26 October 1940.

Keith Ball had three separate spells at Fellows Park, making a total of 48 League appearances for the Saddlers. He joined the club

initially as an amateur in 1957, became a part-professional in January 1959 and a full-timeer in July 1960. Ball was given a free transfer in July 1962 when he joined Worcester City, but after gaining experience in the Southern League, he returned to Fellows Park for a fee of £1,500 in May 1965, staying until November 1968, when he switched to Port Vale. There followed a brief spell with Stourbridge before he came back to Walsall for a third time in November 1972. Ball retired from League football in 1973 but still played in a lot of charity games up to 1987.

JOE BAMBRICK

Centre-forward; 41 apps, 20 goals.

Born: Belfast, 1 November 1907. Died: 27 November1983.

Well built and fearless, Joe Bambrick (first name James incidentally) was an intelligent player, a powerful header of the ball and clever on the ground with a strong right-foot shot. He began scoring at a cracking rate with Linfield in 1925 and in season 1929-30 netted an amazing total of 94 goals, a tally bettered the very next year by Fred Roberts of Glentoran who hit 96. Bambrick was a great success in Ireland and in February 1930 grabbed a double hat-trick (six goals) for his country against Wales at Celtic Park, Belfast – an individual scoring record in a full international. After this game, Fred Keenor, the Welsh captain who had attempted to mark him but who had been given a torrid afternoon, presented Bambrick with the ball. Bambrick went on to gain 11 caps in all and on Christmas Eve 1934 he was secured by Chelsea. At Stamford Bridge he found the English game much more intense but still continued to prosper, hitting 37 goals in 66 games for the Pensioners for whom he contested the centre-forward berth with George Mills. He moved to Walsall in March 1938 and stayed at Fellows Park until the outbreak of World War Two when he returned to his native Ireland. After announcing his retirement in 1945, Bambrick went to live almost next door to the Windsor Park ground in Belfast, and whenever possible enjoyed a round of golf – his favourite other sport. He was aged 76 when he died.

FRED BARBER

Goalkeeper; 189 apps.

Born: Ferryhill, Co Durham, 26 August 1963

An eccentric goalkeeper who often donned a weird mask when he took the field before the start of a game, Fred Barber had a chequered professional career serving, in turn, Darlington (apprentice August, 1979, professional, August 1981), Everton (signed for £50,000, March 1986), Walsall (bought for a fee of £95,000 in October 1986), Peterborough United (on loan October/November 1989), Chester City (on loan October 1990 and April 1991), Blackpool (on loan December 1990), Peterborough United (August 1991), then

Ipswich Town (loan) and Birmingham City (loan) before retiring in May 1996. He made over 150 senior appearances for the Quakers, failed to get a game whilst at Goodison Park, but had 189 outings for the Saddlers and represented the Football League. He was ever-present in 1987-88, playing 61 games in all competitions, and in the penalty competition to decide the venue for the Third Division Play-off Final replay, he saved two spot-kicks. He helped Peterborough United win promotion from the Third Division via the Play-offs, this time at Wembley against Stockport County in 1992, and when he called it a day in 1996 he had amassed 474 senior appearances. He now runs a goalkeeping school in the Midlands.

JIM BARNES

Outside-left; 75 apps, 18 goals.

Born: Atherstone, Warwicks 1905. Deceased.

Jim Barnes (first name James) was an enterprising winger who had a fair amount of pace, good footwork and when he chose to let fly, a strong shot. He began his career with his local club, Atherstone Town, and after showing excellent form he was chosen to represent Birmingham in a Junior 'International' against Scotland in 1927. The following year he signed for Coventry City but in 1929 switched to Walsall, staying at Fellows Park until July 1931 when he was transferred to Watford. After appearing in 76 matches in two seasons for the Vicarage Road club he moved to Exeter City (July 1933) and then did well for York City (1934-35) before retiring in 1936. An ex-miner, Jim owned and raced a greyhound and he was a good golfer with a handicap of 12.

MICK BATES

Midfield; 104+1 apps, 6 goals.

Born: Doncaster, 19 September 1947.

Mick Bates went to Elland Road as a teenager, signing professional forms under Don Revie's management in September 1964. He

developed alongside Johnny Giles, Billy Bremner and Eddie Gray and made over 150 senior appearances for United before transferring to Walsall in June 1976. Bates had two fine seasons at Fellows Park before going back to Yorkshire to sign for Bradford City in June 1978. He made 65 appearances whilst at Valley Parade prior to joining Doncaster Rovers in June 1980. Bates retired in May 1981 with 267 League appearances to his name (nine goals). He was still playing in charity matches in the early 1990s.

LEWIS BEDFORD

Outside-right or left; 147 apps, 13 goals.

Born: Erdington, 26 March 1904. Died: Walsall, 12 May 1975.

A small winger, fast and tricky, Lewis Bedford made his League debut for West Bromwich Albion three days before his 17th birthday (v Arsenal in March 1921). A pupil at Icknield Street School (Hockley), Bedford joined Albion in November 1920 and turned professional in March 1921. He made only three League appearances for the Baggies before setting off on his travels, which took him all around the country including four spells at Fellows Park. His moves went as follows: Walsall (June 1922); Sheffield Wednesday (1925); Walsall again (1926), Nelson (1927); back to Walsall later that same year; to Luton Town (1928); Walsall for the fourth and final time (December 1929).

Two years later he chose to try his luck in non-League football with Bloxwich Strollers and rounded off his career with Walsall Wood, eventually retiring in June 1940 at the age of 36. Bedford accumulated well over 200 senior appearances as a professional.

KENNY BEECH

Midfielder; 88+1 apps, 5 goals

Born: Stoke, l8 March 1958

Kenny Beech was an honest midfield grafter who spent five and a half years as a professional with Port Vale (January 1976 to August 1981) before transferring to Walsall. After two seasons at Fellows Park he went to Peterborough United, retiring from the first-class game in May 1985, but then spent a

time with Stafford Rangers. Beech chalked up a total of 314 League appearances for his three clubs, 175 of them for the Vale, whom he joined as an apprentice from Edensor High School, Longton, Stoke-on-Trent, in June 1974. In 1992 Kenny was still living in Longton and worked at the Michelin Tyre factory near to the Stoke City ground.

JACK BENNETT

Full-back/left-half; 210 apps.

Born: Basford, Notts, February, 1911. Died: July, 1972

Jack Bennett was a strong right-back or wing-half. He played for Birmingham's reserve team from September 1928 but failed to win a place in the senior side and moved to Blackpool in May 1931, before signing for Walsall 12 months later. He did well at Fellows Park, being a regular in the League side for the first four of his six seasons with the Saddlers. Injury interrupted his career, however, and he was eventually replaced at right-back by Jack Shelton. In the summer of 1938 Bennett was transferred to Wellington Town and he rounded off his career playing with Long Eaton United.

STAN BENNETT

Defender; 430+8 apps, 13 goals.

Born: Birmingham, l8 September 1944

Stan Bennett gave Walsall tremendous service for 15 years during which time he chalked up more than 450 senior appearances as a centre-half. He joined the club as a lad in 1959 and remained at Fellows Park until his retirement from the first-class game

in 1974. He eventually took over from the former England international, Trevor Smith, in the heart of the Saddlers' defence, having made his League debut at Notts County in October 1963.

Bennett skippered the Aston Boys team and the Birmingham County Schools XI, and at that time wanted to play on the wing. But he chose to defend rather than attack and became one of the great stalwarts of the Walsall club. He is related to Martyn Bennett who played in a similiar defensive position for West Bromwich Albion (1979-90).

FRED BIDDLESTONE

Goalkeeper; 24 apps.

Born: Pensnett, Dudley, 26 November. 1906. Died: Great Barr, Birmingham, 7 April 1977.

Goalkeeper Fred Biddlestone was nicknamed the 'Councillor'. Standing almost 6ft tall and weighing 12st, he was sound and reliable rather than spectacular and classy, and leapt to stardom after a fine performance for Walsall against Aston Villa in an FA Cup tie in January 1930. He was signed by Villa for £1,750 the following month and went on to appear in 160 senior games for them up to August 1939 when he joined Mansfield Town, retiring in 1944. Initially he played as a centre-half for Bilston Boys' Club and Hickman Park Rangers and thereafter as a goalkeeper for Moxley Wesleyans, Wednesbury Town, Sunbeam Motors FC and Bloxwich Strollers before becoming a professional with the Saddlers in April 1929. He helped Villa win the Second Division championship in 1938 and after retiring he ran a successful boarding house in Blackpool, returning to Birmingham in the 1960s. He guested for Walsall during World War Two.

GEORGE BINKS

Centre-half; 110 apps. one goal

Born: West Bromwich, March 1899. Deceased.

A fearless left-half, George Binks was one of the stars of the Walsall side in the mid-1920s, making well over 100 senior appearances. He was a regular in the first team at Fellows Park in 1922-23 (his first season with the club) and again in 1925-26 and 1926-27. Although he struggled with injuries from time to time, he always battled back.

He started his career with St Andrew's FC, playing next as amateur with Birmingham (December 1919) before transferrring as a professional to Walsall in June 1922. After leaving Fellows Park in the summer of 1928 he played non-League football in the Midlands but was forced to give up the game through injury in 1930.

ALAN BIRCH

Midfielder; 176+15 apps, 24 goals.

Born: West Bromwich, 12 August 1956.

Brother of Paul Birch (of Aston Villa and Wolves fame) Alan Birch arrived at Fellows Park as a 16-year-old in 1972 after having three trial games with West Bromwich Albion. He came through his apprenticeship successfully and turned professional with the Saddlers in August 1973. An enthusiastic performer he quickly settled with Walsall and went on to appear in more than 170 League games (23 goals) before being transferred to Chesterfield for £40,000 in July 1979. Two years later he switched to Wolverhampton Wanderers in a £180,000 deal, but never really adapted himself to the

surroundings of Molineux and within six months he was on his way to Barnsley (February 1982). He then went back to Chesterfield (August 1983), joined Rotherham United (March 1984), had a spell with Scunthorpe United (June 1986 to October 1987) and served with Stockport County until May 1988. He finally pulled out of League action after 506 appearances (107 goals) having spent practically all of his career performing in the lower divisions. He helped Chesterfield win the Anglo-Scottish Cup (v Glasgow Rangers).

SID BIRD

Left-back; 97 apps, 2 goals.

Born: Leamington-on-Tyne, May 1904. Deceased.

A sturdily-built, strong kicking full-back, Sid

Bird perhaps lacked that extra ability to make him a quality defender, although he did well enough to help thwart the Arsenal attack in that epic Cup-tie of 1933. He played for Scotswood FC in the North-East before joining Fulham for £250 in June 1928 but made only 46 first-team appearances for the London club prior to his transfer to Walsall in August 1932. After leaving the Saddlers in the summer of 1935, he returned to the North-East, where he teamed up with Spennymoor United and also played for Brandwood.

ROGER BOLI

Striker; 57 apps, 24 goals.

Born: Adjame, Ivory Coast, 29 June 1965.

A quicksilver striker, signed from the French club Lens on a free transfer in August 1997, Boli, a former French Under-21 international, spent just one season with the Saddlers, but what an impact he had. He netted five goals in his first six games for the club (including a hat-trick in a 3-1 win over

Southend) and went on to register 24 in all competitions (12 in the League) despite having a rather quiet second half to the campaign. His ability to turn his marker in one movement brought him his due rewards and he had the pleasure of scoring a superb goal in Walsall's FA Cup defeat at Old Trafford. He finished second to Barry Hayles (Bristol Rovers) in the Division Two scoring charts and was selected in the PFA Second Division team by his fellow professionals. Boli, who was a big favourite with the fans, left Bescot Stadium for Dundee United in the summer of 1998, but quickly found his way back into the Football League with Bournemouth after failing to settle down north of the border. The Cherries paid £100,000 for his return to English soccer.

ALAN BOSWELL

Goalkeeper; 72 apps.

Born: Wednesbury, 8 August 1943.

Alan Boswell had an excellent career as a professional footballer, serving five clubs over 14 years (1960-74), totalling close on 500 senior appearances, 435 in the League alone. Educated in Walsall, he represented South-East Staffs Schools and joined Walsall

as an amateur in 1958, turning professional in August 1960. He made his League debut for the Saddlers against Norwich City in November 1961 and played in over 70 games for the club before transferring to Shrewsbury Town in August 1963. Boswell spent five years at Gay Meadow (222 League games) and in September 1968 he signed for Wolves, manager Ronnie Allen taking him to Molineux mainly as cover for Phil Parkes. He subsequently replaced the big fellow between the posts but had only ten outings, letting in six goals in one game against Liverpool. He left Molineux for Bolton Wanderers in October 1969, and in August 1972 joined Port Vale. He had two fine seasons in the Potteries (86 League outings) before drifting into non-League football in 1974. Once, while keeping for Port Vale, he lost the ball in the glare of the floodlights and conceded a goal against Walsall. And there was the time he was forced to get changed in a taxi on his way to the ground, arriving just ten minutes before kick-off.

TOMMY BOWEN

Inside-forward; 81 apps, 17 goals.

Born: West Bromwich, January 1900. Deceased.

An exciting inside-forward of the 1920s, Tom

Bowen was a big favourite with the Walsall fans. Forever involved in the action, he had pace and a strong right-foot shot, and always loved to have a crack at goal, from any angle and from all sorts of distances. He once scored from 55 yards playing in a reserve-team game. Only 5ft 6ins tall, Bowen played initially for Bush Rangers, a West Bromwich junior team. He then joined Birmingham as an amateur (1920), switching to Walsall in July 1921. He spent three seasons with the Saddlers before moving to Wolverhampton Wanderers in March 1924. Four years later (June 1928), after scoring 24 goals in 94 appearances for Wolves, he teamed up with Coventry City and in August 1930 left the Football League to play for Kidderminster Harriers. He gained representative honours whilst at Coventry, playing for a selected Birmingham team against an FA XI in September 1925.

TOMMY ('TODDY') BOWEN,

Outside-right; 97 apps, 7 goals.

Born: West Bromwich, 21 August 1924.

Known as Toddy, this dashing right winger came from a footballing stock, being the son of Teddy Bowen (ex-Walsall) and brother of Reg, once of Hereford United. He signed for his home-town club, West Bromwich Albion, in August 1945 but quickly moved away

from The Hawthorns to team up with Newport County in July 1946. He scored six goals in 37 League games for the Welsh club, but after four years there he was desperate to return to the Midlands and was duly transferred to Walsall on 30 June 1950. He went on to serve the Saddlers in almost 100 games until May 1953 when he pulled out of League football to work in a local factory.

BILL BRADFORD

Left-half; 351 apps, 22 goals.

Born: Peggs Green, Nr Coalville, Leicestershire, July 1900. Deceased.

Once a farmer in a Leicestershire village, Bill Bradford, the younger brother of Joe Bradford (of Birmingham and England fame) gave the Saddlers excellent service during the late 1920s when he occupied several positions, including those of inside-left, right-half and left-half as well as centre-half. He joined the Saddlers in May 1926 from Preston North End, having earlier played three League games for Brighton and Hove Albion in 1924-25. He was appointed player-coach at Fellows Park in 1934, retiring from football in 1938, when he went back to working on the farm.

COLIN BRAZIER

Defender/midfield; 144+1 apps, 4 goals.

Born: Solihull, 6 June 1957.

Colin Brazier's career took him from Alvechurch to Northfield Town to Wolverhampton Wanderers (apprentice June 1973, professional August 1975), to Jacksonville Tea Men (June 1981), Birmingham City (October 1982), AP Leamington (March 1983), Lincoln City (April 1983), Walsall (August 1983) and finally to Kidderminster Harriers (October 1986), before he retired in 1990.

A useful squad player at Wolves, being principally a central-defender or defensive midfielder, Brazier was never guaranteed a first-team place and after a spell in America he joined Blues mainly as defensive cover, although he was asked to play as an out-and-striker a few times at St Andrew's. After a disagreement with manager Ron Saunders he left Blues, played a few games for Lincoln City and then came to Walsall where he did well for three seasons before drifting into non-League football with Kidderminster Harriers. Brazier won a League Cup winners' medal with Wolves in 1980 (as a sub) and was capped by England at semi-professional level whilst with Kidderminster. He appeared in a total of 213 Football League games, including 115 for the Saddlers and 78 for Wolves.

JACK BRIDGETT

Forward/Defender; 116 apps, 18 goals.

Born: Walsall, 10 April 1929.

Educated at Wolverhampton Road School, Walsall, Jack Bridgett played on the left wing in Black Country junior football before joining West Bromwich Albion as a professional on 16 May 1947 following a spell as an amateur at The Hawthorns. He suffered two broken ankles playing Services' football for Western Command and worse was to follow when he fractured his left leg in two places shortly after being demobbed. After Bridgett came out of plaster to start his recovery programme, Harry Hibbs secured his signature for Walsall on a free transfer in May 1950 – this after Bridgett had failed to make Albion's first team. He had one or two outings for Walsall Reserves at both centre-half and centre-forward, and finally made his League bow for the Saddlers as leader of the attack at Norwich in September 1950, only to be injured before the end of the game. It was not until 1951-52 that he earned a regular place in the side but once in, he stayed, and was top-scorer in 1952-53 with 11 goals. He was switched to a defensive position for the next campaign and was in fine form until dislocating an elbow in mid-March 1954.

Bridgett went on to play in 108 League games for the Saddlers before being released in May 1955 when he joined Worcester City, being replaced in the number-five shirt by Albert McPherson. At Worcester he linked

up with Jimmy Dunn (ex-Wolves) and Frank Hodgetts (ex-WBA) but still the injury bug persisted, this time a fractured skull after which he reluctantly decided to give up football. In 1958, though, he came out of retirement to enjoy a successful season with Abergavenny in the Welsh football before another broken leg caused him to hang up his boots for good.

Through his employment Bridgett worked with youth clubs and one, in Little Bloxwich, won most of the local honours in their age group, including the Walsall FA's T. J. Botham Trophy four times between 1967 and 1971. He then took over as manager of Blakenhall, leaving them after a short while only to return later for a second spell during which time they won the Walsall FA Senior Cup four times, the Midland Combination title and reached the fifth round of the FA Vase competition. Bridgett, who became chairman of the ex-Walsall Players' Association, then worked as an Education Welfare Officer for the Walsall Metropolitan Borough.

ALLY BROWN

Striker; 46+1 apps, 15 goals.

Born: Musselburgh, Scotland, 12 April 1951.

Ally Brown was a hard-working, enthusiastic and tireless marksman who had a fine career in the game, serving Leicester City (July

1967), West Bromwich Albion (March 1972), Crystal Palace (March 1983), Walsall (August 1983) and Port Vale (July 1984) before retiring in 1986 to become a publican. He also appeared in the NASL for Portland Timbers from May to August 1981 and played in charity matches for WBA All Stars for many years. He was voted Midlands Footballer of the Year (with his colleague Tony Brown) in 1979 when he scored 24 goals for West Brom, whom he helped win promotion from Division Two in 1976 and reach the FA Cup semi-final two years later. Whilst at Filbert Street he won a Second Division championship medal with Leicester and finished up with a fine record of 140 goals in 496 League appearances for his five English clubs, including 72 in 279 outings for West Brom and 31 in 101 starts for Leicester City. In his one season at Fellows Park, 1983-84, Brown was leading League goalscorer with 13 goals from 37 games. He is now steward of the West Bromwich Albion Throstle Club near The Hawthorns.

ALAN BUCKLEY

Striker; 461+22 apps, 202 goals (174 in the Football League).

Born: Mansfield, Notts, 20 April 1951.

Alan Buckley holds the individual scoring record for the Saddlers – 202 goals in all

major competitions – and he is the club's most expensive signing, costing £175,000 when he rejoined Walsall from neighbours Birmingham City in June 1979. He started his career as an apprentice with Nottingham Forest in June 1967, turning pro in April 1968. He came to Walsall first time round in August 1973 and was transferred to Birmingham City in October 1978, but returned to Fellows Park in June of the following year, staying with the Saddlers as a player and/or manager and having four spells in the Fellows Park hot seat.

First he was caretaker during July and August 1978 following Dave Mackay's departure; then from July 1979 to July 1981; with Neil Martin from July 1981 to January 1982 and finally from May 1982 until June 1986. He then briefly assisted both Stourbridge and Tamworth, took charge of Kettering Town (from November 1986) and was appointed manager of Grimsby Town in June 1988. He did well at Blundell Park, leading the Mariners to promotion from the Fourth Division in 1990 and into the Second 12 months later. A short, stocky, blond-haired striker with an eye for goal, Buckley proved to be one of Walsall's finest-ever captures, scoring at a rate of almost a goal every two games during his association with the Saddlers, including 34 League goals in 1975-76 which included a four-timer against Rotherham United. His League career totalled 465 appearances and 183 goals for his three clubs. (*see also Walsall Managers*)

CHARLES BUNYAN

Goalkeeper; 47 apps.

Born: Walsall, April 1878. Died: Brussels, 3 August 1922.

Charles Bunyan must have been quite a strong character because he recovered to enjoy a good career after being the Hyde goalkeeper when they lost 26-0 to Preston in an FA Cup match in October 1887. He was a lively 'keeper, often fly-kicking the ball to safety rather than collecting it with his hands. He also liked to fist the ball away from corners and free-kicks, and when he cleared his lines, he did so forcefully, often getting more height than distance with kicks out of his hands.

He also played for Derby County (in two spells), Chesterfield Town and Sheffield United and gained Amateur international honours for England prior to joining Walsall from Ilkeston Town in November 1896, after Tom Hawkins had been injured and young reserve Dick Towe had conceded ten goals in three games. Bunyan held his position for the remainder of that campaign, and was first choice in 1897-98. Billy Tennent then arrived from Wolves and Bunyan left the club, playing later for New Brompton, Newcastle United and Ripley Athletic, then Willenhall and Bloxwich Strollers before becoming manager of the Tivoli Concert Hall, High Street, Walsall. He died while on a coaching assignment in Belgium at the age of 44. His brother, George, played one game for Walsall in 1896-97.

FRANK BURRILL

Inside-forward; 40 apps, 14 goals.

Born: Manor Park, London, 20 April 1894.
Died: Whitechapel, London, 7 July 1962.

Described as a 'cool, skilful dribbler', Frank Burrill gained recognition as a teenager playing for East London Schools. He was eventually taken on by West Ham United (1911) and in July 1914 joined Southend, transferring to Wolverhampton Wanderers in May 1920. In his three years at Molineux, he scored 17 goals in 69 appearances and won an FA Cup winners' medal in 1921. He was transferred to Charlton Athletic in July 1923, and after 13 League games for the Addicks he switched to Walsall in May 1924. He had one excellent season at Fellows Park, netting 14 goals in 39 Division Three South games before he drifted into non-League football in 1925.

TERRY CARLING

Goalkeeper; 115 apps.

Born Otley, Yorkshire, 26 February 1939.

Terry Carling played works football in Otley, Yorkshire, and for Dawsons FC before join-

ing Leeds United as a professional in November 1956. He spent six seasons as reserve 'keeper at Elland Road, making only six senior appearances before transferring to Lincoln City in July 1962. He had 84 League outings for the Imps prior to transferring to Walsall in a player-exchange deal (involving Malcolm White) on 16 June 1964. He went on to amass over 100 senior appearances for the Saddlers, up to December 1966, when he moved to Chester City. Carling retired from League soccer in 1971 with a total of 389 League appearances under his belt, 199 coming of them for Chester.

BRIAN CASWELL

Utility; 446+12 apps, 19 goals.

Born: Wednesbury, 14 February, 1956.

Brian Caswell had a marvellous 12-year professional career with the Saddlers, making exactly 400 League appearances before transferring to Doncaster Rovers in August 1985. He joined Walsall straight from Wood Green School in June 1971 and turned professional at Fellows Park in September 1973, having already made his senior debut as an apprentice against Chesterfield the previous April in the Third Division. Playing mainly in midfield or defence, he became hugely popular with the fans and was voted Player of the Season in 1976-77.

Early the following season he broke an ankle but quickly regained full fitness and starred in Walsall's FA Cup run which took them into the fifth round where they lost at Highbury. Caswell missed only one match in the 1979-80 promotion season and appeared against Liverpool in the 1983-84 League Cup semi-final. He was a fine club man and the fans were bitterly disappointed when he eventually left the Saddlers for Doncaster Rovers. After just three months at Belle Vue he tried his luck with Leeds United (ten games) before announcing his retirement in the summer of 1987 following a loan spell with Wolves in January of that year. He joined the coaching staff at Birmingham City in 1990 and was still participating in various charity matches in 1992, helping West Brom win the over-35s Cup Final at Wembley along with Ally Brown, Garry Pendrey and Joe Mayo.

MIKE CECERE

Midfield/striker; 118+23 apps, 35 goals.

Born: Chester, 4 January 1968.

Michele Cecere, **a** well-built player, six feet tall and deceptively quick, spent four seasons with Oldham Athletic before joining Huddersfield Town in November 1988 for £100,000. He had a loan spell with Stockport County (March 1990) before switching to Walsall six months later for a fee of £25,000. Cecere signed for the Latics as an apprentice

in June 1984, turning professional at Boundary Park on his 18th birthday in January 1986. He scored ten goals in 63 outings for Oldham; 13 in 71 for Huddersfield and made just one substitute appearance for Stockport He was transferred to Exeter City in January 1994 after scoring 32 goals in 122 League appearances for the Saddlers. From St James's Park he moved to Rochdale in July 1996 and quit League football in May 1997 after scoring 73 goals in 334 appearances.

PHIL CHAPMAN

Centre-forward; 68 apps, 38 goals.

Born: Chasetown, 27 November 1925.

Phil Chapman burst on to the soccer scene in terrific style when he scored 28 goals for Walsall in his first season of competitive League and Cup football. He was signed from Cannock Town in September 1948 to fill the gap left by Dave Massart, who had moved from Fellows Park the previous March. One or two other players had filled the number-nine slot in the last six weeks of that 1947-48 campaign, and in the opening eight games of 1948-49, but none had really stood out and Chapman was seen as the man to do the job. And do it he did – in some style.

His all-action approach was a godsend to the Saddlers and he was a great favourite with the fans. He scored in his first two games and later netted two hat-tricks in suc-

cessive matches against Crystal Palace and Exeter City. He also found the score in eight consecutive matches (six League, two FA Cup) between mid-November and 1 January, and rounded off the season with four goals in four outings. He was troubled by injury in 1949-50 but still managed ten goals from 23 games, and in 1950-51 he appeared in only 11 League games. Jack Winter then arrived on the scene and Chapman was out in the cold after two-and-a-half seasons of truly wonderful marksmanship. He left Fellows Park for Weymouth but later returned to the area to play for Walsall Police.

STEVE CHERRY

Goalkeeper; 94 apps.

Born: Nottingham, 5 August 1960.

An England Youth international, Steve Cherry began his League career with Derby County in 1979-80 having been at the Baseball Ground since 1976 when he signed as an apprentice, turning professional in March 1978. He finally established himself in the Rams' team in 1982-83 following a loan spell with Port Vale, and after 77 League games for Derby he was transferred to Walsall in August 1984, having two pretty useful seasons at Fellows Park prior to moving south to Plymouth Argyle in October 1986. Another loan spell (this time with Chesterfield in 1988) preceded his transfer to Notts County for £70,000 in February 1989 – and at Meadow Lane he helped the Magpies win promotion from the Third to the Second and then to the First Division in successive seasons (1989-90 and 1990-91). Cherry won Player of the Year awards with each of his first three clubs (Derby, Walsall, Plymouth) and his total number of senior appearances eventually exceeded 500. For Notts County he made 266 League appearances and he later played for Watford, Plymouth again (loan) and Rotherham United.

GARY CHILDS

Midfield; 150+14 apps, 23 goals.

Born: Kings Heath, Birmingham, 19 April 1964.

Gary Childs, an inventive midfielder, was a former England Youth international who broke through with West Bromwich Albion, making his League debut in February 1982.

Transferred to Walsall for £15,000 in December 1983 after a month on loan at Fellows Park, in July 1987 he was sold to Birmingham City for £21,500 and two years later switched to Grimsby Town whom he helped win promotion in two successive seasons, from the Fourth to the Second (1990 and 1991). When he was released by Grimsby at the end of the 1996-97 season he had taken his career tally to 502 senior appearances. After a trial with Lincoln City, Childs became player-manager of Wisbech Town and in 1998 joined Boston United.

GORDON CHILVERS

Goalkeeper; 130 apps.

Born: Norwich, 15 November 1933.

A former pupil of Wolverhampton Grammar School, Gordon Chilvers played for Fordhouses Boys' Club before signing as an amateur for Walsall on 25 August 1950, turning professional on 21 April 1952, ten days after having made his League debut against Newport County. He kept goal for the Saddlers up to May 1958 when he pulled out of competitive football, later playing for Weymouth and Glastonbury. Strong and mobile, he did a first-class good job between the posts during a period when things were going badly for the Saddlers.

JOHN CHRISTIE

Goalkeeper; 107 apps.

Born: Fraserburgh, 26 September 1929.

John Christie started off in competitive football with Ayr United in 1946, joining Southampton in January 1951. He played over 200 games for the Saints before transferring to Walsall in June 1959. A good line

'keeper with a safe pair of hands, he went on to appear in more than 100 senior games for the Saddlers, helping them win promotion from Divisions Four and Three in successive seasons (1959-60 and 1960-61). He returned to his native Scotland after retiring in 1964.

TREVOR CHRISTIE

Striker; 120+8 apps, 32 goals.

Born: Cresswell, Northumberland, 28 February 1959.

Trevor Christie started his Football League career in 1977 with Leicester City, then served, in turn, Notts County, Nottingham Forest, Derby County, Manchester City, Walsall and Mansfield Town up to 1991. His best spell came at Meadow Lane (June 1979 to July 1984) during which time he scored 72 goals in 217 competitive games and helped the Magpies into the top flight in 1981. He left for Forest in a £175,000 deal but that move was not a success and a fee of £100,000 took him to Derby, where he helped the Rams to promotion from Division Three in 1985-86, missing only one League game and scoring 15 goals that season. A move to Manchester City was far less successful and Walsall paid £30,000 for his signature in October 1986, after he had made only nine appearances for the Maine Road club. Christie helped the Saddlers to promotion via the Third Division Play-offs in 1988 before leaving Fellows Park for Mansfield in March 1989, later moving into non-League football with Kettering Town and later VS Rugby.

ALLAN CLARKE

Striker; 82 apps, 46 goals.

Born: Short Heath, Willenhall, 31 July 1946.

Allan Clarke was one of the finest marksmen in the Football League during the period from 1963 to 1980. In those 17 years he rattled in no fewer than 275 goals for Walsall, Fulham, Leicester City, Leeds United, Barnsley and England – and won practically every domestic honour in the game whilst at Elland Road: League Championship 1974; FA Cup winners 1972, runners-up 1970 and 1973; European Cup runners-up 1975; UEFA Cup winners 1971. He also played for Leicester City in the 1969 FA Cup Final.

Known affectionately as 'Sniffer' (because of his ability to sniff out goalscoring opportunities) Clarke came to Fellows Park as a teenager on leaving school in 1962 and turned professional on 12 August 1963. He went to Craven Cottage for a then club record fee of £37,500 in March 1966, switched to Leicester for £150,000 in June 1968 and was transferred to Leeds for £166,000 two months after appearing in the 1969 FA Cup Final, ending up with a losers' medal after Neil Young's goal won the trophy for Manchester City, although Clarke was voted Man of the Match by the journalists present at Wembley. Those last two transfers were both British records in terms of cash deals. He spent nine years at Elland Road, netting 151 goals in 364 games, before he rounded off his playing career at Barnsley whom he joined initially as a player in June 1978.

He took his League scoring record up to 223 goals before being appointed manager at Oakwell, but left the Tykes after two years, taking over as manager at his beloved Leeds (1980-82). He then had a good spell in charge of Scunthorpe United, leading the Irons to promotion from Division Four in 1983. He returned to Barnsley for a second spell as manager in July 1985, but lost his position there in 1989. Clarke won 19 full and six Under-23 caps for England and played in the 1970 World Cup finals in Mexico. On his Under-23 debut he scored four goals against Wales. His brothers Derek, Frank, Kelvin and Wayne, all played League football with Derek, Kelvin and Wayne each lining up for the Saddlers like Allan, who himself was voted Walsall's Player of the Year by the supporters in 1964-65, when he topscored with 23 League goals. He finished top scorer again in 1965-66 (with 23 once more) even though he was sold to Fulham in March. After retiring he ran a soccer school on Humberside.

WAYNE CLARKE

Striker; 47+1 apps, 24 goals.

Born: Willenhall, 28 February 1961.

Wayne Clarke followed his elder brother, Allan, to Walsall in July 1992, and quickly got into his stride by scoring in pre-season friendly matches and then whipping in eight

goals in his first ten senior games, including a League hat-trick against Bury when Walsall came back from the dead to win 4-3. At the age of 16, he went to Molineux and after two years as an apprentice was taken on as a pro by Wolves in March 1978. He gained England Youth caps as a teenager and went on to score 33 goals in 170 games for the Wanderers, up to August 1984, when a fee of £80,000 took him across the Midlands to Birmingham City. He did particularly well at St Andrew's and in less than three seasons there netted 43 goals in 105 outings, helping Blues win promotion from Division Two in 1985.

His next transfer took him to Everton, Howard Kendall paying £500,000 for his services in March 1987. He failed to make the same impression at Goodison Park, yet still managed 22 goals in 76 outings, gaining a First Division championship medal in 1987 as well as scoring Everton's winning goal in that year's FA Charity Shield game against Coventry City at Wembley.

He was sold to Leicester City for another £500,000 fee in July 1989, but stayed at Filbert Street barely six months before switching to Manchester City for yet another £500,000 fee in January 1989. However, injuries, loss of form and the fact that younger players were preferred in the front line, meant that he did not have the best of fortunes with the Lancashire club and in October 1990 he went on loan to Shrewsbury Town, scoring a hat-trick in one game against his old club Birmingham City. Two more loan spells followed: in March-April 1991 he was with Stoke City and in September-October 1991 he went back to Wolves (making one appearance). Then along came Kenny Hibbitt – who of course, was a player himself at Molineux when Wayne Clarke first went there in 1977 – and he persuaded his former colleague to become a Saddler. In 1992-93 he was Walsall's leading scorer with 22 League and Cup goals. Clarke left the Bescot Stadium in July 1993, returning to Shrewsbury Town where he stayed for two years before becoming manager of Telford United, a position he held until November 1996. More recently Clarke has worked as a window cleaner.

JOE CONNOR

Inside-forward; 53 apps, 14 goals.

Born: Lochee, Dundee, 14 July 1880. Died: Scotland, 2 August 1934.

Born in Scotland of Irish parents, Joe Connor was a graceful footballer who gained three full caps for Ireland. During a long career in the game he assisted eight different clubs, several being outside the Football League, appearing in well over 200 competitive matches. On leaving Lochee Welfare School, Connor joined Dundee Fereday in 1896, serving next with the Gordon Highlanders before signing for West Bromwich Albion in March 1898. He spent a little over a year with the Baggies, moving to Walsall in June 1899. Two years later he went to Bristol City, had a spell with Woolwich Arsenal (1902), Brentford (1902-03), Fulham (1903-04), New Brompton and Glentoran (1904-05), finally hanging up his boots in 1916. In later years he worked in business insurance.

DAVID COPELAND

Forward; 113 apps, 40 goals.

Born: Ayr, Scotland, 2 April 1875. Died: Erdington, Birmingham, 16 November 1931.

The moustachio'd David Copeland was an enterprising, hard-working footballer who, despite standing only 5ft 7ins tall, was both strong and aggressive with a powerful right-foot shot. He developed with his local club, Ayr Parkhouse, before joining Walsall during the last week of October 1893, making his League debut for the Saddlers in the Second Division match against Liverpool the following month. He quickly established himself in the team and was a regular until suffering a leg injury in a 6-0 defeat at Newton Heath in October 1897.

Copeland came back later in that season, but was never the same player and surprisingly he opted to leave League football and joined Bedminster in July 1898. Twelve months later he was secured by Tottenham Hotspur, then members of the Southern League, and he did well with the London club, helping them win the championship in 1899-1900 and then the FA Cup the following season.

He remained with Spurs until May 1905 (appearing in 226 games and scoring 76 goals) and then teamed up with Chelsea where he became skipper (September 1906) but was injured in only his sixth match and there his career with the London club ended. He netted nine goals in 26 outings for Chelsea who transferred him to Glossop North End in May 1907, staying there until June 1908. He died suddenly while chopping wood in the back garden of his Birmingham home.

NICKY CROSS

Striker; 135+4 apps, 52 goals.

Born: Birmingham, 7 February 1961.

An exceptionally nimble striker with a keen eye for goal, Nicky Cross scored 19 times in 119 appearances for West Bromwich Albion before transferring to Walsall for £48,000 in August 1985. He had signed for the Baggies as a youngster from Woodbank Albion in July 1977, turning professional at The Hawthorns in February 1979 (under Ron Atkinson's management). He was never able to hold down a first-team place with Albion (he made 40 substitute appearances during his stay at the club) but once he had set foot inside Fellows Park he quickly made a name for himself, and became a firm favourite with the supporters. He scored over 50 goals in two and a half seasons with the Saddlers before transferring to Leicester City for £80,000 in January 1988. After 18 months at Filbert Street (during which time he scored 16 goals in 65 senior outings) he moved to Port Vale for £125,000 in June 1989, and did well in the Potteries until injury struck him

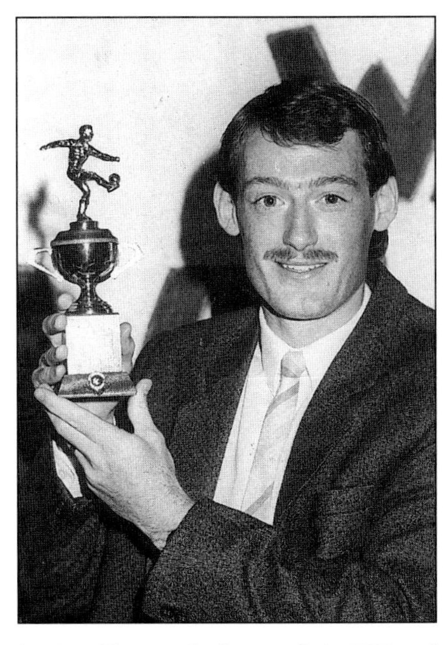

in 1991. He came back strongly in 1992 and was a key figure in Port Vale's side as they won promotion from Division Two in 1993-94. He moved to Hereford in the 1994 close season and two years later quit League football to sign for Solihull Borough. Cross scored 145 goals in 585 senior appearances (91 as a substitute).

RON CRUTCHLEY

Wing-half; 71 apps, 4 goals.

Born: Brownhills, Walsall, 20 June 1922. Died: August 1990.

A determined, wing-half, Ron Crutchley was part of a fine middle line which of Crutchley, Foulkes, Newman. He had a useful spell with the Saddlers, whom he joined towards the end of World War Two, making 42 appearances for the club during the 1944-45 and 1945-46 seasons. He added 62 League appearances to his tally before transferring to

Shrewsbury Town in September 1950 after a series of knee injuries which threatened his career at one stage. Fortunately he had better luck at Shrewsbury and stayed at Gay Meadow until May 1954, accumulating a further 146 League appearances.

In the mid-1950s Crutchley assisted Wellington Town (now Telford United) but although he was an effective and very popular player with the Shropshire club, he expressed the wish that he had stayed to finish his career with Walsall. After retiring from the game he worked with his brother in a toy and fancy goods wholesale business in Littleton Street, Walsall, and attended as many matches as he could at Fellows Park. Like so many other ex-Saddlers during the early part of the war, he played his football with Gil Bromley's Hillary Street Old Boys and he was signed for Walsall by manager Harry Hibbs, initially on a temporary basis as an amateur before becoming full-time in August 1945.

JOEY CUNNINGHAM

Goalkeeper; 53 apps.

Born: Glasgow, Scotland 1904. Deceased.

A tall, agile 'keeper – 6ft 1in tall and weighing 12st 4lbs – Joey Cunningham had two

seasons with Aberdeen before joining Newport County in 1925. Twelve months later he left Somerton Park for QPR and signed for Walsall in 1932. He later played for York City, Dartford and Folkestone, and whilst with Dartford helped them to an FA Cup win over Cardiff City in 1936. The brother of Andrew Cunningham, the former Glasgow Rangers forward and ex-Newcastle United manager, he was also one of Walsall's 11 gallant heroes in their famous 2-0 Cup win over Arsenal in 1933.

ALF DEAN

Outside-right; 75 apps, 36 goals.

Born: West Bromwich, 2 January 1877. Died: June 1959.

A nippy right winger, 5ft 5ins tall Alf Dean had great dribbling skills and could torment opposing defenders. Educated at West Bromwich Baptist School, he first joined Walsall in 1894 but failed to make an impression and left for West Bromwich Albion in May 1896. He scored three goals in only eight games for the Baggies (including one on his debut against Nottingham Forest – his future club) before returning to Walsall in September 1898. After giving the Saddlers exceptionally fine service for two and a half years he switched to Nottingham Forest for a fee of £120 in February 1901. In May that year he was transferred to Grimsby Town; he went to Bristol City in April 1902 (84 League games 37 goals); teamed up with Swindon Town in July 1905; Millwall signed him in May 1906; he played in Scotland with Dundee from May 1907 to May 1908 when he went back to Millwall; and in July 1909 he found his way to Wellington Town where he finished his nomadic career in 1916. He later ran a pub in Walsall. It was said that on his day Alf Dean was 'one of the most dangerous forwards in the country.'

DON DEARSON

Wing-half; 52 apps, 13 goals.

Born: Ynysybwl, Wales, 13 May 1914. Died: Sheldon, Birmingham, 24 December 1990.

Don Dearson played competitive football for 20 years (1932-1952) and during that time he appeared in around 500 matches for clubs and country. Dearson began his career with Llanwit Major Juniors, moving to Barry Town in August 1932. In April 1934 he became a professional with Birmingham and stayed at St Andrew's until February 1947 when he joined Coventry City. For Blues he made more than 300 first-team appearances (136 in League and Cup and 166 during wartime). He helped them win the Football League South championship in 1946 and also gained three full caps for Wales as well as playing in 15 Wartime/Victory internationals. He had earlier won four Amateur caps for his country. He switched from Highfield Road to Fellows Park in March 1950 and after 52 senior games for Walsall, signed for Nuneaton Borough and then Bilston United before hanging up his boots in May 1952. He had guested for Northampton Town and West Brom during the war.

Initially a clever, scheming inside-forward with powerful shot, Dearson was moved into the half-back line by Blues and also filled in at full-back. He was in a restricted occupation during the war, hence he was able to play regularly for Blues. At one time he spent nine weeks in the Birmingham City Police Force, and later worked in the BSA factory, later becoming an employee of British Leyland, Coventry, while also running his own grocery business.

MIAH DENNEHEY

Forward; 145+6 apps, 22 goals.

Born: Cork, Ireland, 29 March 1950.

Jeremiah Dennehey was a skilful winger or inside-forward who played for Cork Hibs prior to joining Nottingham Forest as a professional in January 1973. Dennehey never established himself at the City Ground, and after 41 League games (four goals scored) he left for Walsall in July 1975, staying at Fellows Park until July 1978, when he signed for Bristol Rovers. He scored 22 goals in 128 League games for Saddlers, and six in 52 for

the Pirates. He was capped ten times by the Republic of Ireland and on his day could be quite brilliant, his movement down the touchline being graceful as well as penetrating.

WILL DEVEY

Forward/half-back; 40 apps, 13 goals.

Born: Perry Barr, Birmingham, 12 April 1865. Died: Birmingham, 10 June 1935.

A player who relied on skill rather than strength, Will Devey was not a big man but he possessed a powerful shot and enjoyed a battle. He played initially for Clavendon Montrose, joining Wellington in 1883 and

Aston Villa in 1884. In August 1885 he moved to Birmingham (then Small Heath) and six years later teamed up with Wolverhampton Wanderers before rejoining Aston Villa in December 1892. Walsall Town Swifts took him on in May 1894, and he had a decent spell with Burton Wanderers (1895-97) and also assisted Notts County prior to rejoining Walsall in December 1897. Another stint with Burton Wanderers came next (late 1897); he served Walsall yet again, and then Darlaston before rounding off an interesting career with Birmingham (July 1898 to May 1900).

JOHNNY DEVLIN

Inside-forward; 166 apps, 49 goals.

Born: Airdrie, 11 December, 1917.

Johnny Devlin proved to be one of Walsall's finest-ever signings. A former Glasgow schoolboy player, he emerged with Hibernian and cost the Saddlers a big fee – £7,000 – when he was signed from Kilmarnock in mid-December 1947. But he was worth every penny as he performed in either an inside-forward berth or as a wing-half. Adept at both constructing and finishing off attacks, he scored five goals against Torquay United in September 1949 and went on to strike home almost 50 goals for the Saddlers in more than 160 senior appearances before retiring from the League scene in the summer of 1952.

A charismatic footballer, skilful and versatile, he loved to get inside the penalty area and would try his luck with a shot as soon as he could, from practically anywhere within range of the woodwork. A great club man and fine competitor, Johnny Devlin later played for Bloxwich Strollers and in 1992 was still living in Walsall, following the Saddlers with interest, albeit through the local press, TV and radio.

DON DORMAN

Inside-forward; 124 apps, 34 goals.

Born: Hall Green, Birmingham, 18 September 1922. Died: 1998.

A paratrooper, wounded and captured at Arnhem, Don Dorman's courage and never-say-die attitude was always evident in his play. He turned out for Shirley Juniors before joining Birmingham City in 1945, turning professional in May 1946. He scored seven goals in 65 games for Blues before transferring to Coventry City in September 1951, switching to Walsall in October 1954. In his last season with the Saddlers he skippered the side before retiring in May 1957, soon after representing the Third Division South against the Third Division North in the annual challenge match at Stockport, and duly returned to St Andrew's as scout, rising to chief scout on the death of Walter Taylor. He left Blues for a second time in 1983 and later took over as chief scout of Aston Villa, before retiring in 1985. He was the epitome of the old-fashioned inside-forward, a ball player who could score goals as well as make them.

ANDY DORNAN

Full-back; 147+2 apps, 1 goal.

Born: Aberdeen, 19 August 1961.

Although on the small side Andy Dornan was a fierce competitor. He started his career as a youngster with Aberdeen, playing for the Dons in the European Cup. He moved to Motherwell for £20,000 and appeared in more than 100 games for the Scottish club before switching to Walsall for £17,000 in August 1986, being followed down from Scotland a month or so later by his former Fir Park colleague, Graeme Forbes. Dornan quickly established himself in the Saddlers' side and was the regular right-back for three campaigns before being replaced by Chris Hutchings in 1990. His only goal for the Saddlers came against Rotherham United in May 1990. He also scored another at Fellows Park, a dramatic own-goal for Watford, which duly knocked the Saddlers out of the FA Cup in 1987. On leaving Walsall in May 1990, Dornan moved back to Scotland where he became player-manager of Montrose. He later had spells with Ayr United and Forfar Athletic.

JIMMY DUDLEY

Wing-half- 176 apps, 3 goals.

Born: Gartosh, Lanarkshire, 24 August 1928.

Although born in Scotland, Jimmy Dudley moved to the Black Country at the age of eight. After attending Hill Top School, he had a good spell with Walsall Conduits FC and joined West Bromwich Albion from Albright Youth Club in August 1944, becoming a professional 12 months later on his 17th birthday. He made his League debut for the Baggies three and half years later (against Manchester City) and went on to amass a total of 320 senior appearances for The Hawthorns club (11 goals scored), winning both an FA Cup winners' medal and a Scotland 'B' cap in 1954. He was transferred to Walsall in mid-December 1959, for £4,000, and spent five years at Fellows Park, helping the Saddlers win promotion from the Fourth to the Second Division in successive seasons (1959-60 and 1960-61). Dudley left the club in 1964 (for Stourbridge) after accumulating 176 League and Cup appearances. On retiring in 1965 he went to work at Guest Motors, Carters Green, West Bromwich, staying there until 1993. Originally an inside-forward, he developed into a fine wing-half. His brother, George, also played for West Brom and Walsall.

STEVE ELLIOTT

Striker; 81+1 apps, 24 goals.

Born: Haltwhistle, 15 September 1958.

Steve Elliott was a footballing wanderer who served with seven different League clubs up to 1992. He began his career as an apprentice with Nottingham Forest, signing profession-

al forms for Brian Clough in September 1976. He never established himself at Forest, making only six senior appearances, and in March 1979 was transferred to Preston North End for whom he went on to score 70 goals in 208 League matches, up to July 1984, when he moved to Luton Town. Elliott failed to hit his top form at Kenilworth Road and in December 1984 he was snapped up by Walsall, in a deal involving David Preece. There followed a good spell at Fellows Park which ended in July 1986 when he went off to Bolton Wanderers, later serving with Bury (1988-89) and Rochdale (1989-91). Elliott drew up an impressive League record of more than 130 goals in 400 plus appearances for his seven clubs (21 in 69 for the Saddlers). He joined Guiseley in 1991-92.

ALUN EVANS

Forward; 91+10 apps, 8 goals.

Born: Bewdley, 30 April 1949.

Alun Evans became Britain's first £100,000 teenage footballer when he left Wolves for Liverpool in September 1968. Capped by England at Schoolboy, Youth and Under-23 levels, he was said to be a star of the future when he moved to Anfield. But things never really worked out for Evans, the son of a former Welsh wartime international with West Brom. He spent just under four years with Liverpool, playing for them in the 1971 FA Cup Final (against Arsenal). In June 1972 he left Merseyside for Aston Villa in a £72,000 deal and scored 17 goals in 72 appearances for the Villains before Walsall secured his services in December 1975, nine months after he had gained a League Cup prize (as sub) against Norwich City at Wembley. Evans netted the FA Cup match-winning goal for the Saddlers against Leicester City in January 1977, perhaps his most crucial strike for the club. In July 1978 he left Walsall and went to try his luck in Australia, assisting both South Melbourne (briefly) and then Hellas, retiring in August 1981. Evans' progress at Anfield was marred by a much-publicised night club incident which left him facially scarred – and also by a cartilage operation which eventually led to him hanging up his boots at the age of 32.

HUGH EVANS

Inside-forward; 37 apps, 12 goals.

Born: Ynysbwl, South Wales, 12 December 1919.

Although born and bred in Wales, Hugh Evans was brought up in Luton and had trials with Bedford Town during his last year at St Stephen's School. In 1935 he signed for Redditch United before going off to serve his country in World War Two. In mid-December 1947, shortly after being demobbed, he was snapped up by Birmingham City – just minutes before a scout from Wolverhampton Wanderers turned up. Evans made only 14 senior appearances for the Blues before being transferred to Bournemouth in June 1950. In August 1951 he was taken on at Fellows Park and scored 12 goals in 33 League games for Walsall before leaving the Saddlers for Watford in August 1952. He rounded off his career in non-League circles with Hitchin Town.

MICK EVANS

Defender; 260+3 apps, 8 goals.

Born: West Bromwich, 3 August 1946.

A six-footer who could occupy all five defensive positions, but was perhaps best suited at full-back, Mick Evans represented the Birmingham County FA whilst at West

Bromwich Grammar School, and played for Vono Sports before joining Walsall as an amateur in October 1963, turning professional in May 1964. Well built and physically strong, he possessed a good, strong kick and tackled hard but fair. He made a total of 263 senior appearances for the Saddlers before transferring to Swansea City in December 1972, later serving Crewe Alexandra, from July 1975 to May 1977, when he left League football. He continued to star in local non-League circles, assisting Rushall Olympic, Stafford Rangers and Halesowen amongst others, as well as playing Sunday football for a number of years, starring also in numerous charity matches for the Aston Villa, Walsall and WBA All Stars teams; he won a Cup Final medal with the Albion over 35s at Wembley in 1992. He worked as the Midlands area scout for Crystal Palace, now lives in Kidderminster and works in Tipton.

WAYNE EVANS

Defender; 213+15 apps, 2 goals.

Born: Abermule, mid-Wales, 25 August 1971.

A very consistent and capable full-back who can also play in the centre of the defence, Evans was playing regularly for Welshpool before Walsall recruited him to the Bescot Stadium in August 1993 on a free transfer. A strong tackler, with good positional sense, he settled into the team exceptionally well and was a permanent fixture for five years during which time he massed over 200 first team appearances. When Ray Graydon took over as manager, Evans found it more difficult to get into the side and in 1998-99 he made only a dozen or so first team appearances – but he did help, albeit in a small way to bringing First Division football back to the club.

BILL EVANS

Utility forward; 132 apps, 64 goals.

Born: Cannock, Staffs, 1914. Deceased.

Spotted by Walsall playing as an amateur centre-forward for Cannock Chase Colliery in August 1934, Bill Evans was a strong, forceful player, standing 5ft 11ins tall and weighing over 11st. His progress was rapid and in his five years at Fellows Park he became a big favourite with the fans, scoring on average a goal every two games to finish with an exceptionally fine record in the League of 54 strikes in 115 outings. In his second season (1935-36) he hit 25 goals in competitive action, and following Alsop's transfer to West Brom, he took over the mantle as leading marksman. He left the Saddlers for Tranmere Rovers in June 1939, but the war disrupted his career and he never played top-class soccer after 1945.

JOHN EYRES

Inside-forward; 89 apps, 37 goals.

Born: Northwich, 20 March 1899. Died: Gainsborough, 2 October 1975.

John Eyres played for five major clubs in his career – Stoke, Walsall, Brighton & Hove Albion, Bristol Rovers and York City. He was not a tall man (5ft 9ins and 11st) but he loved a battle in centre-field and always gave a good account of himself. He emerged with Nantwich Town and then progressed with Witton Albion before joining Stoke for £250 in June 1922. He scored 23 goals in 65 games for Stoke before switching to Walsall in May 1929 for a modest fee which, in fact, was handed over to the player for his service with Stoke. He left the Saddlers in 1931, after finishing the season joint top-scorer with 18 League and Cup goals, and after a brief association with Brighton, he joined Bristol Rovers in July 1932, later playing for York City and Gainsborough Trinity.

ROY FAULKNER

Inside-forward; 105 apps, 45 goals.

Born: Manchester, 28 June 1935.

Roy Faulkner remained a part-time professional throughout his career which began at Manchester City in December 1952, having earlier been a junior at Maine Road. Faulkner scored four goals in seven League games for City before transferring to Walsall in March 1958. He did well at Fellows Park, where he teamed up splendidly with Tony Richards, going on to score 45 goals in 105 competitive games. He netted on his debut, a 3-2 victory at Swindon Town, and scored 22 goals in the Fourth Division championship season of 1959-60. After retiring he became a representative for a Midlands firm.

JACK FLAVELL

Full-back; 27 apps.

Born: Wall Heath, 15 May 1929.

Jack Flavell was one of the band of double-sportsman, a footballer/cricketer. He played as a hard-tackling full-back on the soccer pitch and powered in as a right-arm fast bowler on the cricket field. Flavell was spotted by West Brom playing for Lye Town, and joined The Hawthorns semi-professional staff in May 1947. With so many excellent full-backs with Albion at the time he never made their League side and in September 1953 was transferred to Walsall, where he stayed for just a season before pulling out of top-class football to concentrate on his cricket with Worcestershire. He was a versatile footballer who led the Walsall attack in an FA Cup-tie against Lincoln City in January 1953 when he twice almost scored, hitting the woodwork once and then having a header superbly saved by the Imps goalkeeper.

Jack Flavell was a member of the New Road staff from 1949 to 1967, during which time he appeared in 392 matches for Worcestershire and went on two tours with the county – a world tour in 1964-65 and to Jamaica in 1965-66. He also played in four Test matches for England (1961-64).As a bowler he took 1,529 wickets at 21.48 each with his best return coming at Dover in 1955 when he took 9-30 against Kent. He took 100 wickets in a season eight times (171 for an average of 17.79 in 1961 being his best return) and he also claimed 128 catches. At Old Trafford in 1963 he achieved an unusual hat-trick, all his victims being lbw. As a left-hand tailend batsman, he scored 2,032 runs in 453 innings (141 n.o.'s) for an average of 6.51, with his best score being 54.

GRAEME FORBES

Defender; 214 apps, 14 goals.

Born: Forfar, Scotland, 29 July 1958.

A strong, commanding centre-back, 6ft tall and 13st, Graeme Forbes was recruited by Walsall for a fee of £80,000 in September 1986, moving south soon after full-back Andy Dornan joined Walsall from the same Scottish club, Motherwell. Forbes began with Lochee United in 1976 and turned professional at Fir Park in 1980, appearing in 185

League games for the Well before going on to amass a total of 214 senior outings for the Saddlers up to May 1990. Forbes, who skippered the side in 1988-89, moved back north of the border in 1991. In Walsall's 1987-88 promotion season from Division Three he played in 58 competitive games and missed only a handful of League matches.

NORMAN FORSYTH

Utility player; 126 apps, 17 goals.

Born: Walsall, November 1869. Deceased.

Norman Forsyth occupied eight different positions during his stay with Walsall. He came to the club from Darlaston in July 1891 as an inside-left, and played in that position during his first season. But then he switched to left-half and appeared in that position in Walsall's first Football League game, against Darwen on 3 September 1892. He was then pushed into the forward-line and before the

1892-93 campaign closed he had lined up at left-half, inside-left, outside-left, inside-right and centre-forward. He started the 1893-94 season at right-half, but soon settled down in the left-half berth and there he stayed, with the odd exception, until leaving the club for Willenhall in December 1895, having scored nine goals in 78 League appearances for Walsall.

TREVOR FOSTER

Utility forward; 63 apps, 12 goals.

Born: Walsall, 11 January 1941

Trevor Foster became a Walsall player in June 1956, when he signed as an amateur after being spotted scoring goals in Pleck Park. He turned professional in July 1959 and stayed at Fellows Park until May 1965 – his last senior appearance was in December 1964 – when he moved into non-League football. He scored 12 goals in his 62 League outings for the Saddlers and generally did well although he was plagued many times by injury. He filled every forward position for Walsall but preferred the number-seven shirt. At one point during his career with Walsall, manager Bill Moore tried to groom Foster for the centre-forward berth by building up his physique with a diet of steaks, egg and sherry. It didn't work.

REG FOULKES

Centre-half; 175 apps, 6 goals.

Born: Shrewsbury, 23 February 1923.

Reg Foulkes won England Schoolboy honours in 1937, at the age of 14, and also had trials with both Manchester United and Birmingham before joining the groundstaff at Fellows Park in 1938, turning professional with the Saddlers during the war. A fine centre-half, cool and calculated, Foulkes was also a fine skipper. After guesting for

Birmingham and Walsall during the war, he made his senior debut for the Saddlers against Norwich City on 3 November 1945 and went on to record 175 League and Cup appearances for the club (some as an emergency centre-forward when he scored a few goals) before being transferred to Norwich City on 17 May 1950. He went on to serve the Canaries for a further six seasons, making 238 appearances (eight goals) in the heart of their defence. In May 1956 he joined Wisbech Town as player-manager, moving to King's Lynn in May 1957 before winding down his career as a permit player with Ceyms FC. He was living in his native Shrewsbury in 1992.

ROGER FRY

Full-back; 136 apps, 2 goals.

Born: Southampton, 18 August 1948.

A steady defender, Roger Fry spent eight years with Southampton before joining Walsall in July 1973. He first went to The Dell as an apprentice in 1965, turning profession-

al in October 1967. Fry played in 23 League games for the Saints and followed up with 136 senior appearances for the Saddlers, before leaving Fellows Park in May 1977 to team up with Salisbury Town with whom he served for three years. For Walsall, Fry alternated between right and left-back.

MARK GOODWIN

Midfield; 101+13 apps, 3 goals.

Born: Sheffield, 23 February 1960.

Mark Goodwin was a purposeful blond midfielder, who had 91 League outings for

Leicester City (1977-81) and 237 for Notts County (from March 1981) before joining Walsall in July 1987. He spent three seasons at Fellows Park, making a further senior 124 appearances for the Saddlers before drifting into non-League football. He featured in over 40 games as Walsall were promoted to Division Two via the Play-offs in 1987-88 but then experienced successive relegations with the Saddlers. He had joined Leicester as a 16-year-old in July 1976 and went on to play 99 games for the Foxes scoring eight goals. He later helped Notts County win promotion in 1981, alongside Trevor Christie.

RON GREEN

Goalkeeper; 265 apps.

Born: Birmingham, 3 October 1956.

Ron Green's League career spanned 14 years (1977-91). He began with Alvechurch, joined Walsall as a professional in July 1977 and won a regular place in the side at Fellows Park in season 1979-80, appearing in 163 League games for the Saddlers before signing for Shrewsbury Town in June 1984 after a brief spell on loan to West Bromwich Albion. He failed to hold down a first-team place at Gay Meadow and went on loan to Bristol Rovers, signing for the Pirates on a permanent basis in February 1985. He spent two seasons with Scunthorpe United (August 1986 to May 1988), followed this with four League games for Wimbledon (whom he joined for £20,000), 17 outings on loan with his former club Shrewsbury, and a short spell with Manchester City before he returned to Walsall for £20,000 on the transfer deadline in March 1989. Green went on to push his overall appearance tally up in League and Cup to past the 450 mark, before drifting out of the League to sign for Kidderminster Harriers in August 1991. In November 1992 he was drafted back into League action when

he signed for his former colleague, Roy McDonough's Colchester United (four appearances) on loan from Aggborough. He made 220 League appearances for the Saddlers, whom he helped gain promotion from Division Four in 1980.

After leaving Kidderminster in 1993, Green went on to serve Bromsgrove Rovers, Shrewsbury Town (non-contract), Happy Valley FC (Hong Kong), Bromsgrove (again), Hereford United (non-contract), Redditch United, Bromsgrove (for a third time), Moor Green and Oldbury United. In 1999 he was Coventry City's community liaison officer.

BILLY GREEN

Wing-half; 188 apps, 8 goals.

Born: Hull, 9 October 1927.

Billy Green was a Wolves discovery who was transferred to Fellows Park for a modest fee on 11 October 1949, making his League debut four days later at left-half. That was his accepted position although from time to time he showed his versatility by lining up at outside-left and full-back, and even played one game in goal, against Southend United on Boxing Day 1951. He left Walsall for Wrexham in June 1954 after appearing in 188 senior games for the Saddlers, and then added another 60 League games to his tally with the Welsh club before leaving League football in the summer of 1956, moving into non-League circles in the North-East. His days at Fellows Park were gloomy ones for the Saddlers who finished bottom of Division Three South each time, Green missing only one game in those three dreadful campaigns.

FRANK GREGG

Full-back; 439+5 apps, 3 goals.

Born: Stourbridge, 9 October 1942.

Frank Gregg spent his entire playing career with Walsall, accumulating a total of 393 Football League appearances between 1960 and 1973, which sees him in fifth place in the all-time list of appearance makers for the Saddlers. A pupil at Audnam School, Stourbridge, he represented Brierley Hill Schools and Birmingham County Boys before joining the Fellows Park groundstaff, turning professional in October 1959.

Defensively strong, with great anticipation and solid tackle, Gregg made his Third

Division debut at right back at Reading in October 1960 in what was to be a promotion-winning season for the Saddlers. He lined up at right-back that day but with the likes of Grenville Palm, John Sharples and Bill Guttridge competing for places on the defensive flanks, his chances were limited until he finally claimed a regular first-team place midway through 1962-63, the club's second season in Division Two. He played in every game in 1964-65, and was voted Player of the Year in 1966-67 and then in a remarkable 1967-68 campaign he participated in 46 Third Division games, in six FA Cup-ties and two League Cup matches.

Gregg, who perhaps preferred the left-back position, was still going strong in 1971-72 when Micky Evans came to join him at full-back, and together with Stan Jones and Stan Bennett, formed a terrific defensive foursome. He was a fine club man and had a marvellous temperament. His last game for Walsall was against Halifax Town in May 1972 He was not quite 30 but chose to leave Fellows Park, signing for non-League Burton Albion, before retiring in 1975.

ALF GRIFFIN

Outside-left; 88 apps, 34 goals.

Born: Walsall, 3 June 1871. Died: c.1945.

Alf Griffin had two spells with Walsall, his second being by far the best. He began with Brierley Hill Alliance in 1887 and joined Walsall the following year. From July 1892 until 1896 he was a star performer with Wolves, scoring 14 goals in 76 appearances for the Molineux club and collecting an FA Cup winners' medal in 1893. A big favourite with the Wolves' fans, on his return to Walsall he was quickly taken to by the Saddlers supporters as well, and he treated them to some terrific wing play. He was forced to quit football with a bad ankle injury in 1901 after netting over 30 goals in a total of 88 League and Cup appearances for the Saddlers.

ALBERT GROVES

Defender; 124 apps, 24 goals.

Born: Newport, Wales, January 1886. Died: c.1960.

Albert Groves was one of the smallest defenders in the game during the 1920s but he was certainly a star performer for the Saddlers. He started his career with the Welsh club Aberdare Athletic, and in season 1908-09 scored 22 goals for them from inside-forward. This sort of form enticed the Wolves to bring him to the Midlands, and during a lengthy spell at Molineux he scored 20 goals in 221 matches, ten strikes coming in 1912-13 when he played as an emergency inside-right. After serving in the Army and guesting for Bury during World War One, Groves joined the Sunbeam Works team, going back to Molineux in the summer of 1919.

He spent one more season with Wolves and left for Walsall in May 1920, joining the Saddlers as player-manager under club secretary Joe Burchill. He held that position for a season before Burchill took over the running of the team, allowing Groves to concentrate on playing. He went on to serve the Saddlers right up to February 1924 when he suffered a serious knee injury at Southport in a Third Division North game. He was forced him to retire three months later at the age of 38, making him at that time the oldest player to turn out for the club in a League game.

Albert Groves went into the licensing trade, keeping the Hope and Anchor in Bloxwich Road, Willenhall. (*see also Walsall Managers*)

TEDDY GROVES

Utility; 256 apps, 27 goals.

Born: Walsall, July 1900. Deceased.

Another 1920s star – no relation to Albert – Teddy Groves was secured from the Talbot Stead Works team in March 1922 and he made his League debut the following month in a game at Crewe, lining up at right-back.

The following season he started off in the Reserves, came into the first team for one game (at right-half) but was then successfully converted into a centre-forward. He scored 13 goals in 22 games from that position in 1922-23 as the Saddlers finished third in the Division Three North table. Groves, who stood 5ft 10ins tall and weighed 11st 2lbs, continued to prosper and top-scored in 1923-24 before being switched to a defensive role the following term. When Wally Webster left the club for Scunthorpe & Lindsey United in 1925, Teddy Groves was moved to right-back and for two and a half years he did an excellent job there before reverting to to a more central defensive position. In July 1930. After nine years with the Saddlers, he left for Shrewsbury Town and before announcing his retirement in 1933, mainly through injury problems, he had a brief spell with Wellington Town.

BILLY ('CHOPPER') GUTTRIDGE

Full-back; 210 apps.

Born: Darlaston, 4 March 1931.

Known simply as 'Chopper' this tough-tackling full-back gave Walsall great service for almost eight years following his transfer from Wolverhampton Wanderers in November 1954. Guttridge played for Metro-Shaft FC in the Wolverhampton Works League before joining the Molineux club as a professional in March 1948, making his League debut in the local derby against Aston Villa on Christmas Day 1951. Guttridge could never establish himself in the Wolves team and had no second thoughts above switching to Fellows Park. Injury forced him into an early retirement in 1962 after he had appeared in well over 200 games for the Saddlers and enjoyed successive promotions in 1959-60 and 1960-61. He later coached the younger players at the club.

HARRY HADDINGTON

Full-back; 235 apps.

Born: Scarborough, 7 August 1931.

A strong right-back with good positional sense , Harry Haddington made his League debut for Bradford Park Avenue in 1952 after coming through the ranks with the Yorkshire club. He followed his manager Vic Buckingham down to West Brom, teaming up with the Baggies for a modest fee in July 1953 (with his team-mate Derek Kevan). But

unlike Kevan, Haddington failed to make the breakthrough at The Hawthorns, owing to the likes of Stan Rickaby and one or two other defenders, and in July 1955 he was transferred to Walsall. He settled in well at Fellows Park and went from strength to strength, making in all 235 senior appearances before he had the misfortune to suffer a broken leg early in 1960-61, against Chesterfield. Haddington never fully recovered from that mishap and in August 1961 he joined Worcester City and played at a lower level for two years before he finally hung up his boots in 1963. He skippered the Saddlers in their Fourth Division championship-winning season of 1959-60 when he was an ever-present, as he also was in 1957-58.

JOHNNY HANCOCKS

Outside-right or left; 39 apps, 10 goals.

Born: Oakengates, Salop, 30 April 1919. Died: 19 February 1994.

During the first ten years after World War Two, Johnny Hancocks was one of the game's finest goalscoring wingers. Indeed, from 1946 to 1956, he netted 168 goals in 378 matches for Wolves, whom he helped win the FA Cup (1949) and the First Division championship (1954). A tiny winger, standing at 5ft 4ins tall and weighing around 10st, he wore a size-2 boot yet could unleash shots of devastating power, especially from free-kicks. He was also something of a penalty ace.

Hancocks played for Oakengates Town as a 15-year-old and in 1938 turned professional with Walsall, who had monitored his progress since 1934. He made his debut for the Saddlers at outside-right in October 1938, in a 2-2 home draw with Aldershot in the Third Division South. Once in the side, he held his position, and when the season ended he had scored ten goals in 37 matches. During the hostilities he continued to play for Walsall, scoring a further 34 goals in 92 games when he was able to get time off from his duties in the Army where he became a PT instructor. He played several times for the Western Command and Army sides and guested for a handful of other League clubs.

On 11 May 1946, Hancocks was transferred to Molineux for £4,000 and went on to win three full England caps, against Switzerland at Highbury in 1948 when he scored twice, against Wales in 1949 and against Yugoslavia in 1950. He also represented the Football League and was Wolves' top-scorer on three occasions, in 1947-48 (joint), 1954-55 and 1955-56. He left Wolves in the summer of 1957 after spending a season in the Reserves. He then served Wellington Town, initially as player-manager, giving up the managerial tag in September 1959 and quitting as a player three months later. In January 1960 he signed for Cambridge United; in July of that year he switched to Oswestry Town; and he ended his playing days with GKN Sankey's in season 1960-61. In later years he worked full-time at ironfounders Maddock & Sons in his native Oakengates, taking retirement in 1979 on his 60th birthday. Sadly he suffered a stroke but continued to follow the fortunes of both the Saddlers and Wolves until his death.

IAN HANDYSIDES

Midfield; 73+8 apps, 12 goals.

Born: Jarrow, 14 December 1962. Died: Solihull, 17 August 1990.

After showing impressive form playing for Durham Boys, Ian Handysides was hailed as the 'new Trevor Francis' when he arrived at St Andrew's to start his career with Birmingham City, signing apprentice forms in June 1978, and becoming a professional

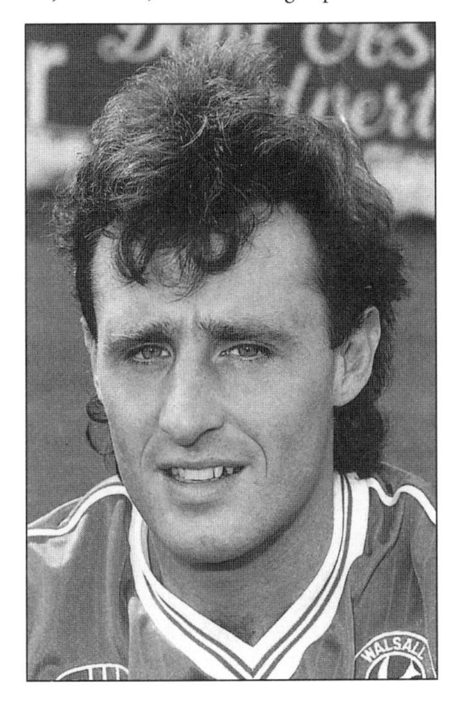

there in January 1980. But these high expectations proved to be a millstone round his neck and, in all fairness, he was a completely different type of player to Francis. In fact, he found it hard to cope with First Division football and in January 1984 moved to Walsall for a fee of £17,000. At Fellows Park, Handysides matured a great deal and it came as a bolt out of the blue when John Bond re-signed him for Birmingham in March 1986. He showed much more consistency in his second spell at St Andrew's although he did have a loan spell with Wolves (September-October 1986). Following a friendly game for Blues against Willenhall in August 1988 when he scored a hat-trick, he complained of severe headaches and shortly afterwards Blues and Walsall supporters, and soccer fans in general, were stunned to hear that a brain tumour had been diagnosed. Ian underwent surgery and for a time it seemed as if he was recovering, but sadly, further tumours developed on his spinal cord, resulting in his tragically early death at the age of 27.

JOHNNY HARRIS

Full-back; 85 apps, 2 goals.

Born: Upper Gornal, near Dudley, 3 April 1939.

Johnny Harris came through the ranks at Molineux where he understudied the likes of his namesake Gerry Harris, Eddie Stuart, George Showell and Bobby Thomson, among others. He joined Wolves as a lad in June 1955, from Sedgley Rovers, and turned professional under Stan Cullis in May 1958. He went on to play in only three League games for Wanderers. His debut came against West Ham United in August 1961 but in his next game, against Aston Villa two days later, he broke a leg. After recovering full fitness, he suffered another fractured limb in season 1963-64. He was subsequently transferred to Walsall on 7 January 1965, making his debut for the Saddlers nine days later against Shrewsbury Town. It was against the

Shrews that he scored his only goals for Walsall, both penalties in a 2-1 win in March 1966. He stayed at Fellows Park for three and a half years, during which time he became club captain while doing well alongside Frank Gregg. John Harris led Walsall to that dramatic FA Cup win at Stoke in January 1966, but injury struck in the first match of the following season and he was eventually forced to retire from competitive football in 1969.

COLIN HARRISON

Full-back/midfield; 508+22 apps, 34 goals.

Born: Pelsall, 18 March 1946.

Colin Harrison is Walsall's record appearance maker and a player who gave the club tremendous service for 19 years; indeed, only two other players, Nick Atthey and Colin Taylor, have played over 500 games for the Saddlers. Signed as an amateur by the Saddlers in June 1961, Harrison turned professional on 13 November 1963, and made his League debut against Southend United the following September, in the outside-left position. During his early days with the club he occupied a number of positions, includ-

ing both wing-halves berths, but it was finally as a full-back where he settled best, going on to become one of Walsall's finest-ever servants. His football for them was played almost exclusively in Division Three. Injury meant he played only once when the Saddlers were in Division Four in 1979-80 but appeared 19 times when Walsall were back in the Third Division the following season. His last appearance was in the number 3 shirt against Chesterfield in September 1981.

For a time Harrison acted as reserve-team trainer at Fellows Park and later had several good seasons playing for Rushall Olympic.

PETER HART

Defender/midfield; 472+2 apps. 13 goals.

Born: Mexborough, 14 August 1957.

Soon after leaving school, Peter Hart joined the staff of Huddersfield Town as a full-back, in August 1972, turning professional at Leeds Road on his 17th birthday two years later, after having made his League debut for the Yorkshire club in March 1974 against Southend United, aged 16 years seven months. He progressed well and after skippering the Terriers to the FA Youth Cup Final established himself in the senior side and went on to appear in 229 League and Cup games for Huddersfield, helping them win the Fourth Division title before transferring to Walsall for £70,000 in August 1980. Hart quickly became a star performer in the

Saddlers defence, assuming the role of team captain and going on to make more than 470 senior appearances for the club, including a club record 35 in the League Cup, reaching a rare level of consistency in his performances

and rarely missing a game. A credit to his profession both on and off the field, Peter Hart duly received a deserved testimonial against West Brom in May 1990 – the last game to be staged at Fellows Park. He ended his senior career with a record of 701 appearances and 21 goals. In August 1992 he was ordained full-time into the church. He played 53 times in 1987-88 when Walsall won promtion via the Play-offs.

PHILIP HAWKER

Defender; 201+20 apps, 16 goals.
Born: Solihull, 7 December 1962.
Phil Hawker played for Langley Green Secondary School as a lad and joined Birmingham City as an apprentice in June 1978, turning pro two years later. A tall, long striding defender, he failed to make his mark at St Andrew's where he acted, in the main, as reserve to Mark Dennis, although it was thought he would make the grade as a centre-half. After a brief spell on loan to Walsall (December 1982) he signed full-time for the Saddlers in March 1983. Hawker had to wait until 1985-86 to establish a regular place with Walsall but he eventually enjoyed some highlights, not least scoring in the epic 4-4 FA Cup fifth-round replay against Watford in February 1987. And in the 1987-88 Play-off Final replay against Bristol City he also netted. That season he played in over half the games but was in and out of the side when Walsall suffered successive relegations in

1988-89 and 1989-90. In 1990 he moved into non-League football with Kidderminster Harriers, following a loan spell with West Brom, and later served Solihull Borough, retiring in 1993 but coming back to play again for Borough in 1996-97.

TOM HAWKINS

Goalkeeper; 99 apps.
Born: West Bromwich, April 1869. Deceased.
A hefty six-footer, strong and courageous, Tom Hawkins played for Great Bridge Unity and Elwells FC before signing for Walsall in 1890. He lined up between the posts in Walsall's first-ever Football League game, against Darwen in September 1892. Hawkins played in every game that season and had a good career with the Saddlers which lasted until 1898 when he moved into local non-League football with Walsall Wood, later serving Bloxwich and Willenhall Olympic. In an emergency in January 1897 he was called up to play at left-back in a League game at Manchester City when Charlie Aston failed to meet the train. Walsall lost 5-0.

SID HELLIWELL

Defender; 104 apps, 8 goals.
Born: Berkshire, 1905. Deceased.
A strong, reliable stopper centre-half, well over 6ft tall with 'tree-trunk legs', Sid Helliwell joined Reading as a youngster in 1925 but made only five League appearances for the Elm Park club (in season 1926-27) before transferring to Tottenham Hotspur in August 1927, mainly as cover for centre-half Harry Skitt. He stayed at White Hart Lane for two years, making 13 senior appearances and scoring one goal, his debut for Spurs coming at Old Trafford in September 1927. In July 1929 he was recruited by Walsall boss Sid Scholey – along with his defensive colleague from Spurs, Tommy Muldoon – and quickly settled into the team, playing alongside Muldoon and Bradford in the middle line. Helliwell had 40 games in his first season with the Saddlers but was restricted to 27 in 1930-31 following injury problems. He was back to full fitness for the next campaign which unfortunately turned out to be his last with the club and in May 1932 he was transferred to Gravesend, later assisting Dover before retiring during World War Two.

KEN HILL

Wing-half; 141 apps, 1 goal.
Born: Walsall, 28 April 1938.
Ken Hill started as a centre-half with North Walsall Boys and then turned out at right-back for North Walsall Schools, but while working on the railway he was moved to right-half with Bescot United, and was invited to join Walsall as a professional in November 1956. He made his debut in the number-two shirt against Hartlepools United in February 1959, the first of 141 senior appearances for the Saddlers in two spells with the club. His first spell ended on 26 July 1963, when he transferred to Norwich City for £17,000, but he returned to Fellows Park in October 1966, staying there until the end of that season when he moved into non-League circles. He played only three times before 1960-61 before establishing himself as the Saddlers won a second successive promotion. The only goal of his career came in a 3-0 Second Division home win over Stoke in March 1962. A hard-working, industrious player who never gave his opponent any room in which to manoeuvre, Hill made 50 appearances for Norwich City.

KEN HODGKISSON

Inside-forward; 351+1 apps, 56 goals.
Born: West Bromwich, 12 March 1933.
Ken Hodgkinson was a scheming inside-forward who learnt his trade with West Bromwich Albion where his fellow inside-forwards were internationals Ronnie Allen, Johnny Nicholls and Reg Ryan. He could never hold down a first-team position at The Hawthorns, though, and after he had scored four goals in 21 games for the Baggies he was transferred to Walsall in December 1955 for £1,600. At Fellows Park he did far better and settled into the Saddlers' front line alongside ace marksman Tony Richards.

Hodgkisson was a key figure in the Fourth Division championship success of 1959-60 when he scored 11 goals (one of five Saddlers players to score reach double figures

that season) and he played a key role as Walsall surged into the Second Division the following campaign. He left the club in July 1966, teaming up with Worcester City. In later years he served with Dudley Town (as a player in 1967-68 then as manager from 1968 to 1971) and Greets Green Prims, before returning to West Brom as a coach in 1975, linking up again with his old Walsall colleague, Albert McPherson. In 1981 he was promoted to youth-team manager at The Hawthorns but when Ron Saunders moved in 1985 he was pushed out. Since then he has scouted for several clubs including Albion and Derby County. He made his League debut for Albion in front of 49,500 fans at Villa Park in April 1953 and he was Walsall's first-ever substitute, coming on against Workington in August 1965. He now lives and works in West Bromwich.

EDDIE HOLDING

Defender/forward; 41 apps, 8 goals.

Born: Wolverhampton, 15 October 1930.

Eddie Holding was equally happy in defence or attack, and once scored a Christmas Day hat-trick against Brighton. He joined Walsall as an amateur in 1947 and turned professional at Fellows Park in January 1949. He made his debut for the Saddlers at right-half at Gillingham in September 1950 – his only game that season – but in 1951-52 he made 25 appearances in the Third Division South, 17 at right-back, mainly as partner to Bill Green. He also lined up in the number-four shirt and took over the centre-forward berth for five games in January/February, when he scored three goals. The following season he was transferred to Derby County where he was a permanent reserve, but he returned to Fellows Park for the 1953-54 campaign and this time he managed 13 games, having the pleasure of cracking in that treble against Brighton when the Saddlers won 3-1 in December 1953. Holding was then transferred to Barrow in July 1954 and after scor-

ing five goals in five League games for the Holker Street club he returned to the Midlands, where he went into business. He is now happily retired and living in Wolverhampton, but still follows the fortunes of the Saddlers with great interest.

SAMMY HOLMES

Forward/wing-half; 381 apps, 108 goals.

Born: Walsall 1870. Deceased.

Sammy Holmes played for the Saddlers in each of their first eight seasons of League football (1892-1901 inclusive). He went on to amass over 380 senior appearances (including a club record 43 in the FA Cup) and scored more than a century of goals. He had tremendous stamina and was always involved in the action. He invariably caused defenders much anxiety with his incisive runs and was as sharp as anyone inside the box. A serious knee injury ended his career with the Saddlers in 1901 although he did play an occasional reserve-team games over the next three years and in 1906 played for Dudley.

TOMMY HOLT

Left-half; 89 apps.

Born: West Bromwich, February 1896. Deceased.

A stern-tackling half-back with strong shoulders and muscular thighs, Tommy Holt was forever involved in the action, never shirked a tackle and was a great inspiration to his colleagues, always giving 100 per-cent. Holt joined Walsall from Bush Rangers, a West Bromwich junior side, in September 1913. He took time to settle with the Saddlers and played in the Reserves for quite some time before finally establishing himself in the first team in season 1923-24. He was plagued by injury in 1924-25, making only five League appearances, but he bounced back in style in 1925-26 and took his total number of appearances past the 80 mark before leaving the club for Dudley Town in the summer of 1927. He later assisted Brierley Hill Alliance and Cradley St Peter's.

SCOTT HOUGHTON

Midfielder; 90+3 apps, 18 goals.

Born: Hitchin, Herts, 22 October 1971.

Scott Houghton is a busy, hard-working midfielder who can play on either side of the park where he always gives 100 per-cent effort. A trainee with Tottenham Hotspur before turning professional at White Hart Lane in August 1990, he failed to establish himself with Spurs who transferred him to Luton Town in August 1993 following loan spells with Ipswich Town, Gillingham and Charlton Athletic. He played in just over 20 games for the Hatters before moving to Walsall for £20,000 in September 1994. Over the next two years he battled hard and long in centre-field for the Saddlers and it came as something of a surprise when he left the club for Peterborough United for £60,000 in July 1996. He did well at London Road before moving on, this time to Third Division strugglers Southend United in 1998. Capped by England at Schoolboy and Youth levels, he helped Spurs win the FA Youth Cup in 1990.

CHARLIE HOULDEY

Full-back; 112 apps.

Born: Birmingham 1902. Deceased.

Charlie Houldey burst on to the soccer scene with Coventry City in 1925 after having played junior football with the Birmingham-based junior side, Harborne Lynwood. A right-back, strong and resourceful, confident on the ball with good vision, he made 62 appearances (two goals scored) during his stay at Highfield Road and he joined Walsall in 1929 for a fee of £400. Apart from his duties at full-back, Charlie appeared in goal for the Saddlers in an FA Cup game at Middlesbrough in 1929 after regular custodian Harry Wait had cried off at the last minute with a boil. Houldey left the Saddlers in the summer of 1931, following the arrival at Fellows Park of Ted Watson from Wolverhampton Wanderers. In 1932-33 he was playing for Lea Hall Rangers and later he worked at the Birmingham Fruit Market.

ROGER HYND

Centre-half; 106 apps, 1 goal.

Born: Falkirk, 2 February 1942.

Roger Hynd was a tough-tackling defender with a distinctive running style which involved a very high knee lift, thus singling him out from the rest of the team. A former

pupil at Lanark Grammar School, Hynd joined Glasgow Rangers in 1961 and six years later played for the Ibrox Park club in the European Cup-winners' Cup Final. He finished on the losing side and promptly tossed his medal into the crowd, disgusted at the result and indeed with his own performance. He left Rangers for Crystal Palace in a £12,000 deal in July 1969 and 12 months later he drove up the M1 to to sign for Birmingham City, £25,000 changing hands this time. He made over 200 senior appearances for Blues before joining Walsall in December 1975 after a brief spell on loan to Oxford United two months earlier. He did well at Fellows Park, missing only three out of a possible 109 games, but when the opportunity arose for him to become a manager, he couldn't turn the offer down, taking over at Motherwell in June 1978 having amassed a grand total of 296 appearances in the Football League (89 for Walsall and 171 for Blues). After pulling out of football in the early 1980s he became a PE teacher in Wishaw. He is the nephew of the late Bill Shankly, hence one of his christian names being Shankly.

CAESAR JENKYNS

Centre-half; 88 apps, 2 goals.

Born: Bulith, Wales, 24 August 1866. Died: Birmingham, 23 July 1941.

A burly player with a fearsome shoulder charge and bone-shattering tackle, nicknamed 'The Mighty Caesar', Jenkyns was the backbone of every defence he played in, a born leader who skippered each of his clubs. He was certainly the inspiration of the rest of the side and it is on record that he could head a ball fully 50 yards, and once sent a free-kick some 100 yards downfield first bounce. Controversial to the last, Jenkyns was certainly a tough character who feared no one and was sent-off a number of times during his career. Capped eight times by Wales, his first major club was Birmingham (Small Heath) whom he joined in 1884. There followed spells, in turn, with Unity Gas FC (1886), Blues again (from July 1888 to April 1895), Woolwich Arsenal, Newton Heath (May 1896), Walsall (November 1897), Coventry City (as first-team coach 1902), Saitley Wednesday (guest in 1904), retiring the following year to become a publican in Moxley, where he took over the George Inn. He later joined the Birmingham City Police Force. He helped Blues win the Second Division championship in 1893 – they lost the resultant test natch and stayed down – and eventual promotion to the First Division in 1894. He was sacked by Blues following a brawl involving a Derby County player.

ROY JOHN

Goalkeeper; 93 apps.

Born: Briton Ferry, near Neath, mid-Glamorgan, 29 January 1911. Died: Fort Talbot, 12 July 1973.

Roy John (whose first names were William Ronald) started as a centre-forward, a position he occupied with Neath Road School, Briton Ferry Schoolboys and Briton Ferry Athletic. He was then switched to left-back by Swansea Town whom he joined in June 1927, initially as an amateur, signing professional before the turn of the year. He then had a trial with Manchester United (1928), but it was with Walsall that he took to goalkeeping, having switched to that role in an emergency. He eventually won 14 caps for Wales in that position, plus one during the war, and he skippered his country in his last full international. He came to Walsall in May 1928 (his first four appearances were at left-back) eventually leaving Fellows Park for Stoke City in April 1932. He saved a penalty on his debut for the Potters (against Bradford PA) and at the end of the following season collected a Second Division championship medal. After 76 senior games for Stoke, he was transferred to Preston and from December 1934 to June 1936 made 28 League appearances for Sheffield United who paid £1,250 for his services. He switched back to Manchester United (£600) and whilst at Old Trafford had 15 League outings. A spell with Newport County followed (March-July 1937 when he made ten League appearances) and up until the outbreak of World War Two he served with Swansea Town, adding 40 more League games to his tally. He guested for Blackburn Rovers, Bolton Wanderers, Burnley, Swansea Town and Southport during the war and played his last game in September 1942, for a Welsh XI against the RAF. He made 145 League appearances all told. He later became a hotel manager and then kept a pub in Swansea, but when this was bombed during the war he worked for British Steel. He was a fine cricketer, playing as a batsman/wicketkeeper for Briton Ferry CC.

CHRIS JONES

Forward; 58+5 apps, 15 goals.

Born: Altrincham, Cheshire, 19 November 1945.

Chris Jones was a soccer nomad who served with nine different clubs between 1964 and 1980. In that time he accumulated 338 League appearances and 97 goals, and in all major competitive matches he registered almost 150 goals in some 500 outings. He started his career as a junior at Maine Road in 1961 after some impressive displays with Cheshire Boys. He turned professional for his boyhood heroes Manchester City in May 1964 and thereafter did the rounds, signing for Swindon Town (July 1968), Oldham Athletic (on loan, January 1972), Walsall (February 1972), York City (June 1973), Huddersfield Town (August 1976),

Doncaster Rovers (July 1977), Darlington (on loan January 1978) and finally Rochdale (December 1978). Jones then went into a lower grade of soccer with Rowntree McIntosh FC in the North East Counties League and later became chairman of the York Soccer Coaches Association. His best spell in the League came when he was with York, for whom he scored 34 goals in 95 League games. In his only full season with Walsall, 1972-73, he was top scorer with 12 League and Cup goals.

PAUL JONES

Midfield/forward; 158+24 apps, 19 goals.

Born: Walsall, 6 September 1965.

A powerfully-built footballer who spent two years as an apprentice at Fellows Park before

turning professional with the Saddlers on his 18th birthday in 1983, by which time he had already made his senior debut. He began to establish a regular place in 1985-86 as Walsall achieved promotion from Division Three via the Play-offs. That season Jones scored 14 goals, eight of them penalties. Towards the end of the 1987-88 campaign he was badly injured in a game against Notts County and this kept him out of another Play-offs. He recovered to make 16 League appearances in 1988-89 and also went on loan to Wrexham before being surprisingly bought by Wolves manager Graham Turner for £15,000. He made 14 appearances for the Molineux club in his first season , but then fell out of favour and eventually left the club in May 1991. He played next for Kettering Town before teaming up with Stafford Rangers in March 1992.

SID JONES

Full-back; 152 apps, 1 goal.

Born: Rothwell, Leeds, 15 February 1921.

Sid Jones was discovered by the great Herbert Chapman playing as a 15-year-old

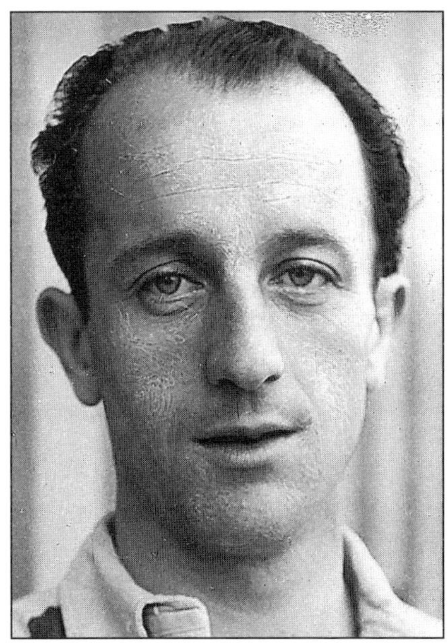

for Kippax Juniors in the Yorkshire League and moved to Arsenal in 1936, turning professional two years later. War disrupted his progress at Highbury and on 14 July 1948, having failed to establish himself as a first-team regular with the Gunners, he joined Walsall for a small fee – and never looked back. He went on to serve the Saddlers well in more than 150 Division Three South and FA Cup matches before retiring from League soccer in 1952. He was an ever-present for Walsall in season 1950-51.

STAN JONES

Centre-half; 263+2 apps, 7 goals.

Born: Highley, Salop, 16 November 1938.

Stan Jones was a strong defender, inspiring, good in the air, hard in the tackle and above all a player who rarely put a foot wrong – although during a disastrous spell in the mid-1960s when with West Brom, he netted three own-goals in the space of five games. Jones had a long and steady career, including two excellent spells at Fellows Park and an

eight-year stay at The Hawthorns. Shortly after leaving school he joined Kidderminster Harriers (1954) and following brief spell as an amateur with both Wolves and Walsall, he signed as a professional for the Saddlers in May 1956. His first stint ended in May 1960 when, after having helped the Saddlers win the Fourth Division championship, he (and his teammate Peter Billingham) were transferred to West Brom for £7,000.

Stan Jones went on to play in 267 games for the Baggies (three goals scored) before returning to Fellows Park in March 1968. He proceeded to give the Saddlers, then a middle-of-the-table Division Three club, another five years' service and was an ever-present in 1970-71. Jones left League football for Burton Albion in July 1973. He became player-manager of Kidderminster Harriers in 1974-75, played briefly for Hednesford Town (from March 1976) and took to coaching with Coleshill Town (1977-80). He then came back to Walsall as trainer for seven years (to 1987); he held a similar position at Burton Albion in 1988 and during the period 1979 to 1989 assisted WBA All Stars in various charity matches. He now runs a successful sports clothing business in Walsall.

MICK KEARNS

Goalkeeper; 322 apps.

Born: Banbury, 25 November 1950.

Standing well over 6ft tall, Mick Kearns was a commanding figure between the posts and throughout his varied career he always produced the goods for both club and country, appearing in 18 full internationals for the Republic of Ireland (15 whilst at Walsall – the club's most-capped player). Brother of Ollie, who was at Fellows Park during his second spell (1982-83), Mick Kearns joined Oxford United on leaving school (1966), turning professional at the Manor Ground two years later. He stayed

with Oxford until July 1973 when he arrived at Fellows Park, having been on loan to Plymouth Argyle (October 1972) and Charlton Athletic (February 1973) in between. He spent six excellent years with the Saddlers, being an ever-present three seasons on the trot (1974 to 1977). Between August 1973 and January 1979 Walsall played a total of 293 competitive games and Kearns missed only five. It came as a surprise to the die-hard Saddlers fans when, in July 1979, Wolves manager John Barnwell signed him as cover for Paul Bradshaw. Three years later (August 1982) Kearns was back at Fellows Park for his second spell – and he even came back again as a non-contract player, appearing in the last five games of 1984-85 while working as a steward at a local working men's club in Aldridge.

In 1990 he was taken on at Fellows Park as the club's official Community Relations Officer. In his League career he amassed 356 appearances – 275 for Walsall. Outside football, he was an exceptionally fine golfer who won the Midland Professional Footballers Golf Championship in 1977; and in May 1992 he scooped an international record for a footballer by holing-in-one at a course in Scotland, having previously done likewise on courses in both England and Ireland.

He was a member of the Walsall side which knocked Manchester United and Newcaste out of the FA Cup in 1974-75 and he helped the Saddlers to the League Cup semi-finals in 1983-84, although he missed the games against Liverpool after playing in all the other rounds.

Mick Kearns and Kevin Wilson were both Walsall players who were born in Banbury; one played for the Republic of Ireland, the other for Northern Ireland.

JOHN KEISTER

Midfielder; 94+31 apps, 2 goals.

Born: Manchester, 11 November 1970.

A strong-tackling constructive midfielder, John Keister, although born in Lancashire, has already won three caps for Sierra Leone as a Saddler and is hoping for more call-ups in the near future. He was signed by Walsall

from Faweh FC in September 1995 and established himself in the first team at the Bescot Stadium during the 1996-97 campaign. After a bright start he suffered cruciate knee ligament damage and didn't figure at all for much of the following season.

DAVID KELLY

Striker; 152+38 apps, 80 goals.

Born: Birmingham, 25 November 1965.

David Kelly was another Republic of Ireland international, a vital member of Jack Charlton's famous Irish squad and by 1999 the winner of 26 full caps. An out-and-out goalscorer, alert, quick – especially inside the box – and possessing good skills and a powerful shot, Kelly joined Walsall as a lad in 1981 and turned professional at Fellows Park in December 1983. His game developed fast and he was top-scorer for the Saddlers in 1986-87 with 26 goals in League and Cup games, and again in 1987-88 when he scored 30 in all games including a dynamic hat-trick in the crucial Play-off game against Bristol City which sealed promotion. This form made the bigger clubs take note and it was no surprise when, in August 1988, he was transferred to West Ham United for £600,000 (the most money ever received by Walsall for a player). Unfortunately Kelly never settled at Upton Park and after scoring 12 goals in 61 outings for the Hammers he was sold to

Leicester City in March 1990 for £300,000. His next move, in December 1991, took him north to Newcastle United for £250,000 and his goals during the second half of that season helped the Geordies stave off the threat of relegation to the Third Division.

Kelly top-scored with 28 goals as Newcastle won the First Division title in 1992-93, but was surprisingly transferred to Wolves for £750,000 in June 1993. After three seasons at Molineux he moved to Sunderland for £900,000 in September 1995, but after only two goals in 40 games for the Wearsiders he went to Tranmere Rovers for £350,000 in August 1997. In 1998-99, Kelly reached 500 League appearances and 200 senior goals.

GEORGE KIRBY

Centre-forward; 86+1 apps, 30 goals.

Born: Liverpool, 20 December 1933.

George Kirby served as a professional with eight Football League clubs, as well as New York Cosmos, between 1952 and 1969. A tall, strong-looking player with useful control, he was good in the air and packed a fair shot in his right foot. He started on the goal trail with Everton whom he served (initially as an amateur) from 1950 to March 1959 when he joined Sheffield Wednesday. In January 1960 he switched to Plymouth Argyle; he had a reasonable spell with Southampton from September 1962 to March 1964); played next with Coventry City up to October 1964 having moved to Highfield Road for £12,000; and he then switched to Swansea Town for £11,500, staying at Vetch Field until May 1965 when he was secured by Walsall for a fee of £10,000. He did well at Fellows Park, scoring a goal on average every three games, but in the summer of 1967 he went off to try

his luck in America with the Cosmos, returning to see out his League career in England with Brentford (October 1968 to May 1969). In all, he netted 120 goals in his 309 League appearances, his best sets of statistics coming with Plymouth (38 in 93 games) and Southampton (28 in 68), while for Walsall it was 25 in 75. In later years he returned to football and managed Halifax Town (two spells) and also Watford (1971-73) before going into business as an insurance broker.

MOSES LANE

Centre-forward; 67 apps, 55 goals.

Born: Willenhall, 17 February 1895. Died: Cannock, 14 July 1949.

Moses Lane's strike record for Walsall was second to none and if he had been able to continue for a few more seasons, who knows

what sort of records he might have created. Surprisingly, though, he was allowed to leave in 1921 after scoring four goals in ten Birmingham League games. When he returned for his second spell which lasted from June 1927 until May 1929, he could not do a thing wrong during the first season and a half. He finally left the scene after a long absence out of the side through injury, when he managed only one game in a little over four months, and was sold to Brierley Hill Alliance for a nominal fee.

He began with Willenhall Pickwick in 1912-13 and during World War One he served in France and Italy, being decorated with the Military Medal. In August 1920 he signed for Willenhall Town, switching to Walsall in December 1920 before going back to Willenhall in May 1921. Birmingham took him on their staff in April 1922, and he managed four goals in 15 games for the Blues before trying his luck with Derby County (June 1924 to May 1925). Unfortunately he only had one outing for the Rams, in an FA Cup-tie against Bradford City, before joining Wellington Town, switching to Worcester City inside 12 months. In the summer of 1927, Walsall manager Jimmy Torrance secured his services for around £150. It was certainly money well spent, and in his first season of League football Lane cracked home 35 goals in 41 matches, including a magnificent effort on his debut, against Bristol Rovers. He blasted four past Gillingham in Walsall's exciting 7-4 win in late September and hat-tricks followed in home matches against Brentford and Luton Town. He and George Robson worked well together and Lane continued to hit the mark in 1928-29, scoring 15 goals in 15 League outings up to Christmas Day, but then after scoring twice against Northampton Town he suffered a niggling knee injury which kept him out of action until mid-March and after which he played in only one more League game. He duly drifted into non-League soccer, first with Brierley Hill and later with Netherton and Dudley Town, retiring altogether in 1933.

JACK LEWIS

Goalkeeper; 286 apps.

Born: Tamworth, 1 May 1920. Died: 10 October 1988.

One of the smallest 'keepers in the game, Jack Lewis served Walsall well for a number of years, amassing well over 280 senior appearances as the last line of defence. Initially spotted by the former England goalie Harry Hibbs, playing for Boldmere St Michael's in 1945, Lewis eventually took over from Bert Williams when he went to Wolves and held his place in the Saddlers side until May 1953 when he moved to Hereford United, then members of the Southern League. His initial trial game in Walsall colours was a pre-season practice match at Fellows Park in August 1945, and on the manager's report, alongside Lewis' name, it stated: 'Shaped well'. He was taken on immediately, and became a star performer who made 130 consecutive appearances for Walsall between 21 September 1946 and 30

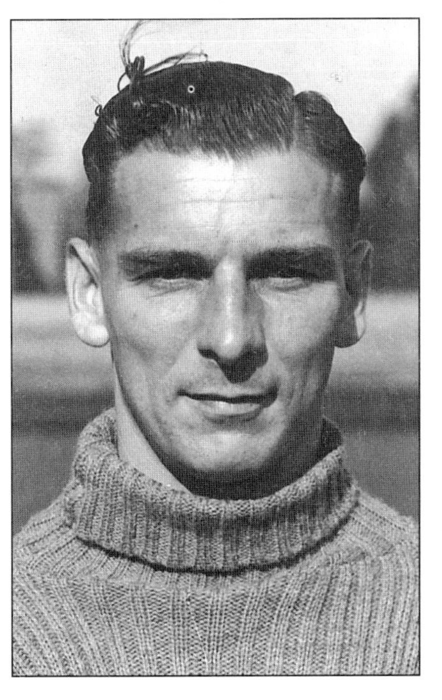

March 1949. He guested for West Bromwich Albion during World War Two and Albion had the chance to sign him on a permanent basis, but never followed it up. In later years Jack Lewis kept a popular public house in Tamworth, from 1962 to 1974.

KYLE LIGHTBOURNE

Striker;189+9 app, 83 goals.

Born: Bermuda, 29 September 1968.

Tall, rangy Bermuda international (26 caps) Kyle Lightbourne top-scored for the Saddlers in three successive seasons, 1993-96. For a big man (6ft 2ins tall and 12st 6lbs in weight) he had electrifying pace, superb finishing power and was a grafter, always working for his side, defending when necessary. He entered League football with Scarborough in December 1992 but remained with the Seaside club for only nine months before transferring to Walsall in September 1993. In his four seasons with the Saddlers he averaged a goal every two-and-a-half games and was certainly a big favourite with the supporters. He left the Bescot Stadium in July 1997, joining Premiership side Coventry City for £500,000. But he never settled at Highfield Road and after a loan spell with Fulham, he moved to Stoke City for £500,000 in February 1998. Unfortunately he couldn't

save the Potters from relegation at the end of that season and in 1998-99 was in and out of the side as Brian Little's men stuttered after an excellent start, in what was to prove a vain attempt to regain their First Division status.

DOUG LISHMAN

Inside-forward; 65 apps, 29 goals.

Born: Birmingham, 14 September 1923. Died: Longton, Staffs, 23 December 1994.

Doug Lishman had an excellent career in League football, amassing a total of 323 appearances for his three clubs (Walsall, Arsenal and Nottingham Forest) and scoring 173 goals. A pupil at St Thomas RC School (Erdington), he played local junior football in Birmingham and after wartime service

with the Royal Marine Commandos (when he took part in the Walcheren Island landing in Holland), he was spotted by Walsall scoring for Paget Rangers. He signed as a professional at Fellows Park in August 1946 and spent two fine seasons with the Saddlers, averaging a goal every two games. In July 1948 he was transferred to Highbury for £3,000. In December 1950 he fractured a leg but regained full fitness and went on to serve the Gunners well, winning a League championship medal in 1953. In all he scored 137 goals in 245 games for Arsenal, for whom he netted eight hat-tricks. He was also capped by England 'B' and represented the Football League. In March 1956 he moved to Forest and prior to his retirement in May 1957 he scored 22 goals in 38 games for them. He then took charge of the family furnishing business in Stoke.

DUGGIE LOCHHEAD

Left-half; 46 apps.

Born: Partick, Glasgow, 16 December 1904. Died: Leeds, 29 August 1968.

Dougald Lochhead was a neat and tidy footballer with a telling shot from well outside the penalty area. He started his career at competitive level with St Johnstone who secured his services from the Glasgow-based junior club, St Anthony's in August 1926. Lochhead left Perth for Walsall in July 1928 and immediately claimed the left-half berth in place of George Binks who had held the position since 1925-26. An ever-present in his only season with Walsall, Lochhead was transferred to Norwich City in June 1929 and at Carrow Road helped the Canaries win promotion from Division Three South in 1933-34. He went on to serve Norwich, in various capacities, for some 20 years. He appeared in 222 games for them (five goals scored) before retiring as a player in May 1935 after being rewarded with a benefit. After a spell as coach-trainer he became assistant manager of Norwich City (23 February 1937) and thereafter did some scouting before taking charge of team affairs in the transitional League season of 1945-46. He was appointment full-time manager on 10 December 1947 and held that position until March 1950. He then became chief scout of the Galatasary Sports Club in Istanbul (October 1950 to October 1952), coached Almelo FC from December 1953 and then returned to the UK as manager of Merthyr Tydfil (June 1956-1958).

ROD McDONALD

Forward; 171+7 apps, 46 goals.

Born: Liverpool, 20 March 1967.

Rod McDonald played consistently well for

Colne Dynamoes before moving to Walsall on 24 August 1990 following the FA's decision not to allow Dynamoes into the GM Vauxhall Conference. Fast, sprightly, alert inside the box, he had an excellent first season with the Saddlers, appearing in 41 games and scoring six goals. He followed up with several more impressive displays during the early 1990s and at one stage there were clear indications that he could be on his way to a more fashionable club as scouts from several First Division clubs were seen checking on his progress. In September 1994, however, it was Partick Thistle who snapped him up. He did well in Scotland before moving to Barrow in 1997-98.

ROY McDONOUGH

Striker; 87+6 apps, 17 goals.

Born: Solihull, 16 October 1958.

A tall, hard-working goalscorer, who always gave 100 per cent at whatever he level he played, Roy McDonough represented Villa Boys as a lad before joining Birmingham as an apprentice in October 1974, turning professional at St Andrew's two years later. He made two first-team appearances for Blues before transferring to Walsall for £15,000 in September 1978. At Fellows Park he did better and hit 15 goals in his 82 League outings, including seven in 45 League games when the Saddlers were promoted from Division Four in 1979-80, prior to making the move to Chelsea in October 1980, also for £15,000. Another £15,000 deal took him to Colchester in February 1981 and his next move was to Southend United for £5,000 in August 1983. He played for Exeter from January to October 1984; for Cambridge United until

August 1985; he returned to Southend for a second spell to May 1990; and then went back to Colchester, taking over as player-manager there in August 1991, in succession to Ian Atkins. McDonough helped Southend win promotion from Division Four in 1990 and then guided Colchester back into the Football League the following year. In his full League career he scored 80 goals in 437 games. In August 1992 as player-manager, he was sent-off playing for Colchester. McDonough lost his job at Layer Road during the latter part of the 1993-94 season.

JIMMY McMORRAN

Midfielder; 118+2 apps, 7 goals.

Born: Muirkirk, Ayr, 29 October 1942.

Jimmy McMorran gained Scottish Schoolboy international honours as a lad and joined Aston Villa at the age of 16, signing professional forms in October 1959. He

struggled to get into Villa's first team and made only 14 appearances before transferring to Third Lanark in February 1963. He was then snapped up by Walsall for £6,000 in November 1964 and spent three and a half years at Fellows Park, during which time he did well in centre-field. In June 1968 he went to Swansea Town. He returned to Walsall for a second spell in November of that same year but at the end of the season he was sold to Notts County (July 1969), transferring to Halifax Town (August 1970), Worcester City (July 1971) and Redditch United (August 1974). McMorran retired in May 1977, but continued to play in charity matches. On his day he was an outstanding ball player, but several defenders attempted to take advantage of his fiery temper by provoking him into retaliation. In his professional career he played in 137 League games and scored 14 goals.

ALBERT McPHERSON

Centre-half; 367 apps, 8 goals.

Born: Salford, Manchester, 8 July 1927.

Albert McPherson was a splendid defender who started his senior career with Bury, signing on as a professional in June 1949. He spent three seasons at Gigg Lane without breaking into their League side, leaving the Shakers after a disagreement. He went out of the big time and signed for the Cheshire

League side, Stalybridge Celtic in August 1952. But after two happy years there he came to Walsall in May 1954 after Celtic's manager, Harry Chapman had told him to 'get back into the Football League'. McPherson remained at Fellows Park for a decade during which time he amassed a grand total of 367 senior appearances, helping the Saddlers win promotion in 1960 and 1961. He certainly gave Walsall superb service as a steady centre-half.

A pupil at Regent Junior School, Salford, he started as a full-back or wing-half at the age of 12 with his senior school after he was evacuated to Askam-in-Furness. In 1944 he returned to Salford and began to play for the Salford Lads' Club, moving to the Aldephi Lads' Club in the Manchester Amateur League in August 1947. He stayed there until February 1948 when he was posted to Detmold, Germany, with the Royal Engineers. In the forces he played three times a week – for the Army, for CCG (a Civil Service side) and as a centre-forward for Detmold in the German National League.

Demobbed in February 1950, he went back to the Adelphi Lads' Club and also assisted Grove Inn, a local Salford club. Spotted by a Bury scout he went for trials with Shakers but it was Major Frank Buckley who took him on at Walsall. His senior debut came against Brighton in October 1954 (when he replaced the injured Jack Bridgett). At the end of that 1954-55 season he was invited to play for Grimsby Town against an All Star XI in a friendly match arranged to open the Blundell Park floodlights. He was in fact on trial but Major Buckley said that he would not leave Fellows Park. After eventually leaving the club in 1964, he became trainer-coach at West Bromwich Albion, a position he held with the first team, the Reserves and also the Youth team, right up to the mid-1980s.

PETER McSEVICH

Goalkeeper; 121 apps.

Born: Stevenston, Ayrshire, 1908. Died: Walsall 1982.

Peter McSevich, who at 5ft 9ins was small for a goalkeeper, began his career with Aberdeen in July 1925. He won two Scottish Junior international caps against England and Wales in his first season at Pittodrie and went on to appear in 36 senior games before having a good spell with Celtic from July 1928, moving to England to join Bournemouth in 1929. After being injured in the Bournemouth against Brighton game at Hove in October 1931, he went to outside-right and scored his side's only goal in a 4-1 defeat. In August 1932, McSevich came to the Midlands, signing for Coventry City for whom he made 38 senior appearances prior to joining Walsall in July 1933. After his retirement through injury in May 1936, McSevich served Walsall for many years as dressing-room attendant and part-time coach. His pastimes included golf, gardening and motoring.

TONY MACKEN

Right-back; 214 apps, 2 goals.
Born: Dublin, 30 July 1950.
Tony Macken was a hard-tackling midfield player who emerged with the Irish League club, Waterford before joining Derby County for £30,000 in August 1974. He had a loan spell with Portsmouth (November 1975 to February 1976) and starred for Washington Diplomats (also on loan from April 1976 to May 1977) and then Dallas Tornadoes (from July 1977) before transferring to Walsall for

a bargain fee of £9,600 in October 1977, former Rams manager Dave Mackay bringing him in to add stability to the defence, in which Macken was converted to full-back. Macken stayed at Fellows Park until June 1982 when he returned home to Waterford, later assisting Home Farm in 1987-88. Capped once by the Republic of Ireland, he had a good League career, making 223 appearances and scoring three goals, one for each of his clubs.

NORMAN MALE

Full-back; 81 apps, 2 goals.
Born: West Bromwich, 27 May 1917. Died: Tividale, Dudley, summer 1992.
Norman Male was an efficient full-back who played consistently in West Bromwich Albion's reserve team before joining Walsall for a bargain fee of £250 in May 1938. He made four League appearances for the Baggies (one goal scored) and in 1935 gained a Junior International cap. At Fellows Park he became a permanent fixture in the Saddlers defence, making over 80 first-team appear-

ances, plus around 180 in wartime football. He was forced to retire in August 1949 and thereafter worked on the club's groundstaff for another 22 years. Educated at Greets Green and Horseley Heath Schools, he was first spotted by Albion playing for Bush Rangers, and joined The Hawthorns club as an amateur in November 1933, turning professional in October 1934. Today he lives in retirement in Tividale, near Dudley. In his very last game for Walsall, November 1948, he was injured, went up into the attack and duly scored twice from the outside-left position against Millwall. Unfortunately he never recovered from that injury which left him with a distinctive limp.

CHRIS MARSH

Defender/midfielder; 388+38 apps, 28 goals.
Born: Sedgley, West Midlands, 14 January 1970.
Chris Marsh, Walsall's longest-serving player when the 1998-99 season ended, was as proud as anyone when promotion was achieved. Indeed it was he who helped secure First Division football for the Saddlers with a splendid goal in the 3-1 home win over Oldham Athletic which guaranteed his side runners-up spot behind Fulham. Marsh first joined the club as a junior in 1986 and turned professional in July 1988. He was granted a deserved testimonial after ten years loyal service during which time he amassed more than 400 senior appearances for the Saddlers and moved into the top ten of the club's all-time appearance makers.

Over the years he has donned practically every numbered shirt for Walsall, including the goalkeeper's, but it has been the left-back

position where he has played in recent times. Indeed, he has performed exceedingly well, putting in many outstanding displays as skipper of the side. A player who enjoys getting forward, Marsh is quick to react, is excellent in recovery and is an exemplary professional.

JIMMY MARTIN

Inside-forward; 103 apps, 33 goals.
Born: Lancaster, September 1875. Deceased.
In a three-year period, 1898 to May 1901, Jimmy Martin netted 28 League goals for the Saddlers in 93 games, having moved to the Midlands club from Blackpool South Shore in May 1898. He made his debut for Walsall at right-half against Loughborough at home in September 1898, setting up three of the goals in his side's 7-0 win. He was switched to inside-right for one game and then settled down in the other inside-forward berth, forming an excellent left wing partnership with Alf Griffin and then Jock Dailly and later with Bert Flynn. Martin left the club for non-League football in 1902 after struggling with a knee injury for 12 months.

DAVE MASSART

Inside/centre-forward; 29 apps, 23 goals.
Born: Yardley, Birmingham, 2 November 1919.
Dave Massart was a never-say-die goalscorer who grabbed a hat-trick in each of his first three home Third Division South League matches for Walsall at the start of the 1947-48 season. He ended up with 23 goals in 27 games that term. A real old fashioned number-nine, Massart started his career with Bells Athletic, joining Blues an an amateur in 1938, turning professional the following

year. He switched from St Andrew's to Walsall in June 1947 after failing to win a regular place with Blues, although he did help them win the League South title in 1946. He went to Bury from Walsall in March 1948 and netted 45 times in 85 League outings for the Shakers before switching to Chesterfield in February 1951. He retired from top-class action in 1952 and later played for Weymouth before going in the hotel business in the 1960s, a career he was still following in 1985.

BILLY MAYS

Centre-forward; 17 apps, 11 goals.

Born: Ynyshir, Merthyr, 12 March 1902. Died: Derby, 3 November 1959.

Billy Mays scored 154 goals for Ynyshir Swallows in two seasons of Welsh football between his duties down the pit and also played for Porth and Wattstown before joining Bristol City in September 1923. Mays hit four goals in 19 League games for City before transferring to Plymouth Argyle in June 1926. Failing to make an impact at Home Park, after 12 months he joined Merthyr Town, scoring 14 goals in his 34 League appearances for them before moving to Wrexham in August 1928.

Mays had a magnificent first season at the Racecourse Ground, scoring 32 goals in 34 games in the Third Division North, as well as winning his only full cap against Northern Ireland when he also found the net. Dubbed 'Amazing Mays' by the Wrexham supporters, he ended his stay there with 41 goals in 54 appearances before transferring to Notts County for £650 in March 1930. After five goals in eight League matches for the Magpies, Burnley bought him in May 1930. That move wasn't successful and in January 1931 Mays was snapped up by Walsall.

An aggressive, two-footed player, he made a terrific start to his career at Fellows Park, netting nine goals in his first seven matches, including the winner on his debut at Torquay and a hat-trick at Exeter City. He finished the season with 11 goals from 17 appearances but was allowed to join Halifax Town in June 1931, much to the annoyance of Walsall's supporters. He scored eight goals in 25 League games for Halifax before signing for non-League Margate Town for whom he played from July 1932 until May 1933. He later worked in the NAAFI offices and was then on the clerical staff at Derby Police Station. His son Abert Mays played 272 League games for Derby County between 1949 and 1959 and 37 for Chesterfield up to 1961.

GEORGE MEEK

Winger; 187 apps, 29 goals.

Born: Glasgow, 15 February 1934.

At 5ft 3ins one of the smallest players of his era, George Meek was spotted by the great Major Frank Buckley while playing inside-left for Hamilton Academical (who had secured his services from Thorniewood United). Major Buckley took Meek to Leeds United as a professional in August 1952. He was loaned to Walsall for 15 months whilst doing his National Service in the Royal

Armoured Corps (23 January 1954 to 30 April 1955) and he made 44 League appearances for the Saddlers during that time of struggle in the Third Division South. After returning to Elland Road – and taking his total of appearances for Leeds up to 200 (19 goals) – he was transferred to Leicester City for £7,000 in August 1960, but made only 13 appearances at Filbert Street before moving to Walsall for a then record fee in July 1961, staying with the Saddlers until March 1965 and adding another 129 League games to his tally, during which time the team were relegated from Division Two. Fast and direct, good on the ball, Meek was a great crowd-pleaser who finished his career with an impressive total of 382 League appearances and 47 goals. After leaving Fellows Park he had a brief spell with Dudley Town and then joined Rushall Olympic in 1966 and continued to turn out in various charity matches right up until he reached the age of 50. He worked as a postman in Walsall for 15 years.

IRVINE METHLEY

Full-back; 121 apps.

Born: Barnsley, 22 September 1925.

Irvine Methley began his playing career with Wolverhampton Wanderers in 1940-41, but failed to breakthrough at Molineux, transferring to Walsall in 1945. He did well for the Saddlers after finding his feet in that transitional season of 1945-46 when he settled down at right-back. He played in that season's Division Three South Cup Final against Bournemouth and went on to appear in well over 100 games before eventually an injury first sustained in January 1948 eventually caused him to quit competitive football in May 1951. Today he lives in retirement in Bloxwich having run a fish and chip shop in Leamore for a number of years immediately following his footballing career. Today, Methley lives in Bloxwich.

COLIN METHVEN

Midfield/defender; 116+1 apps, 3 goals.

Born: India, 10 December 1955.

Although born on the sub-Continent, Colin Methven made his name with East Fife, joining the Scottish League club from Leven Royals in August 1974. He moved south in

October 1979 to team up with Wigan Athletic for whom he went on to play in more than 300 games, helping them win promotion to Division Three in 1982. In July 1986 he was transferred to Blackpool, and for the Seasiders he played in well over 150 League games prior to his move to Walsall in November 1990. Standing 6ft 2ins tall and weighing over 12st, Methven reached the milestone of 700 League appearances during the course of the 1991-92 season (144 with East Fife, 296 with Wigan, 173 with Blackpool and the rest with the Saddlers). He became one of the oldest players ever to make his debut for Walsall in a League game. Injuries forced Methven to retire from competitive football in June 1994. He then became a hotelier in Blackpool.

HARRY MIDDLETON

Centre-forward; 63+3 apps, 30 goals.
Born: Birmingham, 18 March 1937.
Former England Youth international Harry Middleton enjoyed 14 years in League football, from 1955 to 1968 inclusive, during

which time he served six different clubs. He started as an amateur with Wolves and turned professional at Molineux in August 1954, but after only one League game in his five years at the club he was transferred to Scunthorpe United in September 1959. In June 1961, after 11 goals in 29 League games for the Iron, he moved to Portsmouth and then switched to Shrewsbury Town in February 1962. After scoring 37 goals in 85 League games for the Shrews, Middleton signed for Mansfield Town in November 1964. He continued to score regularly for the Stags (24 goals in 46 League outings) before rounding off his cãreer with Walsall, whom he joined in March 1966. Middleton achieved an equally good scoring rate with the Saddlers, helped by 14 goals in 18 games in his first season, four of them coming against Gillingham in only his sixth appearance. He left Fellows Park in May 1968 and later played for Worcester City. His overall League career totalled 236 appearances and 103 goals.

JOHN MORGAN

Centre-half/ left-half; 22 apps.
Born: Penicuik, Edinburgh, 7 March 1900. Died c.1975.
At over 6ft tall and weighing around 12st, Jock Morgan was the ideal build for a defender. After he was spotted doing well with Edinburgh Emmett, Morgan was signed by Birmingham in August 1924, mainly as cover for the likes of Cringan and Hunter. He had only one first-team outing for Blues before transferring to Doncaster Rovers in 1926. He immediately gained a regular place in the Rovers' League side and went on to make 149 appearances for them before spending the 1930-31 season with Bristol City. Just after the opening of the 1931-32 campaign he was transferred to Barrow, where he played in another 66 League games before joining Walsall in July 1933. During his only season in the side at Fellows Park, Walsall finished fourth in the Third Division North, when he appeared 19 times. Morgan pulled out of top-class football in 1935 after suffering an ankle injury the year before.

DAI MORGAN

Right-half/centre-half; 224 apps, 1 goal.
Born: Merthyr, South Wales 1909. Deceased.
Dai Morgan played for Aberdare as a youngster before signing for Charlton Athletic in May 1930. He moved to Bradford City in June 1932, but was basically a reserve at Valley Parade, making only one appearance before switching to Aldershot 12 months later. He signed for the Saddlers in the summer of 1934. Strong in the tackle, Dai was a spirited competitor whose enthusastic approach sometimes found himself at odds with referees. He played for the Saddlers well into World War Two, amassing more than 200 senior appearances before the hostilities and 111 during the conflict. Golf and tennis were two other sports in which he excelled. Walsall enjoyed little League success during his time with them but he did help them to the fifth round of the FA Cup in 1938-39 and played in the 3-0 defeat at First Division Huddersfield, who had reached the Final the previous season.

FRED MORRIS

Outside-right; 230 apps, 49 goals.
Born: Oswestry, 15 June 1929.
Fred Morris played for Oswestry Town in the Birmingham League before transferring to Walsall on 16 May 1950. Morris appeared in five different positions under Major Frank

Buckley, but was at his best as a right winger where he showed great pace, good skill on the ball and a powerful shot to finish. He hit 43 goals in 210 League games for the Saddlers although his days there coincided with Walsall's march towards breaking the record for the number of times a club has had to apply for re-election. Between August 1953 and August 1956 he appeared in 151 consecutive League and FA Cup games for Walsall, and at Brighton on Boxing Day 1954 he scored a hat-trick but Walsall still lost. He moved to Mansfield Town in March 1957 for £1,500. Morris scored 19 goals in 60 games for the Stags and in May 1958 switched to Liverpool for £7,000. The ex-Saddler had two fine seasons at Anfield up to June 1960, scoring 14 goals in 47 League matches, and later he served with Crewe Alexandra to January 1961, Gillingham, for six months, and Chester from July 1961, announcing his retirement from League football in May 1962 with a total of 360 League appearances and 79 goals to his name. He later played briefly for Altrincham and for Oswestry again, whom he also managed. While with Chester he launched his own successful building contractor's business before taking over a garage in his home town of Oswestry where he lives today.

GEOFF MORRIS

Winger or midfield; 195+6 apps, 41 goals.
Born: Birmingham, 8 February 1949.
A busy outside-left, good on the ball with a fair change of pace, Geoff Morris arrived at Fellows Park as a 15-year-old in June 1964, and turned full-time professional in February 1966. He made his League debut

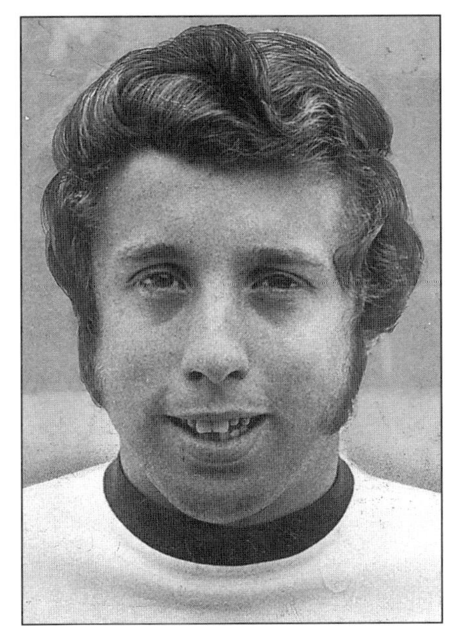

for the Saddlers at the age of 16 in that same season (1965-66) and went on to score 35 goals in 177 League appearances for Walsall. He was leading scorer with 12 League and Cup goals in 1971-72. In January 1973 he was transferred to Shrewsbury Town and rounded off his career at senior level with a spell at Port Vale (August 1975 to April 1976). All told he played in 267 League games and hit 45 goals. He spent two seasons with Kidderminster Harriers after leaving Villa Park.

DEREK MOUNTFIELD

Defender; 117+2 sub apps, 2 goals.
Born: Liverpool, 2 November 1962.
Derek Mountfield, a former England under-21 and 'B' international central defender, joined Walsall in November 1995 at the age of 33, having previously accumulated almost 450 League and Cup appearances while playing, in turn, for Tranmere Rovers (from 1980), Everton (signed for £30,000 in June 1982), Aston Villa (£450,000 in June 1988), Wolverhampton Wanderers (£150,000 in November 1991), Carlisle United (free in August 1994) and Northampton Town (free in October 1995). He added experienced and stability to the Saddlers' defence and re-signed for the club in August 1997, having been released at the end of the previous season. He acted as assistant-manager/coach to Jan Sorensen but when Ray Graydon took

charge Mountfield was released for a second time. Earlier in his career he helped Everton win the FA Cup in 1984, the League championship in 1985 and 1987 and the European Cup-winners' Cup, also in 1985. In 1995 he was in the Carlisle side which gained promotion from Division Three. Altogether he made 563 senior appearances at club level.

KENNY MOWER

Full-back; 487+7 apps, 10 goals.
Born: Bloxwich, 1 December 1960.
A one-club man, Kenny Mower joined the Saddlers as an apprentice in June 1976, from T. P. Riley School via Streetly Youth Club, and turned professional in November 1978, mak-

ing his Football League debut in May 1979. He went on to amass almost 500 senior appearances for the Saddlers (415 coming in the Football League). He made his debut in the last match of the 1978-79 relegation season and played in 48 League and Cup games when the Saddlers were promoted straight back to Division Three the following campaign. He appeared in all nine games when Walsall reached the 1983-84 League Cup semi-finals (and 56 games in all that season), but missed the 1987-88 Play-off games after appearing in the final games of the regular season. His last appearance for Walsall was against Scunthorpe in March 1991 and in June that year he left Fellows Park to join the GM Vauxhall Conference side, Stafford Rangers, later playing for Blakenhall (January 1992).

ALBERT MULLARD

Inside-forward; 67 apps, 13 goals.
Born: Walsall, 22 November 1920. Died: Stoke, 12 April 1985.
During World War Two, Albert Mullard spent four years as a prisoner of the Germans while serving in the Royal Marines. In peacetime he was a tireless inside-forward, always willing to do the fetching and carrying. Mullard joined Walsall as a teenager in July

1938, from Hinckley Athletic, and after the war established himself in the first team, going on to score 12 goals in 63 League games for the Saddlers before transferring to Crewe Alexandra in June 1949, being signed by Arthur Turner who later managed Birmingham City. Mullard proved to be a great asset to the Railwaymen and netted 14 times in 44 Third Division North games before moving to Stoke City for the fee of £8,000 in August 1950.

He spent a little over a season at the Victoria Ground, but still stayed in the Potteries, signing next for Port Vale in September 1951 for the sum of £10,000 plus Alan Martin. He did extremely well at Vale Park after being switched to right-half by manager Freddie Steele. Mullard was a big favourite with the fans, who cheered his 22 goals in 164 League outings. He gained a Third Division North championship medal in 1953-54 and also played in that season's FA Cup semi-final against West Brom at Villa Park. Albert Mullard retired from League football in June 1956, having scored 51 goals in 292 League games during his career. He later played several years for Wednesbury Tube in the Wolverhampton Works League.

JIMMY MURRAY

Centre-forward; 60+4 apps, 15 goals.

Born: Dover, Kent, 11 October 1935.

For some 15 years, from 1955 to 1969 inclusive, Jimmy Murray was one of the best goalscorers in the Football League. In that time he served three clubs – Wolves, Manchester City and Walsall – and netted 211 goals in 404 League matches, a fine return by any standard. Spotted playing schools football in his native Dover by Wolves scout, George Poyser, he arrived at Molineux in 1951 and turned professional in November 1953. He bided his time in the Reserves but when Roy Swinbourne was

injured during the 1955-56 campaign, Murray stepped up to take over the number-nine shirt. He never looked back and went on to crack in 166 goals in 299 senior games for Wolves. He grabbed five hat-tricks, three coming in the space of four weeks in February-March 1958, and was Wolves' top scorer in 1957-58, 1959-60 and 1961-62. He won two League championship medals in the late 1950s, added an FA Cup winners' medal to his collection in 1960 when Wolves beat Blackburn Rovers 3-0 in the Final, was capped twice at Under-23 level by England and also represented the Football League.

After that marvellous career with Wolves, Murray was transferred to Manchester City for £27,000 in November 1963 and he made a great start to his time at Maine Road, with 12 goals in his first six matches including two more hat-tricks. He formed a wonderful strike force with former Albion player Derek Kevan and in his three and a half years with City he scored 43 goals in only 70 appearances. It was May 1967 when Jimmy Murray found his way to Walsall, and he did well at Fellows Park in the two seasons he spent there, hitting 13 goals in his 58 full League outings. In August 1969 he moved to Telford United, finally hanging up his boots in the summer of 1971 after playing for the Shropshire club in successive FA Trophy Finals at Wembley. He then started his own greengrocery business in Tamworth, which he ran until 1990.

WILLIE NAUGHTON

Left-winger; 185+17 apps, 24 goals.

Born: Catrine, Ayrshire, 20 March 1962.

An aggressive left winger whose League career took off with Preston North End, Willie Naughton joined the Deepdale club as an apprentice in June 1978, turning pro in March 1980. He went on to score ten goals in 162 League games for North End before

transferring to Walsall for £35,000 in March 1985. Overall he did well at Fellows Park and was a regular performer in the side until his departure to Shrewsbury Town in July 1989. Naughton suffered with injury and loss of form during the 1986-87 campaign, but was instrumental in helping the Saddlers gain promotion to Division Two in 1988, when he appeared in 41 League games. He came back for a second spell with the Saddlers in season 1990-91, but left for Shrewsbury Town within six months. He later played for Bamber Bridge.

ALBERT ('NUTTY') NEWMAN

Wing-half; 149 apps, 2 goals.

Born: Lichfield, Staffs., 1 March 1915. Died: 25 August 1982.

Albert Newman spent quite some time play-

ing in West Bromwich Albion's reserve side before finally transferring from The Hawthorns to Walsall in May 1945. He was a hard player, with a big heart who loved a battle. He established himself in Walsall's side in season 1945-46 and after the hostilities went on to play in 136 League games before retiring in May 1950. Indeed, after the Football League proper resumed in August 1946, Newman missed only one out of the next 123 League and Cup games. Walsall's best season during his time at Fellows Park was in 1947-48 when the finished third in the Third Division South.

CHARLES NTAMARK

Midfield/Full-back; 314+22 apps, 14 goals.

Born: Paddington, London, 22 July 1964.

Prior to linking up with the English non-League club Boreham Wood, Ntamark had played for Canon Waounde in Cameroon.

He went on to win a total of 31 full caps for his country as well as amassing well over 330 senior appearances for the Saddlers. In his last two seasons with the club he played more as a defensive right-back than an attacking midfielder, but still gave 100 percent effort, as always. He joined Hednesford Town in the summer of 1997, later moving to Bromsgrove Rovers.

MARTYN O'CONNOR

Midfielder; 125 apps, 28 goals.

Born: Walsall, 10 December 1967.

Martyn O'Connor was Walsall's skipper and midfield general for two seasons before he left the Bescot Stadium with Scott Houghton

to join Peterborough United. O'Connor started his career with Bromsgrove Rovers and entered League football with Crystal Palace in 1992 following his £25,000 transfer to Selhurst Park. He was given only four first team outings by the Eagles, who then sold him to Walsall for £40,000 in February 1994 – this after he had been on loan at the Bescot Stadium during March/April 1993. A positive, hard-working player, O'Connor was elected by his fellow professionals in the PFA Division Two side in 1996 – just before he left for London Road in a £350,000 deal. He never settled down with Posh and had no second thoughts when, in November 1996, Trevor Francis asked him to move to St Andrew's for a fee of £500,000. Since then O'Connor has done very well with Blues and in 1998-99 helped them reach the First Division Play-offs, although his season was severely disrupted by injury.

RICHARD O'KELLY

Striker; 231+23 apps, 65 goals.

Born: West Bromwich, 8 January 1957.

Richard O'Kelly had two spells as a professional with Walsall. His first lasted almost seven years from October 1979, after he signed from non-League Alvechurch. He

returned for a second stint towards the end of the 1987-88 campaign, re-signing in February 1988. O'Conner won his place in the Saddlers' forward-line in season 1980-81 and remained a regular in the team, injuries apart, until leaving for Port Vale in July 1986. He scored a hat-trick against Newport in November 1981, played in the 1983-84 League Cup semi-finals and was the Saddlers' top scorer in 1984-85 with 18 goals in League and Cup. Altogether he scored 55 goals in 204 League games for Walsall and added four in 28 games for Vale before returning to Fellows Park. He then switched to Grimsby Town (July 1988) and hit ten goals in 39 League outings for the Mariners before returning to the Potteries to work as the Port Vale community officer in 1990-91. He took up a coaching position at Grimsby Town in 1991-92, when Alan Buckley was manager at Blundell Park, and followed Buckley to The Hawthorns. His overall League career brought him a total of 70 goals in 283 games.

GRENVILLE PALIN

Full-back; 139 apps, 10 goals.

Born: Doncaster, 13 February 1940.

Signed as a professional by Wolves in March 1957, Grenville Palin was in their FA Youth Cup winning side of 1958, but suffered a

broken leg on 28 November 1959 without having played first-team football at Molineux. He recovered and was transferred to Walsall in July 1960, staying at Fellows Park until the summer of 1964, when he joined Worcester City. In his four years at Fellows Park, he played in 140 League and Cup games and helped the Saddlers win promotion to the Second Division in 1960-61. His son, Leigh, played for Aston Villa, Shrewsbury Town, Nottingham Forest, Bradford City and Hull City.

PHIL PARKES

Goalkeeper; 60 apps.

Born: Sedgley, 8 August 1950.

In a quite superb career the giant Phil Parkes

– 6ft 3ins and 14st 9lbs – kept goal in more than 900 senior games for his four Football League clubs and England, gaining caps at four different levels – full (1), 'B' (1), Under-21 (1) and Under-23 (6). He came to Walsall as a 16-year-old from Brierley Hill Reserves and turned professional at Fellows Park in January 1968, going on to make 60 League and Cup appearances for the Saddlers before transferring to QPR for £15,000 in June 1970.

At Loftus Road, Parkes took his appearances tally for the London club to 408 before he was sold to neighbouring West Ham United for £500,000 in late February 1979. At the end of his full first season at Upton Park, he helped the Hammers lift the FA Cup, and in 1981 he collected his second medal when the championship of Division Two was achieved. In August 1990 he joined Ipswich Town on a free transfer as cover for the Canadian international Craig Forrest, staying at Portman Road for a season. By coincidence, Parkes played in 344 League games for both his London clubs.

TED PEERS

Right-back; 75 apps, 2 goals.

Born: Hednesford, June 1896. Deceased.

Ted Peers played his early football with Hednesford Rovers and, after a spell in West Bromwich Albion's reserve team, joined Walsall Town in December 1896, going on to serve the Saddlers for three years during which time he made 73 League appearances. He didn't have the greatest of debuts for the Saddlers, lining up at full-back alongside goalie Tom Hawkins in a 5-0 defeat at Manchester City three weeks after moving to the club. But he missed only a handful of matches up to April 1899 when he was transferred to Nottingham Forest, being replaced at right-back by Bunch. Peers spent two years with Forest and in July 1901 moved to Burton Swifts. Described as a 'huge kicker', Ted Peers was 5ft 9ins tall and 12st 3lbs.

WILLIE PENMAN

Wing-half or inside-forward 130+5 apps. 6 goals.

Born: Wemyss, Fife, Scotland, 7 August 1939.

A highly skilful midfielder who began his career with Dundee in 1957, Willie Penman was transferred to Glasgow Rangers in 1959 and then to Newcastle United for £10,000 in April 1963. He scored 18 goals in 64 games for the Geordies before moving much further south to team up with Swindon Town for £9,800 in September 1966. For the Robins he added another 98 League games to his tally (18 goals) and was then bought by Walsall for £6,000 in August 1970. Penman spent three seasons at Fellows Park, up to May 1973 when he went across to Ireland to play for Dundalk, later returning to Scotland where he finally called it a day with over 300 senior appearances under his belt. In later years he appeared in several charity matches. He won a Second Division championship medal with Newcastle in 1965 and a League Cup winners' prize (as substitute) with Swindon Town in 1969 when the Robins registered a famous 3-1 Wembley victory over Arsenal.

DON PENN

Striker; 148+11 apps, 58 goals.

Born: Smethwick, 15 March 1960.

Don Penn was scoring goals for Newton Albion in the Warley Alliance and for Warley Borough when in 1977 he was recommended to Ron Jukes, then Walsall's chief scout. Penn was brought to Fellows Park and after some excellent displays for the Youth teams and Reserves was asked to sign as a professional in January 1978. He quickly slotted in to the Saddlers style of play and became a great favourite with the fans, scoring an average of a goal every three games before injury forced him into an early retirement in May 1983. In 1979-80, when Walsall returned to the Third Division at the first attempt, he top-scored with 26 League and Cup goals, and in 1981-82 he was again the club's leading scorer, this time with 15. He made only five appearances in 1982-83 but marked his final appearance for the club with a goal, a 1-1 draw at home to Bradford City in May that season. He later played for Harrisons FC

JEAN-FRANCOIS ('JEFF') PERON

Midfielder; 52 apps, 1 goal.

Born: France, 11 October 1965.

Experienced midfielder 'Jeff' Peron put in some outstanding performances during his one and only season with the Saddlers. A player who enjoys a role wide on the left, he joined the club from Lens on a free transfer with Roger Boli in August 1997 and left for First Division Portsmouth in August 1998 after a quite superb campaign. Prior to his association with Lens, Peron had also served with Caen and Racing Club Strasbourg. In 1998-99 he did well in a struggling Pompey side.

DAVID PREECE

Midfield; 131+4 apps, 11 goals.

Born: Bridgnorth, Shropshire, 28 May 1963.

A left-sided midfielder who turned professional with Walsall in July 1980 after serving a two-year apprenticeship, David Preece went on to appear in 111 League games for the Saddlers and helped them reach the League Cup semi-finals before being transferred to Luton Town for £150,000, in a deal which also involved striker Steve Elliott, in December 1984.

Preece became a vital member of the Hatters side and in 1988 helped them bring the League Cup to Kenilworth Road when Arsenal were beaten in the Final at Wembley. He continued to impress, winning three England 'B' caps, and when the 1991-92 season ended he had assembled a pretty useful record with Luton, 260 senior appearances and 12 goals, but his presence in the team failed to keep them in the Premier Division. In August 1995, Preece moved on a free transfer to Derby County but never settled at the Baseball Ground and following loan spells with Birmingham City and Sunderland, he joined Cambridge United in September 1996. In 1999, Preece had tallied almost 650 senior appearances in his career.

ANDY RAMMELL

Striker; 48 apps, 20 goals.

Born: Nuneaton, 10 February 1967.

After starting out with non-League Atherstone United in the mid 1980s, Andy Rammell suddenly found himself on 'cloud nine' when Manchester United boss Alex Ferguson swooped and took him to Old Trafford for £40,000 in September 1989.

Unfortunately Rammell failed to make the breakthrough with the Reds and in September 1990 was transferred to Barnsley for £100,000 without ever pulling on a United first-team shirt. At Oakwell he became an instant success and over the next six years scored 50 goals in 220 first-team appearances for the Tykes. In February 1996 he perhaps surprisingly left the Yorkshire club for Southend United and continued to score well for the Shrimpers (14 goals in 79 games) before moving to Walsall, signed to replace Roger Boli in July 1998 to become one of manager Ray Graydon first recruits. Rammell settled in quickly. The fans took to him at once and he certainly did the business, netting some very important goals to help the Saddlers win promotion to the First Division. A strong, forceful striker, he never shirks a tackle, enjoys a challenge and was certainly a key player in manager Graydon plans throughout 1998-99.

JACK REED

Wing-half; 141 apps, 6 goals.

Born: Walsall 1908. Deceased.

A 'powerhouse' wing-half who gave the

Saddlers excellent service during his five years with the club from February 1932 to May 1937, Jack Reed was signed from Dudley Town having earlier served with Walsall Miners' Welfare, Dudley White Star and Beaverbrook Swifts. He got into the League side almost immediately, lining up at inside-left before taking over at left-half towards the end of the 1931-32 season. Strong and forceful, he was a significant performer in Walsall's famous 1933 Cup win over Arsenal and indeed he was all set to join a First Division club until injury caught up with him in 1936, causing him to pull out of the big time prematurely. He later scouted for Walsall.

MARK REES

Outside-right; 216+58 apps, 42 goals.

Born: Smethwick, 13 October 1961.

An exceptionally quick and strong outside-right who enjoyed taking on defenders, Mark Rees came to the fore in season 1980-81 and was a firm favourite with the Fellows Park

faithful during his time with the Saddlers. Signed initially as an apprentice in 1977, he turned professional in August 1979 and he went on to serve Walsall in various positions, including full-back, right up until 1990, with a brief spell on loan with Rochdale in October 1986 (three League games). Among his best performances in a Walsall shirt was the one at Anfield in the 1984 League Cup semi-final when he raced at the Liverpool defence from deep in his own half, causing all sorts of problems. After leaving the Saddlers he had a stint with Shamrock Rovers and Aldershot, and in 1991-92 he was playing for Dover in the Beazer Homes Premier Division. In August, 1992, he joined forces with Shrewsbury Town, later signing for Solihull Borough in November. Mark Rees holds the club record of having come on most times as substitute.

GEORGE REID

Forward; 55 apps, 37 goals.

Born: Belfast, January 1896. Deceased.

George 'Paddy' Evans was a useful scorer and was leading marksman for the Saddlers in season 1921-22 with 24 goals in League and Cup competitions. But was soon transferred to Cardiff City, in December 1922, marking his debut for the Welsh club with a goal. In March 1923 he gained a full international cap for Ireland against Scotland, helping his team win 1-0 in Belfast. After only seven games for Cardiff (three goals) he moved to Fulham, but failed to impress at Craven Cottage, quickly switching north to Stockport County in July 1924 after only three games for the London club.

TONY RICHARDS

Centre-forward; 358 apps, 198 goals.

Born: Smethwick, 6 March 1934.

One of the greatest goalscorers ever to play for Walsall, Tony Richards was released by his first club, Birmingham City, in May 1952 after having signed as an amateur for Blues in October 1950 from Birmingham FA works team, Hopes, turning professional in December 1951. National Service was the rule of the day for 18-year-olds at that time and Richards spent two years in the Royal Artillery, playing a fair amount of services football and netting a double hat-trick in one game. After demobilisation he had trials with both Tottenham Hotspur and Wolves, but was not retained and was on the point of giving up soccer when he decided to write to Major Frank Buckley, then manager of Walsall, asking if he could have a trial at Fellows Park. He made a big impression and after a fine debut in the Reserves in September 1954, Tony Richards was given his Football League baptism against Bristol City only 12 days later and never looked back.

Richards went on to claim almost 200 goals in 358 matches for the Saddlers including a haul of 185 in 338 League games. He simply enjoyed scoring – it came naturally to him – and he was certainly the spearhead of the Saddlers' attack throughout the late 1950s, then helping the club win the Fourth Division title in 1960 and gain promotion to Division Two the following season. And in both seasons he was the club's top scorer, with 26 League and Cup goals in the first and 36 in the second. Not the most stylish of centre-forwards, he had the knack of being in the right place at the right time. He left

Walsall in March 1963, signing for Port Vale, where he stayed until June 1965, adding another 30 League goals to his tally in 63 appearances. In the mid-1960s he was registered with Nuneaton Borough.

TOM RICHARDS

Defender; 274 apps, 6 goals.

Born: Walsall, 1885. Deceased.

A hard-tackling, reliable 6ft 2in defender, who was perhaps unfortunate to be at his best when the Saddlers were out of the Football League, nevertheless, Tom Richards was a terrific club man. He joined Walsall from Wolves in August 1908, having earlier been with Pleck, and during the next eight years appeared in well over 250 games, up to April 1916 when football – as far as the Saddlers were concerned – eventually came to an end due to World War One. Thereafter Tom spent a couple of seasons with Dudley Town, retiring in 1918.

BILL RICHMOND

Wing-half; 100 apps.

Born: Kirkcaldy, Fife, February 1908. Deceased.

Bill Richmond was with the Saddlers from August 1935 to May 1938, amassing exactly 100 senior appearances (89 in the League). Initially an engineer in a Scottish shipyard, he played for Raith Rovers for quite some time before joining Bournemouth in August 1932. He made only 27 League appearances during his three seasons at Dean Court before transferring to Walsall where he quickly fitted into the middle line, partnering Morgan and Bradford. Able to fill either the right-half or left-half berths, Richmond possessed a strong tackle and was excellent in the air He suffered a knee injury playing against Exeter City in November 1937 which caused him some concern, and after that he managed only a handful of games before leaving the club in May 1938 and returning to Scotland where he assisted St Bernard's FC and Valentine Thistle before hanging up his boots in 1942.

STUART RIMMER

Striker; 103+3 apps, 44 goals.

Born: Southport, 20 October 1964.

Stuart Rimmer was an out-and-out striker who won three England Youth caps whilst with his first club Everton, whom he joined as an apprentice in 1980, turning profession-

al at Goodison Park in October 1982. He made only three League appearances for the Merseysiders before transferring to Chester City for £10,000 in January 1985. At Sealand Road he became an instant success, and went on to register 76 goals in 139 League and Cup games before joining Watford in March 1988 for £205,000. Rimmer did not settle at Vicarage Road despite scoring 12 goals in 12 matches and left there for Notts County in November 1988, quickly switching to Walsall in for £150,000 in February 1989 after netting twice in nine outings for the Magpies.

He settled at Fellows Park and proceeded to excite the fans with his all-action style. He had scored 43 goals in 106 appearances for the Saddlers when, in March 1991, he was surprisingly sold to Barnsley for another £150,000 fee – and it was perhaps more of surprise to the diehard Saddlers supporters when he returned to Chester City for £110,000 in August 1991, having failed to impress at Oakwell. Rimmer had loan spells with Rochdale and Preston North End and was still scoring goals in 1999 and at the same time had also topped the 600 appearance mark in senior competitions having made his debut for Everton back in 1981-82.

DAVE ('SUGAR') ROBINSON

Defender; 179+2 apps, 3 goals.

Born: Bartley Green, Birmingham, 14 July 1948.

Dave 'Sugar' Robinson was an England Schools trialist and keen West Brom fan as a youngster yet his first club was Birmingham

City, who he joined as an apprentice in June 1964, signing as a full-time professional on his 18th birthday two years later. He started off at St Andrew's as an inside-forward, striking up a fine partnership with Phil Summerill in the Blues' Youth team. But after he had been moved back into defence he quickly established himself in the Reserves and was given his League debut against Aston Villa in September 1968. He never looked back and his form prompted Blues manager, Stan Cullis, to say: "He's saved us £80,000."Robinson made 127 appearances for Blues (four goals) before joining Walsall in February 1973. He spent over five and a half years at Fellows Park – up to September 1978 when he switched to Tamworth – and he was certainly an impressive performer in the Saddlers' defence. He became manager of Oldbury Town in 1980.

GEORGE ROBSON

Forward; 83 apps, 27 goals.

Born: County Durham, 1901. Deceased.

A native of the North-East, George Robson was a prolific scorer with New Delaval FC and in one season alone netted over 50 goals, including a seven and a five in successive matches. Fast and adept at turning quickly on his marker, he had an excellent spell with Walsall who secured his services from the Delaval club in December 1926, following an injury to Sarvis. He got into his stride immediately and ended that season with nine goals to his name from 22 games. With the introduction of Moses Lane to the attack for the 1927-28 campaign, Robson's game developed even more and he and Lane became two of the best marksmen outside the First Division, netting 47 goals between them in League matches. Injury then forced Robson to miss the first half of the 1928-29 season and when he returned to action, Lane had left, to be replaced by Attwood. Robson managed nine more goals that term, but his firepower was missing and after struggling early on in 1929-30 (when he lined up at outside-right) he was transferred to Coventry City. He managed only four goals during a brief stay at Highfield Road and in 1931 found his way nearer home, joining forces with Ashington. He retired in 1935.

RON RUSSON

Half-back; 145 apps, 1 goal.

Born: Wednesbury, 10 December 1928. Died: 1995.

A former Wolverhampton Wanderers junior, Ron Russon joined Walsall as a professional in May 1948, from Hednesford Town, and he went on to give the Saddlers great service right up until May 1955. In those seven years, he amassed almost 150 senior appearances and was always a reliable, efficient performer in the heart of the back division. He took over the number-five shirt in March 1954 following an elbow injury to Jack Bridgett, having himself suffered a broken ankle against Brighton 12 months earlier.

STUART RYDER

Defender; 107+17 apps, 5 goals.

Born: Sutton Coldfield, 6 November 1973.

After suffering serious injury problems dur-

ing the 1995-96 and 1996-97 campaigns (he broke his leg in a game against Carlisle United Reserves in a tackle with Steve Hayward) Stuart Ryder re-established himself in the Walsall defence during 1997-98 and passed the personal milestone of 100 League outings for the club with some solid and heart-warming performances. Capped by England as a youth team player, he went on to gain an under-21 cap as a cool, calm and totally reliable central defender. He was released by the club in the summer of 1998 following the arrival of manager Ray Graydon.

KEN SATCHWELL

Utility forward; 60+3 apps, 8 goals.

Born: Birmingham, 17 January 1940.

Former Paget Road School player and Birmingham Works FA star Ken Satchwell

was an amateur with Aston Villa (he scored 90 goals in two seasons for their juniors), Nottingham Forest and Wolves before joining Coventry City in 1957, turning professional at Highfield Road in September 1958. He made his League debut for the Sky Blues after only one reserve game and went on to amass 75 appearances in the senior competitions (24 goals scored) before moving to Nuneaton Borough in 1963 for £2,000. Walsall brought him back into League football on 9 January 1965, paying £1,200 for his services and he went on to make over 60 appearances for the Saddlers, then drifting in the Third Division, before he moved back into non-League football in 1967.

JOHN SAUNDERS

Defender; 102+6 apps, 2 goals.

Born: Newport, Wales, 2 October 1950.

John Saunders was another former Birmingham City youngster who was released from St Andrew's before being asked to sign as a professional. Although disappointed at the time, especially having won Welsh Schoolboy honours, he soon perked up when, in August 1969, he was signed on a full-time basis by Newport County. He went on to make 27 League appearances for County before transferring to Leeds United in July 1971, but after 15 months and no games he decided to leave Elland Road for Walsall in October 1972. There followed a good spell with the Saddlers and his presence in the defence was crucial in so many matches during the mid-1970s, never more so than when he helped them to famous FA Cup victories over Manchester United and Newcastle United in 1974-75. Sadly, a bad injury caused Saunders to call it a day prematurely in November 1975 at the age of only 25.

JOHN SAVAGE

Goalkeeper; 52 apps.

Born: Bromley, Kent, 14 December 1929.

John Savage, who stood 6ft 4ins, could release a huge kick out of his hands and once sent the ball, first bounce, over the crossbar

at the opposite end of the field. After service in the RAF he began his League career with four games with Hull City (from September 1950). In March 1952 he joined Halifax Town and 57 appearances (and, remarkably, one goal) later he was transferred to Manchester City for £4,000 in November 1953, as cover for the legendary Bert Trautmann. His outings were limited at Maine Road (30 games in all, one being at West Brom in 1957 when he let in nine goals) and in January 1958 he was secured by Walsall for £1,000 as a replacement for Gordon Chilvers.

Within a few weeks he was involved in a controversial sending-off incident at Swindon when Walsall went on to win 3-2 after Tony Richards had taken over between the posts and saved a penalty. Savage, who represented the Third Division South against the Third Division North in the annual challenge match shortly after moving to the Saddlers, stayed at Fellows Park until being released in May 1959 having added 51 more League games to his tally. He had a good spell with Wigan Athletic who were then members of the Lancashire Combination.

DAVE SERELLA

Defender; 302+2 apps, 13 goals.

Born; Kings Lynn, 24 September 1952.

A strong, reliable defender who started his career with Nottingham Forest, Dave Serella served a two-year apprenticeship at the City Ground before turning professional there in August 1970. He made 76 appearances for Forest before transferring to Walsall in November 1974. Serella had eight excellent years with the Saddlers, making 267 League appearances before leaving Fellows Park for Blackpool in August 1982. During his time with the Saddlers he saw them relegated in 1978-79 and promoted again the following season. He pulled out of top-class football in 1984 after having chalked up an impressive record of 370 League appearances (15 goals).

CRAIG SHAKESPEARE

Midfield; 347+8 apps, 60 goals.

Born: Great Barr, Birmingham, 26 October 1963.

A keen footballer since he was eight years of age, Craig Shakespeare represented Aston and Birmingham Boys before joining Walsall as an apprentice in 1979, turning professional at Fellows Park in October 1981. He spent seven excellent seasons with the Saddlers, netting 60 goals in more than 350 competitive matches, helping them win promotion to the Second Division and also reach the semi-finals of the League Cup. In July 1988 he was transferred to Sheffield Wednesday but never settled at Hillsborough and in February 1990 moved to The Hawthorns, signing for West Bromwich Albion in a £265,000 deal. He immediately slotted into Albion's midfield and was a consistent performer for the Baggies, taking his career appearance tally to past the 500 mark. A stylish footballer, Shakespeare possessed a strong shot, was a useful exponent of free-kick situations and an ace penalty taker. He skippered West Bromwich Albion in 1991-92 and 1992-93 before leaving The Hawthorns in June 1997 for Grimsby Town in a £100,000 deal. Shakespeare later played for

Scunthorpe United and in 1998-99 was player-assistant manager of Telford United. In his overall senior career he scored 86 goals in 634 appearances.

JOHN SHARPLES

Full-back; 132 apps, 1 goal.

Born: Heath Town, Wolverhampton, 8 August 1934.

John Sharples was an amateur with Walsall in 1951 but was allowed to drift away from Fellows Park to team up with Aston Villa, for whom he signed professional forms in October 1955. He made 13 League appearances for Villa, mainly as deputy to Peter Aldis, but in May 1959 he was placed on the transfer list and subsequently moved back to Walsall on 10 August that year. A strongly-built footballer with good judgement, Sharples could play at centre-half as well as full-back, and he chalked up over 130 senior appearances for the Saddlers before entering the non-League scene in 1964 with Darlaston. In Walsall's two successive promotion seasons he managed only 12 appearances in 1959-60, his first season with the club, but when the Saddlers went up to Division Two the following campaign he appeared in 34 League games.

CHARLIE ('SHINER') SHAW

Right-half/forward; 86 apps, 30 goals.

Born: Walsall, January 1866. Died: Walsall, May 1942.

'Shiner' Shaw was a great footballer who thoroughly enjoyed the rough and tumble of the game during the late 19th century. He loved to mix it with the biggest and bravest players and was never out of his depth. After leaving school, he started his career with Walsall Town in 1885 and played in many of the needle matches against Walsall Swifts over the next three seasons. He played in both the last Walsall Town v Swifts clash in March 1888 and in the first encounter for the newly-formed Walsall Town Swifts against Aston Villa later that same month. He continued to serve the Town Swifts in the Midland Combination in 1888-89 and in the Football Alliance from 1889 to 1892, and then he starred in the early Football League games in Division Two in 1892-93. Playing mainly up front, Shaw was small but often outjumped his bigger opponents to head some smart goals. He represented both the Staffordshire County FA and the Birmingham Association in 1888 and 1889. A harnessmaker by trade, he was employed first by Joe Noake, a Walsall Town FC official, and later by Lickies. He acquired the nickname Shiner from the fine gloss that he put on his harness. He continued to live in Walsall and attended matches at Fellows Park right up until his death during World War Two.

GARY SHELTON

Midfield; 14+15 apps, 1 goal.

Born: Carlton, Notts, 21 March 1958.

A neat footballer and a tireless worker who passed the milestone of 500 senior appearances as a professional during 1991-92, Gary Shelton began his long career with Walsall as an apprentice in June 1974 after having rep-

resented Nottingham & District Schools and Nottingham Boys. He turned professional at Fellows Park in March 1975, making his debut at the age of 18 in April 1976 as a substitute in the last match of the season at Southend. Shelton managed only a handful of games for Walsall before Aston Villa snapped him up for £80,000 in January 1978.

However, he never established himself at Villa and after scoring eight goals in 27 games, and following a loan spell with Notts County (March-April 1980, eight League outings) he was sold to Sheffield Wednesday for £50,000 in April 1982. Five years – and 242 games and 24 goals later – after skippering the Owls to the Second Division title in 1985, he switched to Oxford United for £150,000 in July 1987. He made 79 appearances (three goals) for Oxford and in August 1989 joined Bristol City in a player-exchange deal involving Steve McClaren. Shelton was a key figure in City's promotion winning side from Division Three in 1991 and he also had a good 1991-92 campaign. He left Ashton Gate for Chester City in July 1994 (after a loan spell with Rochdale). In 1998-99, Shelton reached the milestone of 650 senior appearances and 75 goals. He gained one England Under-21 cap as an over-age player and captained the side against Finland in 1985. He was Wednesday's Player of the Year in 1984-85.

JACK SHELTON

Full-back; 118 apps, 7 goals.

Born: Wollaston, Stourbridge, 9 November 1912.

Jack Shelton joined Walsall in 1934 having been an amateur with Wolverhampton Wanderers for the previous two and a half years after going to Molineux from Chase Terrace FC. He appeared fleetingly in the forward line and at half-back in his first two seasons at Fellows Park before settling at full-back to such good effect that after getting into the side in the fourth match of 1936-37 he remained there for the rest of that season and all of the next, making 92 consecutive League and Cup appearances before injury caused him to miss the whole of the last pre-war season. He played in almost 200 games for the Saddlers during World War Two and appeared in the FA Cup in the transitional season of 1945-46. After three appearances in the first proper post-war season of 1946-47, by which time he was in his 30s having lost seven League seasons to the war, his Walsall days came to an end and he later worked for many years behind the scenes at Oxford United. He was the son of Jack Shelton, the former Wolves and Port Vale forward who gained an FA Cup winners' medal in 1908 when Wolves beat Newcastle United.

BILL SHEPPARD

Inside-forward; 82 apps, 29 goals.

Born: Ferryhill, County Durham, 1907. Deceased.

After attending Stockton Grammar School, Bill Sheppard joined Ferryhill Athletic for whom he scored over 60 goals in two seasons before doing even better with Chilton Colliery FC. He then scored well for Crook Town before becoming a professional with Liverpool in December 1925. From Anfield he switched to Watford in July 1927 and three years later he went to QPR, in June 1930. Sheppard was transferred to Coventry City in July 1931 and after scoring seven goals in 21 games for them he moved to Walsall in December 1932. A few weeks later he was a goalscoring hero in the Saddlers' historic 2-0 FA Cup win over Arsenal. After a good spell with the Saddlers, Sheppard, who was a regular penalty-taker, signed for Chester where he wound down an eventful career.

BOBBY SHINTON

Striker; 85+1 apps, 23 goals.

Born: West Bromwich, 6 January 1952.

Bobby Shinton had a fine career in the Football League, finishing up with 99 goals in 392 games for Walsall, Cambridge United, Wrexham, Manchester City, Newcastle United and Millwall. He was spotted by the Saddlers scoring for Lye Town and signed as a professional at Fellows Park in February 1972. Shinton made his debut against Swansea the following month and marked it with a goal; he scored two more the following week, against Bradford City.

In March 1974 he joined Cambridge, for £22,000, and went on to net 25 goals in 99 League appearances for that club before going to Wrexham in July 1976. For the Welsh outfit he claimed 37 goals in his 128 League outings and helped them win the Third Division championship and the Welsh

Cup in 1978 and finish as runners-up in the latter the following season. Then, perhaps surprisingly, he was transferred for £300,000 to Maine Road (2 June 1979) but he had no success with Manchester City and left on 6 March 1980 after only six outings following a loan spell with Millwall (February 1980 – three goals in five games). There followed a 15-month stay with Newcastle United up to March 1982, during which he registered ten goals in 42 League games. He rounded off his career back at The Den, when he hit another four goals in 34 League appearances for Millwall. He pulled out of competitive football in 1982 but still continued to play regularly in charity matches.

TERRY SIMPSON

Wing-half; 58+1 apps, 6 goals.
Born: Southampton, 8 October 1938.
A member of the highly-rated Southampton Boys side in 1953-54, Terry Simpson went to The Dell in February 1955 and after producing some excellent performances for the 'A' team was taken on as a full-time professional in June 1957. He made 22 League appearances for the Saints before transferring to Peterborough United in June 1962, being signed by manager Jimmy Hagan. In June 1963, Hagan, who in the interim period had left London Road for The Hawthorns, then secured Simpson's transfer to West Bromwich Albion with striker Keith Smith joining Posh as part of the deal. Simpson went on to play in 77 games for the Baggies and on 15 March 1967 was bought by Walsall for £2,000. In his only full season at Fellows Park, Walsall finished seventh in the Third Division and he also played in the FA Cup fourth-round tie against Liverpool.

In July 1968 he moved to Gillingham, becoming player-coach at the Priestfield Stadium in 1969. He retired in the summer of 1971 following a broken leg mishap. A durable wing-half who also did a fine job at right-back, Terry Simpson accumulated a total of 226 League appearances for his five clubs. He is now living and working in Southampton.

LEE SINNOTT

Defender; 46 apps, 2 goals.
Born: Pelsall, Walsall, 12 July 1965.
The Saddlers sold Lee Sinnott to Watford for £100,000 in September 1983, having secured his registration for nothing when

taking him on from Rushall Olympic in November 1981. He made his Saddlers debut in March 1982. A compact footballer, able to play at full-back, centre-half or as a sweeper, Sinnott blossomed at Vicarage Road. He went on to gain England Under-21 honours, to add to his Youth caps won earlier, and in 1984 lined up for Watford against Everton in the FA Cup Final. He made 95 senior appearances for the Hornets (two goals) before transferring to Bradford City for £130,000 in July 1987. After four good seasons at Valley Parade during which time he made 213 senior appearances, he went back into the First Division when he signed for Crystal Palace in the summer of 1991 for a fee of £300,000.
From Selhurst Park, he moved to Bradford City in December 1993. Twelve months later he joined Huddersfield Town and in July 1997 he signed for Oldham Athletic, having a loan spell back at Bradford City and a trial with Scunthorpe United in 1998.

JOHN SISSONS

Defender; 105+6 apps, 1 goal.
Born: Chester-le-Street, County Durham, 20 May 1934.
John Sissons moved to Birmingham as a youngster via Sheffield where he had played for Kiveton Boys FC. He assisted Erdington Juniors and Country Girl FC before joining Birmingham City as a professional on 20 June 1954 following his demob from the Army. Sissons played in 106 games for the Blues up to December 1961 when he switched to Peterborough United, transferring to Walsall on 20 November 1964. He retired in 1968 after making over 250 League appearances for his three clubs (exactly of them 100 for the Saddlers). He could play at full-back position, at wing-half or in the pivotal berth.

BILLY SKIDMORE

Defender; 107 apps, 11 goals.
Born: Barnsley, 15 March 1925.
Billy Skidmore had hoped to make the grade with Wolverhampton Wanderers, the club he first played for during the wartime season of 1942-43, but he was never taken on full-time at Molineux, being released without breaking into the League side. He subsequently joined Walsall as a professional in May 1946, and quickly established himself in the side at Fellows Park, where he stayed for five years, making over 100 senior appearances. One of the most powerful strikers of a ball ever seen at Fellows Park, Billy was strong in all aspects of defence and was a penalty king. He later played non-League football back in his native Yorkshire.

PETER SKIPPER

Defender; 99 apps, 3 goals.

Born: Hull, 11 April 1958.

Peter Skipper started his League career in his native city, joining the Tigers from Schultz Youth Club in 1977 and turning professional in January 1979. He made his debut for Hull in 1978-79 but after a loan spell with Scunthorpe United (February 1980) he signed for Darlington (May 1980). He returned to Boothferry Park for £10,000 in August 1982 after making 98 appearances for the Quakers. In his second spell with the Tigers he did tremendously well, helping them win promotion to Division Two in 1985. He added a further 115 League and Cup appearances to his tally with Hull (seven goals scored), and then had a brief spell with Oldham Athletic (1988-89) before joining Walsall in July 1989. In his first season with the Saddlers, however. they were relegated to Division Four in 1989-90 and in his second they struggled to finish 16th in the bottom division.

In September 1991 he signed as a non-contract player for Wrexham and after two appearances for them went to Wigan Athletic on the same basis. After 18 appearances for Wigan he joined Stafford Rangers of the GM Vauxhall Conference.

DAVID SLOAN

Winger; 46+6 apps, 3 goals.

Born: Lisburn, Ireland, 28 October 1941.

A former shipyard worker, David Sloan won Northern Ireland international honours at three different levels: Amateur, Under-23 and full (two caps). He played his early football with Bangor in the Irish League before moving into the Football League with Scunthorpe United as a professional in November 1963. He scored 42 goals in 136 League games for the Iron before going on to claim another 34 goals in exactly 200 League and Cup outings for Oxford United, between February 1968 up to July 1973, when he transferred to Walsall. He left Fellows Park in May 1975 after making over 50 appearances for the Saddlers. Sloan was the first player from Oxford United to be selected for a full international match and he also helped Oxford win the Third Division title in 1967-68. When he left Scunthorpe for the Manor Ground he was succeeded by Kevin Keegan.

GEORGE SMITH

Full-back; 94 apps, 2 goals.

Born: Kent , June 1901. Deceased.

George Smith was a gutsy footballer who gave the Saddlers three years excellent service during the mid-1920s, making almost 100 senior appearances. He was signed in the summer of 1924 from Gillingham, and he lined up in Walsall's first team at the start of 1924-25 season, partnering Wally Webster at full-back. He played with a lot of consistency and confidence, and missed only two games up to May 1926, making 84 out of a possible 86 appearances. Injury then caused him to sit out most of 1926-27, however, and following the arrival of the Welsh international Edward Parry and the signing of Billy Adams from West Bromwich Albion, both of them adequate full-backs, George Smith was allowed to leave the Saddlers for Torquay United in June 1927. He later played for Exmouth Town and Newton Abbot Spurs, retiring in 1932.

TREVOR SMITH

Centre-half; 13 apps.

Born: Brierley Hill, 13 April 1936.

Trevor Smith was a skinny lad when he played alongside Duncan Edwards for Brierley Hill and Sedgley Schoolboys, but he developed into a muscular centre-half who reached international class. After leaving Quarry Bank Secondary Modern School, Smith joined Birmingham City as an amateur in July 1951 and turned professional in April 1953. He appeared in 430 games for the Blues (three goals scored) before transferring to Walsall for £18,000 in October 1964. Whilst at St Andrew's, he helped Blues' Under-18 team win the Switzerland Youth Tournament in 1952, he gained a Second Division championship medal in 1954, an FA. Cup runners-up medal in 1956, a Fairs Cup loser's prize in 1960 and a League Cup winners' tankard in 1963. He also won two full England caps, two at 'B' team level, 15 for

the Under-23's, represented the Football League twice and collected Youth honours as well to go with his England Schoolboy caps.

Alas, he managed only 13 first-team appearances for the Saddlers before breaking down with injury (he later suffered from osteo-arthritis) and there were rumours that Blues had 'cheated' the Saddlers in allowing an injured player to join their ranks. Smith was forced to retire in February 1966 and became a permit player in the Lichfield Sunday League. He was manager of Mile Oak Rovers in 1970-71 and later became a licensee in Tamworth. He then managed a Thresher's wine store in the Bull Ring Centre, Birmingham, before moving in the same line to Dagenham, Essex.

DEREK STATHAM

Left-back; 54+4 apps.

Born: Whitmore Reans, Wolverhampton, 24 March 1959.

Derek Statham was one of the finest full-backs in the Football League during the the period 1978-1982 and if it had not been for Kenny Sansom then he would surely have been England's permanent number 3. As it was Statham had to play second fiddle to the Arsenal man and won only three full caps (against Wales and two against Australia) to show for his efforts. He joined West Brom as a 16-year-old and turned professional at The Hawthorns in April 1976. He made a scoring debut against Stoke City (a future club) eight months later and from that day on he went from strength to strength, making well over 300 senior appearances for the Baggies. After a proposed £250,000 move to Liverpool had fallen through on medical grounds in 1986, he finally left The Hawthorns for Southampton in a £200,000 deal in 1987 and two years later switched to Stoke City for £75,000 plus another £25,000 after he had made 40

appearances for the Potters. He spent two seasons with Stoke and joined Walsall on a free transfer in August 1991. He quit League football in 1993 and joined Telford United, retiring in 1996. As well as his full appearances for England, Statham gained caps at Youth, Under-21 (6) and 'B' team levels and he helped Albion win the FA Youth Cup in 1976 and qualify for the UEFA Cup in 1978, 1979 and 1981.

KEVIN SUMMERFIELD

Forward/midfield; 48+14 apps, 19 goals.

Born: Walsall, 7 January 1959.

A former pupil at Alma Street and Joseph Leckie Schools in Walsall, Kevin Summerfield played for Walsall Town Boys and then joined West Bromwich Albion as an apprentice in July 1975. He helped the Baggies win the FA Youth Cup, against Wolves, in April 1976 and signed professional forms at The Hawthorns the same month. He was a reserve forward with Albion, scoring four goals in 11 games before transferring to Birmingham City in May 1982. Thereafter he had a loan spell with Walsall (December 1982) before joining the Saddlers on a permanent basis in February 1983 – this after he had been recalled to St Andrew's to score the goal which knocked Walsall out of that season's FA Cup. On the other side of the coin he scored for the Saddlers in the League Cup semi-final first leg at Anfield when he came on as a sub.

In May 1984 he moved to Cardiff City, switched to Plymouth Argyle in December 1984 and after helping the Pilgrims win promotion to Division Two in 1986 he went on loan to Exeter City, coming nearer home to sign for Shrewsbury Town in October 1990, going on to captain the Gay Meadow club. He made over 200 appearances in his seven seasons with Shrewsbury, helping them win the Third Division title in 1994. In 1997 he was appointed the Shrews' coach and took up a similar job with Plymouth Argyle in 1998.

GERRY SUMMERS

Wing-half; 48+3 apps, 2 goals.

Born: Small Heath, Birmingham, 4 October 1933.

Gerry Summers was educated at Coventry Road and Hay Mills Schools, joined Erdington Albion in 1948 and moved as an amateur to West Brom in April 1950, turning professional at The Hawthorns in August 1951. He stayed with the Baggies until May 1957, mainly as reserve to the elegant Ray Barlow, making only 25 appearances. Sheffield United signed him for £3,500 and he went on to play in 260 League matches for the Blades, helping them reach the FA Cup semi-finals and win promotion from the Second Division in 1961. In the summer of 1962 he toured the Far East with an FA party, his only representative honour. In April 1964 he was transferred to Hull City for £14,000, and he found his way to Fellows Park in October 1965, when Walsall boss Ray Shaw paid £10,000 for his signature.

Summers became a part-time player-coach with the Saddlers in February 1967 and after retiring as a player, in August that year, he went to Wolves in the same capacity under manager Ronnie Allen, the former England centre-forward, later to manage Walsall; Allen had been a playing colleague at The Hawthorns in the 1950s. In July 1969, Summers was appointed manager of Oxford United, a position he held until October 1975 when he took over at Gillingham, holding that post until May 1981. A month later he became a scout with Southampton and returned to West Brom as coach-scout in October 1981, again under Allen. In October 1982 he was given a coaching job at Filbert Street, staying with Leicester City for over four years, up to December 1986 when he became chief scout and Youth-team manager at Derby County.

JACK TAGGART

Defender; 123 apps. one goal

Born: Belfast, 3 February 1872. Died: 12th May 1927.

Jack Taggart was an Irish international, capped against Wales in 1898-99. He played for West Bromwich Albion in the 1895 FA Cup Final before joining Walsall for a small fee in 1896. He always performed methodically, attempting to keep the ball on the ground rather than hoof it aimlessly into space. Perhaps his sole blemish was his headwork. He was educated at Dundonald and Belmont Schools in Belfast, and starred for Belfast Distillery and Middlesbrough before joining Albion in March 1893. He went on to play in almost 100 games for the Baggies before teaming up with the Saddlers. His career with them were all League seasons – his first saw them just returned after a season in the Midland League and at the end of his last Walsall once more failed to gain re-election in 1901. After a couple of years in local non-League football he was forced to retire through ill-health in April 1903.

LES TALBOT

Inside-forward; 23 apps, 5 goals.

Born: Hednesford, 3 August 1910.

Brother of Alex, the former Aston Villa centre-half, Les Talbot played non League football for Hednesford before joining Blackburn Rovers in August 1930. He stayed at Ewood Park for six seasons but found it hard going to gain a regular place in the side until 1932. Thereafter he did reasonably well and eventually made 86 senior appearances for Rovers (21 goals scored) before transferring to Cardiff City (in a double-deal with Albert Pinxton) in August 1936. He was popular with the Ninian Park fans and had three enjoyable seasons with the Welsh club, making 104 appearances and netting another 21 goals.

In June 1939 he joined Walsall, but the war disrupted his career at Fellows Park and he played in only three League games for the Saddlers early in that ill-fated 1939-40 season. Throughout the hostilities, Les Talbot guested regularly for Bath City and he rejoined Walsall as a professional in 1945, helping the Saddlers reach the League South Cup Final against Bournemouth. He stayed another two years at Fellows Park, retiring from League football in August 1947 at the age of 37. Talbot maintained a keen interest in the game and in the 1970s was coaching in Holland. One pen-picture described him as being 'a big, strong constructive inside-forward with tremendous shot. He could slow a game down superbly and had splendid passing skills. He also had a distinctive knock-kneed crouching run and his broad, beaming smile brightened up many a dark, wet winter's day.'

TED TARRANT

Wing-half; 109 apps, 13 goals.

Born: Stainforth, nr Doncaster, 12 February 1932.

After nine years and 30 League games for Hull City – he initially signed for the Tigers as a 14-year-old in 1944, becoming a registered amateur in July 1946, turning professional in February 1949) – Ted Tarrant was bought by his former boss, Major Frank Buckley, for Walsall on 4 December 1953. A tough-tackling left-half, he went on to make over 100 senior appearances for the Saddlers before pulling out of League football to join Cambridge City in July 1958. Plagued by injuries throughout his career, he suffered a double fracture of the ankle in 1947 and underwent two cartilage operations in 1955-56 as well as damaging a knee, elbow and shoulder. His playing days ended his June 1960, although his last appearance in Walsall's League team came three years earlier, in April 1957. His brother, Brian, played for Leeds and Mansfield.

BRIAN TAYLOR

Full-back; 234+13 apps, 29 goals.

Born: Gateshead, 2 July 1949.

Brian Taylor was a versatile footballer able to occupy a variety of positions including full-back, wing-half and winger. He emerged with Durham City before turning professional with Coventry City in February 1968 but failed to break into the first team at Highfield Road and in May 1971 was transferred to Walsall. Taylor spent six excellent seasons at Fellows Park during which time he amassed almost 250 League and Cup appearances (29 goals scored) before moving to Plymouth Argyle in October 1977. Twelve months later, after he had hit seven goals in 39 games for the Pilgrims, Taylor teamed up with Preston North End and after a loan spell with Wigan Athletic (March-April 1981) he called it a day, pulling out of League competition in May 1982 with over 400 senior appearances. His time at Walsall saw the Saddlers a moderate Third Division side although there was the famous FA Cup run in 1974-75.

BRIAN TAYLOR

Outside-left; 77 apps, 17 goals.

Born: Walsall, 24 March 1937. Died: 10 December 1993.

On leaving school in July 1952, Brian Taylor signed amateur forms for Walsall and became a full-time professional at Fellows Park in September 1954. Four years later he was transferred to Birmingham City for

£10,000 plus Jimmy Cochrane, and went on to make 66 first-team appearances for Blues. A sprightly winger, with a good turn of pace and strong shot, his career suffered a major set-back at St Andrew's when he suffered a fractured leg while playing against Union St Gilloise in the Inter-Cities Fairs Cup semi-final. After returning to action it seemed as if he had lost quite a bit of his speed and he left Blues for Rotherham United in October 1961. He switched to Shrewsbury Town in August 1963, had two seasons with Port Vale (August 1965 to June 1967), spent a year with Barnsley (to July 1968) and rounded off his career by playing for Kidderminster Harriers (to 1970) and for Bromsgrove Rovers (in season 1970-71). In all, Brian Taylor scored 43 goals in a total of 316 League games for his six major clubs.

COLIN TAYLOR

Outside-left; 491+11 apps, 189 goals.

Born: Stourbridge, 24 August 1940.

Ginger-haired Colin Taylor was a great character, famous for his 'cannonball' shooting and who, in his three spells with club (1958-63; 1964-68 and 1969-73) scored some spectacular goals. In 1960-61 he netted 33 from the left wing, a feat matched only by

Arsenal's Cliff Bastin. Taylor first joined the Saddlers on 5 February 1958 after only a handful of Birmingham League games for Stourbridge. He made his reserve-team debut against Worcester City and scored his first goal for Walsall in a reserve game against his former club, Stourbridge, a few weeks later. Taylor entered League football on 28 August 1958, against Millwall, and the fans soon took to him. For the next five years he hardly missed a game, scoring 21 times in Walsall's promotion season of 1959-60 and 33 times when they went up again the following term. In May 1963 he moved to Newcastle United for a fee of £20,000 but came back to Fellows Park in October 1964 for half that amount. His next move took him to Crystal Palace in May 1968 but he returned again to Walsall in November 1969 and wound down his career with a good spell in the forward line for Kidderminster Harriers from August 1973 to 1975 before becoming a painter and decorator in the Midlands. Only Nick Atthey, Colin Taylor and Colin Harrison have appeared in more than 500 competitive games for Walsall.

BILLY TENNANT

Goalkeeper; 112 apps.

Born: Wolverhampton, 12 July 1865. Died: Hull, 6 December 1927.

The moustachio'd Billy Tennant, who nearly always kept goal wearing a short knotted necktie, started off playing rugby at school and occasionally for Moseley, but in 1881 he turned to soccer, keeping goal for Willenhall Pickwick. Tennant later joined Hartshill Unity who eventually sold him to Wolverhampton Wanderers for a £30 fee in January 1896. He quickly made the number-one position his own at Molineux and starred in that year's FA Cup Final defeat by Sheffield Wednesday. He was an ever-present in the Wolves side in 1896-97 but was surprisingly transferred to Walsall for £75 in June 1897, a move which certainly upset diehard Wolves supporters. After making exactly 100 League appearances for the Saddlers, he signed for Grimsby Town in May 1901, but made only 13 appearances for the Mariners before announcing his retirement. He became reserve-team manager at Blundell Park in September 1903 and later ran a fish business in Hull.

KEN TEWKESBURY

Goalkeeper; 84 apps.

Born: Brighton, 10 April 1909. Died: 20 November 1970.

A quiet, bespectacled goalkeeper who won six Amateur caps for England, Ken Tewkesbury attended Birmingham University and signed for Birmingham in October 1929 while studying for a degree which he eventually obtained. After only five games for Blues, Tewkesbury had the first of two spells with Aston Villa and then played for Notts County in 1932 before eventually turning professional at Villa Park in January 1933. Bradford Park Avenue was his next club in July 1935 and he arrived at Walsall in May 1936. The Saddlers were a struggling Third Division South team during his time at Fellows Park and he was an automatic choice only in his last season, 1938-39, when Walsall also reached the fifth round of the FA Cup. Tewkesbury retired in August 1939 and after the war had a job in the Jewellery Quarter in Hockley, Birmingham.

BEN TIMMINS

Full-back; 126 apps.

Born: West Bromwich, August 1898. Died: Birmingham 13 August 1965.

Benniah Timmins played in over 100 League games for the Saddlers before being transferred to neighbouring Wolverhampton Wanderers (with Bowen) in March 1924 for a combined fee of £130. He was a fearsome tackler who could clear his lines with a massive kick. He enjoyed a teenage career playing in West Bromwich for Beeches Road Methodists and Dartmouth Victoria before teaming up with the Saddlers in 1920, when they played in the Birmingham League. When they finished eighth in Division Three North in 1921-22 he missed only one game and in 1922-23, when the Saddlers finished third, five points behind promoted Nelson, he again appeared in all but one League game. Timmins could play equally as well in either the right or left- back positions. He made only 11 appearances for Wolves, leaving Molineux in the summer of 1926 to join non-League Kidderminster, later assisting both Bridgnorth and Aveley.

RAY TRAIN

Midfield; 93+11 apps, 12 goals.

Born: Nuneaton, 10 February 1951.

Ray Train enjoyed over 20 years in the game. He started his career at Fellows Park as an apprentice in June 1966, turned professional in November 1968 and played his last game at competitive level in 1987 having served Walsall, Carlisle United (£15,000, December 1971), Sunderland (£80,000, March 1976), Bolton Wanderers (£80,000, March 1977), Watford (£50,000, November 1978), Oxford United (for £10,000, March 1982), Bournemouth (on loan November-December 1983), Northampton Town (free, March 1984), Tranmere Rovers (free, August 1985) and Walsall again, also on a free transfer, from August 1986 to May 1990 when he was player-coach to the Reserves as well as acting as caretaker manager between Tommy Coakley's departure and John Barnwell's arrival. In 1991-92 he was reserve-team coach at Middlesbrough as they powered into the Premiership, but lost his job at Ayresome Park in 1994.

In all Train totalled 621 senior appearances for his nine clubs and scored 30 goals. He played 154 League matches for Carlisle with whom he had his longest spell (five years) being an ever-present in their first-ever season in Division One (1974-75). He helped Sunderland win the Second Division championship and made 92 appearances for Watford whom he helped win promotion from the Third Division (1979) and to the First (1982). He won a Second Division championship medal with Bolton (1978), while making 57 appearances for the Trotters. He also had 61 games for Oxford.

ADRIAN VIVEASH

Defender; 195 apps, 15 goals.

Born: Swindon, 30 September 1969.

Adrian Viveash is a tall, dominant central defender who has been practically an ever-present in Walsall's ranks since joining the

club from Swindon Town on a free transfer in October 1995. He started his career at the County Ground as an apprentice, turning professional in July 1988. He played 64 times for the Robins and had two separate loans spells with Reading and another with Barnsley prior to signing for the Saddlers. He stands 6ft. 2ins. tall and weighs almost 13 st. – precisely the right build for a dedicated, no-nonsense defender. Certainly a bargain capture, he had an excellent 1998-99 campaign, when he partnered Ian Roper at the heart of the Saddlers' defence and indeed his overall performances at the back went a long way in helping the team win promotion to the First Division.

STEVE WADDINGTON

Midfield; 133+9 apps, 14 goals.

Born: Crewe, 5 February 1956.

Son of the former Stoke City manager Tony Waddington, Steve Waddington was taken on as an apprentice by Stoke at the age of 16 and turned professional at the Victoria Ground in 1974. In September 1978, after 56 games and six goals for the Potters, he was transferred to Walsall for £40,000. Quickly into his stride at Fellows Park, he teamed up down the right with Alan Birch and full-back Tony Macken. Waddington had 33 games in his first season and he followed up with 44 in 1979-80, 36 in 1980-81 and 29 in 1981-82. He started to lose his form in that latter campaign and in the summer of 1982 was sold to Port Vale, later serving Chesterfield, Cape Town City in South Africa, Macclesfield Town, Northwich Victoria, Leek Town, Rocester, Winsford United, Macclesfield Town (again, 1986) and finally Nantwich Town. On the eve of the 1986-87 season he was involved in a car crash on his way to a pre-season friendly for Macclesfield. After a lengthy lay-off he returned to play for Nantwich.

Waddington was often in trouble with referees and in April 1991, after being sent-off for the ninth time in his career, when playing for Nantwich, he was banned *sine die* and fined £200. He was told that his case would not be reviewed for at least five years but he never pursued it anyway and quit competitive football. He is no relation to Paul Waddington, who was with Walsall from 1978-82. The two played together several times, especially in 1980-81, and many people mixed them up.

HARRY WAIT

Goalkeeper; 275 apps.

Born: Darlaston, March 1892. Died: Walsall c.1975.

Harry Wait was a fine clubman who spent 37 years with Walsall, first as a player, then as trainer and finally as groundsman. He was signed as a 31-year-old by Walsall's secretary-manager Joe Burchell in August 1923, having played in goal for Darlaston in the Birmingham and District League, the Birmingham Combination and the Birmingham League for 15 years before that and had helped Darlaston win the Keys Cup. Many doubted the wisdom of such an old goalkeeper moving into Fellows Park, especially one whose experience was limited to non-League football. But Wait, who succeeded Dick Mann and Cyril Houghton, quickly made his mark after his debut at Rotherham County on 25 August 1923 in a Third Division North match.

He missed only one game in his first five seasons and at one stage had a run of exactly 200 consecutive appearances in League and Cup competition, a fantastic achievement considering his age. When he was forced to miss a match it was because of a boil which put him out of a Cup replay at Middlesbrough in January 1929. His long run came to an end following the emergence of the up-and-coming Roy John and the arrival of Fred Biddlestone. After a handful of games as a stand-in he announced his retirement in May 1932, to take over as assistant trainer.

Amazingly, almost four years later – on 14 April 1936 – at the age of 44 he was recalled for first-team duty in an emergency, and his displays proved that the intervening years had not impaired his judgement. Thus he became the oldest player ever to don a Walsall jersey and so was made up his grand total of 264 League and 11 FA. Cup tie appearances in the Walsall goal. He remained the club's trainer right through the war years, up to 1950, when he took over the job of groundsman with the former Wolves defender Jack Nelson assuming Wait's duties as senior trainer. He was groundsman until 1960 and even after that was still a prominent figure at the club, coming along to watch the Walsall teams in action at various levels – he lived almost opposite the ground in Wallows Lane. On 2 May 1957 a testimonial match was staged at Fellows Park between Walsall and a Select Midlands Xl which included several internationals. The Saddlers lost 7-0, but those present were there to pay tribute to a truly wonderful man. During the latter stages of his playing career, his son, Harry junior, registered as a goalkeeper with Walsall and appeared in several reserve-team matches under the watchful eye of his father. It was Harry Wait who forecast that one day a young lad called Bert Williams would 'go places'. He did, winning glory with both Wolves and England.

JIMMY WALKER

Goalkeeper; 263+1 apps.

Born: Sutton-in-Ashfield, Notts, 9 July 1973.

Jimmy Walker ended the 1998-99 season in great form and with a terrific record behind him – that of 153 consecutive appearances

between the posts for the Saddlers: 35 during the latter part of the 1996-97 campaign, 62 in 1997-98 and 56 when Walsall clinched promotion the following year. He was an ever-present in each of the last two campaigns despite being carried off unconscious at Northampton on Boxing Day 1997. He recovered quickly from that mishap against the Cobblers and continued to produce the goods week in week out, often keeping his side in the game. An excellent shot-stopper, Walker, nicknamed 'Whacker' skippered the team on several occasions and over the last two years has been watched by several Premiership clubs. He played for Notts County before joining the Saddlers on a free transfer in August 1993, as cover for Trevor Wood whom he replaced in goal on a permanent basis in November 1996.

MARK WALLINGTON

Goalkeeper; 12 apps.

Born: Sleaford, 17 September 1952.

During his career Mark Wallington appeared in 490 League games between 1971 and 1990. He started his career with Walsall, having joined the staff at Fellows Park as a junior

in 1969, turning professional in October 1971. An England Schoolboy, Amateur, Youth and Under-23 international, he had only a short stay with the Saddlers, until March 1972 when he signed for Leicester City for £30,000, switching to Derby County for £25,000 in July 1985. At the Baseball Ground he helped the Rams to successive promotions from the Third Division into the First before going into non-League soccer in the Conference with Lincoln City in August 1988. He immediately helped the Imps regain Fourth Division status but then called it a day in 1990. Wallington had an unbroken run of 331 senior games between the posts for Leicester (including 294 in the Football League). He helped them win the Second Division championship and skippered them from time to time. All told he appeared in 460 first-class games for the Filbert Street club (412 in the League).

ALBERT WALTERS

Centre/inside-forward; 55 apps, 34 goals.

Born: Derby, May 1902. Deceased.

Albert Walters prospered early in his career with the Derbyshire club Heanor Town before joining Portsmouth in May 1927. He failed to impress at Fratton Park, however, and after a brief association with Aldershot he was signed by Luton Town in July 1928. After 12 months at Kenilworth Road, Walters was signed by Walsall, becoming a Saddler in May 1929 when his colleague, Tommy Roe also moved from the Hatters. During his two-year spell at Fellows Park he found the net regularly, and in his first season scored 29 League and Cup goals, and five the following season when he played only ten times. He left the Saddlers in the summer of 1931, joining Shrewsbury Town.

FRED WALTERS

Utility; 139 apps, 14 goals.

Born: Walsall, May 1901. Died: 10 June 1992.

Fred Walters, no relation to Albert, served Walsall for eight seasons during which time he was willing to play in any position the manager required. A first-class utility player he accumulated a useful record after breaking into the League side in the centre-forward spot at Darlington on 1 November 1924 when Sibbald was an absentee through injury and the forward line was switched around accordingly to accommodate the new man. That was his only game that season, but in 1925-26 – on £6 a-week – he began to establish himself in the team and hit six goals in his 18 League outings, seven of which saw him occupy the inside-left berth. Strong running, Walters was considerably mobile for a big man and caused defenders all sorts of trouble. He teamed up superbly with ex-Fulham star Bert White in 1926-27, but then injuries began to knock him back and he made only 14 appearances in the next two seasons. After making a full recovery he was switched to full-back where he became an instant success, lining up on the right-hand side of defence. He left League football in May 1931, although he did play for a number of local non-League sides before retiring in 1935. In later years Fred Walters, who lived in Handsworth until his death, worked on Saturdays for the *Sports Argus*.

HENRY WALTERS

Wing-half; 266 apps, 2 goals.

Born: Walton-on-Dearne, near Rotherham, 15 March 1925.

Henry Walters tried hard to make the grade at Molineux, having been discovered for Wolves by their former player, Mark Crook. But things didn't work out as planned at Molineux and Walters was eventually persuaded to try his luck with Walsall, signing

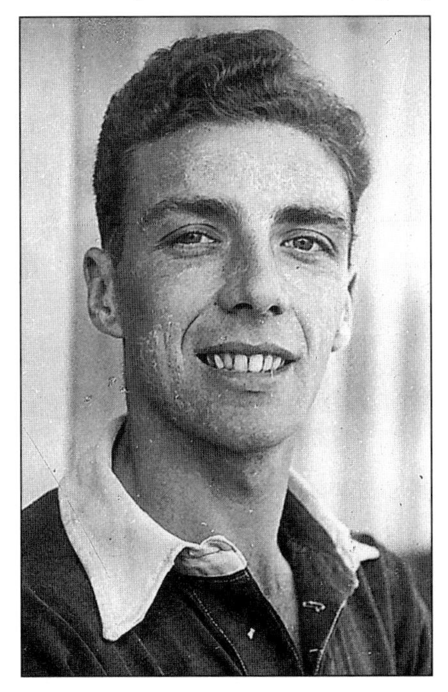

for the Saddlers in June 1946. He proved to be a great capture and became a most successful servant to Walsall whether performing at wing-half – his best position – or at full-back. He went on to make over 260 League and Cup appearances for the club before transferring to Barnsley in July 1953. He added another 160 League games to his overall tally with the Tykes, moving on in 1960 to take over as player-manager of Wombwell, a Yorkshire non-League side. He later worked for many years at the Cortonwood Colliery and played in charity matches well into the 1970s.

ANDY WATSON

Striker; 73+33 apps, 24 goals.

Born: Leeds, 1 April 1967.

Andy Watson was the hero of Walsall's excellent Cup runs during 1997-98, scoring dramatic goals against Nottingham Forest and Sheffield United in the Coca-Cola Cup and versus Peterborough United in the FA Cup which helped set up a trip to Old Trafford in the next round. Ligament trouble prevented him from appearing during the last third of that season but he came back early on in 1998-99 and teamed up superbly in attack with Andy Rammell. Further injuries, how-

ever, severely disrupted his game as the season progressed. Once a goalscorer with Harrogate Town, Watson entered League soccer with Halifax Town in 1988 and he did very well with the Shaymen, scoring 19 goals in 102 games before moving to Swansea City for £40,000 in July 1990. He didn't do too well at the Vetch Field and in September 1991 signed for Carlisle United for a fee of £30,000. With the Cumbrians he did much better and after claiming 28 goals in 64 starts he diverted his attention to Blackpool, joining the Seasiders for £55,000 in February 1993. He continued to score well at Bloomfield Road and after netting 49 times in under 140 appearances, he was recruited by Walsall for £60,000 in September 1996. Five years earlier, he had gained a Welsh Cup winners' medal with Swansea and in 1998-99 helped the Saddlers clinch a place in the First Division with two important goals – one in the home draw with Manchester City and a second in the 2-1 win at York.

TOMMY WATSON

Outside-right or left; 103+3 apps, 22 goals.

Born: Lesmahagow, Scotland, 23 August 1943.

Tommy Watson played his early football north of the border, but in 1964 came to England and signed for Stevenage Town, moving to Peterborough United as a full-time professional in May 1965. He did well at London Road, scoring 20 goals in 75 League matches for Posh before signing for Walsall in September 1967. A winger with good skills and fair pace, Watson had three good years with the Saddlers – scoring 15 goals in 1967-68 and getting both Walsall goals in the 5-2 Cup defeat at Anfield – before rounding off his career with Gillingham (June 1970 to May 1972). In all, he made 210 appearances in the Football League and scored 44 goals.

WALLY WEBSTER

Full-back; 137 apps, 3 goals.

Born: West Bromwich, 22 May 1895. Died: Sheffield, 15 September 1980.

Wally Webster served the Saddlers for three and a half seasons up to May 1925. He started his career with West Bromwich United, joining Walsall in the summer of 1921. He made his League debut later that year (on 21 December at Ashington) and held his place in the side until May 1925, being an ever-present in 1922-23 (as partner to Ben Timmins). He then paired up with George Smith and missed only one match in 1924-25, ironically at Ashington when the Saddlers crashed 6-1. In June 1925 he joined Lincoln City, but remained with the Imps only a short time, switching to the FA Cup holders, Sheffield United, in October that year. Webster spent almost five years at Bramall Lane, basically as a reserve. Indeed, he made only 35 League appearances for the Blades before moving to Scunthorpe United in August 1930. A season later he teamed up with Torquay United, returning to Yorkshire in 1934 to round off his career in non-League football. Wally Webster went into business in Sheffield and lived in that city up until his death.

BOB WESSON

Goalkeeper; 220 apps.

Born: Thornaby, 15 October 1940.

A former railway worker on the Stockton-

Darlington line, Bob Wesson was on Middlesbrough's books as a youngster and also played at weekends for Thornaby BB before being snapped up by Coventry City, who signed him as a full-time professional in December 1958. Wesson made his Football League debut at Newport County in March 1961 but could not keep out Bill Glazier. He regained his place during Glazier's 12 month absence with a broken leg but when Glazier was fit again, Wesson was once more left out in the cold and he subsequently joined Walsall on 30 September 1966 after making 156 League and Cup appearances for the Sky Blues. Either side of Phil Parkes' spell in goal, Wesson was the regular 'keeper and in 1970-71 was ever-present. A strong, confident 'keeper, he went on to give the Saddlers excellent service right through to May 1973, although in February 1970 he had a loan spell with Doncaster Rovers (five League games). He was voted Saddlers Player of the Year in 1968-69. He later played for Burton Albion.

GEORGE WILES

Utility player; 185 apps, 2 goals.

Born: East Ham, London, May 1905. Deceased.

George Wiles played full-back for East Ham and London Schools before joining Sittingbourne in the Kent League. He signed as an amateur for QPR in May 1929, turning professional the following year, and after being converted into a wing-half, he joined Walsall on the transfer deadline in March 1933. Wiles made his League debut for the Saddlers against Crewe Alexandra at home on 18 March 1933 at right-half, switching to left-half for the next game at Rochdale. He played in the last 11 games of that season and Walsall lost only one. The following season he hit his first goal for Walsall, a swirler at home to Tranmere in early March when the Saddlers won 5-3. Injuries caused him to miss a few matches in 1934-35, but he came back with a vengence in 1935-36, having 46 League and Cup outings at left-back. The 1936-37 campaign was one of his best (another 44 games) when he partnered a youthful Jack Shelton, and in his last season at Fellows Park he made 25 appearances. In the summer of 1938 he joined Halesowen.

It was hoped that his brother, Harry, would also make the grade with the Saddlers as a marksman, especially after he had slammed in 64 goals in 1933-34, playing in the Birmingham Combination, the Midland Midweek League and various minor Cup competitions plus a handful of Third Division South games. But he never developed and eventually left Fellows Park in 1935 after only 11 League matches (five goals).

BERT WILLIAMS

Goalkeeper; 28 apps.

Born: Bilston, 31 January 1920.

Bert Williams started his career with Walsall and developed into one of the finest goalkeepers in the game. He played for Thompson's FC in the local Works League after leaving school and in April 1937 joined the Saddlers. During the war he served in the RAF and in September 1945 left Fellows Park for Molineux, the Wolves' boss at the time, Ted Vizard, paying £3,500 for his signature. Williams went from strength to strength, going on to amass a grand total of 449 appearances for the Wolves (381 in the League, 38 in the FA Cup, 29 in that transitional season of 1945-46 and the 1954 FA Charity Shield game against West Bromwich Albion). He gained 24 England caps, his first coming against France in May 1949 and his last against Wales in October 1955. He was England's World Cup goalkeeper in 1950 and was on the losing side in only seven internationals. He collected an FA Cup winners' medal at Wembley in 1949 (against Leicester City) and a League championship medal in 1954.

Bert Williams eventually called it a day in May 1957, handing over his green jersey to Malcolm Finlayson. He became a businessman, running a sports outfitters in Bilston as well as organising a goalkeeping school. Nowadays he lives in Shifnal and is president of the ex-Wolves players' association.

DENNIS WILSHAW

Utility forward; 82 apps, 21 goals.

Born: Stoke, 11 March 1926.

Another player who achieved fame following a spell with the Saddlers, Dennis Wilshaw, like Bert Williams, progressed to the international front with Wolverhampton Wanderers. He was a natural goalscorer who during his career occupied four positions in the front-line, never playing at outside-right. He started hitting the target at Hanley High School (with Ronnie Allen, who was to become Walsall's manager in 1973) and carried on his marksmanship with Packmoor Boys' Club in the North Staffs League. In 1943 he scored ten in one game for the Boys' Club and was immediately whisked away to Molineux where he turned out for Wolves against West Brom in a regional wartime game, lining up with two greats – Stan Cullis and Tom Galley. He was then farmed out to Walsall to gain experience and made his first appearance for the Saddlers in 1945-46. The following season, the first post-war campaign, he was top scorer for the club.

He returned to Wolves in September 1948, after a two-year stint at Fellows Park, and

scored a hat-trick from outside-left on his League debut, against Newcastle United on 12 March 1949.

He became a regular in the Wolves' side in 1952-53 and the following season collected a League championship medal when he finished as the club's top scorer with 26 League and Cup goals. In October 1953 he won the first of 12 England caps, against Wales when he scored twice in a 4-1 win. He played in the World Cup finals in Switzerland in 1954 and in April 1955 smashed in four goals as England whipped Scotland 7-2 in a Home International at Wembley. He also played twice for England 'B', scoring twice in his first game.

In December 1957 he joined Stoke City for £10,000 after scoring 117 goals in 232 senior outings for Wolves. A further 50 goals in 108 games came his way for the Potters but his career came to an abrupt end when he suffered a broken leg playing against Newcastle United in an FA Cup-tie in 1961. During his playing days he had qualified as a schoolteacher, and he eventually became a headmaster in Stoke, later taking over as Head of Service and Community Studies at Crewe and Alsager College before his retirement in 1986.

KEVIN WILSON

Forward; 151+1 apps, 50 goals.

Born: Banbury, 18 April 1961.

Kevin Wilson spent three excellent seasons with Walsall and was then offered the manager's job. He refused and left the Bescot Stadium to sign for Northampton Town on a free transfer in July 1997. Capped 42 times by Northern Ireland, Wilson played initially for his hometown club, Banbury United, before joining Derby County for £20,000 in

December 1979. After more than 140 games for the Rams (41 goals) he was transferred to Ipswich Town for £100,000 in January 1985 and added a further 125 senior appearances and 49 more goals to his tally before leaving Portman Road for Chelsea in a £335,000 deal in June 1987. He went on to play in 191 games for the Londoners (55 goals) up to March 1992 when Notts County enticed him to Meadow Lane. Wilson made over 70 appearances for the Magpies and five on loan with Bradford City, up to August 1994 when he became a Saddler. A purposeful player, totally committed, he looked far younger than he really was during his time at the Bescot Stadium and while a Walsall player he netted the 200th goal of his professional career (club and international competition) and also reached the personal milestone of 700 appearances.

TOMMY WILSON

Centre-forward; 57 apps, 19 goals.

Born: Bedlington, County Durham, 15 September 1930. Died: Brentwood, Essex, April 1992.

Tommy Wilson scored at a prolific rate for his junior club, Cinderhill Colliery, and this prompted Nottingham Forest to sign him as a professional in April 1951. Originally an outside-right – he moved to centre-forward in 1954 – he quickly established himself at the City Ground and went on to score 89 goals in 217 games for Forest, including 75 in 190 League games, before transferring to Walsall in November 1960 and helped them to a second successive promotion season.

Unfortunately injury plagued him at Fellows Park and he was forced to quit in May 1962 after 19 goals in his 53 League outings for the Saddlers. He gained an FA Cup winners' medal with Forest in 1959, scoring one of their goals in a 2-1 win over Luton Town at Wembley. He also helped them gain promotion to the First Division in 1957. He later played for Chelmsford City and retired to live in Essex. Tommy Wilson died in 1992 after a short illness, aged 61.

TREVOR WOOD

Goalkeeper; 83 apps.

Born: St Helier, Jersey, 3 November 1968.

Trevor Wood began his professional career with Brighton & Hove Albion in November 1986. He failed to get a game with the Gulls

and in July 1988 moved to Port Vale on a free transfer, after a trial for the Potteries club. Under John Rudge his game developed considerably and he went on to make exactly 50 first-team appearances for the Valiants before transferring to Walsall in July 1994, also on a free. Over the next two years he did well at the Bescot Stadium and when the Saddlers gained promotion in his first season he played in 39 matches. Then he lost his place to Jimmy Walker which resulted in Wood moving to Third Division Hereford United in January 1997 but was unable to help them avoid dropping into the Conference at the end of that season. Coincidentally the only game he missed after joining them was the last match of the season when they needed to beat Brighton to stay in the League and could only draw 1-1. He later joining the Irish club St Patrick's Athletic. He was capped by Northern Ireland at both senior and 'B' team levels whilst at the Bescot Stadium.

JOHN ('WOODIE') WOODWARD

Striker; 136+9 apps, 29 goals.

Born: Tunstall, Stoke-on-Trent, 16 October 1947.

John Woodward began scoring goals for Tunstall Park as a teenager. He joined Stoke City as an apprentice in June 1962 and turned professional at the Victoria Ground in October 1964. Two years later he was transferred to Aston Villa for £27,500 but suffered a serous ankle injury playing against West Brom that same month. He recovered but after hitting eight goals in 27 games for Villa, he was transferred to Walsall on a free in May 1969. After three seasons in the Third

Division with the Saddlers he switched back to the Potteries in February 1973 to team up with Port Vale, and after a good spell with Scunthorpe United (from July 1975 to May 1977) he ended his playing days with a brief stint with VG Ostend in the Belgian League. His League career saw him play in 281 games played and score 66 goals scored – 23 coming in 116 outings for Walsall and 30 in 99 outings for the Vale.

BEN WOOLHOUSE

Outside-right; 203 apps, 46 goals.

Born: Sheffield, 25 November 1904. Died: Walsall, 3 March 1986.

Reuben Woolhouse did well in Sheffield junior soccer with Newton Chambers FC before attempting to break into League football with Birmingham in the summer of 1927. He failed to impress Blues and had a season with Southend United (1928-29) before playing for Loughborough Corinthians in the Midland League. He returned to League action with Bradford City in May 1930 and spent two seasons at Valley Parade (five goals in 26 games) before moving to Coventry City in July 1932. Injured, he made only 11 appearances during his brief stay at Highfield Road and was transferred to Walsall in June 1933.

Woolhouse was a lanky player (nicknamed 'Sticks') but quick over short distances, had good, close ball control, possessed a neat body-swerve and a strong shot. He proved to be a fine signing by Saddlers boss, Bill Slade. He finally left Fellows Park in August 1938, joining Swindon Town, his last game for Walsall being against Newport County on 7 May 1938 when he scored in a 2-1 win. After one season at the County Ground, under the management of the former Bolton player, Ted Vizard, he decided to hang up his boots after having made almost 300 League and Cup appearances as a professional. During the war he was a PT instructor in the RAF and afterwards worked for some years as a despatch clerk with Hill Top Foundry and AEI Wednesbury, until retiring in 1967. His father played for Sheffield Wednesday and Barnsley in the 1890s and his uncle was in the Wednesday team which was beaten 6-1 by Blackburn Rovers in the 1890 FA Cup Final.

DARREN WRACK

Forward; 56 apps,14 goals.

Born: Cleethorpes, 5 May 1976.

Walsall's second top scorer and an ever-present in 1998-99, Darren Wrack's goals went a long way to helping the Saddlers win promotion from the Second Division in his first campaign at the Bescot Stadium. Signed on a free transfer from Grimsby Town by manager Ray Graydon in July 1998, Wrack – who had played barely an hour's first team football during his last season at Blundell Park – fitted nicely into the right-wing position and his ability to send over precise and measured crosses, his skill on the ball plus his pace and

goalscoring technique was just what the boss ordered – remembering that Graydon himself played in that very same position. Initially a player with Derby County who signed him as a professional in July 1994 after two years as an apprentice, he made 31 appearances for the Rams (27 of them as a sub) before moving to Grimsby Town for £100,000 in July 1996. He never fitted in at Blundell Park and after a loan spell with Shrewsbury Town (February 1997) he moved to Walsall to become one of the bargain captures of the season as far as the Saddlers were concerned.

BERNIE WRIGHT

Centre-forward; 187+9 apps, 48 goals.

Born: Birmingham, 17 September 1952.

Second Division Birmingham City had the chance to secure the services of the ex-Paget Rangers striker Bernie Wright in 1969-70, but after the big, bustling striker had been on amateur forms at St Andrew's, he was released without being offered a profession-

al contract. Then, in September 1971, he was registered as a full-time professional by Walsall. His first spell with the Saddlers, when his speed, headwork and skill on the ball seemed to be the hallmarks of a player with a great future, lasted only six months and in February 1972 he was signed by Everton, only to return to Fellows Park in January 1973 after scoring twice in 11 games for the Merseysiders.

Back with Walsall, Wright became a great favourite with the fans, going on to claim 38 goals in his 152 League outings in the next four years, also scoring the winner against Manchester United in the fifth round of the FA Cup in 1974-75. He moved to Bradford City in February 1977 and at Valley Parade continued to do well. After adding 13 more League goals to his tally, he switched to Port Vale in June 1978, where he netted 23 times in his 76 League matches before moving out of the League in 1980 to sign for Kidderminster Harriers and later played for Trowbridge Town, Cheltenham Town, Worcester City and Gloucester City, retiring in 1992, aged 40.

Walsall's Record in the Football League

			Home					Away						
	DIv	P	W	D	L	F	A	W	D	L	F	A	Pts	Pos
1892-93	2	22	4	3	4	25	24	1	0	10	12	51	13	12
1893-94	2	28	8	1	5	36	23	2	2	10	15	38	23	10
1894-95	2	30	8	0	7	35	25	2	0	13	12	67	20	14
1896-97	2	30	8	2	5	37	25	3	2	10	16	44	26	12
1897-98	2	30	9	3	3	42	15	3	2	10	16	43	29	10
1898-99	2	34	12	5	0	64	11	3	7	7	15	25	42	6
1899-00	2	34	10	5	2	35	18	2	3	12	15	17	32	12
1900-01	2	34	7	7	3	29	23	0	6	11	11	33	27	16
1921-22	3N	38	15	2	2	52	17	3	1	15	14	48	39	8
1922-23	3N	38	13	4	2	32	14	6	4	9	19	30	46	3
1923-24	3N	42	10	5	6	31	20	4	3	14	13	39	36	17
1924-25	3N	42	10	6	5	27	16	3	5	13	17	37	37	19
1925-26	3N	42	9	4	8	40	34	1	2	18	18	73	26	21
1926-27	3N	42	10	4	7	35	22	4	6	11	33	59	38	14
1927-28	3S	42	9	6	6	52	35	3	3	15	23	66	33	18
1928-29	3S	42	11	7	3	47	25	2	5	14	26	54	38	14
1929-30	3S	42	10	4	7	45	24	3	4	14	26	54	34	17
1930-31	3S	42	9	5	7	44	38	5	4	12	34	57	37	17
1931-32	3N	40	12	3	5	42	30	4	0	16	15	55	35	16
1932-33	3N	42	16	4	1	53	15	3	6	12	22	43	48	5
1933-34	3N	42	18	2	1	66	18	5	5	11	31	42	53	4
1934-35	3N	42	11	7	3	51	18	2	3	16	30	54	36	14
1935-36	3N	42	15	2	4	58	13	1	7	13	21	46	41	10
1936-37	3S	42	11	3	7	38	34	2	7	12	25	51	36	17
1937-38	3S	42	10	4	7	34	37	1	3	17	18	51	29	21
1938-39	3S	42	9	6	6	47	23	2	5	14	21	46	33	21
1939-40*	3S	3	1	0	0	1	0	0	1	1	2	3	3	15
1946-47	3S	42	11	6	4	42	25	6	6	9	32	34	46	6
1947-48	3S	42	13	5	3	37	12	8	4	9	33	28	51	3
1948-49	3S	42	9	5	7	34	28	6	3	12	22	36	38	14
1949-50	3S	42	8	8	5	37	25	1	8	12	24	37	34	19
1950-51	3S	46	12	4	7	32	20	3	6	14	20	42	40	15
1951-52	3S	46	11	3	9	38	31	2	2	19	17	63	31	24
1952-53	3S	46	5	9	9	35	46	2	1	20	21	72	24	24
1953-54	3S	46	8	5	10	22	27	1	3	19	18	60	26	24
1954-55	3S	46	9	6	8	49	36	1	8	14	26	50	34	23
1955-56	3S	46	13	5	5	43	28	2	3	18	25	56	38	20
1956-57	3S	46	11	7	5	49	25	5	5	13	31	49	44	15
1957-58	3S	46	10	7	6	37	24	4	2	17	24	51	37	20
1958-59	4	46	13	5	5	56	25	8	5	10	39	39	52	6

			Home					Away						
	Div	P	W	D	L	F	A	W	D	L	F	A	Pts	Pos
1959-60	4	46	14	5	4	57	33	14	4	5	45	27	65	1
1960-61	3	46	19	4	0	62	20	9	2	12	36	40	62	2
1961-62	2	42	11	7	3	42	23	3	4	14	28	52	39	14
1962-63	2	42	7	7	7	33	37	4	2	15	20	52	31	21
1963-64	3	46	7	9	7	34	35	6	5	12	25	41	40	19
1964-65	3	46	9	4	10	34	36	6	3	14	21	44	37	19
1965-66	3	46	13	7	3	48	21	7	3	13	29	43	50	9
1966-67	3	46	12	8	3	37	16	6	2	15	28	'56	46	12
1967-68	3	46	12	7	4	47	22	7	5	11	27	39	50	7
1968-69	3	46	10	9	4	34	18	4	7	12	16	31	44	13
1969-70	3	46	11	4	8	33	31	6	8	9	21	36	46	12
1970-71	3	46	10	1	12	30	27	4	10	9	21	30	39	20
1971-72	3	46	12	8	3	38	16	3	10	10	24	41	48	9
1972-73	3	46	14	3	6	37	26	4	4	15	19	40	43	17
1973-74	3	46	11	7	5	37	19	5	6	12	20	29	45	15
1974-75	3	46	15	5	3	46	13	3	8	12	21	39	49	8
1975-76	3	46	11	8	4	43	22	7	6	10	31	39	50	7
1976-77	3	46	8	7	8	39	32	5	8	10	18	33	41	15
1977-78	3	46	12	8	3	35	17	6	9	8	26	33	53	6
1978-79	3	46	7	6	10	34	32	3	6	14	22	39	32	22
1979-80	4	46	12	9	2	43	23	11	9	3	32	24	64	2
1980-81	3	46	8	9	6	43	43	5	6	12	16	31	41	20
1981-82	3	46	10	7	6	32	23	3	7	13	19	32	53	20
1982-83	3	46	14	5	4	38	19	3	8	12	26	44	64	10
1983-84	3	46	14	4	5	44	22	8	5	10	24	39	75	6
1984-85	3	46	9	7	7	33	22	9	6	8	25	30	67	11
1985-86	3	46	15	7	1	59	23	7	2	14	31	41	75	6
1986-87	3	46	16	4	3	50	27	6	5	12	30	40	75	8
1987-88	3	46	15	6	2	39	22	8	7	8	29	28	82	3
1988-89	2	46	3	10	10	27	42	2	6	15	14	38	31	24
1989-90	3	46	6	8	9	23	30	3	6	14	17	42	41	24
1990-91	4	46	7	12	4	25	17	5	5	13	23	34	53	16
1991-92	4	42	5	10	6	28	26	7	3	11	20	32	49	15
1992-93	3	42	11	6	4	42	31	11	1	9	34	30	73	5
1993-94	3	42	7	5	9	28	26	10	4	7	20	27	60	10
1994-95	3	42	15	3	3	42	18	9	8	4	33	22	83	2
1995-96	2	46	12	7	4	38	20	7	5	11	22	25	69	11
1996-97	2	46	12	8	3	35	21	7	2	14	19	32	67	12
1997-98	2	46	10	8	5	26	16	4	4	15	17	36	54	19
1998-99	2	46	13	7	3	37	23	13	2	8	26	24	87	2

* These three games were played prior to the suspension of League Football owing to the outbreak of World War Two. They were subsequently expunged from the record books.

+ The 3 points-for-a-win rule was introduced for season 1981-82

Divisional Records (1892 to 1999)

	Played	Won	Drawn	Lost	For	Against	Points
Division 2	556	190	127	239	799	923	590
Division 3N	452	175	85	192	720	743	435
Division 3S	830	248	187	395	1228	1500	713
Division 3	1322	506	343	473	1850	1768	1564
Division 4	226	96	67	63	368	280	283
Totals	3386	1215	809	1362	4965	5214	3585

AGAINST OTHER LEAGUE CLUBS

	HOME							AWAY						TOTALS				
	P	W	D	L	F	A	P	W	D	L	F	A	P	W	D	L	F	A
Accrington Stanley	11	7	3	1	36	13	11	3	3	5	22	23	22	10	6	6	58	36
Aldershot Town	23	12	9	2	42	20	23	7	4	12	33	40	46	19	13	14	75	60
Arsenal	7	6	0	1	20	9	7	0	3	4	4	19	14	6	3	5	24	28
Ashington	6	4	2	0	12	4	6	2	0	4	7	16	12	6	2	4	19	20
Aston Villa	2	1	1	0	4	1	2	0	2	0	0	0	4	1	3	0	4	1
Barnet	3	3	0	0	8	0	3	2	0	1	4	4	6	5	0	1	12	4
Barnsley	14	6	6	2	30	19	14	3	5	6	16	22	28	9	11	8	46	41
Barrow	16	10	3	3	35	16	16	4	5	7	20	33	32	14	8	10	55	49
Birmingham	9	3	1	5	14	17	9	0	1	8	7	35	18	3	2	13	21	52
Blackburn Rovers	5	1	1	3	4	7	5	1	2	2	6	9	10	2	3	5	10	16
Blackpool	16	10	5	1	37	15	16	5	2	9	20	25	32	15	7	10	57	40
Bolton Wanderers	8	5	3	0	15	9	8	1	1	6	6	21	16	6	4	6	21	30
Bootle	1	0	1	0	4	4	1	0	0	1	1	7	2	0	1	1	5	11
Bournemouth	46	21	19	6	72	40	46	12	12	22	42	78	92	33	31	28	114	118
Bradford City	11	4	4	3	16	9	11	3	4	4	9	15	22	7	8	7	25	24
Bradford Park Avenue	6	5	0	1	12	7	6	1	1	4	8	24	12	6	1	5	20	31
Brentford	26	13	4	9	55	36	26	4	8	14	26	55	52	17	12	23	81	91
Brighton & HA	34	14	9	11	52	41	34	7	6	21	41	74	68	21	15	32	93	115
Bristol City	24	10	8	6	42	35	24	5	5	14	28	57	48	15	13	20	70	92
Bristol Rovers	40	19	10	11	71	50	40	10	5	25	42	83	80	29	15	36	113	133
Burnley	12	4	4	4	20	18	12	2	4	6	9	16	24	6	8	10	29	34
Burton Swifts	8	6	0	2	29	15	8	3	0	5	18	20	16	9	0	7	47	35
Burton Wds	2	2	0	0	5	1	2	0	0	2	0	8	4	2	0	2	5	9
Bury	20	11	3	6	37	25	20	5	6	9	24	33	40	16	9	15	61	58
Cambridge United	3	2	1	0	8	0	3	1	1	1	2	2	6	3	2	1	10	2
Cardiff City	12	5	2	5	23	20	12	1	4	7	13	23	24	6	6	12	36	43
Carlisle	20	12	4	4	39	17	20	4	7	9	32	33	40	16	11	13	71	50
Charlton Athletic	8	3	2	3	13	11	8	2	3	3	12	19	16	5	5	6	25	30
Chelsea	2	0	0	2	1	12	2	1	0	1	1	2	4	1	0	3	2	14
Chester City	17	12	5	0	30	11	17	2	6	9	12	33	34	14	11	9	42	44
Chesterfield	36	16	12	8	62	43	36	9	9	18	40	59	72	25	21	26	102	102
Colchester United	22	11	6	5	43	30	22	4	8	10	26	39	44	15	14	15	69	69
Coventry City	14	7	5	2	29	13	14	2	3	9	12	28	28	9	8	11	41	41
Crewe Alex	25	16	6	3	57	26	25	9	4	12	35	43	50	25	10	15	92	69
Crystal Palace	26	11	11	4	42	27	26	5	2	19	25	64	52	16	13	23	67	91
Darlington	19	10	8	1	34	14	19	7	4	8	26	31	38	17	12	9	60	45
Darwen	5	4	0	1	25	3	5	1	1	3	3	21	10	5	1	4	28	24
Derby County	4	1	2	1	4	4	4	1	0	3	4	8	8	2	2	4	8	12
Doncaster Rovers	24	17	1	6	45	23	24	6	6	12	27	40	48	23	7	18	72	63
Durham City	6	2	3	1	8	5	6	2	0	4	5	10	12	4	3	5	13	15
Exeter City	30	19	5	6	72	40	30	10	5	15	45	50	60	29	10	21	117	90
Fulham	13	3	7	3	21	18	13	0	5	8	12	31	26	3	12	11	33	49
Gainsborough Trinity	5	3	2	0	14	5	5	0	2	3	1	6	10	3	4	3	15	11
Gateshead	7	4	1	2	17	5	7	0	2	5	5	13	14	4	3	7	22	18
Gillingham	44	23	10	11	77	44	44	11	4	29	45	92	88	34	14	40	122	136
Glossop	2	2	0	0	4	1	2	0	0	2	0	4	4	2	0	2	4	5
Grimsby Town	26	20	5	1	50	16	26	5	4	17	27	58	52	25	9	18	77	74
Halifax Town	22	14	5	3	42	17	22	5	4	13	20	41	44	19	9	16	62	58
Hartlepool United	17	7	5	5	39	20	17	3	6	8	22	38	34	10	11	13	61	58
Hereford United	10	6	4	0	22	11	10	5	2	3	13	11	20	11	6	3	35	22
Huddersfield Town	9	3	5	1	16	10	9	0	4	5	11	20	18	3	9	6	27	30
Hull City	12	4	4	4	15	18	12	1	3	8	8	21	24	5	7	12	23	39
Ipswich Town	12	4	0	8	17	24	12	2	1	9	16	31	24	6	1	17	33	55
Leeds United	3	0	2	1	2	5	3	0	0	3	1	8	6	0	2	4	3	13
Leicester City	7	2	2	3	8	9	7	0	1	6	6	26	14	2	3	9	14	35
Leyton Orient	24	13	2	9	50	39	24	5	8	11	26	38	48	18	10	20	76	77
Lincoln City	31	18	7	6	63	40	31	7	8	16	35	55	62	25	15	22	98	95
Liverpool	2	0	2	0	2	2	2	0	0	2	1	9	4	0	2	2	3	11
Loughborough Town	4	4	0	0	16	1	4	1	2	1	4	4	8	5	2	1	20	5
Luton Town	17	10	2	5	39	16	17	4	1	12	16	39	34	14	3	17	55	55
Macclesfield	1	1	0	0	2	0	1	0	1	0	1	1	2	1	1	0	3	1
Maidstone United	2	0	2	0	1	1	2	1	0	1	4	3	4	1	2	1	5	4
Manchester City	8	2	4	2	18	17	8	0	1	7	6	26	16	2	5	9	24	43
Manchester United	6	1	3	2	7	7	6	0	1	5	1	24	12	1	4	7	8	31
Mansfield Town	25	14	6	5	46	22	25	7	7	11	33	44	50	21	13	16	79	66
Merthyr T	3	1	2	0	9	3	3	1	0	2	5	6	6	2	2	2	14	9
Middlesbrough	6	3	2	1	12	6	6	2	1	3	8	11	12	5	3	4	20	17
Middlesbrough I	1	1	0	0	1	0	1	0	1	0	1	1	2	1	1	0	2	1
Millwall	26	10	7	9	49	42	26	5	5	16	23	48	52	15	12	25	72	90
Newcastle United	6	1	0	5	6	16	6	1	0	5	5	14	12	2	0	10	11	30
New Brighton	12	7	3	2	25	12	12	2	3	7	13	28	24	9	6	9	38	40
Newport County	27	13	8	6	45	33	27	6	6	15	41	58	54	19	14	21	86	91
Nelson	5	3	0	2	12	5	5	0	0	5	3	11	10	3	0	7	15	16
Northampton	34	16	7	11	58	48	34	9	7	18	44	77	68	25	14	29	102	125
Norwich City	18	12	4	2	50	23	18	3	1	14	20	43	36	15	5	16	70	66
Northwich Victoria	2	1	0	1	5	3	2	0	0	2	2	6	4	1	0	3	7	9
Nottingham Forest	2	0	0	2	1	5	2	0	0	2	0	5	4	0	0	4	1	10
Notts County	23	12	8	3	42	33	23	1	4	18	18	56	46	13	12	21	60	89
Oldham Athletic	15	6	6	3	27	18	15	8	1	6	30	24	30	14	7	9	57	42
Oxford United	12	3	3	6	12	20	12	2	2	8	14	32	24	5	5	14	26	52
Peterborough United	14	6	4	4	23	14	14	6	4	4	22	17	28	12	8	8	45	31
Plymouth Argyle	27	9	8	10	30	41	27	3	5	19	27	51	54	12	13	29	57	92
Portsmouth	8	2	4	2	12	12	8	1	3	4	6	11	16	3	7	6	18	23
Port Vale	30	21	6	3	62	23	30	7	12	11	34	44	60	28	18	14	96	67
Preston North End	18	12	3	3	26	14	18	4	1	13	12	26	36	16	4	16	38	40
QPR	20	7	3	10	31	31	20	0	5	15	13	38	40	7	8	25	44	69
Reading	32	17	9	6	68	32	32	9	9	14	33	45	64	26	18	20	101	77
Rochdale	22	11	4	7	30	22	22	6	6	10	29	41	44	17	10	17	59	63
Rotherham United	32	16	6	10	58	33	32	8	4	20	30	66	64	24	10	30	88	99
Scarborough	6	3	2	1	9	6	6	2	1	3	7	10	12	5	3	4	16	16
Scunthorpe United	14	7	6	1	24	11	14	2	3	9	13	29	28	9	9	10	37	40
Sheffield United	4	0	3	1	6	7	4	1	0	3	2	8	8	1	3	4	8	15
Sheffield Wednesday	5	1	3	1	9	7	5	1	2	2	3	4	10	2	5	3	12	11
Shrewsbury Town	30	13	10	7	53	36	30	10	10	10	35	40	60	23	20	17	88	76
Southampton	7	1	4	2	5	8	7	0	2	5	5	16	14	1	6	7	10	24
Southend United	32	15	4	13	64	44	32	3	8	21	26	59	64	18	12	34	90	103
Southport	17	11	5	1	45	13	17	2	4	11	17	35	34	13	9	12	62	48
Stockport County	16	7	3	6	18	16	16	5	3	8	16	27	32	12	6	14	34	43
Stoke City	5	2	1	2	5	4	5	1	0	4	5	11	10	3	1	6	10	15
Sunderland	4	2	1	1	10	8	4	1	1	2	4	9	8	3	2	3	14	17
Stalybridge Celtic	2	1	1	0	4	3	2	0	0	2	0	4	4	1	1	2	4	7
Swansea City	14	6	5	3	22	11	14	2	3	9	14	27	28	8	8	12	36	38
Swindon Town	34	16	9	9	62	31	34	7	9	18	44	75	68	23	18	27	106	106
Thames	1	1	0	0	6	0	1	0	0	1	1	4	2	1	0	1	7	4
Torquay United	33	14	8	11	58	42	33	8	5	20	39	66	66	22	13	31	97	108
Tranmere Rovers	25	18	4	3	51	21	25	7	5	13	24	45	50	25	9	16	75	66
Watford	34	14	9	11	53	41	34	8	5	21	36	71	68	22	14	32	89	112
West Bromwich Albion	1	0	1	0	0	0	1	0	1	0	0	0	2	0	2	0	0	0
Wigan Athletic	12	5	4	3	19	11	12	3	1	8	10	22	24	8	5	11	29	33
Wigan Borough	6	5	0	1	16	6	6	0	1	5	5	14	12	5	1	6	21	20
Wimbledon	2	2	0	0	5	0	2	0	0	2	0	4	4	2	0	2	5	4
Wolverhampton W	2	1	1	0	3	2	2	0	2	0	0	0	4	1	3	0	3	2
Workington	5	2	2	1	9	7	5	2	0	3	5	8	10	4	2	4	14	15
Wrexham	28	14	6	8	50	26	28	4	5	19	23	57	56	18	11	27	73	83
Wycombe W	5	1	2	2	.8	8	5	2	0	3	6	9	10	3	2	5	14	17
York City	23	14	6	3	51	22	23	7	6	10	26	28	46	21	12	13	77	50

SEASON-BY-SEASON RESULTS

SEASON 1888-89

Midland Association

Date		Opponents	Res	Score	Comp	Scorers	Att	Wood G.	Aldridge A.	Jones A.	Morris G.	Tonks J.	Morely	Davis R.	Shaw C.	Holmes S.	Cope G.	Paddock J.	Tapper G.	Brettle J.	Gray F.	Barnett W.	Clarkson D.	Lewis S.	Horton F.	Brown A.	Reynolds T.	Beech J.	Wilson J.	Hicklin W.	Reynolds G.	Selby G.	Holmes C.
Sep 8	(h)	Derby St Lukes	W	6-1	F	Holmes (4), Shaw, Morely	1,200	1	3	2	4		6	7	8	9	10	11		5													
10	(h)	Burnley	W	1-0	F	Cope	1,500	1	3	2	4		6	7	8	9	10	11		5													
15	(a)	Newton Heath	L	1-2	F	Holmes	3,000	1	3	2	4		6		8	9	10	11	7	5													
22	(h)	Crewe Alexandra	D	2-2	MA	Paddock, Brettle	2,000	1	3	2	4		6	7	8	9		10		5	11												
24	(h)	WBA	D	2-2	F	Shaw, Morely	7,000	1	3	2	4		6	7	8	9	10	11		5													
29	(h)	Burslem Port Vale	W	1-0	MA	Shaw	2,000	1	3	2	4		6	7	8	9	10	11		5													
Oct 6	(a)	Derby Junction	W	2-1	MA	Holmes (2)	1,000	1	3	2	4			7	8	9		10		5	11	6											
13	(h)	Small Heath	D	2-2	MA	Shaw, Paddock	3,000	1	3	2	4		6	7	8	9		10		5	11												
20	(a)	Birmingham St Geo	W	3-2	MA	Horton, Davis, Holmes	1,800		3	2	4		6	7	8	9		10		5				1	11								
27	(a)	Long Eaton Rgrs	L	0-2	MA		2,000		3	2	4		6	7	8	9		10		5				1	11								
Nov 3	(h)	Darwen	W	3-0	F	Shaw, Holmes (2)	500		3	2	4		6	7	8	9				5	11			1		10							
10	(a)	Small Heath	L	0-2	MA		3,500		3	2	4		6	7	8	9				5	11			1		10							
17	(a)	Oldbury Town	W	5-0	WC	Cope, Brettle, Gray, Davis, Holmes	800		3	2	4		6	7	8	9	10			5	11			1									
24	(a)	Burslem Port Vale	W	2-1	MA	Cope, Shaw	1,200		3	2	4		6	7	8	9	10			5	11			1									
Dec 1	(h)	Notts Rangers	L	0-4	MA		1,000			2				7		9	10		8	5	11	6		1			3	4					
8	(a)	Nottingham Forest	W	2-1	F	Cope, Shaw	200		3	2	4		6	7	9		10				8		11	1				5					
22	(h)	Long Eaton Rgrs	W	4-3	MA	Cope, Shaw, Gray, Davis	1,000		3	2	4		6	7	8		10	9		5	11			1									
24	(a)	Notts Olympic	W	6-4	BC	Cope, Gray, Shaw (2), Davis, Hicklin	1,200		3	2	4		6	7	9		10			5	11								1	8			
26	(h)	Blackpool Sth Shore	W	4-2	F	Hicklin, Gray (3)	2,000		3	2	4		6	8	9		10			5	11								1	7			
31	(a)	Burnley	L	1-2	F	Davis	1,000		3	2	4		6	7	8	9	10			5	11										1		
Jan 1	(a)	West Manchester	W	3-1	F	Holmes, Shaw,Cope	3,000		3	2	4		6	7	8	9	10			5	11										1		
5	(a)	Stoke	D	1-1	F	Shaw	500		3	2			6		8	9	10	11	7	5								4			1		
12	(h)	Derby Junction	W	3-2	MA	Holmes (3)	1,000		3	2	4		6		8	9	10	11	7	5											1		
19	(a)	Crewe Alexandra	L	1-5	MA	Cope	2,000		3	2	4		6		8	9	10		7	5	11										1		
21	(h)	Birmingham St Geo	W	3-0	MA	Cope, Shaw, Holmes	1,500		3	2	4		6		8	9	10		7		11		5									1	
26	(a)	Notts Rangers	W	5-4	MA	Morris, Gray (2), Shaw, Cope	2,500		3	2	4		6		8	9	10		7		11		5									1	
Feb 2	(h)	Sheffield Heeley	W	5-1	FAC	Cope, Gray, Shaw (2), Morely	1,600		3	2	4		6	7	8	9	10			5	11										1		
9	(a)	Great Bridge Unity	W	2-0	WC	Cope, Morris	600			2	4	3		7			10	11	8	5			6							9	1		
16	(a)	Wolves	L	1-6	FAC	Gray	4,000		3	2	4			7	8	9	10			5	11		6									1	
Mar 9	(h)	Wednesbury O Ath	W	3-0	WC	Shaw, Holmes, Brettle	2,500		3	2	4		6		8	9	10			5	11		7								1		
16	(h)	Stoke	W	3-0	SC	Shaw, Holmes, Gray	4,000		3	2	4		6	7	8	9	10			5	11										1		
23	(h)	Aston Villa	L	1-3	BC	Shaw	5,000		3	2	4		6	7	8	9	10			5	11										1		
Apr 6	(a)	WBA	L	0-5	SC		4,000			2	4		6	7	8	9	10			3	11		5								1		
19	(a)	West Manchester	W	4-1	F	Morely, Davis (2), Shaw	5,000			2		3	6	7	8	9	10			5					11						1		4
20	(a)	Hyde	L	0-1	F		2,000			2		3	6	7	8	9	10			5					11						1		4
27	(h)	Wednesbury O Ath	W	6-2	F	Holmes, Cope (2), Gray, Shaw, Davis	1,000			2	4	3	6	7	8	9	10			5	11										1		

Key:
- **MA** Midland Assoc.
- **WC** Walsall Cup
- **BC** Birmingham Cup
- **SC** Staff Cup
- **FAC** F.A.Cup
- **F** Friendly

F.A. Cup: Apps: Aldridge 2, Brettle 2, Cope 2, Davis R. 2, Gray 2, Holmes S. 2, Jones 2, Morris 2, Shaw 2, Clarkson 1, Morely 1, Reynolds 1, Selby 1: Total 22
Goals: Gray 2, Holmes 2, Cope 1, Morely 1: Total 6
Midland Association: Apps: Jones 14, Aldridge 13, Holmes 13, Morris 13, Shaw 13, Brettle 12, Morely 12, Davis R. 10, Gray 10, Cope 8, Paddock 8, Lewis 6, Tapper 5, Wood 4, Reynolds G 2, Barnett 2, Clarkson 2, Horton 2, Selby 2, Beech 1, Brown 1, Reynolds T 1: Total 154
Goals: Holmes 7, Shaw 6, Cope 5, Gray 3, Davis 2, Paddock 2, Brettle 1, Horton 1, Morris 1: Total 28

SEASON 1889 - 90

Football Alliance

Date		Opponents	Res	Score	Scorers	Att	Edge G.	Jones A.	Holmes C.	Morris	Jones B.	Morely.	Sheldon D.	Shaw C.	Holmes S.	Cope G.	Millington	Reynolds T.	Tapper G.	Ashbourne	Horton	Davis R.	Dyke	Heath	Whittick	Stokes	Tonks	Richards	Tipper G.
Sep 7	(h)	Nottingham F	L	1-3	Millington	3,000	1	2	3	4	5	6	7	8	9	10	11												
14	(a)	Crewe Alexandra	W	3-2	Holmes S, Shaw (2)	1,000	1	2	5	6		4		8	9	10	11	3	7										
21	(h)	Small Heath	D	1-1	Cope	1,500	1	2	5	6		4		8	9	10		3	7	11									
28	(h)	Grimsby Town	D	2-2	Millington, Holmes S.	2,000	1	2	5			6			10		11	3	7		4	8	9						
Oct 19	(h)	Newton Heath	W	4-0	Morely, Holmes C, Holmes S, Davis	600	1	2	5			6			10		11	3	7		4	8		10	9				
Nov 9	(a)	Small Heath	W	2-0	Shaw, Davis	3,000	1	2	5			6			10		11	3	7		4	8			9				
23	(a)	Darwen	L	3-6	Shaw, Holmes S (2)	4,000	1	2	5	6		4		8	10			3	7			11		9					
30	(a)	Grimsby Town	L	0-4		2,000	1	3	5	4		6		10	8			2	11			7		9					
Jan 4	(a)	Long Eaton Rgrs	L	2-3	Shaw, Heath	2,000	1	2	5					8	7	11		3			4		10	9		6			
18	(h)	Long Eaton Rgrs	W	3-1	Holmes S, Tapper, Shaw	1,000	1	2	5			4		8	7			3	10					9		6	11		
Feb 1	(h)	Crewe Alexandra	L	3-4	Tonks, Holmes S (2)	2,500	1	2				4		8	7			3	10		5					6	11	9	
10	(h)	Bootle	W	1-0	Shaw	2,000	1	2	5			4		8	7		11	3	10							6			9
24	(a)	Bootle	L	1-5	Holmes S	1,500	1	2	5	6		4		8	7		11	3	10										9
Mar 1	(h)	Darwen	W	5-3	Tapper (3), Richards, Cope	1,000	1	2	5	6						11		3	10							4	7	8	9
8	(h)	Sunderland Albion	W	3-2	Holmes S, Tapper, Shaw	2,000	1	2	5					8	7	10		3	11							6	4		9
15	(h)	Sheffield Wed	D	2-2	Tipper, Jones	3,500	1	2	5					8	7	11		3	10							6	4		9
22	(h)	Birmingham St G	W	2-1	Richards (2)	4,000	1	2	5			6		10	11	7		3	8							4		9	
29	(h)	Nottingham F	L	0-3		2,000	1	2	5	6				8	7	10		3	11							4		9	
Apr 8	(a)	Sheffield Wed	L	0-4		3,000	1	2	5					9	7	11		3	8							6	4		10
19	(a)	Sunderland Albion	L	2-6	Holmes C, Cope	3,000	1	2	5					8	7	10		3	11							6	4		9
21	(a)	Newton Heath	L	1-3	Cope	1,000	1	2	5					8	7	10		3	11							6	4		9
26	(a)	Birmingham St G	L	3-5	Tipper, Holmes S (2)	4,000	1	2	5					7	8	11		3	10							6	4		9
						Apps	22	22	21	8	1	13	1	18	21	13	7	21	20	1	5	5	2	5	2	13	9	4	9
League position: 9th						Goals		1	2			1		8	12	4	2		5			2		1			1	3	2

F.A. Cup

Date		Opponents	Rd	Score	Scorers	Att	Edge G.	Jones A.	Holmes C.	Morris	Jones B.	Morely.	Sheldon D.	Shaw C.	Holmes S.	Cope G.	Millington	Reynolds T.	Tapper G.	Ashbourne	Horton	Davis R.	Dyke	Heath	Whittick
Oct 5	(h)	Wellington St G	1Q	3-0	Dyke, Davis (2)	2,000	1	2	5			6		4	11		10	3	7			8	9		
26	(a)	Warwick County	2Q	1-1	Tapper (aet)	1,500	1	2	5			6		4	10	11		3	7			8			9
Nov 2	(h)	Warwick County	2QR	2-0	Davis, Tapper	2,500	1	2	5			6		4	10	11		3	7			8			9
16	(a)	Burton Swifts	3Q	6-1	Tapper, Shaw (2), Price (og), Holmes S, Dyke	2,000	1	2	5			6		4	10	11		3	7			8	9		
Dec 7	(a)	Small Heath	4Q	0-4		3,000	1	2	5			6		4	11			3	7			8	10	9	
						Apps	5	5	5			5		5	5	3	1	5	5			5	3	1	2
						Goals								2	1				3			3	2		

Own goal 1

SEASON 1890-91

Football Alliance

Date		Opponent		Score	Scorers	Att	Edge G.	Withington S.	Reynolds T.	Tonks J	Morely J.	Stokes A.	Shaw C.	Holmes S.	Tipper G.	Wilson E.	Gray F.J.S.	Whittick E.A.	Bate G.	Dyke W.	Ball E.	Pinches A.	Kitchley W.S.	Biddulph R.	Walters S.	Edwards T.	Forsyth N.	Clark W.	Selby T.	Bray W.	Proffitt	Hunter
Sep 6	(h)	Small Heath	W	5-2	Shaw, Holmes S (2), Stokes, Gray	5,000	1	2	3	4	5	6	7	8	9	10	11															
20	(a)	Crewe Alexandra	W	2-1	Holmes, Whittick	2,000	1	2	3	4	5	6	8	7		10	11	9														
27	(h)	Sheffield Wed	W	2-1	Holmes, Gray	4,000	1	2	3	4	5	6	7	8		10	11	9														
Oct 11	(a)	Stoke	L	0-1		4,000	1	3	2	4	5		8	7		10	11		6	9												
18	(a)	Small Heath	W	1-0	Shaw	5,000	1	3		6	5	2	8	7		10	11	9			4											
Nov 1	(a)	Birmingham St G	W	2-1	Morely, Whittick	2,000	1	2		4	5	3	7	8		10	11	9			6											
8	(h)	Newton Heath	W	2-1	Holmes, Wilson	1,000	1		3	4	5	2	8	7		10	11	9			6											
22	(a)	Sheffield Wed	D	2-2	Holmes (2)	6,000	1	5	3	4	9	2	7	8			11	10			6											
29	(h)	Crewe Alexandra*	L	1-6	Opponent (og)	2,000	1	4		6	9	2	8	10				7			5	3										
Dec 13	(h)	Birmingham St G	D	1-1	Walters	3,000	1	2					4	7	8			9			6	3		5	10	11						
27	(a)	Sunderland Alb	L	1-11	Walters	4,000	1	2		6			4	10		8	11	7			5	3			9							
Jan 17	(a)	Newton Heath	D	3-3	Wilson, Mitchell (og), Holmes S	2,000	1	2		4				10		11		9	6		5	3	8		7							
24	(a)	Bootle	L	1-6	Whittick	4,500	1	2	3	4				8			11	9			5				7		6	10				
Feb 16	(h	Bootle	W	3-2	Clark, Holmes, Gray	3,000	1	3		4		2	8	7			11	10			6		5					9				
28	(a)	Grimsby Town	L	0-3		1,500		3	2	4	5	6	8	7			10											9	1	11		
Mar 7	(h)	Stoke	L	1-3	Holmes	4,000		3	2	6	5		8	7		11	10				4							9	1			
14	(a)	Nottingham F	L	0-2		3,000	1		3	6	5	2	8	7			10	11									4	9				
21	(h)	Grimsby Town	L	0-1		1,000	1	3	2		5		8	7		11	10				4						6	9				
28	(h)	Sunderland Alb	W	2-0	Shaw, Forsyth	3,000	1			4	5	2	8	7			11					10					6				3	9
30	(h)	Darwen	L	2-3	Shaw, Forsyth	5,000	1			4	5	2	8	7			11					10					6				3	9
Apr 14	(h)	Nottingham F	W	3-2	Holmes, Forsyth (2)	3,000	1	3		4	5	6	7	8			10										11				2	9
18	(a)	Darwen*	L	0-9		3,000	1	3		4	5	6	8	7			10										9				2	
						Apps	20	18	11	20	17	15	20	22	2	11	19	13	2	1	12	6	2	1	4	1	7	6	2	1	4	3
League position: 7th						Goals					1	1	4	11		2	3	3							2		4	1				

* 10 men v Crewe: 29 November
* 10 men v Darwen: 18 April

Own goals: 2

F.A. Cup

Date		Opponent	Rd		Score	Scorers	Att	Edge G.	Withington S.	Reynolds T.	Tonks J	Morely J.	Stokes A.	Shaw C.	Holmes S.	Tipper G.	Wilson E.	Gray F.J.S.	Whittick E.A.	Bate G.	Dyke W.	Ball E.	Pinches A.	Kitchley W.S.	Biddulph R.
Sep 27	(a)	Warmley	1Q	W	12-0	Shaw (2), Whittick (4), Holmes (2) Morley, Gray (2), Wilson	2,200	1	3	2	4	5		8	7			10	9			6			11
Oct 25	(a)	Burslem P Vale	2Q	W	3-2	Shaw (2), Opponent (og).	1,500	1	3		4	5	2	8	7		10	11	9			6			
Nov 15	(h)	Wednesbury O A	3Q	W	5-3	Shaw (2), Gray, Holmes, Ball	4,000	1	3		4	5	2	8	7			11	9			6			10
Dec 6	(a)	Kidderminster H	4Q	L	0-3		2,500	1	5	2	6		3	8	7			10	9			4			11
							Apps	4	4	2	4	3	3	4	4		1	4	4			4			3
							Goals					1		6	3		1	3	4			1			

Own goal: 1

SEASON 1891-92

Football Alliance

Date		Opponent		Score	Scorers	Att	Hawkins T.	Proffitt	Withington	Tonks J.	Stokes A.	Pinches	Holmes S.	Shaw C.	Wood H.	Forsyth N.	Wilson J.	Morely	Pangbourne	Edge	Loynes	Ball E.	Sylvester G.	Clark	Sadler	Morley	Woodward J.	Gray F.J.S.	Dixon S.
Sep 5	(h)	Birmingham St G	L	1-3	Wilson	4,500	1	2	3	4	5	6	7	8	9	10	11												
12	(a)	Nottingham Forest	L	1-5	Pangbourne	2,000	1	3	2		4		7	5	10	8	11	6	9										
19	(a)	Birmingham St G	L	1-6	Wilson	1,000		2	3		6		7	4	10	8	11	5	9	1									
26	(h)	Sheffield Wed	W	2-1	Holmes, Pangbourne	3,000		3	2	4			9	7	10	6	11	5	8	1									
Oct 17	(a)	Small Heath	L	1-4	Forsyth	2,000			4		3		9	6	10	7	11	5	8	1	2								
31	(h)	Grimsby Town	W	2-0	Holmes, Wood	1,500			8	4		3	9	2	10	6	11		7	1		5							
Nov 7	(a)	Ardwick	L	0-6		4,000				6	3	2	9	8	10	4	11		7	1		5							
21	(a)	Sheffield Wed	L	0-4		7,000	1		6		5	3	9	8	10	4	11		7		2								
28	(h)	Newton Heath	L	1-4	Wood	2,500	1		6		5	3	9	8	10	4	11		7		2								
Dec 19	(a)	Lincoln City	W	2-0	Holmes, Wilson	1,500	1		2		6	3	9	8		4	11		10				5	7					
25	(h)	Bootle	W	7-0	Clark (2), Pangbourne (2), Wilson, Shaw, Holmes	2,000	1		2		6	3	9	8		4	11		10				5	7					
Jan 2	(h)	Crewe Alexandra	W	3-1	Wilson, Holmes, Moss (og)	2,000	1		2		6	3	9	8		4	11		10				5	7					
16	(a)	Burton Swifts	L	0-4		2,500	1				6	3	9			4	11		10		2		5	7	8				
30	(h)	Burton Swifts	L	2-3	Shaw, Wilson	3,000	1		2		6	3	9	8		4	11		10				5	7					
Feb 6	(a)	Crewe Alexandra	D	1-1	Holmes	2,000	1		2		6	3	7	8		4	11		10				5			9			
Mar 5	(a)	Newton Heath	L	0-5		3,500	1		2		6	3	7	8		4	11		10				5			9			
19	(a)	Bootle	L	0-3		3,000	1		2		6	3		8		4	11		10				5	9			7		
26	(h)	Ardwick	D	2-2	Shaw, Dixon	2,500	1		2		6	3		8		4			9				5	9			7	11	10
Apr 2	(h)	Nottingham Forest	W	3-0	Clark, Holmes, Pangbourne	4,000	1		2		6	3	9	8		4			10				5	7				11	
9	(h)	Small Heath	L	3-4	Holmes (2), Shaw	4,000	1		2		6	3	9	8		4			10				5	7				11	
15	(a)	Lincoln City	D	1-1	Shaw	3,000	1		2		4	3	9	8		6			10				5	7					11
16	(a)	Grimsby Town	L	0-2*		2,000	1		2		6	3	9	8					10				5	7				11	
						Apps	17	4	20	4	20	18	20	21	9	21	17	4	21	5	4	2	13	11	1	2	2	4	2
League position: 11th						Goals							9	5	2	1	6		5					3					1

** Walsall played with only 10 men*

Own goal : 1

F.A. Cup

Date		Opponent	Rd	Score	Scorers	Att	Hawkins T.	Proffitt	Withington	Tonks J.	Stokes A.	Pinches	Holmes S.	Shaw C.	Wood H.	Forsyth N.	Wilson J.	Morely	Pangbourne	Edge	Loynes
Oct 3	(h)	Wednesbury O.A.	1Q	7-2	Pangbourne (2), Holmes (3), Wood, Morely	3,000			3	4			9	6	10		11	5	8	1	2
24	(h)	Burton Swifts	2Q	2-4	Holmes, Shaw	4,000		2	3	4			9	7	10		11	5	8	1	
						Apps		1	2	2			2	2	2		2	2	2	2	1
						Goals							4	1	1			1	2		

SEASON 1892-93

Division 2

Date	Opponent	Res	Score	Scorers	Att	Alcock J.	Clark H.	Davis W.	Forsyth N.	Gray F.J.S.	Hawkins T.	Haynes A.	Hodson T.	Holmes S.	Marlow T.	Marshall F.A.	Pangbourne	Pinches A.	Robinson H.	Russell J.H.	Sadler J.	Shaw T.	Siddons W.	Turner J.	Whitehouse	Whittick E.A	Withington .	Woodward .
Sep 3 (h)	Darwen	L	1-2	Gray	4,000				6	10	1			8		7	11	3	4					9		5	2	
10 (h)	Small Heath	L	1-3	Turner	2,500		7		6	11	1			10		8		3	4					9			2	5
17 (h)	Ardwick	L	2-4	Marshall, Turner	2,000				6		1			9	11	8	10	3	4			5		7			2	
24 (a)	Darwen	L	0-5		1,500				6	11	1			7	10		9	3	4			5		8			2	
Oct 1 (a)	Ardwick	L	0-2		2,000				6		1			7	11		10	3	4	9		5		8			2	
8 (h)	Lincoln City	W	2-1	Pangbourne, Shaw	2,000		7		6		1			8	11		10	3	4			5		9			2	
22 (h)	Grimsby Town	W	3-1	Holmes, Turner (2)	2,500				10		1			8	11	7		3	4			5		9	6		2	
Nov 5 (a)	Crewe Alex.	W	6-5	Forsyth (2), Marshall Holmes (2), Turner	2,000				10		1			8	11	7		3	4				2	9	6		5	
26 (a)	Northwich Victoria	L	2-5	Forsyth (2)	1,500				10		1			8	11	7		3	4			9	2		6		5	
Dec 17 (a)	Small Heath	L	0-12		2,000			8	10		1	7			11			3	4				2	9	6		5	
24 (h)	Bootle	D	4-4	Forsyth (2), Davis (2)	500			8	6	11	1	7	10					3	4	9		5					2	
31 (a)	Burslem P Vale	L	0-3		2,000			10	11		1	7			9			3	4				2	8	6		5	
Jan 7 (a)	Sheffield United	L	0-3		2,000			10	8		1			11				3	4		7	5		9	6			2
14 (h)	Crewe Alex.	D	3-3	Turner, Davis, Forsyth	1,000			10	8		1			11	7			3	4			6		9			5	2
Feb 4 (a)	Burton Swifts	L	2-3	Marlow, Turner	700			8	7	11	1			6	10			3	4			5		9			2	
11 (h)	Northwich Vic.	L	2-0	Opponent (og), Marlow	500		5	7	6	11	1			8	10			3				4		9				
18 (h)	Burslem P Vale	W	3-0	Holmes, Marlow, Davis	700			7	9	11	1			8	10			3	4			6					5	2
Mar 4 (h)	Burton Swifts	W	3-2	Alcock, Holmes, Davis	1,000	10		7	8		1			9	11			3	4			5					6	2
18 (a)	Bootle	L	1-7	Alcock	600	10		7	8		1			9	11			3	4			5					6	2
31 (a)	Lincoln City	L	1-3	Holmes	1,000	10		7	8		1		11	9				3	4			5					6	2
Apr 1 (a)	Grimsby Town	L	0-3		1,000	10		7	8		1			9	11			3	4			5					6	2
15 (h)	Sheffield United	D	1-1	Holmes	2,000	10		7	6		1			9	11			3	8			5					4	2
					Apps	5	3	13	22	7	22	3	2	19	17	6	5	22	21	2	1	17	4	14	6	1	20	9
League position: 12th					Goals	2		5	7	1				7	3	2	1					1		7				

own goal: 1

F.A. Cup

Date	Opponent	Rd	Score	Scorers	Att	Alcock J.	Clark H.	Davis W.	Forsyth N.	Gray F.J.S.	Hawkins T.	Haynes A.	Hodson T.	Holmes S.	Marlow T.	Marshall F.A.	Pangbourne	Pinches A.	Robinson H.	Russell J.H.	Sadler J.	Shaw T.	Siddons W.	Turner J.	Whitehouse	Whittick E.A	Withington .	Woodward .
Oct 15 (h)	Derby Junction*	1Q	1-0	Holmes (aet)	2,000		7		6		1			8	11		10	3	4			9			5		2	
29 (h)	Stourbridge	2Q	7-0	Marlow (2), Turner, Forsyth (2), Holmes (2)	2,000				11		1			8	10	7		3	4				2	9	6		5	
Nov 19 (h)	Burton Swifts	3Q	1-3	Holmes	3,000				10		1			8	11	7		3	4				2	9	6		5	
					Apps		1		3		3			3	3	2	1	3	3			1	2	2	3		3	
					Goals				2					4	2									1				

* Game v Derby Junction due to be played away but venue switched to Walsall.

SEASON 1893-94

Division 2

Date	Opponent	Res	Score	Scorers	Att	Alcock J	Bailey J.T	Brettle N	Connolly J	Cook R	Copeland D	Cox S	Davies J.W	Davis W	Dunn W	Forsyth N	Gee J.H	Harley C.E	Hawkins T	Hodson A	Holmes S	Leatherbarrow C	Ledbrook L	Lofthouse J. M	McDonald W	McLanesclan A	McWhinnie W	Marlow T	Morton J.W	O'Brien J	Pinches A	Robinson H	Shaw T	Smellie R	Taylor A	Tracey D	Warner J
Sept 2 (h)	Small Heath	L	1-3	Tracey	5,000		3		9	5			6	7		4			1		8							11						2		10	
9 (h)	Burslem PV	L	0-5		3,000		3		10	5			4	11						7					6				1					2	9	8	
11 (a)	Arsenal	L	0-4		2,500		3			5			4	7		6				11	9					1	8							2		10	
16 (a)	Small Heath	L	0-4		2,000	10	3		7							6				11	9				5	1	8						4	2			
23 (h)	Crewe Alex.	W	5-1	Robinson, McWhinnie (2), Alcock, Holmes.	1,500	11				5						6			1		9		10				8				3	7	4	2			
26 (h)	Rotherham T.	W	3-0	McWhinnie, Ledbrook, Holmes.	2,000	11	3			5						6			1		9		10				8					7	4	2			
30 (a)	Grimsby T.	L	2-5	Holmes, Alcock.	1,500	11	2			5						6			1		9		10				8				3	7	4				
Oct 7 (a)	Northwich V.	L	0-1		2,000	11	2		9	5						6			1				10				8					7	4	3			
21 (h)	Middlesbro. I.	W	1-0	Holmes.	2,000		2			5			6	7		4			1		9		10				8	11						3			
Nov 11 (h)	Liverpool	D	1-1	Cox.	4,000		2			5	9	11	6			4			1		7						8			10				3			
18 (h)	Ardwick	L	0-3		2,000		2			5	9	11	6			4			1		7						8			10				3			
Dec 2 (a)	Crewe Alex.	D	1-1	Lofthouse.	1,500		2			5	9				11						4	10		7			8			6				3			1
9 (a)	Liverpool	L	0-3		3,000		2			5	9				11	6					4	10		7			8							3			1
23 (h)	Northwich V.	W	3-0	Copeland, Cooke, McWhinnie.	2,000		2			5	9					6					4	10		7			8			11				3			1
26 (h)	Newcastle U.	L	1-2	Copeland.	3,000		2			5	9					6					4	10		7			8			11				3			1
30 (a)	Middlesbro. I.	D	1-1	Leatherbarrow.	1,500		2			5	10					6					4	9		7			8			11	3						1
Jan 6 (h)	Burton Swifts.	L	3-4	Leatherbarrow (2), Copeland.	2,000		2			5	10					6						9		7			8			11	3	4					1
20 (a)	Notts County	L	0-2		1,500		2			5	9					6					4	8		7			10			11	3						1
Feb 3 (a)	Rotherham T.	L	2-3	Ledbrook, Leatherbarrow.	1,000		2			5	9					6					4	8	10							11	3	7					1
10 (a)	Burslem PV	W	2-1	O'Brien, McWhinnie	1,500		2			5	9					6					4	8		7			10			11	3						1
12 (h)	Arsenal	L	1-2	Holmes.	3,000		2			5	9					6					4	8		7			10			11	3						1
24 (a)	Burton Swifts.	L	5-8	O'Brien (2), Copeland, McWhinnie, opponent (og).	1,200		2			5	9					6					4	8		7			10			11	3						1
Mar 10 (a)	Newcastle U.	L	0-2		3,000		2			5	9					6					4	8		7			10			11	3						1
12 (h)	Notts County	W	2-1	Leatherbarrow (2).	2,000		2			5	9					6			1		4	8		7			10			11	3						
24 (h)	Grimsby T.	W	5-0	O'Brien, Leatherbarrow, Gee, Harley, Holmes.	1,500			5		2						6	8	7	1		4	9					10			11	3						
26 (h)	Lincoln City	W	5-2	Gee (2), McWhinnie, Harley, Leatherbarrow.	2,000			5		2						6	8	7	1		4	9					10			11	3						
Apr 7 (a)	Lincoln City	W	2-0	McWhinnie, Lofthouse.	1,500			5		2	9					6			1		4	8		7			10			11	3						
14 (h)	Ardwick	W	5-2	McWhinnie (3), Copeland, Leatherbarrow.	1,700			5		2	9					6		7	1		4	8					10			11	3						
					Apps	5	23	4	4	27	17	2	6	4	2	26	2	3	13	3	25	17	6	13	2	2	25	2	1	18	15	6	5	14	1	3	12
League position: 10th					Goals	2				1	5	1					3	2			6	9	2	2			11			4		1				1	

Own Goal 1.

F.A. Cup

Date	Opponent	Rd	Score	Scorers	Att	Alcock J	Bailey J.T	Brettle N	Connolly J	Cook R	Copeland D	Cox S	Davies J.W	Davis W	Dunn W	Forsyth N	Gee J.H	Harley C.E	Hawkins T	Hodson A	Holmes S	Leatherbarrow C	Ledbrook L	Lofthouse J. M	McDonald W	McLanesclan A	McWhinnie W	Marlow T	Morton J.W	O'Brien J	Pinches A	Robinson H	Shaw T	Smellie R	Taylor A	Tracey D	Warner J
Oct 14 (a)	Wellington St Geo	1Q	3-0	Marlow (2), Holmes	1,000		2			5			6	7		4			1		9		10				8	11						3			
Nov 4 (a)	Stourbridge	2Q	3-1	Holmes (3)	2,500		2			5	9	10	6			4					7						8			11				3			1
25 (h)	Brierley Hill All	3Q	1-2	Cook	4,000		2			5	9	10	4			6					7						8			11				3			1
					Apps		3			3	2	2	3	1		3			1		3		1				3	1		2				3			2
					Goals					1											4							2									

SEASON 1894-95

Division 2

Date	Opponent	Res	Score	Scorers	Att	Benwell J	Brettle N	Copeland D	Cook R	Cox S	Devey W	Forsyth N	Gee H	Hartley	Hawkins T	Holmes S	Leatherbarrow	Lewis G	Lofthouse J	McWhinnie	O'Brien J	Pinches A	Roberts A.	Roberts W.	Robertson	Salt H	Shaw G.T	Stokes A.W	Taylor W
Sept 1 (a)	Burslem PV	L	0-1		3,000	1	5	9				6		7		4	8			10	11	3			2				
8 (h)	Grimsby T.	W	4-3	O'Brien, Lofthouse, Leatherbarrow, Copeland.	2,000	1	5	9				6				4	8		7	10	11	3			2				
15 (h)	Manchester C.	L	1-2	O'Brien.	2,500	1	5	9				6				4	8		7	10	11	3			2				
22 (h)	Burslem PV	W	2-0	Hartley, Holmes.	1,500	1	5				9	6		7		4	8			10		3		11	2				
24 (h)	Rotherham T.	L	1-2	Brettle.	2,000	1	5	9				6		7		4	8				11	3		10	2				
29 (a)	Crewe Alex.	W	3-2	O'Brien, Gee, opponent (og).	1,500	1	5	10	2		9	6	8			4			7		11	3							
Oct 1 (a)	Burton Swifts.	W	2-1	Copeland (2).	1,000	1	5	10	2		9	6	8	7		4					11	3							
6 (a)	Manchester C.	L	1-6	Leatherbarrow.	3,000	1	5	9				6		7		4	8		11		10	3			2				
27 (h)	Bury	L	0-3		1,500	1	5			10		6	8	7		4					11	3		9	2				
Nov 10 (h)	Arsenal	W	4-1	Devey (2), Leatherbarrow, O'Brien.	3,000	1	5	10			9	6				4	8		7		11	3			2				
17 (a)	Rotherham T.	L	1-6	Lofthouse.	1,500		5				9	6	8		1	4			7		11	3		10	2				
Dec 1 (a)	Darwen.	L	0-2		1,000	1	5				9	10	8			4		6	7		11	3			2				
8 (h)	Leicester F.	L	1-3	O'Brien.	2,000	1	5	10			9	6		8		4			7		11	3			2				
22 (a)	Newcastle U.	L	2-7	Gee (2).	4,000		5	10	2		9	6	8		1	4			7		11	3							
25 (a)	Notts County	L	0-5		2,000	1	5				9	10	8			4		6	7		11	3			2				
26 (h)	Newton H.	L	1-2	Roberts.	3,000		5	10	2		9	6			1	4			7		11	3		8					
29 (h)	Newcastle U.	*L	2-3	Copeland (2).	3,000		5	10	2		9	6			1	4			7		11	3		8					
Jan 5 (a)	Leicester F.	L	1-9	Devey.	2,000	10					9	6	8		1	4		2	7			3	11			5			
12 (a)	Burton W.	L	0-7		1,200	10						6			1	8		4	7			3	11	9		5	2		
26 (h)	Crewe Alex.	W	4-0	W. Roberts, Forsyth, Brettle, Devey.	2,000		5				9	6			1	10		2	7			3	11	8		4			
Feb 16 (a)	Lincoln City	L	0-1		800		5			10	9	6			1	7		2				3	11	8		4			
Mar 16 (a)	Grimsby T.	L	0-1		1,000		5	10			9	6			1	8		2	7			3	11			4			
23 (h)	Burton Swifts.	W	4-1	W. Roberts (2), Taylor, Forsyth.	1,000		5	10			9	6			1	4		2	7			3		8					11
25 (h)	Notts County	W	2-1	Devey, Taylor.	1,500		5	10			9	6			1	4		2	7			3				8			11
Apr 2 (a)	Bury	L	1-4	Taylor.	1,000		5	10				6			1	8		2	7			3		9				4	11
3 (a)	Newton H.	L	0-9		2,000		5	10				9			1	8		2				3		9		4		7	11
12 (a)	Arsenal	L	1-6	Devey.	3,000		5	10			9	7			1	4		2				3		8		6			11
15 (h)	Darwen	W	5-1	W. Roberts (2), Copeland, Taylor (2).	1,000		5	10			9	6			1	7		2				3		8		4			11
16 (h)	Burton W.	W	3-1	Holmes, Devey, Taylor.	700		5	10			9	6			1	7		2				3		8		4			11
20 (h)	Lincoln City	L	1-2	Holmes.	500			10			9	6			1	5		2	7			3		8		4			11
					Apps	15	27	21	5	2	21	30	8	7	17	30	7	15	20	4	16	30	5	16	12	11	1	2	8
League position: 14th				* Game abandoned after 80 minutes, score stood.	Goals		2	6			7	2	3	1		3	3		2		5			6					6

F.A. Cup

Own Goal 1.

Date	Opponent	Rd	Score	Scorers	Att	Benwell J	Brettle N	Copeland D	Cook R	Cox S	Devey W	Forsyth N	Gee H	Hartley	Hawkins T	Holmes S	Leatherbarrow	Lewis G	Lofthouse J	McWhinnie	O'Brien J	Pinches A	Roberts A.	Roberts W.	Robertson	Salt H	Shaw G.T	Stokes A.W	Taylor W
Oct 13 (a)	Burton Wds	1Q	0-3		2,500	1	5	8			9	4	11	10		6			7			3			2				
					Apps	1	1	1			1	1	1	1		1			1			1			1				

Walsall did not play League Football in season 1895-96. They failed to gain re-election to the Second Division at the end of the 1894-95 campaign, and entered the Midland League. But in the summer of 1896 they were re-admitted into Division Two along with Blackpool and Gainsborough Trinity.

SEASON 1895-96

Midland League

Date	Opponent	Res	Score	Scorers	Att	Towe E.J.	Pinches A	Lewis G.	Wilkes	Brettle N.	Forsyth N	Holmes S.	Payton	Copeland D.	Taylor W.	Milner	Cooper	Salt H	Brocksopp A	Horobin D.	Plimmer	Haddon	Edwards	Meredith	Aston C.	Aston J.	Hawkins T.	Brocksopp E.H.	Keeling	Haynes	Roberts W.	Rigby	Wightman
Sep 7 (h)	Matlock	W	7-1	Brettle, Taylor (3), Copeland (2), Holmes (pen)	2,000	1	2	3	4	5	6	7		9	10			4													8	11	
14 (h)	Rushden Town	D	1-1	Copeland	2,500	1		2	3	5	6	7		9	10	11		4															8
21 (a)	Mansfield	W	3-0	Payton, Copeland, Taylor	1,500	1	2	3	4	5	6	7	8	9	10	11																	
23 (h)	Gainsborough T	W	3-2	Holmes , Taylor, Copeland	3,000	1	2	3	4	5	6	7	8	9	10	11																	
28 (a)	Heanor Town	D	4-4	Holmes (2), Cooper, Copeland	3,000	1	3	2	4	5	6	7		8	10	11	9																
Oct 5 (a)	Dresden Utd	W	3-0	Wilkes, Holmes, Copeland	500	1	3	2	7	5	6	8		9	10			4	11														
19 (a)	Rushden Town	D	2-2	Taylor, Wilkes	1,500	1	3	2	4		6	8		9	10			5	11	7													
26 (h)	Ilkeston Tn	W	2-1	Holmes, Copeland	2,000	1	3	2			6	8		9	5			4	11	7	10												
Nov 9 (a)	Kettering	L	2-5	Copeland, Holmes	4,000	1		2	3	4	6	8		9	5				11	7	10												
16 (h)	Barnsley St Peter's	W	5-0	Holmes, Copeland (2), Plimmer, Brocksopp	600	1	3	2		4	6	8		9	5				11	7	10												
30 (a)	Long Eaton Rangers	L	0-3		1,500	1	3		6	2		4		8	5					7	10	9	11										
Dec 7 (h)	Wellingborough	W	6-1	Holmes (2), Plimmer, Copeland (2), Brocksopp A.	200	1	3	2				8		9	5				11	7	10			4	6								
Jan 1 (a)	Barnsley St Peter's	L	1-5	Holmes	4,000	1	3	2	6			4		9					11	7	10				5	8							
4 (a)	Grantham Rovers	D	1-1	Copeland	200	1	3	2	5			4		9					11	7	10				6	8							
11 (h)	Newark	W	5-1	Holmes (3), Horobin, Brocksopp A.	1,500	1	3	2	4			8		9			6		11	7	10				5								
18 (h)	Mansfield	W	4-0	Aston J, Taylor (2), Plimmer	2,500			2				4		9	5		3		11	7	10				6	8	1						
25 (a)	Newark	W	4-3	Plimmer (2), Copeland, Horobin.	200	1	3	2				4		9	5				11	7	10				6	8							
Feb 1 (h)	Doncaster Rovers	W	9-1	Brocksopp A (2), Aston J (3), Holmes (2), Copeland, Horobin	2,000	1	3	2				4		9	5				11	7	10				6	8							
15 (h)	Dresden Utd	W	5-2	Aston J, Copeland (2), Brocksopp A (2)	1,500		3	2				4		9	5				10	7	11				6	8	1						
22 (a)	Gainsborough T	L	1-4	Holmes (pen)	2,000		3	2				4		9	5				11	7					6	8	1	10					
29 (h)	Kettering	W	5-2	Brocksopp A (3), Aston J (2)	3,000		3	2				4		9	5				11	7					6	8	1	10					
Mar 3 (a)	Wellingborough	D	1-1	Brocksopp A	2,000		3	2				4		9	5				11	7					6	8	1	10					
7 (a)	Doncaster Rovers	L	2-3	Copeland, Aston J.	1,500		3	2				4		9					11	7	5				6	8	1	10					
28 (h)	Long Eaton Rangers	W	2-0	Copeland, Fairbrother (og).	2,000		3	2	6			4		9	5				11	7						8	1	10					
Apr 3 (a)	Matlock	W	5-0	Haynes, Brocksopp E (2), Aston J (2)	1,500		3		6			4			5		2		11	7						8	1	10		9			
7 (a)	Ilkeston Town	W	4-2	Aston J, Horobin, Lewis, Brocksopp E	1,000		3	2	6			4		9	5				11	7						8	1	10					
11 (h)	Heanor Town	D	2-2	Brocksopp A (2)	1,500			2				4		9	5				11	7					6	8	1	10	3				
15 (a)	Grantham	W	3-1	Aston J, Copeland, Horobin	800		3	2				4		9	5				11	7					6	8	1	10					
					Apps	17	24	26	15	9	10	28	2	27	24	4	4	5	22	22	13	1	1	1	14	15	11	9	1	1	1	1	1
League position: 3rd					Goals			1	2	1	1	17	1	21	7		1		14	6	5					12		2		1			

F.A. Cup

Own goal 1

Date	Opponent	Rd	Score	Scorers	Att	Towe E.J.	Pinches A	Lewis G.	Wilkes	Brettle N.	Forsyth N	Holmes S.	Payton	Copeland D.	Taylor W.	Milner	Cooper	Salt H	Brocksopp A	Horobin D.	Plimmer	Haddon	Edwards	Meredith	Aston C.	Aston J.	Hawkins T.	Brocksopp E.H.	Keeling	Haynes	Roberts W.	Rigby	Wightman
Oct 12 (h)	Dresden Utd	1Q	1-0	Milner	2,000	1	3	2	7	5	6	8			9	10		4	11														
Nov 2 (h)	Redditch	2Q	4-0	Brettle, Horobin, Holmes, King (og)	2,500	1		2	3	4	6	8		9	5				11		7	10											
23 (a)	Wrockwardine Wood	3Q	1-3	Holmes	2,000	1	3	2		5	6	8		10	9			4	11		7												
					Apps	3	2	3	2	3	3	3		1	3	2		2	3		2	1											
					Goals					1		2				1					1												

SEASON 1896-97

Division 2

Date		Opponent		Score	Scorers	Att	Aston C.L.	Aston J.	Baugh R.	Brocksopp A.	Bunyan C.	Bunyan G.	Copeland D	Davies G.	Griffin A	Hawkins T.	Holmes S.	Horobin D	Johnson G.	Johnson T. W.	Lewis G.	Moore F.	Paddock J.	Peers E.	Pinches A.	Taggart J.	Taylor W.	Towe E.J.	Wilkes A
Sept 5	(h)	Burton Wand.	W	2-0	J. Aston, Griffin.	2,500	4	8					10		9	1		7	11		2				3	6	5		
7	(a)	Newton Heath	L	0-2		2,000		8	2				10		9	1	4		7		3		11			6	5		
12	(a)	Arsenal	D	1-1	Copeland.	4,000		8	2				10		9	1	4	7	11		3					6	5		
19	(h)	Gainsboro. T.	D	1-1	Copeland.	2,000		8	2				10		9	1	4	7	11		3					6	5		
21	(h)	Newton Heath	L	2-3	J. Aston, Lewis.	2,500	6	8	2				10		9	1	4	7	11		3						5		
26	(a)	Gainsboro. T.	L	0-2		1,500	6	8	2				9			1	4	7	11	10	3								5
Oct 5	(a)	Burton Swifts.	W	3-1	Griffin, Holmes (2).	1,000	4	8							9	1	7		11	10	2				3	6	5		
10	(a)	Loughboro.	W	2-1	Griffin (2).	1,000	4	8							9	1	7		11	10	2				3	6	5		
17	(h)	Arsenal	W	5-3	T. Johnson, G. Johnson, Wilkes (3).	2,500	4	8		7									11	10	2				3	6	5	1	9
24	(h)	Small Heath	L	1-6	G. Johnson.	4,000	4	8		7					9				10		2		11		3	6	5	1	
31	(h)	Loughboro.	W	5-1	Griffin (2), J. Aston (2), C. Aston.	2,000	4	8	3				9		11		7		10		2					6		1	5
Nov 14	(a)	Notts. County	L	2-5	Copeland, G. Johnson.	1,500	2	7					8		9		4		10	11	3					6	5		1
23	(h)	Manchester C.	W	3-2	T. Johnson, G. Johnson (2).	2,000	3	7			1		8		9		4		10	11	2					6	5		
28	(a)	Leicester F.	L	1-4	Griffin.	4,000	3	7			1		8		9		4		10	11	2					6	5		
Dec 25	(a)	Small Heath	D	3-3	J. Aston (2), Griffin.	7,500	3	7			1		8		9		4		10	11	2					6	5		
26	(a)	Darwen*	L	0-12		2,000					1	2	8		9					10		4				6			5
Jan 6	(a)	Manchester C.	L	0-5		3,000		7			1		8			3	4		10	11		9		2		6	5		
9	(a)	Burton Wand.	L	0-1		1,700	3	7			1		8		9		4		10	11				2			5		6
16	(h)	Notts. County	L	1-3	G. Johnson.	2,000	3	7			1		8		9		4		10	11				2		6	5		
23	(h)	Burton Swifts.	W	5-2	Davies, G. Johnson (2), T. Johnson (2).	1,500	6	7			1			8	9		4		10	11	3			2			5		
Feb 13	(a)	Blackpool	L	2-3	Griffin, Davies.	2,000	6				1		8	7	9		4		10	11	3			2			5		
27	(h)	Grimsby T.	L	0-1		1,700	3	7			1		8		9		4		10	11				2		6			5
Mar 6	(a)	Newcastle U.	L	0-2		4,000	3	7			1		8		9		4		10	11				2		6			5
13	(a)	Grimsby T.	W	1-0	Griffin.	2,000	3	7			1		8		9		4		10	11				2		6			5
20	(h)	Leicester F.	D	1-1	Wilkes.	2,500	3	7			1		8		9		4		10				11	2		6			5
Apr 3	(h)	Newcastle U.	L	0-2		3,000	3	8			1		10		9		4	7	11					2		6			5
10	(h)	Blackpool	W	2-0	Griffin, G. Johnson.	1,200	3	8			1		10		9		4	7	11					2		6			5
16	(a)	Lincoln C.	L	1-2	J. Aston.	1,000	3	8			1		10		9		4	7	11					2		6			5
17	(h)	Lincoln C.	W	5-0	J. Aston (2), Holmes, G. Johnson, Griffin.	1,000	3	8			1		10		9		4	7	11					2		6			5
21	(h)	Darwen*	W	4-0	J. Aston, Copeland (2), G. Johnson.	1,500	3	8			1		10		9		4	7	11					2		6			5
						Apps	25	28	6	2	18	1	25	2	27	9	26	10	29	17	17	2	3	14	5	25	18	3	15
League position: 12th						Goals	1	10					5	2	12		3		11	4	1								4

* 8 men only fielded in game v. Darwen 26.12.1896.

F.A. Cup

Date		Opponent	Rd	Score	Scorers	Att	Aston C.L.	Aston J.	Baugh R.	Brocksopp A.	Bunyan C.	Bunyan G.	Copeland D	Davies G.	Griffin A	Hawkins T.	Holmes S.	Horobin D	Johnson G.	Johnson T. W.	Lewis G.	Moore F.	Paddock J.	Peers E.	Pinches A.	Taggart J.	Taylor W.	Towe E.J.	Wilkes A
Nov 21	(h)	Dresden Utd	3Q	11-0	T Johnson (4), G Johnson (3), A Griffin (3), J Aston	3,000	3	7					8		9	1	4		10	11	2					6	5		
Dec 19	(h)	Burton Swifts	4Q	1-1	T Johnson	3,000	3	7			1		8		9		4		10	11	2					6	5		
21	(a)	Burton Swifts	4QR	0-1		1,000	3	7			1		8		9		4		10	11	2					6	5		
						Apps	3	3			2		3		3	1	3		3	3	3					3	3		
						Goals		1							3				3	5									

SEASON 1897-98

Division 2

Date		Opponent		Score	Scorers	Att	Aston C.L.	Aston J.	Bunyan C.	Copeland D.	Devey W.	Griffin A.	Hawkins T.	Hitch A.	Hodson E.	Holmes S.	Horobin D.	Izon C.J.	Jenkyns C.A.	Johnson G.	Johnston J.	Loynes J.	Peers E.	Taggart J.	Wedge A.	Wilkes A.
Sept 4	(a)	Loughboro.	L	1-2	Horobin.	2,000	3	8	1	10		9				4	7			11			2	6		5
11	(h)	Newcastle U.	L	2-3	J. Aston (2).	3,000	3	8	1	4		9					7	11		10			2	6		5
18	(a)	Burnley	L	1-4	Griffin	2,500	3		1	8		9				4	7	11		10			2	6		5
25	(h)	Burnley	L	1-2	Johnson	3,000	3	9	1	8						4	7	11		10			2	6		5
27	(h)	Darwen	W	5-0	J. Aston, Wilkes (2), Copeland, Horobin.	2,000	3	8	1	9		11				4	7			10			2	6		5
Oct 2	(a)	Burton Swifts	L	2-3	Johnson, Horobin	1,500	2	8	1	9		11	3				7			10		4		6		5
9	(h)	Loughboro.	W	3-0	Copeland, Johnson (2).	2,000	3	8	1	9		11					7			10		4	2	6		5
16	(a)	Leicester F.	L	1-3	Loynes.	2,500	3	9	1	10		11				8	7					4	2	6		5
23	(h)	Burton Swifts	W	4-0	J. Aston, Griffin, Johnson (2).	2,000	3	8	1			11				9	7			10		4	2	6		5
30	(a)	Newton H.	L	0-6		2,000	3	8	1	10		11				9	7					4	2	6		5
Nov 6	(h)	Arsenal	W	3-2	Griffin, Johnson (2).	3,000		8	1			11	2	4		9	7			10			3	6		5
13	(a)	Arsenal	L	0-4		3,500		8	1			11		5		3	7			10		4	2	6		9
20	(h)	Grimsby T.	D	1-1	Taggart.	2,000	3	8	1			11				9	7			10		4	2	6		5
Dec 4	(a)	Small Heath	L	0-6		3,000	3	8	1							7		9	5		11	4	2	6		10
11	(h)	Newton H.	D	1-1	J. Aston.	2,000	3	8	1			11				7		9	5	10			2	6		4
18	(h)	Small Heath	L	1-2	Griffin.	3,000	3	8	1			11				7		9	5	10			2	6		4
27	(h)	Blackpool	W	6-0	Holmes (3), opponent (og), Aston (2).	2,000	3	8	1			11				7		9	5	10			2	6		4
Jan 1	(a)	Newcastle U.	L	1-2	Johnston	3,000	3	8	1		9	10				7			5		11		2	6		4
3	(a)	Manchester C.	L	2-3	Johnson, Devey.	4,000	3	8	1		9	11				7			5	10			2	6		4
8	(h)	Luton Town	W	5-0	Devey (2), Holmes J., Aston (2).	2,000	3	8	1		9	11				7			5	10			2	6		4
15	(h)	Manchester C.	D	2-2	J. Aston, Jenkyns.	2,500	3	8	1		9	11				7			5	10			2	6		4
22	(a)	Gainsboro. T.	D	1-1	Devey.	1,500	3	8	1		9	11				7			5	10			2	6		4
Feb 5	(a)	Luton Town	L	0-6		2,000	3	8	1		9	11			7				5	10			2	6		4
12	(a)	Darwen	W	2-1	Johnson, Devey.	1,500		8		11	9		1			7			5	10			2	6	3	4
26	(h)	Leicester F.	W	2-1	Johnson, Griffin.	2,000	3		1	8	9	11				7			5	10			2	6		4
Mar 5	(a)	Grimsby T.	W	2-1	Copeland, Griffin.	1,500	3	8		11		9	1			7			5	10			2	6		4
12	(h)	Lincoln C.	W	3-1	J. Aston, Holmes, Wedge.	1,000	3	8			11	9	1			7			5	10				6	2	4
Apr 2	(a)	Blackpool	D	1-1	Griffin.	1,200	3	8	1		11	9				7			5	10			2	6		4
9	(a)	Lincoln C.	W	2-0	J. Aston, Devey.	1,000	3	8			11	9	1			7			5	10			2	6		4
11	(h)	Gainsboro. T.	W	3-0	Jenkyns, Johnson, Holmes.	900	3	8	1	9		11				7			5	10			2	6		4
						Apps	27	28	26	13	11	27	6	2	1	26	13	7	17	26	2	8	28	30	2	30
League position: 10th						Goals		12		3	6	7				6	3		2	12	1	1		1	1	2

Own Goal 1.

F.A. Cup

Date		Opponent	Rd	Score	Scorers	Att	Aston C.L.	Aston J.	Bunyan C.	Copeland D.	Devey W.	Griffin A.	Hawkins T.	Hitch A.	Hodson E.	Holmes S.	Horobin D.	Izon C.J.	Jenkyns C.A.	Johnson G.	Johnston J.	Loynes J.	Peers E.	Taggart J.	Wedge A.	Wilkes A.
Jan 29	(a)	Newton Heath	1	0-1		6,000	3	8	1		9	11				7			5	10			2	6		4
						Apps	1	1	1		1	1				1			1	1			1	1		1

SEASON 1898-99

Division 2

Date	Opponent	Res	Score	Scorers	Att	Aston J.	Davis H.	Dean A.	Flynn J.	Genever E.	Greatwich F.	Griffin A.	Hickinbotham	Holmes S.	Jenkyns C.	Lyons J.W.	Martin J.	Millington E.	Peers E.	Peers H.	Philpott W.	Pratt J.	Smith G.	Taggart J.	Tennant W.	Vail T.	Wedge A.	Yates H.R.
Sep 3	(h) Loughboro.	W	7-0	Griffin (2), Greatwich (2), Vail (2), Peers H.	2,000	8	3				7	11			5		4		2	10				6	1	9		
10	(a) Blackpool	W	2-1	Aston (2).	2,000	8	2				7	11			5					10			4	6	1	9	3	
17	(h) Grimsby T.	W	4-1	Peers H. (2), Martin (2).	2,500		3				7	11			5		8		2	10			4	6	1	9		
24	(a) Newton H.	L	0-1		2,000	8		7			11				5				2	10			4	6	1	9	3	
26	(h) Leicester F.	D	1-1	Griffin	2,500	8		7				11			5				2	10			4	6	1	9	3	
Oct 1	(h) New Brighton	D	1-1	Martin.	2,000	8	3	7				11			5		10		2				4	6	1	9		
8	(a) Lincoln C.	D	1-1	Vail	1,750	8	3	7				11			5		10		2				4	6	1	9		
15	(h) Arsenal	W	4-1	Griffin, Vail, Dean (2).	3,000	8	3	7				11			5		10		2				4	6	1	9		
22	(a) Luton Town	L	2-3	Pratt, Vail.	2,000	8	3	7						4	5		10		2			11		6	1	9		
Nov 5	(a) Darwen	D	1-1	Martin.	1,700	8	3	7						4	5		10	6	2	11					1	9		
12	(h) Gainsboro. T.	W	6-1	Vail, Dean (3), Aston (2).	2,000	8	3	7		11				4			10		2				5	6	1	9		
19	(a) Manchester C.	L	0-2		3,000	8		7				11		3	5		10		2				4	6	1	9		
26	(h) Glossop	W	2-0	Genever, Martin.	2,000	8	3			11		7		4			10							6	1	9	2	5
Dec 3	(a) Barnsley	D	1-1	Vail	2,500	8	3	7		11				4			10		2					6	1	9		5
17	(h) Burslem P.V.	D	1-1	Opponent (og).	3,000	8	3	7	11					4			10		2					6	1	9		5
24	(a) Small Heath	L	1-2	Vail.	6,500	8	3	7				11		4			10		2					6	1	9		5
31	(a) Loughboro.	D	1-1	Peers H.	2,000	8	3	7				11		4			5		2	10				6	1	9		
Jan 7	(h) Blackpool	W	6-0	Griffin, Aston (2), Vail (3).	2,500	8	3	7				11		4			10		2	5				6	1	9		
14	(a) Grimsby T.	L	1-2	Martin.	2,000	8	3	7				11		4			10		2				5	6	1	9		
21	(h) Newton H.	W	2-0	Griffin (2).	1,500	8	3	7				11		4	5		10		2					6	1	9		
28	(a) New Brighton	L	0-6		1,000	8	3	7				11		4	5		10		2					6	1	9		
Feb 4	(h) Lincoln City	W	3-2	Holmes, Dean, Aston.	1,000	8	3	7				11		4	5		10		2					6	1	9		
11	(a) Arsenal	D	0-0		3,000		3	7				11		4	5		10		2	8				6	1	9		
18	(h) Luton Town	W	6-0	Dean (2), Aston, Vail (2), Martin.	2,000	8	3	7				11		4	5		10		2					6	1	9		
25	(a) Leicester F.	D	2-2	Aston (2).	1,700	9	3	7				11	4		5		10		2					6	1	8		
Mar 4	(h) Darwen	W	10-0	Aston (4), Dean (3), Vail (2), Peers E.	2,000	8	3	7		10		11		4	5		6		2						1	9		
11	(a) Gainsboro. T.	D	0-0		1,500	8	3	7				11		4	5		10		2	9				6	1			
18	(h) Manchester C.	D	1-1	Vail.	3,000	8	4	7				11	3		5		10		2					6	1	9		
25	(a) Glossop	L	0-2		1,000	8	2	7	11				3		5	4	10							6	1	9		
31	(a) Burton Swifts.	W	2-0	Martin (2).	1,200	8	3	7	11						5		10		2		4			6	1	9		
Apr 1	(h) Barnsley	D	1-1	Martin	2,000	8	3	7	11					4	5		10		2					6	1	9		
4	(h) Burton Swifts.	W	7-1	Griffin (3), Dean (2), Aston, Peers E.	1,750	8	3	7	11			9		5			10		2		4			6	1			
15	(a) Burslem P.V.	W	1-0	Martin.	2,000	8	3	7	11			9		4	5		10		2					6	1			
22	(h) Small Heath	W	2-0	Aston, Martin.	4,000	8	3	7	11			9		4	5		10		2					6	1			
					Apps	32	31	30	7	4	4	25	3	22	25	1	31	1	31	10	2	1	10	32	34	30	4	4
League position: 6th					Goals	16		13		1	2	10		1			12		2	4		1				16		

Own Goal 1.

F.A. Cup

Date	Opponent	Rd	Score	Scorers	Att	Aston J.	Davis H.	Dean A.	Flynn J.	Genever E.	Greatwich F.	Griffin A.	Hickinbotham	Holmes S.	Jenkyns C.	Lyons J.W.	Martin J.	Millington E.	Peers E.	Peers H.	Philpott W.	Pratt J.	Smith G.	Taggart J.	Tennant W.	Vail T.	Wedge A.	Yates H.R.
Oct 29	(a) Druids	3Q	1-2	Aston	2,000	8	3	7				11			5		10		2				4	6	1	9		
					Apps	1	1	1				1			1		1		1				1	1	1	1		
					Goals	1																						

SEASON 1899-1900

Division 2

Date		Opponent		Score	Scorers	Att	Bunch W.	Connor M.J.	Dailly H.	Davis H.	Dean A.	Griffin A.	Hickinbotham	Holmes S.	Jenkyns C.	Lyons J.	McAuley W.	McLean J.C.	Martin J.	Moffatt J.	Taggart J.	Tennant W.	Timmins S.
Sept 2	(a)	Small Heath	L	2-3	Martin (2).	8,000	2	8	11	3	7			4	5	6			10	9		1	
9	(h)	New Brighton	W	2-1	Dailly, Moffatt.	2,500		8	11	3	7		2	4	5	6			10	9		1	
16	(a)	Grimsby T.	L	2-4	Dean, Moffatt.	2,500		8	11	3	7		2	4	5	6			10	9		1	
23	(h)	Arsenal	W	2-0	Moffatt, Connor.	3,000		8	11	3	7		2	4	5	6			10	9		1	
25	(h)	Leicester F.	L	1-2	Dean.	2,500		8	11	3	7		2	4	5	6			10	9		1	
30	(a)	Barnsley	D	2-2	Connor, Dean.	2,400	2	8	11	3	7			4	5	6			10	9		1	
Oct 14	(a)	Luton Town	L	0-4		2,500	2		11	3	7	9		4	5	6	8		10			1	
21	(h)	Burslem PV	L	0-1		3,000	2		11	3	7			4	5	6	8		10	9		1	
Nov 4	(a)	Middlesbro.	D	1-1	Dailly.	2,000	2	8	11	3				4	5			7	10	9	6	1	
11	(h)	Chesterfield	W	6-3	Moffatt (2), Connor (2), Martin (2).	2,500	2	8	11	3				4	5	6		7	10	9		1	
25	(h)	Bolton W.	D	2-2	Dailly, Martin.	3,500	2		11	3				4	5	6	8	7	10	9		1	
Dec 2	(a)	Loughboro.	D	0-0		2,000	2		11	3				4	5	6	8	7	10	9		1	
16	(a)	Sheffield Wed.	L	0-2		3,500	2		11	3				4	5	6	8	7	10	9		1	
23	(h)	Lincoln City	W	3-1	Connor (2), McAuley.	2,000	2	10	11	3				4	5	6	8	7		9		1	
25	(h)	Barnsley	W	4-2	Holmes, McAuley, Connor, Moffatt.	3,500	2	10	11	3				4	5	6	8	7		9		1	
26	(a)	Lincoln City	L	1-3	Moffatt.	2,000	2	10	11	3				4	5	6	8	7		9		1	
27	(a)	Leicester F.	L	1-2	Dailly	2,500	2		11	3				4	5	6	8	7	10	9		1	
30	(h)	Small Heath	W	1-0	Dailly	3,000	2		11					4	5	6	8	7	10	9	6	1	
Jan 6	(a)	New Brighton	W	1-0	Martin.	1,500	2		11	3				4	5	6	8	7	10	9		1	
13	(h)	Grimsby Town	D	1-1	McAuley	2,000	2		11	3				4	5	6	8	7	10	9		1	
20	(a)	Arsenal	L	1-3	Moffatt	7,000	2		11	3				4	5	6	8	7	10	9		1	
Feb 17	(h)	Luton Town	W	7-3	Griffin, Moffatt (3), McAuley (3).	2,500	2	10		4		11		4	5	6	8	7		9		1	
24	(a)	Burslem PV	L	0-1		2,000	2	10		3		11		4	5	6	8	7		9		1	
Mar 10	(h)	Middlesbro.	D	1-1	Moffatt.	3,000	2		11	3				4	5	6	8	7	10	9		1	
17	(a)	Chesterfield	W	3-1	Martin, Connor, Moffatt.	1,500	2	11						4	5	6	8	7	10	9		1	3
24	(h)	Gainsboro. T.	W	1-0	McAuley.	2,000	2	11						4	5	6	8	7	10	9		1	3
31	(a)	Bolton W.	L	0-2		3,500	2	11						4	5	6	8	7	10	9		1	3
Apr 7	(h)	Loughboro.	W	1-0	Connor.	2,000	2	11							5	4	8	7	10	9	6	1	3
13	(a)	Burton Swifts.	L	1-2	Martin.	1,750	2	11	9	3				6	5	4	8	7	10			1	
14	(a)	Newton H.	L	0-5		2,500	2	11	9	3					5	4	8	7	10		6	1	
16	(h)	Burton Swifts.	W	2-0	Dean, Lyons.	1,000	2	11	9	3	8			4	5	6		7	10			1	
17	(h)	Newton H.	D	0-0		1,500	2	11	8	3	9			4				7	10		6	1	5
21	(h)	Sheffield W.	D	1-1	Dean.	2,000	2		11	3	9			4	5	6	8	7	10			1	
30	(a)	Gainsboro. T.	L	0-2		1,000	2		11	3	9			4	5		8	7	10		6	1	
						Apps	30	21	28	29	12	3	4	32	33	31	24	26	29	27	6	34	5
League position: 12th						Goals		9	5		5	1		1		1	7		8	13			

F.A. Cup

Date		Opponent	Rd	Score	Scorers	Att	Bunch W.	Connor M.J.	Dailly H.	Davis H.	Dean A.	Griffin A.	Hickinbotham	Holmes S.	Jenkyns C.	Lyons J.	McAuley W.	McLean J.C.	Martin J.	Moffatt J.	Taggart J.	Tennant W.	Timmins S.
Oct 28	(h)	Kidderminster H	3Q	6-1	Dailly, Martin, Dean, Connor (2), Griffin	800	2	8	11	3	7	9		4	5	6			10			1	
Nov 23	(h)	Wellington Tn	4Q	2-1	Martin (2), (1 pen)	150	2	8	11	3				4	5	6		7	10	9		1	
Dec 9	(a)	Small Heath	5Q	0-0		6,500	2	9	11	3				4	5	6	8	7		10		1	
14	(h)	Small Heath	5QR	2-0	McLean, Martin (pen)	1,000	2	9	11	3				4	5	6	8	7		10		1	
Jan 27	(h)	W.B.A.	1P	1-1	Dailly	9,106	2		11	3				4	5	6	8	7	10	9		1	
Feb 1	(a)	W.B.A.	1PR	1-6	Martin (pen)	4,892	2		11	3				4	5	6	8	7	10	9		1	
						Apps	6	4	6	6	1	1		6	6	6	4	5	4	5		6	
						Goals		2	2		1	1						1	5				

SEASON 1900-01

Division 2

Date		Opponent	Res	Score	Scorers	Att	Baker G.	Bunch W.	Carver T.	Connor M.J.	Dean A.	Flynn H.	Hayward H.	Holmes S.	Lynex J.	Lyons J.	Jenkyns C.	McLean J.	Martin J.	Pee R.	Philpott W.	Taggart J.	Tennant W.	Thorpe W.T.	Timmins S.	Tuft W.
Sept 1	(h)	Barnsley	W	3-0	Dean, Flynn, Holmes	3,000		2		10	9	11		8			5	7			4	6	1		3	
8	(a)	Arsenal	D	1-1	Dean.	4,000		2		10	9	7		6			5	11	8				1		4	3
15	(h)	Blackpool	L	1-2	Baker.	2,500	11	2		8	9			4			5	7	10				1		6	3
22	(a)	Stockport C.	L	1-4	Opponent (og).	2,000		2		8	9	11		6			5	7	10					1	4	3
24	(h)	Burton Swifts	L	1-5	Dean.	3,000	11	2			9		6	8			5	7	10					1	4	3
29	(h)	Small Heath	D	2-2	Dean, Connor	3,000	11	2		8	9			4				7	10			6	1		5	3
Oct 6	(a)	Grimsby T.	D	0-0		2,500		2		8	9	11		4				7	10			6	1		5	3
13	(h)	Lincoln C.	W	3-0	Dean, Martin, Flynn.	1,500		2		8	9	11		4				7	10			6	1		5	3
20	(a)	Newton H.	D	1-1	Martin.	2,500		2		8	9	11		4				7	10			6	1		5	3
27	(h)	Glossop	W	2-1	McLean, Dean.	2,000		2		8	9	11		4				7	10			6	1		5	3
Nov 10	(h)	Burnley	W	2-0	Dean, Lynex.	2,500		2			9	11		4	8			7	10			6	1		5	3
24	(h)	Leicester F.	W	2-0	McLean, Martin.	3,000		2			9	11		4	8			7	10			6	1		5	3
Dec 1	(a)	New Brighton	L	1-5	Dean.	2,000		2			9	11		4	8			7	10			6	1		5	3
15	(h)	Chesterfield	D	2-2	McLean, Martin	2,500		2		8	9	11		4				7	10			6	1		5	3
22	(a)	Burton Swifts.	L	1-2	Dean.	1,000		2			9	11		4	8			7	10			6	1		5	3
24	(h)	Arsenal	W	1-0	Dean.	3,000		2		8	9	11		4				7	10			6	1		5	3
25	(a)	Burslem PV	D	2-2	Martin, McLean.	2,500		2		8	9	11		4				7	10			6	1		5	3
26	(h)	Gainsboro. T.	D	3-3	Flynn, Connor, Martin.	3,000	10			8	9	11		2				7	4			6	1		5	3
29	(a)	Barnsley	L	1-2	Connor.	2,000		2		8	9	11		4				7	10			6	1		5	3
Jan 12	(a)	Blackpool	L	0-1		1,500		2		8	9	11		4	10			7	6				1		5	3
19	(h)	Stockport C.	L	1-3	Dean.	2,000		2		10	9	11		4	8			7	6				1		5	3
Feb 9	(h)	Grimsby T.	D	0-0		2,000		2		7	9	11		4	8	6			10				1		5	3
16	(a)	Lincoln C.	L	0-2		1,500		2			9	11		4	8	6		7	10				1		5	3
25	(h)	Newton H.	D	1-1	Flynn.	2,000	9					11		4	8	2		7	10			6	1		5	3
Mar 2	(a)	Glossop	L	0-2		1,000		2		10		11		4	8	6		7	9				1		5	3
9	(a)	Middlesbro.	L	1-2	Flynn.	2,500		2		9		11		4	8	5		7	10			6	1			3
16	(a)	Burnley	D	0-0		2,000		2		8		11		4	9	5		7	10			6	1			3
23	(h)	Burslem PV	W	2-1	Martin, Lynex	3,000		2		9		11		4	8	5		7	10			6	1			3
30	(a)	Leicester F.	L	0-5		2,500		2		9		11		4	8	5		7	10			6	1			3
Apr 6	(h)	New Brighton	D	3-3	Martin, McLean, Connor	2,000			9	8		11		5		2		7	10	6	4		1			3
8	(a)	Small Heath	L	1-2	Connor.	7,000		2		8		11		5	9	6		7	10		4		1			3
13	(a)	Gainsboro. T.	L	0-1		2,000	6	2		8		11		5	9			7	10		4		1			3
20	(a)	Chesterfield	D	1-1	Flynn.	1,500		2		8		11		4	9	5		7	10		6		1			3
22	(h)	Middlesbrough	D	0-0		800		2	9	8		11		4		5		7	10	6			2			3
						Apps	6	31	2	27	23	31	1	34	17	12	5	33	33	2	5	20	32	2	25	33
League position: 16th						Goals	1			5	11	6		1	2			5	8							

Own Goal 1.

F.A. Cup

Date		Opponent	Rd	Score	Scorers	Att	Baker G.	Bunch W.	Carver T.	Connor M.J.	Dean A.	Flynn H.	Hayward H.	Holmes S.	Lynex J.	Lyons J.	Jenkyns C.	McLean J.	Martin J.	Pee R.	Philpott W.	Taggart J.	Tennant W.	Thorpe W.T.	Timmins S.	Tuft W.
Nov 3	(a)	Shrewsbury Tn	3Q	1-1	Flynn	3,000		2		8	9	11		4				7	10			6	1		5	3
8	(h)	Shrewsbury Tn	3QR	1-0	Dean	2,000		2			9	11		4	8			7	10			6	1		5	3
17	(a)	Chirk	4Q	1-0	Lynex	2,500		2			9	11		4	8			7	10			6	1		5	3
Dec 8	(h)	Wellington Tn	5Q	6-0	Dean (5), McLean	4,000		2			9	11		4	8			7	10			6	1		5	3
Jan 5	(a)	Chesterfield	Int	0-3		2,500		2			9	11		4	8			7	10			6	1		5	3
						Apps		5		1	5	5		5	4			5	5			5	5		5	5
						Goals					6	1			1			1								

* Walsall failed to gain re-election, being replaced in the League by Bristol City and entered the Midland League for the season 1901-02

SEASON 1901-02

Midland League

Date	Opponent	Res	Score	Scorers	Att	Johnson C.	Waters J.	Lewis, A.E.T.	Holmes S.	Yates H.	Southall W.	Tonks, J	Bastock R	Reece	McIntyre	Baker	Griffiths	Noble	Green	Lester, F.	Purcell	Hayes	Colley, R.	Newman	Tolley	Bidmead	Foster	Clewes	Watson	Thorpe W. T.
Sept 2 (h)	Lincoln City Res	L	1-5	Tonks.	3,000	1	2	3	4	5	6	7	8	9	10	11														
7 (a)	Sheffield Utd Res	L	1-8	Baker.	1,000		2	1	4	9	6	7	10		8	11	3	5												
14 (a)	Barnsley St. Peters	L	1-2	Bastock.	700		2	1	4	5	7		10		8	11	3	6	9											
21 (a)	Newark	D	0-0		500		2	1	4	5	10	7	8		9	11	6			3										
24 (h)	Barnsley St. Peters	L	0-1		1,000		2	1	4	5	10	7			8	11	6		9	3										
28 (a)	Lincoln City Res	L	1-3	Reece.	1,000		2	1	4	5		7	10	9		11				3	6	8								
Oct 5 9h)	Derby County Res	W	4-0	Colley, Reece, Baker (2).	1,000		2	1	4	5	6	7		9		11			10	3			8							
7 (a)	Sheffield Wed. Res	D	2-2	Yates, Baker.	500		2	1	4	5	10	7			9	11		6		3			8							
12 (a)	Worksop Town	D	0-0		1,000		3	1	2	5	6	7			9	11			10		4		8							
19 (h)	Leicester Fosse	W	4-1	Tonks (2), Colley, Green.	3,000			1	2	5	6	7		9		11			10	3	4		8							
26 (h)	Hinckley Town	L	0-1		2,000			1	2	5	6	7			9	11			10	3	4		8							
Nov 9 (a)	Derby County Res	W	2-1	Newman (2).	1,000		2	1	9	5	6	8				11				3	4		7	10						
23 (a)	Coalville Town	W	2-1	Green, Tonks.	1,500		2	1		5		7			9	11			10	3	6		8		4					
Dec 21 (h)	Whitwick White C.	W	1-0	Holmes.	1,000		2	1	9	5	6	7				11			10	3	4		8							
25 (a)	Burton Utd Res.	D	0-0		600		2	1	9	5	6	7				11			10	3	4		8							
26 (h)	Burton Utd Res.	W	3-0	McIntyre, Bidmead (2).	4,000		2	1	8	5	6				7	11				3	4			10		8				
28 (h)	Grimsby Town Res	D	2-2	Bidmead, opponent (og).	2,000		2	1	8	5	6					11				3	4		7	10		8				
Jan 4 (h)	Newark	W	2-0	Green, Baker.	1,200		2	1	7	5	6					11			9		4			10		8	3			
11 (a)	Grimsby Town Res	D	0-0		600		2	1	7	5	6				10	11			9		4					8	3			
18 (h)	Coalville Town	W	7-0	Holmes, Bidmead, Green (3), Colley (2).	2,000		2	1	7	5	6								9	3	4		11	10		8				
Feb 1 (a)	Leicester Fosse R	W	2-1	Lester, McIntyre.	2,000	1	2			5	6				10	11			9	3	4		7			8				
15 (a)	Whitwick White C	D	3-3	Bidmead (2), Green.	600	1	2		4	5	6				11	10			9	3			8			7				
Mar 22 (h)	Sheffield Wed. R.	W	2-0	Green, McIntyre.	500		2	1		5	6				10	11			9	3	4		7			8				
29 (a)	Hinckley Town	W	2-0	McIntyre, Baker.	1,000		2	1		5	6	7			10	11			9	3	4					8				
Apr 1 (h)	Sheffield Utd Res	W	1-0	Green.	2,000		2	1		5	6	7			10	11			9	3	4					8				
5 (h)	Worksop Town	W	4-1	Green (2), McIntyre (2).	1,500		2	1		5	6				10	11			9	3	4		7			8				
19 (a)	Ilkeston Town	L	1-3	McIntyre.	1,000					5	6	7			10				9		4		11			8	3	1	2	
26 (h)	Ilkeston Town	W	3-0	Colley, Green, McIntyre.	300		2				6		8		10	11			9	3	4		7			5				1
					Apps	3	25	24	20	27	26	17	6	4	19	26	4	3	20	21	20	1	17	5	1	13	3	1	1	1
League position: 5th					Goals				2	1		4	1	2	8	6			12	1			5	2		6				

Own goal: 1

F.A. Cup

Date	Opponent	Rd	Score	Scorers	Att	Johnson C.	Waters J.	Lewis, A.E.T.	Holmes S.	Yates H.	Southall W.	Tonks, J	Bastock R	Reece	McIntyre	Baker	Griffiths	Noble	Green	Lester, F.	Purcell	Hayes	Colley, R.	Newman	Tolley	Bidmead	Foster	Clewes	Watson	Thorpe W. T.
Nov 2 (a)	Brierley Hill All.	3Q	1-1	McIntyre	5,000		2	1	9	5	6				8	11			10	3	4		7							
7 (h)	Brierley Hill All.	3QR	2-1	Holmes, Green	1,500		2	1	9	5	6				8	11			10	3	4		7							
16 (h)	Berwick Rangers	4Q	0-0	(Abandoned after 20 mins-fog)	1,000		2	1		5	6	8			9	11			10	3	4		7							
18 (h)	Berwick Rangers	4Q	2-1	McIntyre, Green	1,500		2	1		5	6	8			9	11			10	3	4		7							
Dec 7 (a)	Burslem Pt Vale	5Q	2-1	Southall, McIntyre	1,200		2	1		5	6	8			10	11			9	3	4		7							
14 (h)	New Brompton	IR	2-0	Holmes, Baker	3,000		2	1	10	5	6	8				11			9	3	4		7							
Jan 25 (h)	Burnley	1st	1-0	Colley	9,045		2	1	9	5	6					11			10	3	4		7			8				
Feb 8 (h)	Bury	2nd	0-5		9,551		2	1	10	5	6					11			9	3	4		7			8				
					Apps		7	7	5	7	7	3			4	7			7	7	7		7			2				
					Goals				2		1				3	1			2				1							

SEASON 1902-03

Midland League

Date		Opponents			Scorers	Att	Harris S.	Waters	Lester F.	Pickering	Yates H	Pee	Rogers J	Lloyd T	Bott	Earl	Anson E	Wootton C G.	Hargreaves	Webb	Preedy	Hogg	Clark	Lloyd P	Turnbull	Bromage T.	Nicholls W.	Cobly	Smith	Jones	Fletcher	Bastock R.	Vernon	Hirons JW	Cresser	Lloyd E	Lynex	Clarkson O.	Lord W.
Sept 1	(h)	Sheffield Utd Res	D	1-1	Pickering (pen).	2,000	1	2	3	4	5	6	7	8	9	10	11																						
6	(a)	Worksop Town	L	1-3	Rogers.	1,000	1	2	3	6	5	4	7			11	10	8	9																				
13	(h)	Sheffield Wed Res	W	1-0	Earl.	2,000	1	2	3	4	5	6	7	11		10			9	8																			
20	(a)	Sheffield Wed Res	L	1-4	Earl.	1,500		2	3	4	5	6	7			10	8		9		1	11																	
22	(h)	Worksop Town	W	1-0	Clark.	1,500	1	2	3	4	5	6	7			10	8					11	9																
29	(h)	Chesterfield T Res	L	0-1		1,200	1	2	3	4		6	7			10						11	8	5	9														
Oct 11	(h)	Whitwick White C	W	2-0	Clark, Rogers.	2,000	1	2	3	4		6	11			8	10		5				9		7														
25	(a)	Grimsby Town Res	L	1-5	Hargreaves	750		2	3	4	5	6	7			11	8		9				10			1													
Nov 8	(h)	Denaby United	W	3-2	Lloyd T, Earl, Anson.	500		2	3	4	5	6	7	10		11	9		8							1													
22	(h)	Doncaster Rov R.	W	5-1	Lester, Pickering, Anson, Earl , Hope(og).	500		2	3	8	5	6	7			11	9		10							1	4												
29	(a)	Lincoln City Res	L	0-1		600		2	3	4	5	6	7	10		11	8		9							1													
Dec 20	(a)	Newark	W	2-1	Earl, Anson.	400		2	3			4	7			11	8		5						6	1		9	10										
25	(a)	Gainsboro Trin. R	D	1-1	Turnbull	500		2	3	4		6	7	10		11	8		5						9	1													
27	(a)	Hinckley Town *	L	0-3		600		2	3	4		6		10			8		5						9	1				7									
Jan 3	(a)	Whitwick White C	D	2-2	Bastock (2).	500		2	3	4		6	7	10			9		11							1	5					8							
10	(h)	Grimsby Town R	W	2-0	Bastock, Pickering (pen).	2,000		2	3	5		6		9					10							1	4				7	8	11						
17	(a)	Sheffield Utd Res	L	1-2	Hargreaves.	1,500		2	3	4		6		9			10		7							1	5					8		11					
24	(h)	Barnsley Reserves	W	5-1	Pickering (2 pens), Hargreaves, Anson, Cox (og).	2,000		2	3	5		6		8			10		9							1	4					7		11					
31	(h)	Derby County Res	L	1-2	Bastock	2,500		2	3	5		4	8				10		9							1	6					7		11					
Feb 7	(a)	Leicester Fosse R	D	1-1	Hirons.	1,000		2	3	6		5	8				10		9							1	4					7		11					
14	(h)	Lincoln City Res	W	5-0	Waters (pen), Bastock, Hargreaves(2), Rogers.	1,500		2	3	6		5	11	8			10		9							1	4					7							
21	(h)	Newark	W	2-0	Waters (pen), Anson.	800		2	3	6		5	11	8			10		9							1	4					7							
28	(a)	Burton Utd Res	L	1-2	Waters (pen).	700		2	3	6		5	11	8			10		9							1	4					7							
Mar 14	(a)	Denaby United	L	0-1		400		2	3	6		5	11	8			10		9							1	4					7							
21	(a)	Doncaster Rov R*	L	1-4	Lloyd.	500		2	3	6		5	11	8			10									1	4					7							
28	(h)	Leicester Fosse R	W	5-0	Waters (pen), Hargreaves, Lloyd T. (2), Anson.	500		2		3		5	11	8			10		6							1						7			4	9			
Apr 4	(a)	Derby County Res	L	0-2		2,000			2	3		5	11	8			10		9							1	6					7			4				
11	(h)	Hinckley Town	D	1-1	Pee.	2,000		2	3	6		5	11	8			10		9							1						7			4				
13	(h)	Gainsboro Trin R	W	3-0	Bastock (2), Hargreaves.	1,500		2	3	6		5		8			10		9							1						7			4		11		
14	(h)	Burton United Res	D	2-2	Hargreaves, opponent (og).	700		2	3	6		5		8			11		9							1						7			4			10	
18	(a)	Barnsley Reserves	D	1-1	Bastock.	1,000		2	3	6		5		8			10		9							1						7			4				11
25	(a)	Chesterfield T R.	L	0-4		500		2	3	6		5	11	8			10		9							1						7			4				
						Apps	6	31	31	31	9	32	25	22	1	13	29	1	28	1	1	3	4	1	5	25	13	1	1	1	1	18	1	4	7	1	1	1	1
League position: 8th						Goals		4	1	5		1	3	4		5	6		8				2		1							8		1					

* Walsall fielded only 10 players in these two matches v. Hinckley (27 Dec) and Doncaster (21 March)

Own goals: 3

F.A. Cup

Date		Opponents	Rd	Score		Att	Harris S.	Waters	Lester F.	Pickering	Yates H	Pee	Rogers J	Lloyd T	Bott	Earl	Anson E	Wootton C G.	Hargreaves	Webb	Preedy	Hogg	Clark	Lloyd P	Turnbull	Bromage T.	Nicholls W.	Cobly	Smith	Jones	Fletcher	Bastock R.	Vernon	Hirons JW	Cresser	Lloyd E	Lynex	Clarkson O.	Lord W.
Oct 18	(h)	Brierley Hill All.	2Q	0-2		3,500	1	2	3	4	5	6	7			11	8		10				9																
						Apps	1	1	1	1	1	1	1			1	1		1				1																

This season Walsall played two Midland League games against Ilkeston (won 1-0 at home, won 3-1 away), but Ilkeston were expelled from the League and the results deleted from the record books

SEASON 1903-04

Birmingham League

Date		Opponent	Res	Score	Scorers	Att	Jones, H.	Waters J.	Ore, J.	Nicholls	Pickering G.	Pee	Griffiths W.	Bastock R.	Beale G.	Pember L.	Law, W.	Bywater S.	Lloyd, T.	Burden, F.	Lester, F.	Leadbetter T.	Aston J	Thorpe, W. T.	Philpott, W.	Jones, R.	Brookes	Flavell, J.F.	Franks, A.	Cole, A.
Sept 5	(h)	Brierley Hill All.	D	2-2	Pember (2).	1,500	1	2	3	4	5	6	7	8	9	10	11													
12	(a)	Kidderminster H.*	W	1-0	Law.	1,500	1	2	3	4	5	6	7	8	9		11													
19	(h)	Wellington Town	W	3-1	Waters (pen), Griffiths, Bywater.	2,000	1	2	3	4	5	6	7		9	10	11	8												
21	(h)	Stourbridge	W	1-0	Beale.	1,000	1	2	3	4	5	6	7		9	10	11		8											
26	(a)	W.B.A. Res.	D	0-0		2,000	1	2	3	4	5	6	7		9	10	11		8											
Oct 3	(h)	Small Heath Res	W	3-2	Waters (2 pens), Pickering.	3,000	1	2	3	4	5	6	7		8	10	11			9										
10	(a)	Crewe Alexandra	L	1-2	Pickering	1,000	1	2	3	4	5	6	7		8	10	11			9										
17	(h)	Worcester City	D	2-2	Waters (2 -1 pen).	2,500	1	9	2	4	5	6	7	8		10	11				3									
24	(a)	Dudley	W	2-1	Beale, Law.	1,500	1	2		4	5	6	7		9	10	11				3	8								
Nov 7	(a)	Halesowen	D	2-2	Pember (2).	1,000	1	3		4	6	5	7			9	11		10		2	8								
21	(a)	Aston Villa Res	L	0-3		8,000	1	2		4	5	6	7		9	10	11				3	8								
Dec 5	(a)	Stoke Res.	L	1-5	Bastock.	2,000	1	2	9	4	5	6	7	8		10	11				3									
12	(a)	Wolves Res.	L	1-3	Lewis (og)	1,500	1	2	3	4	5	6	7		9	10	11					8								
19	(h)	Ruabon Druids	W	4-3	Griffiths, Aston, Pember (2).	1,000	1	2		4	5	6	7			10	11				3	8	9							
26	(a)	Coventry City	L	0-2		4,000	1	2		4	5	6	7			10	11				3	8	9							
Jan 2	(a)	Brierley Hill All.	L	1-3	Leadbetter.	2,000	1	2		4	5	6		7	9	10	11				3	8								
9	(h)	Kidderminster H.	D	1-1	Law.	800		2		4	5	6	7		9	10	11				3	8		1						
16	(a)	Wellington Town	L	3-4	Beale, Pember, Law.	500		2			5	6	7		9	10	11		4		3	8		1						
23	(h)	W.B.A. Res.	W	3-2	Nicholls, Lloyd, Law.	1,500	1	2		4	5	6	7		9	10	11		8		3									
30	(a)	Small Heath Res.	W	2-1	Beale, Law.	2,000	1	2		4	5	6	7		9	10	11		8		3									
Feb 20	(h)	Dudley	W	2-0	Griffiths, Pember.	1,500	1	2		4		6	7		9	10	11		8	5	3									
27	(a)	Stourbridge	L	0-4		1,200	1	2		4	5	6	7		9	10	11		8		3									
Mar 5	(h)	Halesowen	W	4-0	Griffiths, Pember (2), Opponent (og).	500	1	2		5		6	7	8		10	11		9		3				4					
12	(a)	Shrewsbury Town	L	0-3		1,000	1	2		4		6	7	8		10	11		9	5	3									
19	(h)	Aston Villa Res.	L	0-3		2,000	1	2		4	5	6	7			10	11		8	9	3									
21	(h)	Stafford Rangers	L	1-2	Nicholls.	200	1	2		4		6	7	9		10	11		8	5	3									
28	(a)	Stafford Rangers	L	0-2		500	1	2		4		6	7			10	11		8	5	3					9				
Apr 2	(h)	Stoke Res.	L	0-1		1,500	1	2		4	5	6	7			9	11		8		3						10			
4	(h)	Crewe Alex.	L	1-4	Opponent (og).	1,500	1	2		4	5		11			9	7		6		3						8	10		
5	(a)	Worcester City	D	1-1	Flavell.	1,000	1	2		4	5	6	11			9	7				3						8	10		
9	(h)	Wolves Res.	L	0-2		500		2		6	5		7			9	11			4	3			1			10	8		
16	(a)	Ruabon Druids	L	1-3	Waters (pen).	600		2		4						9	11			5	3			1			10	8	6	7
18	(h)	Shrewsbury Town	D	1-1	Law.	200		2		4						9	11			5	3			1			10	8	6	7
23	(h)	Coventry City	W	1-0	Waters (pen).	1,000		2		4	3		7			10	11			5				1				8	6	9
						Apps	28	34	10	33	27	29	31	8	17	33	34	1	15	11	25	9	2	6	1	1	6	6	3	3
League position: 13th						Goals		7		2	2		4	1	4	10	7	1	1			1	1					1		

* Walsall only had 10 players v. Kidderminster (12 Sept)

Own goals: 3

F.A. Cup

Date		Opponent	Rd	Score	Scorers	Att	Jones, H.	Waters J.	Ore, J.	Nicholls	Pickering G.	Pee	Griffiths W.	Bastock R.	Beale G.	Pember L.	Law, W.	Bywater S.	Lloyd, T.	Burden, F.	Lester, F.	Leadbetter T.
Oct 31	(a)	Coventry City	3Q	4-2	Lester, Lloyd, Beale (2)	5,000	1	2		4	5	6	7		9	10	11		8		3	
Nov 14	(a)	Stafford Rangers	4Q	2-1	Nicholls, Pember	1,500	1	2		4	5	6		7	9	10	11				3	8
28	(a)	Shrewsbury Town	5Q	0-1		2,000	1	2		4	5	6	7		9	10	11				3	8
						Apps	3	3		3	3	3	2	1	3	3	3		1		3	2
						Goals				1					2	1			1		1	

SEASON 1904-05

Birmingham League

Date	Opponents	Res	Score	Scorers	Att	Thorpe.W.T.	Watson. A.E.	Pickering G.	Ellard. J.	Burden. F	Franks. A	Taylor	Anson. E	Cole	Dickenson	Flavell. J.F.	Corfield. J	Nicholls	Burton. E.C.	Wright R.	Sawyer T.	Ager	Pearson	Clarkson O.	Adams. W.	Middleton	Owen. A.G.	Benton	Shelton	Thomas	Dyer	Watterson	Archer	Jones. C	Thompson	Webster	Bourne	Hanley
Sep 3 (h)	Aston Villa Res.	L	0-3		2,000	1	2	3	4	5	6	7	8	9	10	11																						
10 (a)	Burslem P Vale Res	L	0-3		800	1	2	3	6	5			7	11	10	8	4																					
17 (a)	Coventry City	L	0-2		1,500	1	2	3	6	5								4	7																			
24 (h)	Brierley Hill All	D	1-1	Pickering	1,000	1	3	2	6	5			10	7		8		4		11																		
Oct 8 (h)	Wellington Town	W	3-2	Flavell, Sawyer (2)	1,000	1	2	3	10	5	6					8		4	7		9																	
22 (h)	Crewe Alexandra	D	1-1	Cole	1,500	1		2	10	5	6			11		8		4	7		9	3																
24 (a)	Kidderminster H	W	2-1	Flavell (2)	1,000	1		2	10	5	6			11		8		4	7		9	3																
29 (a)	Stoke Res	L	0-4		2,000	1		2	10	5	6							4	7		9	3	8	11														
Nov 5 (h)	Small Heath Res	W	3-1	Ellard (3)	2,000	1		3	10	5	6					8		4	7		9			11	2													
12 (a)	West Brom Alb Res	L	1-3	Clarkson	2,000	1		3	10	5	6					8			7		9		4	11	2													
19 (h)	Halesowen	W	2-1	Franks, Flavell	2,000	1		3	10	5	6					8		4	7				9	11	2													
26 (a)	Stourbridge	W	2-0	Burton (2)	1,000	1		3	10	5	6					8		4	7		9			11	2													
Dec 3 (h)	Dudley	L	1-3	Pickering	1,500	1		3	10	5	6					8		4	7		9			11	2													
10 (a)	Shrewsbury Tn	L	2-6	Ellard (2)	1,200	1		3	10	5	6					8		4	7		9			11	2													
17 (h)	Stafford Rangers	L	1-3	Franks	800	1		2	9	5	6			10					7					11	3	4	8											
24 (a)	Wolves Res	D	0-0		1,500	1		3	10	4	6					8		5			9			11	2			7										
26 (a)	Worcester City	L	1-4	Clarkson (pen)	1,200	1		3	10	5						8		4	7	6	9			11	2													
31 (a)	Aston Villa Res	L	0-8		5,000	1		3	10	5						8		4	7	6	9			11	2													
Jan 7 (h)	Burslem P Vale Res	W	2-1	Pearson, Ellard	1,000			5	10	6	3					8			7	11			9		2				1	4								
14 (h)	Coventry City	L	1-3	Ellard	1,500			3	10	5	6					8			7	11			9		2				1		4							
21 (a)	Brierley Hill All	L	0-2		1,000	1		3	10	5	6					8			7	4			9	11	2													
28 (h)	Worcester City	L	0-1		1,000	1		3	8		6					4			7				5	11	2							9	10					
Feb 4 (a)	Wellington Town	D	2-2	Burton, Ellard	1,500	1		3	8		6					4			7				5	11	2							9	10					
11 (h)	Kidderminster H	D	0-0		1,500	1		3	6							4			7				5	11	2							9	10	8				
18 (a)	Crewe Alexandra	L	1-2	Pearson	2,000	1		3	8							4			7	6			5	11	2								10	9				
25 (h)	Stoke Res	W	2-1	Burton, Ellard	1.100	1		3	8		6					4			7				5	11	2								10	9				
Mar 4 (a)	Small Heath Res	L	1-7	Jones	2,500	1		3	8		6					4			7				5	11	2								10	9				
11 (h)	West Brom Alb Res	L	0-1		1,000	1		3	8		6					4			7				5	11	2								10	9				
18 (a)	Halesowen	D	1-1	Thompson	1,200	1		3								6			7	4			5	11	2								10		8	9		
25 (h)	Stourbridge	W	2-1	Webster (2)	1,000	1		3	8		6					7				4			5	11	2								10			9		
Apr 1 (a)	Dudley	W	4-3	Pearson, Franks, Flavell, Archer	2,000	1		3	8		6					7				4			5	11	2								10			9		
8 (h)	Shrewsbury Tn	W	3-0	Flavell, Webster, opponent (og)	1,000	1		3	8		6					4							5	11	2		7						10			9		
15 (a)	Stafford Rangers	L	1-4	Archer	500	1		3			6					8							5	11	2								10			9	7	4
22 (h)	Wolves Res	W	4-2	Owen (2), Flavell, Clarkson	1,500	1		3			6					8							5	11	2								10			9	7	4
					Apps	32	5	34	31	21	26	1	3	6	2	31	1	14	25	10	12	3	19	25	26	1	2	1	2	1	1	3	13	5	1	6	2	2
League position: 14th					Goals			2	9		3					7			4		2		3	3									2	1	1	3		

own-goals 1

Also played: Lynch (8), Ravenscroft (9), Snoutt (10), Bott (11) v Coventry 17-09-04. Hill (9) v B.P.Vale 10-09-04: Caswell (9) v B.H.Alliance 24-09-04 and Whitehouse (11) v Wellington T 8-10-04.

F.A. Cup

Date	Opponents	Rd	Score	Scorers	Att	Thorpe.W.T.	Watson. A.E.	Pickering G.	Ellard. J.	Burden. F	Franks. A	Taylor	Anson. E	Cole	Dickenson	Flavell. J.F.	Corfield. J	Nicholls	Burton. E.C.	Wright R.	Sawyer T.	Ager	Pearson	Clarkson O.	Adams. W.	Middleton	Owen. A.G.	Benton	Shelton	Thomas	Dyer	Watterson	Archer	Jones. C	Thompson	Webster	Bourne	Hanley
Oct 1 (h)	Brierley Hill All	Q1	3-0	Flavell, Sawyer (2).	1,000	1	2	3	10	5	6					8		4	7		9																	
Oct 15 (a)	Coventry City	Q2	0-2		3,000	1	2	3	10	5	6					8		4	7		9																	
					Apps	2	2	2	2	2	2					2		2	2		2																	
					Goals											1					2																	

Also played: Whitehouse (11) v B.Hill Alliance 1-10-04; Coventry City 15-10-04

SEASON 1905-06

Birmingham League

Date		Opponent		Score	Scorers	Att	Reddall. J	Adams. W	Hewitt G	Burden. F	Pearson	Franks. A	Owen. A.G.	Holt	Managhan S.	Clarkson O.	Flavell, J.F.	Thorpe. T.W.	Smith.H	Webster	Brookes, D	Kelly	Thompson	Cameron	Maybury, A.E	Aston J.	Farnell	Bolton	Nightingdale	Pickering G.	Maybury, J.	Colclough	Simcox	Bryant	Pemberton	Smith,G.	Ellard J.	Smith, E.	Green, E.H.
Sep 2	(h)	Wellington Town	W	4-1	Owen(2), Holt, Managhan	2,000	1	2	3	4	5	6	7	9	10	11																							
7	(a)	West Brom A Res	L	2-9	Holt, Clarkson	2,500	1	2	3	4	5	6	7	9	10	11	8																						
16	(h)	Birmingham Res	D	2-2	Holt (2)	2,000		2		5	4	6	7	8		11		1	3	9	10																		
23	(a)	Kidderminster H	W	0-1	Thompson	1.000		2			5	6	7	9		11		1	3		10	4	8																
30	(h)	Stourbridge	W	2-1	Franks, Brookes	2,500		2			5	6	7	9		11		1	3		10	4	8																
Oct 7	(a)	Burslen PV Res	W	3-2	Holt(2), Brookes	500		2			5	6	7	9		11		1	3		10	4	8																
14	(h)	Wrexham	L	1-3	Holt	6,000		2		4	5	6	7	9		11		1	3		10		8																
21	(a)	Dudley	L	0-2		1,500		2		5		6	7	9		11	8	1	3			4	10																
28	(h)	Shrewsbury Tn	L	2-3	Owen, Cameron	2,000		2		5	4	6	7	9		11		1	3				10	9															
Nov 4	(a)	Coventry City	L	1-5	Cameron	1,500		2		5		6	7	9					3					10	1	8													
11	(a)	Aston Villa Res	L	0-5		3,000		2	3	5		6	7	9									11		1	8	4	10											
18	(h)	Stafford Rangers	L	0-2		1,000		2	3	5		6	7	9									11		1	8	4	10											
25	(a)	Wolves Res	L	1-7	Owen	1,500		2				6	7			11	10		3				11		1	8			9										
Dec 2	(h)	Brierley H Alliance	L	1-2	Nightingale	1,000		2		4	5		7			11	6			10					1	8			9	3									
16	(h)	Worcester City	D	1-1	Owen	1,000		2		4	5	6	7	8		11									1	9			10	3									
23	(a)	Crewe Alexandra	D	1-1	Holt	2,000		2		4	5			7		11	6								1	8			9	3	10								
27	(a)	Stoke Res	D	1-1	Maybury, J	500		2		4	5			7		11	6								1	8			9	3	10								
30	(a)	Wellinton Town	L	1-4	Holt	1,000		2		4	5			7		11	6								1	8			9	3	10								
Jan 20	(a)	Birmingham Res	L	0-7		2,000		2				6	7	9	8		4	1				5										10	11						
27	(h)	Kidderminster H	L	2-3	Owen, Adams	1,000		9			5	6	7		8		4		3						1					2		10	11						
Feb 3	(a)	Stourbridge	L	2-3	Adams, Holt	600		9		5		6	7	10	8		4		3						1					2			11						
10	(h)	Burslem PV Res	W	3-0	Pickering (pen), Holt (2)	500		2		5		6	7	9	8		4								1					3			11	10					
17	(a)	Wrexham	L	0-1		1,600		2		5		6	7	9	8		4								1					3			11		10				
24	(h)	Dudley	L	1-2	Pemberton	1,500		2		5		6	7	9	8		4								1					3			11		10				
Mar 3	(a)	Shrewsbury Town	L	0-2		1,000		2		5		6	7	8											1					3	10		11	9					
10	(h)	Coventry City	W	2-1	Managhan, Smith,G.	1,000		2		5		6	7	9	8		4								1					3			11			10			
17	(h)	Aston Villa Res	L	0-2		3,000		2		5		6	7	9	8		4								1					3			11				10		
24	(a)	Stafford Rangers	L	1-2	Owen	750		2		5		6	7	9	8		4								1					3			11			10			
31	(h)	Wolves Res	L	0-2		1,500		2		5		6	7	8	10		4								1					3								11	
Apr 2	(h)	West Brom A Res	D	1-1	Holt	2,000		2		5		6	7	8	10		4								1												6	11	9
7	(a)	Brierley H Alliance	L	0-5		800		2		5		6	7	9	8		4								1					3							10	11	
14	(h)	Stoke Res	W	2-1	Owen, Green	1,000		2		5		6	7		8		4			11					1					3				10					9
21	(a)	Worcester City	L	1-3	Green	800		2		5		6	7				4			10					1					3						11			9
28	(h)	Crewe Alexandra	D	3-3	Burden, Walker, Owen.	600		2		5		6	7		9		4								1					3	10					11			
						Apps	2	34	4	28	14	30	31	28	16	15	22	8	11	4	5	5	9	2	24	9	2	2	6	19	5	2	10	3	2	4	3	3	3
League position: 16th						Goals		2		1		1	9	13	2	1					2		1	1					1	1	1				1	1			2

Also played: Bayley (3) v Birmingham 20-1-06: Day (9) v Wolves; 31-3-06: Bywater (8) v Wellington ; 2-9-05: McAlister (4) v Coventry 4-11-05: Mansell (4) v Wolves 25-11-05: Doggettt (5) v Wolves 25-11-05 and (4) v Shrewsbury 3-3-06: Walker (8) v Worcester 21-4-06 and Crewe 28-4-06.

F.A. Cup

Date		Opponent	Rd	Score	Scorers	Att	Reddall. J	Adams. W	Hewitt G	Burden. F	Pearson	Franks. A	Owen. A.G.	Holt	Managhan S.	Clarkson O.	Flavell, J.F.	Thorpe. T.W.	Smith.H	Webster	Brookes, D	Kelly	Thompson	Cameron	Maybury, A.E	Aston J.	Farnell	Bolton	Nightingdale	Pickering G.	Maybury, J.	Colclough	Simcox	Bryant	Pemberton	Smith,G.	Ellard J.	Smith, E.	Green, E.H.
Dec 9	(h)	Stockport County	4Q	3-3	Aston (2); Clarkson	2,000		2		4	5		7	9		11	6						10		1	8				3									
14	(a)	Stockport County	4QR	0-5		1,500		2		4	5	3	7	8		11	6						10		1	9													
						Apps		2		2	2	1	2	2		2	2						2		2	2				1									
						Goals										1										2													

SEASON 1906-07

Birmingham League

Date	Opponents	Res	Score	Scorers	Att	Nix, A.J.	Pickering G.	Smith, H	Bird, J	Burden, F	Flavell, J.F	Brookes	Walker	Adams, W	Pember, L	Hirons, J.W	Smith, G	Managhan	Morris	Wright, E.W	Hunt, A	Parker	Brannan	Gaffney	Boardman	Handley	Whitehouse	Weaver	Bollington	Hartland	Barnard	Harrison	Urmson	Rankle	Cartledge	Jeavons	West	Roberts
Sep 1 (a)	Worcester City	L	0-4		1,000	1	2	3	4	5	6	7	8	9	10	11																						
8 (h)	Stoke Res	W	2-1	Smith, H, Walker	2,000	1	2	3	4	5	6	7	9		10	11	8																					
15 (a)	Brierley H Alliance	L	2-3	Managhan (2)	1,000	1		3	4	5		7		2	6	11	10	8	9																			
22 (h)	Crewe Alexandra	W	2-0	Hunt (2)	2,000	1		3	4	5		7		2		11	10	8		6	9																	
29 (a)	West B Alb Res	L	1-3	Walker	5,000	1	2	3	4	5			9		10	11	7	8		6																		
Oct 13 (a)	Halesowen	L	0-3		1,000	1		3	4	5		7		2		11	10	8		6	9																	
20 (a)	Shrewsbury Town	L	1-2	Wright	1,500	1		3	4	5				2	10		11	7		8	9	6																
27 (a)	Wrexham	L	2-5	Hunt, Smith,G	700	1			4	5				2			11	7		10	9	6	3	8														
Nov 3 (h)	Shrewsbury Town	W	2-0	Hunt, Hirons	1,200	1		3	4	5				2		10		8	7	6	9				11													
10 (a)	Burslem P V Res	W	3-2	Hunt, Smith, G, Hirons	1,000		3		4	5				2		10	11	8		6	9					1	7											
17 (h)	Stourbridge	L	0-1		1,000		3		4	5				2		10	11			6	9					1	7	8										
24 (a)	Dudley	D	1-1	Pickering	500		6	3	9	5				2			11								10	1	7	8	4									
Dec 1 (h)	Aston Villa Res	L	1-3	Wright	2,500		6	3	4	5				2		10	11			7	9					1		8										
8 (h)	Wolves Res	L	1-2	Smith, G	1,500			3	4	5				2			11			6	9					1	7			8	10							
15 (a)	Stafford Rangers	L	1-5	Bird	1,000			3	4	5				2			11				9					1			6	8	10	7						
22 (h)	Coventry City	W	3-1	Hartland, Hunt (2)	1,000	1		3		5				2		7	11			6	9								4	8	10							
26 (h)	Birmingham Res	D	1-1	Hunt	1,000	1		3		5				2		7	11	10		6	9								4	8								
29 (h)	Worcester City	W	4-3	Managhan, Hunt, Hartland, Smith, G	1,500	1		3		5				2		7	11	8		6	9								4	10								
Jan 5 (a)	Stoke Res	L	3-10	Harrison, Managhan (2)	2,000	1		3	5					2		7	11	10		6	9								4			8						
19 (h)	Brierley H Alliance	W	4-3	Hirons, Hunt, Cartledge, opponent (og)	1,254			3	4	5				2		7	11			6	9												1	8	10			
26 (a)	Crewe Alexandra	W	2-1	Cartledge, Hartland	800				4	5				2		6	11						3				7			10			1	8	9			
Feb 2 (h)	West B Alb Res	W	1-0	Rankle	1,200			3	4	5				2		11				6	9						7			10			1	8				
9 (a)	Birmingham Res	L	2-4	Hunt (2)	8,000			3	4	5				2		7	11			6	9									10			1	8				
16 (h)	Halesowen	W	2-1	Hirons, Hartland	3,000			3	4	5				2		7	11			6	9									10			1	8				
23 (h)	Kidderminster H	L	1-3	Hirons (pen)	3,000			3	4	5				2		7	11			6	9									10			1	8				
Mar 2 (h)	Wrexham	W	2-1	Rankle, Hartland	2,800			3	4	5				2		7	11			6	9									10			1	8				
16 (h)	Burslem PV Res	W	6-1	Hartland (2), Burden, Hirons, Rankle, Hunt	1,000			3	4	5				2		7	11			6	9									10			1	8				
23 (a)	Stourbridge	D	1-1	Rankle	600			3	4	5				2		7	11			6	9									10			1	8				
30 (h)	Dudley	W	3-1	Hunt (3)	3,000			3	4	5				2		7	11			6	9												1	8		10		
Apr 2 (a)	Kidderminster H	L	0-2		1,000			3	4	5				2		7	11			6	9									10			1	8				
6 (a)	Aston Villa Res	L	0-5		4,000			3	4	5				2		6	11				9									10			1			8	7	
15 (a)	Wolves Res	W	1-0	Hartland	2,000			3	4	5				2		7	11				9									10			1	8				6
20 (h)	Stafford Rangers	D	1-1	Rankle	2,000			3	5					2		7	11				9									10			1	8			4	6
27 (a)	Coventry City	L	2-4	Rankle, Hartland	1,500				4	5				2		7	11				9									10			1	8			3	6
					Apps	13	7	29	31	32	2	5	3	32	5	29	31	11	2	24	28	2	2	1	2	6	6	3	6	18	3	2	15	14	2	2	3	3
League position: 13th					Goals		1	1	1	1			2			5	2	5		2	14									9		1		6	2			

own goal: 1

F.A. Cup

Date	Opponents	Rd	Score	Att	Nix, A.J.	Pickering G.	Smith, H	Bird, J	Burden, F	Flavell, J.F	Brookes	Walker	Adams, W	Pember, L	Hirons, J.W	Smith, G	Managhan	Morris	Wright, E.W	Hunt, A
Oct 6 (h)	Brierley Hill All.	1Q	0-3	3,000	1	2	3	4	5			8		10	11	7			6	9
				Apps	1	1	1	1	1			1		1	1	1			1	1

SEASON 1907-08

Birmingham League

Date	Opponents	Res	Score	Scorers	Att	Urmson S.	Adams, W.	Moreton T.	Bird, J.	Burden, F.	Williams, R.	Robinson	Bytheway, G.	Pope, F	Newman, E.	Hirons, J.W.	Pickering, G.	Edwards	Newton, C.J.	Crutchley	Wright, E.W.	Hunt, A.	Knight	Corbett W.	Massey	Smith, G	Garrattly, G.	Flavell, J.F.	Fox,H.	Hatton	Grosvenor
Sep 2 (h)	Birmingham Res	L	2-3	Bird, Bytheway (pen)	2,500	1	2	3	4	5	6	7	8	9	10	11															
7 (h)	Worcester City	L	1-4	Bytheway	3,500	1	2	3	4	5	6	7	8		9	11	10														
14 (a)	Crewe Alexandra	L	0-4		1,000	1	2	3	4	5	6	7	8			11		9	10												
28 (a)	Stoke Res	L	2-8	Bytheway, Hunt	3,000		2		4		3	7	8			11	10		5	1	6	9									
Oct 12 (a)	West Brom A Res	L	1-5	Pickering	2,500		2		4	5	6	7	8			11	10					9	1	3							
Nov 2 (h)	Stafford Rangers	W	5-0	Robinson, Pickering, Hirons, opponents: (og 2)	2,000			2	4	5	6	7	8			11	10					9	1	3							
9 (a)	Wrexham	W	3-1	Robinson, Bytheway, Hirons	1,000			2	4	5	6	7	8			11	10					9	1	3							
16 (h)	Stourbridge	W	4-3	Robinson, Bytheway (2, 1 pen) opponent (og)	3,000			2	4	5	6	7	8			11	10					9	1	3							
23 (a)	Shrewsbury Tn	L	3-5	Bytheway, Pickering, Hirons	1,000			2	4		6	7	8			11	10		5			9	1	3							
Dec 7 (a)	Dudley	W	5-2	Robinson, Bytheway, Hunt (2), Pickering	800			2	4	5	6	7	8			11	10					9	1	3							
14 (a)	Burton United	L	1-3	Hunt	1,000			2	4	5	6	7	8			11	10					9	1	3							
21 (h)	Wolves Res	W	4-1	Burden, Robinson (2), Hunt	3,000			2	4	5	6	7	8		10	11						9	1	3							
28 (a)	Kidderminster H	L	0-1		2,000			2	4	5	6		9		10	7			11			8	1	3							
Jan 4 (a)	Worcester City	D	1-1	Massey	1,500			2	4	5	6	7	8		10							9	1	3	11						
11 (h)	Crewe Alexandra	L	0-1		2,650			2	4	5	6	7	8		10							9	1	3	11						
18 (a)	Brierley Hill All	D	1-1	Bytheway	1,000			2	4	5	6	7	8		10	11						9	1	3							
25 (h)	Stoke Res	W	4-2	Bytheway (2), Hunt (2)	3,000		2		4	5	6		8			7	10					9	1	3	11						
Feb 1 (a)	Birmingham Res	W	4-2	Robinson (2), Hunt, Hirons	1,500			2	4	5	6	7	8			11	10					9	1	3							
8 (h)	West Brom A Res	L	2-4	Pickering, opponent, (og)	5,200			2	4	5	6	7	8				10					9	1	3	11						
15 (a)	Halesowen	L	1-2	Bytheway	1,000			2	4	5	6	7	8				10					9	1	3		11					
22 (h)	Coventry City	W	2 1	Moreton, Pickering	1,000			2	4	5	6	7	8			11	10					9	1				3				
29 (a)	Stafford Rangers	L	0-1		1,200				4	5	6	7	8			11	10					9	1	3			2				
Mar 7 (h)	Wrexham	L	2-3	Robinson, Hunt	3,000			2	4	5	6	7	8			11	10					9	1				3				
9 (h)	Aston Villa	L	1-3	Hunt	2,000			2	4	5	6	7	8			11	10					9	1				3				
14 (a)	Stourbridge	W	3-0	Robinson, Hunt, Hirons	1,500			2	4	5		7	8			11	10					9	1				3	6			
21 (h)	Shrewsbury Tn	D	0-0		3,000			2	4	5		7	8			11	10					9	1				3	6			
23 (a)	Coventry City	L	0-3		2,000			2	4	5			8			7							1	9	11	10	3	6			
28 (a)	Aston Villa Res	L	0-6		6,000			2	4	5		7	8		9	11	10						1				3	6			
Apr 4 (h)	Dudley	W	1-0	Robinson	2,000			2	4		6	7	8		10	11	9						1				3		5		
6 (h)	Burton United	W	2-0	Pickering, Newman	1,000		2		4		6	7	8		10		9						1		11		3		5		
18 (a)	Wolves Res	W	3-0	Bytheway, Newman, Massey	2,000		2		4	5	6		7		10		8					9	1		11		3				
20 (h)	Halesowen	W	2-1	Bytheway, Newman	1,500			2	4	5	6	8	7		10							9	1		11		3				
21 (h)	Brierley Hill All	W	5-1	Williams, Hunt (2), Massey (2)	2,000		2		4	5	6	8	7				10					9	1		11		3				
25 (h)	Kidderminster H	W	2-0	Bytheway, Massey	3,000		2		4	5	6		8				10					9	1		11		3			7	
					Apps	3	10	26	34	30	30	29	34	1	12	25	25	1	4	1	1	27	30	18	10	2	14	4	2	1	
League Position: 10th					Goals			1	1	1	1	11	16		3	5	7					12			5						

Own Goals: 4

* On 19th October the Walsall v Halesowen League game was abandoned after 84 minutes due to bad light with Walsall trailing 2-3. And on 30th November fog caused the abandonment of the Walsall v Aston Villa Reserves match after 28 minutes with Villa leading 2-0.

F.A. Cup

Date	Opponents	Rd	Score	Scorers	Att	Urmson S.	Adams, W.	Moreton T.	Bird, J.	Burden, F.	Williams, R.	Robinson	Bytheway, G.	Pope, F	Newman, E.	Hirons, J.W.	Pickering, G.	Edwards	Newton, C.J.	Crutchley	Wright, E.W.	Hunt, A.	Knight	Corbett W.	Massey	Smith, G	Garrattly, G.	Flavell, J.F.	Fox,H.	Hatton	Grosvenor
Sep 21 (h)	Stafford Rangers	1Q	2-5	Bytheway (pen), Robinson	4,000	1	2		4	5	6	7	8	9		11	10														3
					Apps	1	1		1	1	1	1	1	1		1	1														1
					Goals							1	1																		

SEASON 1908-09

Birmingham League

Date	Venue	Opponent	Res	Score	Scorers	Att	Knight	Jones, J.H.	Smith, H.	Richards, T.	Bird, J	Williams, R.	Bourne, R.A.	Bailey, T	Francis S.	Newman, E.	Sheldon D.	Price T.	Lewis	Rochelle W.	Massey	Robinson	Hunt, A	Walker, W	Walker, G	Smith, A.H	Dolman	Urmson	Trinder	Atkins	Fletcher	Davis, W
Sep 5	(a)	Birmingham Res.	L	2-3	Francis, Newman.	2,500	1	2	3	4	5	6	7	8	9	10	11															
12	(h)	Stoke	W	3-0	Francis, Newman, Sheldon	4,200	1	2	3	4	5	6	7	8	9	10	11															
26	(h)	Crewe Alexandra	D	1-1	Bailey	5,000	1	2	3	4	5	6	7	8	9	10	11															
Oct 10	(h)	Kidderminster H	D	1-1	Bailey	4,000	1	2	3	4	5	6	7	8	9	10	11															
17	(a)	Shrewsbury Tn	L	1-2	Francis	1,000		2	3	4	5	6	7	8	9	10	11	1														
24	(h)	Brierley H Alliance	D	2-2	Francis, opponent (og)	2,500	1	2	3	4	5	6	7	8	9	10	11															
31	(a)	Stourbridge	L	2-3	Francis, Lewis (pen)	1,500		2	3	4	5	6	7		9	8	11	1	10													
Nov 7	(h)	Wellington Town	W	3-0	Lewis, Francis, opponent (og)	2,000		3		4	5	6	7	11	9	10		1	8	2												
14	(a)	Stafford Rangers	L	2-3	Bird, Lewis	1,000		2	3	4	5	6	7	9	10			1	8		11											
21	(h)	Worcester City	D	2-2	Francis, Bailey	1,500		2	3	4	5	6	7	10	9	8	11	1														
28	(a)	Wolves Res	L	0-2		4,000		2	3	4	5	6		7	9	10	11	1	8													
Dec 5	(h)	Dudley	W	1-0	Newman	2,000		2	3	4	5	6		11	8	10		1				7	9									
12	(a)	Burton United	L	0-1		1,500		2	3	4	5	6	11	9	8	10		1				7										
19	(h)	West Br Alb Res	D	1-1	Walker, W	1,000		2	3	4	5	6	7	11	8			1					9	10								
26	(h)	Aston Villa Res	D	1-1	Newman (pen)	5,000		2	3	4	5	6		11	9	8		1	7					10								
28	(a)	Aston Villa Res	L	0-4		3,500		2	3	4	5	6		11	9	8		1	7					10								
Jan 2	(h)	Birmingham Res	L	1-3	Walker. G	3,000		2	3	4	5	6			8		11	1	10			7			9							
9	(a)	Stoke	L	0-5		3,000		2	3	4	5	6	11		8			1				7	9		10							
16	(a)	Halesowen	L	0-3		1,000		2	3	4	5	6				10		1			11	9			8	7						
23	(h)	Halesowen	W	3-2	Robinson, Bailey (2)	2,000		2	3	4	5			10	9		11	1				8				7	6					
30	(a)	Crewe Alexandra	L	1-2	Bird	3,000		3	2	6	5			8	9		7	1				10				11	4					
Feb 6	(h)	Wrexham	W	5-0	Bird (2), Robinson, Francis, Massey	3,000			2	4	5	6		10	9			1			11	8				7	3					
13	(a)	Kidderminster H	W	3-2	Robinson (2), Bailey	700			2	4	5	6		10	9			1			11	8				7	3					
20	(h)	Shrewsbury Tn	D	1-1	Francis	4,000		2		4	5	6		10	9			1			11	8				7	3					
27	(a)	Brierley H Alliance	L	0-1		500		2		4	5	6		10	9						11	8				7	3	1				
Mar 13	(a)	Wellington Town	L	1-3	Francis	1,500		2		4	5	6			9	10		1			11	8				7	3					
20	(h)	Stafford Rangers	W	3-0	Jones, Robinson, Massey	2,000		2	3	4	5	6			9	10		1			11	8				7						
27	(a)	Worcester City	L	0-2		2,000		2	3	4	5	6			9	10		1			11	8				7						
Apr 3	(h)	Wolves Reserves	D	0-0		3,000		2	3	4	5	6			9	10		1			11	8				7						
5	(a)	Wrexham	L	0-2		2,000		2	3	4	5	6		10	8			1			11	7							9			
10	(a)	Dudley	W	3-0	Newman (3)	1,000		2	3	4	5	6			9	10					11	8				7		1				
12	(h)	Stourbridge	W	1-0	Francis	2,000		2	3	4		6	5	9	8	10										7		1		11		
17	(h)	Burton United	W	3-1	Robinson (2), Francis	2,000		2	3	4		6		5	9	10					11	8				7					1	
24	(a)	West Br Alb Res	L	0-3		4,000		2	3	4	5	6			9	10					11	8				7		1				
						Apps	5	32	30	34	32	32	14	24	33	23	12	24	7	1	14	19	3	3	3	15	7	4	1	1	1	
League position: 15th						Goals		1			4			6	12	7	1		3		2	7		1	1							

own goals: 2

F.A. Cup

Date	Venue	Opponent	Rd	Score	Scorers	Att	Knight	Jones, J.H.	Smith, H.	Richards, T.	Bird, J	Williams, R.	Bourne, R.A.	Bailey, T	Francis S.	Newman, E.	Sheldon D.	Price T.	Lewis	Rochelle W.	Massey	Robinson	Hunt, A	Walker, W	Walker, G	Smith, A.H	Dolman	Urmson	Trinder	Atkins	Fletcher	Davis, W
Sep 19	(a)	Worcester City.	Pr	2-0	Francis (2)	2,000	1	2	3	4	5	6	7	8	9	10	11															
Oct 3	(a)	Kidderminster H	1Q	1-2	Francis	4,000		2		4	5	6	7	8	9	10	11	1														3
						Apps	1	2	1	2	2	2	2	2	2	2	2	1														1
						Goals									3																	

SEASON 1909-10

Birmingham League

Date	Opponents	Res	Score	Scorers	Att	Urmson S.	Cook, W.J.	Dawson, J.W	Richards, T	Bird, J	Shufflebotham	Brawn	Crump J.	Lyon	Caddick W.	Dilly, T	Cooch, H	Chance, B	Walker, W. R.	Walker, G	Dean G.	Davies, H	Coffey, P	Adams	Coyle	Parsonage H.	Husler, W.T	Lindop, F.W	Hurst, C
Sep 4 (h)	Kidderminster H	L	0-2		4,000	1	2	3	4	5	6	7	8	9	10	11													
11 (a)	Stourbridge	W	4-2	Crump (3), Lyon	2,000		2		4	5		7	8	9	10	11	1	3	6										
25 (a)	Stoke	L	1-5	Bird	7,000		2		4	5		7	9	8	10	11	1	3	6										
Oct 2 (h)	Wellington Town	W	1-0	Caddick	3,000				4	2		7	9	8	10	11	1	3	6	5									
4 (h)	Worcester City	W	3-1	Crump (2, 1 pen), Dilly	2,000				4	2		7	9		10	11	1	3	6	5	8								
9 (a)	Halesowen	W	3-1	Brawn, Caddick (2)	1,500				4	2		7	9		10	11	1	3	6	5	8								
16 (h)	Dudley	W	3-0	Caddick (2), Dilly	3,700				4	2		7	9		10	11	1	3	6	5		8							
23 (a)	Birmingham Res	D	0-0		2,500				4	2		7	9		10	11	1	3	6	5		8							
30 (h)	Stafford Rangers	W	1-0	Caddick	4,000				4	2		7	9		10	11	1	3	6	5		8							
Nov 6 (a)	Brierley H Alliance	D	1-1	Dilly	1,500				4	2			9		10	11	1	3	6	5	8	7							
13 (h)	Wrexham	D	0-0		4,000				4	2			9		10	11	1	3	6	5		7	8						
20 (a)	Burton United	W	3-2	Dilly, Caddick (2)	500				4	2			8		10	9	1	3	6	5		7	11						
27 (h)	Burton United	W	3-1	Chance, Crump, Lyon	2,000				4	2			8	9	10	11	1	3	6	5		7							
Dec 4 (a)	Wolves Reserves	L	2-3	Crump, Lyon	200				4	2			8	9	10	11	1	3	6	5		7							
11 (h)	Shrewsbury Town	W	4-0	Lyon (3), Dilly	2,000		4			2		7		9	10	11	1	3	6	5		8							
18 (a)	West Br Alb Res	D	2-2	Brawn, Davies	1,500				4	2		7	10	9		11	1	3	6	5		8							
26 (a)	Crewe Alexandra	W	1-0	Crump	2,000		6		4	2			10	9	8	11	1	3		5		7							
Jan 1 (a)	Aston Villa Res	L	1-2	Caddick	4,000		6		4	2		7	9		10	11	1	3		5		8							
8 (a)	Kidderminster H	D	2-2	Crump, Lyon	2,000				4	2			8	9	10	11	1	3	6	5		7							
15 (h)	Aston Villa Res	W	1-0	Lyon	4,600				4	2			10	9	8	11	1	3	6	5		7							
22 (h)	Stourbridge	W	4-3	Caddick (2), Crump, Dilly (pen)	3,000				4	2			10	9	8	11	1	3	6	5		7							
29 (a)	Worcester City	W	3-2	Walker G, Caddick, Crump	2,000				4	2			10	9	8	11	1	3	6	5		7							
Feb 5 (h)	Stoke	D	2-2	Caddick, Crump	2,500	1	2		4				10	9	8	11		3	6	5		7							
12 (a)	Wellington Town	W	1-0	Crump	1,500				4	2			10	9	8	11	1	3	6	5		7							
19 (h)	Halesowen	W	7-0	Davies, Caddick (2), Lyon (2), Bird, Crump	2,000		6		4	2			10	9	8	11	1	3		5		7							
26 (a)	Dudley	W	3-2	Walker ,. Walker, W, Caddick	2,000				4	2			10	9	8	11	1	3	6	5		7							
Mar 5 (h)	Birmingham Res	W	3-0	Davies, Caddick (2)	4,500				4	2			10	9	8	11	1	3	6	5		7							
12 (a)	Stafford Rangers	L	1-3	Crump	1,500				4	2			10	9	8	11	1	3	6	5		7							
19 (h)	Brierley H Alliance	L	0-1		3,200				4	2			10	9	8	11	1	3	6	5		7							
26 (a)	Wrexham	D	2-2	Walker G, Crump	2,000				4	2		9	10		8	11	1	3	6	5		7							
Apr 2 (h)	Crewe Alexandra	L	1-2	Dilly	5,000				4	2			10	9	8	11	1	3	6	5		7							
16 (h)	Wolves Reserves	L	0-1		2,000		6		4	2			10			11	1	3				7		5	8	9			
23 (a)	Shrewsbury Town	L	0-2		2,000		6		4	2			9		10	11	1	3				7		5	8				
30 (h)	West Br Alb Res	W	3-0	Lindop (2), Hurst	500				4	2					8	11	1	3				7		5			6	9	10
					Apps	2	10	1	33	33	1	13	32	21	32	34	32	33	27	28	3	28	2	3	2	1	1	1	1
League position: 5th					Goals					2		2	16	10	18	7		1	1	3		3						2	1

F.A. Cup

Date	Opponents	Rd	Score	Scorers	Att	Urmson S.	Cook, W.J.	Dawson, J.W	Richards, T	Bird, J	Shufflebotham	Brawn	Crump J.	Lyon	Caddick W.	Dilly, T	Cooch, H	Chance, B	Walker, W. R.	Walker, G	Dean G.	Davies, H	Coffey, P	Adams	Coyle	Parsonage H.	Husler, W.T	Lindop, F.W	Hurst, C
Sep 18 (h)	Cannock.	PR	1-2	Crump	4,000		2		4	5		7	8	9	10	11	1	3			6								
					Apps		1		1	1		1	1	1	1	1	1	1			1								
					Goals								1																

SEASON 1910-11

Birmingham League

Date		Opponents		Score	Scorers	Att	Moult, J	Bird, J	Chance, B	Richards, T	Adams G.	Husler, W.T	Davies, H	Robinson, W	Bailey, T	Rampton, G	Wedge, J.H	Cook, W J	Caddick W.	Perry, S.H	Mansell	Hurst, C	Bowser, W	Copeland, D	Rogers	Winswood	Price, H	Parsonage, H	Nickless	Wilcox, J	Spier	Smith, R
Sep 3	(a)	Wednesbury O.A	W	2-1	Robinson, Bailey	5,000	1	2	3	4	5	6	7	8	9	10	11															
10	(h)	Brierley H Alliance	D	0-0		4,500	1	2	3	4		6	7	9		10	11	5	8													
24	(h)	Worcester City	L	2-3	Chance, Perry	3,500	1	2	3	4	5	6	7			10	11			8	9											
Oct 8	(h)	West Br Alb Res	W	1-0	Rampton	3,227	1	2	3		5	6		7		11					4	8	9	10								
15	(a)	Stafford Rangers	W	1-0	Rampton	1,000	1	2	3		5	6		7		11				10	4	8		9								
22	(h)	Dudley	L	0-1		2,975	1	2	3		5	6		7		11			9		4	8		10								
29	(a)	Stoke	W	4-3	Caddick, Robinson (2), Rampton	5,000	1	2	3	4	5		7	9		11			8		6	10										
Nov 5	(h)	Stourbridge	L	2-4	Hurst, Rampton	2,885	1	2	3	4	5		7	8		11					6	10			9							
12	(h)	Shrewsbury Town	D	1-1	Hurst	1,343	1	5	3			6	7	8		11		2			4	10			9							
19	(a)	Kidderminster H	W	3-2	Bird, Caddick, Rampton	1,500	1	9	3				7			11		2	10		4				8	5	6					
26	(h)	Wrexham	W	1-0	Rampton	1,292	1	9	3				7			11		2	10		4				8	5	6					
Dec 3	(a)	Aston Villa Res	L	1-3	Bird	3,340	1	9	3				7			11		2	10		4				8	5	6					
10	(h)	Wolves Reserves	W	7-3	Richards, Caddick, Davies, Rampton (2),																											
					Rogers, Parsonage	500	1	5	3	6			7			11		2	10		4				8			9				
17	(a)	Halesowen	W	2-0	Parsonage (2)	1,250	1	5	3	4			7			11		2	10		6				8			9				
24	(h)	Crewe Alexandra	W	2-1	Richards, Parsonage	2,258	1	5	3	4			7			11		2	10		6				8			9				
26	(h)	Wednesbury O. Ath.	W	4-0	Robinson, Parsonage (2), Caddick	4,950	1	5	3	4			7			11		2	10		6				8			9				
Jan 2	(a)	Birmingham Res	W	3-1	Bird, Caddick, Rogers	3,140	1	5	3	4			7	9				2	10		6				8				11			
7	(a)	Brierley H Alliance	W	1-0	Parsonage	2,000	1	5	3	4			7				11	2	10		6				8			9				
14	(a)	Wellington Town	L	0-6		1,500	1	5	3	4			7			11		2	10		6				8			9				
21	(h)	Wellington Town	W	4-1	Robinson (3. 1 pen), Caddick	2,000	1	5		4			7	11				2	10		6				8			9		3		
28	(a)	Worcester City	L	3-4	Parsonage (2), Caddick	2,000	1	5	3	4			7			11		2	10		6				8			9				
Feb 4	(h)	Birmingham Res	D	0-0		2,500	1	5	3	4				7		11		2			6	10			8			9				
11	(a)	West Br Alb Res	W	1-0	Hurst	4,500	1	5	3	4				7		11		2			6	10			8			9				
18	(h)	Stafford Rangers	W	1-0	Mansell	2,462	1	5	3	4			7			11		2			6	10			8			9				
25	(a)	Dudley	W	1-0	Mansell	1,500	1	5	3		4		7			11		2			6	10			8			9				
Mar 4	(h)	Stoke	L	2-4	Bird, Rogers	4,500	1	5	3	4			7			11		2			6	10			8			9				
11	(a)	Stourbridge	W	1-0	Rogers	1,000	1	5	3	4			7			11		2	10		6				8			9				
18	(a)	Shrewsbury Town	W	1-0	Caddick	2,000	1	5	3	4			7			11		2	10		6				8			9				
25	(h)	Kidderminster H	D	0-0		2,356	1	5	3	4			7					2	10		6				8		11	9				
Apr 1	(a)	Wrexham	D	3-3	Parsonage, Caddick, Price	1,700	1	5	3	4			7					2	10		6				8		11	9				
15	(a)	Wolves Reserves	W	2-0	Parsonage, Rampton	2,240	1	5		4			7			11		2	10		6				8			9		3		
17	(h)	Aston Villa Res	D	0-0		8,055	1	5	3	4			7			11		2	10		6				8			9				
22	(h)	Halesowen	W	3-1	Rogers (2), Parsonage	1,000	1	5	3	4			7			10		2			6				8		11	9				
29	(a)	Crewe Alexandra	L	1-2	Parsonage	1,000	1	5	3	4			7					2	10		6				8		11	9				
						Apps	34	34	32	26	8	7	29	12	1	28	4	27	22	2	32	11	1	3	27	3	7	21	1	2		
League position: 3rd						Goals		4	1	2			1	7	1	9			9	1	2	3			6		1	13				

F.A. Cup

Date		Opponents	Rd	Score	Scorers	Att	Moult, J	Bird, J	Chance, B	Richards, T	Adams G.	Husler, W.T	Davies, H	Robinson, W	Bailey, T	Rampton, G	Wedge, J.H	Cook, W J	Caddick W.	Perry, S.H	Mansell	Hurst, C	Bowser, W	Copeland, D	Rogers	Winswood	Price, H	Parsonage, H	Nickless	Wilcox, J	Spier	Smith, R
Sep 17	(h)	Willenhall Swifts.	PR	1-0	Spier.	2,000	1	5	3	4		6	7	8		10	11	2													9	
Oct 1	(a)	Hednesford Tn	1Q	3-4	Robinson, Rampton, Spier	2,500	1	5	3	4		6		7	8	11		2													9	10
						Apps	2	2	2	2		2	1	2	1	2	1	2													2	1
						Goals								1		1															2	

Southern League Div. 2

Date		Opponents		Score	Scorers	Att	Steventon	Cook	Nickless	Smith	Moule	Mansell	Houlston	Perry S.H.	Spier	Caddick	Cooper	Wilcox J.	Bourne R.A.	Bailey	Haywood	Robinson W.	Hollins	Jenkins	Bollington	Davies	Walton	Richards T.	Price	Ronchetti	Husler	Peters J. G.	Adams W.	Chance	Bird	Davenport F.	Rampton G.	Woodward	Hurst	Parsonage
Sep 3	(h)	Salisbury City	W	2-0	Houlston, Spier	1,000	1	2	3	4	5	6	7	8	9	10	11																							
24	(a)	Chesham Town	W	4-0	Houlston, Hollins, Bourne, Haywood	500	1	2					7		10			3	4	5	6	8	9	11																
Oct 8	(a)	Kettering	L	2-3	Walton (2)	3,000	1	2					7					3	4	9	6			11	5	8	10													
15	(h)	Treharris	W	1-0	Davies	1,000	1	2					7					3	4	9				11		8	10	5	6											
22	(a)	Reading	L	0-4		3,000	1	2	11				7	10				3		5	6					8		4		9										
29	(a)	Treharris	L	1-5	Houlston	400	1	2					7					3	4								10		5	9	6	8								
Dec 12	(a)	Stoke	L	0-4		1,200	1									10						9				7		4			6		2	3	5	8	11			
17	(h)	Reading	L	1-3	Houlston	500	1						7						4			9		11	5						6		2			8		3	10	
28	(a)	Croydon Common	L	0-2		1,000	1		11				7						4		6			11	5								2			8		3	10	9
31	(h)	Croydon Common	L	1-3	Rodgers	2,000			11			6				10						9			5	7		4						3	2					
Jan 14	(h)	Ton Pentre	D	1-1	Robinson	1,00	1											2				7			5				4							8		3	10	
28	(h)	Merthyr Town	L	0-1		700	1		11				7					3	4		6	9			5										2					
Feb 11	(h)	Cardiff	D	1-1	Davenport	700	1		11				7			10		3	4						5						6		2			8				
18	(a)	Merthyr Town	L	1-4	Robinson	2,000	1						7	9		10		3	4		11	8			5					6			2							
25	(h)	Kettering	W	4-2	Caddick, Perry, Jenkins, Robinson	150	1		3				7	8		10		2	4		6	9		11	5															
Mar 4	(a)	Cardiff	L	1-2	Perry	2,000	1						7	8		10		3	4		6	9		11	5								2							
11	(h)	Chesham Town	W	6-1	Robinson, Jenkins, Bollington, Bourne,																																			
					Houlston, Perry	300	1						7	8				3	4		6	9		11	5								2						10	
20	(h)	Stoke	W	1-0	Bird	1,000		2				6		10								11				7		4						3	5				10	
25	(a)	Aberdare	D	1-1	Morris	3,000	1						7					3	4					11	5								2							9
Apr 1	(h)	Aberdare	W	6-0	Houlston (2), Lindop (2), Rampton, Robinson	700	1						7					3	4		6	8		11	5								2				10			
15	(a)	Sailisbury	D	3-3	Jenkins, Haywood, Morris	200	1		3				7						4		6			11	5								2							8
29	(a)	Ton Pentre	L	0-1		100	1						7					3	4		6			11	5								2							8
						Apps	20	7	8	1	1	3	18	7	2	7	1	15	16	4	12	12	1	12	15	6	3	5	3	3	4	1	11	3	4	5	2	3	5	4
League position: 9th						Goals							7	3	1	1			2		2	5	1	3	1	1									1	1	1			

Also played: A Rodgers (No 8 matches 10 & 19) (1g); P Gardner (11 in match 11); T Mason (8 in match 12); L Hopkins (9 in match 11); C.D. Frost (6 in match 11); F.W.Lindop (9 in matches 20, 21 & 22) (2g); E Stych (10 in match 12); J Moult (1 in matches 10 & 18); E Hayes (9 in match 13); J Nichols (10 in matches 21 & 22); J Anson (8 in match 19); R Hulse (6 in match 14); F.W.Weston (9 in match 18); T Morris (9 in matches 19 & 21) (2g).

SEASON 1911-12

Birmingham League

Date		Opponent		Score	Scorers	Att	Moult, J	Cook, W.J	Chance, B	Richards, T	Bird, J	Humphries, E	Davies, H	Rogers, J	Stanton, J.W	Nicholls, A	Price, H	Robinson, W	Caddick, W	Freeman, W	Bailey, A.H	Adams, W	Izon, W	Hurst, C	Steventon, E	Mansell, R	Houlston, C.M	Wilcox, J
Sep 2	(h)	Wellington Town	D	1-1	Price	4,128	1	2	3	4	5	6	7	8	9	10	11											
9	(a)	Birmingham Res	D	0-0		2,500	1	2	3	4	5	6	7	10	9		11	8										
16	(h)	Wednesbury O A	W	3-0	Robinson (2), Caddick	4,000	1	2	3	4	5	6	7	8			11	9	10									
23	(a)	Dudley	L	0-1		1,500	1	2	3	4	5	6	7	8			11	10		9								
30	(h)	West Br Alb Res	W	1-0	Price	2,600	1	2	3	4	5	6	7	8			11	10		9								
Oct 7	(a)	Worcester City	D	1-1	Robinson	2,000	1	2	3	4	5	6	7	8			11	10		9								
14	(h)	Stafford Rangers	W	3-0	Freeman, Robinson, Bailey	2,493	1	2	3	4	5	6		8			7	10		9	11							
21	(a)	Brierley H Alliance	W	2-1	Chance, Robinson	1,600	1	2	3	4	5	6		8			7	10		9	11							
28	(h)	Kidderminster H	L	0-1		3,000	1	3	11	4	5	6		8			7	10		9		2						
Nov 4	(a)	Shrewsbury Town	W	3-0	Bird, Stanton, Freeman	2,000	1	2	3	4	5	6	7		8		11	10		9								
11	(h)	Darlaston	W	2-1	Bird, Robinson	6,000	1	2	3	4	5	6	7	8			11	10		9								
25	(a)	Aston Villa Res	L	0-1		10,000	1	2	3	4	5	6	7	8			11	10		9								
Dec 9	(a)	Wolves Res	L	1-2	Izon	2,000	1		3	4	5	6	7				11	10		9		2	8					
16	(h)	Stoke Res	L	1-2	Robinson	1,000	1	2	3	4	5	6		7			11	10		9			8					
23	(a)	Stourbridge	L	2-4	Price (2)	1,200	1	2	3	4	5	6		7			9	11					8	10				
26	(h)	Willenhall Swifts	W	2-1	Davies, Robinson	3,356	1	2	3	4	5	6	7	8			9	11	10									
30	(a)	Wellington Town	D	1-1	Rogers	700		2	3	4	5	6	7	8			9	11						10	1			
Jan 27	(h)	Dudley	W	4-0	Chance, Bird, Rogers, Freeman	1,996	1	2	3	4	5	10		7			11			9			8			6		
Feb 3	(a)	West Br Alb Res	L	1-2	Freeman	1,500	1	2	3	4	5	6		7			11	10		9			8					
10	(h)	Worcester City	L	0-4		3,000	1	2	3	4	5	6	7		10				11				8				9	
17	(a)	Stafford Rangers	W	4-0	Izon, Robinson, Price (2)	800	1	2		4	5	6	7				11	10		9			8					3
24	(h)	Brierley H Alliance	W	3-1	Robinson (2), Chance	2,000	1	2	10	4	5	6	7				11	8		9								3
Mar 2	(a)	Kidderminster H	L	0-1		800	1	2	3	4	5	6		7			11			9			8	10				
9	(h)	Shrewsbury Town	W	1-0	Freeman	1,487	1	2	3	4	5	6		7			11	10		9			8					
16	(a)	Darlaston	W	2-0	Richards, Robinson	4,000	1		3	4	5	6		7			11	10		9		2	8					
21	(a)	Wednesbury O A	W	3-1	Bird, Rogers, Freeman	1,500	1	2	3	4	5	6		7			11	10		9			8					
23	(h)	Birmingham Res	W	3-2	Izon, Freeman (2)	1,147	1	2	3	4	5	6		7			11	10		9			8					
30	(h)	Aston Villa Res	L	0-1		4,000	1	2	3	4	5	6		7			11	10		9			8					
Apr 6	(a)	Willenhall Swifts	W	1-0	Freeman	1,000	1		3	4	5			7				10		9	11	2	8			6		
8	(h)	Stourbridge	W	7-2	Bird, Izon (3), Stanton (2), Robinson	1,681	1		3	4	5			7	9		11	10				2	8			6		
13	(h)	Wolves Res	W	2-1	Stanton, Robinson	2,000			3	4	5		7		9			10			11	2	8		1	6		
20	(a)	Stoke Res	D	1-1	Rogers	6,000	1	2	3	4	5	6		7	9		11						8	10				
24	(a)	Wrexham	D	0-0		300	1	2	3	4	5	6		7	9						11		8	10				
27	(h)	Wrexham	D	1-1	Robinson	1,000	1	2	3	4	5	6		7	9			10			11		8					
						Apps	32	29	33	34	34	31	16	28	9	1	29	28	3	22	6	6	19	5	2	4	1	2
League position: 4th						Goals			3	1	5		1	4	4		6	15	1	8	1		7					

F.A. Cup

Date		Opponent	Rd	Score	Scorers	Att	Moult, J	Cook, W.J	Chance, B	Richards, T	Bird, J	Humphries, E	Davies, H	Rogers, J	Stanton, J.W	Nicholls, A	Price, H	Robinson, W	Caddick, W	Freeman, W	Bailey, A.H	Adams, W	Izon, W	Hurst, C	Steventon, E	Mansell, R	Houlston, C.M	Wilcox, J
Nov 18	(h)	Stoke	4Q	2-1	Rogers, Freeman	6,569	1	2	3	4	5	6	7	8			11	10		9								
Dec 2	(h)	Accrington Stanley	5Q	2-1	Freeman, Robinson (pen)	6,027	1	2	3	4	5	6	7	8			11	10		9								
Jan 13	(a)	Aston Villa	1	0-6		18,000	1	2	3	4	5	6	7	8			11	10					9					
						Apps	3	3	3	3	3	3	3	3			3	3		2			1					
						Goals								1				1		2								

Southern League Div 2

Date		Opponent		Score	Scorers	Att	Moult, J	Cook, W.J	Chance, B	Richards, T	Bird, J	Humphries, E	Davies, H	Rogers J	Stanton, J.W	Caddick W	Jenkins F.	Adams W.	Mansell R	Freeman W.	Robinson W.	Price H.	Wilcox J.	Haywood H.C.	Lewis B.	Steventon E.	Houlston C.	Newbrooke S.	Izon W.	Hurst C.	Daw R.S.	Swaby A.B.	Simcox G	Bailey A.H.	Steventon J.	Lamb R.	Brown W.W.	Stokes H.	Newbrooke W.J.
Sep 4	(h)	Portsmouth	W	1-0	Stanton	550	1	2	3	4	5	6	7	8	9	10	11																						
28	(a)	Mardy	W	4-2	Stanton (2), Jenkins, Davies	200	1	2	3	4	5	6	7	8	9		11				10																		
Oct 30	(a)	Cwm Albion	D	0-0		150	1		3	4	5		7	8				2	6	9	10	11																	
Nov 6	(h)	Mardy	W	3-0	Rogers, Freeman (2)	350	1	2		4	5		7	8		10				9			3	6	11														
20	(a)	Aberdare	L	1-2	Freeman	200	1		3	4	5	6	7	8				2		9	10				11														
27	(h)	Ton Pentre	W	4-2	Bird (3), Caddick	250	1	2		4	5	6	7		8	10				9			3		11														
Dec 11	(a)	Kettering	L	0-3		200	1		3	4	5	6	7					2		9	10	11							8										
18	(a)	Pontypridd	L	1-3	Freeman	150	1			4	5			7				2	6	9			3		11				8	10									
27	(a)	Chesham	W	3-1	Davies, Caddick (2)	400		2	3	4	5	6	7	8		10					11	9				1													
Jan 1	(a)	Portsmouth	L	0-3		4,000		2	3	4	5		7	8		10					11	9		6		1													
10	(a)	Croydon Common	W	2-1	Caddick (2)	300									9	8	11	2	4				3	6		1	7	5		10									
15	(h)	Kettering	W	4-0	Izon (2), Stanton, Newbrooke	500	1	2	3					7	9		11							6			4	5	8	10									
31	(a)	Southend	L	0-2		300	1		3	4	5	6		7				2		9	10	11							8										
Feb 12	(h)	Croydon Common	W	2-1	Robinson, Freeman	200	1	2		4	5	6	7							10	11		3						8		9								
19	(h)	Treharris	W	4-0	Freeman (4)	250	1	2		4	5	6	7							9	10		3						8										11
26	(a)	Treharris	L	0-2		100	1		3	4	5		7					2	6	9	10								8										11
Mar 18	(h)	Cardiff	L	0-3		300	1		3	4	5							2		9	10			6					8			7	11						
25	(h)	Merthyr Town	L	0-1		300		2	6							8		5	4	9	10		3			1	7							11					
Apr 1	(h)	Southend	W	2-1	Hurst, Freeman	300	1	2	3	4	5		8	7			11		6	9										10									
9	(h)	Chesham	W	7-1	Stanton (4), Jenkins, Davies, Richards (pen)	296				4			7		9		11						3	5		1			8			6			2	10			
10	(a)	Cardiff	L	1-5	Izon	5,000	1	2	3		5	6		7					4	9	10	11							8										
11	(a)	Ton Pentre	L	1-5	Hurst	200							7		9	8	11	2	4				3	6		1		10							5				
15	(a)	Merthyr Town	L	0-2		150							7		9	8	11	2	4				3	6		1									5				10
22	(h)	Cwm Albion	W	*	(*scratched to Walsall)																																		
29	(h)	Aberdare	W	2-1	Caddick, Newbrooke.W.	100		2						7		8	11		6		9			3		1						4			5				10
30	(h)	Pontypridd	W	2-0	Stanton, Izon	70	1		3	4	5	6		7	9								2						8								10	11	
						Apps	17	13	15	18	18	11	16	14	9	10	9	11	10	14	14	6	11	9	4	8	3	2	11	5	1	3	1	1	4	1	1	1	4
League position: 6th						Goals				1	3		3	1	9	6	2			10	1							1	4	2									1

SEASON 1912-13

Birmingham League

Date		Opponents		Score	Scorers	Att	Moult, J	Cook, W J	Chance, B	Richards, T	Bird, J	Humphries, E	Bridge	Ogden, S	Davies, J	Robinson, W	Baddeley, A	Jones	Stanton, W J	Johnson, J.W	Wilcox, J	Adams	Richardson	Haywood, M.(	Whitehouse	Price, H	Lester	Mansell	Sanders	Lewis	Johnson, H	Hollinshead	Sivorns	Barnes	Crowe	James	Penton	Evans	Pykitt
Sep 7	(a)	Birmingham Res	L	0-1		5,000	1	2	3	4	5	6	7	8	9	10	11																						
14	(h)	West Br Alb Res	D	0-0		3,700	1	2	3	4	5	6	7		8	10	11	9																					
16	(h)	Dudley	W	2-0	Stanton, Johnson	1,300	1	2	3	4	5	6	7			10		9	8	11																			
21	(a)	Wednesbury O Ath	W	2-0	Davies (2)	600	1	2		4	5	6	7		8	10		9		11	3																		
28	(h)	Stoke Res	W	7-0	Davies (4), Jones, Robinson (2, 1 pen)	3,000	1		3	4	5	6	7		8	10		9		11	2																		
Oct 5	(a)	Shrewsbury Town	L	0-4		2,000	1		3	4	5	6	7		8	10		9		11	2																		
12	(h)	Birmingham Res	L	1-5	Davies	3,000	1		3	4	5	6	7		8		10	9		11		2																	
19	(h)	Kidderminster H	W	3-0	Ogden, Jones, Davies	2,000	1	2	3	4	5	6		8	10			9		11			7																
Nov 2	(h)	Wolves Reserves	D	1-1	Jones	2,000	1	2	3	4	5	6	7		8	10		9		11																			
9	(a)	Aston Villa Res	L	2-4	Johnson, Whitehouse	4,000	1	2		4	5			8		9				7	3			6	10	11													
16	(h)	Darlaston	L	2-3	Bird, Price	2,500		2		4	5	6				11		10		7	3				8	9	1												
23	(a)	Worcester City	L	0-1		2,500	1	2	3	4	5	6				10		9		7					8	11													
Dec 7	(a)	Stourbridge	D	2-2	Baddeley, Price	1,000	1	2	3		5	6			8	9	10			7						11		4											
21	(a)	Wrexham	L	1-3	Mansell	1,000	1		3	4	5	6		8			10			7	2					11		9											
25	(h)	Coventry City Res	W	4-1	Price (2), Sanders (2)	2,000	1		3	4	5					8	10			7	2					11		6	9										
26	(h)	Wednesbury O Ath	W	2-1	Jones, Robinson (pen)	1,500	1			4	5					8	10	9		7	2	3				11		6											
Jan 4	(a)	West Br Alb Res	L	0-2		2,500	1			4	5	6		8		9	10				3	2				11				7									
18	(a)	Willenhall Swifts	W	2-0	Baddeley, opponent (og)	700	1		3	4	5	6		8			10			11	2					9					7								
25	(a)	Stoke Res	L	1-3	Baddeley	2,000	1		3	4	5	6					10	8			2		7			9						11							
Feb 1	(h)	Wellington Town	W	1-0	Bird	1,500	1		3	4	5	6					10				2		7			11							8	9					
8	(h)	Shrewsbury Town	W	1-0	Baddeley	2,000	1		3	4	5	6					10				2		7										8	9	11				
15	(a)	Brierley H Alliance	L	0-3		500	1		3	4	5	6					10				2		7			11							8	9					
22	(a)	Kidderminster H	L	0-4		1,000	1		3	4	5						11				2			6									8	9		10	7		
Mar 1	(h)	Willenhall Swifts	L	1-3	Jones	1,500	1		3	4	9	6				10	11	5			2												8				7		
8	(a)	Wolves Reserves	W	4-1	Jones, Robinson, Baddeley (2)	4,500	1		3			6				8	10	5			2					11		4	9								7		
22	(a)	Darlaston	D	1-1	Robinson	1,000	1		3			6				8	10	5			2					11		4	9								7		
24	(h)	Aston Villa Res	W	7-1	Penton, Robinson, Baddeley (2), Sanders (2), Price	3,500	1		3			6				8	10	5			2					11		4	9								7		
25	(h)	Brierley H Alliance	W	3-0	James, Baddeley (2)	2,060	1		3			6					10	5			2					11		4	9							8	7		
29	(h)	Worcester City	W	4-0	Penton, Baddeley (3)	1,000	1		3			6				8	10	5			2					11		4	9								7		
Apr 5	(a)	Coventry City Res	W	1-0	Baddeley	3,500	1		3			6				8	10	5			2					11		4	9								7		
7	(a)	Dudley	D	1-1	Baddeley	1,000	1		3			6				8	10	5			2					11		4	9								7		
12	(h)	Stourbridge	L	1-2	James	2,000	1		3			6					10	5			2					11		4	9							8	7		
19	(a)	Wellington Town	L	0-5		500	1		3			6				8		5			2					11		4								10	7	9	
26	(h)	Wrexham	W	3-2	Jones, Pykitt, Baddeley	500	1		3	4		6				8	10	5			2					11											7		9
						Apps	33	10	29	24	24	30	8	6	9	23	24	23	1	15	26	3	5	2	3	22	1	13	9	1	1	1	5	4	1	4	12	1	1
League position: 7th						Goals					2			1	8	6	16	7	1	2					1			1								2	2		1

* The initial League game v Willenhall Swifts (played on 26th October) was abandoned at half-time due to heavy rain.

F.A. Cup

Date		Opponents	Rd	Score	Scorers	Att	Moult, J	Cook, W J	Chance, B	Richards, T	Bird, J	Humphries, E	Bridge	Ogden, S	Davies, J	Robinson, W	Baddeley, A	Jones	Stanton, W J	Johnson, J.W	Wilcox, J	Adams	Richardson	Haywood, M.(	Whitehouse	Price, H	Lester	Mansell	Sanders	Lewis	Johnson, H	Hollinshead	Sivorns	Barnes	Crowe	James	Penton	Evans	Pykitt
Nov 30	(h)	Crewe Alexandra	4Q	2-1	Robinson 2 (1 pen)	6,559	1	2	3	4	5	6				9	10			7					8	11													
Dec 14	(h)	Halifax Town	5Q	0-0		6,027	1	2	3	4	5	6			8	9	10			7						11													
19	(a)	Halifax Town	5QR	0-1		3,000	1		3	4	5	6				9	10	8		7	2					11													
						Apps	3	2	3	3	3	3			1	3	3	1		3	1				1	3													
						Goals										2																							

SEASON 1913-14

Birmingham League

Date		Opponents		Score	Scorers	Att	Moult, J	Wilcox, J	Chance, B	Richards, T	Moore	Humphries, E	Penton	Crossley, C	Sanders	Horton	Shingler	Moss, D	Williams	Green, A	Green, J	Allsop	Mansell	Bates, H.J	Wootton	Holt	Rushton	Bishop	Haywood	Haddon	White, A	Labeta, A	Campey, A	Walker, D	Merrick, J	Lane	Kimberley, W	Wilkes	Boycott
Sep 6	(a)	Wrexham	D	1-1	Crossley	1,000	1	2	3	4	5	6	7	8	9	10	11																						
13	(h)	Kidderminster H	D	0-0		2,000	1	2	3	4		6	7	8	9		11	5	10																				
20	(h)	Birmingham Res	W	4-0	Crossley, Green A. (3)	3,000	1	2	3	4		6	7	8		9	11	5		10																			
Oct 4	(h)	Stourbridge	W	2-0	Crossley, Green A.	3,000	1	2	3	4		6	7	8				5		10	9	11																	
18	(h)	Wednesbury O Ath	D	0-0		3,000	1	2	3	4		6	7	8		9		5		10			11																
25	(a)	Coventry City Res	W	1-0	Crossley	2,000	1	2	3	4		6	7	8				5		10				9	11														
Nov 1	(h)	West Br Alb Res	L	1-3	Crossley	4,000	1	2	3	4		6	7	8	10			5						9	11														
8	(a)	Stoke Res	L	1-7	Bates	2,000	1		3	5		6	7	8	4								2	9	11	10													
15	(h)	Coventry City Res	L	1-2	Crossley	500			2	4		6	10	8										9	11		1	3	5										
22	(a)	Shrewsbury Town	L	0-6		2,000			2	4		6	7	8		10		5						9	11		1												
29	(h)	Brierley H Alliance	W	1-0	Crossley	900			3	4		6		10				5						7			1			8	9	11							
Dec 6	(a)	Darlaston	W	3-1	Crossley (3)	1,500			3	4		6		10				5						7			1			8	9	11	2						
13	(h)	Willenhall Swifts	W	1-0	White	3,000			3	4		6	8	10				5						7			1				9	11	2						
20	(a)	Wolves Reserves	L	0-2		3,000			3	4		6		10				5						7			1				9	11	2						
26	(a)	Wednesbury O Ath	W	2-0	Bates, Green J.	1,000			3	4		6		8				5			9			7	11		1						2	10					
27	(h)	Wrexham	W	4-2	Moss (pen), Bates, Crossley, Wootton	3,500			3	4		6		8				5			9			7	11		1						2	10					
Jan 3	(a)	Kidderminster H	D	2-2	Walker (2)	1,500			3	4		6		8				5			9			7	11		1						2	10					
10	(h)	Worcester City	W	3-1	Crossley, Wootton (2)	4,000			3	4		6		8				5						7	11		1				9		2	10					
17	(a)	Birmingham Res	L	2-4	Crossley (2)	5,000			3	4		6	7	8				5			9				11		1						2	10					
24	(h)	Wellington Town	W	2-1	White (2)	2,000			3	4		6	7	8				5							11		1				9		2	10					
31	(a)	Wellington Town	D	2-2	Crossley (2)	1.500			3	4		6	7	8	9			5							11		1						2	10					
Feb 7	(a)	Stourbridge	D	0-0		1,000			3	4		6	7	8				5							11		1				9		2	10					
14	(h)	Dudley	L	0-2		3,000			3	4		6	7					5							11		1						2	10	8	9			
Mar 2	(a)	Dudley	L	1-2	Penton	1,000			3	4			7			6									11		1						2	10	8	9	5		
7	(a)	West Br Alb Res	L	1-6	Walker	2,000			3	4		6	7												11		1						2	10	8	9	5		
14	(h)	Stoke Reserves	W	1-0	Sanders	1,500			3	4		6			8									7	11		1						2	10		9	5		
21	(a)	Worcester City	L	0-5		3,000			3	4	9	6												7	11		1						2	10		8	5		
28	(h)	Shrewsbury Town	D	1-1	Sanders	1,500				4	5	6			9									7	11		1							10		8	3	2	
Apr 4	(a)	Brierley H Alliance	L	2-3	Humphries, Lane	1,000				4		6			9										11		1				7		2	10		8	5	3	
10	(h)	Aston Villa Res	L	0-3		2,000				4		6			9										11		1				7		2	10			5	3	8
11	(h)	Darlaston	L	2-4	Richards, Moore	2,000				4	5	6			9									7	11								2	10			3		8
13	(h)	Aston Villa Res	W	1-0	Campey (pen)	3,000					5	6								10				7	11		1				9		4	8			2	3	
18	(a)	Willenhall Swifts	D	0-0		600					5	6			10									7	11		1				9		4	8			2	3	
25	(h)	Wolves Reserves	W	6-1	Lane (3), Campey, Walker, Wootton	2,000				4	5	6												7	11		1						9	10		8	2	3	
						Apps	8	7	27	32	7	33	18	22	11	5	3	20	1	5	5	1	2	20	25	1	25	1	1	2	11	4	22	20	3	8	11	6	2
League position: 10th						Goals				1	1	1	1	16	2			1		4	1			3	4						3		2	4		4			

Also played: Tustin (1), v Darlaston , 11-04-14, Fieldson (8) v Wolves, 20-12-13, S.J. Davies, (2) v Brierley Hill Alliance, 29-11-13, Reading, (3) v Shrewsbury, 22-11-13, Harrison (7) v Coventry, 15-11-13

F.A. Cup

Date		Opponents	Rd	Score	Scorers	Att	Moult, J	Wilcox, J	Chance, B	Richards, T	Moore	Humphries, E	Penton	Crossley, C	Sanders	Horton	Shingler	Moss, D	Williams	Green, A	Green, J	Allsop	Mansell	Bates, H.J	Wootton	Holt	Rushton	Bishop	Haywood	Haddon	White, A	Labeta, A	Campey, A	Walker, D	Merrick, J	Lane	Kimberley, W	Wilkes	Boycott
Sep 27	(h)	Stafford Rangers	PR	1-0	Green A.	3,000	1	2	3	4		6	7	8	9		11	5		10																			
Oct 11	(a)	Worcester City	1Q	0-7		1,500	1	2	3	4		6	7	8				5		10	9																		
						Apps	2	2	2	2		2	2	2	1		1	2		2	1																		
						Goals														1																			

Also played: Price (11) v Worcester City on 11-10-13

SEASON 1914-15

Birmingham League

Date		Opponents		Score	Scorers	Att	Rushton, G	Campey, A	Wilkes	Richards, T	Walker, W	Humphries, E	Wootton	Goldie	Bowers	Shingler	Pointon. R.S	Cox	Bates, H.J	Bradburn	Austin	Walker, D	Haper	Powell	Corbett, W	Wilcox, J	Wickham	Wilkinson	Penton	Freeman, W	Burnett	Salt	Williams,E. (D)	Chappell, I
Sep 2	(a)	Wrexham	L	0-4		500	1	2	3	4	5	6	7	8	9	10	11																	
5	(h)	Shrewsbury Town	D	0-0		1,000	1		3	2	5	6		8	10		11	4	7	9														
19	(h)	Brierley H Alliance	L	0-1		1,500	1		3	2	5	6				8	11	4	7		9	10												
Oct 3	(h)	Darlaston	L	1-2	Bates	8,000	1	4	3	2	9						11		7	5		10	6	8										
17	(h)	Wolves Reserves	W	3-1	Wootton, Pointon (2)	2,400	1	9	3	4	5		8				11		7	6		10			2									
31	(h)	Worcester City	W	1-0	Wootton	1,500	1	9		4	5		8				11		7			10			2	3	6							
Nov 14	(h)	Stourbridge	W	3-1	Wootton, Walker, D (2)	1,500	1		3	4	5		8				11		7	6		10				2		9						
28	(h)	Dudley	W	4-2	Richards, Bates, Campey, Pointon	1,500	1	9		4	5		8				11		7	6		10			2	3								
Dec 12	(h)	West Br Alb Res	W	2-1	Walker W., Pointon	1,500	1	9		4	5		8				11		7	6		10			2	3								
19	(a)	Willenhall Swifts	D	0-0		1,000	1	9		4	5		8				11		7	6		10			2	3								
25	(a)	Coventry City Res	W	2-1	Bates, Campey	2,500	1	9	2	4	5		8				11		7	6		10			3									
26	(h)	Coventry City Res	W	5-0	Wootton, Campey (3), Pointon	3,000	1	9	3	4	5		8				11		7	6		10			2									
28	(a)	Wednesbury Old Ath	W	3-1	Penton, Walker D. (2)	1,500	1	9	3	2	5		11						7	6		10						4	8					
Jan 9	(a)	Wellington Town	W	2-1	Campey (2)	1,200	1	9		4	5		8				11		7	6		10			2	3								
16	(h)	Wrexham	W	2-0	Wootton, Pointon	1,000	1	9	3	4	5		8				11		7	6		10				2								
23	(a)	Brierley H Alliance	L	0-2		1,250	1			4	5		8				11		7	6		10			3	2				9				
30	(h)	Kidderminster H	W	3-1	Walker W., Walker.D. (2)	2,000	1	9	3	4	5						11			6		10				2			7	8				
Feb 6	(a)	Darlaston	W	2-0	Campey, Pointon	2,500	1	9	2	4	5						11		7	6		10				3				8				
13	(h)	Aston Villa Res	W	4-1	Bradburn, Freeman, Campey, Walker D.	2,000	1	9	3	4	5						11		7	6		10				2				8				
20	(a)	Wolves Reserves	D	2-2	Freeman, Walker D.	5,000	1	9	3	4	5						11		7	6		10				2				8				
27	(h)	Stokes Reserves	L	0-2		4,000	1	9	3	4	5						11		7	6		10				2				8				
Mar 6	(a)	Worcester City	W	2-1	Wootton, Walker D.	700	1	9	3	4	5		7				11			6		10				2				8				
13	(h)	Wellington Town	W	5-2	Wootton (2), Campey (3)	2,000	1	9		4	5		7				11			6		10				2				8	3			
20	(a)	Stourbridge	D	0-0		1,400	1	9		4	5		7				11			6		10				2				8	3			
22	(a)	Stoke Reserves	W	1-0	Campey	2,500	1	9		4	5		7				11			6		10				2				8	3			
27	(h)	Wednesbury Old Ath	W	4-0	Walker W., Wootton, Campey, Pointon	2,000	1	9		4	5		7				11			6		10				2				8	3			
Apr 3	(a)	Dudley	L	1-3	Campey	1,000	1	9		4	5		7				11			6						2			10	8	3			
5	(a)	Aston Villa Res	D	0-0		3,000	1			4	5		9				11		7	6		10				2				8	3			
6	(a)	Kidderminster H	W	2-1	Wootton, Pointon	1,500	1		3	4	5		9				11		7	6		10				2				8				
10	(h)	Birmingham Res	W	3-1	Bates, (2), Walker. D	4,000	1			4	5		7				11		9	6		10				2				8	3			
12	(a)	Birmingham Res	L	0-6		2,000	1			4	5		7				11		9	6		10				2				8	3			
17	(a)	West Br Alb Res	L	1-5	Williams	3,000	1		3	4			7				11		9	6						2				10		5	8	
24	(h)	Willenhall Swifts	W	5-1	Walker W., Wootton, Campey (3)	1,500	1	9		4	5		8				11		7	6		10				2					3			
29	(a)	Shrewsbury Town	W	3-1	Campey (2), Freeman	1,000	1	9		4	5		11						7	6		10			3	2				8				
						Apps	34	25	18	34	33	3	26	2	2	2	32	2	26	31	1	30	1	1	10	26	1	2	3	18	9	1	1	
League position: 3rd						Goals		20		1	4		11				9		5	1		10							1	3			1	

F.A. Cup

Date		Opponents	Rd	Score	Scorers	Att	Rushton, G	Campey, A	Wilkes	Richards, T	Walker, W	Humphries, E	Wootton	Goldie	Bowers	Shingler	Pointon. R.S	Cox	Bates, H.J	Bradburn	Austin	Walker, D	Haper	Powell	Corbett, W	Wilcox, J	Wickham	Wilkinson	Penton	Freeman, W	Burnett	Salt	Williams,E. (D)	Chappell, I
Sep 12	(h)	Willenhall Pickwick	EXP	4-0	Bates, Bradburn, Walker D., Pointon	500	1		3	2	5	6		8			11	4	7	9		10												
26	(h)	Cannock	PR	2-1	Shingler, Pointon	1,500	1	4	3	2	5				8	9	11	6	7			10												
Oct 10	(h)	Hednesford Town	1Q	3-1	Campey (3)	2,000	1	9	3	4	5		8				11		7	6		10												2
24	(h)	Crad Heath St Lukes	2Q	5-2	Campey (5)	1,000	1	9	3	4	5		8				11		7	10						2	6							
Nov 7	(h)	Stoke	3Q	1-0	Campey	3,500	1	9		4	5		8				11		7			10			2	3	6							
21	(h)	Wrexham	4Q	2-1	Campey (2)	3,000	1	9		4	5		8				11		7	6		10			2	3								
Dec 5	(a)	Shrewsbury Town	5Q	1-2	Bates	3,500	1	9		4	5		8				11		7	6		10			2	3	2							
						Apps	7	6	4	7	7	1	5	1	1	1	7	2	7	5		6			3	4								1
						Goals		11								1	2		2	1		1												

SEASON 1915-16

Walsall & District Combination

Date		Opponents		Score	Scorers	Att	Rushton G.	Garrattly W.	Brownett J.	Moule	Moss	Hadley	Chambers	Crossley C.	Davies	Perry	Radford	Brooks	Wootton C.	Peers E.	Dyall	Richards T.	Bollington	Collins E.	Buttery	Campey A.	Millington C.	Beebee	Hill J.	Penton	Needham	Wilkes	Garrattly J.	Clark	Cook
Oct 9	(a)	Wednesbury O Ath	W	2-0	Ward (og), Davies	500	1	2	3	4	5	6	7	8	9	10	11																		
16	(h)	Walsall Wood	D	3-3	Crossley (2), Perry	1,000	1	3			5	6	4	8	9	10	11	2	7																
23	(a)	Willenhall Pickwick	L	2-3	Crossley (pen), Moss	250		3		4	5	6	7	8	9	10	11	2		1															
30	(a)	Walsall Wood	D	1-1	Crossley	300		2			5			8	9	10	7	3	11		1	4	6												
Nov 6	(h)	Hednesford Tn	L	0-2		400		2			5	6		8		10	7	3	11	1		4	9												
13	(h)	Willenhall Pickwick	W	3-1	Perry, Crossley, Campey	300		3					6	8	7	10			11		1		5	2	4	9									
27	(a)	Bloxwich Strollers	L	1-6	Perry	1,000		2			6			7		10			11		1	4	5	3	9		8								
Jan 22	(h)	Wednesbury O Ath	L	1-2	Needham	200		2					6			9	8		11			4	5	3					1	7	10				
29	(a)	Bilston	L	2-3	Penton, Buttery	300		2				6				8			11			4	5	3	9				1	7	10				
Feb 5	(h)	Bilston	W	2-1	Buttery, Penton	150	1	2								10	6		11			4	5	3	9				1	7					
12	(a)	Darlaston	W	1-0	Perry	200	1	2								8	6		11			4		3						7	10	5	9		
19	(h)	Wednesbury O Pk	W	6-1	Perry (3), Wootton, Penton, Garrattly	150	1									9			11			4	5	3				2		7	10		8	6	
Mar 11	(h)	Bloxwich Strollers	D	1-1	Perry	200		2				6		8		10	9		11			4	5	3					1					7	
25	(h)	Wednesbury O Pk	W	5-1	Radford (2), Clark, Needham, Perry	300						6				9	8		11			4	5	3					1		10	2		7	
Apr 1	(h)	Darlaston	D	1-1	Perry	100						6				9	10		11			2	5					8	1			3		7	4
15	(a)	Hednesford Tn	L	0-1		200								8		9	10		11			2	5					3	1			6		7	4
22	(a)	Cannock	W	7-1	Clark (3), Radford (2), Perry, Wootton	200	1							8		9	7		11			2	6					3				5		10	4
29	(h)	Cannock	W	7-1	Collins (5), Clark, Bollington	250		2									10		11			4	5	9				3	1		8	6		7	
						Apps	6	13	1	2	6	8	5	10	5	17	14	4	16	2	3	14	14	10	4	1	1	5	8	5	6	6	2	7	3
League position: 5th						Goals					1			5	1	11	4		2				1	5	2	1				3	2		1	5	

Own goal: 1

SEASON 1919-20

Birmingham League

Date	Opponent	Res	Score	Scorers	Att	Steventon. E	Clark	Smith, F	Wilkins, E	Lazenby, T	Bates, F	Benton, G	Weate	Wainwright, G	Dunn, J	Buttery, H	Corbett, W	Williams, T	Whittaker	Randall, W	Arrowsmith	Green	Radford, J	Parsonage, H	Renneville, W	Bird, W	Fletcher	Merrick, J	Fellows	Upton	Johnson, H	Lote	Hayes	Ingram, S	Edwards, E J	Clark	Willmott	Blower. A.L.
Aug 30 (h)	Shrewsbury Town	L	1-2	Weate	2,000	1	2	3	4	6	7	8	9	10	11																							
Sep 6 (a)	Shrewsbury Town	L	1-4	opponent (og)	1,500	1		2	4		7	8		11		5																						
13 (a)	Wolves Reserves	L	1-2	Wainwright	2,500	1		2			7			10		4	3	5	6	8	11																	
20 (h)	Wolves Reserves	D	1-1	Benton	5,000	1		3	8		7	9		11		5	2	4	6			10																
27 (h)	Wednesbury O. A.	W	2-0	Radford, Benton	4,000	1		3	4			9		10			2	5	6	7	11		8															
Oct 4 (a)	Wrexham	L	2-4	Benton, Parsonage	1,500	1		3				9		11		5	2	4	6	7			8	10														
18 (a)	Wellington Town	W	3-2	Renneville, Radford, Bird	1,000	1	2		4			9				5	3	6					8	10	7	11												
25 (h)	Stourbridge	D	2-2	Radford (2)	3,550	1	2	3	4			9				5							8	10	7	11	6											
Nov 1 (a)	Wednesbury O. A.	L	0-1		1,000	1	2	3	4			9					6						8	10		11	5											
15 (a)	West Brom A Res	D	1-1	Parsonage	3,500				4			9				5	2		6				8	10	7	11		1										
29 (a)	Stourbridge	W	5-3	Benton (2), Radford, Parsonage, opponent (og)	1,200			3	4			8				5	2		6				9	10		11		1	7									
Dec 13 (h)	Kidderminster H	W	4-1	Whittaker (pen), Bates, Bird (2)	2,000				4		7	8					2		6				9	10		11		1		3	5							
20 (a)	Darlaston	W	2-1	Fellows, Radford	1,500		2		4		7								6				9	10		11		1	8	3	5							
25 (a)	Willenhall	D	1-1	Radford	1,200		2		4			8					3		6				9	10		11		1	7		5							
26 (h)	Willenhall	W	2-1	Whittaker (pen) Radford	3,200		2	7	4							5	3		6				9	10		11		1										
27 (h)	Darlaston	W	3-2	Benton, Parsonage, Bird	5,415			3	4		7	8					2		6				9	10		11		1			5							
Jan 10 (h)	Wrexham	D	1-1	Wilkins	3,500				4			8					2		6				9	10		11		1			5	3	7					
17 (h)	Wellington Town	L	1-2	Whittaker (pen)	2,000				4			8					2		6				9	10		11		1			5	3	7					
24 (a)	Brierley H Alliance	D	0-0		1,600				4			8				2	3		5				9	10		11		1	7		6							
31 (h)	Brierley H Alliance	W	7-0	Wilkins, Fellows (2), Parsonage, Benton,																																		
				Radford (2)	2,958			3	4			8					2		6				9	10		11		1	7		5							
Feb 7 (h)	West Brom A Res	L	0-2		4,700			3	4			8					2		6				9	10		11		1	7		5							
21 (a)	Nuneaton Town	L	0-2		2,000			3	4			8				5	2												10		6		11	7				
28 (h)	Nuneaton Town	W	3-0	Whittaker, Benton, Bird	3,176			3	4			10					2		6				9			11		1			5			7	8			
Mar 6 (a)	Birmingham Res	W	3-2	Ingram, Bird (2)	2,500			3	4			6					2						9	10		11		1			5			7	8			
13 (h)	Birmingham Res	L	0-1		3,500		2	3	4			6											9	10		11		1			5			7	8			
20 (a)	Worcester City	L	1-4	Edwards	1,800		2	3	4			6											9	10		11		1			5			7	8			
27 (h)	Worcester City	W	3-0	Corbett (pen), Radford (2)	2,500			3	4					11			2						9	10		6		1			5			7	8			
Apr 2 (a)	Hednesford Town	L	0-2		1,800			3	4			11					2						9	10		6		1			5			7	8			
3 (a)	Stoke Reserves	L	0-4		2,500			3	4			11					2						9	10		6		1			5			7	8			
5 (h)	Hednesford Town	L	0-1		7,736			3	4			11					2							10				1			5				8	7		
10 (h)	Stoke Reserves	L	1-3	Edwards	4,000			3	4			6					2							10				1			5			7	9			
17 (a)	Coventry Cty Res	L	0-2		2,500			3	4			8					2							10		11		1			5			7	9		6	
24 (h)	Coventry Cty Res	L	1-4	Edwards	3,200			3	10			6					2						9			11		1			5			7	8		4	
May 1 (a)	Kidderminster H	L	1-4	Ingram	1,200			3								5	2					9				7					4			11		6		8
					Apps	9	9	26	31	1	7	29	1	7	1	12	28	5	17	3	2	2	26	25	3	25	2	23	7	2	22	2	3	12	11	2	2	1
League Position:- 16th					Goals				2		1	8	1				1		4				12	5	1	7			3					2	3			

Own goals: 2

Also played: Powner (5) v Shrewsbury 30-8-19: Dennis (3), O'Connor (6), Campey (9), Dentley (10) v Shrewsbury 6-9-19: O'Connor (6): Henshall (9) v Wolves 13-9-19: Harrington (7) v Wednesbury OA 1-11-19:Tough (3) v WBA 15-11-19: Parkes (8) v Willenhall 26-12-19: Palmer (1) v Nuneaton 21-2-20: Allcock (6) v Hednesford 5-4-20: Blower (8),Davies (11) v Stoke 10-4-20,; Truelove (1), Burton (10) v. Kidderminster 1-5-20.

F.A. Cup

Date	Opponent	Rd	Score	Scorers	Att	Steventon. E	Clark	Smith, F	Wilkins, E	Lazenby, T	Bates, F	Benton, G	Weate	Wainwright, G	Dunn, J	Buttery, H	Corbett, W	Williams, T	Whittaker	Randall, W	Arrowsmith	Green	Radford, J	Parsonage, H	Renneville, W	Bird, W	Fletcher	Merrick, J	Fellows	Upton	Johnson, H	Lote	Hayes	Ingram, S	Edwards, E J	Clark	Willmott	Blower. A.L.
Nov 22 (h)	Worcester City	4Q	3-1	Benton (3)	3,400	1		3	4		7	8				5	2		6				9	10		11												
Dec 6 (a)	Hednesford Town	5Q	2-4	Radford, Parsonage	6,000			3	4			8				5	2		6				9	10		11		1	7									
					Apps	1		2	2		1	2				2	2		2				2	2		2		1	1									
					Goals							3											1	1														

SEASON 1920-21

Birmingham League

Date	Opponent	Res	Score	Scorers	Att	Wyke, C	Corbett, W	Mackenzie, J	Johnson, H	Groves, A	Kinsella, J	Ingram, S	Bowyer, T	Edwards, E.J	Mann, J	Rogers, T	Wilkins, E	Allan	Houghton, J	Smith, J	Lane	Hughes	Timmins	Fessey	Swann	Walters	Duggan	Leedham	Ireland
Aug 29 (a)	Wednesbury Old Ath	W	2-0	Mann, Rogers	5,000	1	2	3	4	5	6	7	8	9	10	11													
Sep 4 (h)	Wednesbury Old Ath	W	3-1	Bowyer, Edwards (2)	8,000	1	2	3	4	5	6	7	8	9	10	11													
11 (a)	Worcester City	W	4-0	Groves, Bowyer, Edwards, Mann	1,500	1	2	3		5	6	7	8	9	10	11	4												
18 (h)	Worcester City	W	4-1	Groves, Bowyer (2), Rogers	6,000	1	2	3		5	6	7	8	9	10	11	4												
Oct 2 (h)	Stourbridge	W	4-3	Groves, Edwards (2), Mann	5,000	1	2	3		5	6	7	8	9	10	11		4											
16 (a)	Darlaston	W	4-2	Bowyer (2), Mann (2)	3,000	1	2	3		5		7	9	8	10	11	4	6											
23 (h)	Kidderminster H	W	2-0	Edwards (2)	8,000	1	2	3		5	4	7		8	10	11	6	9											
30 (h)	Wrexham	D	0-0		10,000		2	3		5	6	7		8	10	11	9	4	1										
Nov 6 (a)	Shrewsbury Town	L	1-4	Mann	2,000		2	3		5	6	7	9	8	10	11		4	1										
13 (h)	Shrewsbury Town	W	2-0	Edwards, Bowyer	7,500		2	3		5	6	7	9	8	10	11		4	1										
20 (a)	Wrexham	L	0-2		5,000		2	3		5	6	7	9	8	10	11		4	1										
27 (a)	Kidderminster H	D	2-1	Allan, Groves	1,500		2	3		5	9	7	10	8		11	6	4	1										
Dec 11 (a)	Stourbridge	L	0-4		2,500			3		5	6	7	8	9	10	11		4	1	2									
18 (a)	Wolves Reserves	W	2-1	Edwards, Bowyer	2,500		2	3	4	5	6	7	10	9		11			1		8								
25 (a)	Willenhall	W	4-1	Lane, Edwards, Bowyer (2)	1,500		2	3		5	6	7	10	9		11	4		1		8								
26 (h)	Willenhall	W	3-1	Lane, Edwards (2)	11,500		2	3		5	6	7	10	9		11		4	1		8								
Jan 1 (h)	Wolves Reserves	L	1-3	Edwards	6,000		2	3		5	4	7	10	9		11	6		1		8								
8 (h)	Darlaston	W	6-0	Ingram, Lane, Edwards (3), Rogers	7,000		2	3		5		7	10	9	6	11	4		1		8								
15 (a)	Stoke Res	W	2-1	Lane, Bowyer	2,500		2	3		5		7	10	9	6	11	4		1		8								
22 (h)	Stoke Res	L	0-1		10,224		2	3		5		7	10	9	6	11		4	1		8								
29 (a)	Birmingham Res	L	1-4	Bowyer	20,122		2	3		5			10	9	6	11	4		1		8	7							
Feb 5 (h)	Birmingham Res	L	0-2		7,742			3		5	4		10	8	6	11			1				2	7	9				
12 (a)	Coventry City Res	D	1-1	Hughes	7,000			3		5	4		10	8	6	11			1			7	2		9				
19 (h)	Coventry City Res	D	1-1	Groves (pen)	6,000			3		5	4		7	8	10	11		6	1				2		9				
26 (a)	Nuneaton Town	L	1-2	Groves	5,000			3		9	5		7	8	6	11		4	1		10		2						
Mar 12 (a)	Brierley H Alliance	W	3-0	Groves, Edwards, Walters	4,000			3		5			8	9	6	11		4	1			7	2			10			
19 (h)	Brierley H Alliance	W	5-1	Edwards (2), Leedham (3)	6,000			3		5			10	8	6	11		4	1				2				7	9	
25 (a)	Hednesford Town	L	0-2		9,630			3		5			10	8	6	11		4	1			7	2					9	
26 (a)	Wellington Town	L	1-6	Bowyer	5,000			3		5		7	10	8	6	11		4	1				2					9	
28 (h)	Hednesford Town	D	0-0		4,000			3		5		7	8		6	11		4	1				2			10		9	
Apr 2 (h)	Wellington Town	W	2-0	Edwards (2)	10,000		2			5		7	8	9	6	11		4	1				3					10	
9 (h)	West Br Alb Res	W	4-0	Wilkins (2), Leedham (2)	4,000		2	3		5		7	8		6	11	9	4	1									10	
16 (a)	West Br Alb Res	D	0-0		6,500		2			5		7	8	9	6	11		4	1				3					10	
23 (h)	Nuneaton Town	W	3-1	Ireland (2) opponent (og)	4,733		3	2					7		6	11		4	1		8		5					10	9
					Apps	7	24	32	3	33	20	25	32	31	29	34	12	22	27	1	10	4	12	1	3	2	1	8	1
League position: 5th					Goals					7		1	13	21	6	3	2	1			4	1				1		5	2

own goals 1

F.A. Cup

Date	Opponent	Rd	Score	Scorers	Att	Wyke, C	Corbett, W	Mackenzie, J	Johnson, H	Groves, A	Kinsella, J	Ingram, S	Bowyer, T	Edwards, E.J	Mann, J	Rogers, T	Wilkins, E	Allan	Houghton, J	Smith, J	Lane	Hughes	Timmins	Fessey	Swann	Walters	Duggan	Leedham	Ireland
Sep 25 (h)	Birmingham Tramways	PR	3-0	Groves (pen), Bowyer, Rogers	5,500	1	2	3		5	6	7	8	9	10	11		4											
Oct 9 (a)	Shrewsbury Town	1Q	0-1		3,000	1	2	3		5	6	7	8	9	10	11		4											
					Apps	2	2	2		2	2	2	2	2	2	2		2											
					Goals					1			1			1													

SEASON 1921 - 22

Division 3 (N)

Date	Opponent	Res	Score	Scorers	Att	Merrick	Timmins	Mackenzie	Christie	Groves A.	Barber	Bowyer	Wall, L	Reid	Butler	Spence	Jackson	Eden	Ellis	Bowen, T	Wilson	Webster	Franklin	Houghton	Leedham	Harper	Foster	Rogers	Beck	Evans	Bytheway, G	Groves E.	Ramsay
Aug 27	(a) Lincoln	L	0-1		6,000	1	2	3	6	4	10	7	5	9	8	11																	
Sept 3	(h) Lincoln	W	3-0	Reid (2), Barber	10,627	1	2	3	6	4	10	7	5	9	8	11																	
6	(a) Grimsby T.	L	1-3	Barber.	8,000	1	2	3	6	4	8	7	5		10	11									9								
10	(a) Tranmere R.	W	1-0	Reid.	8,000	1	2		4	5		7		9	10	11	3	6		8													
17	(h) Tranmere R.	W	2-0	Butler, Bowen.	9,815	1	2		4	5		7		9	10	11	3	6		8													
24	(a) Stalybridge C.	L	0-2		7,000	1	2		4	5		7		9	10	11	3	6		8													
Oct 1	(h) Stalybridge C.	D	2-2	Bowyer, Butler.	9,089	1	2		4	5		7		9	10	11	3	6		8													
8	(a) Wigan Boro.	L	2-4	Spence, Butler.	11,000	1	2		4	5		7		9	10	11	3	6		8													
15	(h) Wigan Boro.	W	4-1	Bowen, Butler, Reid, Spence.	8,606	1	3		4	5		7		9	10	11	2	6		8													
22	(h) Hartlepool U.	W	3-1	Bowyer, Spence (2).	7,422	1	3		4	5		7		9		11	2	6		8					10								
29	(a) Hartlepool U.	L	0-1		8,000	1	3		4	5		7		9	10	11	2	6		8													
Nov 5	(a) Southport C.	L	0-3		5,000	1	3		4	5		7			10	11	2	6		8	9												
12	(h) Southport C.	W	4-1	Groves, Butler (2,) Reid.	7,371	1	3		4	5	6	7		8	10	11	2			9													
26	(a) Stockport C.	L	1-3	Bowen.	10,000	1	3		4	5	6	7		8	10	11	2			9													
Dec 10	(h) Grimsby T.	W	2-1	Reid (2).	9,000	1	3		6	5		7		9	10		2		4	8								11					
24	(a) Rochdale	L	0-7		5,000	1	3	2	6	5		7		9	10	11				8	4												
27	(h) Wrexham	D	2-2	Groves, Beck.	9,372	1	3		6	5		7			10	11	2			8	4								9				
31	(a) Halifax T.	W	3-1	Christie, Bowyer, Butler.	5,000	1	3		6			7			10	11	2			8	4					9			5				
Jan 2	(a) Darlington	L	0-5		7,000	1	3		4					7		11	2			8	10					9	6		5				
14	(h) Halifax T.	W	4-1	Reid (2), Groves (2).	4,667	1	3		6	5		7		9	10	11	2			8	4												
16	(h) Stockport C.	L	0-2		3,480	1	3		6	5		7		9	10	11	2				4					8							
21	(a) Ashington	W	3-2	Butler, Groves (2).	4,000	1	3		6	5		7		9	10	11					4	2	8										
28	(h) Ashington	W	6-2	Franklin (4), Reid (2).	7,000	1	3		4	5		7		9	10	11					6	2	8										
Feb 4	(h) Barrow	W	3-1	Butler (2), Bowyer.	4,770	1	3		6	5		7		9	10	11					4	2	8										
11	(a) Barrow	L	0-3		5,000	1	3		4	5		7		9	10							2	8				6			11			
18	(a) Durham C.	L	0-2		2,000	1			6	5		7		9		11	3			10	4	2	8										
25	(h) Durham C.	W	2-0	Butler, Reid.	6,801	1	3		6	5		7		9	10	11				8	4	2											
Mar 4	(a) Wrexham	L	0-4		5,000	1	2		6	5				9	10	11				8	4	3									7		
18	(h) Nelson	W	2-0	Reid, Bowyer.	5,500		3			5		7		9	10	11					4	2	8	1	6								
Apr 1	(h) Chesterfield	W	2-1	Reid, Bowen.	5,000		3			5		7		9		11				8	4	2		1	6	10							
8	(a) Chesterfield	L	0-1		3,000		3			5		7		9		11				8	4	2		1	6	10							
15	(h) Crewe Alex.	W	1-0	Groves.	6,000		3			5		7		9		11				8	4	2		1	6	10							
17	(h) Darlington	L	0-1		8,738		2			5		7		9		11				8		3		1	4	10	6						
18	(h) Rochdale	W	4-0	Groves, Harper, Butler, Reid.	5,000		2			5		7		9	10	11						3		1	4	8	6						
21	(a) Crewe Alex.	L	0-2		6,000		3			5				9	10	7					4			1	6	8						2	11
25	(a) Nelson	L	0-1		3,000		3			5				9		7				8	4	2		1	6	10							11
29	(a) Accrington St.	D	3-3	Reid (3).	5,000		3		4	5		7		9		11				8		2		1	6	10							
May 6	(h) Accrington St.	W	6-1	Reid (3), Harper (2), Crawshaw (og).	5,000		3		4	5		7		9		11				8		2		1	6	10							
					Apps	28	37	4	30	36	5	34	3	34	28	36	18	9	1	27	19	16	6	10	12	12	4	1	3	1	1	1	2
League position: 8th					Goals				1	8	2	5		21	12	4				4			4			3			1				

Own Goal 1.

F.A. Cup

Date	Opponent	Rd	Score	Scorers	Att	Merrick	Timmins	Mackenzie	Christie	Groves A.	Barber	Bowyer	Wall, L	Reid	Butler	Spence	Jackson	Eden	Ellis	Bowen, T	Wilson	Webster	Franklin	Houghton	Leedham	Harper	Foster	Rogers	Beck	Evans	Bytheway, G	Groves E.	Ramsay
Nov 19	(a) Shrewsbury T	4Q	1-0	Butler.	4,000	1	3		4	5	6	7		8	10	11	2			9													
Dec 3	(h) Chesterfield	5Q	2-0	Bowen, Christie.	9,206	1	3		6	5		7		9	10	11	2		4	8													
17	(a) Mansfield	6Q	1-1	Butler.	10,586	1	3		6	5		7		9	10		2		4	8								11					
22	(h) Mansfield	6QR	4-0	Wilson, Bowen, Reid (2).	6,798	1	3		6	5		7		9	10	11	2			8	4												
Jan 7	(h) Bradford C.	1	3-3	Butler, Groves, Reid.	15,340	1	3		6	5		7		9	10	11	2			8	4												
11	(a) Bradford C.	1R	0-4		16,990	1	3		6	5		7		9	8	11	2		4		10												
					Apps	6	6		6	6	1	6		6	6	5	6		3	5	3							1					
					Goals				1	1				3	3					2	1												

SEASON 1922-23

Division 3(N)

Date	Venue	Opponents	Res	Score	Scorers	Att	Houghton	Webster	Timmins, B	Binks	Groves A.	Bradburn, E	Spence, D	Cullum	Reid	Archer	Cameron, E	Bowen, T	Walton	Leedham	Groves,E	Roberts	Mann	Langenove	Harper	Bedford, L	Potts	Lyons	Ceney
Aug 26	(h)	Hartlepool U.	D	2-2	Cullum (2).	9,627	1	2	3		5	6	7	8	9	10	11		4										
Sept 2	(a)	Hartlepool U.	D	2-2	Bowen, Reid.	6,000	1	2	3		5	6	7		9	10	11	8	4										
9	(h)	Chesterfield	L	0-1		9,781	1	2	3		5	6	7		9	10	11	8	4										
11	(a)	Chesterfield	L	0-6		8,000	1	2	3			5			9	10	11	7		6	4	8							
23	(a)	Bradford PA	D	2-2	A. Groves, Archer.	8,000	1	2	3	4	5	6	7	8		10	11					9							
30	(h)	Bradford PA	W	1-0	Cullum.	7,884		2	3		5	6		8		10	11	7	4			9	1						
Oct 7	(h)	Crewe Alex.	D	1-1	Reid	7,073		2	3	4	5	6	11		9	10	7						1	8					
14	(h)	Rochdale	D	0-0		6,178		2	3	4	5	6	11		9		7						1	8	10				
21	(a)	Darlington	L	0-2		3,588		2	3	4	5	6			9	11		8					1		10	7			
28	(h)	Darlington	D	2-2	Reid, Harper.	5,984		2	3	4	5	6	11		9								1		10	7	8		
Nov 4	(a)	Tranmere R.	W	3-2	Reid (2), A. Groves.	4,000		2	3	4	5	6	11		9	8							1		10	7			
11	(h)	Tranmere R.	W	2-1	Archer, Reid	5,841		2	3	4	5	6			9	8	11						1		10	7			
18	(a)	Grimsby T.	W	2-1	Reid (2).	8,000		2	3	5					9	8	11		4	6			1		10	7			
25	(h)	Grimsby T.	W	1-0	Reid.	6,300		2	3	5					9	8	11	10	4	6			1			7			
Dec 9	(a)	Durham C.	W	2-0	Turnbull (og), Reid.	2,000		2	3	5	8				9		11		4	6			1		10	7			
23	(a)	Accrington S.	L	1-2	Walton	3,000		2	3	5	8						11		4	6	9		1		10	7			
25	(a)	Lincoln City	W	2-0	Bowen, E. Groves.	6,000		2	3	5				8			11	10	4	6	9		1			7			
26	(h)	Lincoln City	W	2-0	E. Groves (2).	8,954		2	3	5				8			11	10	4	6	9		1			7			
30	(a)	Wigan Boro.	L	0-1		5,000		2	3	5				8			11	10	4	6	9		1			7			
Jan 6	(h)	Wigan Boro.	W	3-1	Bowen, E. Groves (2).	6,732		2	3	5				8			11	10	4	6	9		1			7			
20	(a)	Halifax T.	W	2-1	Bowen, E. Groves.	8,000		2	3	5				8			11	10	4	6	9		1			7			
27	(h)	Halifax T.	W	2-1	Cullum, E. Groves.	7,068		2	3	5				8			11	10	4	6	9		1			7			
Feb 3	(a)	Wrexham	L	0-1		5,000		2	3	5				8			11	10	4	6	9		1			7			
10	(h)	Wrexham	W	1-0	Cullum.	5,103		2		5				8			11	10	4	6	9		1			7		3	
24	(a)	Rochdale	W	2-0	E. Groves (2).	4,000		2	3	5				8			11	10	4	6	9		1			7			
Mar 3	(h)	Barrow	W	3-1	Cullum (2), Leedham.	7,059		2	3	5				8			11	10	4	6	9		1			7			
10	(a)	Barrow	D	0-0		4,000		2	3	5				8			11	10	4	6	9		1			7			
17	(a)	Ashington	L	0-3		5,000		2	3	5				8			11	10	4	6	9		1			7			
24	(h)	Ashington	W	2-1	E. Groves (2).	6,000		2	3	5				8			11	10	4	6	9		1			7			
30	(a)	Crewe Alex.	D	0-0		8,000		2	3	5				8			11	10	4	6	9		1			7			
31	(a)	Southport C.	L	1-2	Cullum.	5,000		2	3	5				8			11	10	4	6	9		1			7			
Apr 2	(h)	Accrington	L	0-2		10,000		2	3	5				8			11	10	4	6	9		1			7			
3	(h)	Durham C.	W	2-0	Cameron, Harper.	4,814		2	3		5			8			11		4	6	9		1		10				7
7	(h)	Southport C.	W	1-0	Ceney.	5,081		2	3	5							9	10	4	6	8		1			11			7
14	(a)	Stalybridge L.	L	0-2		2,000		2	3	5				8			11	10	4	6	9		1						7
21	(h)	Stalybridge L.	W	2-1	Cameron, Cullum.	4,031		2	3	5				8		10	11		4	6			1		9				7
28	(a)	Nelson	L	0-3		7,000		2	3	5							11	10	4	6	9		1		8				7
May 5	(h)	Nelson	W	5-0	E. Groves (2), Bedford, A. Groves (pen), Bowen.	2,500		2	3		5						11	10	4	6	9		1		8	7			
						Apps	5	38	37	31	15	12	8	22	13	13	35	26	30	27	23	3	33	2	12	26	1	1	5
League position: 3rd						Goals					3			9	10	2	2	5	1	1	13				2	1			1

Own Goal 1.

F.A. Cup

Date	Venue	Opponents	Rd	Score	Scorers	Att	Houghton	Webster	Timmins, B	Binks	Groves A.	Bradburn, E	Spence, D	Cullum	Reid	Archer	Cameron, E	Bowen, T	Walton	Leedham	Groves,E	Roberts	Mann	Langenove	Harper	Bedford, L	Potts	Lyons	Ceney
Dec 2	(a)	Wellington St G.	5Q	5-0	Reid 3, Harper, Cameron	4,328		2	3	5	8				9		11		4	6			1		10	7			
16	(h)	Wigan Boro.	6Q	1-3	Harper.	9,689		2	3	5	8				9		11		4	6			1		10	7			
						Apps		2	2	2	2				2		2		2	2			2		2	2			
						Goals									3		1								2				

SEASON 1923-24

Division 3(N)

Date		Opponent			Scorers	Att	Wait H	Webster W	Timmins B	Walton	Groves A.	Leedham	Dolphin	Bowen T	Groves E.	Bedford L	Cameron E	Bancroft	O'Doherty	Archer	Binks	Holt	Bratt	Harper	Robinson	Lloyd	Marshall	Birch	Wainwright	Ceney	Day
Aug 25	(a)	Rotherham C.	W	2-0	Bowen, Dolphin.	11,000	1	2	3	4	5	6	7	10	9		11		8												
27	(h)	Wrexham	L	1-2	E. Groves.	7,911	1	2	3	4	5	6	7	10	9		11		8												
Sept 1	(h)	Rotherham C.	D	1-1	E. Groves.	6,565	1	2	3	4	5	6	7	10	9		11		8												
5	(a)	Wrexham	D	0-0		10,500	1	2	3	4	5	6	7		9	11				10				8							
8	(a)	Durham C.	L	0-1		5,000	1	2	3	4	5	6			9		11			10				8				7			
15	(h)	Durham C.	D	1-1	Archer.	5,139	1	2	3	4	5	6			9		11			10				8				7			
22	(a)	Crewe Alex.	L	0-2		6,000	1	2	3	4	5	6	7		9		11	8		10											
29	(h)	Crewe Alex.	W	1-0	E. Groves.	4,382	1	2	3	4	5	6	7		9	10	11	8													
Oct 6	(a)	Accrington S.	W	3-0	E. Groves (2), A. Groves (pen).	5,000	1	2	3	4	5	6	7		9	10	11	8													
13	(h)	Accrington S.	W	2-0	Bedford, E. Groves.	5,655	1	2	3	4	5	6	7		9	10	11	8													
20	(h)	Halifax T.	W	2-0	E. Groves (2).	6,307	1	2	3	4	5	6	7	8	9	10	11														
27	(a)	Halifax T.	L	0-3		6,000	1	2	3	4	5	6	7		9	10	11	8													
Nov 3	(h)	Chesterfield	L	0-1		4,336	1	2	3	4	5	6	7		9	10	11	8													
10	(a)	Chesterfield	L	0-7		8,000	1	2	3	4		6	7	8	9	10	11				5										
17	(a)	Grimsby T.	L	0-1		8,000	1	2	3	6	5			8	9	7	11		10			4									
24	(h)	Grimsby T.	W	2-0	A. Groves, Cameron.	5,000	1	2	3	6	5			8	9	7	11		10			4									
Dec 8	(a)	New Brighton	L	0-1		5,000		2	3	6	5		7	8	9	11			10			4	1								
22	(a)	Wolves	D	0-0		16,000	1	2	3	6	5			8	9	7	11		10			4									
25	(h)	Wigan Boro.	W	3-0	Bowen (2), A. Groves (pen).	7,178	1	2	3		5	6		8	9	7	11		10			4									
26	(a)	Wigan Boro.	L	1-2	O'Doherty.	10,000	1	2	3		5	6		8		7	11		10			4		9							
29	(h)	Hartlepool U.	W	2-0	Bowen, Cameron.	5,000	1	2	3	4	5	6		8		7	11		10					9							
Jan 1	(a)	Ashington	L	1-3	Bowen.	6,000	1	2	3	6	5			8			11		10			4			9			7			
5	(a)	Hartlepool	W	1-0	Robinson.	4,000	1	2	3	6	5			8		7	11		10			4			9						
12	(h)	New Brighton	W	3-0	Bowen, A. Groves, Bedford.	4,182	1	2	3	4	5			8		7			10			6			9				11		
19	(a)	Doncaster R.	L	0-3		6,500	1	2	3	4	5			8		7			10	11		6			9						
26	(h)	Doncaster R.	W	5-2	E. Groves (2), Harper (2), Bowen.	4,593	1	2	3	4	5			8	9	7	11					6		10							
Feb 2	(a)	Rochdale	L	0-1		5,000	1	2	3	4	5			8	9	7	11					6		10							
9	(h)	Rochdale	L	0-1		5,116	1		3	4	5			8	9	7	11					6		10		2					
16	(a)	Southport	D	1-1	O'Doherty.	4,000	1		3	4	5			8	9	7	11		10			6				2					
23	(h)	Southport	L	0-1		9,543	1		3	4				8	9	7	11		10		5	6				2					
Mar 1	(a)	Darlington	L	2-4	Archer, Bedford.	4,000	1					6				10	11	9		8	5	4				2	3			7	
8	(h)	Darlington	W	2-1	Archer (2).	3,883	1	2		4		9				7	11			10	5	6		8			3				
15	(h)	Barrow	D	1-1	Leedham.	4,019	1	2		4		9				11				10	5	6		8			3			7	
22	(a)	Barrow	W	1-0	Harper.	3,000	1	2		4						11		9		10	5	6		8			3	7			
29	(h)	Lincoln	D	0-0		2,953	1	2		4						11		9		10	5	6		8			3	7			
Apr 5	(a)	Lincoln	L	0-2		4,000	1	2		4					8	11			10		5	6					3	7			9
7	(h)	Wolves	W	2-1	Archer, Harper.	12,281	1	2		4		6			9	11				10	5			8			3	7			
12	(h)	Tranmere R.	L	0-4		3,200	1	2		4		6			9	11				10	5			8			3	7			
19	(a)	Tranmere R.	L	1-3	Archer.	4,000	1	2		4		6			9	11				10	5			8			3	7			
21	(h)	Ashington	D	1-1	Archer.	3,245	1			4		6			3	11		9		10	5			8		2		7			
26	(h)	Bradford PA	L	2-3	E. Groves (pen), Archer.	1,887	1	2		4		6			9	11				10	5			8			3	7			
May 3	(a)	Bradford PA	L	0-5		5,000		2		4		6			9	11			10	8	5		1				3	7			
						Apps	40	37	30	39	28	26	13	21	31	35	28	10	18	16	14	21	2	17	4	5	11	12	1	2	1
League position: 17th						Goals					4	1	1	7	11	3	2		2	8				4	1						

F.A. Cup

Date		Opponent	Rd		Scorers	Att	Wait H	Webster W	Timmins B	Walton	Groves A.	Leedham	Dolphin	Bowen T	Groves E.	Bedford L	Cameron E	Bancroft	O'Doherty	Archer	Binks	Holt	Bratt	Harper	Robinson	Lloyd	Marshall	Birch	Wainwright	Ceney	Day
Dec 1	(h)	Stalybridge C.	5Q	3-1	Bowen, O'Doherty, Cameron.	4,287		2	3	6	5		7	8	9		11		10			4	1								
15	(a)	Aberdare Ath.	6Q	0-1		5,000	1	2	3	6	5		7	8	9		11		10			4									
						Apps	1	2	2	2	2		2	2	2		2		2			2	1								
						Goals								1			1		1												

SEASON 1924-25

Division 3(N)

Date	Opponents	Res	Score	Scorers	Att	Wait	Webster	Smith G.H.	Pendleton	Bowser	Hill	Tetlow	Burrill	Sibbald	Duggins	Bedford	Thomas	Higgs	Noakes	Higham	Birch	Boswell	Williams	Binks	Holt	Groves E.	Walters F.	Spencer
Aug 30	(a) Wigan Boro.	D	0-0		10,000	1	2	3	4	5	6	7	8	9	10	11												
Sept 6	(h) Crewe Alex.	D	0-0		8,336	1	2	3	4	5	6	7	8	9	10	11												
8	(a) Chesterfield	L	0-1		6,000	1	2	3	4	5	6	7	8	9	10	11												
13	(a) Durham C.	W	2-0	Webster (pen), Tetlow.	3,000	1	2	3	4	5	6	8	10	9		11					7							
20	(h) Doncaster R.	W	4-0	Burrill, Tetlow, Webster (2 pens).	6,751	1	2	3	4	5	6	8	10	9		11					7							
27	(a) Southport	L	0-1		5,000	1	2	3	4	5	6	8	10	9		11					7							
Oct 2	(a) Tranmere R.	W	1-0	Noakes.	6,000	1	2	3	4	5	6	8	10	9		7			11									
4	(h) Ashington	W	1-0	Burrill.	7,420	1	2	3	4	5	6		10	9		7			11						8			
11	(a) Nelson	L	1-2	Sibbald.	7,000	1	2	3	4	5	6	8	10	9		7			11									
18	(h) Barrow	W	1-0	Burrill.	6,735	1	2	3	4	5	6	8	10	9		7			11									
25	(h) Rochdale	L	0-2		6,183	1	2	3				4	10	8		7			11					5	6	9		
Nov 1	(a) Darlington	L	0-3		6,000	1	2	3			6	4	10			11					7			5		8	9	
8	(h) Bradford PA	L	0-2		4,187	1	2	3	4			8	10	7		11								5	6	9		
15	(a) Wrexham	D	1-1	Burrill.	6,000	1	2		5		6	4	9	7	10				11							3		8
22	(h) Rotherham C.	L	0-1		4,044	1	2		5			4	10	7	9				11						6	3		8
Dec 6	(h) Accrington S.	D	1-1	Burrill.	3,837	1	2	3	4	5			10	8	9	11	6				7							
13	(a) Halifax T.	D	1-1	Sibbald.	3,000	1	2	3	4	5			10	9		11	6	8			7							
20	(h) New Brighton	W	2-1	Burrill (2).	4,000	1	2	3	4	5			10	9		11	6	8			7							
25	(a) Grimsby T.	L	1-2	Sibbald (pen).	8,000	1	2	3	4	5			10	9		11	6	8			7							
26	(h) Grimsby T.	W	2-0	Sibbald (2).	7,428	1	2	3	4	5				9	10	11	6	8			7							
27	(h) Wigan Boro.	W	3-1	Sibbald (2, 1 pen), Higgs.	3,000	1	2	3	4	5			10	9		11	6	8			7							
Jan 1	(a) Hartlepool U.	L	1-3	Burrill.	3,000	1	2	3	4	5			10	9			6	8	11		7							
3	(a) Crewe Alex.	D	1-1	Sibbald.	6,000	1	2	3	4				10	9		11	6	8			7					5		
10	(h) Tranmere R.	W	2-0	Burrill (2).	4,085	1	2	3	4				10	9		11	6	8			7					5		
17	(h) Durham City	D	2-2	Higgs, Burrill.	4,500	1	2	3	4				10	9		11	6	8			7					5		
24	(a) Doncaster R.	L	1-2	Sibbald.	5,000	1	2	3	4	5	7		10	9			6	8	11									
31	(h) Southport	D	0-0		3,893	1	2	3	4	5	7		10	9			6	8	11									
Feb 7	(a) Ashington	L	1-6	Hamilton (og).	4,000	1		3	4	5	6		10	9				8	11	2	7							
14	(h) Nelson	L	1-2	Burrill	4,077	1	2	3	4	5			10	9		7	6	8	11									
21	(a) Barrow	L	2-3	Sibbald (2, 1 pen).	3,000	1	2	3	4				10	9		11	6				7	5	8					
28	(a) Rochdale	L	0-3		3,000	1	2	3	4	5			10	9		11	6				7		8					
Mar 7	(h) Darlington	W	2-1	Williams, Bedford.	4,683	1	2	3	4				10	9		11	6				7	5	8					
14	(a) Bradford PA	L	0-2		7,000	1	2	3	4				10	9		11	6				7	5	8					
21	(h) Wrexham	W	3-0	Burrill (2), Birch.	2,869	1	2	3	4				10	9		11	6				7	5	8					
28	(a) Rotheram C.	L	0-2		3,500	1	2	3	4				10	9		11	6				7	5	8					
Apr 4	(h) Chesterfield	D	0-0		3,029	1	2	3	4				10	9		11	6				7	5	8					
10	(a) Lincoln C.	W	1-0	Boswell.	7,000	1	2	3	4	5			10	9	11	7	6					8						
11	(a) Accrington S.	D	1-1	Sibbald.	4,000	1	2	3	4	5			10	9	11	7	6					8						
13	(h) Lincoln City	W	2-0	Tetlow (2).	4,193	1	2	3	4	5		8		9	11	7	6									10		
18	(h) Halifax Town	L	0-2		2,583	1	2	3	4	5		8		9	11	7	6									10		
25	(a) New Brighton	L	2-3	Tetlow (2).	5,000	1	2	3	4	5		8	10		11	7	6									9		
May 2	(h) Hartlepool	D	1-1	Tetlow.	1,775	1	2	3				8	10			11				4	7			5	6	9		
					Apps	42	41	40	39	27	15	18	39	39	12	36	25	13	12	2	23	8	7	4	5	12	1	2
League position: 19th					Goals		3					7	14	12		1		2	1		1	1	1					

Own Goal 1.

F.A. Cup

Date	Opponents	Rd	Score	Scorers	Att	Wait	Webster	Smith G.H.	Pendleton	Bowser	Hill	Tetlow	Burrill	Sibbald	Duggins	Bedford	Thomas	Higgs	Noakes	Higham	Birch	Boswell	Williams	Binks	Holt	Groves E.	Walters F.	Spencer
Nov 29	(h) Coventry C.	1	1-2	Pendleton	9,772	1	2	3	4	5			10	8	9	11	6				7							
					Apps	1	1	1	1	1			1	1	1	1	1				1							
					Goals				1																			

SEASON 1925-26

Division 3(N)

Date		Opponent			Scorers	Att	Wait	Groves E.	Smith G.H.	Holt	Binks	Adams	Potter	Clark	Pitt	Profitt	Alcock	Lawley	Timms	Felix	Crockford	Bowen D.	Smith H.	Walters F.	Martin	Gibbons	Hayward	Maloney	Phillips	Edwards H.	White	Raynes	Mutch	Thompson	Torrance	Kelly
Aug 29	(h)	Accrington S.	D	3-3	Profitt, Alcock, Walters.	4,752	1	2	3	4			7	8		10	11	6					5	9												
31	(a)	Grimsby T.	L	1-5	Clark.	8,000	1		3	4				8		10	7	11					5	9	2	6										
Sept 5	(a)	Durham	L	1-4	Alcock.	3,300	1	2	3	4	5		7	8		10	11	6						9												
7	(h)	Grimsby T.	D	2-2	Pitt, Alcock	3,580	1	2	3		5	6	7	8	9	10	11										4									
12	(h)	Hartlepool	L	1-2	Pitt.	5,000	1	2	3	4	5	6	7	8	9	10	11																			
14	(a)	Bradford	L	0-8		8,000	1	2	3		5	6		8	9	10	11	4	7																	
19	(a)	Rochdale	L	0-2		4,000	1	2	3	6			7	8		10	11	4					5	9												
24	(h)	Bradford	W	3-1	Alcock, Clark, Potter.	3,000	1	2	3	6			7	8		10	11	4					5	9												
26	(h)	Tranmere R.	L	1-3	Alcock.	3,981	1	2	3	6			7	8		10	11	4					5	9												
Oct 3	(a)	Crewe Alex.	L	1-2	Walters.	6,000	1	2	3	6	5		7	8		10	11	4						9												
10	(a)	Chesterfield	L	0-4		6,000	1	2	3	6	5	4	7	8		10	11							9												
17	(h)	New Brighton	W	3-1	Walters, Profitt, Alcock.	2,358	1	2	3		6		7	8		10	11	4						9				5								
24	(a)	Wigan Boro.	L	0-2		5,000	1	2	3		6		7	8	9	10	11	4										5								
31	(h)	Southport	D	2-2	Phillips, Lawley.	2,747	1	2	3		6		7			4	11	10							9			5	8							
Nov 7	(a)	Lincoln C.	L	1-5	Alcock.	2,000	1	2	3		6		7	8		4	11	10					5							9						
14	(h)	Nelson	L	0-2		2,461	1	2	3	4	6		7					11		8	9		5							10						
21	(a)	Coventry	L	0-2		13,000	1	2	3	4	6		7				11	10		8			5							9						
Dec 5	(a)	Doncaster R.	D	1-1	Crockford	4,000	1	5	3	4	6	2		8		10		11		7	9															
12	(h)	Ashington	W	2-0	Crockford (pen), Lawley.	1,879	1	5	3	4	6	2		8		10		11		7	9															
19	(a)	Barrow	L	2-5	Crockford (2).	1,000	1	5	3	4	6	2		8		10		11		7	9															
26	(a)	Halifax	L	0-5		9,000	1	2	3	4	6	5		8				11		7	9					10										
Jan 2	(a)	Accrington	L	2-5	Crockford (2).	5,000	1	2	3	4	6	5		8			10			7	9	11														
9	(h)	Wrexham	W	5-1	Clark (2), Alcock (2), Crockford.	1,825	1	2	3	4	6	5		8			10			7	9	11														
16	(h)	Durham C.	L	0-1		2,007	1	2	3	4	6	5		8			10	11		7	9															
23	(a)	Hartlepool U.	L	3-9	Felix, Crockford (2).	3,000	1	2	3	4	6	5		8			10	11		7	9															
25	(h)	Halifax Town	W	3-1	Lawley, Clark, Crockford (pen).	1,047	1	2	3	4		5		8		6	10	11		7	9															
30	(h)	Rochdale	L	1-5	Crockford.	2,000	1	2	3	4		5		8		6	10	11		7	9															
Feb 6	(a)	Tranmere R.	L	1-2	Binks	4,000	1	2	3	4	6	5		8			11	10		7	9															
13	(h)	Crewe Alex.	L	0-3		3,680	1	2	3	4	6	5		8				11		7	10			9												
20	(h)	Chesterfield	W	3-1	Crockford, Dennis (og), White.	3,758	1	2	3	4	5						11			7	9					10	6				8					
27	(a)	New Brighton	L	2-3	Crockford (2).	4,000	1	2	3	4	5						11			7	9					10	6				8					
Mar 6	(h)	Wigan Boro.	L	0-1		5,608	1	9	3	4	5					6	11	7													8	2	10			
13	(a)	Southport	D	1-1	White	4,000	1	2	3		6						11			7				9							8		10	4	5	
20	(h)	Lincoln C.	D	0-0		4,906	1	2	3	4	6							11		7	9										8		10		5	
27	(a)	Nelson	L	0-2		5,000	1	2	3	4	6						11			7	9										8		10		5	
Apr 3	(h)	Coventry	W	4-1	Felix, Alcock, Crockford, White.	5,039	1	2	3	4	6						11			7	9			10							8				5	
5	(h)	Rotherham U.	W	4-1	Crockford, White, Felix, Jackson (og).	5,645	1	2	3	4	6						11			7	9			10							8				5	
6	(a)	Rotherham U.	L	1-4	Walters (pen).	4,000	1	2	3	4	6						11			7	9			10							8				5	
10	(a)	Wrexham	W	1-0	Walters.	1,825	1		3	4	6		7				11				9			10							8	2			5	
17	(h)	Doncaster R.	W	2-1	Walters, Crockford.	3,203	1	2	3	4	6						11			7	9			10							8				5	
24	(a)	Ashington	L	0-2		3,000	1	2	3	4	6						11			7	9			10							8				5	
May 1	(h)	Barrow	L	1-2	White.	1,990	1	2	3		6									7	9			10							8	4			5	11
						Apps	42	40	42	34	35	16	16	26	4	21	34	26	1	25	24	2	8	18	2	4	3	3	1	3	13	3	4	1	10	1
League position: 21st						Goals					1		1	5	2	2	10	3		3	17			6					1		5					

Own Goals 2.

F.A. Cup

Date		Opponent	Rd	Score	Att	Wait	Groves E.	Smith G.H.	Holt	Binks	Adams	Potter	Clark	Pitt	Profitt	Alcock	Lawley	Timms	Felix	Crockford	Bowen D.	Smith H.	Walters F.	Martin	Gibbons	Hayward	Maloney	Phillips	Edwards H.	White	Raynes	Mutch	Thompson	Torrance	Kelly
Nov 28	(h)	Grimsby Town	1	0-1	4,982	1	2	3		6	4	7				11	8			9		5							10						
					Apps	1	1	1		1	1	1				1	1			1		1							1						

SEASON 1926-27

Division 3(N)

Date	Opponent	Res	Score	Scorers	Att	Wait	Groves E.	Parry	Walker D	Torrance	Binks	Rawlings	White	Bancroft	Bradford W	Scholes	Pumford	Holt	Beck	Walters F	Alcock	Kelly	Bedford	Smith G.H.	Hadlington	Sarvis	Robson	Edwards W	Adams	Harker	Abrahams	Raynes
Aug 28	(a) Doncaster R.	D	2-2	Bancroft, Bradford.	5,000	1	2	3	4	5	6	7	8	9	10	11																
Sept 4	(h) Stoke City	L	0-1		9,670	1	2	3	4	5	6	7	8		10	11	9															
6	(h) Ashington	D	0-0		4,951	1	2	3		5		7	8	9	10	11		4	6													
11	(a) Rotherham U.	L	1-4	White.	6,000	1	2	3		5		7	8				9	4	6	10	11											
15	(a) Wrexham	W	2-1	Walters, White.	5,000	1	2	3		5		7	9	8				4	6	10		11										
18	(h) Bradford P A.	W	1-0	White.	8,022	1	2	3		5		7	9	8				4	6	10			11									
25	(a) Halifax Town	D	1-1	White.	7,000	1		2		5		7	9	8				4	6	10			11	3								
27	(h) Wrexham	L	0-1		8,000	1		2		5		7		8	10			4	6	9			11	3								
Oct 2	(a) Nelson	L	2-3	Baker (og), Bedford.	3,000	1	9	3		2	6	7	8		10			4	5				11									
9	(h) Chesterfield	L	0-1		6,000	1	2			5		7		9	10			4	6				11	3	8							
16	(h) Accrington S.	W	5-1	Walters (2), Bedford, White (2)	5,612	1	2	3		5		7	9					4	6	10			11			8						
23	(a) Lincoln City	D	3-3	McConville (og), White (2)	3,000	1	2	3		5		7	9					4	6	10			11			8						
30	(h) Barrow	W	1-0	Walters	6,352	1	2	3		5		7	9					4	6	10			11			8						
Nov 6	(a) Crewe Alex.	D	1-1	White.	5,000	1	2	3		5		7	9					4	6	10			11			8						
13	(h) Hartlepool U.	D	2-2	White. (2)	3,802	1	2	3		5		7	9					4	6	10			11			8						
20	(a) Stockport C.	W	2-0	Sarvis, White.	5,000	1	2	3		5		7	9					4	6	10			11			8						
Dec 4	(a) Rochdale	D	4-4	White (3), Walters.	5,000	1	2	3		5		7	9					4	6	10			11			8						
18	(a) Durham City	L	0-3		1,500	1	2	3		5		7	9					4	6	10			11			8						
25	(h) Wigan Borough	W	3-2	Sarvis, Walters, White.	7,000	1	2	3		5		7	9					4	6	10			11			8						
27	(a) Wigan Borough	L	2-5	Bedford, White.	5,000	1	2	3		5		7	9					4	6	10			11				8					
Jan 15	(h) Doncaster R.	W	1-0	White.	4,011	1	2	3		5	6	7	9					4		10			11				8					
22	(a) Stoke City	L	1-4	Walters.	6,000	1	2	3		5		8	9		4				6	10			11					7				
24	(h) Tranmere R.	W	5-1	White, Robson, Bedford, Walters (2).	1,512	1	2	3		5	6		9		4					10			11				8	7				
29	(h) Rotherham U.	W	3-2	Bedford, Pumford, Smith (pen).	3,739	1	2			5	6				4		10			9			11	3			8	7				
Feb 5	(a) Bradford P A	L	1-5	Robson.	10,000	1				2	6	7	9					4		10			11	3			8		5			
12	(h) Halifax Town	L	0-1		3,394	1	2	3			6		9		4					10							8	7	5	11		
19	(h) Nelson	W	4-1	Edwards, White (2, 1 pen), Robson.	3,025	1	2	3			6		9		4				5	10			11				8	7				
26	(a) Chesterfield	L	0-2		5,000	1	2	3			6		9		4				5	10			11				8	7				
Mar 5	(a) Accrington S.	W	5-3	Walters, White (3), Bedford.	2,000	1	2				6		9					4	5	10			11	3			8	7				
12	(h) Lincoln City	L	1-2	Smith (pen).	3,897	1	2			5	6				4		10			9				3			8	7			11	
19	(a) Barrow	L	0-1		4,000	1	2	3		5	6				4					10							8	7	9		11	
26	(h) Crewe Alex.	L	2-3	Walters, Robson.	1,738	1	2	3		5					4			6		10							8	7	9		11	
Apr 2	(a) Hartlepool U.	D	2-2	Robson (2).	3,000	1	2		4		6				5					10	9						8	7	3		11	
4	(a) Ashington	W	2-0	Edwards, Alcock	2,000	1	2		4		6				5					10	9						8	7	3		11	
9	(h) Stockport C.	W	1-0	Alcock	3,525	1	2		4		6									10	9			3			8	7	5		11	
15	(a) New Brighton	L	1-3	Robson	4,000	1	2		4		6									10	9			3			8	7	5		11	
16	(a) Southport	L	1-6	Pumford	6,000	1	2		4		6						10				9			3			8	7	5		11	
18	(h) New Brighton	L	0-1		3,600	1	2		4		6						10		5		9						8	7	3		11	
23	(h) Rochdale	W	4-1	Alcock, Edwards, Robson, Raynes.	1,948	1	2		4		6				5						10						8	7	3		11	9
25	(h) Southport	D	1-1	Robson.	1,249	1	2		4		6				5						10						8	7	3		11	9
30	(a) Tranmere R.	L	0-6		7,000	1	2		4		6				5	9					10						8	7	3		11	
May 7	(h) Durham City	D	1-1	Adams (pen).	2,000	1	2		4		6			9	5						10						8	7	3		11	
					Apps	42	39	27	12	28	23	23	26	8	21	4	6	23	22	31	11	1	23	10	1	9	22	20	14	1	13	2
League position: 14th					Goals								24	1	1		2			11	3		6	2		2	9	3	1			1

Own Goals 2.

F.A. Cup

Date	Opponent	Rd	Score	Scorers	Att	Wait	Groves E.	Parry	Walker D	Torrance	Binks	Rawlings	White	Bancroft	Bradford W	Scholes	Pumford	Holt	Beck	Walters F	Alcock	Kelly	Bedford	Smith G.H.	Hadlington	Sarvis	Robson	Edwards W	Adams	Harker	Abrahams	Raynes
Nov 27	(h) Bradford PA	1	1-0	White.	10,995	1	2	3		5		7	9					4	6	10			11			8						
Dec 11	(h) Mansfield T.	2	2-0	White, Sarvis.	12,899	1	2	3		5		7	9					4	6	10			11			8						
Jan 8	(h) Corinthians	3	0-3		16,607	1	2	3		5		7	9					4	6	10			11			8						
					Apps	3	3	3		3		3	3					3	3	3			3			3						
					Goals								2													1						

SEASON 1927-28

Division 3(S)

Date		Opponent		Score	Scorers	Att	Wait	Groves E	Adams	Staley	Caesar W	Bradford W	Edwards W	Robson	Lane	Hughes	Springell	Walters F	Beck	Fairhurst	Walker J.D.	White	Hill	Reeve	Plunkett	Fereday	Lake W	Lansdale	Bedford	McClure
Aug 27	(a)	Bristol Rovers	L	2-5	Robson, Lane.	9,000	1	2	3	4	5	6	7	8	9	10	11													
29	(h)	Watford	W	2-0	Edwards, Lane.	7,000	1	2	3	4	5	6	7	8	9		11	10												
Sept 3	(h)	Plymouth Argyle	W	2-1	Hughes, Robson.	13,047	1	2	3	4		6	7	8	9	10	11		5											
7	(a)	Watford	L	0-4		6,000	1	2	3		4	6	7	8	9	10	11		5											
10	(a)	Merthyr Town	L	2-3	Lane, Walters.	3,000	1	2	3		4	6	7	8	9		11	10	5											
17	(h)	Norwich City	D	1-1	Lane.	9,148	1	2	3	4		6	7	8	9		11	10	5											
24	(h)	Gillingham	W	7-4	Hebdon (og), Hughes (2), Lane (4).	6,186	1	2	3	4		6	7	8	9	10	11		5											
Oct 1	(a)	Coventry City	W	1-0	Edwards.	14,000	1	2	3	4		6	7	8	9	10	11		5											
8	(h)	Newport County	L	0-3		11,001	1	2	3	4		6	7	8	9	10	11		5											
15	(a)	Swindon Town	L	0-5		7,000	1	2		4		6	7	8	9		11		5	3	10									
22	(a)	Brighton & H.A.	D	0-0		5,000	1	3		4	5	6	7		9		11	10		2	8									
29	(h)	Southend Utd.	L	0-1		7,000	1	3		4	5	6	7		10		11			2	8	9								
Nov 5	(a)	Northampton	L	0-10		11,000	1	3		4	5	6	7	8			11			2	10	9								
12	(h)	Bournemouth Utd.	L	2-3	Blair (og), Lane.	3,180	1		5		4		7	10	9		11		6	2		8	3							
19	(a)	Brentford *	Abd	1-4	Robson.	5,000	1	5	3		4		7	8	9	10	11		6	2										
Dec 3	(a)	Millwall Athletic	L	1-7	Springell.	15,000	1	5	3			4		8	9	10	11		6	2				7						
5	(a)	Brentford	L	2-3	Lake, Lane.	2,000	1	5		4				8	9				6	2					3	7	10	11		
10	(h)	Torquay Utd.	W	4-0	Lake (2), Lane (2).	2,832	1	5		4				8	9				6	2					3	7	10	11		
17	(a)	Exeter City	L	0-3		5,000	1	5		4					9			8	6	2					3	7	10	11		
27	(h)	Charlton Athletic	W	1-0	Lane.	5,000	1	5		4					9		11		6	2	8				3	7	10			
31	(h)	Bristol Rovers	L	1-2	Walker.	4,000	1	5		4					9				6	2	8				3	7	10	11		
Jan 7	(a)	Plymouth Argyle	L	1-2	Lane.	7,000	1	5		4					9				6	2	8				3	7	10	11		
14	(h)	Crystal Palace	D	1-1	Walker.	5,000	1	5		4					9		11		6	2	8				3	7	10			
21	(h)	Merthyr Town	D	2-2	Lansdale, Lane.	4,000	1	5		4					9				6	2	8				3	7	10	11		
28	(a)	Norwich City	W	4-1	Lane (2), Lake, Robson.	5,000	1	5	3	4		6		8	9		11			2						7	10			
Feb 4	(a)	Gillingham	L	0-2		5,000	1	5	3	4		6		8	9		11			2						7	10			
9	(a)	Charlton Athletic	W	3-1	Lane (2), Robson.	4,000	1	5		4		6		8	9		11			2					3		10		7	
11	(h)	Coventry City	W	7-0	Lane (2), Lake, Bradford (2), Robson (2).	5,141	1	5		4		6		8	9		11			2					3		10		7	
18	(a)	Newport County	L	1-4	Lane.	7,000	1	5		4		6		8	9		11			2					3		10		7	
25	(h)	Swindon Town	L	1-2	Robson.	6,854	1	5		4		6		8	9		11			2					3		10		7	
Mar 3	(h)	Brighton & H.A.	D	3-3	Robson, Lane (2, 1 pen).	5,433	1	5				6		8	9	4	11			2					3		10		7	
10	(a)	Southend United	L	1-2	Robson.	6,000	1	5				6		8	9	4	11			2		10			3				7	
17	(h)	Northampton T.	D	1-1	Lane.	8,000	1	4				6		8	9		11			2		10			3				7	5
24	(a)	Bournemouth U.	L	1-3	Lake.	5,000	1	4				6		8	9		11			2					3		10		7	5
31	(h)	Brentford	W	4-2	Lane (3), Bradford (pen).	5,000	1	4				6		8	9	10	11			2					3				7	5
Apr 7	(a)	Crystal Palace	L	1-5	Lane (pen).	16,000	1	4				6		8	9	10	11			2					3				7	5
9	(a)	Q.P.R.	D	1-1	Hughes.	10,000	1	4	2			6		8	9	10	11								3				7	5
10	(h)	Q.P.R.	D	2-2	Lane (2).	6,000	1	4	2			6		8	9	10		7							3			11		5
14	(h)	Millwall	L	2-5	Robson, Lane.	5,606	1	4				6		8	9	10				2					3			11	7	5
21	(a)	Luton Town	L	1-4	Hughes.	7,000	1	4				6		7	9	10				2	8				3				11	5
23	(h)	Luton Town	W	4-1	Lane (3, 1 pen), Robson.	4,000	1	4				6		8	9	10	11			2					3				7	5
28	(h)	Exeter City	W	5-1	Walker (3), Lane, Bedford.	6,000	1	4				6		8	9		11			2	10				3				7	5
May 5	(a)	Torquay United	D	1-1	Walker.	4,000	1	4				6		8	9		11			2	10				3				7	5
						Apps	42	41	15	25	8	33	14	34	41	16	33	6	18	31	12	5	1	1	25	10	16	8	16	11
League position: 18th						Goals						3	2	11	36	5	1	1			6						6	1	1	

* Match abandoned, bad light after 79 minutes.

Own Goals 2.

F.A. Cup

Date		Opponent	Rd	Score	Scorers	Att	Wait	Groves E	Adams	Staley	Caesar W	Bradford W	Edwards W	Robson	Lane	Hughes	Springell	Walters F	Beck	Fairhurst	Walker J.D.	White
Nov 26	(a)	Bristol Rovers	1	2-4	White, Groves.	8,000	1	5	3	4			7	8		10	11		6	2		9
						Apps	1	1	1	1			1	1		1	1		1	1		1
						Goals		1														1

SEASON 1928-29

Division 3(S)

Date		Opponent		Score	Scorers	Att	Wait	Fairhurst	Wragge	Bradford W	O'Brien	Lochhead	Moffatt	Walker D.J	Lane	Bell R	Thompson D.	Lake	Walters F.	Groves E	Smith	Thompson N.	Gough	Narrowmore	John	Houldey	Hunter	Attwood	Murphy	Johnstone	Robson	Hague
Aug 25	(a)	Newport County	L	1-3	Lane.	9,000	1	2	3	4	5	6	7	8	9	10	11															
27	(h)	Bristol Rovers	L	1-3	Lane.	6,300	1	2	3	4	5	6	7	8	9		11	10														
Sep 1	(h)	Crystal Palace	W	3-1	Lane (3).	6,609	1	2			5	6	7	8	9			10	3	4	11											
8	(a)	Swindon Town	L	1-5	Lane.	8,000	1	2			5	6	7		9			10	3	4	11	8										
12	(a)	Bristol Rovers	L	1-4	McCaig (og)	7,000	1	2			5	6	7		9			10	3	4	11	8										
15	(h)	Torquay Utd	W	1-0	Lane.	5,000	1	2		6	5	4	7		9					3	11	8	10									
22	(a)	Gillingham	W	4-1	Lake (2), Smith, Lane (pen).	5,000	1	2		6	5	4	7		9			10		3	11	8										
29	(h)	Plymouth Arg.	D	1-1	Smith.	8,207	1	2		6		4	7		9			10		3	11	8		5								
Oct 6	(a)	Fulham	L	1-5	Lane (pen).	10,000	1	2		6		4	7		9			10		5	11	8			3							
13	(h)	Q.P.R.	W	3-1	N. Thompson (2), Lane.	10,000	1	2				6	7		9			10		4	11	8				3	5					
20	(h)	Coventry City	D	0-0		13,335	1	2				6	7		9			10		4	11	8				3	5					
27	(a)	Luton Town	L	1-3	Lane.	10,000	1			10		6	7		9				2	4	11	8				3	5					
Nov 3	(h)	Brentford	W	2-0	N. Thompson, Attwood.	7,000	1			10		6	7						2	4		8	11			3	5	9				
10	(a)	Bournemouth	W	2-1	Moffatt, Attwood.	5,000	1			10	5	6	7							4		8	11			2	3	9				
17	(h)	Merthyr Town	D	1-1	Gough.	6,000	1				5	6	7	10						4		8	11			2	3	9				
Dec 1	(h)	Exeter City	W	7-2	Bradford (2), Attwood, Groves, N. Thompson (3).	6,000	1			10	5	6	7							4		8	11			2	3	9				
15	(h)	Norwich City	D	3-3	Lane (2), N. Thompson.	3,000	1			10	5	6	7		9					4		8	11			2	3					
22	(a)	Charlton Ath.	L	0-5		5,000	1	2		10		6	7		9				4			8				3	5		11			
25	(h)	Northampton T.	W	4-3	Lane (2), Smith (2).	7,785	1	2			5	6	7		9					4	11	8				3				10		
26	(a)	Northampton T.	L	2-4	Attwood (2).	12,000	1	2			5	6	7							4	11	10				3		9			8	
29	(h)	Newport County	W	3-1	Attwood (2), N. Thompson.	6,000	1	2			5	6	7							4	11	10				3		9			8	
Jan 5	(a)	Crystal Palace	D	1-1	Attwood.	10,000	1	2			5	6	7							4	11	10				3		9			8	
19	(h)	Swindon Town	D	1-1	Attwood.	7,000	1	2			5	6	7							4	11	10				3		9			8	
26	(a)	Torquay Utd	L	2-3	N. Thompson, Robson.	5,000	1	2			5	6	7							4		10	11			3		9			8	
Feb 2	(h)	Gillingham	W	4-0	Robson, Attwood (2), Moffatt (pen).	3,143	1	2			5	6	7							4		8	11			3		9			10	
9	(a)	Plymouth Arg.	D	2-2	Attwood, Robson.	9,000	1	2			5	6	7							4		8	11			3		9			10	
16	(h)	Fulham	D	2-2	Moffatt (pen), Robson.	6,000	1	2			5	6	7							4		8	11			3		9			10	
20	(a)	Southend Utd.	L	1-3	Moffatt.	3,000	1	2			5	6	7							4		8				3		9	11		10	
23	(a)	Q.P.R.	D	2-2	Moffatt, Attwood.	12,000	1	2			5	6	7							4		8				3		9	11		10	
Mar 2	(a)	Coventry City	D	1-1	N. Thompson.	12,000	1			4	5	6	7							2		8				3			11	9	10	
9	(h)	Luton Town	D	0-0		8,000	1			4	5	6	7							2		8	9			3			11		10	
16	(a)	Brentford	L	0-1		8,000	1	2			5	6	7		9					4		8	11			3					10	
23	(h)	Bournemouth	W	2-1	Walters (2).	6,000	1	2			5	6	7						9	4		8				3			11		10	
29	(a)	Watford	L	1-4	Murphy.	12,000	1			4	5	6	7							2		8	10	9		3			11			
30	(a)	Merthyr Town	L	0-1		2,000	1			4	5	6								2	7	8	10	9		3			11			
Apr 1	(h)	Watford	W	4-0	N. Thompson, Gough (2), Murphy.	6,000	1			4	5	6	7							2		8	9			3			11		10	
6	(h)	Southend Utd.	W	4-1	Robson (2), Gough, N. Thompson.	5,000	1			4	5	6	7						2			8	9		3				11		10	
13	(a)	Exeter City	D	1-1	Walker.	5,000	1			4	5	6	7	9						2		8			3				11		10	
20	(h)	Brighton & H.A	L	1-2	N. Thompson.	4,000	1			4		6	7	9						2		8			3		5		11		10	
27	(a)	Norwich City	L	1-2	Robson.	8,000	1			4	5	6	7	9						2		8				3			11		10	
May 1	(a)	Brighton & H.A	L	1-2	Hague.	7,000	1			4	5	6	7							2						3			11	8	10	9
4	(h)	Charlton Ath.	L	0-2		6,000	1			4	5	6	7	9						2		8				3			11		10	
						Apps	42	25	2	23	34	42	41	8	16	1	2	9	8	38	16	38	16	3	4	30	10	14	15	3	21	1
League position: 14th						Goals				2			5	1	15			2	2	1	4	13	4					13	2		7	1

Own Goal 1

F.A. Cup

Date		Opponent	Rd	Score	Scorers	Att	Wait	Fairhurst	Wragge	Bradford W	O'Brien	Lochhead	Moffatt	Walker D.J	Lane	Bell R	Thompson D.	Lake	Walters F.	Groves E	Smith	Thompson N.	Gough	Narrowmore	John	Houldey	Hunter	Attwood	Murphy	Johnstone	Robson	Hague
Nov 24	(h)	Worcester C.	1	3-1	Groves, N. Thompson, Gough.	8,423	1			10		6	7						2	4		8	11			3	5	9				
Dec 8	(h)	Sittingbourne	2	2-1	Gough, Moffatt.	7,809	1			10	5	6	7							4		8	11			2	3	9				
Jan 12	(h)	Middlesbrough	3	1-1	N. Thompson.	14,980	1	2			5	6	7							4	11	10				3		9			8	
21	(a)	Middlesbrough	3R	1-5	Gough.	14,917		2			5	6	7							4		10	11			1	3	9			8	
						Apps	3	2		2	3	4	4						1	4	1	4	3			4	3	4			2	
						Goals							1							1		2	3									

SEASON 1929-30

Division 3(S)

Date	Opponents	Res	Score	Scorers	Att	Biddlestone	Walters F.	Houldey	Muldoon	Helliwell	Bradford W.	Lanyon	Roe	Walters A.V.	Eyres	Barnes	Groves E.	Robson	Murphy	Harris	Prince	Cooper T.A.	Wait	Bedford	Mason	Johnson	Lewis	Hague	Capewell	John	Archer
Aug 31 (a)	Gillingham	L	1-2	Walters A.	8,000	1	2	3	4	5	6	7	8	9	10	11															
Sept 5 (a)	Q.P.R.	D	2-2	Walters A., Roe	8,000	1	2	3		5	6	7	8	9	10	11	4														
7 (h)	Northampton T.	L	1-2	Barnes.	9,369	1	2	3	4	5	6	7	8	9	10	11															
9 (h)	Q.P.R.	W	4-0	Eyres (2), Roe (2).	7,000	1	2	3		5	6		8	9	10	11	4	7													
14 (a)	Exeter City	W	2-0	Eyres, Walters A.	5,000	1	2	3		5	6		8	9	10	11	4	7													
16 (a)	Norwich City	L	0-3		10,000	1	2	3		5	6		8	9	10	11	4	7													
21 (h)	Southend Utd.	L	1-3	Walters A.	8,000	1	2	3	4	5	6		8	9	10	7			11												
23 (h)	Swindon Town	W	4-0	Eyres (2), Walters A, Murphy.	5,000	1	2	3		5	6		8	9	10		4		11	7											
28 (a)	Luton Town	W	3-2	Murphy, Eyres, Harris.	8,000	1	2	3		5	6		8	9	10		4		11	7											
Oct 5 (h)	Bournemouth U.	D	2-2	Bradford (pen), Eyres.	6,500	1	2	3		5	6		8	9	10		4		11	7											
11 (a)	Clapton Orient	D	1-1	Eyres.	15,000	1	2	3	4	5	6	7	8	9	10	11															
19 (h)	Coventry City	W	3-2	Eyres, Helliwell, Roe.	15,000	1	2	3	4	5	6	7	8	9	10	11															
26 (a)	Watford	L	1-2	Eyres.	8,000	1	2	3	4	5	6		8		10	11				9	7										
Nov 2 (h)	Newport County	W	2-1	Walters A. (2).	5,000	1	2	3	4		6		8	9	10	11				7		5									
9 (a)	Torquay United	L	2-5	Barnes, Walters A.	5,000	1	2	3	4		6		8	9	10	11				7		5									
16 (h)	Merthyr Town	W	6-0	Lanyon (2), Walters A (3), Barnes.	3,309	1	2	3	4	5	6	7	8	9	10	11															
23 (a)	Plymouth Arg.	D	1-1	Walters A.	11,000	1	2	3	4	5	6	7	8	9	10	11															
Dec 7 (a)	Brighton & H. A.	L	0-4		7,000	1	2	3	4	5	6	7	8	9	10	11															
21 (a)	Brentford	L	2-6	Roe, Walters A.	5,000			3	4	5	6	7	8	9	10	11	2						1								
25 (h)	Crystal Palace	D	0-0		4,800			3	4	5	6	7	8	9	10	11	2						1								
26 (a)	Crystal Palace	L	1-5	Barnes.	25,000			3	4	5	6		8	9	10	11	2						1	7							
28 (h)	Gillingham	L	1-2	Walters A.	4,000		2	3	4		6		8	9	10	11	5						1	7							
Jan 4 (a)	Northampton T.	L	0-1		10,000	1	2	3	6		5		8	9	10		4		11						7						
18 (h)	Exeter City	W	5-2	Roe, Walters A, Barnes, Mason, Eyres.	7,000	1	2	3	4	5	6		8	9	10	11									7						
Feb 1 (h)	Luton Town	W	1-0	Walters A.	6,000	1		3	4	5	6		8	9	10		2		11						7						
8 (a)	Bournemouth U.	D	1-1	Walters A.	4,000			3	4	5	6		8	9	10		2		11								1	7			
15 (h)	Clapton Orient	L	0-1		6,000			3	4	5	6		8	9	10	11	2						1						7		
19 (a)	Southend Utd	L	0-1		3,000			3	4	5	6		8	9	10	11	2										1		7		
22 (a)	Coventry City	L	0-4		15,000			3	4	5	6			8	10	11	2						1					7	9		
Mar 1 (h)	Watford	L	1-2	Barnes.	5,000		2	3	4		6		8	9	10	11						5							7	1	
8 (a)	Newport County	L	2-3	Barnes, Walters A.	5,000		2	3	4	5	6		8	9	10	11							1						7		
22 (a)	Merthyr Town	W	3-2	Eyres, Walters A, Roe.	2,000		2	3	4	5	6		8	9	10	11							1						7		
29 (h)	Plymouth Arg.	L	1-3	Eyres.	8,000		2	3	4	5	6		8	9	10	11							1						7		
Apr 5 (a)	Swindon Town	L	1-3	Walters A.	4,000		2	3	4	5	6		8	9	10	11								7						1	
10 (h)	Torquay Utd.	W	7-0	Eyres (3), Helliwell (2), Bedford, Walters A.	4,000		2	3	4	5	6		8	9	10	11								7						1	
12 (h)	Brighton & H. A.	W	2-0	Walters A, Eyres.	5,000		2	3	4	5	6		8	9	10	11								7						1	
19 (a)	Bristol Rovers	L	1-3	Bradford.	5,000		2	3	4	5	6		8	9	10	11								7						1	
21 (a)	Fulham	L	2-3	Walters A., Roe.	18,000		2		4		5		8	9	10		3		11									7		1	6
22 (h)	Fulham	D	2-2	Eyres (pen), Walters A.	6,000		2		4	5	6		8	9	10		3		11									7		1	
26 (h)	Brentford	L	1-2	Walters A.	2,288		2	3	4	5	6		8	9	10				11									7		1	
30 (h)	Bristol Rovers	D	0-0		4,000		2	3	4	5	6		8	9	10				11									7		1	
May 3 (h)	Norwich City	W	1-0	Bradford.	4,000		2	3	4	5	6		8	9	10				11									7		1	
					Apps	21	34	40	35	36	42	10	41	41	42	31	19	3	12	6	1	3	9	6	3		2	7	7	10	1
League position: 17th					Goals					3	3	2	8	25	18	7			2	1				1	1						

F.A. Cup

Date	Opponents	Rd	Score	Scorers	Att	Biddlestone	Walters F.	Houldey	Muldoon	Helliwell	Bradford W.	Lanyon	Roe	Walters A.V.	Eyres	Barnes	Groves E.	Robson	Murphy	Harris	Prince	Cooper T.A.	Wait	Bedford	Mason	Johnson	Lewis	Hague	Capewell	John	Archer
Nov 30 (h)	Exeter City	1	1-0	Roe.	7,989	1	2	3	4	5	6		8	9	10	11	7														
Dec 14 (a)	Newport County	2	3-2	Walters A (3).	4,121			3	4	5	6	7	8	9	10	11	2						1								
Jan 11 (h)	Swansea Town	3	2-0	Eyres, Walters A.	12,715	1	2	3	4	5	6		8	9	10	11									7						
25 (a)	Aston Villa	4	1-3	Johnson.	74,626	1	2	3	4	5	6		8	9	10										7	11					
					Apps	3	3	4	4	4	4	1	4	4	4	3	2						1		2	1					
					Goals								1	4	1											1					

SEASON 1930-31

Division 3(S)

Date		Opponents		Score	Scorers	Att.	Gretton	Walters F.	Bradford B.	Godfrey	Helliwell	Bradford W.	Lanyon	King	Cooper	Eyres	Barnes	Walters A.V.	Shaw	John	Brown	Wilson	Parle	Muldoon	Houldey	Archer	Brookes	Bartley	Hurst	Murphy	Edgar	Bell J	Mays
Aug 30	(h)	Clapton Orient	W	4-2	Cooper (3), Eyres.	7,841	1	2	3	4	5	6	7	8	9	10	11																
Sept 3	(a)	Swindon Town	L	3-4	Eyres (2), Walters A.	7,000	1	2	3	4	5	6	7	8		10	11	9															
6	(a)	Thames	L	1-4	Walters A.	9,000	1	2	3	4	5	6	7	8			11	9	10														
8	(h)	Bournemouth Utd	D	3-3	Godfrey, King, Eyres.	6,000		2	3	4	5	6	7	8		10			9	1	11												
13	(h)	Norwich City	W	7-0	King, Barnes (3), Cooper (3).	6,000			3	4	5	6		8	9	10	11			1		2	7										
17	(a)	Bournemouth Utd	W	2-0	King, Eyres.	4,000			3	4	5	6		8	9	10	11			1		2	7										
20	(a)	Q.P.R.	L	0-3		9,000			3	4	5	6		8	9	10	11			1		2	7										
27	(h)	Torquay United	L	0-4		5,000			3		5	6		8	9	10	11			1		2	7	4									
Oct 4	(h)	Coventry City	L	1-2	Cooper.	12,000		2		4	5		7	8	9	6	11		10	1					3								
11	(a)	Fulham	L	2-5	Helliwell (pen), Cooper.	18,000		2		4	5		7		9	10	11	8		1					3	6							
18	(a)	Northampton T.	L	0-3		9,000				4	5		7		8	10	11	9		1		2			3	6							
25	(h)	Brentford	L	1-4	Cooper.	2,378		4			5			8	9	10	11			1		2			3	6	7						
Nov 1	(a)	Crystal Palace	L	3-6	Walters A. (2), Helliwell.	16,000				4	5	10	7		8	6	11	9		1		2			3								
8	(h)	Southend United	L	1-3	Barnes	6,000				4	5	10	7			6	11	9		1		2			3	8							
15	(a)	Luton Town	D	0-0		7,000		2		4	5	8				10	11	9		1			7	6	3								
22	(h)	Bristol Rovers	W	4-2	Eyres, Barnes, Bradford W. Helliwell (pen).	5,000		2		4	5	8				10	11	9		1			7	6	3								
Dec 6	(h)	Gillingham	D	2-2	King, Barnes.	4,127		2		4	5	8		9		10	11			1			7	6	3								
20	(h)	Brighton & Hove A	D	0-0		6,000		2		4	5	8				10	11			1			7	6	3				9				
25	(h)	Watford	D	2-2	Cooper (2)	6,227		2		4		5			9	10				1			7	6	3			8		11			
26	(a)	Watford	D	2-2	Lanyon, Eyres.	6,000		2		4		5				10				1			7	6	3			8	9	11			
27	(a)	Clapton Orient	W	5-2	Eyres, Barnes (2), Cooper (2).	6,000				4		5			9	10	11			1		2	7		3	6			8				
Jan 3	(h)	Thames	W	6-0	Hurst (2), Eyres (3), Cooper.	6,000				2		5			9	10	11			1			7	4		6			8		3		
17	(a)	Norwich City	L	1-3	Cooper.	8,000				2	5	6			9	10	11						7	4	3				8			1	
22	(a)	Newport County	D	1-1	Walters (A).	4,000			3		5					10	11	9					7	4		6			8		2	1	
24	(h)	Q.P.R.	L	0-2		5,000			3		5		7			10	11			1			8	4		6			9		2		
31	(a)	Torquay Utd	W	1-0	Mays.	3,000				2		5				10	11			1				4	3	6			7		8		9
Feb 7	(a)	Coventry City	L	1-2	Barnes.	10,000				2		5				10	11			1				4	3	6			7		8		9
14	(h)	Fulham	W	2-0	Mays (2).	6,000				2		5				10			11	1			7	4	3	6					8		9
18	(a)	Exeter City	W	5-2	Mays (3), Barnes, Parle	4,000				2		5				10	11		8	1			7	4	3	6							9
21	(h)	Northampton T.	L	2-6	Mays (2).	6,000				2		5					11		10	1			7	4	3	6			8				9
28	(a)	Brentford	L	1-6	Bradford W.	8,000				4		8				10	11			1				6	3	5			7		2		9
Mar 7	(h)	Crystal Palace	W	2-1	Mays, Godfrey.	4,000		2		4		5					11		10	1			7		3	6		8					9
14	(a)	Southend United	L	0-2		7,000		2		4		5				10	11			1			7		3	6		8					9
21	(h)	Luton Town	L	0-1		6,000		2		4		5				10	11			1			7		3	6		8					9
28	(a)	Bristol Rovers	W	2-1	Mays, Shaw.	6,000		2		4		5				10	11		8	1			7		3	6							9
Apr 3	(a)	Notts County	L	1-6	Eyres.	13,000		2		4		5				10	11		8	1			7		3	6							9
4	(h)	Newport County	W	1-0	Barnes.	2,750		2		4		5				10	11		8	1			7		3	6							9
6	(h)	Notts County	W	2-1	Bradford W, Brookes.	4,622		2		4	5	8				10	11			1					3	6	7						9
11	(a)	Gillingham	L	0-2		5,000		2		4	5	8				10	11			1					3	6	7						9
18	(h)	Exeter City	W	2-1	Bradford W. (2).	2,316			3	4	5	8				10	11			1						6	7				2		9
25	(a)	Brighton & Hove A	D	3-3	Eyres (3).	5,000		2		4	5	8				10				1					3	6	7			11			9
May 2	(h)	Swindon Town	D	2-2	Mays, Eyres.	2,496				4	5	8				10	11			1					3	6	7				2		9
						Apps	3	22	11	38	26	36	10	11	14	39	37	9	10	37	1	9	24	17	30	25	6	5	11	3	9	2	17
League position: 17th						Goals				2	3	5	1	4	15	16	11	5	1				1				1		2				11

F.A. Cup

Date		Opponents	Rd	Score	Scorers	Att.	Gretton	Walters F.	Bradford B.	Godfrey	Helliwell	Bradford W.	Lanyon	King	Cooper	Eyres	Barnes	Walters A.V.	Shaw	John	Brown	Wilson	Parle	Muldoon	Houldey	Archer	Brookes	Bartley	Hurst	Murphy	Edgar	Bell J	Mays
Nov 30	(h)	Bournemouth	1	1-0	Eyres.	4,113		2		4	5	8				10	11	9		1			7	6	3								
Dec 13	(h)	Newport County	2	4-0	Cooper (3), Bartley.	7,676		2		4		5			9	10	11			1			7	6	3			8					
Jan 10	(a)	Blackburn Rovers	3	1-1	Eyres.	18,819				2		5	7		9	10	11			1				4	3	6			8				
15	(h)	Blackburn Rovers	3R	0-3		18,170				2		5			9	10	11			1			7	4	3	6			8				
						Apps		2		4	1	4	1		3	4	4	1		4			3	4	4	2		1	2				
						Goals									3	2												1					

SEASON 1931-32

Division 3(N)

Date	Opponent	Res	Score	Scorers	Att	John	Hunter A.E.	Watson	Henry	Helliwell	Bradford W.	Bushell	Scott	Pointon	Prentice	Turner	Walters F.	Brookes	Alsop	Phillipson	Rotton	Vaughan	Cooper T.	Livingstone	Wheeler	Ball	Poole	Reed	Long	Olney
Aug 29	(h) Barrow	L	1-2	Phillipson.	6,500	1	2	3	4	5	6		8	7						9	10	11								
31	(h) Gateshead	L	1-2	Rotton	4,152	1	2	3		5	6	7		8						9	10	11	4							
Sept 5	(h) Hull City	L	1-4	Rotton.	3,500	1	2	3			6			8		11	4	7		9	10		5							
9	(a) New Brighton	W	1-0	Rotton.	3,000	1	2	3		5	6		4	8		11		7		10	9									
12	(a) Lincoln City	L	0-3		6,000	1	2	3		5	6		4	8		11		7		10	9									
14	(h) New Brighton	W	3-0	Phillipson (2), Pointon	3,000	1	2	3		5	6		4	8		11		7		10	9									
19	(h) Chester	D	1-1	Helliwell (pen).	6,000	1	2	3		5	6		4	8		11		7		10	9									
26	(a) Hartlepool Utd.	L	3-4	Pointon, Bushell, Turner.	4,000	1	2	3		5	6	7	4	9	10	11								8						
Oct 10	(a) Darlington	L	0-2		5,000	1	2	3	4	5	8	7	6	9	10	11														
17	(h) Doncaster Rov.	W	2-0	Alsop, Prentice.	4,000	1	2	3	4	5	8		6	7	10	11			9											
24	(a) Rochdale	W	1-0	Pointon.	3,000	1	2	3	4	5	8		6	7	10	11			9											
31	(h) Crewe Alex.	W	2-1	Bradford, Alsop.	5,000	1	2	3	4	5	8		6	7	10	11			9											
Nov 7	(a) Carlisle Utd.	L	0-4		4,000	1	2	3	4	5	8		6	7	10	11			9											
14	(h) Wrexham	W	2-0	Turner (2).	5,000	1	2	3	4	5	8	7	6		10	11			9											
21	(a) Accrington S.	L	0-1		3,000	1	2	3	4		5	8	6	7	10	11			9											
Dec 5	(a) Rotherham Utd.	L	0-3		2,000	1	2	3	4	5	8	7	6		10	11			9											
12	(h) York City	D	2-2	Prentice, Turner.	5,000	1	2	3	4	5	6	7			10	11			9						8					
19	(a) York City	L	0-2		5,000	1	2	3	4	5	6	7		9	10	11									8					
25	(a) Southport	L	1-5	Wheeler.	7,000	1	2	3	4	5		7	6		10	11			9						8					
26	(h) Southport	W	2-1	Turner, Pointon.	6,000	1	2	3	4	5		7	6	9	10	11		8												
Jan 2	(a) Barrow	L	1-7	Brookes.	4,309	1	2	3	4			7	6	9	10	11	5	8												
9	(h) Stockport Co.	W	3-1	Helliwell (pen), Turner, Bushell.	6,000	1	2		4	5		7	6		10	11	3	8	9											
16	(a) Hull City	L	0-3		5,000	1	2		4	5		7	6		10	11	3	8	9											
23	(h) Lincoln	L	0-3		5,300	1	2	3	4	5	10	7	6			11			9						8					
30	(a) Chester	L	1-5	Alsop.	5,000	1	2	3	4	5	6	7	10		11	9			8											
Feb 6	(h) Hartlepool Utd.	L	2-3	Alsop, Turner.	3,000	1		3		5	4	7	6		10	11	2	8	9											
18	(h) Tranmere Rov.	W	2-1	Alsop, Turner.	4,000	1	2	3		5	6	7	4			11			9							8	10			
20	(h) Darlington	W	1-0	Alsop.	2,840	1	2	3		5	6	7	4			11			9							8		10		
27	(a) Doncaster Rov.	L	1-2	Turner.	3,000	1	2	3		5		7	4			11			9							8	6	10		
Mar 5	(h) Rochdale	W	2-1	Turner, Reed.	3,000	1	2	3		5		7	4			11	6		9							8		10		
12	(a) Crewe Alex.	L	1-2	Scott.	6,000	1	2	3		5		7	4			11	6		9							8		10		
19	(h) Carlisle United	W	3-1	Turner (2), Wheeler.	3,000	1	2	3		5		7	4			11	6		9						10	8				
26	(a) Wrexham	L	1-5	Bushell.	4,000	1	2	3		5		7	4			11	6		9							8		10		
28	(a) Halifax Town	W	2-1	Alsop, Turner.	3,000	1	2			5		7	4			11			9						10	8		6	3	
29	(h) Halifax Town	W	4-2	Bushell, Alsop (3).	4,000	1	2			5		7	4			11			9						10	8		6	3	
Apr 2	(h) Accrington S.	D	5-5	Prentice, Alsop (3), Scott.	3,000	1	2					7	4		8	11			9				5		10			6	3	
9	(a) Stockport Co.	W	1-0	Wheeler.	3,000	1		3		5		7	4		8	11	2		9						10			6		
16	(h) Rotherham Utd.	W	3-0	Alsop (2), Prentice.	3,000			3		5		7	4		8	11	2		9						10			6		1
23	(a) Tranmere Rov.	L	1-4	Turner.	4,000			3		5		7	4		8	11	2		9						10			6		1
May 7	(a) Gateshead	L	0-2		2,000			3		5		7	4		10	11	2		9							8		6		1
					Apps	37	35	35	18	36	23	30	36	17	23	38	13	10	28	7	7	2	3	1	11	10	2	12	3	3
League position: 16th					Goals					2	1	4	2	4	4	14		1	15	3	3				3			1		

Void League game

Date	Opponent	Res	Score	Scorers	Att	John	Hunter A.E.	Watson	Henry	Helliwell	Bradford W.	Bushell	Scott	Pointon	Prentice	Turner
Oct 3	(h) Wigan	W	3-0	Helliwell (pen), Pointon, Turner.	4,000	1	2	3	4	5	6	7	8	9	10	11
					Apps	1	1	1	1	1	1	1	1	1	1	1
					Goals					1				1		1

F.A. Cup

Date	Opponent	Rd	Score	Att	John	Hunter A.E.	Watson	Henry	Helliwell	Bradford W.	Bushell	Scott	Pointon	Prentice	Turner	Walters F.	Brookes	Alsop
Nov 28	(a) Darlington	1	0-1	5,377	1	2	3	4	5	8	7	6		10	11			9
				Apps	1	1	1	1	1	1	1	1		1	1			1

SEASON 1932-33

Division 3(N)

Date		Opponents		Score	Scorers	Att	Cunningham	Bird	Langford	Scott	Leslie	Bennett	Lee	Turner	Alsop	Ball	Coward	Reed	Salt	Sheppard	Walker	Bradford W.	Taylor	Devlin T.	Bell J.	Wiles G.H.
Aug 17	(h)	Hull City	W	1-0	Lee.	6,854	1	3	2	6	5		11		9	8	7		4				10			
29	(a)	Doncaster Rov.	L	2-3	Alsop (2).	4,000	1	3	2	6	5		11		9	8	7		4				10			
Sept 3	(a)	Barnsley	L	1-2	Lee.	5,000	1	3	2	6	5		11		9	8	7		4					10		
5	(h)	Doncaster Rov.	W	2-0	Alsop, Turner.	5,000	1	3	2	6	5		11	10	9	8	7		4							
10	(h)	Hartlepool Utd	W	4-1	Alsop (2), Turner, Lee.	6,000	1	3	2	6	5	4	11	10	9	8	7									
17	(a)	Halifax Town	L	0-4		7,000	1	3	2	4	5		11	10	9	8	7								6	
21	(a)	Chester	L	0-1		9,000	1	3	2	4	5		11		9	8	7							10	6	
24	(h)	Tranmere Rov.	W	3-2	Coward, Ball, Alsop.	6,234	1	3	2	4	5		11		9	8	7							10	6	
Oct 1	(a)	Wrexham	L	0-3		5,000	1	3	2	6	5			11	9	8	7	4				10				
8	(h)	Barrow	D	1-1	Ball.	5,000	1	3	2		5		11	10	9	8	7	4	6							
15	(h)	Gateshead	W	2-0	Alsop, Turner.	5,276	1	3	2		5	6	11	10	9	8	7	4								
22	(a)	Carlisle	D	1-1	Ball.	4,000	1	3	2		5	6	11	10	9	8	7	4								
29	(h)	York City	W	4-2	Ball (2), Alsop, Turner.	3,410	1	3	2		5	6	11	10	9	8	7	4								
Nov 5	(a)	Crewe Alex.	L	1-2	Alsop.	7,000	1	3	2		5	6	11	10	9	8	7	4								
12	(h)	Rochdale	W	2-1	Bird (2, 1 pen).	5,000	1	3	2		5	6	11	10	9	8	7	4								
19	(a)	Southport	L	1-2	Lee.	5,000	1	3	2		5	6	11	10	9	8	7	4								
Dec 3	(a)	Rotherham	L	1-4	Alsop.	2,000	1	3	2		5	6	11		9	8	7	4					10			
12	(h)	Accrington S.	W	1-0	Alsop.	4,000	1	3	2		5	6	11		9	8	7	4					10			
17	(a)	New Brighton	D	2-2	Langford (pen), Turner.	3,000	1	3	2		5	6		11	9	8	7	4						10		
24	(h)	Chester	W	3-1	Lee, Alsop (2).	6,000	1	3	2		5	6	11	10	9		7	4					8			
26	(a)	Stockport	L	0-5		5,000	1	3	2		5	6	11	10	9		7	4					8			
27	(h)	Stockport	D	0-0		9,000	1	3	2		5	6	11	10	9	8						4	7			
31	(a)	Hull City	D	0-0		10,000	1	3	2		5	6	11		9	8	7	4		10						
Jan 7	(h)	Barnsley	D	1-1	Alsop	6,080	1	3	2		5	6	11		9	8	7	4		10						
19	(h)	Mansfield Town	W	8-1	Lee (2), Alsop (4), Coward (2).	2,658	1	3			5	2	11		9	8	7	4	6	10						
21	(a)	Hartlepool Utd.	L	0-2		4,000	1	3			5	2	11		9	8	7	4	6	10						
Feb 4	(a)	Tranmere Rov.	W	3-1	Sheppard, Lee, Taylor.	3,000	1	3			5	2	11			8		9	4	10		6	7			
9	(h)	Halifax Town	W	4-0	Turner, Alsop (2), Taylor.	3,000	1	3			5	2	11	10	9	8			4			6	7			
11	(h)	Wrexham	L	2-3	Lee, Alsop.	8,722	1	3			5	2	11	10	9	8			4			6	7			
18	(a)	Barrow	W	2-1	Ball, Sheppard.	5,000	1	2			5		11		9	8				10	4	6	7		3	
Mar 4	(h)	Carlisle United	W	5-0	Taylor, Alsop (2), Ball, Lee.	5,324	1	3			5	2	11		9	8				10	4	6	7			
11	(a)	York City	L	2-4	Sheppard, Ball.	6,000	1	3			5	2	11		9	8				10		6	7			4
18	(h)	Crewe Alex.	W	2-1	Sheppard, Coward.	5,000	1	3			5	2	11		9	8	7	4		10						6
25	(a)	Rochdale	D	1-1	Alsop.	2,000	1	3			5	2	11		9	8	7	4		10						6
Apr 1	(h)	Southport	W	3-1	Coward (3).	4,555	1	3				2	11		9	8	7	4		10					5	6
8	(a)	Mansfield	L	0-2		4,000	1	3			5	2	11		9		7	4		10			8			6
14	(a)	Darlington	D	1-1	Alsop.	5,000	1	3			5	2	11		9		7	4		10			8			6
15	(h)	Rotherham	W	1-0	Sheppard.	5,000	1	3			5	2	11		9		7	4		10			8			6
17	(h)	Darlington	W	4-0	Turner, Alsop (2), Taylor.	5,000	1	3			5	2		11	9		7			10		4	8			6
22	(a)	Accrington S.	W	3-1	Alsop, Coward, Lee.	1,200	1	3			5	2	11		9		7			10		4	8			6
29	(h)	New Brighton	D	0-0		3,843	1	3				2	11		9		7	4		10		5	8			6
May 3	(a)	Gateshead	D	1-1	Lee.	3,000	1	3				2	11		9		7	4		10			8		5	6
						Apps	42	42	24	9	39	32	39	18	41	33	35	26	10	18	2	11	20	4	6	11
League position: 5th						Goals		2	1				12	7	28	8	8			5			4			

F.A. Cup

Date		Opponents	Rd		Score	Scorers	Att	Cunningham	Bird	Langford	Scott	Leslie	Bennett	Lee	Turner	Alsop	Ball	Coward	Reed	Salt	Sheppard	Walker	Bradford W.	Taylor	Devlin T.	Bell J.	Wiles G.H.
Nov 26	(h)	Mansfield	1		4-1	Lee (2), Taylor, Ball.	9,838	1	3	2		5	6	11		9	8	7	4					10			
Dec 10	(h)	Hartlepool Utd.	2		2-1	Lee, Ball.	8,311	1	3	2		5	6	11		9	8	7	4					10			
Jan 14	(h)	Arsenal	3		2-0	Alsop, Sheppard (pen).	11,149	1	3			5	2	11		9	8	7	4	6	10						
28	(a)	Manchester City	4		0-4		52,085	1	3			5	2	11		9	8	7	4	6	10						
							Apps	4	4	2		4	4	4		4	4	4	4	2	2			2			
							Goals							3		1	2				1			1			

SEASON 1933-34

Division 3(N)

Date		Opponent		Score	Scorers	Att	McSevich	Bennett	Bird	Reed	Leslie	Morgan J.	Woolhouse	Ball	Alsop	Sheppard	Lee	Wiles G.H.	Bradford W.	Cunningham	Edwards	Plummer	Wiles H.S.	Caldicott	Whitehouse W	Whitehouse F
Aug 26	(a)	York City	D	2-2	Ball, Alsop.	5,000		2	3	4	5		7	8	9	10	11	6		1						
30	(a)	New Brighton	L	0-2		4,500		2	3	4	5		7	8	9	10	11	6		1						
Sept 2	(h)	Chester	W	5-0	Alsop (4), Woolhouse.	8,590		2	3	4	5		7	8	9	10	11	6		1						
4	(h)	New Brighton	W	2-1	Alsop (2).	6,211		2	3	8	5	4	7		9	10	11	6		1						
9	(a)	Doncaster Rov.	L	0-4		4,000		2	3	4	5		7	8	9		11	6		1	10					
16	(h)	Barrow	L	2-4	Sheppard (pen), Woolhouse.	7,000		2	3	4	5		7	8	9	10	11	6		1						
23	(a)	Carlisle Utd.	L	2-3	Alsop, Sheppard.	5,000	1	4	3		5		7	8	9	10	11	6				2				
30	(h)	Stockport	W	2-0	Bradford, Wiles H.S	5,453	1	2	3		5		7		9	10	11	6	4				8			
Oct 7	(a)	Halifax Town	L	0-2		8,000	1	2	3		5		7		9	10	11	6	4				8			
14	(h)	Crewe Alex.	W	5-1	Woolhouse (2), Sheppard (2, 1 pen), Alsop.	4,778	1	2	3		5		7	8	9	10	11	6	4							
21	(h)	Barnsley	W	5-1	Alsop (2), Ball, Sheppard (2).	6,000	1	2	3		5	6	7	8	9	10	11		4							
28	(a)	Tranmere Rov.	L	0-1		5,000	1	2	3		5	6	7	8	9	10	11		4							
Nov 4	(h)	Rochdale	W	2-0	Sheppard (pen), Alsop.	6,000	1	2	3		5	6	7	8	9	10	11		4							
11	(a)	Chesterfield	W	2-1	Alsop (2).	13,000	1	2	3	4	5	6	7	8	9	10	11									
18	(h)	Accrington S.	W	5-0	Alsop (3), Lee, Leslie.	5,473	1	2	3	4	5	6	7	8	9	10	11									
Dec 2	(h)	Darlington	W	3-0	Ball, Woolhouse, Reed.	4,797	1	2	3	4	5	6	7	8	9	10	11									
16	(h)	Wrexham	W	3-1	Sheppard, Woolhouse (2).	3,116	1	2	3		5	6	7	8	9	10	11	4								
23	(a)	Hartlepool	W	1-0	Wiles H.S	3,000	1	2	3	4		5	7	8		10	11	6					9			
25	(a)	Mansfield	W	2-1	Ball, Wiles H.S	8,000	1	2	3	4		5	7	8		10	11	6					9			
26	(h)	Mansfield	D	0-0		9,955	1	2	3	4		5	7			10	11	6	8				9			
30	(h)	York City	W	1-0	Caldicott.	5,543	1	2	3		5		7	4	9	10	11	6						8		
Jan 6	(a)	Chester	W	1-0	Alsop	5,000	1	2	3	4	5		7	8	9	10	11	6								
13	(a)	Darlington	L	1-2	Woolhouse.	4,000	1	2	3	4	5		7	8	9	10	11	6								
17	(a)	Gateshead	L	1-2	Alsop.	1,000	1	2	3	4	5		7	8	9	10	11	6								
20	(h)	Doncaster Rov.	W	2-0	Lee (2).	6,000	1		3		5	6	7	4	9	10	11					2			8	
27	(a)	Barrow	D	5-5	Lee (3), Alsop (2).	4,000	1	2	3		5	6	7	4	9	10	11								8	
Feb 3	(h)	Carlisle Utd.	W	3-2	Alsop (2), Sheppard (pen).	6,000	1	2	3	8	5		7	4	9	10	11	6								
10	(a)	Stockport C.	L	2-3	Ball, Woolhouse.	8,000	1		3	4	5	6	7	8	9	10	11					2				
17	(h)	Halifax Town	W	2-0	Whitehouse W, Alsop.	5,500	1		3	4	5	6	7	8	9		11	2							10	
24	(a)	Crewe Alex.	W	4-1	Ball, Reed, Sheppard, Alsop	4,000	1	2	3	4	5		7	8	9	10	11	6								
Mar 3	(a)	Barnsley	D	1-1	Alsop.	12,000		2	3	4	5		7	8	9	10	11	6		1						
10	(h)	Tranmere Rov.	W	5-3	Lee, Sheppard, G. Wiles, Woolhouse, Alsop.	5,530	1	2	3	4	5		7	8	9	10	11	6								
17	(a)	Rochdale	D	3-3	Sheppard, Alsop, Leslie.	2,000	1	2	3	4	5		11	8	9	10		6								7
20	(a)	Southport	L	1-3	Alsop.	1,000	1	2	3	4	5		11	8	9	10		6								7
24	(h)	Chesterfield	D	2-2	Alsop (2).	10,636	1	2	3	4	5		11	8	9	10		6					7			
30	(h)	Rotherham Utd	W	3-1	Lee, Reed, Ball.	5,988	1	2	3	4	5		7	8	9	10	11	6								
31	(a)	Accrington S.	L	0-1		3,000	1	2	3	4	5		7	8	9	10	11	6								
Apr 2	(a)	Rotherham Utd	D	1-1	Sheppard.	4,000	1	2	3	4	5		11	8	9	10		6					7			
7	(h)	Gateshead	W	5-1	Lee (2), Alsop (2), Ball.	5,441	1	2	3	4		5	7	8	9	10	11	6								
21	(h)	Southport	W	4-1	Alsop (2), Lee, Ball.	4,934	1	2	3	4		5	7	8	9	10	11	6								
28	(a)	Wrexham	L	2-6	Sheppard (2).	3,000	1	2	3	4		5	7	8	9	10	11	6								
May 5	(h)	Hartlepool Utd	W	5-0	Alsop (4), Woolhouse.	4,390	1	2		4		5	7	8	9	10	11	3	6							
						Apps	35	39	41	31	35	19	42	38	39	40	38	33	8	7	1	3	7	1	3	2
League position: 4th						Goals				3	2		11	9	39	15	11	1	1				3	1	1	

F.A. Cup

Date		Opponent	Rd	Score	Scorers	Att	McSevich	Bennett	Bird	Reed	Leslie	Morgan J.	Woolhouse	Ball	Alsop	Sheppard	Lee	Wiles G.H.	Bradford W.	Cunningham	Edwards	Plummer	Wiles H.S.	Caldicott	Whitehouse W	Whitehouse F
Nov 25	(h)	Spennymoor Utd.	1	4-0	Alsop, Woolhouse (2), Sheppard.	9,336	1	2	3	4	5	6	7	8	9	10	11									
Dec 9	(h)	Clapton Orient	2	0-0		11,277	1	2	3	4	5	6	7	8	9	10			11							
14	(a)	Clapton Orient	2R	0-2		8,147	1	2	3	4	5	6	7	8	9	10	11									
						Apps	3	3	3	3	3	3	3	3	3	3	2		1							
						Goals							2		1	1										

SEASON 1934-35

Division 3(N)

Date	Venue	Opponent	Res	Score	Scorers	Att	Higgs	Tilford	Bird	Reed	Grice	Morgan L.	Woolhouse	Ball	Alsop	Haddleton G.	Wiles G.H.	McSevich	Bennett	Bradford W.	Bate	Pearson G.	Leslie	Sheppard	Lee	Evans	Shelton	Readman	Whitehouse F.	Wiles H.S.	Griffith	Jones
Aug 25	(h)	Hartlepool Utd	L	1-2	Wiles G	9,031	1	2	3	4	5	6	7	8	9	10	11															
29	(a)	Wrexham	L	2-4	Alsop (2).	6,000			3	4	5		11	8	9	10	6		2									1	7			
Sept 1	(a)	Chesterfield	L	0-2		7,000			3	4		5	11		9	10	6	1	2								8		7			
3	(h)	Wrexham	D	0-0		5,000			3			5	7	4	9	10	6	1	2						11		8					
8	(h)	Mansfield T.	D	2-2	Alsop, Woolhouse.	3,000			3			5	11	4	9		6	1	2		10						8		7			
15	(a)	Barrow	L	1-3	Wiles H.	5,000			3	4		5	11	8	9		6	1	2								10			7		
17	(a)	Halifax Town	D	1-1	Alsop.	5,000			3	4		5	11	8	9			1	2	6							10			7		
22	(h)	Carlisle Utd	W	1-0	Alsop.	3,980		3		4		5	11	8	9			1	2	6							10			7		
29	(a)	Rochdale	L	0-1		3,000		3		4		5		8	9			1	2	6	7	11					10					
Oct 6	(h)	Lincoln	D	0-0		4,500		3		4		5			9		10	1	2	6	7	11					8					
13	(a)	Tranmere Rov.	L	0-4		8,000		3		4		5	7	8	9		10	1	2	6		11										
20	(h)	Doncaster Rov.	L	0-2		5,648		3		4		5	7	8	9			1	2	6						11	10					
27	(a)	Southport	L	2-3	Alsop (2).	3,000		3		4		5			9			1	2	6	7			10		11	8					
Nov 3	(h)	Chester	D	1-1	Sheppard.	6,305		3				6			9	7	4	1	2			11	5	10			8					
10	(a)	New Brighton	D	2-2	Sheppard (2).	4,000		3		8	4	6	7		9			1	2			11	5	10								
17	(h)	York City	L	2-3	Shelton, Sheppard.	5,825	1	3		4		6			9				2			11	5	10			8				7	
Dec 1	(h)	Accrington S.	W	6-0	Alsop (3), Wiles H, Sheppard, Griffith.	5,500		3		4		5			9		6	1	2			11		10						8	7	
15	(h)	Stockport Co	W	3-1	Ball, Alsop, Bate.	5,559		3			4	5		8	9			1	2	6	10	11									7	
22	(a)	Crewe Alex.	L	0-1		5,000		3			4	5		8	9		6	1	2		10	11									7	
25	(h)	Rotherham Utd	W	5-2	Alsop (2), Woolhouse (2), Bate.	8,000		3				5	11	8	9		6	1	2	4	10										7	
26	(a)	Rotherham Utd	L	2-4	Alsop, Bate.	6,000		3				5	7	8	9		6	1	2	4	10	11										
29	(a)	Hartlepool Utd.	L	1-2	Woolhouse.	3,000		3				5	11	8	9		6	1	2	4				10							7	
Jan 5	(h)	Chesterfield	W	2-1	Alsop (2).	6,000		3					11	8	9		6	1	2	4	10		5								7	
16	(a)	Darlington	D	2-2	Alsop, Sheppard.	7,000		3		4		5	11	8	9			1	2	6				10							7	
19	(a)	Mansfield	L	2-4	Alsop, Bate.	5,000		3				5	11	8	9	7	6	1	2	4	10											
26	(h)	Barrow	W	5-0	Alsop (4), Bate.	5,000		3		4		5	7	8	9			1	2	6	10					11						
Feb 2	(a)	Carlisle	W	6-1	Alsop (4), Bate (2).	3,000		3		4		5	7		9			1	2	6	8	11		10								
9	(h)	Rochdale	D	0-0		6,548		3		4		5	7	8	9			1	2	6	10	11										
16	(a)	Lincoln	L	1-5	Woolhouse.	2,000				4		3	7		9			1	2	6	8		5	10	11							
23	(h)	Tranmere Rov.	W	3-0	Woolhouse, Sheppard, Evans.	4,921				4		3	7	8	9			1	2	6			5	10		11						
27	(a)	Gateshead	L	0-1		3,000				4		3	7	8	9			1	2	6			5	10		11						
May 2	(a)	Doncaster Rov.	L	0-4		12,000				4		3	7	8	9			1	2	6			5	10		11						
9	(h)	Southport	D	2-2	Evans, Shelton.	3,602				4		3	7		9			1	2	6	10		5			11	8					
16	(a)	Chester	L	1-2	Haddleton.	5,000		3		4		5		8	9	7		1	2	6				10		11						
23	(h)	New Brighton	W	5-1	Alsop (3), Haddleton, Lee.	2,149				4		3		8	9	7		1	2	6	10		5		11							
30	(a)	York City	L	1-4	Bate.	3,000				4		3		8	9	7		1	2	6	10		5		11							
Apr 6	(h)	Darlington	D	0-0		3,611		3		4		5			9	7	6	1	2	10	8				11							
13	(a)	Accrington S.	D	3-3	Alsop (3).	3,000		3		4		5		8	9	7		1	2	6	10				11							
20	(h)	Gateshead	W	5-0	Bate (2), Alsop (2), Haddleton.	3,506				4		5		8	9	7	3	1	2	6	10				11							
22	(h)	Halifax Town	W	4-1	Alsop (2), Woolhouse, Bradford.	6,000				4		5		8	9	7	3	1	2	6	10				11							
27	(a)	Stockport Co.	W	3-0	Alsop (2), Ball.	3,730				4		5	11	8	9	7	3	1	2	6	10											
May 4	(h)	Crewe Alex.	W	4-0	Alsop, Ball, Woolhouse, Haddleton.	5,000				4		5	11	8	9	7	3	1		6	10											2
						Apps	2	25	7	32	5	40	27	31	42	15	21	39	40	31	23	12	11	13	8	8	13	1	3	4	8	1
League position: 14th						Goals							8	3	39	4	1			1	10			7	1	2	2			2	1	

F.A. Cup

Date	Venue	Opponent	Rd	Score	Scorers	Att	Higgs	Tilford	Bird	Reed	Grice	Morgan L.	Woolhouse	Ball	Alsop	Haddleton G.	Wiles G.H.	McSevich	Bennett	Bradford W.	Bate	Pearson G.	Leslie	Sheppard	Lee	Evans	Shelton	Readman	Whitehouse F.	Wiles H.S.	Griffith	Jones
Nov 24	(a)	Crewe Alex.	1	2-1	Alsop (2).	6,796		3		4		5			9		6	1	2			11		10								
Dec 8	(a)	Watford	2	1-1	Alsop.	12,786		3		4		5			9		6	1	2			11		10								
13	(h)	Watford	2R	1-0	Ball.	8,924		3		4		5		8	9		6	1	2			11		10								
Jan 12	(h)	Southampton	3	1-2	Alsop.	14,475		3				5		8	9		6	1	2	4	11			10								
						Apps		4		3		4		2	4		4	4	4	1	1	3		4								
						Goals								1	4																	

Northern Section Cup

Date	Venue	Opponent	Rd	Score	Scorers	Att	Higgs	Tilford	Bird	Reed	Grice	Morgan L.	Woolhouse	Ball	Alsop	Haddleton G.	Wiles G.H.	McSevich	Bennett	Bradford W.	Bate	Pearson G.	Leslie	Sheppard	Lee	Evans	Shelton	Readman	Whitehouse F.	Wiles H.S.	Griffith	Jones
Jan 28	(h)	Lincoln City	1	1-1	Bradford	992		3		4		5	7		9			1	2	6	10					11	8					
Feb 6	(a)	Lincoln City	1R	3-2	Alsop (3).	1,200		3		4		5	7		9			1	2	6	8	11		10								
Mar 13	(a)	Chesterfield	2	1-1	Alsop.	2,000				4		3	7		9			1	2	6	8		5	10		11						
Apr 4	(h)	Chesterfield	2R	1-0	Lee.	880		3		4		5			9	7	6	1	2	10	8				11							
29	(a)	Crewe Alex.	SF	1-0	Alsop.	2,000				4		5		8	9	7	3	1	2	6	10				11							
May 1	(n)	Stockport *	F	0-2		4,035				4		5	11	8	9	7	3	1	2	6	10											
						Apps		3		6		6	4	2	6	3	3	6	6	6	6	1	1	2	2	2	1					
* At Maine Road, Manchester.						Goals									5					1					1							

SEASON 1935-36

Division 3(N)

							McSevich	Bennett	Wiles G.H.	Reed	Morgan	Richmond	Woolhouse	Collins	Alsop	Stevenson	Poxton	Bradford W.	Cunningham	Evans	Bate	Pearson C.	Leslie	Wilmot	Shelton	Jones T.	Smith J.	Cherry	Blackham	Bryan	Dunderdale	Dover	Wood	Wait
Aug 31	(h)	Gateshead	W	2-0	Alsop, Woolhouse (pen).	10,136	1	2	3	4	5	6	7	8	9	10	11																	
Sept 4	(a)	Darlington	D	1-1	Collins.	6,000	1	2	3	4	5	6	7	8	9	10	11																	
7	(a)	Tranmere Rovers	L	1-3	Collins.	8,000	1	2	3	4	5	6	7	8	9	10	11																	
9	(h)	Darlington	W	4-1	Alsop (3), Woolhouse (pen).	6,475	1	2	3	4	5		7	8	9			6	10	11														
14	(h)	Chesterfield	D	1-1	Bradford.	10,354	1	2	3		5		7	8	9			6	10	11			4											
16	(a)	Halifax Town	D	1-1	Collins.	7,000	1	2	3		5	4	7	8	9			6	10	11														
21	(h)	Carlisle United	W	3-0	Woolhouse, Evans (2).	7,000	1	2	3	4	5		7	8	9			6		11	10													
28	(a)	Hartlepool Utd	L	0-5		4,000	1	2	3	4	5		7	8	9			6		11	10													
Oct 5	(h)	Mansfield Town	W	7-0	Bate, Evans (5), Reed.	7,500	1	2	3	4	5		7	8			11	6		9	10													
12	(a)	Rotherham Utd	L	0-2		7,000	1	2	3	4	5		7	8			11	6		9	10													
19	(a)	Stockport County	W	1-0	Evans	4,000	1	2	3	4	5		7	8			11	6		9		10												
26	(h)	Crewe Alex.	W	4-1	Evans (2), Collins, Woolhouse.	8,495	1	2	3		5	4	7	8			11	6		9		10												
Nov 2	(a)	Accrington S.	L	1-3	Collins	5,000	1	2	3	4	5		7	8			11	6		9		10												
9	(h)	Southport Central	W	3-1	Alsop, Evans, Woolhouse.	7,462	1		2		5		7	8	9			6		11		10		3	4									
16	(a)	Chester	L	0-2		7,000	1	2	3		5		7	8	9			6		11		10			4									
23	(h)	Lincoln City	W	4-1	Evans, Collins (2), Bate.	7,764	1	2			5	4	7	8				6		9	11	10		3										
Dec 7	(h)	York City	W	6-0	Collins (4), Poxton (2).	6,000	1	2	3		5	4	7	8			11	6		9	10													
21	(h)	New Brighton	L	1-2	Collins.	5,128	1	2	3		5	4	7	8			11	6		9	10													
25	(h)	Wrexham	W	5-0	Evans (2), Collins (2), Poxton.	8,000	1	2	3		5	4	7	8			11	6		9	10													
26	(a)	Wrexham	D	1-1	Evans.	6,000	1	2	3	4	5	6	7	8			11			9	10													
28	(a)	Gateshead	D	2-2	Evans, Woolhouse.	3,000	1		2	4	5	6	7	8			11			9	10			3										
Jan 4	(h)	Tranmere Rov.	D	0-0		11,207	1		3		5	4	7	8			11	6		9	10					2								
18	(a)	Chesterfield	L	0-3		6,839	1	2	3	6	5	4	7				11			9	10						8							
25	(a)	Carlisle United	L	1-2	Smith J.	5,000	1	2	3	8	5	4					11			9					6		10	7						
Feb 1	(h)	Hartlepool Utd	W	6-0	Woolhouse (2), Evans (3), Blackham.	5,653	1	2	3	8	5	4	7					6		9							10		11					
8	(a)	Mansfield Town	D	2-2	Reed, Blackham.	3,000	1	2	3	8	5	4	7					6		9							10		11					
15	(h)	Rotherham Utd	L	0-1		6,651	1	2	3	8	5	4	7					6		9							10		11					
22	(h)	Stockport County	Ab	0-0	(Abandoned 34 mins. blizzard.)	3,000	1	2	3		5	4	7					6		9	10				8				11					
29	(a)	Southport Central	L	0-1		1,600	1	2	3	8	5	4	7					6		9	10								11					
Mar 7	(h)	Accrington S.	W	2-0	Smith J. Evans.	3,572		2	3		5	4	10				11	6		9							8		7	1				
14	(a)	Crewe Alex.	L	3-4	Smith J. Woolhouse, Blackham.	6,000		2	3		5	4	11					6		9		10					8		7	1				
21	(h)	Chester City	W	1-0	Poxton.	5,000		2	3		5	4	7				11	6				10					8			1	9			
28	(a)	Lincoln City	L	1-4	Dunderdale.	5,000		2	3		5	4	7				11	6				10					8			1	9			
31	(a)	Rochdale	L	4-6	Evans, Woolhouse (2), Smith J.	3,000		2			3	4	7					6		11			5				8			1	9		10	
Apr 4	(h)	Rochdale	W	1-0	Wood.	3,097		2	3		5	4	7				11	6									8			1		9	10	
10	(h)	Oldham Athletic	L	1-2	Dunderdale.	3,000		2	3			4	7					6		11			5				8			1	9		10	
11	(a)	York City	D	0-0		5,000		2	3	8		4	7				6	5		11										1	9		10	
13	(a)	Oldham Athletic	L	1-2	Dunderdale.	5,000		2	3	8		4	11				6	5			10									1	9	7		
14	(h)	Stockport County	L	0-1		3,700		2	3			4	8				11	5			10				6						9	7		1
18	(h)	Barrow	W	5-1	Evans (3), Poxton (pen), Bate.	2,802		2	3			4	7				6	5		9	10						8		11					1
20	(a)	Barrow	L	0-1		2,000		2	3			4	7				6	5		9	10						8		11					1
25	(a)	New Brighton	D	1-1	Bate.	2,000		2	3	8		4	7					5		9	10				6				11					1
May 2	(h)	Halifax Town	W	2-1	Blackham, Cunningham.	2,740		2	3	8		4	7					5	10	9					6				11					1
						Apps	28	39	40	22	34	32	41	22	10	3	25	35	4	34	18	9	3	3	6	1	14	1	10	9	7	3	4	5
League position: 10th						Goals				2			11	14	5		5	1	1	24	4						4		4		3		1	

F.A. Cup

			Rd				McSevich	Bennett	Wiles G.H.	Reed	Morgan	Richmond	Woolhouse	Collins	Alsop	Stevenson	Poxton	Bradford W.	Cunningham	Evans	Bate	Pearson C.	Leslie	Wilmot	Shelton	Jones T.	Smith J.	Cherry	Blackham	Bryan	Dunderdale	Dover	Wood	Wait
Nov 30	(h)	Lincoln City	1	2-0	Collins, Evans.	11,707	1	2	3		5	4	7	8			11	6		9	10													
Dec 14	(a)	Chesterfield	2	0-0		12,409	1	2	3		5	4	7	8			11	6		9	10													
19	(h)	Chesterfield	2R	2-1	Richmond, Bate.	9,006	1	2	3		5	4	7	8			11	6		9	10													
Jan 11	(h)	Newcastle Utd	3	0-2		19,982	1	2	3		5	4	7	8			11	6		9	10													
						Apps	4	4	4		4	4	4	4			4	4		4	4													
						Goals						1		1						1	1													

Northern Section Cup

			Rd				McSevich	Bennett	Wiles G.H.	Reed	Morgan	Richmond	Woolhouse	Collins	Alsop	Stevenson	Poxton	Bradford W.	Cunningham	Evans	Bate	Pearson C.	Leslie	Wilmot	Shelton	Jones T.	Smith J.	Cherry	Blackham	Bryan	Dunderdale	Dover	Wood	Wait
Feb 10	(a)	Chesterfield	2	0-0		500	1	2	3	8	5	4								9					6		10	7	11					
24	(h)	Chesterfield	2R	1-2	Shelton.	755	1	2	3			4	7					6		9	10		5		8				11					
						Apps	2	2	2	1	1	2	1					1		2	1		1		2		1	1	2					
						Goals																			1									

SEASON 1936-37

Division 3(S)

Date		Opponents		Score	Scorers	Att	Leckie J.	Jones T.	Wiles G.H.	Richmond W.	Morgan L.	Bradford W.	Woolhouse R.	Landells J.	Evans W.	Harwood I.	Bulger C.	Bell J.	Cunningham G.	Shelton J.	Green J.	Dunderdale W.	Walker F.	Hunt H.	Reed J.	Tewkesbury K.	Carter J.	Dover H.	Bewick J.	Bennett J.	Bate T.
Aug 29	(h)	Cardiff City	W	1-0	Harwood.	10,029	1	2	3	4	5	6	7	8	9	10	11														
31	(h)	Luton Town	L	0-1		8,786	1	2	3	4	5	6	7	8	9	10	11														
Sept 5	(a)	Crystal Palace	L	1-3	Bulger.	10,000	1	2	3	4	5	6			9	10	11	7	8												
7	(a)	Luton Town	L	0-2		11,000	1		3	4	5	6				8	11	7	9	2	10										
12	(h)	Exeter City	W	4-2	Bulger, Cunningham, Bradford, Woolhouse.	4,422	1		3	4	5	6	7	8			11		10	2		9									
19	(a)	Reading	W	2-0	Landells, Dunderdale.	10,000	1		3	4	5	6	7	8		10	11			2		9									
26	(h)	Q.P.R.	L	2-4	Morgan, Bulger.	9,000	1		3	4	5	6	7	8		10	11			2		9									
Oct 1	(a)	Notts County	D	3-3	Evans, Bulger (2).	12,000	1		3	4	5	6		8	9	10	11	7		2											
3	(a)	Bristol City	D	0-0		10,000	1		3	4	5	6		8	9	10	11	7		2											
10	(h)	Torquay Utd	W	1-0	Evans	7,103	1		3	4	5	6		8	9	10	11	7		2											
17	(h)	Brighton & H.A.	L	1-4	Evans (pen).	5,915	1		3	4	5	6	7	8	9	10	11			2											
24	(a)	Bournemouth	L	2-3	Evans (2).	11,000	1		3	4	5		7	8	9					2	10		6	11							
31	(h)	Northampton T.	D	2-2	Bulger, Russell (og).	5,000	1		3	4	5			8			11			2	10	9	6	7							
Nov 7	(a)	Bristol Rovers	L	0-3		8,000	1		3		5	6		8	9	10	11			2				7	4						
14	(h)	Millwall Ath.	L	0-3		6,499			3	4	5	6		10	9		11			2				7		1	8				
21	(a)	Swindon Town	L	0-2		8,000			3	4	5		7			6	11			2	10					1	8	9			
Dec 5	(a)	Gillingham	D	2-2	Evans, Woolhouse.	7,000	1		3	4	5	6	7	8	9		11		10	2											
19	(a)	Southend United	L	0-3		6,000	1		3	4		6	7		9		11		10	2							8		5		
25	(h)	Clapton Orient	W	3-2	Evans (2), Bulger.	8,002	1		3	4	5	6	7		9	10	11			2							8				
26	(a)	Cardiff City	D	2-2	Evans, Harwood.	33,000	1		3	4	5	6	7	8	9	10	11			2											
28	(a)	Clapton Orient	D	2-2	Carter, Woolhouse.	3,500	1		3	4	5	6	7	8	9	10	11			2											
Jan 2	(h)	Crystal Palace	W	1-0	Carter.	5,803	1		3	4	5	6	7		9	10	11			2							8				
9	(a)	Exeter City	L	0-3		4,000	1		3	4	5	6	7		9	10	11			2							8				
21	(h)	Aldershot	D	0-0		1,946	1		3	4	5	6	7	8	9	10	11			2											
Feb 4	(a)	Q.P.R.	L	0-2		4,000	1		3	4		6	7			10	11			2		9					8		5		
6	(h)	Bristol City	L	1-5	Dunderdale (pen).	5,000	1			4	5	6	7	8		10		11		3		9								2	
13	(a)	Torquay United	L	1-3	Woolhouse.	5,000				4			7		9	10			8	3			6	11		1			5	2	
20	(a)	Brighton & H.A.	L	0-3		9,000				4	5	6	7			8				3	10	9		11		1				2	
27	(h)	Bournemouth	D	1-1	Evans.	2,418	1		3		5	6	11		9	10				4							8	7		2	
Mar 6	(a)	Northampton	L	3-6	Woolhouse (2), Dunderdale.	6,000	1	3		4		6	7		11					5		9					8			2	10
13	(h)	Bristol Rovers	W	5-2	Woolhouse, Dunderdale (2), Evans, Carter.	3,293			3	4	5	6	7		11					2		9				1	8				10
20	(a)	Millwall Athletic	L	1-3	Woolhouse.	20,000			3	4	5	6	7		11					2		9				1	8				10
26	(h)	Watford	W	3-1	Dunderdale (3, 1 pen).	3,349			3	4	5	6	7		11					2		9				1	8				10
27	(h)	Swindon Town	W	5-2	Bate (3), Woolhouse, Bradford.	4,000			3	4	5	6	7		11					2		9				1	8				10
29	(a)	Watford	D	0-0		10,000			3	4	5	6	7		11					2		9				1	8				10
30	(h)	Reading	L	0-1		5,390			3	4	5	6	7		11					2		9				1	8				10
Apr 3	(a)	Aldershot	D	4-4	Harwood, Evans (2), Dunderdale.	4,000			3	4	5	6	7		11	8				2		9				1					10
10	(h)	Gillingham	W	2-1	Dunderdale, Bradford.	6,000			3	4	5	6	7		11					2		9				1	8				10
17	(a)	Newport County	W	2-1	Harwood (2).	9,000			3	4	5	6	7		9	10				2						1	8				11
24	(h)	Southend Utd	W	3-0	Evans (2, 1 pen), Carter.	5,000			3	4	5	6	7		9	10				2						1	8				11
26	(h)	Newport County	L	1-2	Bate.	2,000			3	4	5	6	7		9	10				2						1	8				11
May 1	(h)	Notts County	W	2-1	Mills (og), Harwood.	5,560			3	4	5	6	7	8	9	10				2						1					11
						Apps	26	4	38	40	38	38	34	19	33	28	24	6	6	39	5	16	3	6	1	16	19	2	3	5	13
League position: 17th						Goals					1	3	9	1	15	6	7		1			10					4				4

Own Goals 2

F.A. Cup

Date		Opponents	Rd	Score	Scorers	Att	Leckie J.	Jones T.	Wiles G.H.	Richmond W.	Morgan L.	Bradford W.	Woolhouse R.	Landells J.	Evans W.	Harwood I.	Bulger C.	Bell J.	Cunningham G.	Shelton J.	Green J.	Dunderdale W.	Walker F.	Hunt H.	Reed J.	Tewkesbury K.	Carter J.	Dover H.	Bewick J.	Bennett J.	Bate T.
Nov 28	(h)	Scunthorpe Utd	1	3-0	Evans (3, 1 pen).	6,450	1		3	4	5	6	7		9		11		10	2							8				
Dec 12	(h)	Yeovil & Petters	2	1-1	Woolhouse.	3,924	1		3	4	5	6	7		9		11		10	2							8				
17	(a)	Yeovil & Petters	2R	1-0	Bulger.	5,308	1		3	4	5	6	7		9		11		10	2							8				
Jan 16	(h)	Barnsley	3	3-1	Harwood, Evans (2).	13,339	1			4	5	6	7		9	10	11			3							8			2	
30	(a)	Grimsby Town	4	1-5	Evans.	10,607	1			4	5	6	7		9	10	11			3							8			2	
						Apps	5		3	5	5	5	5		5	2	5		3	5							5			2	
						Goals							1		6	1	1														

Southern Section Cup

Date		Opponents	Rd	Score	Scorers	Att	Leckie J.	Jones T.	Wiles G.H.	Richmond W.	Morgan L.	Bradford W.	Woolhouse R.	Landells J.	Evans W.	Harwood I.	Bulger C.	Bell J.	Cunningham G.	Shelton J.	Green J.	Dunderdale W.	Walker F.	Hunt H.	Reed J.	Tewkesbury K.	Carter J.	Dover H.	Bewick J.	Bennett J.	Bate T.
Oct 5	(a)	Millwall Athletic	1	2-5	Evans (2, 1 pen).	1,000	1		3	4	5	6		8	9	10	11	7		2											
						Apps	1		1	1	1	1		1	1	1	1	1		1											
						Goals									2																

SEASON 1937-38

Division 3(S)

Date		Opponent	Res	Score	Scorers	Att	Tewkesbury K.	Shelton J.	Wiles G.H.	Richmond W.	Morgan L.	Simpson W.	Woolhouse R.	Knott H.	Dodd	Robinson	Bulger C.	Bradford W.	Bate T.	Evans W.	Dunderdale W.	Redwood	Bennett J.	Williams	Harper	Askew	Payne	Prew J.
Aug 28	(a)	Torquay United	L	0-1		4,000	1	2	3	4	5	6	7	8	9	10	11											
30	(h)	Mansfield Town	Ab.	0-0	Abandoned after 33 minutes.	5,500	1	2	3	4	5	6	7	8	9	10	11											
Sept 4	(h)	Clapton Orient	W	2-0	Dodd (2).	7,817	1	2	3	4	5	10	7		9		11	6	8									
8	(a)	Mansfield Town	L	1-3	Bate	8,000	1	2	3	4	5	10	7				11	6	8	9								
11	(a)	Southend United	L	0-1		6,000	1	2	3	4	5	10	7			8	11	6			9							
13	(h)	Newport County	W	3-1	Simpson, Knott, Dunderdale.	4,000	1	2	3	4	5	10		7		8	11	6			9							
18	(h)	Q.P.R.	L	0-3		8,000	1	2	3	4	5	10		7		8	11	6			9							
20	(a)	Millwall	L	0-4		8,000	1	2	3	4	5	10				9	11	6	8			7						
25	(a)	Brighton & Hove	L	0-1		6,000	1	2	3	4	5	6	7	8		10				9		11						
Oct 2	(h)	Bournemouth	W	2-0	Knott, Redwood.	6,000	1	2	3	4	5	6	7	8	9				10			11						
9	(a)	Cardiff City	L	1-3	Redwood.	20,000	1	2		4	5	6		9	7			10	8			11	3					
16	(a)	Bristol City	L	1-3	Redwood.	10,000		2		4	5	6	7	9				10	8			11	3	1				
23	(h)	Watford	W	3-1	Evans (2), Dunderdale.	4,595		2		4	5	6	7						8	10	9	11	3	1				
30	(a)	Gillingham	L	0-3		4,000		2		4	5	6	7	9					8	10		11	3	1				
Nov 6	(h)	Exeter City	L	0-2		4,262	1	2		4	5	6	7	8					10		9	11	3					
13	(a)	Swindon Town	D	1-1	Shelton.	10,000	1	8			5	10	7		9			6				11	3		2	4		
20	(h)	Aldershot	W	2-0	Redwood, Dodd.	3,761	1	8			5	10	7		9			6				11	3		2	4		
Dec 4	(h)	Reading	L	2-5	Dodd, Askew.	1,708	1	8			5	10	7		9			6				11	3		2	4		
18	(h)	Notts County	W	1-0	Dodd.	4,215		8	3		5		7		9			6		10		11		1	2	4		
20	(a)	Bristol Rovers	L	2-5	Redwood, Dodd.	10,000		8	3		5		7		9			6		10		11		1	2	4		
27	(h)	Bristol Rovers	W	5-2	Evans (2), Dodd, Harper, Redwood.	7,598		8			5	6	7		9			3		10		11		1	2	4		
Jan 1	(h)	Torquay United	D	0-0		4,000		8			5	6	7		9			3		10		11	2	1		4		
15	(a)	Clapton Orient	D	2-2	Bate, Dodd.	4,500		2			5	6	7		9			3	8	10		11		1		4		
22	(h)	Southend United	L	1-5	Bate.	3,268		2		4	5	6	7		9			3	8	10		11		1				
29	(a)	Q.P.R.	L	1-3	Dodd.	12,000		2			5	4	7		9	8	11			10			3	1			6	
Feb 5	(h)	Brighton & Hove	L	0-3		4,172		2		4	5				9	8				10		11	3	1			6	7
12	(a)	Bournemouth	L	0-5		4,591		2	6	4	5		8		9	10						11	3	1				7
19	(h)	Cardiff City	W	1-0	Askew.	4,370		2			5		8			10				9		11	3	1		4	6	7
26	(h)	Bristol City	L	2-8	Evans (2).	4,368		2			5		8			10				9		11	3	1		4	6	7
Mar 5	(a)	Watford	L	1-2	Shelton.	10,000		8	3		5	6	7				11		10	9			2	1		4		
12	(h)	Gillingham	W	3-1	Evans, Woolhouse (pen), Bate.	3,397		8	3		5	6	7				11		10	9			2	1		4		
16	(a)	Crystal Palace	L	1-3	Woolhouse.	5,242		8			5	6	7				11		10	9			2	1		4	3	
19	(a)	Exeter City	L	2-3	Brown (og), Bulger.	4,000		8			5	6	7				11		10	9			2	1		4	3	
26	(h)	Swindon Town	L	2-3	Bate, Evans.	2,993		8	3		5	6	7				11		10	9			2	1		4		
Apr 2	(a)	Aldershot	L	0-1		4,000		8	3		5	6	7						10	9		11	2	1		4		
9	(h)	Millwall	D	1-1	Dunderdale.	3,883	1	8	3		5	6	7			11				10	9		2			4		
15	(h)	Northampton T.	D	1-1	Robinson.	3,531	1	8	3		5	6	7			11				10	9		2			4		
16	(a)	Reading	L	1-2	Bate	6,000	1	8	3		5	6	7		9	11			10				2			4		
18	(a)	Northampton T.	D	1-1	Shelton.	7,000	1	8	3		5	6	7			11			10	9			2			4		
23	(h)	Crystal Palace	D	1-1	Woolhouse (pen).	3,707	1	8	3		5	6	7				11		10	9			2			4		
30	(a)	Notts County	L	1-3	Dunderdale (pen).	3,000	1	8	3		5	6	7				11			10	9		2			4		
May 2	(h)	Mansfield Town	W	2-0	Dunderdale (2, 1 pen).	1,754	1	8	3		5	6	7				11			10	9		2			4		
7	(a)	Newport County	W	2-1	Evans, Woolhouse.	3,000	1	8	3		5	6	7		9		11			10					2	4		
						Apps	22	42	24	17	42	36	37	9	18	15	17	17	20	27	9	22	27	20	7	24	6	4
League position: 21st						Goals		3				1	4	2	9	1	1		6	9	6	6			1	2		

Own Goal 1

F.A. Cup

Date		Opponent	Rd	Score	Scorers	Att	Tewkesbury K.	Shelton J.	Wiles G.H.	Richmond W.	Morgan L.	Simpson W.	Woolhouse R.	Knott H.	Dodd	Robinson	Bulger C.	Bradford W.	Bate T.	Evans W.	Dunderdale W.	Redwood	Bennett J.	Williams	Harper	Askew	Payne	Prew J.
Nov 27	(h)	Gateshead	1	4-0	Dodd (2), Shelton, Simpson.	7,825	1	8			5	10	7		9			6				11	3		2	4		
Dec 11	(a)	Watford	2	0-3		10,303		8			5	10	7		9			6				11	3	1	2	4		
						Apps	1	2			2	2	2		2			2				2	2	1	2	2		
						Goals		1				1			2													

Southern Section Cup

Date		Opponent	Rd	Score	Scorers	Att	Tewkesbury K.	Shelton J.	Wiles G.H.	Richmond W.	Morgan L.	Simpson W.	Woolhouse R.	Knott H.	Dodd	Robinson	Bulger C.	Bradford W.	Bate T.	Evans W.	Dunderdale W.	Redwood	Bennett J.	Williams	Harper	Askew	Payne	Prew J.
Sept 29	(a)	Aldershot	1	1-1	Redwood.	1,500	1	2	3	4	5	6	7	8	9					10		11						
Oct 18	(h)	Aldershot	1R	2-1	Evans, Bulger.	200		2		4	5	6	7	8			10			9		11	3	1				
Jan 10	(h)	Bristol City	2	1-2	Redwood.	500		2			5	6	7		9		10	3	8			11		1		4		
						Apps	1	3	1	2	3	3	3	2	2		2	1	1	2		3	1	2		1		
						Goals											1			1		2						

SEASON 1938-39

Division 3(S)

Date		Opponents		Score	Scorers	Att	Tewkesbury K.	Beeson G.	Male N.	Godfrey T.	Morgan L.	Simpson	Davies E.	Hill	Bambrick J.	Buttery	Redwood	Evans W.	Bate T.	Davies T.	Smith	Bulger C.	Askew	Hancocks J.	Brown	Payne	Harper	Alsop G.	Woodward	Williams B.F.
Aug 27	(a)	Brighton & H.A.	L	1-3	Bambrick.	9,000	1	2	3	4	5	6	7	8	9	10	11													
29	(h)	Ipswich Town	L	0-1		13,728	1	2	3	4	5	6	7	8	9	10	11													
Sept 3	(h)	Bournemouth	L	1-2	Davies E.	11,409	1	2	3	4	5	6	7	8	9	10	11													
5	(a)	Cardiff City	L	1-2	Godfrey	18,000	1	2	3	4	5	6	7	8	9		11	10												
10	(a)	Watford	L	2-4	Bambrick (2).	9,000	1	2	3	4	5	6	7		9	10	11		8											
17	(a)	Mansfield Town	D	0-0		5,000	1	2	3	5		6	7			10		9		4	8	11								
24	(h)	Q.P.R.	L	0-1		8,647	1	2	3	5		6	7			10		9	8			11	4							
Oct 1	(a)	Southend United	L	0-2		9,000	1	2	3	4	5	6	7		9			11	8			10								
8	(h)	Exeter City	L	1-2	Bambrick.	6,666	1	2		4	5	6	7		9			11	8			10				3				
15	(h)	Crystal Palace	D	1-1	Simpson.	7,582	1	2	3	4	5	10	7		8			9				11				6				
22	(a)	Port Vale	L	1-5	Evans.	8,600	1		3	4	5	10	7			8		9				11				6	2			
29	(h)	Aldershot	D	2-2	Evans, Bambrick.	7,078	1	2	3	4	5	10			8			9				11		7		6				
Nov 5	(a)	Notts County	D	0-0		6,000	1		3	4	5	10						8				11		7		6	2	9		
12	(h)	Northampton T.	W	1-0	Bulger.	8,852	1		3		5	10						8				11		7		6	2	9	4	
19	(a)	Newport County	L	1-2	Evans.	9,000	1		3		5	10						9				11	8	7		6	2		4	
Dec 3	(a)	Torquay United	W	1-0	Harper.	5,000	1		3		5	10			9							11		7		6	2	8	4	
17	(a)	Bristol City	L	1-2	Bambrick.	6,200	1		3		5	10			9							11		7		6	2	8	4	
24	(h)	Brighton & H.A.	L	0-2		4,500	1		3		5	10			9							11		7		6	2	8	4	
26	(a)	Reading	D	1-1	Hancocks (pen).	7,000	1		3		5	10			9							11		7		6	2	8	4	
27	(h)	Reading	W	3-0	Bambrick, Buttery, Alsop.	8,691	1	2	3	5					9	10						11		7		6		8	4	
31	(a)	Bournemouth	L	1-3	Hancocks.	4,635	1	2	3	5					9	10						11		7		6		8	4	
Jan 12	(h)	Clapton Orient	W	5-1	Bambrick (2), Simpson (2), Alsop.	3,000	1	2	3		5	10			9							11		7		6		8	4	
14	(h)	Watford	W	2-0	Alsop, Bambrick.	7,000	1	2	3		5	10			9							11		7		6		8	4	
28	(a)	Q.P.R.	L	0-3		10,000	1	2	3		5	10			9							11		7		6		8	4	
Feb 2	(h)	Mansfield Town	D	0-0		2,605	1	2	3		5	10			9							11		7		6		8	4	
4	(h)	Southend United	L	0-2		8,084	1	2	3		5	10			9							11		7		6		8	4	
15	(a)	Exeter City	L	2-3	Evans, Brown (og).	2,500	1	3		6	5	10	7					9				11					2	8	4	
18	(a)	Crystal Palace	L	0-4		13,906		3		4	5	6			9			10				11		7			2		8	1
25	(h)	Port Vale	W	4-0	Alsop, Hancocks (pen), Bulger, Bambrick.	5,000		2	3	6	5	10			9							11		7				8	4	1
Mar 4	(a)	Aldershot	D	3-3	Hill, Alsop, Hancocks (pen).	3,500		2	3	6	5			8	9							11		7				10	4	1
11	(h)	Notts County	D	3-3	Bambrick (2), Hancocks (pen).	6,000		2	3	6	5			8	9							11		7				10	4	1
18	(a)	Northampton T.	L	1-4	Hill.	6,000		2	3	6	5			8	9							11		7				10	4	1
25	(h)	Newport County	D	1-1	Alsop.	7,125	1	2	3		5	6		8	9							11		7				10	4	
Apr 1	(a)	Clapton Orient	D	1-1	Hancocks.	8,000	1	2	3		5	10			9							11		7		6		8	4	
7	(a)	Bristol Rovers	L	0-2		12,000	1	2	3		5	10			9							11		7		6		8	4	
8	(h)	Torquay United	W	5-0	Alsop (4), Hancocks (pen).	5,362	1	2	3		5	10			9							11		7		6		8	4	
10	(h)	Bristol Rovers	D	2-2	Alsop (2).	7,349	1	3		6	5				9	10						11		7			2	8	4	
15	(a)	Swindon Town	W	4-1	Alsop (3), Buttery.	6,716	1	3		6	5				8	10						11		7			2	9	4	
22	(h)	Bristol City	W	5-0	Alsop (3), Buttery (2).	5,000	1	3		6	5				8	10						11		7			2	9	4	
24	(h)	Swindon Town	W	5-0	Alsop (4), Bambrick.	5,000	1	3		6	5				8	10						11		7			2	9	4	
29	(a)	Ipswich Town	L	0-1		12,000	1	3		6	5				8	10						11		7			2	9	4	
May 6	(h)	Cardiff City	W	6-3	Bambrick, Hancocks (2) Beeson, Bulger, Alsop.	5,869	1	2	3	6	5				8	10						11		7				9	4	
						Apps	37	34	34	27	38	31	12	8	35	15	5	13	4	1	1	37	2	30		21	15	28	29	5
League position: 21st						Goals		1		1		3	1	2	15	4		4				3		9			1	23		

Own Goal 1

F.A. Cup

Date		Opponents	Rd	Score	Scorers	Att	Tewkesbury K.	Beeson G.	Male N.	Godfrey T.	Morgan L.	Simpson	Davies E.	Hill	Bambrick J.	Buttery	Redwood	Evans W.	Bate T.	Davies T.	Smith	Bulger C.	Askew	Hancocks J.	Brown	Payne	Harper	Alsop G.	Woodward	Williams B.F.
Nov 26	(h)	Carlisle United	1	4-1	Bambrick (3), Alsop.	11,036	1		3		5	10			9							11		7		6	2	8	4	
Dec 10	(h)	Clapton Orient	2	4-2	Bambrick, Bulger, Simpson, Hancocks.	13,570	1		3		5	10			9							11		7		6	2	8	4	
Jan 7	(a)	Newport County	3	2-0	Bambrick, Alsop.	9,645	1	2	3		5	10			9							11		7		6		8	4	
21	(a)	Notts County	4	0-0		34,462	1	2	3		5	10			9							11		7		6		8	4	
26	(h)	Notts County	4R	4-0	Alsop (4).	9,563	1	2	3		5	10			9							11		7		6		8	4	
Feb 11	(a)	Huddersfield T.	5	0-3		33,543	1	2	3		5	10			9							11		7		6		8	4	
						Apps	6	4	6		6	6			6							6		6		6	2	6	6	
						Goals						1			5							1		1				6		

Southern Section Cup

Date		Opponents	Rd	Score	Att	Tewkesbury K.	Beeson G.	Male N.	Godfrey T.	Morgan L.	Simpson	Davies E.	Hill	Bambrick J.	Buttery	Redwood	Evans W.	Bate T.	Davies T.	Smith	Bulger C.	Askew	Hancocks J.	Brown	Payne	Harper	Alsop G.	Woodward	Williams B.F.
Sep 16	(a)	Port Vale	1	0-4	2,500	1	2	3	5		6				10		9				11	4	7	8					
					Apps	1	1	1	1		1				1		1				1	1	1	1					

SEASON 1939-40

Division 3(S)

Date	Venue	Opponent	Res	Score	Scorers	Att	1	2	3	4	5	6	7	8	9	10	11
Aug 26	(a)	Southend Utd	L	2-3	Alsop, Bulger	6,000	Strong	Beeson	Male	Richards	Thayne	Godfrey	Hancocks	Walton	Alsop	Talbot	Bulger
30	(a)	Torquay Utd	D	0-0		5,000	"	Harper	"	"	"	"	"	"	"	"	"
Sep 2	(h)	QPR	W	1-0	Bulger	5,000	"	"	"	"	"	"	"	"	"	"	"

Regional League (Midland Division)

Date	Venue	Opponent	Res	Score	Scorers	Att	1	2	3	4	5	6	7	8	9	10	11
Oct 21	(a)	Leicester City	L	1-6	Alsop	2,500	Williams	Beeson	"	"	Morgan	"	Taylor	Brown	"	Beattie	"
28	(h)	Birmingham	L	1-2	Taylor	4,554	"	Shelton	"	"	"	"	"	Beattie	"	Brown	"
Nov 4	(a)	Wolves	L	1-4	Brown	4,517	"	"	"	"	"	"	"	"	"	"	"
11	(h)	Northampton	D	1-1	Bulger	2,730	"	"	"	"	"	"	"	Brown	"	Buttery	"
18	(h)	Luton Town	L	4-6	Brown, (3) Alsop	2,347	"	"	Fisher	"	"	"	"	Grosv'nor	"	Brown	"
25	(a)	Coventry City	L	3-4	Taylor, Alsop (2)	2,000	"	"	Male	"	"	"	"	Wood	"	"	"
Dec 2	(h)	West Brom Alb	L	0-2		4,815	"	"	"	"	"	"	"	"	"	"	"
9	(h)	Leicester City	W	4-3	Alsop (2), Wood, Bulger	1,645	"	"	"	"	"	"	"	"	"	"	"
16	(a)	Birmingham	L	1-2	Brown	2,464	"	"	"	"	"	"	Hancocks	"	"	"	"
23	(h)	Wolves	L	3-5	Brown, Wood, Alsop	5,448	"	"	"	"	"	"	"	Adams	"	"	Beesley
30	(a)	Northampton	L	1-6	Alsop	6,929	"	Godfrey	"	"	"	Wood	"	Beattie	"	"	Bulger
Jan 6	(a)	Luton Town	L	0-1		529	"	"	"	"	Thayne	"	"	"	"	"	"
13	(h)	Coventry City	L	0-2		1,710	"	Shelton	"	"	"	"	"	"	"	"	"
20	(a)	West Brom Alb	L	2-7	Male, Brown	1,831	"	"	"	Wood	"	Godfrey	"	"	"	"	"
Feb 24	(h)	Luton Town	D	4-4	Starling, Alsop (3)	1,794	"	"	"	"	"	"	"	"	"	Starling	"
Mar 2	(a)	Coventry City	L	1-4	Alsop	1,528	"	"	"	"	"	"	Edwards	"	"	"	"
9	(h)	West Brom Alb	D	1-1	White (og)	3,012	"	"	"	"	Morgan	"	Hancocks	Edwards	"	"	"
16	(h)	Leicester City	W	3-2	Alsop (2), Edwards	2,509	"	"	"	"	"	"	"	"	"	"	"
25	(a)	Birmingham	L	1-2	Alsop	3,241	"	"	"	"	"	"	"	"	"	"	"
30	(h)	Wolves	L	1-2	Brown	6,106	"	"	Thayne	"	"	"	"	Hickman	"	Brown	"
Apr 6	(a)	Northampton	D	2-2	Hancocks, Brown	3,022	"	"	"	"	"	"	"	"	"	"	Dryden
May 4	(a)	Luton Town	W	4-3	Brown, Alsop, Bulger, Hancocks	1,212	Biddlestone	Thayne	Male	Richards	"	"	"	Wood	"	"	Bulger
11	(h)	Northampton	W	1-0	Alsop	2,000	"	"	"	"	"	"	"	"	"	"	"
14	(a)	West Brom Alb	W	3-2	Wood (2), Alsop	1,567	"	"	"	"	"	"	"	"	"	"	"
18	(a)	Wolves	W	5-1	Bulger, Alsop (3), Wood	5,038	"	"	"	"	"	"	"	"	"	"	"
25	(h)	Coventry City	W	2-1	Alsop, Wood	2,700	"	"	"	"	"	"	Taylor	"	"	"	"
Jun 1	(a)	Leicester City	D	0-0		4,000	"	"	"	Wood	"	"	Hancocks	Hickman	"	Clarke	"
8	(a)	Birmingham	L	1-8	Alsop	1,000	"	Godfrey	"	Richards	"	Wood	"	n	"	Brown	"
League position: 8th																	

League Cup

Date	Venue	Opponent	Res	Score	Scorers	Att	1	2	3	4	5	6	7	8	9	10	11
Apr 13	(a)	Port Vale	D	2-2	Alsop (2)	2,483	Williams	Shelton	"	Wood	"	Godfrey	"	"	"	"	Dryden
15	(h)	Port Vale	W	6-0	Dryden (2), Alsop (2), Hancocks, Hickman	883	"	Thayne	"	"	"	"	"	"	"	"	"
20	(a)	Swansea T	L	0-2		5,040	Biddlestone	"	"	"	"	"	"	"	"	"	"
27	(h)	Swansea T	W	2-1	Brown, Wood	3,821	"	"	"	"	"	"	"	Brown	"	Richards	"

Appearances: (All games); Adams, R. 1; Alsop G 35; Beattie, J.M 8; Beesley, J.H 1; Beeson, G 2; Biddlestone, T.F 9; Brown, W.S 26; Bulger, C.G 29; Buttery, A 1; Clarke, I 1; Dryden, J 5; Edwards, G.R 4; Fisher, F.T 1; Godfrey, C 34; Grosvenor, A.T 2; Hancocks, J 25; Harper, K 2; Hickman, J.A 7; Male, N.A 32; Morgan, L.D 26; Richards, D 23; Shelton, J.B.T 19; Starling, R.W 5; Strong, G.J 3; Talbot, F.L 3; Taylor, T 9; Thayne, W 20; Walton, G 3; Williams, B.F 23, Wood, T 26.

Goals: Alsop, 28; Brown 11; Wood, 7; Bulger, 6; Hancocks, 3; Dryden, 2; Taylor, 2; Edwards, 1; Hickman, 1; Male, 1; Starling, 1; opponent, 1 Total 64

SEASON 1940-41

Regional League (South)

Date		Opponent			Scorers	Att	1	2	3	4	5	6	7	8	9	10	11
Aug 31	(a)	West Brom Alb.	L	1-3	Vinall.	2,966	G Jones	Thayne	Male	Richards	Morgan	Godfrey	Hancocks	Wood	Vinall	Starling	Rowley
Sep 7	(h)	West Brom Alb	L	0-2		2,968	Biddlestone	"	"	"	"	"	Bulger	"	"	"	"
14	(a)	Bristol City	L	0-2		2,000	"	Shelton	"	"	"	"	Brown	"	"	"	Beesley
21	(h)	Bristol City	W	4-1	Walton, Beesley, Vinall (2)	1,546	"	"	"	"	Godfrey	Wood	"	Walton	"	"	"
28	(a)	Nottingham For	L	0-2		1,546	"	"	"	Wood	"	Richards	"	"	"	"	"
Oct 5	(h)	Nottingham For	W	4-3	Beesley, Starling, Walton, Vinall	1,500	"	"	"	Richards	"	Wood	"	"	"	"	"
12	(h)	Notts County	W	3-2	Starling, Vinall (2)	3,000	"	"	"	Wood	"	Richards	"	"	"	"	"
19	(a)	Notts County	L	2-4	Vinall, Beesley	1,500	"	"	"	"	"	"	"	"	"	"	"
26	(h)	Mansfield	D	6-6	Vinall (2), Beesley, Hancocks (2), Richards	1,500	"	"	"	"	"	"	Hancocks	Brown	"	"	"
Nov 2	(a)	Mansfield	L	1-3	Brown	520	"	"	"	"	"	"	"	"	"	"	"
7	(h)	Notts County	W	11-4	Rowley (4), Brown (2), Vinall (4), Wood	427	"	"	"	"	Morgan	"	"	"	"	"	Rowley
16	(a)	Notts County	L	1-2	Brown	1,053	"	"	"	"	"	"	"	"	"	"	"
23	(h)	Leicester City	W	5-0	Hancocks (2), Brown, Rowley (2)	1,472	"	"	"	"	"	Godfrey	"	"	"	"	"
30	(a)	Leicester City	D	1-1	Brown	600	"	"	"	"	"	"	"	"	"	"	"
Dec 21	(a)	Stoke City	D	2-2	Starling, Rowley	540	"	"	"	"	"	"	"	"	"	"	"
25	(h)	Birmingham	W	6-3	Vinall (2), Rowley (4)	2,891	"	"	"	Richards	"	"	"	"	"	"	"
28	(h)	Stoke City	W	5-1	Vinall (3), Rowley (2)	3,518	"	"	"	"	"	"	"	"	"	"	"
Mar 29	(a)	West Brom Alb	L	1-4	Wood	1,412	"	"	"	"	"	"	"	Wood	"	"	Dryden
Apr 5	(h)	West Brom Alb	D	3-3	Hancocks (2), Vinall	1,850	"	"	"	"	"	"	"	Brown	"	"	Wood
19	(h)	Mansfield Tn	D	1-1	Hancocks	1,495	"	"	"	"	"	"	"	"	"	Wood	Dryden
26	(a)	Mansfield Tn	D	2-2	Hancocks (2)	522	"	"	"	Godfrey	"	Wood	"	"	Thayne	Starling	Beesley
May 10	(h)	Leicester City	W	3-1	Brown, Thayne, Hancocks	1,250	"	"	"	Wood	"	Godfrey	"	"	"	"	"
24	(h)	Nottingham For	L	6-7	Rowley (4), Vinall, Hancocks	1,038	"	"	Thayne	"	"	"	"	Vinall	Rowley	"	"
31	(h)	West Brom Alb	W	10-3	Beesley (2), Vinall, Rowley (4),												
					Hancocks (2), Starling	1,512	"	"	"	"	"	"	"	"	"	"	"
League Position: 12th																	

Midland Cup

Date		Opponent			Scorers	Att	1	2	3	4	5	6	7	8	9	10	11
Jan 4	(a)	Luton Town	L	2-6	Vinall, Rowley	517	"	"	Male	Richards	"	"	"	Brown	Vinall	"	Rowley
11	(h)	Luton Town	W	3-2	Vinall (2), Rowley	2,500	"	"	"	Wood	"	"	"	"	"	"	"
Feb 8	(h)	West Brom Alb	W	4-3	Hancocks, Vinall, Brown (2)	3,135	Williams	"	"	"	"	"	"	"	"	"	"
Mar 1	(a)	Stoke City	D	1-1	Brown	1,045	Biddlestone	"	"	"	"	"	"	"	"	"	Dryden
8	(h)	Stoke City	W	7-3	Brown (2), Starling (2), Dryden (2), Vinall	1,616	"	"	"	"	"	"	"	"	"	"	"
15	(a)	Northampton T	W	3-1	Wrigglesworth, Starling, Vinall	2,500	"	"	"	"	"	"	"	"	"	"	Wrigglesworth
22	(h)	Northampton T	W	2-0	Hancocks, Dryden	2,566	"	"	"	Richards	"	"	"	Wood	"	"	Dryden
May 3	(a)	Leicester City	L	0-2	(FINAL)	6,562	"	"	"	Wood	"	"	"	Brown	Thayne	"	Beesley

League Cup

Date		Opponent			Scorers	Att	1	2	3	4	5	6	7	8	9	10	11
Feb 15	(h)	Nottingham F	W	3-2	Brown, Alsop, Brodie (og)	2,910	Biddlestone	"	"	"	"	"	"	"	Alsop	"	Dryden
22	(a)	Nottingham F	L	1-8	Starling	1,520	"	"	Thayne	"	"	"	"	"	"	"	"

Appearances: (All games); Alsop, G 2; Beesley, J.H 13; Biddlestone, T.F 32; Brown, W.S 28; Bulger, C.G 1; Dryden, J 7; Godfrey, C 32; Hancocks, J 27; Jones, G.T 1; Male, N.A 31; Morgan, L.D 27; Richards, D 19; Rowley, J.F 14; Shelton, J.B.T 32; Starling, R.W 33; Thayne, W 8; Vinall, E.J 29; Walton, G 5; Williams, B.F 1; Wood, T.F 31; Wrigglesworth, W 1.

Goals: Vinall 27; Rowley 23; Hancocks 15; Brown 13; Starling 8; Beesley 6; Dryden 3; Walton 2; Wood 2; Alsop 1; Richards 1; Thayne 1; Wrigglesworth 1; opponent (og) 1 Total 104

SEASON 1941-42

Football League (South)

Date		Opponent		Score	Scorers	Att	1	2	3	4	5	6	7	8	9	10	11
Aug 30	(a)	Northampton T	L	2-3	Dennison (og), Vinall	2,016	Biddlestone	Shelton	Thayne	Godfrey	Morgan	Wood	Hancocks	Brown	Vinall	Starling	Beesley
Sep 6	(h)	Northampton T	D	2-2	Starling, Brown	2,508	"	"	Male	Wood	"	Godfrey	Bulger	"	"	"	"
13	(a)	Swindon Town	W	7-4	Beesley (2), Wood, Vinall, Shelton, Brown (2)	4,000	"	"	"	"	"	"	Auckland	"	"	"	"
20	(h)	Swindon Town	W	4-2	Brown (2), Vinall, Beesley	2,500	"	"	Thayne	"	"	"	"	"	"	"	"
27	(h)	West Brom Alb	W	2-1	Shell, Francis	4,494	"	"	"	"	"	"	Beesley	"	Shell	"	Batty
Oct 4	(a)	West Brom Alb	L	0-4		4,135	"	"	"	"	"	"	"	"	"	"	"
11	(h)	Nottingham For	W	8-2	Starling, Wood (2), Batty (2), Hancocks (2), Vinall	2,500	"	"	Male	"	"	"	Hancocks	Shell	Vinall	"	"
18	(a)	Nottingham For	L	0-4		1,063	"	"	"	Godfrey	"	Beesley	Shell	Wood	"	"	"
25	(a)	Wolves	L	0-1		3,527	"	"	"	Wood	"	Godfrey	Hancocks	Brown	"	"	Shell
Nov 1	(h)	Wolves	W	4-1	Brown (2), Ashley, Shell	2,408	"	"	"	"	"	Thayne	Ashley	"	Shell	"	Beesley
8	(h)	Leicester City	W	2-1	Wood, Hancocks	3,000	"	"	"	"	"	Godfrey	Hancocks	"	Vinall	"	"
15	(a)	Leicester City	L	0-6		4,000	"	"	"	"	"	"	Beesley	"	"	"	Batty
22	(h)	Bristol City	W	5-0	Vinall (3), Beesley, Batty	2,000	"	"	"	"	"	"	Batty	"	"	"	Beesley
29	(a)	Bristol City	L	2-4	Vinall, Wood	2,500	"	"	"	"	"	"	Ashley	Wilkie	"	Lord	"
Dec 6	(a)	Luton Town	W	2-1	Ashley, Wilkie	1,000	"	"	"	"	"	"	Wilkie	Ashley	"	Roberts	"
13	(h)	Luton Town	W	5-3	Beesley (2), Ashley, Vinall (2)	1,500	"	"	"	"	"	"	Hancocks	"	"	Starling	"
20	(h)	Wolves	L	1-2	Vinall	1,520	"	"	"	"	"	"	Batty	"	"	"	"
25	(a)	Wolves	L	3-4	Vinall (2), Beesley	3,895	"	"	Lane	"	"	"	"	"	"	"	"
Apr 11	(h)	Stoke City	W	1-0	Vinall	1.047	"	"	Tranter	Lewis	"	Jarvis	Newsome	Wood	"	Dudley	"
18	(a)	Stoke City	W	3-2	Dudley, Newsome, Ashley	1,500	"	"	"	"	"	"	"	"	"	Ashley	Dudley
May 23	(a)	West Brom Alb	L	1-3	Newsome	1,695	"	"	"	Wood	"	"	"	Vinall	Beesley	Dudley	Coles
League position: 7th																	

League Cup

Date		Opponent		Score	Scorers	Att	1	2	3	4	5	6	7	8	9	10	11
Dec 27	(h)	Stoke City	L	1-4	Vinall	3,000	"	"	Male	Ashley	"	Batty	Bulger	Wood	Vinall	Starling	Beesley
Jan 3	(a)	Stoke City	L	0-8		3,000	"	"	"	Lewis	"	"	Hancocks	"	"	"	"
10	(a)	Northampton	L	1-6	Vinall	3,000	"	"	Godfrey	Wood	Lewis	"	Ashley	Vinall	Beesley	"	Bulger
17	(h)	Northampton	L	1-3	Beesley	1,500	"	"	"	"	"	"	"	"	"	"	"
31	(a)	Chester	L	3-4	Alsop, Embleton, Duffy	1,000	Williams	"	Ashley	Dyall	Jarvis	Holland	Ball	Alsop	Embleton	Duffy	Beesley
Feb 14	(h)	Chester	L	0-2		1,059	"	"	Male	"	"	"	"	Bulger	Vinall	"	"
21	(a)	Wrexham	L	0-1		996	Biddlestone	"	"	Jarvis	Morgan	"	"	"	"	"	"
28	(h)	Wrexham	W	2-0	Vinall (2)	1,055	"	"	"	Dyall	Jarvis	"	"	Vinall	Richardson	Evans	Bulger
Mar 21	(h)	Mansfield	W	1-0	Newsome	874	"	"	Arnold	"	Morgan	Jarvis	Bulger	Newsome	Dudley	Wood	
28	(a)	Mansfield	L	0-2		627	"	"	Smith	Wood	"	"	Newsome	Ashley	Alsop	Bulger	Dudley

Appearances: (All games) Alsop, G 2; Arnold, J 1; Ashley, H 12; Auckland, D.W 2; Ball, G 4 Batty, S.G 12; Beesley, J.H 26; Biddlestone, T.F 29; Brown, W.S 11; Bulger, C.G 9; Coles, V 1; Dudley, G; 5; Duffy, C 3; Dyall, S.E 4; Embleton, E 1; Evans, C.J 1; Godfrey, C 19; Hancocks, J. 6; Holland, R. 4; Jarvis, L 9; Lane, H 1; Lewis, J 5; Lord, I. 1; Male, N.A 18; Morgan, L.D. 26; Newsome, R. 5; Richardson, W.G 1; Roberts, F. 1; Shell, F.H. 6; Shelton, J.B.T. 31; Smith, A.J. 1; Starling, R.W. 20 Thayne, W. 5; Tranter, A.R. 3; Vinall, E.J. 25; Wilkie, C.H 2; Williams, B.F 2; Wood, T 27

Goals: Vinall 18; Beesley 9; Brown 6; Wood 5; Ashley 4; Batty 3; Hancocks 3; Newsome 3; Starling 3; Shell 2; Alsop 1; Brown 1; Dudley 1; Embleton 1; Shelton 1; Wilkie 1; Opponent (og) 1

SEASON 1942-43

Football League (N) 1st Comp.

Date		Opponent		Score	Scorers	Att	1	2	3	4	5	6	7	8	9	10	11
Aug 29	(h)	Coventry City	W	1-0	Wood (pen)	2,500	Williams	Shelton	Male	Wood	Morgan	Jarvis	Hancocks	Hickman	Vinall	Hann	Beesley
Sep 5	(a)	Coventry City	L	0-1		6,356	"	"	"	"	"	Ashley	"	"	"	"	"
12	(a)	Northampton	L	2-4	Alsop, Brown	2,337	"	"	"	Lewis	"	Wood	Ashley	Brown	Alsop	Vinall	"
19	(h)	Northampton	L	0-2		2,042	"	"	"	Wood	"	Jarvis	"	"	Vinall	Hann	Dudley
26	(a)	Aston Villa	D	2-2	Vinall, Wood	7,500	Bilton	"	"	Lewis	"	Tranter	Newsome	"	"	Wood	"
Oct 3	(h)	Aston Villa	W	3-0	Brown, Newsome (2)	4,500	"	"	"	"	"	"	"	"	"	"	"
10	(a)	Wolves	L	2-3	Brown (2)	6,105	"	"	"	"	"	"	"	"	"	"	"
17	(h)	Wolves	W	5-2	Vinall (2), Newsome, Dudley, Brown	4,950	"	"	"	Jarvis	"	"	"	"	"	Ashley	"
24	(h)	Northampton	W	6-0	Ashley, Newsome (2), Wood, Brown (2)	2,000	"	"	"	Lewis	"	"	"	"	Ashley	Wood	Beesley
31	(a)	Northampton	D	2-2	Vinall, Tranter	4,000	"	"	"	"	"	"	Vinall	"	"	"	Dudley
Nov 7	(a)	Birmingham	L	3-4	Wood (2, 1 pen), Brown	4,000	"	"	"	Jarvis	Lewis	"	Ashley	"	Vinall	"	"
14	(h)	Birmingham	W	1-0	Brown	2,500	Williams	"	"	Lewis	Morgan	"	Colquhoun	"	"	Mitchell	"
21	(a)	West Brom Alb	D	0-0		2,783	"	"	"	"	"	Wood	Collins	"	"	"	"
28	(h)	West Brom Alb	W	2-0	Lewis, Ireland	3,412	"	"	"	"	"	Ashley	Newsome	"	Ireland	Vinall	"
Dec 5	(h)	Coventry	D	1-1	Vinall	2,500	"	"	"	"	"	Tranter	"	Halliday	Symons	"	"
12	(a)	Coventry	L	0-1		6,111	"	"	"	"	"	"	"	Lindley	Vinall	Mason	Mitchell
19	(a)	Stoke City	L	1-7	Nicholls	519	Hird	"	"	"	"	"	"	"	Nicholls	Emmanuel	Ireland
25	(h)	Stoke City	D	2-2	Tranter(2)	2,229	Williams	"	"	"	"	"	"	Ball	"	"	Beesley
Mar 6	(h)	Birmingham	L	1-2	Arnold	1,500	"	Ashley	Vause	Jarvis	"	Featherstone	"	Arnold	"	Reid. M.W	Batty
13	(a)	Birmingham	L	1-2	Nicholls	700	"	"	Male	"	"	Vause	"	Brown	"	"	"
20	(a)	Northampton	W	4-2	Nicholls (2), Dudley, Martin	1,500	"	"	Tranter	"	Vause	Watts	Batty	Martin	"	Clarke	Dudley
27	(h)	Northampton	L	2-5	Martin, Nicholls	955	"	"	Batty	"	"	Featherstone	Haycock	"	"	"	Grainger
Apr 17	(a)	West Brom Alb	L	0-4		1,575	"	Shelton	"	Watts	Morgan	Wood	Dickie	Brown	Martin	Streten	Wilkinson
24	(h)	West Brom Alb	L	1-2	Streten	1,500	"	"	"	"	Vause	"	"	"	Reid. M	"	"

League position: 24th

Football League (N) 2nd Comp.

Date		Opponent		Score	Scorers	Att	1	2	3	4	5	6	7	8	9	10	11
Dec 26	(a)	Coventry City	L	0-2		10,359	"	"	Emmanuel	Wood	Lewis	Tranter	Newsome	Watts	Nicholls	Timms	Beesley
Jan 2	(h)	Coventry City	L	1-3	Nicholls	1,997	"	"	Male	"	"	"	"	Nicholls	Emmanuel	Dickie	Batty
9	(a)	Northampton	D	2-2	Doherty (2)	4,000	"	"	Tranter	Lewis	Morgan	Powell	Wood	Doherty	Nicholls	"	"
16	(h)	Northampton	W	2-0	Nicholls, Mason	2,500	"	"	Powell	"	"	Russell	Hancocks	Mason	"	"	"
23	(h)	Birmingham	D	1-1	Tranter	3,000	"	"	Male	Tranter	Lewis	Powell	Dudley	Newsome	Vinall	Batty	Dudley
30	(a)	Birmingham	L	0-1		1,000	"	"	"	Lewis	Harper	Wood	Dunkley	"	Nicholls	Dickie	Batty
Feb 6	(a)	Stoke City	L	1-2	Ashley	4,000	"	"	"	"	Morgan	Harper	"	"	Ashley	Emmanuel	"
13	(h)	Stoke City	W	4-1	Nicholls (3), Newsome	3,000	"	"	"	"	Harper	Vause	"	"	"	Nicholls	"
20	(a)	Aston Villa	L	1-2	Nicholls	12,000	"	"	Emmanuel	"	Rist	Timms	"	"	"	"	"
27	(h)	Aston Villa	L	1-4	Ashley	7,000	"	"	Male	"	Morgan	Featherstone	"	"	"	"	"

League position: 52nd

Appearances: (All games) Alsop, G 1; Arnold, J 1; Ashley, H 16; Ball, G 1; Batty, S.G 15; Beesley, J.H 6; Bilton, D.H 7; Brown, W.S 15; Bullock, A.E 1; Clarke, I 2; Collins, G.E 1; Colquhoun, D.M 1; Dickie, M.M 2; Dickie, P 3; Doherty, P 2; Dudley, G 14; Dunkley, M 4; Emmanuel, D.L 6; Featherstone, J 3; Grainger, D 1; Halliday, G 1; Hancocks, J 3; Hann, L 3; Harper, K 3; Haycock, F 1; Hickman, A 2; Hird, E 1; Ireland, H.W 2; Jarvis, L 8; Lewis, J 24; Lindley, W.M 2; Male, N.A 25; Martin, E 3; Mason, D.W 1; Mason, W.S 1; Mitchell, T.G 3; Morgan, L.D 24; Newsome, R 21; Nicholls, H 14; Powell, I.V 3; Reid, M 1; Reid, M.W 2; Rist, F.H 1; Russell, D.W 1; Shelton, J.B.T 30; Streten, B,R 2; Symons, R 1; Timms, C 2; Tranter, A.R 35; Vause, P.G 6; Vinall, E.J 16; Watts, J 4; Wilkinson, H 2; Williams, B.F 25; Wood, T 17

Goals: Nicholls 11; Brown 9; Newsome 6; Wood 6; Tranter 4; Vinall 4; Ashley 3; Doherty 2; Dudley 2; Martin 2; Alsop 1; Arnold 1; Ireland 1; Lewis 1; D Mason 1; Streten 1; Total 55

SEASON 1943-44

Football League (North)

Date	Venue	Opponent	Res	Score	Scorers	Att	1	2	3	4	5	6	7	8	9	10	11
Aug 28	(a)	Northampton	L	0-2		3,000	Williams	Shelton	Male	Lewis	Morgan	Jarvis	Dudley	Brown	Alsop	Nicholls	Batty
Sep 4	(h)	Northampton	D	0-0		3,000	"	"	"	Childs	Rist	Featherstone	Alsop	"	Read	Penrose	"
11	(a)	Coventry City	D	3-3	Brown (2), Alsop	6,341	"	"	"	Lewis	"	"	"	"	"	"	"
18	(h)	Coventry City	D	1-1	Penrose	2,750	"	"	"	Nicholls	Lewis	Batty	Newsome	"	Alsop	"	Streten
25	(h)	Aston Villa	L	0-2		7,000	"	"	"	Lewis	Rist	Wood	Nicholls	"	Jones	Streten	Batty
Oct 2	(a)	Aston Villa	D	4-4	Alsop (2), Wood, Morby (og)	12,000	"	Male	Shelton	Emmanuel	"	Lewis	Batty	Wood	Alsop	Brown	Maund
9	(a)	Northampton	L	0-2		4,000	"	Shelton	Male	Lewis	"	Emmanuel	Maund	Brown	Streten	Wood	Batty
16	(h)	Northampton	D	0-0		3,000	"	"	"	"	"	"	"	"	"	"	"
23	(h)	Wolves	L	1-3	Reid	3,794	"	"	"	Nicholls	Lewis	Wood	Hancocks	"	Reid	Batty	Maund
30	(a)	Wolves	D	1-1	Alsop	11,829	"	"	"	Lewis	Rist	Emmanuel	"	"	Alsop	Hinsley	Batty
Nov 6	(h)	Birmingham	L	2-4	Brown, Hinsley	3,500	"	"	"	Dudley	"	"	"	"	"	"	"
13	(a)	Birmingham	L	1-5	Dudley	3,000	"	"	"	Lewis	"	"	Batty	"	Rickman	Cooper	Dudley
20	(h)	West Brom Albion	W	2-0	Hinsley, Rickman	4,297	"	"	"	"	"	"	Roberts	Hinsley	"	"	"
27	(a)	West Brom Albion	W	4-1	Hinsley (3), Brown	4,550	"	"	"	"	"	"	"	"	"	Brown	Batty
Dec 4	(a)	Coventry City	W	3-1	Brown (2), Hinsley	3,606	"	"	"	"	"	"	"	"	"	"	Dudley
11	(h)	Coventry City	D	0-0		2,957	"	"	"	"	"	"	"	"	"	"	Batty
18	(h)	Stoke City	W	4-2	Batty, Roberts, Brown (2)	1,147	"	"	"	"	"	"	"	"	Tranter	"	"
25	(a)	Stoke City	W	1-0	Brown	6,022	"	"	"	"	"	Jarvis	"	Wood	Cooper	"	"
Mar 11	(h)	Notts County	W	2-1	Hinsley, Lewis	2,500	"	"	"	Dougall	Lewis	Lowery	Mullen	Hinsley	Alsop	Emmanuel	"
18	(h)	Nottingham For	D	0-0		1,984	"	"	"	Lowery	"	Emmanuel	Griffiths	"	"	Brown	Dudley
25	(a)	Nottingham For	L	0-2		5,638	"	"	"	Lewis	Rist	Lowery	"	"	Wright	"	Batty
Apr 1	(h)	West Brom Albion	D	2-2	Bulger, Hinsley	2,120	"	"	"	"	"	"	"	"	Taylor	Bulger	"
8	(a)	West Brom Albion	L	0-1		5,588	"	"	"	"	"	"	Mullen	"	Hayward	Hardy	"
15	(h)	Birmingham City	D	2-2	Harper, McCormick	2,000	"	"	"	"	"	Emmanuel	"	McCormick	Harper	Robinson	"
22	(a)	Birmingham City	L	0-5		4,000	"	"	"	Lowery	"	Jarvis	McCormick	Lewis	Rickman	Dudley	"

League position: 25th

Football League Cup

Date	Venue	Opponent	Res	Score	Scorers	Att	1	2	3	4	5	6	7	8	9	10	11
Dec 26	(a)	Coventry City	L	0-3		12,950	"	"	"	Lewis	"	Emmanuel	Roberts	Hinsley	Dudley	Brown	"
Jan 1	(h)	Coventry City	W	3-0	Dudley (3)	4,000	"	"	"	"	"	"	Rickman	"	Vause	"	Dudley
8	(h)	West Brom Albion	D	2-2	Hinsley, Dudley	5,993	"	"	"	"	"	Vause	Roberts	"	Dudley	"	Batty
15	(a)	West Brom Albion	L	1-7	Batty	4,000	"	"	Emmanuel	"	"	"	"	"	"	"	"
22	(h)	Northampton	W	3-0	Welsh (2), Hinsley	3,000	"	"	Batty	Dougall	Lewis	Emmanuel	Mulligan	"	Welsh	"	Tully
29	(a)	Northampton	L	0-2		3,000	"	"	"	"	"	"	"	Turley	"	"	Dudley
Feb 5	(a)	Stoke City	L	1-5	Brown	4,000	"	"	"	"	"	"	Mullen	Hinsley	"	"	"
12	(h)	Stoke City	L	0-2		1,986	"	"	"	Lowery	"	"	"	"	Dougall	"	"
19	(h)	Wolves	D	0-0		2,188	"	"	Male	"	Morgan	"	"	"	Dudley	Dougall	Batty
26	(a)	Wolves	D	1-1	Hinsley	3,085	"	"	"	Lewis	Rist	"	McCormick	"	Jackson	"	"

Appearances: (All games) Alsop, G 9; Batty, S.G 31; Brown, W.S 27; Bulger, C.G 1; Childs, F 1; Cooper, T 3; Dougall, C 7; Dudley, G 18; Emmanuel, D.L 23; Featherstone, J 2; Griffiths, E.O 3; Hancocks, J 3; Hardy, R 1; Harper, K 1; Hayward, L.E 1; Hinsley, G 21; Jackson, G.A 1; Jarvis, L 3; Jones, B 1; Lewis, J 31; Lowery, H 8; Male, N.A 30; Maund, J 4; McCormick, J 2; Morgan, L.D 2; Mullen, W 6; Mulligan, E 2; Newsome, R 1; Nicholls, H 4; Penrose, N 3; Reed, W.M 3; Rickman, F 7; Rist, F.H 25; Roberts, N.E 9; Robinson, G 1; Shelton J.B.T 35; Streten, B.R 4; Taylor, J 1; Tranter, A.R 1; Tully, J 1; Vause, P.G 3; Welsh, A 3; Williams, B..F 35; Wood, T 4; Wright, E.V 1

Goals: Hinsley 11; Brown 10; Dudley 5; Alsop 4; Batty 2; Welsh 2; Bulger 1; Harper 1; Lewis 1; McCormick 1 Penrose 1; Reid 1; Rickman 1; Roberts 1; Wood 1; opponent (og) 1; Total 44

SEASON 1944-45

Football League (North)

Date	Venue	Opponents	Res	Score	Scorers	Att	1	2	3	4	5	6	7	8	9	10	11
Aug 26	(h)	Coventry City	L	2-3	Boonham (2)	4,800	Williams	Shelton	Male	Lewis	Rist	McKenna	White	Lycett	Boonham	Vinall	Batty
Sep 2	(a)	Coventry City	L	1-2	Rickman	2,900	"	"	"	Lowery	"	Rickman	"	Hinsley	Vinall	Lycett	Beesley
9	(a)	Leicester City	W	3-2	Beech, Kernick, White	7,000	"	"	Smythe	"	Morgan	Vinall	"	"	Harper	Kernick	"
16	(h)	Leicester City	L	0-1		5,000	"	"	Male	Lewis	Rist	Lowery	"	"	Vinall	Harper	"
23	(a)	Aston Villa	D	1-1	Hinsley	18,000	"	"	"	"	"	"	Mullen	"	"	Gallon	Haigh
30	(h)	Aston Villa	L	0-2		13,570	"	"	"	"	"	"	"	Layton	"	Buckingham	Hobbis
Oct 7	(h)	Stoke City	D	1-1	Vinall	4,629	"	"	"	"	"	"	White	Hinsley	Armstrong	Vinall	"
14	(a)	Stoke City	W	2-0	Vinall, Morris	4,000	"	"	"	"	"	Vinall	"	"	"	Peace	"
21	(a)	Wolves	D	1-1	Vinall	11,388	"	"	"	"	"	Lowery	Houghton	"	"	Vinall	Redwood
28	(h)	Wolves	L	1-2	Armstrong	7,225	"	"	"	"	"	"	White	"	"	"	Jessop
Nov 4	(a)	Northampton	D	1-1	Shelton	3,000	"	"	""	"	"	"	Houghton	"	"	Peace	Redwood
11	(h)	Northampton	W	3-2	Hinsley, Armstrong (2)	2,000	"	"	"	"	"	"	"	"	"	"	"
18	(h)	Birmingham	W	4-1	Armstrong (2)), Mulligan, Peace	4,500	"	"	"	"	"	"	"	Mulligan	"	"	Alsop
25	(a)	Birmingham	D	2-2	Armstrong, Mulligan	5,000	Bilton	"	"	"	Vinall	"	"	"	"	"	"
Dec 2	(a)	West Brom Albion	L	0-3		8,902	Williams	"	"	"	Rist	Vinall	"	"	"	"	"
9	(h)	West Brom Albion	L	1-2	Hinsley	5,303	Streten	Gregory	"	"	Shelton	Lowery	Kendrick	"	"	Hinsley	Little
16	(h)	Port Vale	D	2-2	Alsop (2)	2,957	Williams	Shelton	"	"	Rist	"	Houghton	"	Alsop	"	"
23	(a)	Port Vale	W	2-0	Ratcliffe, Bownham	4,882	Billingsley	"	"	"	Vinall	Smith	Alsop	"	Boonham	Forrester	Ratcliffe
Mar 10	(a)	Wrexham	L	0-1		5,250	Streten	"	"	Crutchley	Morgan	"	Meath	Archibald	Alsop	Peace	Beech
24	(a)	Port Vale	L	2-3	Archibald, Alsop	6,000	"	Barker	"	"	Lewis	Vinall	Allan	"	"	"	"
31	(h)	Port Vale	W	2-0	Peace, Lewis	1,500	"	Stone	"	"	Lowe	"	Archibald	Lewis	"	"	"
Apr 2	(a)	Mansfield	L	0-2		4,001	Williams	"	"	"	Lewis	"	Meath	Alsop	Price	Male. G	"
7	(a)	West Brom Albion	D	1-1	Beech	5,227	Streten	"	"	"	"	"	"	Jarvis	Alsop	Peace	"
14	(h)	West Brom Albion	L	1-2	Snape	1,780	Williams	Kelly	"	"	"	"	Alsop	"	Snape	"	"
May 3	(h)	Mansfield	W	4-2	Alsop (4)	525	Clough	Rickman	Beck	"	"	"	Meath	Goffin	Boonham	Male. G	Alsop
League position: 32nd																	

League Cup

Date	Venue	Opponents	Res	Score	Scorers	Att	1	2	3	4	5	6	7	8	9	10	11
Dec 26	(a)	Wolves	D	1-1	Boonham	11,042	Williams	Shelton	Male	Lewis	Morgan	Vinall	Meath	Brown	"	Lycett	Alsop
30	(a)	Birmingham	L	1-3	Boonham	10,000	Billingsley	"	"	"	Rist	Lowery	Brown	Mulligan	Hinsley	"	"
Jan 6	(a)	Northampton	L	1-2	Alsop	5,000	Williams	"	"	"	Vinall	"	Alsop	"	Boonham	Peace	Morris
13	(h)	Northampton	L	0-1		2,000	"	"	"	"	Rist	"	Meath	Russell	Alsop	"	Bulger
20	(h)	Coventry City	W	6-5	Russell (2), Peace (2) Alsop (2)	1,095	Billingsley	"	Batty	Russell	Vinall	Johnson	"	Jenkins	"	"	"
27	(a)	Coventry City	W	2-0	Meath, Pearson	2,667	Williams	"	Stone	Lewis	Rist	Vinall	"	Cromwell	Rickman	"	Pearson
Feb 3	(a)	West Brom Albion	W	2-0	Pearson (2)	6,334	"	"	Male	Vinall	"	Batty	"	Jenkins	Alsop	"	"
10	(h)	West Brom Albion	D	0-0		6,376	"	"	"	Lewis	"	Vinall	"	"	"	Hinsley	Bulger
17	(a)	Aston Villa	L	1-6	Alsop	10,000	"	"	"	"	"	"	"	"	"	Hall	"
24	(h)	Aston Villa	L	0-2		9,894	"	"	"	Vinall	Morgan	Flack	"	"	"	McKenzie	Batty
Mar 3	(h)	Birmingham City	L	0-2		4,000	"	"	"	Lewis	Rist	Vinall	"	"	"	Peace	"

Appearances: (All games); Alsop, G.A. 21; Archibald, C. 3; Armstrong, M. 10; Barker, J. 1; Batty, S.G. 5; Beech, G. 7; Beesley, 3; Beck, H. 1; Billingsley, G. 3; Bilton, D. 1; Boonham G. 5; Brown J. 2; Buckingham G. 1; Bulger C.G. 4; Clough J 1; Cromwell T. 1; Crutchley R. 7; Flack W. 1; Forrester G. 1; Gallon J. 1; Goffin W. 1; Gregory A. 1; Haigh W. 1; Hall A. 1; Harper J. 2; Hinsley G. 14; Hobbis H. 3; Houghton R. 7; Jarvis 2; Jenkins R. 6; Jessop W. 1; Johnson J. 1; Kelly F. 1; Kendrick K. 1; Kernick D. 1; Layton W. 1; Lewis J. 30; Little J. 2; Lowe G. 1; Lowery H. 17; Lycett T. 4; Male G. 2; Male N.A. 32; McKenna M. 1; McKenzie J 1; Meath G. 13; Morgan L.D. 4; Morris J. 1; Mullen J. 2; Mulligan E. 8; Peace H. 17; Pearson T 2; Price S. 1; Ratcliffe J. 1 Redwood D. 3; Rickman F. 3; Rist F. 21; Russell D. 2; Shelton J.B.T. 30; Smith A. 2; Smythe G. 1; Snape H. 1; Stone C. 4; Streten B. 5; Vinall E.J. 28; White F.H. 7; Williams B.F. 26.
Goals: Alsop 11; Armstrong 6; Boonham 5; Peace 4; Hinsley 3; Pearson 3; Vinall 3; Beech 2; Mulligan 2; Russell 2; Archibald 1; Kernick 1; Lewis 1; Meath 1; Morris 1; Ratcliffe 1; Rickman 1; Shelton 1; Snape 1; White 1: Total 51

SEASON 1945-46

Division Three (S) (North)

Date		Opponents			Scorers	Att	1	2	3	4	5	6	7	8	9	10	11
Aug 25	(a)	Northampton Tn	D	1-1	Alsop	4,000	Williams	Stone	Male	Crutchley	Sankey	Payne	Hancocks	Acquaroff	Alsop	Finch	Beech
Sept 1	(a)	Northampton Tn	L	0-1		6,000	Lewis	"	Smith	"	"	"	"	Brown	"	Harvey	"
8	(a)	QPR	L	0-4		7,780	"	Sankey	Peck	"	Lowery	"	"	"	"	Peace	Bulger
12	(h)	Ipswich Town	W	3-0	Barratt, Alsop, Jenkins	10,605	"	"	Screen	"	Lewis	Lowery	"	Jenkins	"	Barratt	"
15	(h)	QPR	D	1-1	Hancocks	7,000	Williams	Stone	"	"	Sankey	"	"	Hinsley	"	Heaselgrave	"
19	(a)	Mansfield Tn	L	1-6	Vinall	4,000	Lewis	"	"	Sankey	Lewis	McNab	"	Jenkins	Vinall	"	Beech
22	(h)	Clapton Orient	W	5-3	Darby (3), Alsop, Hancocks	5,000	"	Sankey	"	Crutchley	Lowery	"	"	"	Darby	Clarke.G	Alsop
27	(h)	Mansfield Tn	W	2-0	Bennett (2)	3,000	"	Pritchard	Skidmore	"	Sankey	Methley	"	"	Bennett	"	"
29	(a)	Clapton Orient	L	0-1		4,089	"	Harding	Screen	"	"	Peck	Rowlinson	"	"	"	"
Oct 6	(a)	Watford	L	1-2	Bennett	4,700	"	Shelley	"	"	"	Vinall	Alsop	"	"	Mullard	Peace
13	(h)	Watford	L	0-3		4,000	"	Kelly	"	"	Vinall	Gedders	Hancocks	Peace	"	"	Alsop
Nov 3	(a)	Norwich City	L	1-2	Alsop	7,000	"	Forder	Vinall	"	Foulkes	Newman	Bulger	Walton	Alsop	Talbot	Clarke.J
10	(h)	Norwich City	L	1-2	Bulger	4,000	Strong	Vinall	Male	"	"	"	Hancocks	"	"	"	Bulger
Dec 1	(a)	Southend Utd	W	1-0	Goffin	6,000	Lewis	Shelton	"	"	"	"	Goffin	Mullard	Kelly	"	Alsop
8	(h)	Southend Utd	W	6-0	Alsop (2), Kelly (4)	3,000	"	"	"	"	"	"	Hancocks	"	"	"	"
22	(h)	Notts County	D	3-3	Mullard, Kelly, Hancocks	2,553	"	"	"	"	"	"	"	"	"	"	"
24	(a)	Notts County	L	0-2		7,000	Hinks	Harper	"	"	"	"	"	"	"	"	"
25	(h)	Port Vale	L	1-5	Kelly	2,176	Lewis	Shelton	"	"	Newman	Wood	Alsop	"	"	Peace	Wilkie
26	(a)	Port Vale	W	1-0	Foulkes	5,500	"	Paxton	Walker	"	Foulkes	Newman	"	Jenkins	"	Brown	Evans
29	(a)	Ipswich Town	L	3-5	Evans, Kelly (2)	3,589	"	Harding	Male	"	Newman	Jarvis	"	Mullard	"	Talbot	"
League position: 9th																	

Division Three (S) (North) Cup

Date		Opponents			Scorers	Att	1	2	3	4	5	6	7	8	9	10	11
AJan 5	(h)	Clapton Orient	W	4-3	Hancocks, Kelly, Talbot, Alsop	4,000	Lewis	Shelton	Male	Crutchley	Foulkes	Newman	Hancocks	Mullard	Kelly	Talbot	Alsop
12	(h)	Port Vale	W	3-1	Alsop, Kelly, Hancocks	5,000	"	Walker	"	"	"	"	"	"	"	"	"
19	(a)	Port Vale	L	0-1		4,000	"	Methley	Shelton	"	"	"	"	"	"	"	"
26	(h)	Mansfield Town	D	2-2	Hancocks (2)	4,152	"	"	Male	"	"	"	"	"	"	"	"
Feb 2	(a)	Mansfield Town	W	2-1	Kelly, Mullard	2,500	"	"	"	"	"	"	Mullard	Jenkins	"	"	White
9	(h)	Notts County	W	2-0	Hancocks, Wilshaw	5,144	"	"	"	"	"	"	Hancocks	Mullard	Wilshaw	"	Evans
16	(a)	Notts County	L	0-1		12,116	"	"	"	"	"	"	"	"	Kelly	"	"
23	(a)	Clapton Orient	W	1-0	Kelly	10,096	"	"	"	Hamers	"	"	"	"	"	"	"
Mar 9	(h)	Southend Utd	D	2-2	Hancocks, Alsop	6,000	"	"	Shelton	Crutchley	"	"	"	"	"	"	Alsop
16	(a)	Southend Utd	W	2-0	Alsop, Hancocks	8,228	"	"	"	"	"	"	"	"	Wilshaw	"	"
23	(h)	Aldershot	D	1-1	Talbot	3,547	"	"	"	"	"	"	"	"	"	"	"
30	(a)	Aldershot	W	3-1	Talbot, Hancocks (2)	9.232	"	"	"	"	"	"	"	Talbot	Kelly	Wilshaw	"
Apr 6	(h)	Norwich City	W	4-2	Talbot, Hancocks, Mullard, Alsop	9,449	"	"	"	"	"	"	"	"	Mullard	"	"
13	(a)	Norwich City	D	1-1	Wilshaw	10,422	"	"	"	"	"	"	"	"	"	"	"
20	(a)	Northampton Tn	W	4-1	Mullard (2), Talbot, Wilshaw	8,000	"	"	"	"	"	"	"	"	"	"	"
22	(h)	Northampton Tn	W	3-1	Mullard (3)	13,146	"	"	"	"	"	"	"	"	"	"	"
27	(a)	Bristol Rovers	W	3-1	Hancocks, Wilshaw, Talbot	14,673	"	"	"	"	"	"	"	"	"	"	"
May 4	(n)	Bournemouth	L	0-1	(at Stamford Bridge)	19,715	"	"	"	"	"	"	"	"	"	"	"

Appearances: (League & Cup): Acquaroff J, 1; Alsop G.A. 33; Barratt H. 1; Beech G. 3; Bennett S. 4; Brown W.S. 3; Bulger C.G. 5; Clarke G. 3; Clarke J. 1; Crutchley R. 36; Darby D. 1; Evans A. 5; Finch L; 1 Forder J. 1; Foulkes R. 25; Gedders E. 1; Goffin W.C. 1; Hamers L. 1; Hancocks J. 30; Harding E. 2; Harper K. 1; Harvey E. 1; Heaselgrave S. 2; Hinks H. 1; Hinsley G. 1; Jarvis J. 1; Jenkins R. 8; Kelly F. 17; Lewis J. 2; Lewis J (goal). 34; Lowery H. 4; Male N.A. 15; Methley I. 17; Mullard A. 25; Newman A. 27; Paxton J. 1; Payne L. 3; Peace H. 4; Peck W. 2; Pritchard R. 1; Rowlinson H. 1; Sankey J. 10; Screen J. 7; Shelley A . 1; Shelton J.B.T. 16; Skidmore W. 1; Smith E. 1; Stone C. 4; Strong G.J. 1; Talbot F.L. 25; Vinall E.J. 5; Walker R. 2; Walton G. 2; White F.H. 1; Wilkie W 1; Williams B.F 2; Wilshaw D.J. 10; Wood T. 1
Goals: Hancocks 14; Kelly 12; Alsop 11; Mullard 8; Talbot 6; Wilshaw 4; Bennett 3; Darby 3; Barratt 1; Bulger 1; Evans 1; Foulkes 1; Goffin 1; Jenkins 1; Vinall 1; Total 68

F.A. Cup

Date		Opponents	Rd		Scorers	Att											
Nov 17	(a)	Shrewsbury Tn	1/1	0-5		6,531	Strong	Kelly	Male	Crutchley	Foulkes	Newman	Hancocks	Walton	Alsop	Talbot	Bulger
24	(h)	Shrewsbury Tn	1/2	4-1	Mullard, Bennett, Talbot, Alsop	3,500	"	"	Shelton	"	"	Jarvis	"	Mullard	Bennett	"	Alsop

Appearances: Alsop 2; Bennett 1; Bulger 1; Crutchley 2; Foulkes 2; Hancocks 2; Jarvis 1; Kelly 2; Male 1; Mullard 1; Newman 1; Shelton 1; Strong 2; Talbot 2; Walton 1.
Goals: Alsop 1; Bennett 1; Mullard 1; Talbot 1; Total: 4.

SEASON 1946-47

Division 3(S)

Date		Opponents		Score	Scorers	Att.	Lewis J.	Methley I.	Shelton J.	Crutchley R.	Foulkes R.	Newman A.	Mullard A.	Talbot F.L.	Darby	Wilshaw D.	Davies	Vinall	Kimberley K.	Horton	Skidmore W.	Walters H.	Campbell	Walsh W.	Lishman D.	Robinson	Maund J.	Male N.	Brown W.S.	Alsop G.	Kelly F.	Blincow E.
Aug 31	(a)	Southend Utd	L	1-3	Talbot	11,500	1	2	3	4	5	6	7	8	9	10	11															
Sep 4	(a)	Torquay Utd	L	0-2		5,000	1	2	3	4	5	6	7		9	10	11	8														
7	(h)	Q.P.R	L	0-2		13,994	1	2			5	6	9		10		11	4			3								8	7		
9	(h)	Mansfield Town	D	0-0		9,047	1	2		4	5	6	9		10		11				3								8	7		
14	(a)	Leyton Orient	L	0-1		8,297	1	2		4	5	6	9	8		10	11				3								7			
18	(a)	Mansfield Town	D	1-1	Wilshaw	7,368	1	2		4	5	6	9	8		10	11				3								7			
21	(h)	Ipswich Town	W	4-2	Brown (2), Mullard, Davies	10,596		2		4	5	6	9	8		10	11		1		3								7			
28	(a)	Watford	W	2-0	Mullard, Talbot	10,000	1	2		4	5	6	9	8		10	11				3								7			
Oct 5	(h)	Northampton	W	2-0	Brown, Wilshaw	12,521	1	2		4	5	6	9	8		10	11				3								7			
12	(h)	Reading	D	2-2	Davies, Mullard	13,399	1	2	4		5	6	9	8		10	11				3								7			
18	(a)	Aldershot	W	2-1	Davies, Mullard	5,000	1	2		4	5	6	9	8		10	11				3								7			
26	(h)	Brighton	D	1-1	Talbot	8,834	1	2		4	5	6	9	8		10	11				3								7			
Nov 2	(a)	Exeter City	D	2-2	Maund (2)	9,102	1	2		4	5	6	9	8		10	11				3						7					
9	(h)	Port Vale	W	4-1	Wilshaw, Maund, Darby, Davies	12,171	1	2		4	5	6		8	9	10	11				3						7					
16	(a)	Bristol City	W	2-1	Darby, Skidmore (pen)	25,819	1	2		4	5	6		8	9	10	11				3						7					
23	(h)	Swindon Town	L	0-1		14,291	1	2		4	5	6		8	9	10	11				3						7					
Dec 7	(h)	Cardiff City	L	2-3	Wilshaw (2)	16,386	1	2		4	5	6		8	9	10	11				3						7					
21	(h)	Notts County	W	2-0	Wilshaw, Lishman	8,801	1	2		4	5	6				9	11				3				10		7		8			
25	(a)	Bristol Rovers	D	2-2	Wilshaw, Mullard	6,624	1	2		4	5	6				9	11				3				10		7		8			
26	(h)	Bristol Rovers	W	2-0	Wilshaw, Alsop	14,554	1	2		4	5	6	8			9					3				10		7			11		
28	(h)	Southend Utd	D	2-2	Maund, Alsop	14,000	1	2		4	5	6				9					3				10		7		8	11		
Jan 4	(a)	Q.P.R	L	0-1		15,993	1	2		4	5	6				10	11				3		7						8	9		
15	(a)	Bournemouth	W	3-2	Brown, Lishman, Skidmore	6,000	1	2		4	5	6		8			11				3				10				7		9	
18	(h)	Leyton Orient	W	3-1	Talbot, Kelly, Skidmore (pen)	12,131	1	2		4	5	6		8			11				3				10				7		9	
25	(a)	Ipswich Town	L	1-2	Foulkes	12,000	1	2		4	5	6	8	10							3								7	11	9	
Feb 1	(h)	Watford	L	1-3	Kelly	8,000	1	2		4		6	8	10						5	3								7	11	9	
Mar 1	(a)	Brighton	L	0-2		6,000	1	2		4	5	6	8								3				10				7		9	11
15	(a)	Port Vale	D	2-2	Wilshaw, Lishman	10,000	1	2			5	6			9	11					3			8	10	4	7					
22	(h)	Bristol City	W	3-0	Newman, Maund, Wilshaw	12,000	1	2			5	6			9	11					3			8	10	4	7					
29	(a)	Swindon Town	L	1-4	Walsh	15,000	1	2				5	6		9	11					3			8	10	4	7					
Apr 4	(a)	Crystal Palace	D	1-1	Wilshaw	12,650	1	2		4	5	6			9	11					3			8	10		7					
5	(h)	Bournemouth	W	3-0	Lishman, Wilshaw, Darby	9,666	1	2		4	5	6			9	11					3			8	10		7					
7	(h)	Crystal Palace	D	3-3	Walsh, Wilshaw, Darby	13,326	1	2		4	5	6			9	11					3		7	8	10							
8	(a)	Northampton	W	8-0	Lishman (2), Wilshaw (3), Mullard (3)	5,000	1	2		4	5	6	9			11					3		7	8	10							
12	(a)	Cardiff City	L	0-3		45,234	1	2		4	5	6	9			11					3		7	8	10							
19	(h)	Norwich City	D	2-2	Walsh, Crutchley	10,250	1	2		4	5	6			9	11					3		7	8	10							
26	(a)	Notts County	L	1-3	Mullard	10,350	1	2		4	5	6	9			11							7	8	10			3				
May 10	(h)	Aldershot	W	2-0	Lishman, Sheppard (og)	5,642	1	2		4	5	6	9			11					3			8	10		7					
17	(a)	Norwich City	W	2-0	Wilshaw, Maund	16,002	1	2			5	6	9			11					3	4		8	10		7					
24	(h)	Exeter City	W	2-1	Lishman, Mullard	9,743	1	2			5	6	9			11					3	4	7	8	10							
26	(a)	Reading	D	1-1	Campbell	7,030	1	2			5	6	9			11					3	4	7	8	10							
31	(h)	Torquay	W	2-1	Wilshaw, Skidmore	7,491	1	2			5	6	9			11					3	4		8	10	7						
						Apps	41	42	3	33	40	42	26	18	15	35	22	2	1	1	39	4	8	15	22	4	16	1	19	7	5	1
League position: 6th						Goals				1	1	1	10	4	4	18	4				4		1	3	8		6		4	2	2	

own goal: 1

F.A. Cup

Date		Opponents	Rd	Score	Scorers	Att.	Lewis J.	Methley I.	Shelton J.	Crutchley R.	Foulkes R.	Newman A.	Mullard A.	Talbot F.L.	Darby	Wilshaw D.	Davies	Vinall	Kimberley K.	Horton	Skidmore W.	Walters H.	Campbell	Walsh W.	Lishman D.	Robinson	Maund J.	Male N.	Brown W.S.	Alsop G.	Kelly F.	Blincow E.
Nov 30	(a)	Leytonstone	1	6-1	Wilshaw (2), Maund, Darby, Davies (2)	6,065	1	2		4	5	6		8	9	10	11				3						7					
Dec 14	(h)	Ipswich Town	2	0-0		11,438	1	2		4	5	6	9	8		10	11				3						7					
18	(a)	Ipswich Town	2R	1-0	Lishman	11,521	1	2		4	5	6				9	11				3				10		7		8			
Jan 11	(h)	Liverpool	3	2-5	Kelly, Wilshaw	18,370	1	2		4	5	6		8		11					3				10					7	9	
						Apps	4	4		4	4	4	1	3	1	4	3				4				2		3		1	1	1	
						Goals									1	3	2								1		1				1	

SEASON 1947-48

Division 3(S)

Date		Opponent		Score	Scorers	Att	Lewis J.	Methley I.	Skidmore. W	Walters H.	Foulkes R.E.	Newman A.	Maund J.	Walsh W.	Massart D.	Lishman D.	Wilshaw D.	Mullard A.	Male N.A.	Campbell J.	Guest W.	Brown W.S.	McGowan K.J.	Robinson J.	Crutchley R.	Devlin J.	Condie J.	Kelly F.C.	Humphries C.W.	Davies K.
Aug 23	(h)	Exeter City	W	4-0	Massart (3), Lishman	15,096	1	2	3	4	5	6	7	8	9	10	11													
27	(h)	Leyton Orient	W	3-1	Massart (3)	16,804	1	2	3	4	5	6	7	8	9	10	11													
30	(a)	Newport County	L	2-4	Maund, Lishman	16,000	1	2	3	4	5	6	7	8	9	10	11													
Sep 4	(a)	Leyton Orient	W	1-0	Lishman	12,708	1	2	3	4	5	6	7	8	9	10	11													
6	(h)	Southend Utd	W	6-0	Massart (3), Wilshaw (2), Lishman	18,213	1	2	3	4	5	6	7	8	9	10	11													
11	(h)	Reading	D	0-0		17,523	1	2	3	4	5	6	7	8	9	10	11													
13	(a)	Notts County	L	0-1		18,000	1	2	3	4	5	6	7	8	9	10	11													
17	(a)	Reading	W	1-0	Wilshaw	11,319	1	2	3	4	5	6			9		10	8		7	11									
20	(h)	Swansea Town	W	2-1	Paul (og), Wilshaw	17,996	1	2	3	4	5	6			9		10	8		7	11									
27	(a)	Bournemouth	D	1-1	Lishman	19,500	1	2		4	5	6			9	8	10		3	7	11									
Oct 4	(h)	Ipswich Town	L	1-2	Lishman	18,394	1	2		4	5	6		8	9	10	11		3	7										
11	(h)	Northampton	W	2-0	Wilshaw, Massart	14,988	1	2		4	5	6		8	9	10	11		3	7										
18	(a)	Bristol Rovers	W	3-2	Lishman (2), Massart	17,573	1	2		4	5	6	7	8	9	10	11		3											
25	(h)	Norwich City	W	3-2	Massart (2), Walsh	15,934	1	2		4	5	6	7	8	9	10	11		3											
Nov 1	(a)	Brighton	W	4-0	Massart (4)	10,000	1	2		4	5	6	7	8	9	10	11		3											
8	(h)	Watford	W	2-0	Massart, Lishman	18,004	1	2		4	5	6	7	8	9	10	11		3											
15	(a)	QPR	L	1-2	Lishman	26,100	1	2		4	5	6	7	8	9	10	11		3											
22	(h)	Port Vale	L	1-2	Massart	15,359	1	2		4	5	6		7	9	10	11		3			8								
Dec 6	(h)	Crystal Palace	D	1-1	McGowan	10,669	1	2		4	5	6	7	8		10	11		3				9							
25	(h)	Aldershot	W	3-0	Devlin, McGowan, Crutchley	16,608	1	2		4	5	6					11		3	7			9		8	10				
27	(a)	Aldershot	L	1-3	Devlin	6,400	1	2		4	5	6	7				11		3				9		8	10				
Jan 3	(h)	Newport County	D	1-1	Wilshaw	16,847	1	2		4	5				9		11		3		10			6		8	7			
17	(a)	Southend Utd	D	1-1	Lishman	9,000	1	2		4	5	6			9	10	11		3				7			8				
24	(a)	Crystal Palace	W	3-2	Massart (2), Crutchley	11,600	1	2		4	5	6			9	10	11		3				7		8					
31	(h)	Notts County	W	2-1	Devlin, McGowan	20,383	1	2			5	6			9	10	11		3				7		4	8				
Feb 7	(a)	Swansea Town	D	1-1	Massart	15,000	1				5	6	7		9	10	11								4	8		2	3	
14	(h)	Bournemouth	D	0-0		18,153	1			2	5	6	7		9	10	11		3						4	8				
21	(a)	Ipswich Town	L	1-3	Massart	7,897	1			2	5	6			9	10	11		3						4	8	7			
28	(a)	Northampton	L	1-2	Devlin	8,000	1			2	5	6			9	10	11		3						4	8	7			
Mar 6	(h)	Bristol Rovers	W	2-0	Davies, Devlin	13,442	1			4	5	6				10			3				9			8	7	2		11
13	(a)	Norwich City	L	0-1		22,880	1			4	5	6			9	10			3							8	7	2		11
20	(h)	Brighton	D	0-0		11,765	1			4	5	6				9	10		3							8	7	2		11
26	(a)	Bristol City	D	0-0		24,520	1			3	5	6		8		10									9	4	7	2		11
27	(a)	Watford	L	0-2		16,000	1			3	5	6		8		10									9	4	7	2		11
29	(h)	Bristol City	W	2-0	Devlin (pen), Kelly	12,743	1		3	4	5	6				10					11					8	7	9	2	
Apr 3	(h)	QPR	L	0-1		17,872	1		3	4	5	6				10							9			8	7		2	11
10	(a)	Port Vale	W	1-0	Lishman	13,000	1		3	4	5	6				10	11						9			8	7		2	
15	(h)	Torquay	W	1-0	Lishman	11,914	1		3	4	5	6				10	11						9			8	7		2	
17	(h)	Swindon Town	W	1-0	Wilshaw	10,094	1		3	4	5	6				10	11									8	7	9	2	
21	(a)	Exeter City	W	6-0	Wilshaw, Lishman, Kelly (2), Devlin (2)	6,500	1		3	4	5	6				10	11		2							8	7	9		
24	(a)	Torquay	L	2-3	Lishman (2)	7,000	1		3	4	5	6				10	11		2							8	7	9		
28	(a)	Swindon	W	3-0	Lishman (2), Kelly	8,000	1		3	4	5	6				10	11		2							8	7	9		
						Apps	42	25	17	40	42	41	16	18	27	37	36	2	25	6	5	1	10	1	10	22	16	11	6	6
League position: 3rd						Goals							1	1	23	18	8						3		2	8		4		1

Own goal: 1

F.A. Cup

Date		Opponent	Rd	Score	Scorers	Att	Lewis J.	Methley I.	Skidmore. W	Walters H.	Foulkes R.E.	Newman A.	Maund J.	Walsh W.	Massart D.	Lishman D.	Wilshaw D.	Mullard A.	Male N.A.	Campbell J.	Guest W.	Brown W.S.	McGowan K.J.	Robinson J.	Crutchley R.	Devlin J.	Condie J.	Kelly F.C.	Humphries C.W.	Davies K.
Nov 29	(a)	Vauxhall Motors	1	2-1	Maund, Walsh (pen)	11,721	1	2		4	5	6	7	8	9	10	11		3											
Dec 12	(a)	Norwich City	2	2-2	McGowan, Lishman	24,343	1	2		4	5	6	7			8	11		3				9	10						
20	(h)	Norwich City	2R	3-2	Crutchley, Wilshaw, Lishman	13,464	1	2	3	4	5	6				10	11			7			9		8					
Jan 10	(a)	Coventry City	3	1-2	Lishman	34,278	1	2		4	5	6	7		9	10	11		3							8				
						Apps	4	4	1	4	4	4	3	1	2	4	4		3	1			2	1	1	1				
						Goals							1	1		3	1						1	1						

SEASON 1948-49

Division 3(S)

Date		Opponent		Score	Scorers	Att	Lewis J.	Jones S.	Male N.	Walters H.	Foulkes R.	Newman A.	Condie J.	Devlin J.	Mullard A.	Morgan A.S.	Tinkler L.	Wilshaw D.	Aldred A.	McLaughlin J.	Skidmore W.	Ross L.	McGowan K.	Chapman P.E.	Clark T.	Methley I.	Milligan D.	Haynes A.E.	Crutchley R.	Russon R.	Giles P.	Heseltine G.	Smith J.	Davis C.	Steel A.
Aug 21	(a)	Norwich City	W	2-1	Tobin (og), Condie	27,269	1	2	3	4	5	6	7	8	9	10	11																		
26	(a)	Notts County	L	0-2		36,566	1	2	3	4	5	6	7	8	9	10		11																	
28	(h)	Torquay United	D	1-1	Wilshaw	18,026	1	2	3	4	5	6		8	9	10		11	7																
Sep 2	(h)	Notts County	W	3-2	Devlin (3, 1 pen)	16,036	1	2		4	5	6	7	8		10		11		9	3														
4	(a)	Bristol Rovers	L	0-3		17,244	1	2		4	5	6	7	8		10	11			9	3														
8	(a)	Bournemouth	L	0-2		14,771	1	2		4	5	6	7	8		10			11	9		3													
11	(h)	Newport County	W	3-1	Morgan, Devlin (2)	12,711	1	2		4	5	6	7	8		10	11			9		3													
16	(h)	Bournemouth	D	0-0		13,631	1	2		4	5	6	7	8		10	11			9		3													
18	(a)	Swansea Town	L	1-3	McGowan	27,780	1	2	3	4	5	6	7		8	10	11						9												
25	(h)	Reading	W	2-0	Chapman, Devlin	13,368	1	2		4	5	6		8			11		7			3		9	10										
Oct 2	(a)	Crystal Palace	W	3-1	Devlin (2), Chapman	16,400	1	2		4	5	6		8			11		7			3		9	10										
9	(a)	Exeter City	L	1-2	Devlin	10,844	1	2	3	4	5	6		8			11		7					9	10										
16	(h)	Bristol City	L	0-1		13,979	1		3	4	5	6	7	8		10						11				2	9								
23	(a)	Aldershot	W	1-0	Mullard	8,868	1		3	4	5	6		10	8		11									2	9	7							
30	(h)	Brighton	D	0-0		11,407	1		3	4	5	6			8		11									2	9	7	10						
Nov 6	(a)	Port Vale	W	2-0	Newman, Aldred	10,924	1		3	4	5	6		10	8		11		7					9		2									
13	(h)	Millwall	L	5-6	Condie, Chapman (2), Male (2)	9,604	1		3	4	5	6	11	10	8				7					9		2									
20	(a)	Swindon Town	L	1-2	Chapman	13,037	1			4	5	6	11	10	8				7		3			9		2									
Dec 18	(h)	Norwich City	W	4-1	Chapman (2), Low (og), Devlin	9,728	1	2		4	5	6		10	8		11		7		3			9											
25	(h)	Ipswich Town	W	2-1	Mullard, Chapman	12,956	1	2		4	5	6	7	10	8		11				3			9											
27	(a)	Ipswich Town	L	2-3	Chapman (2)	10,432	1	2		4	5	6	7	10	8		11				3			9											
Jan 1	(a)	Torquay United	L	1-5	Chapman	4,992	1	2		4	5	6	7	10	8		11				3			9											
15	(h)	Bristol Rovers	L	0-1		11,111	1	2		3	5	6	11	10	8				7					9					4						
22	(a)	Newport County	D	1-1	Chapman	14,500	1	2		3	5	6	11	10	8				7					9					4						
Feb 5	(h)	Swansea Town	W	2-1	Milligan, Chapman	14,634	1	2		3	5	6	11		8									7	10	4	9								
12	(a)	Northampton Tn	W	1-0	Clark	8,800	1	2		3	5	6	11		8									7	10	4	9								
19	(a)	Reading	L	0-1		15,367	1	2		3	5	6	7		8		11							9	10	4									
26	(h)	Crystal Palace	W	3-1	Chapman (3)	12,955	1	2		4	5		7	6	8									9	10	3							11		
Mar 5	(h)	Exeter City	W	4-3	Devlin, Chapman (3)	6,028	1	2		4	5	6	7	10	8									9		3							11		
12	(a)	Bristol City	D	2-2	Clark, Chapman	11,726	1	2		4	5	6	7	10	8									9	11	3									
19	(h)	Aldershot	D	0-0		11,314	1	2		4	5		11	8	7									9	10	3				6					
26	(a)	Brighton	W	2-1	Chapman, Mullard	13,514	1	2		4	5	6	7	8	10		11				3			9											
Apr 2	(h)	Port Vale	D	1-1	Skidmore (pen)	9,767	1	2		4	5	6	7	8	10		11				3			9											
6	(a)	Southend Utd	L	0-2		8,860	1	2		4	8	6			7						3	11		9					10	5					
9	(a)	Millwall	L	1-2	Crutchley	17,527	1	2		4	8	6			7							3		9					10	5	11				
15	(h)	Watford	L	0-2		10,955	1	2		4	5	6	7	8	10									9		3					11				
16	(h)	Swindon Town	L	0-1		9,831	1	2		4	5		7		8									9		3			10	6	11				
18	(h)	Watford	L	0-1		7,167	1	2		4	9	6		10	7									8		3				5	11				
23	(a)	Leyton Orient	D	1-1	Chapman	9,412	1	2		4	5			10	7									9		3				6	11	8			
28	(h)	Leyton Orient	L	2-3	Chapman (2)	4,533	1	2		4	5			10	7									9		3				6	11	8			
30	(h)	Southend Utd	L	0-3		4,144	1	2		4	5		11	10	7											3				6		8		9	
May 7	(h)	Northampton Tn	W	2-0	Jones, Chapman	5,995		2		4	5			10	7									9		3			6		11	8			1
						Apps	41	36	10	42	42	35	28	34	33	10	18	3	11	5	10	8	1	29	9	20	5	2	7	8	7	4	2	1	1
League position: 14th						Goals		1	2			1	2	11	3	1		1	1		1		1	25	2		1		1						

Own goals: 2

F.A. Cup

Date		Opponent	Rd	Score	Scorers	Att	Lewis J.	Jones S.	Male N.	Walters H.	Foulkes R.	Newman A.	Condie J.	Devlin J.	Mullard A.	Morgan A.S.	Tinkler L.	Wilshaw D.	Aldred A.	McLaughlin J.	Skidmore W.	Ross L.	McGowan K.	Chapman P.E.	Clark T.	Methley I.	Milligan D.	Haynes A.E.	Crutchley R.	Russon R.	Giles P.	Heseltine G.	Smith J.	Davis C.	Steel A.
Nov 27	(h)	Bristol Rovers	1	2-1	Chapman, Aldred	14,660	1	2		4	5	6	11	8	10				7		3			9											
Dec 11	(h)	Gainsboro Tn	2	4-3	Chapman (2), Walters, Condie	11,471	1	2		4	5	6	11	10	8				7		3			9											
Jan 8	(a)	Fulham	3	1-0	Devlin	24,308	1	2		3	5	6	11	10	8				7					9					4						
29	(a)	Luton Town	4	0-4		26,422	1	2		3	5	6	11	8	10				7					9					4						
						Apps	4	4		4	4	4	4	4	4				4		2			4					2						
						Goals				1			1	1					1					3											

SEASON 1949-50

Division 3(S)

Date		Opponent	Res	Score	Scorers	Att	Lewis J.	Jones S.	Methley I.	Walters H.	Foulkes R.E.	Newman A.	Medd G.E.	Whitehouse J.E.	Chapman P.E.	Devlin J.	Condie J.	Morris G.	Russon R.	McLaughlin J.	Giles P.	Steel A.	Betts E.	Crutchley R.	Atkinson P.	Skidmore W.	Green W.	Hewitt R.	McMorran R.	Heseltine G.V.	Corbett A.B.	Dearson D.
Aug 20	(h)	Aldershot	D	0-0		13,890	1	2	3	4	5	6	7	8	9	10	11															
24	(a)	Torquay Utd	L	1-2	Devlin	11,500	1	2	3	4	5	6	7	8	9	10		11														
27	(a)	Nottingham For	L	0-1		26,888	1	2	3	4	5		7		9	10			6	8	11											
Sep 1	(h)	Torquay Utd	W	7-1	Devlin (5), Whitehouse, Russon	10,996	1	2	3	4	5		11	8	9	10			6	7												
3	(h)	Northampton	L	1-3	Devlin	14,066		2	3	4	5		7	8	9	10			6			1	11									
7	(a)	Crystal Palace	L	0-2		12,202	1	2	3	4	5		11		9	10			6	7				8								
10	(a)	Norwich City	L	2-3	Chapman, Devlin	25,429	1	2	3	4	5		7		9	10			6	8	11											
17	(h)	Newport	W	2-0	Chapman (2)	10,846	1	2	3	4	5		7		9	10			6	8			11									
24	(a)	Bristol City	L	1-2	Morris	19,020	1	2	3	4	5		7		9	10		8	6				11									
Oct 1	(h)	Brighton	W	4-2	Medd, Whitehouse (2), Chapman	10,709	1	2	3	4	5		7	8	9			10	6				11									
8	(h)	Bournemouth	D	1-1	Whitehouse	12,224	1	2	3	4	5	6	7	8	9			10					11									
15	(a)	Bristol Rovers	D	1-1	Devlin	14,185	1	2	3	4	5		7	9		10		8					11				6					
22	(h)	Southend	D	1-1	Morris	9,909	1		2	4	5		7	9		10		8					11			3	6					
29	(a)	Notts County	D	1-1	Medd	42,676	1		2	4	5		7	8		9							11			3	6			10		
Nov 5	(h)	Port Vale	W	1-0	Devlin	9,605	1		2	4	5	6	7	8		9							11			3				10		
12	(a)	Ipswich	W	5-1	Hewitt (2), Devlin (2), Whitehouse	10,749	1		2	4	5	6		10		9							11			3		7		8		
19	(h)	Exeter City	W	3-0	Whitehouse (2), Betts	8,702	1		2	4	5	6		10		9							11			3		7		8		
Dec 3	(h)	Reading	W	2-0	Chapman, Betts	8,140	1		2	4	5	6	7		9	10							11			3		8				
17	(a)	Aldershot	L	0-1		4,034	1	2		4	5	6		8	9	10							11			3		7				
24	(h)	Nottingham For	L	1-3	Devlin	10,910	1	2		4	5	6		10		9				8			11			3		7				
26	(h)	Millwall	L	0-1		10,409	1			2	5	6	7	10		9				8			11			3	4					
27	(a)	Millwall	D	1-1	Chapman	27,012	1			2	5	6		8	9	10			4				11			3		7				
31	(a)	Northampton	L	0-2		12,349	1			2	5	6	7	8	9	10			4				11			3						
Jan 14	(h)	Norwich	D	1-1	Corbett	9,960	1	2		4	5	6			9						11		10			3		7			8	
21	(a)	Newport	L	1-2	Corbett	8,840	1	2		4	5	6			9						11		10			3		7			8	
28	(a)	Orient	D	2-2	Corbett, Chapman	7,251	1	2		3					9	6			5	7			11	4			10				8	
Feb 4	(h)	Bristol City	D	1-1	Devlin	9,060	1	2		3					9	6			5	7			11	4			10				8	
11	(a)	Watford	L	0-3		10,768	1	2		3					9	6			5				11	4			10		7		8	
18	(a)	Brighton	D	1-1	Devlin	12,357	1	2		3			11	9		6			5					4			10		7		8	
25	(a)	Bournemouth	D	1-1	Corbett	11,911	1	2		3	9	6	11						5					4			10		7		8	
Mar 4	(h)	Bristol Rovers	W	3-1	Foulkes, Devlin, Betts	9,179	1	2		3	9					10			5				11	4			6		7		8	
11	(a)	Southend Utd	D	2-2	McMorran, Devlin	9,510	1	2		3	9					10			5				11	4			6		7		8	
18	(h)	Notts County	D	3-3	Devlin (2), Foulkes	19,589	1	2		3	9					10			5				11	4			6		7			8
25	(a)	Port Vale	L	0-2		10,040	1	2		3					9	10			5				11	4			6		7			8
Apr 1	(h)	Ipswich	L	1-3	Devlin	8,765	1	2		3					9	10			5				11	4			6		7			8
7	(h)	Swindon Town	D	0-0		8,305	1	2		3	9					10	7		5				11	4			6					8
8	(a)	Exeter City	L	1-2	Devlin	9,291	1	2		4	9					10	7		5				11			3	6					8
10	(a)	Swindon Town	L	3-4	Dearson, Foulkes, Devlin	10,218	1	2		4	9					10	7		5				11			3	6					8
15	(h)	Orient	L	1-2	Chapman	7,347	1	2		4	5		11		9	10	7		6							3						8
22	(a)	Reading	D	1-1	Foulkes	10,693		2		4	9	6	7			10			5						1	3	11					8
29	(h)	Watford	D	1-1	Foulkes	4,017	1	2		4	9	6		7		10			5							3	11					8
May 6	(h)	Crystal Palace	W	3-1	Dearson (2), Whitehouse	5,379	1	2		4	9			7		10			5							3	11				10	8
						Apps	40	33	18	42	36	17	22	20	23	37	5	6	27	9	4	1	30	12	1	19	20	8	8	4	10	10
League position: 19th						Goals					5		2	8	8	22		2	1				3					2	1		4	3

F.A. Cup

Date		Opponent	Rd	Score	Scorers	Att	Lewis J.	Jones S.	Methley I.	Walters H.	Foulkes R.E.	Newman A.	Medd G.E.	Whitehouse J.E.	Chapman P.E.	Devlin J.	Condie J.	Morris G.	Russon R.	McLaughlin J.	Giles P.	Steel A.	Betts E.	Crutchley R.	Atkinson P.	Skidmore W.	Green W.	Hewitt R.	McMorran R.	Heseltine G.V.	Corbett A.B.	Dearson D.
Nov 26	(a)	Mansfield	1	1-4	Skidmore	16,300	1	2		4	5	6	8	10		9							11			3		7			8	
						Apps	1	1		1	1	1	1	1		1							1			1		1			1	
						Goals																				1						

SEASON 1950-51

Division 3(S)

Date	Opponents	Res	Score	Scorers	Att	Lewis J.	Jones S.	Walters H.	Devlin J.	Russon R.	Green W.	Morris F.	Millard R.	Sutcliffe F.W.J.	Dearson D.	Allison J.	Chapman P.E.	Skidmore W.	Bowen T.H.	Corbett A.B	Knowles H.F	Methley I.	Holding E.	Hughes J.	Bridgett J.	Dean G.	Winter J.	O'Neill W.A.
Aug 19 (a)	Reading	L	1-2	Allison (pen)	21,793	1	2	3	4	5	6	7	8	9	10	11												
24 (h)	Plymouth Argyle	D	1-1	Chapman	14,270	1	2	3	4	5	6	7	8		10	11	9											
26 (h)	Southend Utd	L	1-2	Chapman	11,178	1	2	4		5			10	8	6	11	9	3	7									
30 (h)	Plymouth Argyle	D	1-1	Corbett	12,015	1	2	4		5			10		6	11	9	3	7	8								
Sep 2 (a)	Exeter City	L	0-1		10,712	1	2	3	10	5	6				4	11	9		7	8								
7 (h)	Norwich City	L	0-1		10,831	1	2	3	10	5	6				4	11	9		7	8								
9 (h)	Bournemouth	L	0-1		8,787	1	2	3		5	6	7	8		10		9			4	11							
13 (a)	Norwich	L	0-1		28,204	1	2	3		5	6	7	8		10		9			4	11							
16 (a)	Gillingham	L	1-4	Knowles	14,626	1	2			5	6	7		9	10					8	11	3	4					
23 (h)	Bristol City	W	3-1	Morris, Dearson (2)	8,593	1	2	4	10	5	6	7			9				8		11	3						
30 (a)	Millwall Ath	L	0-2		24,012	1	2	4	10	5	6	7			9				8		11	3						
Oct 7 (a)	Northampton	D	1-1	Dearson	12,190	1	2	4	10	5	6	7			9				8		11	3						
14 (h)	Port Vale	W	2-0	Morris, Hughes	9,686	1	2	4	9		6	7			5				8		11	3		10				
21 (a)	Nottingham For	L	0-4		26,366	1	2	4	9		6	7			5				8		11	3		10				
28 (h)	Torquay Utd	W	3-1	Dearson, (pen) Devlin, Hughes	7,793	1	2	4	9		6	7			5				8		11	3		10				
Nov 4 (a)	Aldershot	L	0-3		7,056	1	2	4	9		6	7			5	11			8			3		10				
11 (h)	Swindon Town	W	1-0	Millard	7,795	1	2	3	4	5	6		7		8	11	9							10				
18 (a)	Colchester	W	1-0	Chapman	9,554	1	2	3	4	5	6				8	11	9		7	10								
Dec 2 (a)	Crystal Palace	L	0-1		12,083	1	2	3	4	5	6	11			8				7	10					9			
16 (h)	Reading	L	1-2	Dearson	3,677	1	2	3	10	5	6	11			4				7	8					9			
23 (a)	Southend Utd	W	1-0	Devlin	8,064	1	2	3	10	5	6	11			4				7	8					9			
25 (h)	Newport Co	D	0-0		8,009	1	2	3	10	5	6				4				7	8				11	9			
26 (a)	Newport Co	L	0-3		14,870	1	2	3	10	5					6				7	8				11	9	4		
30 (h)	Exeter	L	0-2		4,275	1	2	3	10	5		7	8		6		9							11		4		
Jan 6 (a)	Ipswich	L	1-3	Devlin	9,530	1	2	3	10	5		7	8				9			6				11		4		
13 (a)	Bournemouth	L	1-3	Dearson	10,683	1	2	3	10	5					8	11			7	6					9	4		
20 (h)	Gillingham	W	2-1	Winter (2)	8,817	1	2	4	6	5				8		11		3	7								9	10
27 (h)	Ipswich Town	W	2-0	Dearson, Rees (og)	9,334	1	2	4	6	5					8	11		3	7								9	10
Feb 3 (a)	Bristol City	D	3-3	Dearson (2), Skidmore (pen)	15,512	1	2	4	6	5					8	11		3	7								9	10
10 (h)	Aldershot	W	3-1	O'Neill (2), Skidmore (pen)	9,967	1	2	4	6	5					8	11		3	7								9	10
15 (h)	Bristol Rovers	L	1-2	Winter	6,090	1	2	4	6	5					8	11		3	7								9	10
17 (h)	Millwall Ath	W	4-0	Skidmore (2, 1 pen), Devlin, Dearson	8,781	1	2	4	6	5					8	11		3	7					10			9	
24 (h)	Northampton	W	1-0	Bowen	11,941	1	2	4	6	5					8	11		3	7								9	10
Mar 3 (a)	Port Vale	D	1-1	Walters	13,110	1	2	4	6	5					8	11		3	7								9	10
10 (h)	Nottingham For	L	0-2		14,247	1	2	4	6	5					8	11		3	7								9	10
17 (a)	Torquay Utd	L	2-3	Winter, O'Neill	5,500	1	2	4	6	5					8	11		3	7								9	10
23 (a)	Leyton Orient	L	1-2	Winter	9,027	1	2	4	6	5					8	11		3	7								9	10
26 (h)	Leyton Orient	D	1-1	Skidmore (pen)	8,437	1	2	4	6	5					8	11		3	7								9	10
31 (a)	Swindon	D	1-1	Hughes	7,044	1	2	4	6	5					3	11			7					8			9	10
Apr 7 (h)	Colchester	W	4-2	Winter (3), Hughes	7,907	1	2	4	6	5					3	11			7					8			9	10
14 (a)	Bristol Rovers	D	1-1	Hughes	13,896	1	2	4	6	5					3	11			7					8			9	10
19 (h)	Watford	W	1-0	O'Neill	9,070	1	2	4	6	5					3	11			7					8			9	10
21 (h)	Crystal Palace	D	0-0		7,830	1	2	4	6	5					3	11			7					8			9	10
28 (a)	Brighton	L	0-1		9,887	1	2	4	6	5	3					11			7					8			9	10
May 3 (h)	Brighton	W	1-0	Bowen	5,669	1	2	4	6	5	3					11			7	8							9	10
5 (a)	Watford	W	3-1	Winter (2), Walters	6,524	1	2	4	6		3		8			11			7					10	5		9	
					Apps	46	46	45	41	41	23	17	10	4	41	30	11	14	38	15	9	8	1	17	7	4	20	18
League position: 15th					Goals			2	4			2	1		10	1	3	5	2	1	1			5			10	4

Own goal: 1

F.A. Cup

Date	Opponents	Rd	Score	Scorers	Att	Lewis J.	Jones S.	Walters H.	Devlin J.	Russon R.	Green W.	Morris F.	Millard R.	Sutcliffe F.W.J.	Dearson D.	Allison J.	Chapman P.E.	Skidmore W.	Bowen T.H.	Corbett A.B	Knowles H.F	Methley I.	Holding E.	Hughes J.	Bridgett J.	Dean G.	Winter J.	O'Neill W.A.
Nov 25 (a)	Newport Co	1	2-4	Corbett (2)	13,800	1	2	3	4	5	6				8	11	9		7	10								
					Apps	1	1	1	1	1	1				1	1	1		1	1								
					Goals															2								

Festival of Britain game

May 7 (h) R.C. Haarlem W 1-0 Hughes 5,597 Team: Lewis; Jones; Green; Walters; Bridgett; Devlin; Bowen; Millard; Winter; Hughes; Allison.

SEASON 1951-52

Division 3(S)

Date	Venue	Opponent	Res	Score	Scorers	Att	Lewis J.	Jones S.	Green W.	Walters H.	Russon R.	Devlin J.	Bowen T.H	O'Neill W.	Winter J.	Evans H.	Allison J.	Bridgett J.	Holding E.	Morris F.	Hughes J.	Aston P.	Giles P.	Dean G.	Atkinson P.	Stockin R.	Millington J.H.	Barber J.	Chilvers G.	Montgomery A.
Aug 18	(h)	Bristol Rovers	W	1-0	Evans	10,798	1	2	3	4	5	6	7	8	9	10	11													
23	(h)	Aldershot	W	1-0	Evans	10,104	1	2	3	4	5	6	7	8	9	10	11													
25	(a)	Plymouth Argyle	L	0-3		12,991	1	2	3	4	5	6	7	8	9	10	11													
29	(a)	Aldershot	L	1-3	Devlin	6,873	1	2	3	4	5	6	7	8	9	10	11													
Sept 1	(h)	Norwich City	W	4-0	Evans (3), O'Neill	10,600	1	2	3	4	5	6	7	8		10	11	9												
3	(a)	Shrewsbury Tn	W	2-1	O'Neill, Evans	10,414	1	2	3	4	5	6	7	8		10	11	9												
8	(a)	Exeter City	L	0-1		8,500	1	2	3	4	5	6	7	8		10	11	9												
13	(h)	Shrewsbury Tn	L	0-4		12,216	1	2	3	4	5	6	7	8		10	11	9												
15	(h)	Colchester Utd	L	1-3	O'Neill	7,327	1	3	9	4	5	6		8		10	11		2	7										
19	(a)	Leyton Orient	L	0-3		7,926	1	3	9	4	5	6		8		10	11		2	7										
22	(a)	Crystal Palace	L	1-2	Evans	15,819	1		9	3	5	6		8		10	11		2	7		4								
29	(h)	Swindon Town	D	0-0		8,004	1		3	6	5		7	8	9	10	11		2			4								
Oct 6	(h)	Bournemouth	D	2-2	Evans (2)	8,242	1		3	6	5		7	8	9	10	11		2			4								
13	(a)	Millwall	L	1-2	Winter	20,005	1		3	6	5	8	7		9	10	11		2			4								
20	(h)	Brighton	D	1-1	Hughes	6,309	1		3	6	5	4	7		9	10	11		2		8									
27	(a)	Gillingham	L	1-4	Devlin	14,500	1		3	6	5	4	7		9	10	11		2		8									
Nov 3	(h)	Torquay Utd	L	2-3	Evans (2)	4,963	1		3	6	5		7			10	11	9	2			4	8							
10	(a)	Ipswich Town	W	1-0	Bridgett	10,070	1		3	6	5		7	8		10		9	2				11	4						
17	(h)	Bristol City	W	2-0	Bridgett, Giles	6,549	1		3	6	5		7	8		10		9	2				11	4						
Dec 1	(h)	Northampton Tn	W	3-0	Bowen, O'Neill, Bridgett	7,676	1		3	6	5		7	8		10		9	2				11	4						
8	(a)	Reading	L	0-3		12,034	1		3	6	5	4	7	8		10		9	2				11							
22	(h)	Plymouth Argyle	L	2-5	Bridgett (2)	7,991	1		3	6	5		7	10		8		9	2			4	11							
25	(h)	Southend Utd	W	2-0	O'Neill, Bridgett	7,484	1		3	44	5		7	8		10		9	2			6	11							
26	(a)	Southend Utd	L	0-3		15,000			1	3	5		7	8		10		9	2		6	4	11							
29	(a)	Norwich City	L	0-8		18,661			3	4	5		7					9	2		10	6	11		1	8				
Jan 5	(h)	Exeter City	L	1-2	O'Neill (pen)	8,717	1	2	3	4	5		7	8		10		9				6	11							
19	(a)	Colchester Utd	L	2-3	Stockin, Giles	7,240	1	2	6	3	5		7		9	10			4				11			8				
24	(h)	Leyton Orient	L	2-4	Stockin, O'Neill (pen)	2,023	1	2	6	3	5		7	10	9				4				11			8				
26	(h)	Crystal Palace	W	3-0	Holding, Giles, Bowen	4,666	1	2	3	4	5		7			10			9				11			8	6			
Feb 2	(h)	Watford	W	3-1	Stockin, Holding, Giles	6,581	1	2	3	4	5		7			10			9				11			8	6			
9	(a)	Swindon Tn	D	1-1	Holding	10,270	1	2	3	4	5	6							9		10		11			8		7		
16	(a)	Bournemouth	L	1-2	Hughes	8,763	1	2	3	4	5		7	10					9		8		11				6			
23	(a)	Watford	L	0-2		8,636	1	2	3	4	5		7	10		8			9				11				6			
Mar 1	(h)	Millwall Ath	L	1-2	Morris	7,069	1	2	3		5			10					4	9	8		11				6	7		
8	(a)	Brighton	L	1-5	Green	15,757	1	2	3	4	5	10			8					9			11				6	7		
15	(h)	Gillingham	W	1-0	Winter	6,942	1	2	5			8		10	9					7			11	4			6			3
22	(a)	Torquay Utd	D	1-1	Devlin	7,594	1	2	5			8	7	10	9									4			6	11		3
29	(h)	Ipswich Town	L	1-3	O'Neill	3,173	1	2	5			8	7	10	9									4			6	11		3
Apr 5	(a)	Bristol City	L	0-2		6,842	1	2	5	4		10	7		9									8			6	11		3
11	(a)	Newport County	L	2-4	O'Neill, Giles	9,600		2	5	4			7	8	9	10							11				6		1	3
12	(h)	Port Vale	W	3-0	O'Neill (2), Evans	7.518		2	5	6			7	8	9	10							11	4					1	3
14	(h)	Newport County	L	0-1		7,725		2	5	6			7	8	9	10							11	4					1	3
19	(a)	Northampton Tn	L	1-4	Devlin	8,311		2	5	6		8	7		9	10							11	4					1	3
21	(a)	Port Vale	L	0-1		8,500		2	5	6		8	7		9	10							11	4					1	3
26	(h)	Reading	W	2-0	Devlin, Hughes	6,533		2	5	6		9	7	8		10					11			4					1	3
28	(a)	Bristol Rovers	L	1-5	O'Neill	9,309		2	5	6		9	7	8		10					11			4					1	3
						Apps	37	31	46	42	35	25	39	33	21	36	17	14	25	6	9	10	25	13	1	6	11	6	7	11
League position: 24th						Goals			1			5	2	12	2	12		6	3	1	3		5			3				

F.A. Cup

Date	Venue	Opponent	Rd	Score	Att	Lewis J.	Jones S.	Green W.	Walters H.	Russon R.	Devlin J.	Bowen T.H	O'Neill W.	Winter J.	Evans H.	Allison J.	Bridgett J.	Holding E.	Morris F.	Hughes J.	Aston P.	Giles P.	Dean G.
Nov 14	(a)	Reading	1	0-1	17,673	1		3	6	5		7	8		10		9	2				11	4
					Apps	1		1	1	1		1	1		1		1	1				1	1
					Goals																		

SEASON 1952-53

Division 3(S)

Date	Opponent	Result	Scorers	Att	Lewis J.	Rowe N.	Montgomery	Godderidge A.	Green W.	Walters H.	Morris F.	Knight J.W	Ealing W.H.	Driver A.	Hughes J.	Chilvers G.M	Freeman H.G.	Boyden J.	Dean G.	Bridgett J.	Russon. R	Milington J.H.	Horne L.	Howarth S.	Bowen T.	Duggins J.	McIntosh W.I	Wright G.D.	Scarlett	Giles P.	Edwards W.T.
Aug 23 (a)	Millwall Ath	L 0-3		22,228	1	2	3	4	5	6	7	8	9	10	11																
28 (h)	Newport County	L 1-3	Bridgett	10,062	1	2	3	4	5	6	7	8		10	11					9											
30 (h)	Bristol Rovers	L 3-5	Giles, Bridgett, Morris	8,023	1	2			5	6	7			8				3	4	9								10		11	
Sep 4 (a)	Newport County	L 2-3	Morris, Bridgett	8,731	1	2			5	6	7			8				3	4	9								10			11
6 (a)	Exeter City	L 1-6	Bridgett	11,955	1	2			5	4	7			8				3		9		6						10		11	
8 (a)	QPR	L 2-4	Dean, Morris	7,023					2	3	7			9		1			4	5		6				8		10			11
13 (h)	Coventry City	D 1-1	Driver	8,915	1	2			5	3	7			10					4	9		6				8					11
18 (h)	QPR	D 1-1	Dean	7,023	1	2			5	3	7			10					4	9		6				8					11
20 (a)	Norwich City	L 0-3		24,694	1	2			5		7			4				3		9		6				8		10			11
25 (h)	Reading	W 2-0	Bridgett, Driver	4,910	1	2			5	3	7			10					4	9				6		8					11
27 (h)	Colchester Utd	L 0-3		7,736	1	2			5	3	7			10					4	9				6		8					11
Oct 1 (a)	Swindon Town	W 2-1	Bridgett, Duggins	4,279	1	2			5	3	7			8					4	9				6		10					11
4 (a)	Aldershot	L 0-2		6,725	1	2			5	3	7			8					4	9				6		10					11
11 (a)	Crystal Palace	L 1-4	Morris	13,685	1	2			5	3	7			8					4	9				6		10					11
18 (h)	Bristol City	D 3-3	Morris, Bridgett, Giles	7,229	1				5	3	7						2		4	9				6	8	10				11	
25 (a)	Torquay Utd	W 3-0	Duggins (2), Giles	6,513	1				5	3	7			6			2		4	9					8	10				11	
Nov 1 (h)	Northampton Tn	L 1-5	Giles	8,420	1				5	3	7			6			2		4	9					8	10				11	
8 (a)	Leyton Orient	L 1-4	Bridgett	7,581	1		3		5		7			6			2		4	9						10	8			11	
15 (h)	Ipswich Town	L 1-3	Green (pen)	5,724					5	3	7			6		1	2		4	9							8		10	11	
Dec 6 (a)	Southend Utd	L 1-2	Green	8,079			3		6	4	7			10		1	2			9			5				8			11	
13 (h)	Watford	D 0-0		3,251			3		6	4	7					1	2			9			5				8		10	11	
20 (h)	Millwall Ath	L 0-2		3,357			3		6	4	7			10		1	2			9			5			8				11	
26 (a)	Gillingham	L 1-3	Green	9,326			3		10		9					1	2			4	6		5		7	8				11	
27 (h)	Gillingham	L 1-3	Giles	6,898			3		10	4	9					1	2		8		6		5		7					11	
Jan 3 (a)	Bristol Rovers	L 0-2		24,171			3		6		7			10		1	2			9	4		5				8				11
10 (a)	Watford	L 0-3		10,545			3		6		7			10		1	2			9	4		5				8				11
15 (h)	Shrewsbury Tn	D 4-4	McIntosh (2), Giles (2)	3,330			3		6		7			8	10	1	2				4		5				9			11	
17 (h)	Exeter City	D 2-2	McIntosh, Giles	6,775			3		6		7			8	10	1	2				4		5				9			11	
24 (a)	Coventry City	L 1-3	McIntosh	13,881	1				6	3	7			8	10		2				4		5				9			11	
Feb 5 (a)	Shrewsbury Tn	L 0-1		3,653	1				6	3	7			8	10		2				4		5				9			11	
7 (h)	Norwich City	W 3-2	Freeman, Green, McIntosh	6,850	1				6	3	7				10		2				4		5				9	8		11	
14 (a)	Colchester Utd	L 1-6	McIntosh	5,102	1				6	3	7				10		2				4		5				9	8		11	
21 (h)	Aldershot	D 0-0		6,545	1				6	3					10		2				4		5		7		9	8		11	
28 (h)	Crystal Palace	L 2-4	Bowen, Wright	5,931	1				6	3					10		2				4		5		7		9	8		11	
Mar 7 (a)	Bristol City	L 1-6	Green	16,702	1	2			6	3		8										4	5		7		9	10		11	
14 (h)	Torquay Utd	W 2-0	Dean, McIntosh	4,584		2			6	3		8				1			4				5		7		9	10		11	
21 (a)	Northampton Tn	L 1-2	McIntosh	9,717		2			6	3					10	1			4				5		7		9	8		11	
28 (h)	Leyton Orient	W 1-0	Morris	3,282		2			6	3	7				10	1			4				5				9	8		11	
Apr 3 (a)	Brighton	L 2-4	Bowen, Hughes	13,161		2			6	3					10	1				4			5		7		9	8		11	
4 (a)	Ipswich Town	L 0-5		6,801		2			6	3	7				10	1				4			5				9	8		11	
6 (h)	Brighton	W 3-0	Hughes, McIntosh, Green	4,513		2	3		8	4					10	1						6	5		7		9			11	
11 (a)	Reading	D 0-0		9,703		2	3		8	4					10	1				5		6			7		9			11	
18 (a)	Bournemouth	L 1-5	Giles	8,456		2	3	5	8	4					10	1				9		6			7					11	
23 (h)	Swindon Town	L 1-2	Bridgett	6,512		2	3		8	4					10	1				9		6	5		7					11	
25 (h)	Southend Utd	D 1-1	Bridgett	5.997		2	3		11	4						1				9		6	5		7			8		11	
30 (h)	Bournemouth	D 2-2	Bowen, Bridgett	3,857		2	3		10	4						1				9		6	5		7	8				11	
				Apps	24	25	18	3	46	39	34	4	1	26	18	22	20	4	19	31	12	12	25	6	17	16	22	16	2	32	12
League position: 24th				Goals					6		6			2	2		1		3	11					3	3	9	1		9	

F.A. Cup

Date	Opponent	Rd	Result	Scorers	Att	Lewis J.	Rowe N.	Montgomery	Godderidge A.	Green W.	Walters H.	Morris F.	Knight J.W	Ealing W.H.	Driver A.	Hughes J.	Chilvers G.M	Freeman H.G.	Boyden J.	Dean G.	Bridgett J.	Russon. R	Milington J.H.	Horne L.	Howarth S.	Bowen T.	Duggins J.	McIntosh W.I	Wright G.D.	Scarlett	Giles P.	Edwards W.T.
Nov 22 (a)	Newport County	1	1-2	Giles	9,253			3		6	4	9					1	2			5					7		8	10		11	
					Apps			1		1	1	1					1	1			1					1		1	1		1	
					Goals																										1	

SEASON 1953-54

Division 3(S)

Date	Opponent	Result	Scorers	Att	Chilvers	Horne L.	Green W.	Russon R.	Bridgett J.	Woodward H.	Grubb A.J.	Bromley T.	Morris F.	Nicholls R.	Lloyd P.	Holding E.	Dean G.	Scarlett J.	Flack D.	Finlay J.	Perry L.	Flavell J.	Slynn F.	Burgess R.	McCreadie E.	Allsopp N.	Jeffries R.	Jones G.	Tarrant J.	Colombo D.	Meek G.	Baldwin H.	Davis L.	Fort S.M	McClean W.G.	Bicknell J.B.	Lewis K.
Aug 19 (h)	Ipswich Town	L 0-2		13,075	1	2	3	4	5	6	7	8	9		11		10																				
22 (h)	Exeter City	D 1-1	Scarlett	10,428	1	9	3		5	6	7	8	11			2	4	10																			
27 (h)	Bristol City	D 0-0		15,158			3		5	6	7	8	11			2	4	10	1	9																	
29 (a)	Newport County	L 2-4	Bromley, Bridgett	7,784		9	3	4	5	6		8	11			2		10	1	7																	
Sep 1 (a)	Bristol City	L 1-4	Morris	14,502		2	6		5		7	8	11				4	10	1	9	3																
5 (h)	Norwich City	L 1-4	Morris	11,048		2	6		5		7	8	11				4	10	1	9	3																
10 (h)	Swindon Town	L 0-1		7,784			6		5	10		8	7		11		4		1		3	2															
12 (a)	QPR	L 0-2		12,266		2	9		5			8	11	6			4	10	1	7		3															
16 (a)	Swindon Town	L 0-3		8,832		2	6		5		7		11	10		4	8			9		3															
19 (h)	Southampton	W 1-0	Horne	9,666		5	4				7	10	11			2	8		1			3	6														
21 (a)	Shrewsbury Tn	L 1-4	Dean	7,727		5	4		9		7	10	11			2	8		1			3	6														
26 (a)	Colchester Utd	D 1-1	Burgess	8,992	1	2	4		5				7		11		8					3	6	9	10												
Oct 1 (h)	Shrewsbury Tn	D 0-0		8,031	1	2	4		5				7		11			10		8		3	6	9													
3 (h)	Crystal Palace	W 1-0	Morris	11,020	1	2	4		5			10	9				8			7		3	6		11												
10 (h)	Reading	L 1-3	Dean	10,944	1	2	5					10	9			4	8			7		3	6		11												
17 (a)	Leyton Orient	L 1-2	Dean	7,694	1	2	6		5		7	10	11			4	8					3			9												
24 (h)	Millwall Ath	L 0-2		10,178	1	2	4		5		7		9				8					3	6			10											
31 (a)	Ipswich Town	L 0-3		15,026		2	4	6	5				9		7		8		1			3	11			10											
Nov 7 (h)	Bournemouth	W 1-0	Morris	7,613	1	2	4	6	5				7				8					3	11			10	9										
14 (a)	Coventry City	L 0-2		11,064	1	2	4	6	5				7				8					3	11			10	9										
28 (a)	Northampton Tn	L 1-5	Green	12,561	1	2	4	6	5		11		7			9						3				10		8									
Dec 5 (h)	Torquay Utd	L 1-3	Morris	6,848	1	2	8	6	5		7		11									3					9	10	4								
19 (a)	Exeter City	L 1-2	Morris	6,500	1	2	6		5		7		11			9	4					3						10	8								
25 (h)	Brighton	W 3-1	Holding (3)	9,404	1	2	6		5				7			9	4		1			3						10	8	11							
26 (a)	Brighton	L 3-5	Morris (3)	17,512	1	2	6		5				7			9	4		1			3						10	8	11							
Jan 2 (h)	Newport County	L 0-1		6,187	1	2	6		5				7			9	4					3						10	8	11							
16 (a)	Norwich City	L 0-3		14,193	1		3		5		4		7							8		9						10	6	11							
23 (h)	QPR	W 2-0	Dean, Meek	8,734	1	2	3	5					9				4					3				8		10	6	11	7						
30 (h)	Aldershot	L 0-2		8,104	1	2			5				9				4									8		10	6	11	7						
Feb 13 (h)	Colchester Utd	L 2-3	Davis, Meek	9,819		2	3		5		6		7				4											10	8		11	1	9				
20 (a)	Crystal Palace	L 0-1		10,370			3		5				4																6		7	1	9	2	8	10	
24 (a)	Watford	L 1-3	Dean	3,748			3		5				4				10												6	11	7	1	9	2	8		
27 (a)	Reading	W 2-0	Dean (2)	9,721			3		5				4				8												6	11	7	1	9	2		10	
Mar 6 (h)	Leyton Orient	W 4-2	Colombo, Tarrant, Davis, Dean	9,759			3		5				4				8												6	11	7	1	9	2		10	
13 (a)	Gillingham	L 0-3		9,473			3		5				4				8												6	11	7	1	9	2			
17 (a)	Southampton	D 0-0		8,782			3	5					4				10												6	11	7	1	9	2			8
20 (h)	Northampton Tn	L 0-1		10,032			3	5					4				10												6	11	7	1	9	2			8
27 (a)	Bournemouth	D 1-1	Scarlett	7,567			3	5					4				10	11											6		7	1	9	2			8
Apr 3 (h)	Coventry City	W 1-0	Dean	8,728			3	5					4				10												6	11	7	1	9	2			8
7 (a)	Aldershot	L 1-3	Davis	4,089			3	5					4				10												6	11	7	1	9	2			8
10 (a)	Torquay Utd	L 1-3	Dean	5,524			3	5					4				8												6	11	7	1	9	2			10
16 (a)	Southend Utd	L 1-3	Allen	8,500			3	5					4				8												6	11	7	1	9	2			10
17 (h)	Watford	D 0-0		7,154			3	5					4				8												6	11	7	1	9	2			10
19 (h)	Southend Utd	W 2-0	Morris, Lewis	6,987			3	5					4													10			6	11	7	1	9	2			8
24 (a)	Millwall Ath	L 0-3		9,130			3	5					7							6						10				11		1	9	2			8
29 (a)	Gillingham	D 1-1	Tarrant	6,683			3	5					4																6	11	7	1	10	2			8
				Apps	17	27	45	19	32	5	15	13	46	2	5	13	37	8	11	11	3	22	10	2	4	9	3	10	24	20	18	17	17	16	2	3	11
League position: 24th				Goals		1	1		1			1	10			3	10	2						1					2	1	2		3				1

Also played: Smith G. (9) v QPR 12-9-53; Pidcock F. (1) v Swindon Town 16-9-53; Bailey A (9) v Southampton 19-9-53; Smith A. (11) v Millwall 24-10-53; Haddington J (11) v Crystal Palace 20-2-54; O'Shaunessey B (10) v Gillingham 13-3-54; Allen G v Southend 16-4-54 (1 goal) and (9) v Gillingham 29-4-54; Jones B. (2) v Norwich 16-1-54 and (4) v Millwall 24-4-54.

F.A. Cup

Date	Opponent	Rd	Result	Scorers	Att	Chilvers	Horne L.	Green W.	Russon R.	Bridgett J.	Woodward H.	Grubb A.J.	Bromley T.	Morris F.	Nicholls R.	Lloyd P.	Holding E.	Dean G.	Scarlett J.	Flack D.	Finlay J.	Perry L.	Flavell J.	Slynn F.	Burgess R.	McCreadie E.	Allsopp N.	Jeffries R.	Jones G.	Tarrant J.	Colombo D.	Meek G.	Baldwin H.	Davis L.	Fort S.M	McClean W.G.	Bicknell J.B.	Lewis K.
Nov 21 (a)	Bath City	1	3-0	Allsopp, Dean, Morris	10,700	1	2	4	6	5		11		7				10					3							8	9							
Dec 2 (h)	Crewe Alexandra	2	3-0	Holding (2), Jones G.	12,877	1	2	6		5		7		11			9	4					3							8		10						
Jan 9 (a)	Lincoln City	3	1-1	Finlay	13,870	1	2	3		5		4		7							8		9									10	6	11				
14 (h)	Lincoln City	R	1-1	Morris	16,536	1	2	3		5		4		7							8		9									10	6	11				
18 (n)	Lincoln City	2R*	1-2	Finlay	12,365	1		3		5		4		7				9			8		2									10	6	11				
					Apps	5	4	5	1	5		5		5			1	3			3		5							2	1	4	3	3				
* 2nd replay v. Lincoln City played at Nottingham Forest					Goals									2			2	1			2									1		1						

SEASON 1954-55

Division 3(S)

Date		Opponent		Score	Scorers	Att	McBride V.	Fort S.	Vinall A.	Ferriday L.	Bridgett J.	Tarrant J.E.	Meek G.	Lewis K.	Morris F.	Myerscough W.	Goffin W.	McGairy T.	Davis L.	Chilvers G.	McPherson	Baldwin H.	Taylor B.	Pritchett D.	Hall R.	Maher J.	Russon R.	Richards A.	Dorman D.	Beddow R.	Crook W.	Guttridge W.	Cousans W.E.	Knott W.	Love J.	Webb R.
Aug 21	(a)	Reading	D	2-2	Morris (2)	12,852	1	2	3	4	5	6	7	8	9	10	11																			
25	(a)	Brighton	L	0-3		17,211	1	2	3	4	5	6	7	8	9	10	11																			
28	(h)	Gillingham	L	0-1		15,484	1	2	3	4	5	6			7	10	11	8	9																	
Sep 2	(h)	Brighton	L	0-2		13,056		2	3	8	9	6	7		4	10	11			1	5															
4	(a)	Leyton Orient	L	0-1		12,104		2	3	4	5	6	11		7	10		8	9			1														
8	(a)	Torquay Utd	L	0-2		7,102		2	3	4	5	6			7	10	11	8	9			1														
11	(h)	Millwalll Ath	D	1-1	Meek	8,560		2	3	4	5	6	11		7	10		8	9			1														
16	(h)	Torquay Utd	L	2-4	Tarrant, Morris	8,715		2	3	4	5	6	7	10	9	8						1	11													
18	(a)	Southampton	L	1-2	Tarrant	14,533	1	2		4	5	10	11		7				9					3	6	8										
21	(a)	Bristol City	L	3-5	Davis, Tarrant, Goffin	20,110	1	2	3	4	5	10			9	7	11		8								6									
25	(h)	Coventry City	D	1-1	Tarrant	13,909	1	2	3	4	5	10	11		9	7			8								6									
30	(h)	Bristol City	L	1-3	Davis	8,911	1	2	3	6		10	11		4	7			8		5							9								
Oct 2	(a)	Brentford	W	2-0	McGairy, Richards	12,610	1		3		2	6	11	7	4		10	8			5							9								
9	(a)	Aldershot	L	0-4		6,661	1		3		2	6	11	7	4		10				5							9	8							
16	(h)	Swindon Town	L	1-2	Morris	9,010	1		3		5	6	11	7	4			10			2							9	8							
23	(a)	Crystal Palace	L	1-3	Tarrant	11,378	1		3			6	11	7	9			10									5		8	2	4					
30	(h)	Colchester Utd	W	3-1	Richards (2), Meek	11,117			3	2	5	6	11		7	10						1						9	8		4					
Nov 6	(a)	Watford	L	0-4		6,244			3	2	5	6	11		7	10						1						9	8		4					
13	(h)	Bournemouth	W	6-1	Tarrant (pen), Myerscough, Morris (2), Richards (2)	10,152			3	2	5	6	11		7	10						1						9	8		4					
27	(h)	Newport County	D	3-3	Dorman, Richards, Ferriday	12,059			3	10	5	6	11		7							1						9	8		4	2				
Dec 4	(a)	Exeter City	D	1-1	Richards	7,910			3	10	5	6	11		7							1						9	8		4	2				
18	(h)	Reading	W	4-0	Richards (3), Myerscough	12,070			3			6	11		7	10					5	1						9	8		4	2				
25	(h)	Shrewsbury Tn	W	4-0	Richards, Myerscough (2), Meek	17,054			3			6	11		7	10					5	1						9	8		4	2				
27	(a)	Shrewsbury Tn	D	2-2	Morris, Richards	12,506			3			6	11		7	10					5	1						9	8		4	2				
Jan 1	(a)	Gillingham	L	2-3	Tarrant (pen), West (og)	9,741			3			6			7	10					5	1						9	8		4	2	11			
22	(a)	Millwall Ath	L	0-1		7,818			3	10		6	11		7						5	1						9	8		4	2				
29	(a)	Southend Utd	L	1-2	Dorman	8,022			3			6	11		7	10					5	1						9	8		4	2				
Feb 5	(h)	Southampton	D	0-0		13,292			3			6	11		7	10					5	1						9	8		4	2				
12	(a)	Coventry City	L	3-5	Dorman, Meek, Crook	14,333			3			6	11		7						5	1						9	8		4	2		10		
19	(h)	Brentford	D	2-2	Crook, Dorman	9,028			3		5	6	10		7							1						9	8		4	2	11			
Mar 5	(a)	Swindon Tn	D	2-2	Dorman (2)	5,148			3		5	6			7							1						9	8		4	2	11		10	
12	(h)	Crystal Palace	L	1-4	Cousans	10,773			3		5	6			7							1						9	8		4	2	11		10	
19	(a)	Colchester Utd	D	2-2	Webb, Myerscough	7,361			3	4		6			11	8				1	5										10	2			9	7
26	(h)	Watford	L	0-1		4,011			3	4		6			11	8				1	5										10	2			9	7
31	(h)	Aldershot	D	2-2	Richards (2)	3,751			3	4		6			11					1	5							9			10	2			8	7
Apr 2	(a)	Bournemouth	D	1-1	Dorman	6,353			3	4		6			11					1	5							9	8			2			10	7
4	(h)	Nothampton Tn	W	6-1	Dorman (2), Webb (2), Richards, Patterson (og)	5,159			3	4		6			11					1	5							9	8			2			10	7
9	(h)	QPR	W	4-1	Richards (3), Dorman	13,018			3	4		6			11					1	5							9	8			2			10	7
11	(a)	Norwich City	L	1-2	Tarrant (pen)	19,034			3	4		6			11					1	5							9	8			2			10	7
12	(h)	Norwich City	W	2-1	Richards (2)	17,173			3	4		6			7	11				1	5							9	8			2			10	
16	(a)	Newport County	L	0-1		7,193			3	4		6		7	11					1	5							9	8			2			10	
23	(h)	Exeter City	W	1-0	Richards	10,193			3	4		6			7					1	5							9	8			2			10	11
25	(a)	QPR	D	1-1	Love	5,159			3	4		6			11					1	5							9	8			2			10	7
30	(a)	Northampton Tn	D	1-1	Dorman	6,842			3	4		6			7	10				1	5							9	8			2			11	
May 2	(h)	Southend Utd	W	4-1	Morris, Dorman, Myerscough, Love	12,456			3	4		6			7	10				1	5							9	8			2			11	
5	(h)	Leyton Orient	L	1-4	Richards	17,508			3	4		6			7	10				1	5							9	8			2			11	
						Apps	11	12	45	32	22	46	26	8	46	26	8	7	8	15	27	20	1	1	1	1	3	32	30	1	20	27	4	1	16	9
League Position: 23rd						Goals				1		8	4		8	6	1	1	2									22	12		2		1		2	3

Own goals: 2

F.A. Cup

Date		Opponent	Rd	Score	Scorers	Att	McBride V.	Fort S.	Vinall A.	Ferriday L.	Bridgett J.	Tarrant J.E.	Meek G.	Lewis K.	Morris F.	Myerscough W.	Goffin W.	McGairy T.	Davis L.	Chilvers G.	McPherson	Baldwin H.	Taylor B.	Pritchett D.	Hall R.	Maher J.	Russon R.	Richards A.	Dorman D.	Beddow R.	Crook W.	Guttridge W.	Cousans W.E.	Knott W.	Love J.	Webb R.
Nov 20	(h)	Shrewsbury Tn	1	5-2	Meek, Morris, Richards (2), Dorman	18,311			3	2	5	6	11		7	10						1						9	8		4					
Dec 11	(a)	Wrexham	2	2-1	Richards (2)	16,047			3		5	6	11		7	10						1						9	8		4	2				
Jan 8	(a)	Chelsea	3	0-2		40,020			3		5	6	11		7	10						1						9	8		4	2				
						Apps			3	1	3	3	3		3	3						3						3	3		3	2				
						Goals							1		1													4	1							

SEASON 1955-56

Division 3(S)

Date		Opponent		Score	Scorers	Att	Chilvers	Guttridge	Vinall	Crook	McPherson	Gallier	Morris F.	Billingham P.	Walsh D.	McLaren	Davies R.	Dorman D	Love J.	Richards A.	Haddington H.	Moore	Tarrant	Dyas	Dews G	Watson	Hall	Davidson	Taylor B	Hodgkisson K.	Payne	Cooper	Taylor D.
Aug 20	(h)	Leyton Orient	L	0-2		18,786	1	2	3	4	5	6	7		9	11		8										10					
24	(a)	Brighton	L	0-3		8,963		2	3		5		7		9	11	1	4	6	8								10					
27	(a)	Torquay Utd	L	2-3	Towers (og), McLaren	6,224		2	3		5		7			10	1	4	8	9	6	11											
Sep 1	(h)	Brighton	D	2-2	Richards, McLaren	13,147			3		5		7			11	1	4	8	9	2	11	6										
3	(h)	Newport County	D	3-3	McLaren, Walsh, Richards	14,442			3		5		7		10	11	1	4	8	9	2		6										
7	(a)	Ipswich Town	L	2-5	Richards, Walsh	13,527			3		5		7		10	11	1	4	8	9	2		6										
10	(a)	Swindon Town	W	2-1	Walsh (2)	7,576		2			5		7		10	11	1	4		9	3			6	8								
15	(h)	Ipswich Town	L	1-3	McLaren	12,496		5		3			7		10	11	1	4		9	2			6	8								
17	(h)	QPR	D	2-2	Morris, McLaren	12,427		2	5	3			7		10	11	1	4		9				6	8								
21	(a)	Southampton	L	1-4	Love	7,980		2	5	3			7			10	1	4	8	9		11		6									
24	(a)	Northampton Tn	L	1-3	McLaren	14,242	1	2	5	6			7			11		8	10	9	3			4									
28	(a)	Crystal Palace	L	0-2		7,298	1	2	5	6			7			10		4	8		3							9	11				
Oct 1	(h)	Aldershot	W	4-2	Richards (2), Love, Morris	11,090	1	2	5	6			7			11		4	10	9	3				8								
8	(h)	Norwich City	W	2-0	Love (2)	12,784	1		3	6	5		7			11		4	10	9	2				8								
15	(a)	Bournemouth	L	0-2		7,171	1		3		5		7			11		4	10	9	2			6	8								
22	(h)	Gillingham	W	2-1	Dews, McLaren	11,469	1		3		5		7	6		11		4	10	9	2				8								
29	(a)	Millwall Ath	L	2-3	Love, Richards	8,776	1		3	6	5		7					4	10	9	2	11			8								
Nov 5	(h)	Reading	W	1-0	McPherson (pen)	11,261			3		5		7	6	9		1	4	10		2	11						8					
12	(a)	Watford	L	2-4	Morris, Dorman	7,810			3		5		7		9		1	4		8	2	11			10		6						
26	(a)	Coventry City	L	0-1		17,618				6	5	3	7		9	10	1				2	11		4									
Dcc 3	(h)	Southend Utd	W	3-1	Richards, Love, Taylor	11,878					5	3	7			11	1	4	10	9	2			6									8
17	(a)	Leyton Orient	L	0-4		11,455					5	3	7				1	4	10	9	2	11						6					8
24	(h)	Torquay Utd	L	1-4	Moore	11,688					5	3	7			10	1	4		9	2	11		6									8
26	(a)	Shrewsbury Tn	L	1-2	Richards	13,887			5	4		3	7			10	1	8		9	2	11		6									
27	(h)	Shrewsbury Tn	W	1-0	Richards	17,486			5			3	7			10	1	4	8	9	2	11		6									
31	(a)	Newport County	L	0-2		8,008					5	3	7		8	11	1	4		9	2			6						10			
Jan 14	(h)	Swindon Town	W	4-0	Richards, Morris, Walsh (2)	10,961	1			6	5	3	7		8			4		9	2									10			11
21	(a)	QPR	L	2-3	Morris, Dorman	6,527	1			6	5	3	7		8	11		6		9	2									10			
28	(a)	Exeter City	D	1-1	Hodgkisson	7,147			3	6	5		7		8	11	1	4		9	2									10			
Feb 11	(a)	Aldershot	L	1-2	Morris	3,327			3	6	5		7		8	11	1	4		9	2									10			
25	(h)	Bournemouth	D	0-0		9,090			3	6	5		7		8	11	1	4		9	2									10			
Mar 3	(a)	Gillingham	W	1-0	Taylor	5,190			3	6	5		7		8	11	1	4			2									10			9
10	(h)	Millwall Ath	W	2-1	McLaren, Morris	13,229			3	6	5		7		8	11	1	4			2									10			9
17	(a)	Reading	L	0-2		6,257			3	6	5		7		8	11	1	4			2									10			9
26	(h)	Watford	W	2-1	Taylor, Cooper	10,879			3	6	5		7				1	4		9	2									10		11	8
30	(a)	Colchester Utd	D	1-1	Cooper	9,130			3	6	5		7				1	4	8		2									10		11	9
31	(a)	Brentford	D	2-2	Richards, Morris	5,017		6	3		5		7				1	4		8	2									9		11	10
Apr 2	(h)	Colchester	D	0-0		15,179		6	3		5		7				1	4		8	2									9		11	10
7	(h)	Coventry	W	2-0	Richards, Dorman	14,750		6	3		5		7				1	4	10	9	2									8			11
12	(a)	Norwich City	L	2-3	Love, Hodgkisson	6,981		6	3		5		7			11	1	4	10		2									8	9		
14	(a)	Southend	L	2-3	Hodgkisson, Love	6.908		6	3		5		7			11	1	4	10	9	2									8			
16	(h)	Northampton Tn	W	2-0	McPherson (2 pens)	11,934			3	6	5		7		9		1	4	10		2									8			11
21	(h)	Exeter City	W	3-1	Mitchell (og), Hodgkisson, Taylor	13,656	1	3		6	5		7					4	10		2									8		11	9
26	(a)	Crystal Palace	W	4-0	Richards (2),Taylor, Morris	9,663		3		6	5		7				1	4		9	2	11								8			10
28	(h)	Southampton	L	1-3	Richards	13,469	1	3		6	5		7					4		9	2	11								8			10
May 3	(h)	Brentford	L	1-2	Love	9,033	1				5		7	6				4	10	9	2					3				8			11
						Apps	13	18	33	25	38	10	46	3	20	31	33	45	24	35	42	13	3	12	9	1	1	5	1	21	1	5	18
League position: 20th						Goals					3		10		6	8		3	9	15		1			1					4		2	5

Own goals: 2

F.A. Cup

Date		Opponent	Rd	Score	Scorers	Att	Chilvers	Guttridge	Vinall	Crook	McPherson	Gallier	Morris F.	Billingham P.	Walsh D.	McLaren	Davies R.	Dorman D	Love J.	Richards A.	Haddington H.	Moore	Tarrant	Dyas	Dews G	Watson	Hall	Davidson	Taylor B	Hodgkisson K.	Payne	Cooper	Taylor D.
Nov 19	(a)	Margate	1	2-2	Morris, McLaren	6,800			3	6	5		7		8	10	1	4		9	2	11											
24	(h)	Margate	1R	6-1	Richards (2), Walsh (3), McLaren	9,601			3	6	5		7		8	10	1	4		9	2	11											
Dec 10	(h)	Southampton	2	2-1	Morris, Moore	17,021					5	3	7				1	4	10	9	2	11		6									8
Jan 7	(h)	Port Vale	3	0-1		21,811				6	5	3	7		10		1	4		9	2	11											8
						Apps			2	3	4	2	4		3	2	4	4	1	4	4	4		1									2
						Goals							2		3	2				2		1											

SEASON 1956-57

Division 3(S)

Date		Opponent		Score	Scorers	Att	Davies R.	Haddington	Perkins E.	Dorman D.	McPherson	Tarrant	Morris F.	Johnston	Richards	Brown	Taylor B.	Leverton	Hodgkisson	Taylor D.	Moore	Guttridge	Rawlings	Chilvers	Jarman	Billingham
Aug 18	(a)	Millwall Ath	L	0-1		14,301	1	2	3	4	5	6	7	8	9	10	11									
22	(h)	Torquay Utd	L	0-1		13,831	1	2	3	4	5	6				10		7	8	9	11					
25	(h)	Brighton	W	3-2	Morris, Taylor D. Dorman	10,082	1	2	3	4	5	6	7			10		11	8	9						
29	(a)	Torquay Utd	L	0-2		8,105	1	2	3	4	5	6	7			10		11	8	9						
Sep 1	(a)	Gillingham	L	1-2	Morris	8,661	1		3	4		5	7		9	10		8			11	2	6			
6	(h)	Ipswich Town	W	2-0	Leverton, Richards	9,399	1		3	4		5	7		9	10		8		11		2	6			
8	(h)	Swindon Town	L	1-2	Leverton	12,763	1		3	4		5	7		9	10		8		11		2	6			
12	(a)	Ipswich Town	D	2-2	Dorman, Richards	10,389	1		3	4		5	7		9			8	10	11		2	6			
15	(a)	Brentford	L	2-6	Morris (2)	11,480	1		3	4		5	7					8	10	9	11	2	6			
19	(a)	Bournemouth	D	2-2	Morris (2)	8,865	1	2	3	4			7		9	8			10	11		5	6			
22	(h)	Aldershot	W	5-1	Dorman, Morris, Brown, Taylor D. Hodgkisson	11,154	1	2	3	4			7		9	10			8	11		5	6			
27	(h)	Bournemouth	D	0-0		8,769	1	2	3	4			7		9	10		11	8			5	6			
29	(a)	Watford	L	0-1		11,352	1	2	3	4			7		9	10		11	8			5	6			
Oct 6	(h)	Newport County	D	0-0		10,894	1	2	3			6	7	8	9			11	10			5	4			
13	(a)	Reading	L	0-3		9,989	1	2	3	8		6	7	10				9	11			5	4			
20	(h)	Plymouth Argyle	W	1-0		10,113	1	2	3	4	5		7	8			11	10		9			6			
27	(a)	QPR	L	0-1		9,425	1	2	3	4	5	6	7		9	10	11	8								
Nov 3	(h)	Northampton Tn	D	2-2	Taylor B. Taylor	9,842	1	2	3	4	5		7				11	8		9	10		6			
10	(a)	Southend Utd	L	0-2		7,941	1	2	3	4	5		7				11	8	10	9			6			
24	(a)	Exeter City	W	1-0	Moore	4,617		2	3	8	5				9		11	10			7		6	1	4	
Dec 1	(h)	Southampton	D	1-1	Taylor B.	8,571		2	3	8	5				9	10	11				7		6	1	4	
8	(a)	Coventry City	D	2-2	Richards, Perkins	10,099		2	3	8	5				9		11		10		7		6	1	4	
15	(h)	Millwall Ath	W	7-1	Dorman (3), Richards, Jarman, Taylor B. Hodgkisson	7,073		2	3	8	5				9		11		10		7		6	1	4	
22	(a)	Brighton	W	3-1	Dorman (2), Brown	6,773		2	3	8	5				9	10	11				7		6	1		4
25	(h)	Shrewsbury Tn	D	1-1	Richards	12,716		2	3	8	5				9	10	11				7		6	1		4
29	(h)	Gillingham	D	2-2	Rawlings, Richards	12,150		2	3	8	5				9		11		10		7		6	1	4	
Jan 5	(a)	Norwich City	D	2-2	Richards, Brown	9,789		2	3	8	5				9	10	11				7		6	1	4	
12	(a)	Swindon Town	W	2-1	Dorman, Brown	8,948		2	3	8	5				9	10	11				7		6	1	4	
19	(h)	Brentford	W	7-0	Moore (3), Richards (3), Dorman	13,892		2	3	8	5				9	10	11				7		6	1		4
26	(h)	Norwich City	W	6-3	Dorman (2), Richards (2), Moore, Brown	16,169		2	3	8	5				9	10	11				7		6	1		4
Feb 2	(a)	Aldershot	L	1-4	Dorman	5,630		2	3	8	5				9	10	11				7		6	1		4
9	(h)	Watford	W	2-0	Taylor B. (2)	14,758		2	3	8	5				9	10	11				7	4	6	1		
16	(a)	Newport County	D	2-2	Richards, Brown	9,115		2	3	8	5				9	10	11				7		6	1	4	
23	(h)	Reading	W	3-2	Moore, Dorman, Richards	7,771		2	3	8	5				9	10	11				7		6	1	4	
Mar 2	(a)	Plymouth Argyle	W	4-2	Moore, Dorman, Brown, Taylor B.	13,638		2	3	8	5				9	10	11				7		6	1	4	
9	(h)	Coventry City	D	1-1	Richards	14,758		2	3	8	5				9	10	11				7		6	1	4	
16	(a)	Northampton Tn	W	3-2	Jarman, Hodgkisson, Taylor B.	9,177		2	3		5					10	11		8	9	7		6	1	4	
23	(h)	Southend Utd	L	0-1		15,312		2	3	8	5				9	10	11		4		7		6	1		
30	(a)	Crystal Palace	L	0-3		9,338		2	3	8	5				9	10	11		4		7		6	1		
Apr 6	(h)	Exeter City	W	2-0	Dorman, Hodgkisson	10,507		2	3	8	5				9		11		10		7		6	1	4	
13	(a)	Southampton	L	1-3	Dorman	11,499		2	3	8	5				9		11		10		7		6	1	4	
19	(a)	Colchester Utd	L	1-2	Richards	12,770		2	3	8	5				9				10	11	7		6	1	4	
20	(h)	QPR	L	0-2		10,914		2	3		5				9	8			10	11	7		6	1	4	
22	(h)	Colchester Utd	W	2-1	Johnston, Richards	9,414		2			5	6		8	9		11		10	7		3		1		4
27	(h)	Crystal Palace	L	1-2	Taylor B.	9,748		2			5	6		8	9		11		10	7		3	4	1		
29	(a)	Shrewsbury Tn	L	2-3	Dorman Skeech (og)	6,369	1	2		8	5	6		10			11		9	7		3	4			
						Apps	20	41	43	41	35	15	18	7	36	29	30	17	25	18	28	15	40	26	16	6
League position: 15th						Goals			1	18			7		17	7	8	3	4	3	7		1		2	

Own goal 1

F.A. Cup

Date		Opponent	Rd	Score	Att	Davies R.	Haddington	Perkins E.	Dorman D.	McPherson	Tarrant	Morris F.	Johnston	Richards	Brown	Taylor B.	Leverton	Hodgkisson	Taylor D.	Moore	Guttridge	Rawlings	Chilvers	Jarman	Billingham
Nov 17	(h)	Newport Co	1	0-1	12,085	1	2	3	4	5		7				11	8	10	9			6			
					Apps	1	1	1	1	1		1				1		1	1			1			
					Goals																				

SEASON 1957-58

Division 3(S)

Date		Opponent			Scorers	Att	Chilvers	Haddington	Perkins	Jarman	McPherson	Rawlings	Stewart	Hodgkisson	Richards	Davie W.	Evans K.	Savage J.	Guttridge	Billingham	Tarrant	Jones S.	Moore S.	Murray J.	Faulkner	Taylor B.	Brownlee T.	Brown T.
Aug 24	(h)	Northampton Tn	W	2-1	McPherson (pen), Richards	13,059	1	2	3	4	5	6	7	8	9	10										11		
28	(a)	Southampton	L	1-4	Taylor	17,142	1	2	3	4	5	6	7	8	9	10										11		
31	(a)	Watford	D	1-1	Richards	9,567	1	2	3	4	5	6	7	8	9	10										11		
Sep 5	(h)	Southampton	D	1-1	Tarrant	12,085	1	2	3	4	5	6	7	8		10					9					11		
7	(h)	Crystal Palace	W	2-1	Tarrant, Taylor	11,758	1	2	3	4	5	6	7	9		10					8					11		
12	(a)	Newport County	L	0-2		8,000	1	2	3	4	5	6	7	9		10					8					11		
14	(a)	Torquay Utd	L	1-2	Richards	8,000	1	2	3	4	5	6	7	10	9						8					11		
19	(h)	Newport County	W	3-0	Richards (2), Stewart	7,688	1	2	3	4	5	6	7	10	9						8					11		
21	(h)	Brentford	L	0-2		10,775	1	2	3	4	5	6	7		9	10					8					11		
28	(a)	Colchester Utd	D	1-1	Brown	7,366	1	2	3		5	6	7							4	8					11	9	10
Oct 5	(h)	Norwich City	W	2-1	Brownlee, Taylor	9,376	1	2	3					4	8						6	5	7			11	9	10
12	(h)	Brighton	L	2-3	McPherson (pen), Richards	11,080	1	2	3		5		7	8	9					4	6					11		10
19	(a)	Southend Utd	L	1-4	Taylor	10,500	1	2	3	4	5	6	7	10							8					11	9	
26	(h)	QPR	L	1-2	Stewart	7,560		2	3	4	5	6	7	10	9		1						8			11		
Nov 2	(a)	Exeter City	L	1-2	Richards	8,272		2			5	6		8	9		1		3	4			7			11		10
9	(h)	Gillingham	D	1-1	Stewart	6,452	1	2			5	6	10	8	9				3	4			7			11		
23	(h)	Swindon	D	1-1	Hodgkisson	6,539	1	2		4		6	7	8	10				3			5				11	9	
30	(a)	Aldershot	W	3-1	Brownlee, Stewart, Richards	4,782	1	2		4		6	7	8	10				3			5				11	9	
Dec 14	(a)	Port Vale	L	1-2	Richards	8,827	1	2		4		6	7	8	10				3			5				11		9
21	(a)	Northampton Tn	L	0-3		7,048	1	2		4		6	7	8	10				3			5				11	9	
25	(h)	Shrewsbury Tn	L	0-1		9,808	1	2		4		6	7	8	10				3			5				11	9	
26	(a)	Shrewsbury Tn	L	0-2		12,186	1	2		4	5	6	7		10				3	8						11	9	
28	(h)	Watford	L	1-3	Richards	8,943	1	2		4	5	6	7	8	10				3				11				9	
Jan 4	(a)	Bournemouth	W	2-1	Moore, Hodgkisson	9,866	1	2			5	6	7	10	9				3	4			8			11		
11	(a)	Crystal Palace	L	1-4	Richards	10,280	1	2				6	7	10	9				3	4		5	8			11		
18	(h)	Torquay Utd	D	0-0		8,325		2		4	5	6		10	9			1	3				7	8		11		
25	(a)	Millwall Ath	W	3-1	Murray, Richards, Hodgkisson	8,904		2		4	5	6		10	9			1	3				7	8		11		
Feb 1	(a)	Brentford	L	1-2	Richards	9,120		2		4	5	6		10	9			1	3				7	8		11		
8	(h)	Colchester Utd	W	3-0	Rawlings, Richards (2)	7,639		2			5	6			9			1	3	4			7	8		11		10
15	(a)	Norwich	L	1-2	Brown	16,792		2			5	6	7		9			1	3	4				8		11		10
22	(a)	Brighton	L	0-2		12,303		2			5	6	7		9			1	3		4			8		11		10
Mar 1	(h)	Southend Utd	D	1-1	Brownlee	7,658		2			5	6		8				1	3	4			7			11	9	10
3	(h)	Plymouth Argyle	L	0-2		9,393		2			5	6		8	10			1	3	4			7	9		11		
8	(a)	QPR	L	0-1		6,484		2			5	6		8	10			1	3	4			7			11	9	
10	(h)	Coventry City	W	4-1	Richards (3), Brownlee	6,600		2			5	6		8	10			1	3	4			7			11	9	
15	(h)	Exeter City	W	3-0	Brownlee, Richards, Taylor	8,903		2			5	6		8	10			1	3	4			7			11	9	
22	(a)	Swindon Town	W	3-2	Faulkner, Taylor, Bingley (og)	11,202		2			5	6		8	9			1	3	4			7		10	11		
24	(a)	Coventry City	L	1-4	Moore	8,182		2			5	6		8	9			1	3	4			7		10	11		
29	(h)	Port Vale	W	3-0	Faulkner (2), Richards	8,613		2			5	6			10			1	3	4			7		8	11	9	
Apr 4	(a)	Reading	L	1-3	Brownlee	12,366		2			5	6			10			1	3	4			7		8	11	9	
5	(a)	Gillingham	L	0-3		5,081		2			5	6			10			1	3	4			7		8	11	9	
7	(h)	Reading	D	0-0		9,071		2			5	6			10			1	3	4			7	8		11	9	
12	(h)	Aldershot	D	0-0		7,470		2			5	6			10			1	3	4			7		8	11	9	
19	(a)	Plymouth Argyle	L	1-2	Faulkner	19,081		2				6	7		9			1	3	4	5			8	10	11		
24	(h)	Bournemouth	W	3-1	Richards, Faulkner, Taylor	7,203		2				6	7		9			1	3	4	5			8	10	11		
26	(h)	Millwall Ath	W	4-2	Murray, Faulkner, Taylor (2)	6,618		2				6	7		9			1	3	4	5			8	10	11		
						Apps	23	46	14	21	36	44	28	32	40	7	2	21	32	24	14	7	23	11	9	45	18	9
League position: 20th						Goals					2	1	4	3	21						2		2	2	6	9	6	2

Own goal 1

F.A. Cup

Date		Opponent	Rd	Score	Scorers	Att	Chilvers	Haddington	Perkins	Jarman	McPherson	Rawlings	Stewart	Hodgkisson	Richards	Davie W.	Evans K.	Savage J.	Guttridge	Billingham	Tarrant	Jones S.	Moore S.	Murray J.	Faulkner	Taylor B.	Brownlee T.	Brown T.
Nov 16	(a)	Brighton	1	1-2	Tarrant	15,325	1	2	3	4	5	6		10	9						8		7			11		
						Apps	1	1	1	1	1	1		1	1						1		1			1		
						Goal															1							

SEASON 1958-59

Division 4

Date		Opponents			Scorers	Att	Woodward T.P	Haddington	Guttridge	Billingham	McPherson	Rawlings S.	Askey C.	Cochrane J.	Richards A.	Davies J.R.	Metcalfe J	Savage J.	Murray J.	Hodgkisson	Taylor C	Faulkner	Brownlee	Perkins	Jones S.	Ball K.	Hill K.	Walker A.	Wright A.	Kelly J.	Edwards P
Aug 23	(a)	Exeter City	L	0-3		8,950	1	2	3	4	5	6	7	8	9		11					10									
28	(h)	Millwall Ath	W	2-1	Richards (2)	11,259		2	3	4	5	6	7		9			1	8	10	11										
30	(h)	Gillingham	L	1-2	McPherson (pen)	10,131		2	3		5	6	7		9			1	8	4	11	10									
Sep 1	(a)	Millwall Ath	W	3-1	Cochrane, Brownlee (2)	13,709		2	3		5	6	7	8	10			1		4	11		9								
6	(a)	Carlisle Utd	D	1-1	Brownlee	7,000		2	3		5	6	7	8	10			1		4	11		9								
11	(h)	Chester	D	2-2	Richards, Mason (og)	11,791			2		5	6		8	10		7	1		4	11		9	3							
13	(h)	Barrow	W	3-1	Brownlee, Richards (2)	9,691		2		4	5	6	7		10			1		8	11		9	3							
17	(a)	Chester	L	0-2		7,780		2			5	6	7	8	10			1		4	11		9	3							
20	(a)	Oldham Ath	W	4-1	Hodgkisson (2), Brownlee, Richards	6,129		2		4	5	6	7		10			1		8	11		9	3							
25	(h)	Darlington	D	0-0		11,047		2		4	5	6	7		10			1		8	11		9	3							
27	(h)	Gateshead	L	0-1		10,529		2		4	5	6	7		10			1		8	11		9	3							
Oct 1	(a)	Darlington	W	3-2	Faulkner, Billingham, Henderson (og)	3,199		2		4	5	6	7					1	9	10	11	8		3							
4	(a)	Aldershot	W	5-0	Askey(2), Richards (2), Taylor	3,398		2		4	5	6	7		10			1		8	11	9		3							
9	(h)	Shrewsbury Tn	L	2-3	Richards, Hodgkisson	14,614		2		4	5	6	7		10			1		8	11	9		3							
11	(a)	Hartlepool Utd	D	1-1	Richards	6,179		2		4	5	6	7		9			1		10	11	8		3							
18	(h)	Southport	W	5-1	Faulkner (2), Richards, Askey, Hodgkisson	9,992		2	3	4	5	6	7		9			1		10	11	8									
25	(a)	Torquay Utd	W	2-1	McPherson, Faulkner	5,253		2	3	4	5	6	7		9			1		10	11	8									
31	(h)	Crewe Alexandra	W	6-0	Faulkner (2), Brownlee, Taylor, Askey, Richards	16,142		2	3	4			7		10			1		6	11	8	9		5						
Nov 8	(a)	Northampton Tn	L	2-3	Hodgkisson, Brownlee	11,858		2	3	4		6	7		10			1		8	11		9		5						
22	(a)	York City	L	2-3	Brownlee, Taylor	7,403	1	2	3	4		6	7		10					8	11		9		5						
29	(h)	Bradford Pk Ave	W	3-2	Billingham (pen), Richards, Taylor	6,702	1	2	3	4		6	7		10					8	11		9		5						
Dec 13	(h)	Crystal Palace	L	0-2		5,361	1	2	3	4		6	7		9					10	11	8			5						
26	(h)	Watford	W	3-2	Richards, Taylor, Faulkner	10,324	1	2	3	4		6	7		9					10	11	8			5						
27	(a)	Watford	W	2-1	Askey, Taylor	11,921		2	3	4		6	7		9			1		10	11	8			5						
Jan 3	(a)	Gillingham	L	2-4	Askey, Richards	6,123		2	3	4		6	7		9			1		10	11	8			5						
23	(a)	Port Vale	L	1-2	Taylor	11,500	1	2	3	4	5	6	7		9					10	11	8									
31	(a)	Barrow	D	0-0		3,566	1	2	3	4	5	6		8	9	7				10	11										
Feb 7	(h)	Oldham Ath	W	3-0	Hodgkisson (2), Richards	7,180	1	2	3		5	6			10	7				8	11				4					9	
14	(a)	Gateshead	L	1-2	Richards	2,650	1	2	3	4	5	6			10	7				8	11									9	
21	(h)	Aldershot	L	2-4	Richards, Davies	6,706	1	2	3	4	5	6			10	7				8	11									9	
28	(h)	Hartlepool Utd	D	0-0		7,385	1		3		5	6			10	7				4		8					2			9	11
Mar 7	(a)	Southport	D	1-1	Kelly	4,106	1		3	4	5	6			10	7				8	11				2					9	
14	(h)	Torquay Utd	D	2-2	Billingham, Richards	5,125	1		3	4	5	6			10	7				8	11				2					9	
17	(h)	Exeter City	W	3-0	Davies, Faulkner, Taylor	5,616		2	3	4		6			9	7				10	11	8				1		5			
21	(a)	Crewe Alexandra	L	3-5	Evans (og), Faulkner, Wright	7,279		2		3		6			9	7				4	11	10				1		5	8		
28	(h)	Northampton Tn	W	2-1	Richards (2)	5,091		2	3	4	5	6			9	7		1		10	11	8									
30	(h)	Coventry City	W	3-0	Hodgkisson, Taylor, Rawlings	10,949		2	3	4	5	6				7		1		10	11	8								9	
31	(a)	Coventry City	D	0-0		19,523		2	3	4	5	6				7		1		10	11	8								9	
Apr 4	(a)	Workington Tn	W	1-0	Taylor	4,506			3	2	5	6			9	7		1		10	11	8						4			
9	(h)	Workington Tn	W	3-0	Richards, Faulkner, Billingham (pen)	8,272			3	2	5	6			9	7		1		10	11	8						4			
11	(h)	York City	W	5-0	Taylor, Davies, Richards (3)	8,202		2	3	4	5	6			9	7		1		10	11	8									
14	(h)	Carlisle Utd	W	5-0	Richards, Faulkner (2), Hodgkisson, McPherson (pen)	10,087		2	3		5	6			9	7		1		10	11	8						4			
18	(a)	Bradford Pk Ave	L	2-3	Hodgkisson, Taylor	6,054		2	3	4	5	6			9	7		1		10	11	8									
20	(a)	Shrewsbury Tn	L	0-2		10,878		2	3	4	5	6			9	7		1		10	11	8									
25	(h)	Port Vale	D	1-1	Faulkner	6,626		2	3	4	5	6			9	7		1		10	11	8									
29	(a)	Crystal Palace	W	3-1	Faulkner, Richards (2)	8,888		2	3	4	5	6			9	7				10	11	8				1					
						Apps	13	40	36	38	36	45	25	6	43	20	2	30		45	44	28	12	10	11	3	1	5	1	8	1
League position: 6th						Goals				4	3	1	6	1	28	3				10	12	14	8						1	1	

own goals: 3

F.A. Cup

Date		Opponents	Rd			Att																									
Nov 15	(h)	QPR	1	0-1		5,123		2	3	4		6	7		9			1		10	11	8			5						
						Apps		1	1	1		1	1		1			1		1	1	1			1						
						Goals																									

SEASON 1959-60

Division 4

Date		Opponent	Res	Score	Scorers	Att	Christie	Haddington	Guttridge	Billingham	McPherson	Rawlings	Davies J.	Faulkner	Richards	Hodgkisson	Taylor C.	Jones S.	Rowe	Sharples	Walker	Askey C.	Dudley J.	Ball K.	Hill K.	Foster
Aug 22	(h)	Crewe Aleandra	W	3-1	Faulkner, Hodgkisson, Taylor	10,385	1	2	3	4	5	6	7	8	9	10	11									
25	(h)	Hatlepools Utd	D	2-2	Faulkner, Hodgkisson	11,244	1	2	3	4	5	6	7	8	9	10	11									
29	(a)	Chester	W	3-1	Faulkner (2), Richards	7,406	1	2	3	4		6	7	8	9	10	11	5								
31	(a)	Hartlepools Utd	W	2-1	Faulkner (2)	6,677	1	2	3	4		6	7	8	9	10	11	5								
Sep 5	(h)	Crystal Palace	W	3-0	Richards (2), Faulkner	11,826	1	2	3	4		6	7	8	9	10	11	5								
10	(h)	Carlisle Utd	L	0-1		15,403	1	2	3	4	5	6	7	8	9	10	11									
12	(a)	Bradford Pk Ave	W	3-1	Billingham (pen), Taylor, McCalman (og)	8,048	1	2	3	4		6		8	9	10	11	5	7							
15	(a)	Carlisle Utd	D	1-1	Taylor	7,833	1	2	3	4		6	7	8	9	10	11	5								
19	(h)	Stockport Co	W	3-1	Faulkner, Richards, Taylor	11,309	1	2	3	4		6	7	8	9	10	11	5								
22	(h)	Darlington	W	1-0	Faulkner	13,124	1	2	3	4	6		7	8	9	10	11	5								
26	(a)	Exeter City	W	2-1	Hodgkisson, Taylor	8,142	1	2		4	5		7	8	9	10	11			3	6					
30	(a)	Darlington	W	2-0	Richards (2)	5,253	1	2		4	5	6	7	8	9	10	11			3						
Oct 3	(h)	Watford	L	3-4	Davies (2), Richards	12,699	1	2		4	5	6	7	8	9	10	11			3						
10	(h)	Rochdale	W	4-2	Billingham (pen), Davies, Richards (2)	8,552	1	2	3	4	5	6	7	8	9	10	11									
12	(h)	Oldham Ath	W	2-1	Billingham, Taylor	12,685	1	2	3	4		6	7		9	10	11	5				8				
17	(a)	Workington	W	3-0	Faulkner, Richards, Hodgkisson	4,406	1	2	3	4	5	6	7	8	9	10	11									
24	(h)	Doncaster Rov	W	5-2	Davies (2), Richards (2), Taylor	9,294	1	2		4	5	6	7	10	9	8	11			3						
31	(a)	Northampton Tn	W	1-0	Faulkner	13,041	1	2		4	5	6	7	10	9	8	11			3						
Nov 7	(h)	Torquay Utd	W	3-2	Davies, Richards (2)	13,743	1	2		4	5	6	7	10	9	8	11			3						
21	(h)	Southport	W	8-0	Taylor (3), Davies (2), Hodgkisson, Faulkner (2)	12,840	1	2	3		5	6	7	10	9	8	11			4						
28	(a)	Gillingham	L	0-2		5,853	1	2	3		5	6	7	10	9	8	11				4					
Dec 12	(h)	Aldershot	W	1-0	Hodgkisson	9,121	1	2	3		5	6	7	8	9	10	11						4			
19	(a)	Crewe Alexandra	W	5-1	Davies, Faulkner, Hodgkisson, Taylor, Richards	7,958	1	2	3		5	6	7	8	9	10	11						4			
26	(h)	Gateshead	D	2-2	Davies, Faulkner	13,191	1	2	3		5	6	7	8	9	10	11						4			
Jan 2	(h)	Chester	W	2-1	Faulkner, Richards	9,731	1	2	3		5	6	7	8	9	10	11						4			
9	(a)	Millwall	D	1-1	Taylor	16,008	1	2	3		5	6	9	8	10		11					7	4			
16	(a)	Crystal Palace	W	2-1	Faulkner, Richards	14,925	1	2	3		5	6	7	8	9	10	11						4			
23	(h)	Bradford Pk Ave	W	2-1	Davies, Faulkner	8,630	1	2	3		5	6	7	8	9	10	11						4			
29	(h)	Barrow	W	2-1	Davies, Faulkner	6,945	1	2	3		5	6	7	8	9	10	11						4			
Feb 6	(a)	Stockport Co	L	0-2		8,356	1	2	3		5	6	7	8	9	10	11						4			
27	(a)	Rochdale	W	2-0	Richards, Dudley	4,468	1	2	3		5	6	7	8	9	10	11						4			
Mar 5	(h)	Workington	D	2-2	Richards, Hodgkisson	10,912	1	2	3		5	6	7	8	9	10	11						4			
12	(a)	Doncaster Rov	D	1-1	Taylor	8,720		2			5	6	7	8	9	10	11			3			4	1		
19	(h)	Northampton Tn	L	1-2	Richards	9,852	1	2	3		5	6	7	8	9	10	11						4			
22	(h)	Exeter City	D	2-2	Askey, Hodgkisson	10,568	1	2	3		5	6	7	8	9	10	11						4			
26	(a)	Torquay Utd	L	1-2	Hodgkisson	9,200	1	2	3		5	6	11	8	9	10						7	4			
Apr 2	(h)	MillwallAth	W	2-1	Billingham, Taylor	9,703	1	2	3	4	5		9		10	8	11					7	6			
9	(a)	Southport	W	4-1	Dudley, Richards, Taylor (2)	3,942	1	2		4	5			8	9	10	11			3		7	6			
12	(a)	Oldham Ath	W	4-2	Askey, Faulkner, Taylor (2)	21,264	1	2		4	5			8	9	10	11			3		7	6			
16	(h)	Gillingham	L	2-3	Billingham (pen), Hodgkisson	10,529	1	2		4	5			8	9	10	11			3		7	6			
18	(a)	Notts County	L	1-2	Hodgkisson	22,788	1	2		4	5		9		10	8	11			3		7	6			
19	(h)	Notts County	D	2-2	Taylor, Faulkner	14,752	1	2	3		5			8	9	10	11					7	6		4	
23	(a)	Barrow	W	3-2	Dudley, Richards, Taylor	6,093	1	2	3	8		6			9	10	11	5				7	4			
25	(a)	Gateshead	L	0-3		2,366	1	2	3	6				8	9	10	11	5				7	4			
30	(a)	Aldershot	W	2-0	Faulkner, Richards	6,724		2	3	4				8	9		11	5				7	6	1		10
May 3	(a)	Watford	D	2-2	Richards, Taylor	20,734		2	3	6			7	8	9	10	11	5						1	4	
						Apps	43	46	35	28	35	35	38	42	46	44	45	12	1	12	2	12	24	3	2	1
League position: 1st (Champions)						Goals				5			12	22	24	11	21					2	3			

own goal: 1

F.A. Cup

Date		Opponent	Rd	Score	Scorers	Att	Christie	Haddington	Guttridge	Billingham	McPherson	Rawlings	Davies J.	Faulkner	Richards	Hodgkisson	Taylor C.	Jones S.	Rowe	Sharples	Walker	Askey C.	Dudley J.	Ball K.	Hill K.	Foster
Nov 14	(a)	Swindon Town	1	3-2	Richards, Davies (2)	15,123	1	2	3	4		6		8	9	10	11	5				7				
Dec 5	(h)	Peterborough Utd	2	2-3	Richards, Billingham	20,585	1	2	3	4	5	6	7	8	9	10	11									
						Apps	2	2	2	2	1	2	1	2	2	2	2	1				1				
						Goals				1			2		2											

SEASON 1960-61

Division 3

Date		Opponent		Score	Scorers	Att	Christie	Haddington	Guttridge	Dudley	McPherson	Rawlings	Askey	Faulkner	Richards	Hodgkisson	Taylor C.	Sharples	Hill	Palin	Gregg	Eden	Davies	Foster	Rowe	Wilson
Aug 20	(a)	Port Vale	D	1-1	Richards	15,434	1	2	3	4	5	6	7	8	9	10	11									
23	(h)	Southend Utd	W	5-1	Richards, Hodgkisson (2), Taylor, Whale (og)	11,032	1	2	3	4	5	6	7	8	9	10	11									
27	(h)	Torquay Utd	W	3-0	Faulkner, Richards, Taylor	10,512	1	2	3	4	5	6	7	8	9	10	11									
29	(a)	Southend Utd	W	2-1	Richards, Taylor	10,821	1	2	3	4	5	6	7	8	9	10	11									
Sep 3	(a)	Swindon Town	L	0-1		13,427	1	2	3	4	5	6	7	8	9	10	11									
6	(h)	Newport County	D	2-2	Taylor (2)	6,700	1	2	3	4	5	6	7	8	9	10	11									
10	(h)	Brentford	W	4-0	Richards (2), Hodgkisson, Taylor	10,864	1	2	3	4	5	6	7	8	9	10	11									
15	(a)	Newport County	L	2-4	Richards (2)	5,585	1	2	3	4	5	6	7	8	9	10	11									
17	(a)	Watford	L	0-2		14,581	1	2	3	4	5	6	7	8	9	10	11									
20	(h)	Chesterfield	W	2-1	Richards (2)	11,043	1	2	3	4	5	6	7	8	9	10	11									
24	(h)	Tranmere Rovers	W	3-1	Taylor (3)	10,721	1	2	3	4	5	6		8	9		11						7	10		
26	(a)	Chesterfield	W	2-1	Faulkner, Taylor	5,500	1		3	4	5	6	7	8	9		11	2						10		
Oct 1	(a)	Halifax Town	L	0-1		7,253	1		3		5	6		8	9		11	2	4				7	10		
3	(h)	Shrewsbury Town	W	3-2	Foster, Davies, Taylor	12,141	1		3	4		6		8	10		11	2		5			9	7		
8	(a)	Grimsby Town	L	1-3	Taylor	9,846	1			4		6	7	8	10		11	3	2	5			9			
15	(h)	Hull City	W	1-0	Richards	10,125	1		3	4	5	6	7	8	9	10	11	2								
22	(a)	Reading	L	2-3	Taylor, Rawlings	6,092	1				5	6	7	8	9	10	11	2	4		3					
28	(h)	Coventry City	D	1-1	Hodgkisson	13,053	1		3		5	6	7	8	9	10	11	2	4							
Nov 12	(h)	QPR	W	4-3	Richards (3), Wilson	10,344	1		3	6	5		7		10	8		2	4						11	9
19	(a)	Notts County	L	1-3	Wilson	12,574	1			6	5		7		10	8		3	4	2					11	9
Dec 10	(h)	Barnsley	W	1-0	Wilson	6,707	1			6	5		7		10	8	11	3	4	2						9
17	(h)	Port Vale	W	6-2	Richards (4, 1 pen), Hodgkisson, Taylor	8,381	1			6	5		7		10	8	11	3	4	2						9
23	(h)	Bury	W	1-0	Richards	10,702	1			6	5		7		10	8	11	3	4	2						9
26	(a)	Bury	W	4-3	Hodgkisson, Wilson, Richards, Taylor	13,102	1			6	5		7		10	8	11	3	4	2						9
31	(a)	Torquay Utd	L	0-3		6,680	1			6	5		7	8				3	4	2			11	10		9
Jan 9	(h)	Bournemouth	W	2-0	Hodgkisson, Richards (pen)	6,238	1			6	5		7		10	8		3	4	2				11		9
21	(a)	Brentford	L	1-3	Richards	6,250	1			6	5		7		10	8		3	4	2				11		9
Feb 4	(h)	Watford	W	5-2	Richards (2), Wilson, Taylor, Askey	10,465	1			6	5		7		10	8	11	3	4	2						9
11	(a)	Tranmere Rovers	W	4-1	Askey, Wilson, Richards, Taylor	9,611	1			6	5		7		10	8	11	3	4	2						9
18	(h)	Halifax Town	D	0-0		12,567	1			6	5		7		10	8	11	3	4	2						9
21	(a)	Bristol City	L	0-2		11,783	1			6	5		7		10	8	11	3	4	2						9
25	(h)	Bradford City	W	4-0	Richards, Wilson, Taylor (2)	8,216	1			6	5		7		10	8	11	3	4	2						9
Mar 4	(a)	Hull City	L	1-2	Taylor	7,118	1		3	6	5		7		10	8	11	2	4							9
11	(h)	Reading	D	2-2	Wilson, Taylor	9,455	1		3	6	5		7		10		11	2	4					8		9
14	(a)	Bradford City	W	2-1	Richards (2)	5,803	1			6					10	8	11	3	4	2		5			7	9
18	(a)	Coventry City	W	2-1	Wilson, Taylor	14,387	1			6					10	8	11	3	4	2		5			7	9
21	(h)	Swindon Town	W	2-1	Richards (2, 1 pen)	12,102	1			6					10	8	11	3	4	2		5			7	9
25	(h)	Bristol City	W	4-0	Faulkner, Richards (2), Thresher (og)	10,115	1			6				8	10		11	3	4	2		5	7			9
31	(a)	Colchester Utd	W	4-0	Wilson, Richards, Taylor (2)	5,480	1			6	5			8	10		11	3	4	2			7			9
Apr 1	(a)	QPR	L	0-1		14,125	1			6	5		7		10	8	11	3	4	2						9
3	(h)	Colchester Utd	W	3-0	Richards, Taylor (2)	12,985	1			6	5		7		10	8	11	3	4	2						9
8	(h)	Notts County	W	2-1	Taylor (2)	14,508	1			6	5		7		10	8	11	3	4	2						9
15	(a)	Bournemouth	W	3-0	Taylor (3)	10,535	1			6	5		7		10	8	11	3	4	2						9
22	(h)	Grimsby Town	W	2-1	Richards (pen), Taylor	16,446	1			6	5		7		10	8	11	3	4	2						9
26	(a)	Shrewsbury Town	W	2-1	Taylor, Askey	18,917	1			6	5		7		10	8	11	3	4	2						9
29	(a)	Barnsley	D	2-2	Askey, Richards	6,051	1			6	5		7		10	8	11	3	4	2						9
						Apps	46	11	19	43	40	18	38	21	45	37	41	35	32	27	1	4	7	8	5	28
League position: 2nd (Promoted)						Goals						1	4	3	36	7	33						1	1		10

own goals: 2

F.A. Cup

Date		Opponent	Rd	Score	Scorers	Att	Christie	Haddington	Guttridge	Dudley	McPherson	Rawlings	Askey	Faulkner	Richards	Hodgkisson	Taylor C.	Sharples	Hill	Palin	Gregg	Eden	Davies	Foster	Rowe	Wilson
Nov 5	(h)	Yeovil Town	1	0-1		11,887	1		3	4	5	6	7	8	9	10	11	2								
						Apps	1		1	1	1	1	1	1	1	1	1	1								
						Goals																				

League Cup

Date		Opponent	Rd	Score	Scorers	Att	Christie	Haddington	Guttridge	Dudley	McPherson	Rawlings	Askey	Faulkner	Richards	Hodgkisson	Taylor C.	Sharples	Hill	Palin	Gregg	Eden	Davies	Foster	Rowe	Wilson
Oct 31	(a)	Everton	1	1-3	Davies	14,137	1		3		5	6	7	8		10		2	4	9			11			
						Apps	1		1		1	1	1	1		1		1	1	1			1			
						Goals																	1			

Walsall won promotion this season - and so returned to the Second Division for the first time in 60 years.
The average home League attendance at Fellows Park in 1960-61 was 10,670.

SEASON 1961-62

Division Two

Date		Opponents		Score	Scorers	Att	Christie	Palin	Sharples	Hill	McPherson	Dudley	Askey	Hodgkisson	Wilson	Richards	Taylor C.	Meek	Younger	Guttridge	Ball	Gregg	Boswell	Partridge	Rawlings	Beaman	Foster	Eden	Rowe
Aug 19	(h)	Sunderland	W	4-3	Richards (3), Wilson	18,420	1	2	3	4	5	6	7	8	9	10	11												
23	(a)	Newcastle Utd	L	0-1		33,821	1	2	3	4	5	6	7	8	9	10	11												
26	(a)	Derby County	W	3-1	Hodgkisson, Younger, Taylor	26,318	1	2	3	4	5	6		8	9		11	7	10										
29	(h)	Newcastle Utd	W	1-0	Younger	25,453	1	2	3	4	5	6		8	9		11	7	10										
Sep 2	(h)	Leyton Orient	L	1-5	Younger	15,963	1	2		4	5	6	7	8	9		11		10					3					
6	(a)	Southampton	D	1-1	Richards	15,074	1	2		4	5	6	7	8	9	10	11			3									
9	(a)	Preston Nth End	W	3-2	Richards, Wilson, Hodgkisson	12,631	1	2		4	5	6		8	9	10	11	7		3									
16	(h)	Plymouth Argyle	W	1-0	Taylor	14,848	1	2		4	5	6		8	9	10	11	7		3									
19	(h)	Southampton	L	0-2		18,689	1	2		4	5	6		8	9	10	11	7		3									
23	(a)	Huddersfield Tn	L	2-4	Younger, Wilson	15,100	1	2	3	4	5	6			9	10	11	7	8										
30	(h)	Swansea Town	D	0-0		12,640		2	3	4	5	6			9	10	11	7	8		1								
Oct 7	(h)	Rotherham	W	5-0	Wilson (2), Meek, Taylor, Richards	12,028		2	3	4	5	6		8	9	10	11	7			1								
14	(a)	Liverpool	L	1-6	Yeats (og)	14,229		2	3	4	5	6		8	9	10	11	7			1								
21	(h)	Charlton Athletic	D	2-2	Richards, Hodgkisson	11,709		2	3	4	5	6	7	8	9	10	11				1								
24	(a)	Bury	L	1-2	Hodgkisson	8,863		2	3	4	5	6		8	9	10	11	7			1								
Nov 4	(h)	Brighton	D	2-2	Wilson, Richards	9,963	1	2	3	4	5	6		8	9	10	11	7											
11	(a)	Stoke City	L	1-2	Wilson	28,000	1	2	3	4	5	6		8	9		11	7	10										
18	(h)	Norwich City	W	5-0	Taylor (2), Palin, Meek, Younger (pen)	10,971		9	2	4	5	6		8			11	7	10	3			1						
25	(a)	Leeds Utd	L	1-4	Richards	10,999		9	2	4	5	6		8		10	11	7		3			1						
Dec 2	(h)	Bristol Rovers	D	0-0		9,429			2	4	5	6			9	10	11	7	8	3			1						
16	(a)	Sunderland	L	0-3		30,690			2	4	5	6	10	9		8	11	7		3			1						
23	(h)	Derby County	W	2-0	Meek, Taylor	9,641			2	4	5	6		8	9	10	11	7		3			1						
26	(h)	Luton Town	W	2-0	Wilson (2)	9,609			2	4	5	6		8	9	10	11	7		3			1						
Jan 13	(a)	Leyton Orient	L	0-3		15,113			2	4	5	6		8			11	7		3			1			9	10		
20	(h)	Preston Nth End	W	2-1	Meek, Taylor	10,284		9	2	4	5	6		8		10	11	7		3			1						
Feb 3	(a)	Plymouth Argyle	L	1-2	Richards (pen)	12,044		2		4	5	6	7	10		9	11	8		3			1						
10	(h)	Huddersfield Tn	D	2-2	Taylor (2)	10,864		2		4	5	6		8		10	11	7		3			1				9		
17	(a)	Swansea Town	W	3-1	Meek, Foster, Taylor	10,000		2	3	4	5	6		8		10	11	7					1				9		
24	(a)	Rotherham Utd	D	2-2	Meek, Richards	7,751		2	3	4	5	6		8		10	11	7					1				9		
Mar 3	(h)	Liverpool	D	1-1	Hodgkisson	13,660		2	3	4	5	6		8		10	11	7					1				9		
6	(a)	Scunthorpe Utd	L	1-2	Foster	7,023		2	3	4	5	6		8		10	11	7					1				9		
10	(a)	Charlton Athletic	D	3-3	Taylor (2), Sewell (og)	14,451		2		4	5	6		8		10	11	7		3			1				9		
17	(h)	Bury	W	3-0	Richards (2), Taylor	10,184		2	3	4	5	6		8		10	11	7					1				9		
24	(a)	Brighton	L	2-3	Taylor (2)	9,912		2	3	4	5	6		8	9	10	11	7					1						
30	(h)	Stoke City	W	3-1	Hill, Taylor, Allen (og)	16,750		2	3	4	5	6		8	9	10	11	7					1						
Apr 7	(a)	Norwich City	L	1-3	Richards	14,206		2	3	4	5	6		8	9	10	11	7					1						
11	(a)	Luton Town	L	0-2		6,123		2	3	4	5	6		8	9	10	11	7					1						
14	(h)	Leeds Utd	D	1-1	Meek	9,005		2	3	4	5	6		8		10	11	7					1				9		
21	(a)	Bristol Rovers	D	2-2	Meek, Palin	10,445		9	3	4	5	6		8		10	11	7				2	1						
23	(h)	Middlesborough	L	1-2	Taylor	9,664		2		4	5	6		8	9	10	11	7		3			1						
24	(a)	Middlesborough	L	0-3		18,238				4	5	10	7			9	11	8				2	1	3	6				
28	(h)	Scunthorpe Utd	W	4-1	Meek, Hodgkisson, Richards, Rawlings	7,173		3		4	5	6		8		9	11	7				2	1		10				
						Apps	12	36	31	42	42	42	8	38	25	36	42	37	8	16	5	3	25	2	2	1	9		
League position: 14th						Goals		2		1				6	9	15	17	9	5						1		2		

own goals: 3

F.A. Cup

Date		Opponents	Rd	Score	Scorers	Att	Christie	Palin	Sharples	Hill	McPherson	Dudley	Askey	Hodgkisson	Wilson	Richards	Taylor C.	Meek	Younger	Guttridge	Ball	Gregg	Boswell	Partridge	Rawlings	Beaman	Foster	Eden	Rowe
Jan 6	(a)	Bristol City	3	0-0		22,523			2	4		6		8	9	10	11	7		3			1					5	
9	(h)	Bristol City	3R	4-1	Richards (2), Taylor, Hodgkisson	15,420			2	4	5	6		8	9	10	11	7		3			1						
27	(a)	Fulham	4	2-2	Richards (2, 1 pen)	30,030		2		4	5	6		8		10	11	7		3			1						9
30	(h)	Fulham	4R	0-2		24,045		2		4	5	6		8		10	11	7		3			1						9
						Apps		2	2	4	3	4		4	2	4	4	4		4			4					1	2
						Goals								1		4	1												

League Cup

Date		Opponents	Rd	Score	Scorers	Att	Christie	Palin	Sharples	Hill	McPherson	Dudley	Askey	Hodgkisson	Wilson	Richards	Taylor C.	Meek	Younger	Guttridge	Ball	Gregg	Boswell	Partridge	Rawlings	Beaman	Foster	Eden	Rowe
Sep 13	(a)	Millwall Ath	1	2-1	Wilson, Richards	7,902	1	2		4	5	6	7	8	9	10		11		3									
Oct 4	(a)	Sunderland	2	2-5	Taylor (2)	29,558		2	3	4	5	6		8	9	10	11	7			1								
						Apps	1	2	1	2	2	2	1	2	2	2	1	2		1	1								
						Goals									1	1	2												

SEASON 1962-63

Division Two

Date		Opponents			Scorers	Att	Boswell	Gregg	Palin	Hill	McPherson	Dudley	Meek	Hodgkisson	Richards	Wills	Taylor C.	Christie	Sharples	Partridge	Roper	Rawlings	Eden	Smith	Pearson	Foster	O'Neill	Wiggin	Newton
Aug 18	(a)	Portsmouth	L	1-4	Richards	18,469	1	2	3	4	5	6	7	8	9	10	11												
21	(h)	Huddersfield Tn	D	1-1	Richards	13,505	1	2	3	4	5	6	7	8	9	10	11												
25	(h)	Preston Nth End	W	4-1	Meek (2), Hodgkisson, Richards	10,259	1	2	3	4	5	6	7	8	9	10	11												
29	(a)	Huddersfield Tn	L	0-4		12,310	1	2	3	4	5	6	7	8	9	10	11												
Sep 1	(a)	Plymouth Argyle	L	0-3		16,543	1		2	4	5	6	7	8		10	11		3							9			
4	(h)	Middlesbrough	W	1-0	Foster	10,691	1		2	4	5	6	7	8	10		11		3							9			
8	(h)	Grimsby Town	W	4-1	Hodgkisson (2), Foster, Richards	9,929	1		2	4	5	6	7	8	10		11		3							9			
12	(a)	Middlesbrough	W	3-2	Meek, Pearson, Foster	18,436	1		2		5	6	7	10			11		3		4				8	9			
15	(a)	Norwich City	L	1-2	Sharples	17,818	1		2		5	6	7	10			11		3		4				8	9			
22	(h)	Rotherham Utd	W	1-0	Meek	10,616	1		2	4	5	6	7	10	9		11		3						8				
29	(h)	Newcastle Utd	L	0-6		10,336	1	2		4		6	7	10	9		11			3			5			8			
Oct 6	(a)	Charlton Athletic	L	2-3	Richards, Taylor	13,070	1		2	4	5	6	7	8	10		11		3									9	
13	(h)	Stoke City	D	0-0		15,862	1		2	4	5	6	7	8	10		11		3			9							
20	(a)	Sunderland	L	0-5		36,750	1		2		5	6	7	8	9	10	11		3			4							
27	(h)	Leeds Utd	D	1-1	Taylor	7,353	1		2		5	6	7	8	9	10	11		3			4							
Nov 3	(a)	Swansea	L	0-3		9,003	1		2	4	5	6	7	8	10		11		3			9							
10	(h)	Chelsea	L	1-5	Taylor	8,492	1	2	3	4	5	6	7	8	9		11												10
17	(a)	Luton Town	L	3-4	Meek (2), Taylor	5,479		2		4	5	6	7	8	9		11	1	3										10
24	(h)	Southampton	D	1-1	Wiggin	8,005	1	3		2	5	4	7	10			11					6				8		9	
30	(a)	Scunthorpe Utd	L	0-2		7,074	1	3		2	5	4	7	10			11					6				8		9	
Dec 8	(h)	Bury	W	3-1	Richards (2), Eastham (og)	5,451	1	3		2	5	4	7	8	10		11					6						9	
15	(h)	Portsmouth	L	3-5	O'Neill (2), Taylor	8,825	1	3		2	5	4	7	8	10		11					6					9		
Mar 2	(a)	Stoke City	L	0-3		25,456	1	3		4	5		7	8	10		11		2			6					9		
9	(h)	Sunderland	L	2-3	Taylor (2)	7,234	1	3		4	5	6	7	8	10		11		2								9		
13	(a)	Leeds Utd	L	0-3		17,077	1	3		4	5	6	7	8	10		11		2								9		
16	(h)	Derby County	L	1-3	Taylor	7,867	1	3		4	5	6	7	8	10		11		2								9		
19	(a)	Preston Nth End	L	2-4	Palin (pen), Hodgkisson	10,605	1	3	2	4		6		8		10	11						5	7			9		
23	(h)	Swansea Town	L	0-1		7,609	1		2	4		6		8		10	11		3				5	7			9		
26	(h)	Plymouth Argyle	D	2-2	Meek, Taylor	7,846	1		2	4		6	7	10			11		3				5				8	9	
30	(a)	Chelsea	W	1-0	O'Neill	19,625	1		2	4		6	7	10			11		3				5				8	9	
Apr 6	(h)	Luton Town	D	1-1	Palin (pen)	8,960	1		2	4		6	7	10		11			3				5				8	9	
13	(a)	Southampton	L	0-2		18,048	1		2	4		6	7	8			11		3				5				9	10	
15	(a)	Cardiff City	D	2-2	Hodgkisson, Newton	11,599	1	3	2	4		5	7	8			11						6					9	10
16	(h)	Cardiff City	W	2-1	O'Neill, Newton	10,381	1	3	2	4	5	6	7	8			11										9		10
20	(h)	Scunthorpe Utd	D	1-1	Newton	6,828	1	3	2	4		6	7	8			11						5				9		10
24	(a)	Derby County	L	0-2		11,549	1	3	2	4			7	8			11					6	5				9		10
27	(a)	Bury	D	0-0		7,422	1		2	4	5		7	8			11		3			6					9		10
30	(a)	Grimsby Town	L	1-3	Palin (pen)	12,502	1		2	4	5		7	8			11		3			6					9		10
May 4	(a)	Rotherham Utd	W	2-1	O'Neill, Newton	7,740	1		2	4	5		7	8			11		3			6					9		10
8	(a)	Newcastle Utd	W	2-0	O'Neill, Newton	21,797	1	3	2	4	5		7	8			11					6					9		10
14	(h)	Norwich City	W	3-1	Meek, O'Neill, Newton	13,414	1	3	2	4	5		7	8			11					6					9		10
24	(h)	Charlton Athletic	L	1-2	Taylor	16,761	1		2	4	5		7	8			11		3			6					9		10
						Apps	41	22	32	38	32	34	40	42	21	10	41	1	25	1	2	16	10	2	3	8	20	9	12
League position: 21st						Goals			3				8	5	7		10		1						1	2	7	1	6

own goal: 1

F.A. Cup

Date		Opponents	Rd			Att	Boswell	Gregg	Palin	Hill	McPherson	Dudley	Meek	Hodgkisson	Richards	Wills	Taylor C.	Christie	Sharples	Partridge	Roper	Rawlings	Eden	Smith	Pearson	Foster	O'Neill	Wiggin	Newton
Mar 6	(h)	Manchester City	3	0-1		11,553	1	3		4	5	6	7	8	10		11		2								9		
						Apps	1	1		1	1	1	1	1	1		1		1								1		

League Cup

Date		Opponents	Rd		Scorers	Att	Boswell	Gregg	Palin	Hill	McPherson	Dudley	Meek	Hodgkisson	Richards	Wills	Taylor C.	Christie	Sharples	Partridge	Roper	Rawlings	Eden	Smith	Pearson	Foster	O'Neill	Wiggin	Newton
Sep 25	(h)	Stoke City	1	1-2	Taylor	10,583	1		2	4	5	6	7		9	10	11		3						8				
						Apps	1		1	1	1	1	1		1	1	1		1						1				
						Goals											1												

SEASON 1963-64

Division 3

							White	Palin	Sharples	Dudley	McPherson	Wills	Meek	Hodgkisson	Foster	Newton	Fell	Tennant	Roper	Gregg	Kletzenbauer	Bennett	Howells	Atthey	Smith R	Matthews	Mason	Clarke A.	Wiggin	O'Neill	Llewellyn
Aug 24	(a)	Luton Town	L	0-1		9,079	1	2	3	4	5	6	7	8	9	10	11														
27	(h)	Colchester Utd	D	1-1	Fell	9,489	1	2	3	4	5		7			10	11						6			8			9		
31	(h)	Coventry City	L	0-3		17,440	1	2	3	4	5		7	8		9	11						6			10					
Sep 7	(a)	Mansfield Town	L	1-2	Fell	8,407	1	2		4	5	6		10		9	11			3					7	8					
9	(a)	Colchester Utd	D	0-0		5,419	1	2		4	5	6	8	9			11			3					7	10					
14	(h)	Brentford	D	2-2	Fell, Matthews	6,448	1	2		4	5	6	7	8	9		11			3						10					
18	(a)	Reading	W	1-0	Fell	8,296	1	4				6	7	10	9		11		2	3			5			8					
21	(a)	Shrewsbury Town	L	1-2	Hodgkisson	8,447	1	4				6	7	10	9		11		2	3			5			8					
28	(h)	Bristol City	D	1-1	Smith	6,312	1	4				6				10	11		2	3			5		7	8				9	
Oct 1	(h)	Reading	D	1-1	Wills	5,939	1	4				6				10	11		2	3			5		7	8		9			
5	(a)	Port Vale	D	2-2	Matthews, Newton	12,760	1	4				6				10	11		2	3			5		7	8				9	
8	(a)	Crewe Alexandra	W	1-0	O'Neill	6,616	1	4				6				10	11		2	3			5		7	8				9	
11	(h)	Barnsley	D	4-4	Matthews (2), O'Neill, Palin (pen)	9,847	1	4				6				10	11		2	3			5		7	8				9	
14	(h)	Crewe Alexandra	W	2-1	Newton (2)	9,861	1	4				6				10	11		2	3			5		7	8				9	
19	(a)	Peterborough Utd	W	2-1	Newton, O'Neill	11,732	1	4				6				10	11		2	3			5		7	8				9	
24	(a)	Notts County	W	1-0	Matthews	6,548	1	4				6				10	11		2	3		5			7	8				9	
26	(h)	Oldham	D	1-1	Palin (pen)	10,336	1	4				6				10	11		2	3		5			7	8				9	
29	(h)	Notts County	W	2-1	Smith, Matthews	10,598	1	4				6				10	11		2	3		5			7	9	8				
Nov 2	(a)	Bristol Rovers	L	0-3		10,840	1	4				6				10	11		2	3		5			7	9	8				
9	(h)	QPR	L	0-2		7,961	1	4				6	7				11		2	3			5			10	8			9	
23	(h)	Bournemouth	L	0-2		6,398	1	4	2	6				10		9	11			3		5			7	8					
30	(a)	Hull City	L	1-3	Palin	7,578	1	4	3			6	11	10		9			2			5			7	8					
Dec 7	(h)	Southend Utd	W	2-0	Hodgkisson, Matthews	4,566	1	4	3		5	6	7	10	11				2							8			9		
14	(h)	Luton Town	W	4-0	Wiggin (2), Foster, Fincham (og)	3,863	1	4	3		5	6	7	10	11				2							8			9		
21	(a)	Coventry City	L	0-1		19,563	1	4	3		5	6	7	10	11	9			2							8					
26	(a)	Watford	L	3-5	Palin, Foster, Wiggin	11,053	1	4	3		5	6	7	10	11				2							8			9		
28	(h)	Watford	L	1-3	Foster	6,926	1	4			5	6	7		11				2	3						8		10	9		
Jan 4	(a)	Wrexham	L	0-4		7,153	1	4	3		5		7	10	11				2				6			8			9		
11	(h)	Mansfield Town	W	3-1	Matthews (2), Roper	4,376			3	6	5		7	10	11			1	4	2						8			9		
18	(a)	Brentford	D	1-1	Wiggin	10,650			3	6	5		7	10	11			1	4	2						8			9		
Feb 1	(h)	Shrewsbury Town	D	1-1	Matthews	6,662			3	6	5		7	10	11			1	4	2						8			9		
8	(a)	Bristol City	L	1-5	Wiggin	7,523			3	6	5		7		11			1	4	2						8	10		9		
15	(h)	Port Vale	W	2-1	Matthews, Meek	7,056			3	6	5		11	10				1	4	2					7	8					9
22	(a)	Barnsley	W	3-1	Llewellyn (3)	4,696			2	6	5		11	10				1	4	3					7	8					9
28	(h)	Millwall	L	0-2		9,518			3	6	5		11	10				1	4	2					7	8					9
Mar 7	(a)	Oldham Athletic	W	4-2	Hodgkisson, Matthews, Foster, Meek	5,553			3	6	5		11	10	7			1	4	2						8					9
14	(h)	Bristol Rovers	L	2-3	Meek, Llewellyn	3,681			3	6	5		11	4	10			1	2						7	8					9
18	(a)	Crystal Palace	L	0-1		12,784			3	6	5		11	10				1	4		2				7	8					9
21	(a)	Millwall	L	1-2	Roper	8,440			3	6	5		11	10	7			1	4		2					8					9
28	(h)	Wrexham	L	0-2		4,706			3	6	5		11	8	10			1	4		2				7						9
30	(h)	Crystal Palace	D	2-2	Foster, Palin	5,356		2		6	5		11	10	7			1			3	4				8					9
Apr 4	(a)	Bournemouth	D	1-1	Matthews	10,080		2		6	5			10	11			1			3	4				7		8			9
11	(h)	Hull City	D	1-1	Matthews	5,093		2		6	5		11	10	8			1			3	4				7		9			
18	(a)	Southend Utd	D	1-1	Foster	7,467		2		6	5			10	11			1			3	4			7	8		9			
25	(h)	Peterborough Utd	W	2-0	Matthews, Meek	5,611		2		6	5	11	7	10	9			1			3	4				8					
May 1	(a)	QPR	L	0-3		5,539		2			5		11	10	9			1			3	4		6	7	8					
						Apps	28	34	22	24	30	25	31	31	24	18	21	18	33	27	9	12	13	1	23	44	4	5	10	9	10
League position: 19th						Goals		5				1	4	3	6	4	4		2						2	15			5	3	4

own goals: 1

F.A. Cup

			Rd				White	Palin	Sharples	Dudley	McPherson	Wills	Meek	Hodgkisson	Foster	Newton	Fell	Tennant	Roper	Gregg	Kletzenbauer	Bennett	Howells	Atthey	Smith R	Matthews	Mason	Clarke A.	Wiggin	O'Neill	Llewellyn
Nov 16	(a)	Southport	1	1-2	Newton	4,768	1	4				6	11			9	10		2	3			5		7	8					
						Apps	1	1				1	1			1	1		1	1			1		1	1					
						Goals											1														

League Cup

			Rd				White	Palin	Sharples	Dudley	McPherson	Wills	Meek	Hodgkisson	Foster	Newton	Fell	Tennant	Roper	Gregg	Kletzenbauer	Bennett	Howells	Atthey	Smith R	Matthews	Mason	Clarke A.	Wiggin	O'Neill	Llewellyn
Sep 25	(a)	Ipswich Town	2	0-0		8,750	1	4				6				10	11		2	3			5		7	8				9	
Oct 3	(h)	Ipswich Town	2R	1-0	Newton	6,632	1	4				6				10	11		2	3			5		7	8				9	
16	(a)	Halifax Town	3	0-2		4,617	1	4				6				10	11		2	3			5		7	8				9	
						Apps	3	3				3				3	3		3	3			3		3	3				3	
						Goals										1															

SEASON 1964-65

Division 3

Date		Opponent		Score	Scorers	Att	Carling	Gregg	Kletzenbauer	Roper	Leedham	Chadwick	Smith R.	Matthews	O'Neill	Hodgkisson	Meek	Clarke A.	Llewellyn	Foster T.	West	Atthey	Bennett	Smith T.	Harrison	Taylor C.	Tennant	Sissons	Harris J.	Meath	Ford C.	Satchwell	McMorran
Aug 22	(h)	Gillingham	L	0-1		6,825	1	2	3	4	5	6	7	8	9	10	11																
26	(a)	Hull City	L	0-2		10,605	1	2	3	4	5	6	7		9	10	11	8															
29	(a)	Bristol City	L	1-5	Matthews	9,479	1	2	3	4	5			8		6	7	10	9	11													
Sep 5	(h)	QPR	W	4-0	Matthews, Llewellyn (2), Malcolm (og)	4,190	1	3		2	5	4	7	8		6	11	10	9														
11	(a)	Shrewsbury Town	L	1-3	Clarke	8,500	1	3			5	4		8		6	7	10	9	11	2												
15	(h)	Workington Town	L	1-4	Clarke	5,085	1	3			5	4		8			7	10	9	11	2	6											
19	(h)	Reading	W	4-1	Clarke (3), Matthews	3,681	1	3		6	5	4	7	8			10	9		11	2												
26	(a)	Southend Utd	D	0-0		5,868	1	3		6	5	4	7	8			10	9			2				11								
29	(a)	Watford	L	0-3		7,003	1	3		6	5	4	7	8			10	9			2				11								
Oct 3	(h)	Barnsley	D	1-1	Matthews	5,047	1	3		6	5	4	7	8			10	9		11	2												
6	(h)	Watford	L	0-4		4,463	1	3		4	5		7	8			10		9	11	2		6										
10	(h)	Grismby Town	W	1-0	Clarke	5,157	1	3		6			7	8			10	9		11	2		5		4								
13	(a)	Scunthorpe Utd	L	0-4		4,013	1	3		6			7	8			10	9		11	2		5		4								
17	(a)	Peterborough Utd	L	2-3	Clarke, Foster	9,372	1	3		6			7		8		10	9		11	2		5		4								
20	(h)	Scunthorpe Utd	L	1-2	O'Neill	5,471	1	3		6			7		8		10	9		11	2		5		4								
24	(h)	Bournemouth	L	0-1		6,631	1	3		6			7	8			10	9			2		5		4	11							
27	(a)	Carlisle Utd	L	1-2	Clarke	10,183	1	3		2	4		7				10	9				6	5		8	11							
28	(a)	Workington Town	L	1-3	Meek	5,743	1	3		2	4		7		8		10	9				6	5		11								
31	(a)	Exeter City	W	1-0	O'Neill	6,600	1	3		2			7		9		8	10				6	4	5	11								
Nov 7	(h)	Oldham Athletic	L	1-2	Clarke	10,108	1	3		2					9		7	10				6	4	5		11							8
21	(h)	Brentford	W	4-3	Taylor (3), Clarke	8,227		2						8				9		7		6		5		11	1	3		4			10
28	(a)	Colchester Utd	L	1-2	Clarke	3,394	1	2						8				9		7		6	5			11		3		4			10
Dec 5	(h)	Carlisle Utd	W	1-0	Taylor	5,578	1	2					7	8				9				6		5		11		3		4			10
12	(a)	Gillingham	L	0-4		5,867	1	2						8				9				6		5		11		3		4	7		10
19	(h)	Bristol City	L	2-4	Matthews (2)	5,213	1	2						8				9		7		6		5		11		3		4			10
26	(h)	Mansfield Town	W	2-1	Taylor (2)	6,900	1	3						7		8		9				6		5	2	11		4					10
28	(a)	Mansfield Town	L	0-2		5,207	1	3						7		8		9				6	5		2	11		4					10
Jan 1	(a)	QPR	L	0-1		4,844	1	3						7		8		9				6	5		2	11		4					10
16	(h)	Shrewsbury Town	D	1-1	Taylor	8,253	1	2						8				9				6		5		11		4	3			7	10
23	(a)	Reading	W	2-0	Clarke (2)	6,582	1	2										8	9			6		5		11		4	3			7	10
30	(h)	Port Vale	D	0-0		7,324	1	2										8	9			6		5		11		4	3			7	10
Feb 6	(h)	Southend Utd	L	2-3	O'Neill, Taylor	5,916	1	2							9							6		5		11		4	3		8	7	10
13	(a)	Barnsley	W	1-0	Satchwell	2,711	1	2										8				6	5			11		4	3		9	7	10
20	(a)	Grimsby Town	D	2-2	Clarke (2)	4,830	1	2										8				6	5			11		4	3	9		7	10
27	(h)	Peterborough Utd	L	0-1		8,857	1	2										8				6	5			11		4	3	9		7	10
Mar 13	(h)	Exeter City	W	2-1	Clarke (2, 1 pen)	6,463	1	2							9			8				6	5			11		4	3			7	10
16	(a)	Bristol Rovers	W	1-0	McMorran	13,717	1	2					7			9		8				6	5			11		4	3				10
20	(a)	Oldham Athletic	W	3-1	Clarke, Hodgkisson, Satchwell	4,651	1	2								9		8				6	5			11		4	3			7	10
27	(h)	Bristol Rovers	W	2-0	Taylor (2)	7,509	1	2								9		8				6	5			11		4	3			7	10
Apr 3	(a)	Brentford	D	0-0		7,508	1	2								8		9				6	5			11		4	3			7	10
6	(h)	Hull City	D	3-3	Clarke (2), Satchwell	12,097	1	2								9		8				6	5			11		4	3			7	10
10	(h)	Colchester Utd	W	2-1	Clarke, Hodgkisson	8,766	1	2								9		8				6	5			11		4	3			7	10
16	(a)	Luton Town	W	3-1	Clarke (2), Taylor	9,353	1	2								9		8				6	5			11		4	3			7	10
17	(a)	Bournemouth	L	0-4		6,153	1	2								9		8				6	5			11		4	3			7	10
19	(h)	Luton Town	L	0-1		7,482	1	2								9		8				6	5			11		4	3		10	7	
26	(a)	Port Vale	L	1-2	Taylor	3,521	1	2						8				9				6	5			11		4	3			7	10
						Apps	45	46	3	18	13	9	18	23	9	17	20	43	7	13	12	31	27	11	13	29	1	26	18	7	4	17	26
League position: 19th						Goals								6	3	2	1	23	2	1						12						3	1

own goal: 1

F.A. Cup

Date		Opponent	Rd	Score	Scorers	Att	Carling	Gregg	Kletzenbauer	Roper	Leedham	Chadwick	Smith R.	Matthews	O'Neill	Hodgkisson	Meek	Clarke A.	Llewellyn	Foster T.	West	Atthey	Bennett	Smith T.	Harrison	Taylor C.	Tennant	Sissons	Harris J.	Meath	Ford C.	Satchwell	McMorran
Nov 16	(h)	Bristol Rovers	1	0-2		10,756	1	3		2						10	8	9				6	4	5	7	11							
						Apps	1	1		1						1	1	1				1	1	1	1	1							

League Cup

Date		Opponent	Rd	Score	Scorers	Att	Carling	Gregg	Kletzenbauer	Roper	Leedham	Chadwick	Smith R.	Matthews	O'Neill	Hodgkisson	Meek	Clarke A.	Llewellyn	Foster T.	West	Atthey	Bennett	Smith T.	Harrison	Taylor C.	Tennant	Sissons	Harris J.	Meath	Ford C.	Satchwell	McMorran
Sep 2	(h)	Oxford Utd	1	1-1	Matthews	4,356	1	3		4	5		7	8		6	11	10	9		2												
7	(a)	Oxford Utd	1R	1-6	Llewellyn	7,126	1	3		2	5	4	7	8		6	11	10	9														
						Apps	2	2		2	2	1	2	2		2	2	2	2		1												
						Goals								1					1														

SEASON 1965-66

Division 3

Date	Opponent	Res	Score	Scorers	Att	Carling	Gregg	Harris J.	Sissons	Bennett	Atthey	Satchwell	Clarke A.	Kirby	McMorran	Taylor C.	Hodgkisson	Morris	Ford	Meath	Holbutt	Harrison	Summers	Evans	Harris G.	Smith T.	Riley	Middleton
Aug 21 (a)	Bournemouth	W	1-0	Clarke	9,094	1	2	3	4	5	6	7	8	9	10	11												
24 (h)	Workington Town	D	1-1	Satchwell	9,427	1	2	3	4	5	6*	7	8	9	10	11	12											
28 (h)	Southend Utd	W	3-0	Clarke (2, 1 pen), Kirby	8,450	1	2	3	4	5	6	7	8	9		11	10											
Sep 4 (a)	Swindon Town	D	0-0		13,734	1	2	3	4	5	6	7	8	9	10	11												
11 (h)	Shrewsbury Town	W	3-0	Clarke, Kirby, Taylor	13,603	1	2	3	4	5	6	7	8	9	10	11												
14 (h)	Peterborough Utd	W	2-0	Clarke (2)	16,643	1	2	3	4	5	6	7	8	9	10			11*	12									
18 (a)	Grimsby Town	L	1-3	McMorran	5,074	1	2	3	4	5	6	7	8	9	10	11												
25 (h)	Brentford	D	1-1	Sissons	8,384	1	2	3	4	5	6	7		9	10	11				8								
Oct 2 (a)	Bristol Rovers	L	0-3		9,357	1	2	3	4	5	6	7			10	11	8			9*	12							
4 (a)	Peterborough Utd	L	1-3	Clarke	9,309	1	2	3	4	5	6	7	9		10	11	8											
9 (h)	Reading	W	3-0	Clarke (2), Harrison	8,970	1	2	3	4	5	6	7	8	9		11						10						
16 (a)	Hull City	L	2-3	Kirby (2)	15,931	1	2	3	4	5	6		8	9	10	11						7						
23 (h)	Mansfield Town	W	2-1	Kirby, McMorran	9,334	1	2	3		5	6	7	8	9	10*	11			12				4					
30 (a)	QPR	L	1-2	Kirby	5,228	1	2	3	4*	5	11	7	8	9					12			10	6					
Nov 6 (h)	Brighton	W	2-1	Kirby (2)	8,529	1	2	3		5	6	7	8	9	10				11				4					
20 (h)	Watford	W	3-0	Clarke (2), Taylor	7,264	1	2	3		5	6	7	8	9	10	11							4					
Dec 11 (a)	Millwall	D	1-1	Kirby	10,460	1		3	2	5	6	7	8	9	10	11							4					
17 (h)	Hull City	L	2-4	Clarke (2 pens)	8,610	1		2		5	6	7	8	9	10	11							4	3				
27 (a)	Oxford Utd	L	1-7	Kirby	9,707	1		3	2	5	6	7	8	9	10	11							4					
Jan 1 (a)	Reading	L	0-3		6,991	1		3	2		6		8	9		11			7			10	4			5		
8 (h)	Scunthorpe Utd	W	3-0	Atthey, Riley, Taylor	7,059	1	2*	3	4	5	6		8	9	10	11						12					7	
15 (a)	Mansfield Town	W	3-0	Clarke (2), McMorran	4,027	1		3	4	5	6		8	9	10	11						2					7	
29 (h)	Bournemouth	W	2-1	Clarke, Kirby	10,047	1	2	3	4	5	6		8	9		11							10				7	
Feb 5 (a)	Southend Utd	L	3-5	Clarke (2), Taylor	6,310	1	2	3	4	5	6		8	9		11							10				7	
19 (h)	Swindon Town	W	5-0	Riley (2), Satchwell, Taylor (2)	9,367	1	2	3	4	5	6	9		8		11							10				7	
Mar 5 (h)	Swansea Town	D	1-1	Taylor	10,911	1	2	3	4	5	6		9	10		11							8				7	
12 (h)	Grimsby Town	W	1-0	Taylor	9,228	1	2	3	12	5	6	9	8	10		11							4*				7	
15 (a)	Oldham Athletic	W	2-1	Kirby, Satchwell	14,085	1	2	3	4	5	6	9		8		11						10					7	
19 (a)	Brentford	D	2-2	Kirby, Taylor	7,900	1	2	3	4		6			9		11				5		10					7	8
24 (a)	Shrewsbury Town	W	2-1	Harris J (2 pens)	8,924	1	2	3	4	5	6			9		11						10					7	8
26 (h)	Bristol Rovers	D	1-1	Middleton	8,485	1	2	3	4*	5	6			10		11						8	12				7	9
30 (a)	Workington Town	L	0-1		2,719	1	2	3		5	6	7		9		11						10	4					8
Apr 2 (a)	Brighton	L	1-2	Kirby	10,757	1	2	3		5	6			9		11						10	4				7	8
9 (h)	Gillingham	W	6-1	Middleton (4), Taylor (2)	6,632	1	2	3		5*	6			10	8	11						12	4				7	9
11 (h)	Exeter City	D	1-1	Middleton	9,478	1	2	3	12	5	6*			9	10	11							4				7	8
13 (a)	Exeter City	W	2-0	Middleton, Taylor	4,458	1	2	3	4	5				9		11						10	6				7	8
16 (a)	Watford	W	1-0	Taylor	4,715	1	2	3	4	5				9*	10	11						12	6				7	8
23 (h)	Oldham Athletic	D	2-2	Middleton (2)	8,822	1	2	3	4	5					10*	11				8		12	6				7	9
25 (a)	York City	W	3-0	Middleton, Taylor (2)	2,894	1	2	3	4	5*	6					11				12		8	10				7	9
30 (a)	Gillingham	L	0-1		6,628	1	2	3	5		6	12				11			9*			10	4				7	8
May 4 (h)	Oxford Utd	D	1-1	Middleton	8,419	1	2	3	4	5	6					11			9			10					7	8
7 (h)	Millwall	L	1-4	Middleton (pen)	11,224	1	2*	3	4	5	12	9				11						10	6				7	8
17 (h)	York City	W	2-0	Taylor, Baker (og)	6,931	1		2	4	5		12			10	11				9*			6		3		7	8
21 (a)	Scunthorpe Utd	L	2-4	Middleton (2)	3,289	1	2		4	5	6			9		11							10		3		7	8
24 (a)	Swansea Town	L	0-1		6,019	1	2	3	4	5		7*		9	10	11				12			6					8
28 (h)	QPR	L	0-1		8,103	1	2	3	4	5					10	11				9			6				7	8
					Apps	46	40	45	37	43	39	24	24	37	25	43	3	1	4	6		16	27	1	2	1	24	18
					Sub				2		1	2					1		3	2	1	4	1					
League position: 9th					Goals			2	1		1	3	18	14	3	16						1					3	14

own goal: 1

F.A. Cup

Date	Opponent	Rd	Score	Scorers	Att	Carling	Gregg	Harris J.	Sissons	Bennett	Atthey	Satchwell	Clarke A.	Kirby	McMorran	Taylor C.	Hodgkisson	Morris	Ford	Meath	Holbutt	Harrison	Summers	Evans	Harris G.	Smith T.	Riley	Middleton
Nov 13 (h)	Swansea Town	1	6-3	Clarke (2, 1pen), Summers, Satchwell, Kirby (2)	11,651	1	2	3		5	6	7	8	9	10	11							4					
Dec 4 (a)	Aldershot	2	2-0	Taylor, Clarke	6,813	1		3	2	5	6	7	8	9	10	11							4					
Jan 22 (a)	Stoke City	3	2-0	Kirby, Clarke (pen)	32,676	1	2	3	4	5	6		8	9	10	11											7	
Feb 12 (a)	Norwich City	4	2-3	Kirby, Taylor	28,754	1	2	3	4	5	6		8	9		11							10				7	
					Apps	4	3	4	3	4	4	2	4	4	3	4							3				2	
					Goals							1	4	3		2							1				1	

League Cup

Date	Opponent	Rd	Score	Scorers	Att	Carling	Gregg	Harris J.	Sissons	Bennett	Atthey	Satchwell	Clarke A.	Kirby	McMorran	Taylor C.
Sep 1 (a)	QPR	1	1-1	Kirby	3,529	1	2	3	4	5	6	7	8	9	10	11
7 (h)	QPR	1R	3-2	Kirby, Gregg, Clarke (pen)	12,376	1	2	3	4	5	6	7	8	9	10	11
22 (a)	West Brom Alb	2	1-3	Taylor	41,188	1	2	3	4	5	6	7	8	9	10	11
					Apps	3	3	3	3	3	3	3	3	3	3	3
					Goals		1						1	2		1

SEASON 1966-67

Division 3

Date		Opponent			Scorers	Att	Carling	Gregg	Harris J.	Meath	Bennett	Atthey	Baker	Middleton	Kirby	McMorran	Taylor	Harris G.	Sissons	Pace	Evans	MacEwan	Summers	Wesson	Ball	Harrison	Coton	Hill	Simpson	Cross	Satchwell	Murray	Ford	Smith	Jackson	Gough R.	Morris
Aug 20	(h)	Mansfield Town	L	1-2	Richardson (og)	10,287	1	2	3*	4	5	6	7	8	9	10	11	12																			
27	(a)	Grimsby Town	L	1-3	Pace	5,883	1	2		6	5		7	8		10	11	3	4	9																	
Sep 3	(a)	Gillingham	D	0-0		6,343	1	2		6	5*		8	10	9		11		4	12	3	7															
6	(h)	Workington Town	W	2-0	Middleton, Taylor	9,785	1	2		6			8	10	9		11		4		3	7	5														
10	(h)	Peterborough Utd	D	1-1	Middleton	9,236	1	2		4*		12	8	10	9		11		5		3	7	6														
17	(a)	Torquay Utd	L	2-5	Meath, Taylor	5,999	1	2		6	5		8	10	9		11		4		3	7															
24	(h)	Brighton	W	2-1	Kirby, Taylor	8,117	1	2		6	5		8	10*	9		11		4		3	7	12														
28	(a)	Workington Town	L	0-4		5,425	1	2			5	6	8	9	12	10	11		4		3												7*				
Oct 1	(a)	Darlington	W	1-0	Atthey	5,780		2			5	6	8	9		10	11		4		3			1										7			
8	(h)	Scunthorpe Utd	W	2-0	Kirby, McMorran (pen)	9,326		2			5	6	8		9	10	11		4		3			1										7			
11	(h)	Gillingham	W	3-0	Kirby (2), Taylor	10,236		2			5	6	8		10		11		4	9	3			1							7						
15	(a)	Oldham Athletic	L	2-6	Gregg (pen), Baker	10,265		2		4	5	6	8		10		11			9	3			1							7						
18	(h)	Swindon Town	D	1-1	Gregg (pen)	9,017		2			5	6*	8		9		11		4		3		12	1										7		10	
22	(h)	Oxford Utd	W	2-0	Baker (pen), Kirby	8,607		2			5		8		9		11		4		3	7	6	1										10			
29	(a)	Bristol Rovers	L	2-4	Middleton, Taylor	8,963	1	2				6	8	10	9		11		4		3	7	5														
Nov 4	(h)	Colchester Utd	W	1-0	Kirby	8,152	1	2			5	12	8	7	9	10*	11		4		3		6														
12	(a)	Shrewsbury Tn	W	2-1	Baker (2)	7,798		2			5*		8	7	9	10	11		12		3		6	1				4									
19	(h)	Middlesbrough	W	2-1	Kirby, Taylor	8,967		2					8		9	10	11		5		3	7	6	1				4									
Dec 3	(h)	Bournemouth	W	3-0	Kirby, Taylor, McEwan	6,835		2					8		9	10	11		4		3	7	5	1				6									
12	(a)	Mansfield Town	L	1-4	Baker	8,782		2					8		9	10	11		5		3	7	6	1				4									
26	(h)	Reading	W	3-1	Baker, Kirby (2)	10,557		2					8		9	10	11		5		3		6	1				4			7						
27	(a)	Reading	L	1-3	Baker	10,071		2			12		8		9	10	11		5				6	1		3		4*			7						
31	(h)	Grimsby Town	W	1-0	Summers (pen)	8,872		2			5		8		9				3				6	1				4			7			10			11
Jan 14	(a)	Peterborough Utd	L	1-2	Kirby	7,330		2			5		8	11	9	10					3		6	1				4			7						
21	(h)	Torquay Utd	L	0-1		9,401		2		12			8		9	10	11		5	7	3		6	1				4*									
Feb 4	(a)	Brighton	W	3-2	Meath, Satchwell, Middleton	13,411		2		4		6	8	10					5		3			1		11					9		7				
11	(a)	Darlington	D	1-1	Meath	8,647		2		4		6	8	10					5		3			1		11					9		7				
18	(a)	Watford	L	1-2	Meath	11,294		2		6	5		8*	12	9		11		4		3			1		7					10						
24	(a)	Scunthorpe Utd	L	0-2		4,839		2		4		6		10	9		11		5		3			1							7				8		
Mar 3	(h)	Oldham Athletic	D	1-1	Jackson	8,727		2		6			8		9				4		3			1		11*				5	12			7	10		
11	(h)	Watford	L	0-1		7,772		2		4	5	6			9	12	11				3				1						8*			7	10		
18	(a)	Oxford Utd	W	2-1	Baker (2)	6,770		2				6	8	9		10	11				3				1				4	5					7		
25	(h)	Bristol Rovers	D	1-1	Jackson	7,408		2			5	6	8	9		10	11				3				1				4						7		
27	(h)	Doncaster Rovers	W	4-0	Jackson, Taylor, Sykes (2,ogs)	6,696		2			5		8		10		11				3				1	6			4		9				7		
28	(a)	Doncaster Rovers	L	1-2	Harrison	4,831		2			5		8	9	10		11				3				1	6			4						7		
Apr 1	(a)	Colchester Utd	L	1-5	Baker	4,809		2*		9			8		10		11		5		3				1	6			4					12	7		
8	(h)	Shrewsbury Town	D	2-2	Simpson, Jackson	5,708					5	6	8		9		11				3				1		2		4					10	7		
11	(h)	QPR	W	2-0	Simpson, Jackson (pen)	11,881					5	6	8		9	10	11				3				1			2	4						7		
15	(a)	Middlesbrough	W	2-0	Baker, Taylor	18,090					5	6	8		9	10	11				3				1			2	4						7		
18	(a)	Swindon Town	L	2-3	Baker, Taylor	14,459					5	6	8		9	10	11				3				1			2	4						7		
22	(h)	Swansea	D	1-1	Taylor	7,262					5	6	8		9	10	11				3				1			2	4						7		
25	(a)	QPR	D	0-0		11,860					5		8	10	9		11		4		3				1			2							7		
29	(a)	Bournemouth	L	0-3		4,551					5	6	8	10	9		11				3				1			2	4						7		
May 6	(h)	Leyton Orient	D	1-1	Middleton	5,464					5	6	8	10	9		11				3				1	2			4						7		
13	(a)	Swansea	L	1-4	Baker	4,785				10	5	6	8				11				3				1	2			4			9			7		
19	(a)	Leyton Orient	W	2-0	Taylor (2)	3,650				10		6	8				11		12		3			1		2			4	5	7	9*					
						Apps	10	36	1	17	30	23	44	22	37	20	41	1	28	4	42	10	14	21	15	11	1	15	15	3	13	2	3	8	17	1	1
						Sub				1	1	2		1	1	1		1	2	1			2								1			1			
League position: 12th						Goals		2		4		1	13	5	11	1	13			1		1	1			1			2		1				5		

Own goals 3

F.A. Cup

Date		Opponent	Rd		Scorers	Att	Carling	Gregg	Harris J.	Meath	Bennett	Atthey	Baker	Middleton	Kirby	McMorran	Taylor	Harris G.	Sissons	Pace	Evans	MacEwan	Summers	Wesson	Ball	Harrison	Coton	Hill	Simpson	Cross	Satchwell	Murray	Ford	Smith	Jackson	Gough R.	Morris
Nov 26	(h)	St Neots	1	2-0	Baker, Taylor	10,429		2					8		9	10	11		5		3	7	6	1				4									
Jan 7	(h)	Gillingham	2	3-1	Taylor (2), Baker	10,418		2			5		8		9	10	11				3		6	1				4			7						
28	(a)	Bury	3	0-2		14,244		2		4		6	8		9	10	11		5		3			1										7			
						Apps		3		1	1	1	3		3	3	3		2		3	1	2	3				2			1			1			
						Goals							2				3																				

League Cup

Date		Opponent	Rd		Scorers	Att	Carling	Gregg	Harris J.	Meath	Bennett	Atthey	Baker	Middleton	Kirby	McMorran	Taylor	Harris G.	Sissons	Pace	Evans	MacEwan	Summers	Wesson	Ball	Harrison	Coton	Hill	Simpson	Cross	Satchwell	Murray	Ford	Smith	Jackson	Gough R.	Morris
Aug 23	(a)	Port Vale	1	3-1	Middleton (2), Taylor	9,186	1	2		6			7	8		10	11	3	4	9			5														
Sep 13	(h)	Stoke City	2	2-1	Taylor, Middleton	13,600	1	2		6	5		8	10	9		11		4		3	7															
Oct 5	(a)	Exeter City	3	2-1	Baker, Meath	5,487	1	2		12	5	6		8	9*	10	11		4		3													7			
26	(a)	Sheffield Utd	4	1-2	Taylor	13,910	1	2		12		6	8	7*	9		11		4		3		5											10			
						Apps	4	4		2	2	2	3	4	3	2	4	1	4	1	3	1	2											2			
						Sub				2																											
						Goals				1			1	2			3																				

SEASON 1967-68

Division 3

Date		Opponent			Scorers	Att	Ball	Gregg	Evans	Simpson	Bennett	Atthey	Middleton	Jackson	Murray	McMorran	Taylor	Baker	Watson	Wesson	Sissons	Harrison	Harris G	Meath	Cross	Clarke. D.	Morris	Harris J.	Jones	Biggs
Aug 19	(a)	Watford	W	2-1	Murray, Taylor	8,861	1	2	3	4	5	6	7	8	9	10*	11										12			
26	(h)	Gillingham	W	3-0	Middleton, Baker, Murray	8,288	1	2	3	4	5	6	7		9	10	11	8												
Sep 2	(a)	Grimsby Town	L	0-3		4,794	1	2	3	4	5	6	7		9	10	11	8												
5	(h)	Orient	W	5-0	Middleton (2), Baker (2), Murray	7,476	1	2	3	4	5	6	7		9	10	11	8												
9	(h)	Torquay utd	D	1-1	Taylor	9,907	1	2	3	4	5	6	7		9	10	11	8												
16	(a)	Reading	D	2-2	Murray, Taylor	10,864	1	2	3	4	5	6		7	9	10	11	8												
23	(h)	Swindon Town	W	3-2	Murray (2), Taylor	9,132	1	2	3	4	5	6		7	9	10	11	8												
25	(a)	Orient	L	0-2		3,481	1	2	3	4	5	6		7	9	10	11	8												
30	(a)	Shrewsbury Town	W	1-0	Baker	8,475	1	2	3	4	5	6			9	10	11	8	7											
Oct 3	(h)	Tranmere Rovers	W	5-1	Watson, Baker, Murray, Taylor, Martin (og)	7,250	1	2	3	4	5	6			9	10	11	8	7											
7	(a)	Scunthorpe Utd	W	5-2	Watson, Taylor (3), Jackson (pen)	4,047	1	2	3	4	5	6		12	9*	10	11	8	7											
14	(h)	Oldham Athletic	W	3-1	McMorran (pen), Baker, Taylor	10,366	1	2	3	4	5	6			9	10	11	8	7											
21	(a)	Bristol Rovers	W	3-2	Watson (2), Murray	7,912	1	2	3	4	5	6			9	10	11	8	7											
23	(a)	Tranmere Rovers	L	0-2		7,817	1	2	3	4	5	6		10	9		11	8	7											
28	(h)	Barrow	W	4-0	Murray, Jackson, Taylor (2)	11,276	1	2	3	4	5	6		10	9		11	8	7											
Nov 4	(a)	Oxford Utd	L	0-4		7,383	1	2	3	4	5	6		10	9		11	8	7											
11	(h)	Bury	W	2-1	Bennett, Middleton	12,169	1	2	3	4	5	6	12	10*	9		11	8	7											
14	(h)	Grimsby Town	W	2-0	Watson (2)	13,480	1	2	3	4	5	6		10	9		11	8	7											
18	(a)	Bournemouth	D	1-1	Murray	6,206		2	3	4	5	6		10	9		11	8	7	1										
25	(h)	Colchester Utd	D	1-1	Simpson	10,011		2	3	4	5	6		10	9		11	8	7	1										
Dec 2	(a)	Peterborough Utd	L	1-2	Baker	9,479		2	3	4	5	6*	12		9	10	11	8	7	1										
16	(h)	Watford	D	1-1	Simpson	9,409		2	3	4	5	6		7	9	10	11	8		1										
23	(a)	Gillingham	W	1-0	Middleton	8,013		2	3	4	5	6	10		9*		11	8	7	1	12									
26	(h)	Stockport County	L	0-1		15,470		2	3	4*	5	6	10		9		11	8	7	1		12								
29	(a)	Stockport County	D	0-0		11,415		2		10	5	6	9				11	8	7	1			3	4						
Jan 13	(a)	Torquay Utd	L	1-4	Harris	8,342		2		10		6	9				11	8	7	1			3	4	5					
20	(h)	Reading	D	2-2	Murray, Atthey	9,703		2			5	6		10	9		11	8	7	1		12	3	4*						
Feb 3	(a)	Swindon Town	L	0-3		17,111		2		4	5	6		10			11	8	7	1		12	3			9*				
10	(h)	Shrewsbury Town	L	1-2	Watson	14,166		2		4	5	6		10	9		11	8	7	1			3							
24	(h)	Scunthorpe Utd	D	0-0		8,987		2		4	5			12	9*	10			7	1	6		3	8			11			
28	(a)	Brighton	L	0-1		6,447		2		12	5				9	10	11	8	7	1	4*		3	6						
Mar 2	(a)	Oldham Athletic	W	3-0	Watson, McMorran (2,1 pen)	3,881		2	3	4	5		9	8*		10	11		7	1				12				6		
9	(a)	Northampton Tn	L	0-3		8,356	1	2	3	4	5	12		8		10	11		7							9		6*		
16	(h)	Bristol Rovers	W	2-1	Watson, McMorran (pen)	7,341		2			10	6	9			8	11		7	1		4	3						5	
23	(a)	Barrow	D	1-1	Middleton	5,396		2			4	6	8*			10	11		7	1			3	12					5	9
29	(h)	Oxford Utd	L	0-1		11,004		2			4	6*				10	11	8	7	1		12	3						5	9
Apr 2	(h)	Northampton Tn	W	4-0	Morris (2), Middleton, Biggs	5,520		2	3	4	5		8						7	1		10					11		6	9
6	(a)	Bury	L	1-2	Middleton	9,106		2		4	5	3	8						7	1		10					11		6	9
13	(h)	Bournemouth	D	1-1	Harrison	6,815		2	6*	4	5	3	8					7		1		10		12			11			9
15	(a)	Southport	L	0-2		6,994		2		3*			8						7	1		10	12	4	5		11		6	9
16	(h)	Southport	D	1-1	Biggs	5,531		2						3					7	1		10		4	5	9	11		6	8
20	(a)	Colchester Utd	D	2-2	Clarke, Morris	2,764		2			4	12		10*					7	1		6			3	9	11		5	8
23	(h)	Mansfield Town	W	2-1	Biggs (pen), Watson	5,598		2	3		9	6						12	7	1		10		4*			11		5	8
27	(h)	Peterborough Utd	W	3-2	Meath, Biggs (2)	5,620		2	3		9	6						12	7	1		10		4*			11		5	8
May 6	(a)	Mansfield Town	W	3-0	Meath, Bennett, Clarke	5,072		2	3		8	6						12	7	1		10		4		9	11		5*	
11	(h)	Brighton	L	1-2	Bennett	5,385		2	3		5*	6							7	1		10		4		9	11		12	8
						Apps	19	46	32	35	43	38	16	19	28	22	35	31	36	27	2	11	10	11	4	6	11	2	11	11
						Sub				1		2	2	2				3			1	4	1	3			1		1	
League position: 7th						Goals				2	3	1	8	2	11	4	11	7	10			1	1	2		2	3			5

own goal: 1

F.A. Cup

Date		Opponent	Rd		Scorers	Att	Ball	Gregg	Evans	Simpson	Bennett	Atthey	Middleton	Jackson	Murray	McMorran	Taylor	Baker	Watson	Wesson	Sissons	Harrison	Harris G	Meath	Cross	Clarke. D.	Morris	Harris J.	Jones	Biggs
Dec 9	(a)	Leytonstone	1	1-0	Watson	3,411		2	3	4	5	6			9	10	11	8	7	1										
Jan 6	(a)	Exeter City	2	3-1	Meath, Watson, Simpson	10,133		2		10	5	6	9*				11	8	7	1		12	3	4						
27	(h)	Crystal Palace	3	1-1	Taylor	15,333		2		4	5	6		10			11	8	7	1			3			9				
31	(a)	Crystal Palace	3R	2-1	Simpson, Jackson	27,414		2		4	5	6		10			11*	8	7	1		12	3			9				
Feb 17	(h)	Liverpool	4	0-0		21,066		2		4	5	6		10			11	8*	7	1			3	12		9				
19	(a)	Liverpool	4R	2-5	Watson (2)	39,113		2		4	5	6		10			11	8*	7	1			3	12		9				
						Apps		6	1	6	6	6	1	4	1	1	6	6	6	6			5	1		4				
						Sub																2		2						
						Goals				2				1			1		5					1						

League Cup

Date		Opponent	Rd		Scorers	Att	Ball	Gregg	Evans	Simpson	Bennett	Atthey	Middleton	Jackson	Murray	McMorran	Taylor	Baker	Watson	Wesson	Sissons	Harrison	Harris G	Meath	Cross	Clarke. D.	Morris	Harris J.	Jones	Biggs
Aug 22	(h)	Shrewsbury Tn	1	4-2	Taylor (2), Murray, Baker	9,834	1	2	3	4	5		7		9	10	11	8						6						
Sep 13	(h)	West Ham United	2	1-5	Jackson (pen)	17,755	1	2	3	4	5	6	7*	12	9	10	11	8												
						Apps	2	2	2	2	2	1	2		2	2	2	2						1						
						Sub								1																
						Goals								1	1		2	1												

In February 1968, three Clarke brothers wore the No.9 shirt for their respective clubs on the same day; the eldest Frank for Shrewsbury, the youngest Derek for Walsall and the costliest of the trio, Allan, for Fulham.

SEASON 1968-69

Division 3

Date		Opponent		Score	Scorers	Att	Wesson	Gregg	Evans	Atthey	Jones	Bennett	Baker	Murray	Biggs	Tindall	Morris	Watson	Meath	Wilson	Harrison	Trevis	Train	Cross	Harris J.	McMorran	Stephens	Bullock	Parkes
Aug 10	(a)	Shrewsbury Town	W	1-0	Jones	7,978	1	2	3	4	5	6	7	8	9	10	11												
17	(h)	Bristol Rovers	D	2-2	Watson, Biggs	7,593	1	2	3	4	5	6		8	9	10	11	7											
23	(a)	Stockport County	D	2-2	Watson, Biggs	8,034	1	2	3*	4	5	6	8		9	10	11	7	12										
27	(a)	Watford	D	0-0		9,361	1	2	3	4	5	6	8*	12	9	10	11	7											
31	(h)	Northampton Tn	L	0-1		7,768	1	2	3	4	5	6	12	8	9	10*	11	7											
Sep 7	(h)	Reading	D	2-2	Wilson, Atthey	6,945	1	2	3	4	5	6	7	12	9			11		8*	10								
14	(a)	Swindon Town	L	0-1		10,594	1	2	3	4	5	6			9	10	11	7		8									
18	(a)	Plymouth Argyle	L	0-1		11,118	1	2	3	4	5	6			9	10	11	7*		8	12								
20	(h)	Crewe Alexandra	D	1-1	Wilson	5,570	1	2	3	4	5	6	7*		9		11		10	8	12								
28	(a)	Bournemouth	L	0-1		8,645	1	2	3		5	6			9		11	7		8	10	4							
30	(a)	Torquay Utd	L	2-4	Biggs (2)	7,565	1	2	3		5	10		9	12		11	7*	4	8	6								
Oct 5	(h)	Southport	W	3-0	Wilson, Morris (2)	5,731	1	2	3	6	5	10		9			11			8	12	4*	7						
8	(h)	Watford	D	0-0		6,074	1	3		6	5	10		9*			11			8	12	4	7	2					
12	(a)	Barnsley	D	0-0		11,314	1			6	5	10			9		11			8	12	4	7	2*	3				
19	(h)	Oldham Athletic	W	2-1	Wilson (2)	5,552	1			6	5	10			9		11	7*		8	2	4	12		3				
25	(a)	Tranmere Rovers	L	1-2	Morris	6,800	1			6	5	10	8	12			11			9*	2	4	7		3				
Nov 2	(h)	Rotherham Utd	D	0-0		4,857	1			6	5	10	8	7*			11			9	2	4	12		3				
5	(h)	Luton Town	W	2-0	Murray, Morris	5,381	1			6	5	10	8	7			11			9	2	4			3				
9	(a)	Gillingham	L	0-4		4,857	1			6	5	10	8	7			11			9	2	4			3				
23	(a)	Barrow	D	1-1	Morris	4,602	1			6	5	10	8				11	7		9	2	4			3				
30	(h)	Brighton	W	4-0	Everitt (og), Wilson, Atthey, Morris	4,892	1			6	5	10	8				11	7		9	2	4			3				
Dec 16	(h)	Barnsley	W	3-0	Baker (2), Morris	5,159	1		3		5	6	8				11	7		9	2	4				10			
20	(a)	Oldham Athletic	L	0-1		2,086	1		3		5	6	8				11	7		9	2	4				10			
26	(a)	Southport	L	1-2	Wilson	6,578	1	2	3		5	6	8				11	7		9		4				10			
Jan 11	(a)	Rotherham Utd	W	1-0	Morris	7,199	1	2	3	4	5	6	7				11			9		8				10			
25	(a)	Luton Town	L	0-1		15,205	1	2	3	4	5	6	12				11			9		8				10*	7		
28	(h)	Gillingham	W	2-1	Baker, Morris	6,256	1	2	3	4	5	6	8				11			9		10					7		
Feb 1	(a)	Orient	D	0-0		5,309	1	2	3	4	5	6	8				11	7		9		10							
15	(a)	Brighton	L	0-3		10,018	1	2	3	4	5	6	7	12			11			9		8				10*			
22	(a)	Torquay Utd	L	0-1		5,239	1	2	3	4	5	6	7*				11			12		8				10		9	
25	(h)	Barrow	D	1-1	McMorran (pen)	4,826	1	2	3		5	6	12	9*				7		8						4	11	10	
Mar 1	(h)	Shrewsbury Town	W	2-0	Baker, Train	4,826	1	2	3		5	6	4	10				7				8*	11			12		9	
8	(a)	Bristol Rovers	W	1-0	Baker	7,199	1	2	3	4	5	6	11	9				7					8					10	
11	(h)	Orient	W	2-1	Baker, Train	5,622	1	2	3	4	5	6	10	8				7					11					9	
15	(h)	Stockport County	W	2-0	Bennett, Watson	5,802	1	2	3	4	5	6	8	9				7	12				11*					10	
22	(a)	Northampton Tn	L	1-3	Train	5,763	1	2	3	4	5	6	10	8				7		12			11					9*	
25	(h)	Tranmere Rovers	D	1-1	Meath	4,412	1	2	3		5	6	10	8				7	9			4	11						
28	(a)	Reading	D	2-2	Meath, Baker	4,041	1	2	3		5	6	10	8				7	9			4	11						
Apr 1	(h)	Mansfield Tn	W	3-1	Watson, Meath, Train (pen)	5,285		2	3	6	5		10					7	9	8		4	11						1
4	(a)	Hartlepools Utd	D	1-1	Wilson	6,696		2	3	6	5			10				7	9	8		4	11						1
5	(h)	Bournemouth	D	0-0		5,850		2	3	6	5		10	7*				12	9	8		4	11						1
7	(h)	Plymouth Argyle	D	1-1	Jones	5,335		2	3	4	5*	6		8			11	7	9			12	10						1
11	(a)	Crewe Alexandra	W	1-0	Murray	4,500		2	3	4		6	10	8			11		9		7			5					1
15	(h)	Harlepools Utd	W	1-2	Meath	5,003		2	3	4	5	6*		8			11		9		7		12			10			1
19	(h)	Swindon Town	L	0-2		10,654		2	3	6	5		10	8			11	7	9*		4			12					1
25	(a)	Mansfield Town	L	1-2	Wilson	5,862		2	3	4	5	10					11			9	6	8	7						1
						Apps	38	36	37	37	45	42	30	23	12	7	34	28	11	29	16	27	16	3	8	9	3	7	8
						Sub							3	4	1			1	2	2	5	1	3	1		1			
League position: 13th						Goals				2	2	1	7	2	4		9	4	4	9			4			1			

own goal:1

F.A. Cup

Date		Opponent	Rd	Score	Scorers	Att	Wesson	Gregg	Evans	Atthey	Jones	Bennett	Baker	Murray	Biggs	Tindall	Morris	Watson	Meath	Wilson	Harrison	Trevis	Train	Cross	Harris J.	McMorran
Nov 16	(a)	Leytonstone	1	1-0	Baker	1,900	1			6	5	10	8	7			11			9	2	4			3	
Dec 7	(a)	St Albans	2	1-1	Trevis	4,867	1			6	5	10	8				11	7		9	2	4			3	
10	(h)	St Albans	2R	3-1	Gibbs (og), Watson, Wilson	10,626	1		12	6*	5		8				11	7		9	2	4			3	10
Jan 4	(h)	Tottenham	3	0-1		18,779	1	2	3		5	6	8				11	7		9		4				10
						Apps	4	1	1	3	4	3	4	1			4	3		4	3	4			3	2
						Sub			1																	
						Goals							1					1		1		1				

own goal:1

League Cup

Date		Opponent	Rd	Score	Scorers	Att	Wesson	Gregg	Evans	Atthey	Jones	Bennett	Baker	Murray	Biggs	Tindall	Morris	Watson	Meath	Wilson	Harrison	Trevis	Train	Cross	Harris J.
Aug 13	(h)	Shrewsbury Tn	1	2-0	Murray, Biggs (pen)	9,168	1	2	3	4	5	6		8	9	10	11	7							
Sep 3	(h)	Swansea Town	2	1-1	Biggs	7,462	1	2		4	5	6		8	9		11*	7			10			12	3
9	(a)	Swansea Town	2R	2-3	Biggs (2)	10,942	1	2	3	4	5	6	8	10	9		11	7							
						Apps	3	3	2	3	3	3	1	3	3	1	3	3			1				1
						Sub																		1	
						Goals								1	4										

SEASON 1969-70

Division 3

Date	Opponent	Res	Score	Scorers	Att	Parkes	Gregg	Harrison	Atthey	Jones	Bennett	Train	Woodward	Wilson	Baker	Morris	Watson	Taylor	Trevis	Evans	Meath	Stephens	Crowe	Deakin	Wesson	Seal	Cross	Gough
Aug 9 (a)	Brighton & H.A.	D	1-1	Wilson	11,250	1	2	3	4	5	6	7	8	9	10	11												
16 (h)	Southport	W	4-0	Jones, Harrison (2), Meath	5,989	1	2	3	4	5	6	10		8		11	7				9							
23 (a)	Mansfield T.	D	0-0		6,695	1	2	3	4	5	6	10	8	9	7	11												
27 (a)	Bradford C.	L	0-3		7,586	1	2	3	4	5	6	7	8	9	10	11												
30 (h)	Rochdale	L	1-4	Woodward.	6,666	1	2	3	4	5	6	7	8		10*	11					9	12						
Sep 6 (a)	Barnsley	L	0-2		9,492	1	2	3	4	5	6	12	8			11			10		9		7*					
13 (h)	Rotherham U.	L	0-2		4,862	1	2	3	10	5	6	11	8				7				9		4					
16 (h)	Barrow	W	1-0	Train (pen).	5,031	1	2	3	6	5	10	8					7	11			9		4					
20 (a)	Torquay U.	D	0-0		7,547	1	2	3	6		10		8				7	11	5		9		4					
27 (h)	Tranmere R.	D	0-0		5,533	1	2	3	6		10		9			12	7	11	5		8*		4					
30 (h)	Luton Town	L	1-3	Taylor.	7,567	1	2	3	4	5		10	9			7		11	6				8					
Oct 4 (a)	Reading	W	3-2	Crowe, Morris, Harrison.	5,684	1	2	3	6	12	4	10	9			7		11	5				8*					
8 (a)	Southport	W	1-0	Taylor.	3,760	1	2	3	4	5	8	11	9			7		10	6									
11 (h)	Halifax T.	W	2-1	Jones, Taylor.	6,328	1	2	3	4	5	8	10	9			7*		11	6				12					
18 (h)	Bournemouth	W	2-1	Watson, Woodward.	5,388	1	2	3	4	5	8*	10	9				7	11	6				12					
25 (a)	Plymouth Arg.	L	0-1		7,977	1	2	3	4		10		9				7	11	5				8	6				
31 (h)	Doncaster R.	L	1-3	Harrison (pen).	7,319	1	2	3			6	10	9		8			11	5			7		4				
Nov 8 (a)	Gillingham	W	3-1	Bennett, Watson, Woodward.	4,358	1	2	3	6	5	10		9		12	11	7*	8	4									
22 (a)	Bury	L	2-4	Taylor, Jones.	3,560	1	2	3	6	5	10*		9			11	7	8	4				12					
24 (a)	Leyton Orient	L	0-2		6,943		2		6		10		9			11	7	8	5	3			4		1			
29 (h)	Shrewsbury	W	3-2	Woodward, Taylor, Baker.	4,350	1	2		6	5	10		9		8		7	11	4	3								
Dec 13 (a)	Rotherham	L	1-4	Woodward.	7,303	1	2	12	6	5	10		9		8*		7	11	4	3								
20 (h)	Barnsley	W	3-2	Baker (2), Taylor.	4,461	1	2	12	6	5	10	7			8			11	4	3			9*					
26 (h)	Mansfield T.	W	1-0	Train.	7,499	1	2	6		5	10	12	9			11	7*	8	4	3								
Jan 10 (h)	Torquay U.	L	0-1		3,344	1	2	3	6	5	10	7	9		8			11	4									
17 (a)	Tranmere R.	D	0-0		4,460	1	2	3	6	5	10	7	9		8			11	4									
27 (h)	Fulham	L	1-3	Train.	6,215	1	2	3	6	5	10	8	9*		7		12	11	4									
Feb 23 (a)	Barrow	W	1-0	Seal	4,164	1	2	3	6	5	10		9				7	11	4							8		
25 (h)	Brighton & H.A.	L	0-3•		7,535	1	2	3	6	5	10		9		12		7	11	4							8*		
28 (a)	Doncaster T.	D	0-0		4,374	1	2	3	6	5	4		7			11		8		9				10				
Mar 3 (a)	Bristol Rovers	L	1-3	Trevis	11,527	1	2*	3	6	5	4		9			11		7	8	12				10				
14 (a)	Shrewsbury T.	D	1-1	Taylor.	4,640	1	2	3	6	5	4		9			11		7	12					10*		8		
18 (a)	Fulham	L	0-4		7,310	1	2	3	6	5			9			11		7	4					10		8		
21 (h)	Bristol Rovers	W	2-1	Trevis, Seal.	4,442	1		2	6	5	4					11		7	8	3				10		9		
24 (h)	Bury	D	1-1	Trevis.	3,990	1		2	6	5	4					11		7	8	3				10		9		
27 (a)	Bournemouth	D	2-2	Seal, Bennett.	5,172	1		2	6	5	4		12			7		11*	8	3				10		9		
28 (a)	Stockport Co.	D	2-2	Seal (2).	1,783	1	12	2		5			9		10	11	7		4	3				6*		8		
31 (h)	Gillingham	L	0-1		4,295	1		2	6	5			9		10	11			4	3		7				8		
Apr 4 (h)	Bradford C.	W	2-0	Trevis (2).	3,780	1	12	2	6	5	4				10	11*	7		8	3						9		
7 (h)	Leyton Orient	W	2-0	Bennett, Morris.	5,432	1		2	6	5	4				10	11	7		8	3						9		
9 (a)	Rochdale	W	2-1	Taylor, Woodward.	4,404	1	12	2	6	5	4*		7			10		11	8	3						9		
11 (a)	Luton Town	L	0-3		17,893	1	2	4	6	5			9		12	11		7	10	3						8*		
14 (h)	Reading	W	4-1	Harrison, Taylor, Seal (2).	4,921	1		2	6	5			9		10	11		7	4	3						8		
17 (h)	Plymouth Arg.	D	2-2	Trevis, Seal	5,061	1		2	6	5	4				10	7		11	9	3						8		
22 (h)	Stockport C.	D	0-0		3,366	1		2	6	5					10	11	7	8	4	3						9		
24 (a)	Halifax T.	W	1-0	Watson.	1,812		2	4							10*	11	7			3		8		6	1	9	5	12
• Played at the Hawthorns (W.B.A.)					Apps	44	35	42	42	39	38	17	35	4	19	31	20	34	36	19	7	3	10	11	2	17	1	
					Subs		3	2		1		2	1		3	1	1		1	1		1	3					1
League position: 12th					Goals			5		3	3	3	6	1	3	2	3	9	6		1		1			8		

F.A. Cup

Date	Opponent	Rd	Score	Scorers	Att	Parkes	Gregg	Harrison	Atthey	Jones	Bennett	Train	Woodward	Wilson	Baker	Morris	Watson	Taylor	Trevis	Evans
Nov 15 (h)	Leyton Orient	1	0-0		5,683	1	2	3	6	5	10		9			11	7	8	4	
17 (a)	Leyton Orient	R	2-0	Woodward, Taylor.	10,646	1	2	3	6	5	10		9			11	7	8	4	
Dec 6 (a)	Brighton & H.A.	2	1-1	Bennett	10,231	1	2		6	5	10		9		8		7	11	4	3
8 (h)	Brighton & H.A.	R	1-1	(aet) Taylor	9,621	1	2		6	5	10		9		8		7	11	4	3
15 (a)	Brighton & H.A.•	2R	0-0	(aet)	4,299	1	2	10	6	5	8		9				7	11	4	3
17 (h)	Brighton & H.A.+	3R	2-1	Taylor (2)	2,241	1	2		6	5	10		9		8	12	7*	11	4	3
Jan 3 (a)	Crystal Palace	3	0-2		17,015	1	2	10	6	5		7*	9		8		12	11	4	3
					Apps	7	7	4	7	7	6	1	7		4	2	6	7	7	5
					Subs											1	1			
• Played at Coventry; + played at Fulham					Goals						1		1					4		

League Cup

Date	Opponent	Rd	Score	Att	Parkes	Gregg	Harrison	Atthey	Jones	Bennett	Train	Woodward	Wilson	Baker	Morris	Watson
Aug 13 (a)	Shrewsbury Town	1	0-2	6,971	1	2	3	4	5	6		8	9	10	11	7
				Apps	1	1	1	1	1	1		1	1	1	1	1

SEASON 1970-71

Division 3

Date	Venue	Opponents	Res	Score	Scorers	Att	Wesson	Harrison	Evans	Bennett	Jones	Atthey	Morris	Baker	Woodward	Penman	Taylor	Deakin	Train	Gough	Johnston	Gregg	Simmons	Lowery S.	Seal
Aug 15	(h)	Bradford C.	L	1-2	Taylor (pen).	5,112	1	2	3	4	5	6	7	8	9	10	11								
22	(a)	Reading	W	2-1	Woodward, Taylor.	8,434	1	2	3	4	5	6	7	8	9	10	11								
29	(h)	Fulham	W	3-2	Woodward, Taylor (2, 1 pen).	6,146	1	2	3	4	5	6	7	8*	9	10	11	12							
Sept 1	(h)	Barnsley	L	1-2	Taylor (pen).	6,755	1	2	3	4	5	6*	7		9	8	11	10	12						
5	(a)	Halifax T.	L	1-2	Lennard (og).	3,255	1	2	3	4	5	6	7		9	8	11	10							
12	(h)	Tranmere R.	W	2-0	Baker, Train.	4,291	1	2	3	4	5	6		8	9	10	11		7						
19	(a)	Bristol Rov.	L	0-3		8,545	1	2	3	4	5	6			9	10	11		7	8					
26	(h)	Port Vale	W	3-1	Evans, Woodward, Taylor.	5,456	1	2	3	4	5	6			9	10	11		7		8				
29	(h)	Chesterfield	W	2-1	Train, Taylor (pen).	5,454	1	2	3	4	5	6			9	10	11		7		8				
Oct 3	(a)	Rotherham U.	L	0-1		7,337	1	2	3	4	5	6			9	10	11		7		8				
10	(h)	Torquay U.	L	1-4	Train.	5,370	1	2	3	4	5	6			9	10	11	12	7		8*				
14	(a)	Mansfield T.	D	2-2	Penman, Harrison.	6,911	1	2	3	4	5	6			9	8	11	10	7						
17	(a)	Bradford C.	D	0-0		5,174	1	2	3	4	5	6			9	8*	11	10	7			12			
21	(a)	Gillingham	L	1-2	Evans.	2,965	1	3	10		5	6	11		9		8	4	7			2			
23	(a)	Doncaster R.	W	2-1	Johnston, Woodward.	4,762	1	2	3		5	6	11		9		7	10			8	4			
31	(h)	Rochdale	L	0-3		4,667	1	2	3		5	6	12		8		11	10	7*			4	9		
Nov 7	(a)	Swansea C.	D	1-1	Atthey.	7,554	1	3		4	5	6	7		8	10	11					2	9		
9	(a)	Wrexham	L	1-2	Simmons.	7,352	1	3		4	5	6	7		8	10	11		12			2	9*		
14	(h)	Shrewsbury T.	L	0-1		4,666	1	3	12	4	5	6	7		8		11		10			2*	9		
28	(h)	Brighton & H.A.	W	1-0	Taylor.	3,957	1	2	3	4	5	6	7		9*	8	11	12	10						
Dec 5	(a)	Plymouth A.	L	1-3	Simmons.	5,947	1	2	3		5	6	7		8	4	11		10				9*	12	
19	(h)	Reading	L	1-2	Wagstaff, B. (og).	4,371	1	2	3	6	5	4	11		9	8		10	7*					12	
26	(a)	Bury	D	1-1	Taylor.	4,185	1	12	3	6	5	4	7		8*		11	10				2			9
Jan 2	(h)	Aston Villa	W	3-0	Morris (2), Taylor (pen).	19,203	1		3	6	5		7		8	4	11	6				2			9
9	(a)	Chesterfield	D	1-1	Morris.	10,256	1		3	6	5		7		8	4	11	10				2			9
16	(h)	Gillingham	W	3-0	Seal, Woodward (2).	3,752	1		3	6	5	12	7		10	4	11	8*				2			9
27	(h)	Preston N.E.	L	0-1		6,435	1		3	6	5	10	7		9	4	11					2			9
30	(a)	Brighton & H.A.	D	2-2	Morris, Seal.	8,333	1		3	6	5	10	7		8	4	11					2			9
Feb 6	(h)	Plymouth A.	W	1-0	Atthey.	3,951	1	12	3	6	5	10	7		8	4	11					2*			9
13	(a)	Preston N.E.	L	0-1		11,540	1	2	3	6	5	10	11		8	4			7						9
20	(h)	Wrexham	W	3-1	Seal (2), Morris.	4,039	1		3	6	5	10	11		8	4			7*	12		2			9
27	(a)	Rochdale	L	0-2		4,369	1		3		5	6	7		8	4	11	10				2			9
Mar 6	(h)	Doncaster R.	L	1-2	Seal.	3,054	1		3		5	6	7*		8	4	11	10	12			2			9
9	(h)	Mansfield T.	L	0-1		3,364	1		3	10	5	6			8	4	11		7			2			9
13	(a)	Shrewsbury T.	D	1-1	Morris.	4,150	1	12	3	10*	5	6	7		8	4			11			2			9
17	(a)	Aston Villa	D	0-0		37,642	1	12	3		5	6	11		8	4*		10	7			2			9
19	(h)	Swansea C.	L	0-1		3,451	1	2	3		5	6	7		8		11	10	4						9
27	(h)	Halifax T.	D	0-0		3,824	1	2	3	10	5	6	7		8	4*	11	12							9
Apr 3	(a)	Fulham	L	0-1		8,429	1	2	3	10	5	6	7		12		11	4	8						9*
9	(a)	Tranmere R.	D	0-0		4,723	1	2	3	6	5	10	11		7	8		4							9
10	(h)	Bury	W	3-0	Evans, Taylor, Morris.	3,775	1		3	6	5	10	7			8	11	4				2			9
13	(h)	Rotherham U.	L	0-1		4,857	1		3	6	5	10	7			8	11	4				2			9
16	(a)	Torquay U.	W	2-1	Woodward, Seal.	3,639	1		3		5	10	7		8	4	11	6				2			9
24	(h)	Bristol Rov.	L	1-2	Evans.	3,916	1		3	8	5	10	7			4	11	6				2			9
27	(a)	Barnsley	W	2-1	Atthey, Taylor.	3,705	1	11	3	4	5	10*	7			8	12	6				2			9
May 1	(a)	Port Vale	D	1-1	Taylor.	5,758	1		3	4	5	10	7			8	11	6				2			9
						Apps	46	28	43	37	46	43	36	4	40	39	39	24	21	1	5	25	5		24
						Subs		4	1			1	1		1		1	4	3	1		1		2	
League position: 20th						Goals		1	4			3	7	1	7	1	13		3		1		2		6

Own Goals 2

F.A. Cup

Date	Venue	Opponents	Rd	Score	Scorers	Att	Wesson	Harrison	Evans	Bennett	Jones	Atthey	Morris	Baker	Woodward	Penman	Taylor	Deakin	Train	Gough	Johnston	Gregg	Simmons	Lowery S.	Seal
Nov 21	(h)	Plymouth Argyle	1	3-0	Morris (2), Woodward.	4,614	1	2	3	4	5	6	7		9	10	11*	12	8						
Dec 12	(a)	Brentford	2	0-1		8,517	1	2	3	4	5	6	7		9	10	11							8	
						Apps	2	2	2	2	2	2	2		2	2	2		1					1	
						Subs												1							
						Goals							2		1										

League Cup

Date	Venue	Opponents	Rd	Score	Scorers	Att	Wesson	Harrison	Evans	Bennett	Jones	Atthey	Morris	Baker	Woodward	Penman	Taylor
Aug 16	(a)	Port Vale	1	1-0	Woodward	6,605	1	2	3	4	5	6	7	8	9	10	11
Sept 9	(a)	Portsmouth	2	0-1		15,750	1	2	3	4	5	6	7	8	9	10	11
						Apps	2	2	2	2	2	2	2	2	2	2	2
						Goal									1		

SEASON 1971-72

Division 3

Date		Opponent		Score	Scorers	Att	Wesson	Gregg	Evans	Harrison	Jones, S.	Deakin	Smith	Woodward	Manning	Penman	Taylor C.	Bennett	Morris	Atthey	Wallington	Train	Taylor B.	Wright	Gough	Thomson	Jones, C.	Shinton	Dainty
Aug 14	(a)	Barnsley	L	2-4	Manning, Woodward.	5,941	1	2	3	4	5	6	7	8	9	10	11												
21	(h)	Aston Villa	D	1-1	Manning.	13,051	1	2	3	6	5		11	8	9	10		4	7										
28	(a)	Oldham A.	W	3-1	Morris, Penman, Woodward.	8,477	1	2	3	4	5		7	9	10	8			11	6									
Sept. 1	(a)	Shrewsbury T.	L	1-4	Manning.	6,873	1	2	3	6	5		8	7	9	4			11	10									
4	(h)	Notts. County	L	1-2	Manning.	6,780	1	2	3	4	5		7*	9	10	8	12		11	6									
11	(a)	Torquay U.	D	2-2	Morris, Taylor, C. (pen).	5,950		2		3	5		8		9	10	11	6	7	4	1								
13	(a)	Plymouth A.	L	2-3	Smith, Manning.	10,393		2		3	5		8	12	9	10	11	6	7	4*	1								
18	(h)	Blackburn R.	D	0-0		4,235		2		3	5		8	12	9*	4	11	6	7		1	10							
25	(a)	York City	L	0-2		5,294		2*	11	3	5		9	10		4	12	6	7		1	8							
28	(h)	Chesterfield	D	1-1	Morris.	3,664	1	2		3	5	6	8		9			4	11			10	7						
Oct 2	(h)	Port Vale	W	2-0	Taylor, B., Wright.	4,642		2		3	5	6*	9	12				4	11		1	8	7	10					
9	(a)	Bradford C.	L	0-3		4,729			3	2	5		9	8*		12		6	11		1	4	7	10					
16	(h)	Barnsley	D	1-1	Taylor, B.	2,721	1		3	2	5	6			9	4			11			8	7	10					
18	(a)	Wrexham	L	1-3	Taylor, B.	4,566	1		3	2	5	6	8			4	12		11			10	7	9*					
23	(h)	Brighton & H.A.	L	0-1		3,719	1		3	2	5	6		9	10				11			4	7		8				
30	(a)	Rotherham U.	D	1-1	Woodward.	7,997	1			3	5	6		9		10		4				8	2	11	7				
Nov 6	(h)	Bristol Rov.	W	2-0	Morris, Train (pen).	3,978	1			3	5			9		4		6	11			7	2	10	8				
13	(a)	Swansea C.	L	0-2		6,407	1			2		6		9		4		5	12			7*	11	10	8	3			
26	(h)	Rochdale	W	3-0	Jones, Woodward, Wright.	3,575	1	2		3	5			8		4			11	6		10	7	9					
Dec 4	(a)	Halifax T.	L	1-3	Jones.	3,421	1	2		3	5			9		4		6	12	10		11	7*	8					
18	(a)	Notts County	L	0-3		11,775	1	2	3	4	5			9*		8			11	6			7	10	12				
27	(h)	Mansfield T.	W	2-1	Morris, Taylor, C.	7,001	1	2	3	10	5			8			12	6	11				7*	9		4			
Jan 1	(a)	Blackburn R.	D	1-1	Thomson.	10,113	1	2	3	10	5			8*		12	11	6	7					9		4			
8	(h)	Oldham A.	L	2-3	Morris, Harrison.	3,751	1	2	3	5				7*	12	8	11	4	10					9		6			
22	(a)	Chesterfield	D	1-1	Manning.	7,743	1		3	6		4		8	9	7		5	11					10		2			
29	(h)	Wrexham	W	2-1	Harrison (pen), Taylor, B.	3,635			3	6		4		8	9	7		5	11*		1		12	10		2			
Feb 12	(a)	Brighton & H.A.	W	2-1	Bennett, Taylor, B.	14,437		2	3	4	5	9		7		11		6			1		12		8*	10			
19	(h)	Rotherham U.	D	0-0		4,506		2	3	4	5			8		11					1		7		10	6	9		
23	(a)	Bournemouth	D	0-0		10,016	1	2	3	6	5			8		10			11						7	4	9		
26	(a)	Bristol Rov.	L	1-2	Morris.	8,665		2	3	4	5			10		6			11		1		7		8		9		
Mar 4	(h)	Swansea C.	W	4-0	Harrison, Penman, Shinton, Morris.	3,808		2	3	4	5					10		6	11		1		7				9	8	
11	(h)	Bradford C.	W	3-0	Shinton (2), Jones, C.	4,100	1		3	4	5					10		6	11				2				9	8	7
14	(h)	Bournemouth	D	1-1	Morris.	10,828	1	2	3	4	5					10		6	11				7				9	8	
18	(a)	Aston Villa	D	0-0		45,953	1	2	3	4	5					10	12	6	11*				7				9	8	
22	(a)	Bolton W.	W	1-0	Harrison.	6,785	1	2	3	4	5					10	12	6	11				7				9*	8	
25	(h)	Torquay U.	W	1-0	Bennett.	5,511	1	2	3	4	5					10	12	6	11				7*				9	8	
27	(a)	Tranmere R.	D	3-3	Shinton, Morris, Harrison (pen).	2,320	1	2	3	4	5					10		6	11				7				9	8	
Apr 1	(a)	Mansfield T.	D	1-1	Jones, C.	5,770	1	2	3	4	5					10		6	11				7				9	8	
3	(a)	Port Vale	D	1-1	Evans.	5,250	1	2	3	4	5					10*		6	11				7		12		9	8	
4	(h)	York City	W	2-1	Taylor, B., Harrison.	7,661	1	2	3	4	5					10		6	11				7				9	8	
8	(h)	Bolton W.	D	1-1	Taylor, B.	4,735	1	2	3	4	5					10			11	12			7		6*		9	8	
11	(h)	Plymouth Arg.	W	1-0	Harrison.	5,804	1	2	3	4	5					10	9	6	11				7				8		
15	(a)	Rochdale	D	0-0		3,027	1	2	3	4	5					10	9	6	11				7				8		
18	(h)	Tranmere R.	W	4-1	Shinton, Taylor, B., (2), Morris.	5,629	1	2	3	4	5					10*		6	11				7				9	8	12
21	(h)	Halifax T.	D	0-0		6,096	1	2	3	4	5								11	6			7		10		9	8	
25	(h)	Shrewsbury T.	W	4-1	Shinton, Jones, C., Harrison (pen), Evans.	6,697	1	2	3	4	5			7					11	6			10				9	8	
						Apps	35	36	36	46	42	11	13	24	13	38	8	31	40	10	11	13	31	15	10	9	19	14	1
						Subs								3	1	2	7		2	1			2		2				1
League position: 9th						Goals			2	8	2		1	4	6	2	2	2	11			1	9	2		1	3	6	

F.A. Cup

Date		Opponent	Rd	Score	Scorers	Att	Wesson	Gregg	Evans	Harrison	Jones, S.	Deakin	Smith	Woodward	Manning	Penman	Taylor C.	Bennett	Morris	Atthey	Wallington	Train	Taylor B.	Wright
Nov 20	(h)	Dagenham	1	4-1	Woodward, Wright, Taylor, Morris	4,247	1	2		3				8		4		5	11	6		10	7	9
Dec 11	(a)	Brighton & H.A.	2	1-1	Woodward.	12,797	1	2	3	8	5			9		4			11	6		7		10
14	(h)	Brighton & H.A.	2R	2-1	Train, Wright.	8,014	1	2	3	4	5			8		7			11	6		10		9
Jan 15	(h)	Bournemouth	3	1-0	Wright.	9,185	1	2	3	6		4		7	9	8		5	11					10
Feb 5	(a)	Everton	4	1-2	Evans.	45,462		2	3	11	5	6		8	9	4					1		7	10
						Apps	4	5	4	5	3	2		5	2	5		2	4	3	1	3	2	5
						Goals			1					2					1			1	1	3

League Cup

Date		Opponent	Rd	Score	Att	Wesson	Gregg	Evans	Harrison	Jones, S.	Deakin	Smith	Woodward	Manning	Penman	Taylor C.	Bennett	Morris
Aug 18	(a)	Stockport C.	1	0-1	3,052	1	2	3	6	5		10	8	9		11	4	7
					Apps	1	1	1	1	1		1	1	1		1	1	1

SEASON 1972-73

Division 3

Date	Opponent		Score	Scorers	Att	Wesson	Gregg	Evans	Harrison	Jones S.	Atthey	Taylor B.	Shinton	Jones C.	Penman	Morris G.	Devlin	Woodward	Mayo	Bennett	Saunders	Dainty	Taylor C.	Smith	Birch	Johnson	Wright	Andrews	Turner	Robinson	Osborne	Peacock	Caswell	Ball	Inger	Pountney
Aug 12	(h) Charlton A.	W	3-2	Jones, C., Evans, Harrison (pen).	4,675	1	2	3*	4	5	6	7	8	9	10	11	12																			
19	(a) Swansea C.	L	1-2	Taylor, B.	4,211	1	2	3	6		5	7*	8	9	10	11	4	12																		
26	(h) Tranmere R.	W	2-0	Jones, C. Harrison.	3,298	1	2		3	5	6	7	8	9	10	11	4																			
29	(a) Scunthorpe U.	L	1-2	Taylor, B.	4,159	1	2	3	4	5	6	7	8	9	10	11																				
Sept 2	(a) Notts Co.	D	1-1	Mayo	9,554	1	2	3	4	5	6	7	8	9	10*	11			12																	
9	(h) Grimsby T.	W	1-0	Woodward.	4,174	1	2	3	4	5	6	7	8*	9		11		10	12																	
16	(a) Halifax T.	W	1-0	Jones, C.	2,923	1	2	3	4	5	6	7		9	10	11		8																		
19	(h) Southend U.	W	3-1	Harrison, Morris, Woodward.	5,662	1	2	3	4	5	6	7		9	10	11*		8	12																	
23	(h) Port Vale	W	2-0	Gregg, Harrison (pen).	8,159	1	2	3	4	5	6	7		9	10	11		8																		
25	(a) Rochdale	L	1-2	Morris.	4,749	1	2	3	4	5	6	7*		9	10	11		8		12																
30	(a) Plymouth A.	W	2-0	Woodward, Jones, C.	5,257	1	2	3	4	5	6	7	10	9	8	11*		12																		
Oct 7	(h) Bolton W.	W	3-2	Shinton, Woodward, Jones, C.	7,631	1	2	3	4	5		7	10	9	11			8		6																
10	(h) Wrexham	W	2-0	Woodward, Shinton.	6,323	1	2	3	4	5		7*	10	9	11			8		6	12															
14	(a) Brentford	L	0-2		9,490	1	2	3	4	5			10	9*	11			7		6	12	8														
21	(h) Rotherham U	W	1-0	Taylor, B.	6,136	1	2	3	4	5		7	8		10			9		6			11													
25	(a) Blackburn R.	L	0-2		5,943	1	2	3	4	5	6	7	9*	12	10			8					11													
28	(a) York City	D	0-0		3,530	1	2	3	4	5	6	7	8*	9	10	11		12																		
Nov 4	(h) Rochdale	L	0-2		5,682	1	2	3	4	5	6	7		9	10			8						11												
10	(a) Southend U.	L	0-2		6,973		2	3	4	5	10	7		9	12		6	8						11*										1		
25	(h) Watford	L	1-3	Morris.	4,718		2		3	5*	6	7		9	12	11	10	8		4														1		
Dec 2	(a) Chesterfield	L	0-3		5,483	1		3	2	5	6*		8	9	12	11	10	7		4																
16	(a) Oldham A.	L	1-2	Penman.	7,500	1	3*		10			2	9	8	4	11	7		12	6	5															
23	(h) Bournemouth	W	1-0	Woodward.	4,601	1			3		10	2	9	8	4	11*	7	12		6	5															
26	(a) Port Vale	W	2-1	Jones, C., Harrison (pen).	6,787	1			3		10	2	9	8	4		7	11		6	5															
Jan 5	(a) Tranmere R.	L	1-3	Penman.	7,718				3		10	2*	9	8	4		7	11		6	5		12			1										
13	(h) Blackburn R.	L	0-2		3,836				3		6	2	10	9	4	7	8*	11			5			12		1										
23	(h) Notts County	L	1-3	Worthington (og).	4,391		2		3		10	7*	9	12	4	11			5	6						1	8									
27	(a) Grimsby T.	L	2-6	Andrews, Harrison (pen).	11,142	1	2		3		11*	7	8	12	4				5	6							9	10								
Feb 3	(a) Wrexham	L	1-2	Andrews.	3,167				2		10*	7	9		6				12	4	5						8	11	1	3						
16	(a) Charlton A.	D	1-1	Shinton.	5,078		2		3			7	9*		4		10			6			12				8	11	1	5						
19	(h) Swansea C.	D	1-1	Wright.	4,262		2		3			7*	9		4		10			6			12				8	11	1	5						
24	(h) Oldham A.	W	3-0	Saunders, Wright, Jones C.	4,515		2		3		10		9*	12	4		7				6						8	11		5	1					
Mar 3	(a) Bolton W.	L	1-3	Shinton.	14,924		2		3		6*		9	10	4		7			12	11						8			5	1					
6	(a) Shrewsbury T.	D	1-1	Shinton.	3,449		2		3		6	11*	9	12	4						7						8	10		5	1					
10	(h) Brentford.	W	3-0	Harrison (pen), Taylor, B., Shinton.	4,190		2		3		6	11	8	10	4						7						9			5		1				
17	(a) Rotherham U.	L	0-2		3,204		2		3	5	11	7*	9	10	4		12				6						8					1				
19	(h) Bristol R.	W	4-3	Shinton, Jones, C. (2), Wright.	4,595		2		3		6		8*	10	4					5	7	11			12		9					1				
24	(h) York City	D	0-0		4,051		2		3		4	11*		9	6		7				5				12		8	10				1				
31	(a) Watford	L	0-1		5,325		2		3		6	7	8		11					12	5	10					9			4*		1				
Apr 7	(h) Chesterfield	W	3-2	Wright, Shinton, Penman.	3,629		2		6		4	7	9	10	11						5						8					1	3			
14	(a) Bristol Rov.	L	1-2	Wright.	6,285				2		3		9	10	4		12			5	7				11		8					1	6*			
20	(a) Bournemouth	W	1-0	Wright.	10,741				2		3	12	8	10	4					5	7*				11		9					1	6			
21	(h) Shrewsbury T.	W	1-0	Jones, C.	4,020				2		3	10	8	9	6						4		11		7					5		1				
25	(h) Plymouth A.	L	1-3	Harrison.	4,179				2		3	10	8*		4					12	7		11		6			9		5		1				
28	(h) Scunthorpe U.	D	1-1	Jones, C.	3,402		2		4		3		9	10							7				6			11		5					1	8
May 1	(h) Halifax T.	L	0-1		3,989		2		6		3	11*	8	9	4					10					7					5			12		1	
					Apps	23	36	19	46	21	39	38	38	35	41	18	15	17	2	19	20	3	4	2	6	3	16	9	3	12	3	10	3	2	2	1
					Subs							1		5	3		3	4	5	4	2		3	1	2								1			
League position: 17th					Goals		1	1	8			4	8	11	3	3		6	1		1						6	2								

Own Goal 1.

F.A. Cup

Date	Opponent	Rd	Score	Scorers	Att	Wesson	Gregg	Evans	Harrison	Jones S.	Atthey	Taylor B.	Shinton	Jones C.	Penman	Morris G.	Devlin	Woodward	Mayo	Bennett
Nov 18	(h) Kettering	1	3-3	Morris (2), Woodward.	5,961	1		3	2	5	6	7		9	4	11	10	8		
22	(a) Kettering	1R	2-1	Atthey, Jones C.	9,143	1	2		3	5	6	7		9		11	10	8		4
Dec 12	(h) Charlton A.	2	1-2	Morris.	5,641	1	2	3	10	5		7	9	8	6	11				4
					Apps	3	2	2	3	3	2	3	1	3	2	3	2	2		2
					Goals						1			1		3		1		

League Cup

Date	Opponent	Rd	Score	Scorers	Att	Wesson	Gregg	Evans	Harrison	Jones S.	Atthey	Taylor B.	Shinton	Jones C.	Penman	Morris G.	Devlin
Aug 15	(a) Southport	1	1-4	Shinton.	2,663	1	2	3	4	5	6	7*	8	9	10	11	12
					Apps	1	1	1	1	1	1	1	1	1	1	1	
					Subs												1
					Goals								1				

Walsall used seven different goalkeepers in 1972-73: Keith Ball, Jimmy Inger, Glen Johnson, John Osborne, Dennis Peacock, Ian Turner and Bob Wesson.

SEASON 1973-74

Division 3

Date	Venue	Opponent	Res	Score	Scorers	Att	Kearns	Fraser	Fry	Saunders	Robinson	Harrison	Wright	Birch	Shinton	Bennett	Buckley	Caswell	Pollock	Taylor B.	Andrews	Corrigan	Atthey	Young	Sloan	Wharton	Brown	Morgan G.
Aug 25	(a)	Wrexham	L	0-2		5,379	1	2	3	4*	5	6	7	8	9	10	11	12										
Sept 1	(h)	Rochdale	D	0-0		7,211	1	2	3	5	6	4	8	7	9		10	11*	12									
8	(a)	Aldershot	L	0-1		3,544	1	2	3		6*	4	12	7	9	5	10	11	8									
10	(a)	York City	D	1-1	Buckley.	3,506	1	2	3	12		8*	1	4		5	9	6		7	11							
15	(h)	Bournemouth	L	1-2	Wright.	5,220	1	2				8	10	4		5	7	6		12	9*	3	11					
17	(h)	Huddersfield	W	3-0	Shinton (3).	5,491	1	8	3			2	10		9	5	11	6		4			7					
22	(a)	Plymouth A.	L	1-2	Taylor.	7,268	1	8	3			2	11		10	5	9	6		4			7					
29	(h)	Blackburn R.	W	2-0	Fazackerley (og), Buckley.	4,896	1	4	3			2	9	6	8	5	11			7			10					
Oct 9	(a)	Huddersfield T.	D	2-2	Wright, Birch.	4,436	1	8	3	5		2	10	4	9		11	6					7					
13	(h)	Charlton A.	W	4-0	Wright, Buckley (2), Bennett	4,800	1	8	3			2	10		9	5	11			7			6	4				
16	(h)	York City	D	0-0		5,569	1	8	3			2	10		9	5	11			7			6	4				
19	(a)	Southport	D	1-1	Taylor.	1,939	1	8	3			2	10		9	5	11			7			6	4				
27	(h)	Oldham A.	D	1-1	Wright.	6,403	1	8	3			2	10	12	9	4	11			7*			5	6				
Nov 2	(a)	Tranmere R.	L	0-3		3,502	1	8	3			2	10		9	5	11			4			7	6				
6	(a)	Grimsby T.	L	0-1		7,689	1	8	3		4	2	10			5	11				12		7	6*	9			
10	(h)	Bristol Rov.	D	0-0		6,058	1	9	3		6	2	10		12	5	11						7	4	8*			
13	(h)	Brighton & HA	L	0-1		5,116	1	8	3		6	2	9			5	10			12			11	4	7*			
17	(a)	Southend U.	L	1-2	Wright.	6,235	1	8	3	6*	5	2	9	4	7		10	12					11					
Dec 1	(a)	Hereford U.	L	1-3	Andrews.	7,747	1		3	12	5	2*	10	4		6	11			8	9		7					
8	(h)	Shrewsbury T.	W	2-0	Buckley (pen), Andrews.	3,037	1		2		5		8	4		6	10			3	9		7			11		
22	(a)	Blackburn T.	W	2-0	Buckley (2).	7,323	1		3	5	6				10		11			7	9		4		8		2	
26	(h)	Cambridge U.	W	3-0	Buckley (2), Shinton.	4,591	1	2	3	5	4				8		10			11	9		6		7*		12	
29	(h)	Aldershot	W	3-2	Andrews, Buckley, Saunders.	4,330	1	8	3	2	5				10	6	11			7	9		4					
Jan 1	(a)	Rochdale	W	1-0	Hanvey (og).	2,117	1	7	3	2	4				8	5	10			11	9		6					
12	(a)	Bournemouth	L	0-1		8,647	1	7*	3	2	4				8	5	10			11	9		6		12			
20	(h)	Wrexham	W	3-0	Buckley (2, 1 pen), Sloan.	9,035	1		3	2	4				8	5	10			11	9		6		7			
26	(a)	Watford	W	3-1	Andrews (2), Shinton.	7,281	1		3	4	5	2			10		11			8	9		6		7			
Feb 3	(a)	Halifax T.	L	1-3	Taylor.	3,378	1		3	5	4	2			8	12	10			11	9		6*		7			
10	(h)	Plymouth A.	L	0-4		4,926	1		3	2	4	11			8	5	10			12	9		6*		7			
17	(a)	Charlton A.	W	1-0	Buckley.	5,748	1		3	2	4	6			8	5	10			11	9				7			
23	(h)	Grimsby T.	W	3-1	Buckley (2), Taylor.	4,071	1		3	2	4	6			8	5	10			11	9				7			
Mar 3	(a)	Cambridge U.	D	0-0		4,569	1		3	2	4	6			8	5	10			11	9				7			
9	(a)	Oldham A.	L	1-2	Shinton.	9,488	1		3	6	5	2			10		11			8	9		4		7			
17	(h)	Southport	W	2-0	Buckley, Andrews.	4,537	1		3	5	4	2					10	7		11	9		6		8			
19	(h)	Halifax T.	D	2-2	Sloan, Harrison.	3,960	1		3	2	4	7				5	10			11	9		6		8			
23	(a)	Bristol Rov.	W	2-0	Buckley (2, 1 pen).	11,370	1		3	2	5	10	12			4*	11			8	9		6		7			
25	(a)	Port Vale	D	1-1	Boswell (og).	3,659	1		3	5	4	2	8				10			11	9		6		7			
30	(h)	Tranmere R.	L	0-1		3,752	1		3	5	4	2	9	8			11				10		6		7			
Apr 2	(h)	Watford	D	2-2	Robinson, Wright.	3,799	1		3	5	4	6	8				10	2		11	9				7			
6	(a)	Brighton & HA	L	1-2	Buckley.	10,574	1		3	6	5	2	10				11	12		8	9		4		7*			
13	(h)	Southend U.	L	1-2	Taylor.	3,165	1	12	3	5		6	8				10	2		11	9		4		7*			
15	(h)	Chesterfield	W	2-0	Wright, Buckley.	3,775	1	2	3	5		6	8				10			11	9		4		7			
17	(a)	Chesterfield	L	0-1		4,883	1	2		5	4	3	8				10			11	9		6		7			
20	(a)	Shrewbury T.	D	0-0		3,182	1	2			5	6		11			10	3		8	9		4		7			
27	(h)	Hereford U.	W	3-1	Buckley, Taylor (2).	4,168	1	2		5	4	8					11	3		10	9		6		7			
30	(h)	Port Vale	D	0-0		4,227			3	5	4	6		11			10			8	9				7		2	1
						Apps	45	26	42	29	33	39	26	13	26	27	46	12	1	35	30	1	37	8	26	1	2	1
						Subs		1		2			2	1	1	1		3	1	3	1				1		1	
League position: 15th						Goals				1	1	1	7	1	6	1	21			7	6				2			

Own Goals: 3.

F.A. Cup

Date	Venue	Opponent	Rd	Score	Scorers	Att	Kearns	Fraser	Fry	Saunders	Robinson	Harrison	Wright	Birch	Shinton	Bennett	Buckley	Caswell	Pollock	Taylor B.	Andrews	Corrigan	Atthey	Young	Sloan	Wharton	Brown	Morgan G.
Nov 24	(h)	Swansea C.	1	1-0	Andrews	3,975	1		3	6	5	2	10	4			11			8	9		7					
Dec 15	(a)	Plymouth A.	2	0-1		7,322	1		3	2	6		12	8	10*	5	11			4	9		7					
						Apps	2		2	2	2	1	1	2	1	1	2			2	2		2					
						Subs							1															
						Goals															1							

League Cup

Date	Venue	Opponent	Rd	Score	Scorers	Att	Kearns	Fraser	Fry	Saunders	Robinson	Harrison	Wright	Birch	Shinton	Bennett	Buckley	Caswell	Pollock	Taylor B.	Andrews	Corrigan	Atthey	Young	Sloan	Wharton	Brown	Morgan G.
Aug 29	(h)	Shrewsbury T.	1	6-1	Buckley (3), Shinton (2), Harrison.	4,722	1	2	3		6	4	8	7	9	5	10	11										
Oct 2	(h)	Manchester C.	2	0-0		12,943	1	8	3			2	10		9	5	11	6		4			7					
22	(a)	Manchester C.	2R	0-0	(a.e.t.)	19,428	1	8	3			2	10		9	5	11			4			7	6				
30	(a)	Manchester C.	2R2	0-4		13,646	1	8	3			2	10		9	5	11			4			7	6				
						Apps	4	4	4		1	4	4	1	4	4	4	2		3			3	2				
						Goals						1			2		3											

SEASON 1974-75

Division 3

Date		Opponents		Score	Scorers	Att	Kearns	Saunders	Fry	Robinson	Bennett	Atthey	Harrison	Andrews	Wright	Buckley	Taylor B.	Sloan	Spinner	Caswell	Brown A.	Jenkins	Serella	Birch	Clarke
Aug 17	(a)	Gillingham	D	2-2	Shipperley (og), Wright (pen).	6,141	1	2	3	4	5	6	7	8	9	10	11								
24	(h)	Halifax T.	D	1-1	Robinson.	3,280	1	2	3	4	5	6	7	8*	9	10	11	12							
31	(a)	Preston N.E.	L	2-3	Buckley, Wright.	7,446	1	2	3	6	5	4	11*	9	7	10	8	12							
Sept 7	(h)	Hereford U.	W	3-1	Buckley (2), Atthey.	3,328	1	2	3	4	5	6		8	9	10	11	7							
14	(a)	Wrexham	D	0-0		4,824	1	5	3	4		6	2	9	10	11	8*	7	12						
16	(a)	Southend U.	L	0-3		6,966	1	5	3	4		6	2	8	9	10			7*	11				12	
21	(h)	Tranmere R.	W	1-0	Wright.	2,927	1	5	3	4		6	2	8	9	10		7		11					
24	(h)	Swindon T.	W	2-0	Buckley, Atthey.	3,595	1	5	3	4		6	2	8	9	10		7		11					
28	(a)	Colchester U.	W	2-1	Buckley (2).	4,877	1	5	3	4	12	6	2	9	10	11		8		7*					
Oct 1	(h)	Brighton & HA	W	6-0	Buckley (2, 1 pen), Wright (2), Fry, Andrews.	5,291	1	5	3	4		6	2	8	9	10		7		11					
5	(a)	Plymouth Arg.	L	1-2	Andrews.	5,765	1	5	3	4		6	2	8	9	10		7		11					
8	(h)	Port Vale	D	0-0		6,507	1	5	3	4		6	2	8	9	10	12	7*		11					
11	(h)	Aldershot	W	3-0	Buckley (2), Wright.	5,280	1	5	3	4		6	2	8	9	10	12	7*		11					
19	(a)	Crystal P.	L	0-1		15,029	1	5	3	4		6*	2	8	9	10		7		11	12				
26	(h)	Blackburn R.	L	1-3	Andrews.	6,618	1	5	3	4		6	2	8	9	10		7		11					
Nov 2	(a)	Chesterfield	D	2-2	Sloan, Harrison.	4,142	1	5	3	4	12	6	2	8	9	10		7		11*					
4	(a)	Port Vale	D	1-1	Buckley.	4,859	1		3	4	5	11	2	8	9	10		7				6			
9	(h)	Bournemouth	W	2-0	Buckley, Caswell.	4,219	1	5	3		6	4	2	8	9	10		7		11					
16	(a)	Charlton A.	L	2-4	Harrison, Buckley.	6,715	1	5	3			4	2	8	9	10		7		11			6		
30	(a)	Bury	L	0-2		4,724	1		3	4	6	11	2	8	9	10		7					5		
Dec 7	(h)	Peterboro. U.	L	0-1		4,208	1		3	6	5	11	2	8	9	10	12	7*					4		
21	(a)	Huddersfield T.	L	2-3	Buckley, Andrews.	3,627	1		3	4	5	6	2	8	9	10	11	7							
26	(h)	Wrexham	W	2-1	Atthey, Wright.	4,345	1	2		4	5	6*	3	8	9	10	7	12						11	
28	(a)	Grimsby T.	D	0-0		6,051	1	2		4	5		3	8	9	10	7*	12				6		11	
Jan 11	(a)	Peterboro U.	D	0-0		8,671	1	2		4	5	6	3	8	9	10	7							11	
14	(h)	Grimsby T.	W	2-0	Atthey, Buckley.	5,036	1	2		4	5	6	3	8	9	10	7							11	
18	(h)	Bury	W	3-0	Andrews, Buckley, Wright.	10,251	1	2		4	5	6	3	8	9	10	7							11	
Feb 1	(a)	Bournemouth	W	1-0	Hague (og).	6,075	1	2		4	5	6	3	8	9	10	7							11	
4	(h)	Southend U.	W	3-0	Buckley (2), Harrison.	9,894	1	2		4	5	6	3	8	9	10	7							11	
8	(h)	Chesterfield	D	2-2	Taylor, Andrews.	10,248	1	2		4	5	6	3	8	9	10	7							11	
19	(h)	Watford	W	2-0	Bennett, Harrison.	7,177	1	2		4	5	6	3	8	9	10	7							11	
22	(h)	Charlton Ath.	L	0-1		8,971	1	2*		4	5	6	3	8	9	10	7		12					11	
28	(h)	Preston N.E.	W	2-0	Andrews (2).	10,151	1		2	4	5	6	3	8	9	10	7							11	
Mar 8	(a)	Swindon T.	L	0-3		8,562	1		2	4	5	6	3	8	9	10	7							11	
15	(h)	Colchester U.	W	5-2	Atthey, Bennett, Andrews, Harrison, Buckley.	4,914	1		2	4	5	6	3	8	9	10	7							11	
18	(h)	Gillingham	D	1-1	Andrews.	6,390	1		2	4	5	6	3	8	9	10	7							11	
22	(a)	Hereford U.	L	0-2		6,848	1		2	4	5	6	3	8	9	10	7							11	
28	(a)	Tranmere R.	L	0-3		3,305	1		2	4	5	6	3	8	9*	10	11		7	12					
29	(h)	Huddersfield T.	W	2-0	Buckley, Birch.	4,104	1			4	5	6	3	9		10			8	7	2			11	
Apr 5	(a)	Blackburn R.	D	3-3	Birch, Spinner, Andrews.	12,002	1			4	5	6	3	8		10			9	7	2			11	
9	(a)	Brighton & HA	L	0-1		10,898	1			4	5	6	3	9		10			8	7	2			11	
12	(h)	Plymouth A.	D	0-0		7,404	1	5		4		6	3	8	9	10				7	2			11	
19	(a)	Aldershot	D	0-0		4,850	1	5		4		6	3	8	9	10				7	2			11	
22	(a)	Halifax T.	L	0-1		2,030	1	5		4		6	3	8	9	10				7	2			11	
25	(h)	Crystal P.	W	3-0	Andrews, Buckley, Spinner.	6,001	1	5	2	4		6	3	8		10			9	7				11	
29	(a)	Watford	W	3-2	Andrews, Spinner (2).	9,472	1		2	4*	5		3	8		10			9	7		6		11	12
						Apps	46	32	30	44	29	44	45	46	41	46	22	18	7	21	6	3	3	23	
						Subs					2						3	4	2	1	1			1	1
League position: 8th						Goals			1	1	2	5	5	13	8	21	1	1	4	1				2	

Own Goals 2.

F.A. Cup

Date		Opponents	Rd	Score	Scorers	Att	Kearns	Saunders	Fry	Robinson	Bennett	Atthey	Harrison	Andrews	Wright	Buckley	Taylor B.	Sloan	Spinner	Caswell	Brown A.	Jenkins	Serella	Birch	Clarke
Nov 27	(a)	Ashford	1	3-1	Buckley 2, Fry	2,700	1		3	4	5	6	2	8	9	10		7		11					
Dec 14	(a)	Newport	2	3-1	Taylor, Wright, Buckley.	4,764	1		3	4	5	6	2	8	9	10	7	11							
Jan 4	(a)	Manchester U.	3	0-0		43,353	1	2		4	5	6	3	8	9	10	7							11	
7	(h)	Manchester U.	3R	3-2	(a.e.t.) Wright, Buckley (2, 1 pen).	18,105	1	2		4	5	6	3	8	9	10	7							11	
24	(h)	Newcastle U.	4	1-0	Andrews	19,998	1	5	3	4		6	2	8	9	10	7							11	
Feb 15	(a)	Birmingham C.	5	1-2	Taylor.	43,841	1	2		4	5	6	3	8	9	10	7							11	
						Apps	6	4	3	6	5	6	6	6	6	6	5	2		1				4	
						Goals			1					1	2	5	2								

League Cup

Date		Opponents	Rd	Score	Scorers	Att	Kearns	Saunders	Fry	Robinson	Bennett	Atthey	Harrison	Andrews	Wright	Buckley	Taylor B.	Sloan	Spinner	Caswell	Brown A.	Jenkins	Serella	Birch	Clarke
Aug 21	(a)	Chester	1	1-2	Buckley	3,583	1	2	3	4	5	6	7	8*	9	10	11	12							
						Apps	1	1	1	1	1	1	1	1	1	1	1								
						Subs												1							
						Goals										1									

SEASON 1975-76

Division 3

Date		Opponent		Score	Scorers	Att	Kearns	Fry	Harrison	Robinson	Atthey	Caswell	Dennehy	Andrews	Wright	Buckley	Taylor B.	Spinner	Saunders	Birch	Serella	Clarke	Hynd	Evans A.	Shelton
Aug 16	(a)	Peterboro. U.	D	0-0		7,174	1	2	3	4	5	6	7	8	9	10	11								
23	(h)	Swindon T.	D	1-1	Buckley.	5,146	1	2	3	5	4	6	7	8*	9	10	11	12							
30	(a)	Halifax T.	L	1-2	Harrison.	2,076	1	2	3	4	6		7	8	9	10		11*	5	12					
Sept 6	(h)	Southend U.	L	2-3	Buckley (pen), Dennehy.	4,380	1	2	3	4	6*		7	8	9	10		12	5	11					
10	(a)	Brighton & HA	W	2-1	Wright, Andrews.	8,592	1	2	3	4		6	7	8	9	10	12		5	11*					
13	(a)	Preston N.E.	L	1-3	Buckley.	7,015	1	2	3*	4		6	7	8	9	10			5	11	12				
16	(h)	Crystal P.	D	1-1	Wright.	5,496	1	2	3*	4		6	7	9	12	10	8			11	5				
20	(h)	Bury	L	0-1		4,845	1	2		4		6	7	8	12	10	9			11*	5	3			
22	(h)	Shrewsbury T.	W	2-0	Taylor, Buckley (pen).	4,866	1	3		4		2	7	8	9	10	6			11	5				
27	(a)	Mansfield T.	L	1-4	Wright.	5,450	1	3		4		2	7	8	9	10	11			6	5				
Oct 4	(h)	Grimsby T.	W	2-0	Buckley (pen), Spinner.	4,113	1	3		4		2*	7	8	9	10	11	12		6	5				
11	(a)	Colchester U.	L	0-2		2,980	1	3	6	4		2	7		9	10	11	8*		12	5				
18	(h)	Chester	W	1-0	Buckley.	4,146	1	2	3	4	6*		7	12	8	10	11			9	5				
21	(h)	Millwall	D	1-1	Wright.	4,884	1	2	3	4			7	8	9	10	6			11	5				
25	(a)	Gillingham	W	3-2	Wiltshire (og), Buckley, Andrews.	5,942	1	2	3	4			7	8	9	10	6			11	5				
Nov 4	(a)	Cardiff C.	D	0-0		8,884	1	2	3	4			7	8	9	10	6		12	11	5*				
8	(a)	Rotherham U.	L	1-3	Buckley.	4,454	1	2	3	4			7		9	10	8	12	6	11	5*				
15	(h)	Chesterfield	W	1-0	Wright.	4,175	1	2	3	4			7	8	9	10	11		5	6					
29	(a)	Aldershot	L	2-3	Dennehy, Wright.	4,010	1	2	3	4		12	7	8*	9	10	6	11			5				
Dec 2	(h)	Sheffield W.	D	2-2	Buckley, Wright.	4,148	1	2	3	4		12	7	8*	9	10	6			11	5				
6	(h)	Port Vale	W	3-1	Andrews, Birch, Wright.	4,526	1	2	3	4			7	8	9	10	6			11			5		
20	(h)	Brighton & HA	W	2-0	Buckley (2).	5,435	1	2	3	4			7*	8	9	10	6			12			5	11	
26	(a)	Hereford U.	W	3-1	Evans, Buckley (2).	10,891	1	2	3	4			7	8	9	10	6						5	11	
27	(h)	Wrexham	D	2-2	Dennehy, Buckley.	9,028	1	2	3	4			7*	8	9	10	6			12			5	11	
Jan 6	(a)	Crystal P.	W	1-0	Dennehy.	16,181	1	2	3	4			7	8	9	10	6						5	11	
10	(h)	Halifax T.	W	2-0	Robinson, Wright.	7,167	1	2	3	4			7	8	9	10	6						5	11	
17	(a)	Bury	D	1-1	Andrews.	8,068	1	2	3			12	7	8	9	10	6		4				5	11*	
24	(h)	Preston N.E.	W	3-1	Evans, Buckley (2).	6,721	1	2	3	4			7	8	9	10	6						5	11	
31	(a)	Millwall	L	1-2	Dennehy.	4,747	1	2	3	4			7	8	9	10	6						5	11	
Feb 7	(h)	Cardiff C.	L	2-3	Buckley (2).	7,109	1	2	3	4			7	8*	9	10	6			12			5	11	
13	(h)	Rotherham U.	W	5-1	Buckley (4), Dennehy.	4,989	1	2	3	4			7	8	9	10	6			11			5		
21	(a)	Chesterfield	L	1-2	Andrews.	4,595	1	2	3	4			7	8	9	10	6			11*			5	12	
24	(a)	Shrewsbury T.	D	1-1	Wright.	9,085	1	2	3	4			7	8	9	10	6						5	11	
27	(h)	Gillingham	W	4-0	Buckley (3, 1 pen), Andrews.	5,493	1	2	3	4			7	8	9	10	6						5	11	
Mar 6	(a)	Sheffield W.	L	1-2	Hynd	9,713	1		3	4			7	8	9	10	6		2				5	11	
9	(a)	Grimsby T.	W	2-1	Dennehy, Taylor.	5,300	1		3	4		11	7	8		10	6		2				5	9	
13	(h)	Colchester U.	D	1-1	Andrews.	5,371	1		3	4		11*	7	8	12	10	6		2				5	9	
16	(a)	Chester	D	1-1	Buckley.	4,059	1		3	4	6	11	7	8		10			2				5	9	
20	(h)	Aldershot	W	4-1	Buckley (3), Andrews.	5,206	1		3	4	6	11*	7	9	12	10			2				5	8	
27	(a)	Port Vale	W	2-1	Atthey, Buckley.	4,863	1		3	4	6		7	8	9	10			2				5	11	
Apr 3	(h)	Peterboro. U.	D	2-2	Wright, Andrews.	6,266	1	2	3	4	6		7	8	9	10							5	11	
6	(h)	Mansfield T.	L	0-1		6,481	1	2	3	4	6		7	9	12	10	11*						5	8	
9	(a)	Southend U.	D	2-2	Buckley (2).	3,723	1	2	3	4	6			8	9	10							5	7	11
17	(h)	Hereford U.	D	0-0		9,225	1	2	3	4	6		7	8	9	10				12			5	11*	
19	(a)	Wrexham	W	3-0	Dennehy, Wright, Buckley.	5,482	1	2	3	4	6		7	8*	9	10						12	5	11	
24	(a)	Swindon T.	L	1-5	Buckley (pen).	7,363	1	2	3		6*		7	8	9	10						4	5	11	12
						Apps	46	40	42	44	14	14	45	43	39	46	34	3	13	18	13	2	26	23	1
						Subs						3		1	5		1	4	1	6	1	1		1	1
League position: 7th						Goals			1	1	1		8	9	12	34	2	1		1			1	2	

Own Goal: 1.

F.A. Cup

Date		Opponent	Rd	Score	Scorers	Att	Kearns	Fry	Harrison	Robinson	Atthey	Caswell	Dennehy	Andrews	Wright	Buckley	Taylor B.	Spinner	Saunders	Birch	Serella	Clarke	Hynd	Evans A.	Shelton
Nov 22	(h)	Huddersfield T.	1	0-1		5,506	1	2	3	4			6	8	9	10	11*		12	6	5				
						Apps	1	1	1	1			1	1	1	1	1			1	1				
						Subs													1						

League Cup

Date		Opponent	Rd	Score	Scorers	Att	Kearns	Fry	Harrison	Robinson	Atthey	Caswell	Dennehy	Andrews	Wright	Buckley	Taylor B.	Spinner	Saunders	Birch	Serella	Clarke	Hynd	Evans A.	Shelton
Aug 18	(h)	Shrewsbury T.	1/1	0-0		5,910	1	2	3	5	4	6	7	8*	9	10	11	12							
25	(a)	Shrewsbury T.	1/2	1-2	Buckley.	5,933	1	2	3	4		6	7	8	9	10		11	5						
						Apps	2	2	2	2	1	2	2	2	2	2	1	1	1						
						Subs												1							
						Goals										1									

In the final League game of the season, Trevor Anderson scored a hat-trick of penalties for Swindon Town against Walsall.

SEASON 1976-77

Division 3

Date		Opponent		Score	Scorers	Att	Kearns	Fry	Harrison	Serella	Hynd	Andrews	Dennehy	Bates M.J.	Atthey	Wright	Buckley	Caswell	Robinson	Evans	Taylor	Birch	Shelton	Clarke
Aug 21	(a)	Sheffield W.	D	0-0		12,046	1	2	3	4	5	6	7	8	9	10	11							
28	(h)	Gillingham	L	1-2	Buckley.	5,787	1	2	3	4	5	6*	7	8	11	9	10	12						
Sept 4	(a)	Reading	L	1-2	Wright.	6,036	1	2	3	4	5		11	8		9	10		6	7				
11	(h)	Shrewsbury T.	D	3-3	Atthey, Buckley (2).	5,320	1	2	3	5			7	8	6	9	10		4*	11	12			
14	(h)	Lincoln C.	L	1-3	Dennehy.	5,356	1	2	3		5		7	8	6	9	10		4*	11	12			
18	(a)	Wrexham	L	0-1		5,923	1		2		5	9	7	8	6*		10	3	4	11		12		
25	(a)	Northampton T.	W	1-0	Starling (og).	5,656	1		2		5	9*	7	8	6		10	3	4	11		12		
Oct 2	(h)	Port Vale	W	3-1	Atthey, Harrison, Buckley.	5,459	1		2		5	8	7		6	9	10	3	4	11				
5	(a)	Brighton & H.A.	L	0-7		14,128	1		2		5	8	7		6	9	10	3	4	11				
9	(a)	Portsmouth	D	1-1	Buckley	7,779	1		3	5	2		7		6	9	10	8	4	11				
16	(h)	Swindon T.	W	2-0	Taylor, Buckley.	5,529	1		3	5	2		7		12	9	10	6	4	8	11*			
23	(a)	Chesterfield	L	0-1		4,516	1		3	5	2		7	12		9	10	6*	4	8	11			
30	(h)	Crystal P.	D	0-0		6,033	1		3	5	2		7	8		9	10		4	11	6			
Nov 2	(h)	Oxford U.	D	2-2	Wright, Bates.	5,228	1		3	5			7*	6	2	9	10	12	4	8	11			
6	(a)	Chester	L	0-1		3,899	1		3	5	2		7	6	12	9	10*		4	8	11			
13	(h)	York City	L	1-2	Evans.	5,297	1		3*	5	2		12	4		9		8	6	11	7	10		
27	(a)	Rotherham U.	L	0-1		6,180	1			5*	2	8	7	10	6	9		3	4	12	11			
Dec 3	(h)	Peterboro. U.	D	1-1	Caswell.	3,848	1			5		11*	7	8	6	9	10	3	4	12	2			
18	(a)	Bury	W	2-0	Wright, Buckley.	4,326	1			5	4		7	8	6	9	10	3		11	2			
27	(h)	Preston N.E.	L	0-1		8,769	1			5	4		7	8	6	9	10	3		11	2			
28	(a)	Tranmere R.	D	0-0		3,510	1			5	4		7	8	6	9	10	3		11	2			
Jan 3	(a)	Crystal P.	L	0-3		17,614	1			5	4	12	7	8	6	9	10	3		11*	2			
18	(a)	Lincoln C.	L	1-4	Buckley.	5,223	1			5	4		7	8	6	9	10	3			2	11		
22	(h)	Sheffield W.	W	5-1	Birch, Caswell, Wright (2), Dennehy.	7,297	1			5	4		7	8	6	9	10	3			2	11		
Feb 1	(h)	Grimsby T.	W	1-0	Buckley (pen).	4,405	1			5	4		7	8	6	9	10	3*		12	2	11		
5	(a)	Gillingham	L	0-1		4,717	1			5	4		7	8	6		10	3		9	2	11		
12	(h)	Reading	W	6-1	Buckley, Andrews (2), Dennehy (3).	4,534	1				5	9	7	8	6		10	3	4		2	11		
19	(a)	Shrewsbury T.	W	2-1	Andrews, Buckley.	6,697	1				4	9	7	8	6		10	3	5		2	11		
26	(h)	Wrexham	L	2-3	Buckley (pen), Birch.	5,893	1				5	9	7*	8	6		10	3	4	12	2	11		
28	(a)	Mansfield T.	L	0-3		8,029	1			12	5	9	7	8	6		10	3	4		2	11*		
Mar 5	(h)	Northampton T.	L	0-3		4,806	1	2		5	6	9		8	12		10	3*	4		7		11	
11	(a)	Port Vale	D	0-0		4,819	1			5	4	9	7	8	6		10	3	12	11*	2			
19	(h)	Portsmouth	D	1-1	Andrews.	4,871	1			5	4	9	7	8	6		10	3			2	11		
22	(h)	Chester	W	1-0	Buckley.	4,247	1			4	5	9	7	8			10	3	6		2	11*	12	
26	(a)	Swindon T.	D	2-2	Dennehy, Buckley.	7,534	1			4	5	9	7	8			10	3	6		2	11		
Apr 2	(h)	Chesterfield	D	2-2	Andrews, Birch.	4,482	1			5	6	9	7	8			10	3	4		2	11		
9	(h)	Tranmere R.	W	2-0	Buckley (pen), Serella.	4,403	1			5	6	9	7*	8			10	3	4		2	11	12	
11	(a)	Preston N.E.	W	1-0	Buckley.	7,850	1			5	4	9	7	8			10	3	6		2	11		
12	(a)	Oxford U.	D	0-0		4,008	1			4	5	9	7	8	3		10		6		2	11		
16	(h)	Brighton & H.A.	W	1-0	Atthey.	7,591	1			5	6	9	7	8	3		10		4		2*	11	12	
19	(h)	Mansfield T.	L	1-2	Buckley (pen).	7,601	1			5	4	9	7	8	2		10	3	6*			11	12	
23	(a)	York City	D	0-0		2,279	1			5	4	9	7	8	2*		10	3	6			11	12	
30	(h)	Rotherham U.	L	0-1		5,399	1	2		5	4	9	7*	8			10	3	6			11	12	
May 3	(a)	Grimsby T.	D	2-2	Buckley, Serella.	3,500	1	2		5	4	9		8			10	3				11	7	6
7	(a)	Peterboro. U.	W	5-3	Andrews (2), Birch (3).	3,933	1			5	4	9	12	8	6*		10	3			2	11	7	
14	(h)	Bury	D	3-3	Buckley (2, 1 pen), Andrews).	4,738	1			5	4	9	7	8			10	3			2	11	6	
						Apps	46	8	16	37	43	28	42	41	31	23	44	36	31	20	32	23	4	1
						Subs				1		1	2	1	3			2	1	4	2	2	6	
League position: 15th						Goals			1	2		8	6	1	3	5	20	2		1	1	6		

Own Goal: 1.

F.A. Cup

Date		Opponent	Rd	Score	Scorers	Att	Kearns	Fry	Harrison	Serella	Hynd	Andrews	Dennehy	Bates M.J.	Atthey	Wright	Buckley	Caswell	Robinson	Evans	Taylor	Birch	Shelton	Clarke
Nov 20	(h)	Bradford City	1	0-0		5,868	1			5	2	12	7	8	6	9		3	4	10*	11			
24	(a)	Bradford City	R	2-0	Taylor, Wright.	7,399	1			5	2	10	7	8	6	9		3	4		11			
Dec 11	(a)	Chesterfield	2	1-1	Hunter (og).	8,239	1			5	4	11	7	8	6		10	3		9	2			
14	(h)	Chesterfield	R	0-0	(a.e.t.)	6,323	1			4	5	9	7	8	6	12	10	3		11	2*			
21	(n)	Chesterfield *	2R	1-0	Wright.	5,990	1			5	4		7	8	6	9	10	3		11	2			
Jan 8	(a)	Manchester U.	3	0-1		48,870	1			5	4	11	7	8	6	9	10	3			2			
						Apps	6			6	6	4	6	6	6	4	4	6	2	4	6			
						Subs						1				1								
* Played at Derby						Goals										2					1			

Own Goal: 1.

League Cup

Date		Opponent	Rd	Score	Scorers	Att	Kearns	Fry	Harrison	Serella	Hynd	Andrews	Dennehy	Bates M.J.	Atthey	Wright	Buckley	Caswell	Robinson	Evans	Taylor	Birch	Shelton	Clarke
Aug 16	(a)	Shrewsbury	1/1	1-0	Buckley	5,553	1	2	3	5	4		7	8	6	9	10		12		11*			
18	(h)	Shrewsbury	1/2	1-0	Buckley	6,748	1	2	3	5	4	6	7	8	11	9	10							
31	(h)	Nottm. Forest	2	2-4	Buckley, Wright.	6,748	1	2	3	4	5		7	8	6*	9	10	11			12			
						Apps	3	3	3	3	3	1	3	3	3	3	3	1			1			
						Subs													1		1			
						Goals										1	3							

SEASON 1977-78

Division 3

Date	Opponent	Res	Score	Scorers	Att	Kearns	Taylor B.	Caswell	Newton	Hynd	Serella	Shelton	Bates	Evans A.	Buckley	Birch	Clarke	Wood	Dennehy	Robertson	Harrison	Green	Moseley	Macken	King	Austin	Paul	Penn
Aug 20 (h)	Exeter C.	L	1-3	Taylor.	5,174	1	2	3	4	5	6	7*	8	9	10	11	12											
24 (a)	Lincoln C.	D	2-2	Buckley (pen), Evans.	3,723	1	2	3	6	4	5	7	8	9	10	11												
27 (a)	Sheffield W.	D	0-0		10,634	1	2	3	4	5	6	7	8		10	11		9										
Sept 3 (h)	Swindon T.	W	2-0	Serella, Dennehy.	4,717	1	2	3	4	5	6	12		8	10	11		9*	7									
10 (h)	Bury	L	1-2	Buckley (pen).	4,611	1	2	3	4	5		12	8	9*	10	11			7	6								
13 (a)	Plymouth Arg.	D	3-3	Buckley, Craven (og), Caswell.	5,958	1	2	3	6	4	5		8	12	10	11*			9	7								
17 (a)	Shrewsbury T	D	0-0		4,635	1	2	3	6*	5	4		8	12	10	11			9	7								
24 (h)	Port Vale	W	2-0	Wood, Dennehy.	4,892	1	2	3	6	4	5		8		10	11		9*	12	7								
27 (h)	Preston NE	D	0-0		5,138	1	2		6*	4	5		8	12	10	11			9	7	3							
Oct 1 (a)	Peterboro. U.	D	0-0		5,389	1	2			4	5		8	6	10	11		9		7	3							
4 (a)	Rotherham U.	L	0-3		4,843		2			4	5		8	6	10	11		9		7	3	1						
8 (h)	Portsmouth	D	1-1	Evans.	4,764		2		3	4	5	12	8	6	10	11*		9		7			1					
15 (a)	Chesterfield	W	1-0	Buckley.	4,856				3	5	6		8	4	10	11			9	7			1	2				
22 (h)	Wrexham	L	0-1		5,502				3	5	6		8	4	10	11		9*	12	7			1	2				
28 (a)	Tranmere R.	W	1-0	Birch.	4,848	1			3	4	5		8		10	11			9	7	6			2				
Nov 5 (h)	Colchester U.	W	4-2	Serella, Dennehy, Buckley (2).	4,231	1			3	4	5		8	6	10	11			9	7	2							
12 (a)	Hereford U	L	2-3	Birch, Buckley (pen).	5,655	1			3	5	6		8	4	10	11*		12	9	7				2				
19 (h)	Oxford U	W	2-1	Buckley, Bates.	4,453	1			3*	4		12	8	6	10	11			9	7	5			2				
Dec 3 (a)	Gillingham	L	1-3	Buckley.	5,243	1		3		4	5		8	6*	10	11		9	12	7				2				
10 (h)	Bradford C.	D	1-1	Buckley.	4,218	1		3		4	5	12	8	6	10			9	11	7*				2				
26 (a)	Carlisle U.	L	0-2		10,323	1		3			5		8	6	10			9	7		4			2	11			
27 (h)	Chester	W	3-0	Buckley (2, 1 pen), Wood.	4,990	1		3			5	6	8		10			9	7		4			2	11			
31 (h)	Cambridge U	D	0-0		5,086	1		3			5	4	8*	12	10			9	7		6			2	11			
Jan 2 (a)	Colchester U	D	1-1	Buckley.	6,039	1		3			5	6	8		10			9	7		4			2	11			
14 (a)	Exeter C	D	1-1	Buckley (pen).	5,149	1		3			5	4	8		10			9	7		6			2	11			
17 (h)	Tranmere T.	D	0-0		6,072	1		3			5		8	6*	10	12		9	7		4			2	11			
Feb 7 (h)	Lincoln C.	W	3-1	King, Evans, Buckley.	5,082	1		3			5		8	6	10			9	7		4			2	11			
11 (h)	Shrewsbury T	W	3-0	Dennehy, Buckley (pen), Serella.	8,341	1		3			5		8	6	10			9	7		4			2	11			
25 (h)	Peterboro. U.	W	1-0	Caswell.	5,408	1		3			5		8	6	10			9	7		4			2	11			
28 (a)	Port Vale	D	2-2	Buckley (2, 1 pen).	4,682	1		3			5		8	6	10			9	7		4			2	11			
Mar 4 (a)	Portsmouth	W	2-1	Caswell, Dennehy.	9,536	1		3			5		8	6	10			9	7		4			2	11			
7 (h)	Plymouth Arg.	W	1-0	Buckley.	6,722	1		3			5		8	6	10			9	7		4			2	11			
11 (h)	Chesterfield	D	2-2	Buckley (2, 1 pen).	7,426	1		3*			5		8	6	10			9	7		4			2	11	12		
14 (a)	Bury	W	1-0	Dennehy.	3,695	1		3			5		8		10	6		9	7*		4			2	11	12		
18 (a)	Wrexham	L	0-1		13,683	1		3			5		8	6*	10			9	7		4			2	11	12		
25 (h)	Carlisle U	D	0-0		5,907	1		3			5		8	6	10			12	7		4			2	11*	9		
27 (a)	Chester	D	1-1	Buckley.	4,671	1		3			5		8	6	10	11			7		4			2		9		
Apr 1 (a)	Cambridge U.	L	1-2	Birch.	5,849	1		3			5			8	10	11		4	7		6			2		9		
4 (a)	Preston NE	L	0-1		11,239	1		3			5			8	10	11		4	7		6*					9	2	12
8 (h)	Hereford U.	W	2-0	Austin, Bates.	5,152	1		3			5		8	6	10	11			7		4					9	2	
11 (a)	Swindon T.	W	3-2	Buckley, Austin, Prophett (og).	3,925	1		3			5		8	6	10	11	12		7*		4					9	2	
15 (a)	Oxford U.	L	1-3	Austin.	4,610	1		3			5		8	6	10	11		12			4			7*		9	2	
22 (h)	Gillingham	W	2-1	Birch, Dennehy.	4,707	1		3			5		8	6	10	11			7		4			2		9		
25 (h)	Sheffield W.	D	1-1	Buckley.	5,232	1		3			5		8	6	10	11			7		4			2		9		
29 (a)	Bradford C.	W	3-2	Evans, Austin, Bates.	5,110	1		3			5		8	6	10	11			7		4			2		9		
May 1 (h)	Rotherham U.	W	3-1	Austin (2), Dennehy.	4,364	1		3			5		8	6	10	11			7		4			2		9		
					Apps	42	12	36	16	20	44	7	43	35	46	30		26	36	16	32	1	3	30	16	11	4	
					Subs							5		4		1	2	3	3							3		1
League position: 6th					Goals		1	3			3		3	4	24	4		2	8						1	6		

Own Goals: 2.

F.A. Cup

Date	Opponent	Rd	Score	Scorers	Att	Kearns	Taylor B.	Caswell	Newton	Hynd	Serella	Shelton	Bates	Evans A.	Buckley	Birch	Clarke	Wood	Dennehy	Robertson	Harrison	Green	Moseley	Macken	King	Austin	Paul	Penn
Nov 26 (h)	Dagenham	1	1-0	Wood	5,518	1				4		3	8	6	10	11		9*	12	7	5			2				
Dec 17 (h)	Port Vale	2	1-1	Wood	5,978	1		3*		4	5	12	8	6	10			9	7	11				2				
19 (a)	Port Vale	R	3-1	King, Shelton, Bates.	7,051	1				4	5	12	8	6	10			9	7		3			2	11*			
Jan 6 (h)	Swansea C.	3	4-1	Buckley (3), King.	7,705	1					5	3	8*	4	10	12		9	7		6			2	11			
28 (h)	Leicester C.	4	1-0	Evans.	17,421	1		3			5		8	6	10	12		9	7		4			2*	11			
Feb 18 (a)	Arsenal	5	1-4	Buckley.	43,736	1		3			5		8	6	10			9	7		4			2	11			
					Apps	6		3		3	5	2	6	6	6	1		6	5	2	5			6	4			
					Subs							2				2												
					Goals							1	1	1	4			2							2			

League Cup

Date	Opponent	Rd	Score	Scorers	Att	Kearns	Taylor B.	Caswell	Newton	Hynd	Serella	Shelton	Bates	Evans A.	Buckley	Birch	Clarke	Wood	Dennehy	Robertson	Harrison	Green	Moseley	Macken	King	Austin	Paul	Penn
Aug 13 (a)	Bristol Rovers	1/1	2-1	Evans, Bater (og)	3,467	1	2	3	4	6	5		8	9	10	11			7									
16 (h)	Bristol Rovers	1/2	1-0	Bater (og)	5,445	1	2	3	6	4	5		8	9	10	11	12		7*									
29 (h)	P.N.E.	2	0-0		5,380	1	2	3	6	4	5	12	8*		10	11		9	7									
Sep 6 (a)	P.N.E.	R	1-0	(aet) Buckley.	7.079	1	2	3	6	4	5		8*	12	10	11			9	7								
Oct 25 (a)	Sheffield Wed.	3	1-2	Wood.	18,350	1			3	4	5		8	6*	10	11		12	9	7				2				
					Apps	5	4	4	5	5	5		5	3	5	5		1	5	2				1				
					Subs							1		1			1	1										
					Goals									1	1			1										

Own Goals: 2.

SEASON 1978-79

Division 3

Date	Opponent	Res	Score	Scorers	Att	Kearns	Paul	Caswell	Harrison	Serella	King	Birch	Macken	Austin	Buckley	Kelly J.	Clarke	Waddington S	McDonough	Sbragia	Penn	Waddington P	Turner	Jones	Rees	Williams	Syrett	Green	Mower
Aug 19 (h)	Watford	L	2-4	Austin (2).	6,423	1	2	3	4	5	6	7	8	9	10	11													
23 (a)	Chester	L	1-2	Kelly	4,257	1	2	3	4	5	6	7	8	9	10	11													
26 (a)	Carlisle U.	L	0-1		4,781	1	2*	3	4	5	6	7	8	9	10	11	12												
Sept 2 (h)	Shrewsbury T.	D	1-1	Austin.	4,269	1		3	4	5	6	7	2	9	10	11	8												
9 (h)	Swindon T.	W	4-1	Birch (2, 1 pen), Austin, King.	5,024	1		3	4	5	6	7	2	9		11		8	10										
12 (a)	Hull City	L	1-4	McDonough.	6,784	1		3	4	5	6	7	2	9	10			8	11										
16 (a)	Blackpool	L	1-2	Kelly.	8,153	1		3	4	5	6	7	2	9	10	12		8	11*										
23 (h)	Colchester U.	D	2-2	Buckley, King.	4,052	1		3	4	5	6	7	2	9	10	11			8										
26 (h)	Peterboro. U.	W	4-1	McDonough (2), Austin (2).	4,835	1		3	4	5	6	7	2	9	10			8	11										
29 (a)	Lincoln C.	D	1-1	Waddington S.	3,371	1		3	4	5	6	7	2	9	10			8	11										
Oct 7 (h)	Southend U.	D	1-1	Buckley (pen)	4,911	1		3*		5	6	7	2	9	10	12		8	11	4									
14 (a)	Mansfield T.	W	3-1	Buckley (2), Austin.	6,066	1			3	5	6	7	2	9	10			8	11	4									
17 (a)	Bury	D	1-1	McDonough.	4,443	1			3	5	6	7	2	9	10			8	11	4									
21 (h)	Plymouth A.	W	2-1	Buckley, Sbragia	5,552	1			3	5	6	7	2	9	10			8	11	4									
28 (a)	Sheffield W.	W	2-0	King, Blackhall (og).	12,019	1		12	3	5	6	7	2*	9		11		10		4	8								
Nov. 4 (h)	Rotherham U.	L	0-1		5,456	1		10	3	5	6	7	2	9		11				4	8								
10 (a)	Shrewsbury T.	D	1-1	McDonough.	7,615	1		8	3	5	6	7	2	9		11*			10	4	12								
18 (h)	Carlisle U.	L	1-2	Birch.	4,441	1		8	3	5	6	7	2	9		11*			10	4	12								
Dec 2 (a)	Brentford	L	0-1		5,130	1	2	3	6			7	4			11		8	10	5*	9	12							
9 (h)	Tranmere R.	W	2-0	Penn, Birch (pen).	2,954	1	2	3	6		11	7	4	9				8	5		10								
26 (a)	Exeter C.	L	1-3	Austin.	4,159	1	2	3	4	5		7	6	9		11		8	10										
30 (a)	Oxford Utd	L	1-2	Serella.	4,231	1	2	3	4	5	6	7	11	9				8	10										
Jan 6 (h)	Hull City	L	1-2	Caswell.	4,061	1	2	3	6	5		7	4	9		11		8	10										
16 (a)	Swindon T.	L	1-4	Austin.	7,282		2*	3	4	5		7	11	9		12		8	10	6			1						
Feb 3 (a)	Peterboro. U.	W	3-0	Austin (2), McDonough.	4,466			3	2	5		7	4	9				8	11	6			1	10					
6 (h)	Blackpool	W	2-1	Austin, McDonough.	3,711			3	2	5		7	11	9				8	10	6			1	4					
20 (h)	Swansea C.	D	1-1	Birch (pen).	4,335			2	3	5		7	11	9				8	10	6			1	4					
24 (h)	Mansfield T.	D	1-1	Birch.	4,157			3	2*	5		7	11	9		12		8	10	6			1	4					
27 (a)	Colchester U.	L	0-2		3,135			3	2	5	12	7	11	9*				8	10	6			1	4					
Mar 3 (a)	Plymouth A.	L	0-1		6,487			3	2	5	7		11	9				8	10	6			1	4					
10 (h)	Sheffield W.	L	0-2		5,120			3	2	5	10	7	11*	9				8	12	6			1	4					
13 (h)	Lincoln C.	W	4-1	Penn, Austin, Birch, Sbragia.	2,794					5	4	7	2	9		12		8	10*	6	11		1	3					
20 (h)	Gillingham	L	0-1		3,084	1		3		5	8	7	2	9		12			10*	6	11			4					
24 (h)	Chester	W	2-1	Birch (pen), Penn.	2,795		2	3		5	8	7		9		11*				6	10		1	4	12				
27 (a)	Watford	L	1-3	Serella.	11,891			3		5	7	8	2			11*		10		6	9		1	4	12				
31 (a)	Chesterfield	D	0-0		3,322			3		5		7	2					8*	10	6	11		1	4		12	9		
Apr 7 (h)	Brentford	L	2-3	Williams, Kruse (og).	3,840			3		5		7	2					11	8	6	10		1	4*		12	9		
10 (a)	Gillingham	L	1-3	Syrett.	7,342			3		5		7	2					10		6			1	4	11	8	9		
14 (h)	Exeter C.	D	2-2	Sbragia, Birch.	3,118			3		5	4	7						8		6			1	2	11	10	9		
17 (a)	Swansea C.	D	2-2	Syrett (2).	18,096			3		5	4	7	2					10	12	6			1		11*	8	9		
21 (h)	Oxford Utd.	L	0-1		3,396			3		4	6	7	2*					10	12	5			1		11	8	9		
24 (h)	Bury	L	0-1		2,573		2	3			4	7				8			5	6	12		1		11*	10	9		
27 (a)	Tranmere R.	D	0-0		1,453		12	3		5	4	7	2					8	10	6			1		11*		9		
30 (a)	Southend U.	L	0-1		2,887		8	3		5	4*	7	2			12			10	6			1		11		9		
May 5 (h)	Chesterfield	L	0-1		2,625		10	2		5	4	7	3*			11				6			1		12	8	9		
14 (a)	Rotherham U.	L	1-4	Waddington S.	1,996			3		5	4	7				11		8		6		12				10*	9	1	2
					Apps	24	13	41	30	43	34	45	42	33	13	18	1	33	31	32	10		21	15	7	7	11	1	1
					Subs		1	1			1					7	1		3		3	2			3	2			
League position: 22nd					Goals			1		2	3	9		13	5	2		2	7	3	3					1	3		

Own Goals : 2.

F.A. Cup

Date	Opponent	Rd	Score		Att	Kearns	Paul	Caswell	Harrison	Serella	King	Birch	Macken	Austin	Buckley	Kelly J.	Clarke	Waddington S	McDonough	Sbragia	Penn
Nov 25 ((h)	Torquay	1	0-2		4,445	1	2		3	5*	6	7	8	9		11			10	4	12
					Apps	1	1		1	1	1	1	1	1		1			1	1	
					Subs																1

League Cup

Date	Opponent	Rd	Score	Scorers	Att	Kearns	Paul	Caswell	Harrison	Serella	King	Birch	Macken	Austin	Buckley	Kelly J.	Clarke
Aug 12 (h)	Halifax Town	1/1	2-1	Buckley, Birch.	4,589	1	2	3*	6	5	11	7	4	9	10	8	12
15 (a)	Halifax Town	1/2	2-0	Paul, Buckley.	2,276	1	2	3	4	5	6	7	8	9	10	11	
29 (h)	Charlton Ath.	2	1-2	Buckley (pen).	4,519	1		3	4	5	6	7	2	9	10	11	8
					Apps	3	2	3	3	3	3	3	3	3	3	3	1
					Subs												1
					Goals		1					1			3		

SEASON 1979-80

Division 4

Date	Opponent	Res	Score	Scorers	Att	Turner	Macken	Mower	Sbragia	Serella	Paul	Penn	Waddington S.	McDonough	Buckley	Kelly J.	Caswell	Rees	Green	Harrison	Williams J.	Broadhurst	Horne	Williams G.	Syrett
Aug 18	(h) Stockport C.	W	2-1	Penn, Kelly.	3,786	1	2	3	4	5	6	7	8	9	10	11									
21	(a) Bournemouth	D	1-1	Paul.	4,833	1	2	3	4	5	6	7	8	9*	10		11				12				
25	(a) Northampton T.	W	2-1	Penn (2).	3,136	1	2	3	5	4	9	7	8	10	11		6								
Sept 1	(h) Hereford Utd	W	3-2	Buckley (2, 1 pen), Serella.	4,527	1	2	3	4	5	6	7	8	9	10		11								
8	(a) Rochdale	D	1-1	Caswell.	2,494	1	2	3	4	5	6	7	8	9	10		11								
15	(h) Hartlepool U.	W	3-1	Waddington, Buckley (2).	4,203	1	2	3	4	5	6	7*	8	9	10		11	12							
18	(h) Lincoln C.	W	3-0	McDonough, Penn (2).	5,193		2	3	4	5	6	7	8	9	10		11		1						
22	(a) Darlington	W	3-1	Penn, Buckley (2).	1,609		2	3	4	5	6	7	8	9	10		11		1						
29	(h) Aldershot	D	1-1	Buckley	5,137		2	3	4	5	6	7*	8	9	10		11	12	1						
Oct 3	(a) Lincoln C.	D	2-2	McDonough, Penn.	4,197		2	3	4	5	6	7	8	9	10		11		1						
6	(a) Scunthorpe U.	D	2-2	Penn, Caswell.	2,492		2	3	6	5		7	4		10		11	9	1	8*	12				
9	(h) Bournemouth	D	0-0		4,895		2	3	4	5	6	7	8	9	10		11		1						
13	(h) Torquay Utd	D	1-1	Caswell.	4,233		2	3	4	5	6	7	8*	9	10		11		1		12				
20	(a) Halifax T.	L	1-2	Penn.	3,184		2	3	4	5	6	7	8	9	10*		11		1		12				
24	(a) Crewe Alex.	W	2-1	Caswell (pen), Serella.	3,502		2	3	4	5	6	7	8*	9	12		11		1		10				
27	(h) Port Vale	W	2-1	McDonough, Penn.	4,976		2	3	4	5	6	7		9	10		11		1		8				
Nov 2	(a) Stockport C.	L	0-1		3,323		2	3	4	5		7	6	9	10		11		1		8				
6	(h) Crewe Alex.	W	1-0	Penn.	4,125		2	3	4	5		7	6	9*	10		11	12	1		8				
10	(h) Portsmouth	D	1-1	McDonough.	7,468			3	4	5	2	7		9	10		11		1		8	6			
17	(a) Peterboro. T.	W	3-1	Penn, Waddington, McDonough.	4,019			3	4	5	2	7	10	9			11		1		8	6			
Dec 1	(a) Bradford C.	W	1-0	Paul.	5,824		2		4	5	6	7	8*	9	10		3		1		12	11			
8	(h) Wigan Ath.	D	1-1	Penn.	5,261		2		4	5	6	7	8	9	10		3		1		11				
21	(a) York City	W	1-0	Williams.	1,990		2	3	4		6	7	8	9	10		11		1		5				
26	(h) Doncaster R.	W	3-1	McDonough, Penn, Waddington.	5,449		2	3	4		6	7	8	9	10		11		1		5				
29	(a) Newport C.	W	1-0	Paul.	7,452		2*	3	4		6	7	8	9	10		11	12	1		5				
Jan 5	(h) Huddersfield T.	D	1-1	Buckley.	7,639			2	4	5	3	7	8	9	10		11		1		6				
12	(a) Hereford U.	W	1-0	Penn.	4,814			3	4	5	6	7	8	9	10		11		1		2				
26	(h) Northampton T.	W	5-1	Penn, Paul, Caswell, Buckley, Rees.	5,646		2*	3	4	5	6	7		9	10		11	12	1		8				
Feb 2	(a) Hartlepool U.	D	2-2	Buckley, Penn.	4,576		2	3	4	5	6	7*		9	10		11	12	1		8				
9	(h) Darlington	D	1-1	Caswell.	5,505		2	3	4	5	6	7		9	10		11		1		8				
16	(a) Aldershot	D	1-1	Buckley.	4,421		2	3	4	5	6	7		9	10		11		1		8				
19	(h) Rochdale	W	2-0	Paul, Waddintgon.	6,007	1	2	3	4	5	6	7	8	9	10		11*				12				
23	(a) Torquay U.	W	1-0	Penn.	4,459		2	3	4	5	6	7	8	9	10		11		1						
Mar 1	(h) Halifax T.	W	2-0	McDonough, Buckley.	5,859		2	3	4	5*	6	7	8	9	10		11		1		12				
4	(a) Tranmere R.	W	1-0	Penn.	2,903		2	3	4		6	7	8	9	10		11		1		5				
8	(a) Port Vale	D	2-2	Rees, Penn.	6,856		2	3	4		6*	7	8	9	10		11	12	1		5				
15	(h) Scunthorpe U.	D	1-1	Buckley (pen).	5,078		2	3	4			7	8	9	10		11	12	1		5*		6		
22	(a) Portsmouth	W	2-1	Macken, Buckley (pen).	21,785		2	3	4			7*	8		10		11	9	1		5		12	6	
29	(h) Peterboro. U.	L	2-3	Rees, Penn.	5,704		2	3	4			7	8		10		11	9	1		5			6	
Apr 1	(h) York City	W	3-1	Penn (2), Sbragia.	4,897		2	3	4			7*	8	12	10		11	9	1		5			6	
5	(a) Doncaster R.	D	1-1	Waddington.	3,784		2	3	4	5		7	8		10		11	9	1					6	
7	(h) Tranmere R.	W	2-0	Mower, Serella.	5,810		2	3	4	5	8		12	9	10		11*	7	1					6	
12	(a) Huddersfield T.	D	1-1	Penn.	17,233		2	3	4*	5	8	9		12	10		11	7	1					6	
19	(h) Bradford C.	D	1-1	Buckley.	6,937		2	3		5	4*	7	8	9	10		11	12	1					6	
26	(a) Wigan Ath.	L	0-3		7,720		2	3	4	5	7	8		9	10*		11	12	1					6	
May 3	(h) Newport C.	L	2-4	Buckley (pen), Penn.	9,251		2	3	4	5		7*	8	9	10		11	12	1					6	
					Apps	7	42	44	45	37	37	45	37	40	44	1	45	7	39	1	22	3	1	9	
					Subs								1	2	1			11			7		1		
League position: 2nd (Promoted)					Goals		1	1	1	3	5	25	5	7	16	1	6	3			1				

F.A. Cup

Date	Opponent	Rd	Score	Scorers	Att	Turner	Macken	Mower	Sbragia	Serella	Paul	Penn	Waddington S.	McDonough	Buckley	Kelly J.	Caswell	Rees	Green	Harrison	Williams J.	Broadhurst	Horne	Williams G.	Syrett
Nov 24	(h) Stockport C.	1	2-0	Penn, Paul.	4,959		2	3	4	5	6	7	8	9	10		11		1						
Dec 15	(h) Halifax T.	2	1-1	Buckley (pen).	4,651		2	3	4	5	6	7	8	9*	10		11		1		12				
18	(a) Halifax T.	2R	1-1	(a.e.t.) Buckley.	3,641		2	3	4	5*	6	7	8	9	10		11		1		12				
24	(a) Halifax T.	2R2	0-2	(a.e.t.)	6,530		2	3	4		6	7	8	9*	10		11	12	1		5				
					Apps		4	4	4	3	4	4	4	4	4		4		4		1				
					Subs													1			2				
					Goals						1	1			2										

League Cup

Date	Opponent	Rd	Score	Scorers	Att	Turner	Macken	Mower	Sbragia	Serella	Paul	Penn	Waddington S.	McDonough	Buckley	Kelly J.	Caswell	Rees	Green	Harrison	Williams J.	Broadhurst	Horne	Williams G.	Syrett
Aug 1	(a) Chester City	1/1	1-2	Serella.	3,872	1	2	3	4	5	8	7	6	9	10	11									
14	(h) Chester City	1/2	0-0		3,611	1	2		4	5	6	7	8*	9	10	11	3								12
					Apps	2	2	1	2	2	2	2	2	2	2	2	1								
					Subs																				1
					Goals					1															

SEASON 1980-81

Division 3

Date	Venue	Opponent	Res	Score	Scorers	Att	Turner	Macken	Mower	Serella	Baines	Hart	Penn	O'Kelly	McDonough	Buckley	Caswell	Waddington S.	Freeman	Rees	Paul	Connealy	Smith	Harrison	Horne	Green	Waddington P.	Preece
Aug 16	(a)	Reading	L	0-2		4,369	1	2*	3	4	5	6	7	8	9	10	11	12										
20	(h)	Burnley	W	3-1	Penn, Baines, Buckley.	4,714		2	3	4	5	6	7	8*	9	10	11	12	1									
23	(a)	Colchester U.	D	1-1	O'Kelly.	1,979		2	3	4	5	6	7	8	9	10	11*	12	1									
30	(h)	Brentford	L	2-3	Hill (og), Buckley.	4,586		2	3	4	5	6	7	8	9	10		11	1									
Sept 6	(a)	Hull City	W	1-0	Buckley.	4,121		2	3	4	5	6	7	8		10	11		1	9								
13	(h)	Portsmouth	W	2-0	Rees, Buckley.	5,738		2	3	4	5	6	7	8		10	11		1	9								
16	(h)	Rotherham U.	L	0-2		4,500		2	3	4	5	6	7*	8	12	10	11		1	9								
20	(a)	Fulham	L	1-2	Buckley.	4,573		2	3*	4	5	6	7	8		10	11		1	9	12							
27	(h)	Blackpool	D	2-2	Rees, McDonough.	4,227		2*		4	5	6	7	8	9	10	11		1	12	3							
30	(a)	Rotherham U.	L	1-2	Paul.	6,842			3	4	5	6	9	8		10	2			11	7	1						
Oct 4	(h)	Carlisle U.	W	4-3	Penn (2), McVitie (og), Baines.	3,815		2	12	4	5	6	7	8		10	3*			9	11	1						
7	(a)	Charlton A.	L	0-2		3,359		2	3	4	5	6	7	8		10				9	11	1						
11	(a)	Oxford U.	D	1-1	Penn.	3,123	1	2	3	4		6	7	8		10		5		9	11							
18	(h)	Newport C.	W	1-0	Hart.	4,335	1	2	3	4	5*	6	7	8		10		11		9			12					
21	(h)	Exeter C.	L	1-3	Rees.	3,703	1	2	3	4	5	6	7			10*		8		9	11		12					
25	(a)	Chesterfield	W	2-1	O'Kelly, Baines.	7,870	1	2		4	5	6		8		10	3	7			11		9					
28	(a)	Millwall	W	1-0	O'Kelly	2,785	1	2		4	5	6	7	8		10	11						9	3				
Nov 1	(h)	Gillingham	D	3-3	Hart, Paul, O'Kelly.	4,060	1	2		4	5	6		8		10	3	7			11		9					
4	(h)	Charlton A.	D	2-2	Waddington S., Smith.	4,287	1	2		4	5	6		8		10	3	7			11		9					
8	(a)	Plymouth A.	L	0-2		5,022	1	2		4	5	6		8		10	3*	7			11		9	12				
11	(a)	Burnley	D	0-0		5,570	1	2		4		6	10	8				7		12	11		9*	3	5			
15	(h)	Reading	D	2-2	Paul (2).	3,583	1	2		4		6	9	8				7			11		10	3	5			
29	(h)	Sheffield U.	D	4-4	Buckley (pen), Penn (2), Mower.	4,931		2*	3	4		6	12	8		10		7			11		9	5		1		
Dec 6	(a)	Chester	L	0-1		2,215		2	3	4	5	6	8			10		7			11		9			1		
19	(a)	Swindon T.	L	1-3	Buckley.	4,523		2	3	5			7	6		10	11	8		12			9*	4		1		
26	(h)	Huddersfield T.	D	2-2	Buckley, O'Kelly.	5,906		2	3	4	5	6	7*	9		10	11	8		12						1		
27	(a)	Barnsley	L	0-3		14,958		2	3	4	5	6		9		10	11	8*		7						1	12	
Jan 3	(h)	Millwall	D	0-0		3,918		2	3*	4	5	6		12		10	11	8					9			1	7	
10	(a)	Exeter C.	W	3-0	O'Kelly, Hart, Buckley.	4,590		2*		4	5	6		9		10	8	7						3	12	1	11	
17	(h)	Chester	W	2-1	Waddington S., Baines.	3,483				4	5	6	10	9			3	8		7*				2		1	11	12
24	(a)	Brentford	L	0-4		5,500				4	5	6		9			3	7		8*				2	12	1	11	10
31	(h)	Colchester U.	W	3-1	Waddington S., Mower, Smith.	3,195			3	4	5	6				10	2	7					9			1	11	8
Feb 7	(a)	Portsmouth	L	0-2		11,921			3	4	5	6	12			10	8	7					9*	2		1	11	
14	(h)	Hull City	D	1-1	Buckley.	3,914			3		5	6	9	12		10	8	7						2		1	11*	4
21	(a)	Blackpool	L	0-1		3,895				4	5	6	7	9		10	3	8						2		1		11
Mar 1	(h)	Fulham	L	1-2	Smith.	4,958				4	5	6*	7	8		10	3						9	2		1	11	12
7	(a)	Carlisle U.	D	1-1	Hart.	4,485			3	5		6	7*	12		10							9	2	4	1	11	8
14	(h)	Oxford U.	L	0-3		3,185			3	5		6	12			10	4	7					9*	2		1	11	8
28	(h)	Chesterfield	W	4-3	Rees (2), O'Kelly, Hart.	4,044		2	3		5	6	10	9			8	12		7				4		1	11*	
Apr 3	(a)	Gillingham	L	0-1		4,112		2	3	5	9	6	10	8				12		7*				4		1	11	
7	(a)	Newport C.	D	1-1	Caswell	5,446		2	3	5	12	6	10	9			8			7				4		1	11*	
11	(h)	Plymouth A.	L	1-3	Penn.	3,556		2	3	5		6	10	9		12	8*			7				4		1	11	
18	(h)	Barnsley	D	1-1	Buckley (pen).	6,026		2	3	4*	5	6	9	11		10		8		7					12	1		
21	(a)	Huddersfield	D	1-1	Waddington S.	9,463		2	3		5	6	9			10	11	8		7					4	1		
25	(h)	Swindon T.	W	2-1	Penn, Rees.	3,429		2	3		5	6	9			10	11	8		7					4	1		
May 2	(a)	Sheffield U.	W	1-0	Penn (pen).	16,001		2	3	4	5	6*	9			10	11	8		7					12	1		
						Apps	11	36	32	42	37	45	34	35	5	38	34	28	8	21	14	3	16	18	5	24	14	6
						Subs			1		1		3	3	1	1		5		4	1		2	1	4		1	2
League position: 20th						Goals			2		4	5	9	7	1	11	1	4		6	4		3					

Own Goals : 2.

F.A. Cup

Date	Venue	Opponent	Rd	Score	Scorers	Att	Turner	Macken	Mower	Serella	Baines	Hart	Penn	O'Kelly	McDonough	Buckley	Caswell	Waddington S.	Freeman	Rees	Paul	Connealy	Smith	Harrison	Horne	Green	Waddington P.	Preece
Nov 22	(h)	Stafford R	1	3-0	Buckley, Penn, Waddington S.	6,898		2	3	4		6	9	8		10		7			11			5		1		
Dec 13	(a)	Carlisle U.	2	0-3		4,778		2	3	4		6	8			10	9	7		12	11*			5		1		
						Apps		2	2	2		2	2	1		2	1	2			2			2		2		
						Subs														1								
						Goals							1			1		1										

League Cup

Date	Venue	Opponent	Rd	Score	Scorers	Att	Turner	Macken	Mower	Serella	Baines	Hart	Penn	O'Kelly	McDonough	Buckley	Caswell	Waddington S.	Freeman	Rees	Paul	Connealy	Smith	Harrison	Horne	Green	Waddington P.	Preece
Aug 8	(h)	Blackpool	1/1	2-3	McDonough, Penn.	5,496	1		3	4	5	6	7	8*	9	10	11	12			2							
13	(a)	Blackpool	1/2	1-3	Buckley.	9,781	1	2	3	4	5	6	7	12	9	10	11				8*							
						Apps	2	1	2	2	2	2	2	1	2	2	2				2							
						Subs								1				1										
						Goals							1		1	1												

SEASON 1981-82

Division 3

Date	Opponents		Score	Scorers	Att	Green	Macken	Caswell	Beech	Serella	Hart	Rees	O'Kelly	Penn	Buckley	Preece	Waddington P.	Loveridge	Waddington S.	Harrison	Round	Mower	Smith	Horne	Lowery	Sinnott	Teasdale	Baines
Aug 29 (h)	Southend U.	L	0-1		3,419	1	2	3	4	5	6	7	8*	9	10	11	12											
Sept 5 (a)	Brentford	D	0-0		5,315	1	2	3	4	5	6	7		9	10	11		8*	12									
12 (h)	Chesterfield	D	1-1	Waddington S.	3,280	1	2	11	4	5	6			9	10*		12		8	3	7							
19 (a)	Oxford U.	W	1-0	Caswell	3,685	1	2	11	4	5	6	7		9*	10				8		12	3						
23 (a)	Chester	D	0-0		1,978	1	2	11	4	5	6	7		9	10				8			3						
26 (h)	Wimbledon	W	1-0	Penn.	3,027	1	2	11	4	5	6	7		9	10*				8		12	3						
29 (h)	Lincoln C.	W	2-1	Buckley, Penn.	3,653	1	2	11	4	5	6	7		9	10				8			3						
Oct 3 (a)	Bristol C.	W	1-0	Penn.	6,033	1	2	11	4	5	6*	7		9	10			12	8			3						
11 (a)	Millwall	L	0-2		6,289	1	2	11	4	5	6	7		9	10			12	8			3*						
17 (h)	Portsmouth	W	3-1	Beech, Serella, Buckley.	4,408	1	2	3	4	5	6	7	12	9	10			8*	11									
20 (h)	Swindon T.	W	5-0	Buckley (2, 1 pen), Loveridge, Rees (2).	6,010	1	2	3	4	5	6	7	12	9	10			8	11*									
24 (a)	Carlisle U.	L	1-2	Loveridge.	3,956	1	2	3	4	5	6	7*	12	9	10			8	11									
31 (h)	Plymouth A.	L	0-1		4,549	1	2	3	4	5	6		12	9	10			8	11				7*					
Nov 4 (a)	Reading	D	0-0		4,057	1	2	10	4	5	6		7	9				8	11			3						
7 (h)	Newport C.	W	3-1	O'Kelly (3, 1 pen).	4,169	1	2	10	4	5	6		7	9	12			8	11*			3						
14 (a)	Fulham	D	1-1	Penn.	6,168	1	2	10	4	5	6		7	9				8	11			3						
28 (h)	Bristol Rov.	W	2-1	Rees (2).	4,311	1	2	10	4	5	6	7	11	9				8				3						
Dec 5 (a)	Gillingham	W	4-1	O'Kelly (2), Penn, Rees.	5,845	1	2	10	4	5	6	7	11	9				8				3						
Jan 16 (a)	Exeter C.	L	0-2		3,118	1	2	10	4	5	6	7	11	9		12		8*				3						
19 (h)	Brentford	W	3-0	O'Kelly, Penn, Round.	3,853	1		10*	4	5	6	7	11	9				8			12	3		2				
23 (a)	Southend U.	L	2-3	Horne, Caswell.	4,684	1	2	10	4	5	6	7		9		11*		8				3		12				
30 (h)	Oxford U.	L	1-3	Penn.	4,573	1	2	10	4	5	6	7	11	9		12						3*		8				
Feb 6 (a)	Chesterfield	L	0-1		5,989	1	2	11	4	5	6	7		9*	10						12	3			8			
9 (h)	Chester	W	2-1	Lowery, Buckley.	3,668	1	2	11	4	5	6	7		9	10							3			8			
13 (h)	Bristol C.	L	0-1		4,020	1	2*	11	4	5	6	7		9	10						12	3			8			
16 (h)	Huddersfield T.	D	1-1	Waddington S.	3,362	1	2	11	4	5	6	7			10				12		9	3			8*			
20 (a)	Lincoln C.	D	1-1	Hart	3,243	1	2	11	4	5	6	7		9	10				8			3						
27 (h)	Millwall	D	1-1	Penn.	3,731	1	2	8*	4	5	6	7		9	10				11			3			12			
Mar 2 (h)	Burnley	D	1-1	Round.	4,196	1	2		4	5	6	7	9					8	11		10	3*			12			
6 (a)	Portsmouth	L	0-1		7,133	1	2		4	5	6	11	9	8	12			7	10*							3		
9 (a)	Swindon T.	D	2-2	Penn (pen), Caswell.	4,446	1	2	11	4	5	6	7	10*	9	12			8								3		
13 (h)	Carlisle U.	D	1-1	Beech.	3,507	1	2	11	4	5	6	7	12	9	10*			8								3		
16 (h)	Reading	L	1-2	Buckley.	2,789	1	2	3	4	5	6	7	11*	9	10			8			12							
20 (a)	Plymouth A.	L	1-4	Penn.	5,134	1		8	4*	5	6	7	10	9				12	11					2		3		
27 (a)	Newport C.	D	2-2	Penn (2).	3,484	1	2	11		5	6	7	12	9	10			4*				3					8	
Apr 3 (h)	Fulham	D	1-1	Buckley (pen).	3,120	1	4			5			9		10	11		7			12	3		2			8*	6
10 (a)	Huddersfield T.	L	1-2	Teasdale.	6,572	1	2			5	4		7	12	10	11*		8				3					9	6
13 (h)	Preston N.E.	L	0-3		3,507	1	2			5	4	12	11*	9	10			7				3					8	6
17 (h)	Gillingham	W	1-0	Serella.	2,684	1		8	4	5	2	7	11		10							3					9	6
20 (a)	Doncaster R.	L	0-1		3,903	1		8	4	5	2	7	11*	12	10							3					9	6
24 (a)	Bristol Rov.	L	1-2	Baines.	3,677	1		8	4	5	2	11	12	9				7				3					10*	6
27 (a)	Preston N.E.	L	0-1		4,930	1		8	4	5	2	7		10					11			3					9	6
May 1 (h)	Exeter C.	W	2-1	Penn (2).	2,487	1	2	8		5	6	7		9	10	11*			4		12	3						
4 (a)	Wimbledon	L	0-2		1,503	1	2	8		5	6	7	12		10				11		9*	3						4
8 (a)	Burnley	L	1-2	Rees.	8,543	1	2	8		5	6	7	9		10				11			3						4
15 (h)	Doncaster R.	D	0-0		3,799	1	2	8*	12	5	6	7	10	9					11			3						4
					Apps	46	40	41	38	46	45	38	21	38	30	6		23	24	1	4	34	1	4	4	4	8	10
					Subs				1			1	8	2	3	2	2	3	2		8			1	2			
League position: 20th					Goals			3	2	2	1	6	6	14	7			2	2		2			1	1		1	1

F.A. Cup

Date	Opponents	Rd	Score	Scorers	Att	Green	Macken	Caswell	Beech	Serella	Hart	Rees	O'Kelly	Penn	Buckley	Preece	Waddington P.	Loveridge	Waddington S.	Harrison	Round	Mower
Nov 21 (a)	Blyth Spartans	1	2-1	Macken, Caswell.	3,440	1	8	3	4	5	6	12	11*	9				2	7			10
Jan 2 (a)	Peterboro. U.	2	1-2	Butler (og).	5,421	1	2	10	4	5	6*	7	11	9	12			8				3
					Apps	2	2	2	2	2	2	1	2	2				2	1			2
					Subs							1			1							
					Goals		1	1														

Own goal: 1.

League Cup

Date	Opponents	Rd	Score	Scorers	Att	Green	Macken	Caswell	Beech	Serella	Hart	Rees	O'Kelly	Penn	Buckley	Preece	Waddington P.	Loveridge	Waddington S.	Harrison	Round	Mower
Sept 1 (a)	Bristol C.	1/1	0-2		3,906	1	2	8	4	5	6			9	10	11			7			3
14 (h)	Bristol C.	1/2	1-0	Penn	2,830	1	2	11	4	5	6	7		9	10				8		12	3*
					Apps	2	2	2	2	2	2	1		2	2	1			2			2
					Subs																1	
					Goals									1								

SEASON 1982-83

Division 3

Date	Venue	Opponent	Res	Score	Scorers	Att	Green	Arthur	Mower	Beech	Marshall	Hart	Rees	O'Kelly	Kearns O.	Buckley	Preece	Round	Teasdale	Sinnott	Caswell	Shakespeare	Pendrey	Bates	Kearns M.	Penn	Hawker P.	Summerfield	Jones
Aug 28	(a)	Bournemouth	L	0-3		5,330	1	2	3	4	5	6	7	8*	9	10	11	12											
Sept 4	(h)	Portsmouth	L	0-3		2,922	1	2	3	4	5	6			9*	10	11	12	7	8									
7	(h)	Preston N.E.	W	2-1	Teasdale (2).	2,060	1	2	3	4		6			9	10	11*	12	7	5	8								
11	(a)	Huddersfield T.	D	2-2	Preece, Pendrey.	4,282	1		3	4		6			9	10	11		7*	5	2	12	8						
18	(h)	Cardiff C.	L	1-2	Buckley (pen).	3,161	1		3*	4		6	12		9	10	11		7	5	2	8							
25	(a)	Gillingham	L	0-3		3,501	1		3	4		6			9	10	11		7	5	2	12	8*						
29	(a)	Bradford C.	D	1-1	Kearns O.	4,642	1		3	4	5	6			9	10	11				2	7	8						
Oct 2	(h)	Brentford	W	2-1	Kearns O., Shakespeare.	2,723	1		3	4	5	6			9	10	11	12			2	7	8*						
9	(h)	Sheffield U.	D	0-0		5,369	1	8	3	4	5	6			9	10	11				2	7							
16	(a)	Oxford U.	L	2-4	Beech, Buckley.	4,732	1	8	3	4	5	6			9	10	11	12			2	7*							
19	(h)	Chesterfield	L	0-1		2,462	1	12	3	4	5	6		7		10	11	9			2*		8						
23	(a)	Millwall	D	2-2	Kearns O, (2).	3,294	1		3	4	5	6		7	9*	10	11	12			2		8						
30	(h)	Wrexham	D	1-1	Kearns O.	2,473	1		3	4	5	6		7	9	10	11	12			2*		8						
Nov 2	(a)	Orient	L	1-2	O'Kelly.	1,935	1		3	4	5	6		7	8	10	11	12					8*	2					
6	(a)	Exeter City	L	3-4	Buckley (2), Round.	2,614	1		3	4*		6		7	9	10	11	12		5	8			2					
13	(h)	Reading	W	2-1	Kearns O., Beech.	2,343	1		3	4		6		7*	9	10	8	12		5	11			2					
27	(h)	Southend U.	L	1-3	Buckley.	2,453			3	2		6	12	4*	9	10	8			5	11				1	7			
Dec 4	(a)	Bristol Rov.	L	0-2		4,822			3	2		6	7	4	9	10	8			5	11				1				
18	(a)	Newport C.	D	1-1	Penn	3,572	1		3	4		6	12			10*	8				2	11				7	5	9	
27	(h)	Lincoln C.	D	1-1	Summerfield.	5,284	1		3	4		6		8	12	10					2	11*				7	5	9	
29	(a)	Wigan Ath.	W	3-1	Buckley, Summerfield, Preece.	4,564	1		3	4		6	7	11		10	8				2						5	9	
Jan 1	(h)	Doncaster R.	W	1-0	Buckley.	3,859	1		3	4		6	7	11		10	8			5	2							9	
15	(h)	Bournemouth	W	3-1	Kearns 0, (2, 1 pen), Buckley.	2,735	1		3	4		6	7		9	10	8			5	2	11							
22	(a)	Cardiff C.	L	1-3	Beech.	6,237	1		3	4		6	7*	11	9	10	8			5	2	12							
29	(h)	Huddersfield T.	W	2-0	Kearns O., O'Kelly.	3,922	1		3	4		6		11	9	10	8			5	2	7							
Feb 5	(h)	Gillingham	D	0-0		2,608	1	2	3	4		6		11	9	10	8			5		7*							12
8	(a)	Plymouth A.	D	0-0		3,148	1		3	4		6		11	9	10*	8	12		5	2	7							
15	(h)	Orient	W	2-0	Buckley, O'Kelly.	2,328	1		3	4		6	7	11	12	10	8			5	2*							9	
19	(a)	Sheffield U.	L	1-3	Shakespeare.	11,070	1	2*	3	4		6	7	11	12	10				5		8						9	
26	(h)	Oxford Utd.	W	1-0	Summerfield.	3,104	1		3	4		6	7	11	12	10*				5	2	8						9	
Mar 1	(a)	Chesterfield	D	0-0		2,216	1		3	4		6		11	7	10				5	2	8						9	
5	(h)	Millwall	W	4-0	Kearns O., Summerfield, Lovell (og), O'Kelly.	2,779	1		3	4		6		11	7	10	8			5	2*	12						9	
12	(a)	Wrexham	L	0-4		2,748	1		3	4		6		11	9	10*	8			5	2	12							7
19	(h)	Exeter City	W	3-2	Kearns O., Summerfield (2).	2,669	1	2	3	4		6		11	7	10	8*			5		12						9	
25	(a)	Reading	D	1-1	Summerfield.	3,107	1		3	4		6		11	7	10*	8			5	2	12						9	
29	(a)	Preston N.E.	L	0-1		4,013	1		3	4		6		11	7	10	8			5	2							9	
Apr 2	(h)	Wigan Ath.	W	2-0	O'Kelly, Summerfield.	2,829	1*		3	4		6		11	7	12	8			5	2	10						9	
4	(a)	Lincoln C.	L	1-2	Buckley.	4,671			3	4		6		11	7	12	8			5	2	10*			1			9	
9	(h)	Bristol Rov.	W	5-0	Sinnott, Mower, Summerfield, Buckley, Shakespeare.	4,559			3			6	7	11	12	10*	8			5	2	4			1			9	
16	(a)	Brentford	W	3-2	Rees (2), Sinnott.	4,868			3	6			7	11	12	10*	8			5	2	4			1			9	
23	(h)	Newport C.	W	2-1	O'Kelly, Shakespeare.	5,141			3			6	7	11	9	10	8			5	2	4			1				
29	(a)	Southend U.	D	1-1	O'Kelly.	1,904			3			6	7	11		10	8			5	2	4			1			9	
May 2	(h)	Plymouth A.	W	2-0	Buckley, Penn.	3,473			3			6		11		10	8			5	2	4			1	7		9	
7	(h)	Bradford C.	D	1-1	Penn.	3,322			3	2		6		11*	12	10	8			5		4			1	7		9	
10	(a)	Portsmouth	L	0-1		22,244			3			6	7	11		10	8				2	4			1		5	9	
14	(a)	Doncaster R.	W	3-1	Rees, Buckley, O'Kelly.	1,507						6	7	11		10	8				3	4		2	1		5	9	
						Apps	35	8	45	40	10	45	15	35	31	44	42	1	5	32	39	24	8	4	11	5	5	21	1
						Subs		1					3		7	2		11				7							1
League position: 10th						Goals			1	3			3	8	11	13	2	1	2	2		4	1			3		9	

Own Goal: 1.

F.A. Cup

Date	Venue	Opponent	Rd	Score	Scorers	Att	Green	Arthur	Mower	Beech	Marshall	Hart	Rees	O'Kelly	Kearns O.	Buckley	Preece	Round	Teasdale	Sinnott	Caswell	Shakespeare	Pendrey	Bates	Kearns M.	Penn	Hawker P.	Summerfield	Jones
Nov 20	(h)	Kettering	1	3-0	Kearns, Preece, Buckley.	3,471	1		3	4		6		7	9	10	8			5	11			2*		12			
Dec 11	(a)	North Shields	2	3-0	Round, Buckley, Caswell.	3,200			3	4		6				10	8	9		5	2	11			1	7			
Jan 8	(h)	Birmingham C.	3	0-0		12,967	1		3	4		6	7	11		10	8			5	2					9			
11	(a)	Birmingham C.	3R	0-1	(a.e.t.)	14,774	1		3	4		6	7	11	9*	10	8	12		5	2								
						Apps	3		4	4		4	2	3	2	4	4	1		4	4	1		1	1	2			
						Subs												1								1			
						Goals									1	2	1	1			1								

Milk Cup

Date	Venue	Opponent	Rd	Score	Scorers	Att	Green	Arthur	Mower	Beech	Marshall	Hart	Rees	O'Kelly	Kearns O.	Buckley	Preece	Round	Teasdale	Sinnott	Caswell	Shakespeare	Pendrey	Bates	Kearns M.	Penn	Hawker P.	Summerfield	Jones
Aug 30	(h)	Preston N.E.	1/1	0-1		2,490	1	2	3*	4	5	6	7		9	10	11	12		8									
Sept 14	(a)	Preston N.E.	1/2	1-1	Preece.	3,137	1		3	4		6			9	10	11	12	7	5	2	8*							
						Apps	2	1	2	2	1	2	1		2	2	2		1	2	1	1							
						Subs												2											
						Goals											1												

SEASON 1983-84

Division 3

Date		Opponents	Res	Score	Scorers	Att	Kearns	Hawker	Mower	Shakespeare	Sinnott	Hart	Rees	Brown	Summerfield	Preece	Brazier	Buckley	Green	Bates	Jones	O'Kelly	Caswell	Godden	Childs	Handysides	Bamber	Kelly
Aug 27	(a)	Exeter C.	W	1-0	Hart.	4,742	1	2	3	4	5	6	7	8	9	10*	11	12										
Sept 3	(h)	Orient	L	0-1		3,003		2	3	4	5	6	7		9	8	11	10	1									
6	(h)	Sheffield U.	L	1-2	Summerfield.	4,711		6	3	4*	5	2	7	8	9	10	11	12	1									
10	(a)	Bolton W.	L	1-8	Brown.	4,375			3	4	5	6		8	9	10	11	7*	1	2	12							
17	(h)	Newport C.	W	3-2	Summerfield (2), O'Kelly.	2,818		5	3	4		2	12	8	9	7	6	10*	1			11						
24	(a)	Southend U.	D	0-0		3,061			3	4		6	7	8*	9	10	5	12	1			11	2					
28	(a)	Oxford Utd	L	3-6	Brown (2), Shakespeare.	5,720			3	4		6	7	8	9	10	5	12	1			11*	2					
Oct 1	(h)	Port Vale	W	2-0	Summerfield, Shakespeare.	3,757			3	4		6	7	8	9	11	5	10	1				2					
8	(a)	Rotherham	W	1-0	Brown (pen).	3,540			3	4		6	7	8		10	5					9	2	1	11			
15	(h)	Wimbledon	W	4-0	Rees (2), Brown, O'Kelly.	2,546			3	4		6	7	8		10	5					9	2	1	11			
18	(h)	Bournemouth	W	3-1	Brown (pen), O'Kelly (2).	3,782			3	4		6	7	8		10	5					9	2	1	11			
22	(a)	Bradford C.	D	0-0		2,474			3	4		6	7	8*	12	10	5					9	2	1	11			
29	(h)	Bristol Rov.	W	2-1	O'Kelly (pen), Rees.	4,964			3	4		6	7		9	10	5					8	2	1	11			
Nov 1	(a)	Hull City	D	2-2	O'Kelly, Brown.	8,375			3	4		6*	7	8	12	10	5					9	2	1	11			
5	(a)	Scunthorpe U.	D	0-0		2,932			3	4		6		8	9	10	5					7	2	1	11			
12	(h)	Gillingham	W	3-1	Brown (2), Preece.	4,639	1		3	4		6	7	8	12	10	5					9	2*		11			
26	(a)	Wigan Ath.	W	1-0	Rees	3,485	1		3	4		6	7	8	12	10*	5					9	2		11			
Dec 3	(h)	Millwall	D	1-1	O'Kelly.	5,329	1	5	3	4		6	7	8	12	10						9	2		11*			
17	(h)	Brentford	W	1-0	Brown (pen).	3,965	1		3	4		6	7*	8	11	10	5			2	12	9						
26	(a)	Lincoln C.	L	1-2	O'Kelly.	4,886	1		3	4		6	7	8	12	10	5					9	2		11*			
27	(h)	Burnley	D	1-1	Rees.	8,131		2	3	4		6	7	8*	12	10	5		1			9			11			
31	(a)	Preston N.E.	W	1-0	Childs.	6,226		3*		4		6	7	8	10		5	12	1			9	2		11			
Jan 2	(h)	Plymouth A.	W	3-2	Hart, Summerfield, O'Kelly.	4,856			3	4		6	7*	8	10		5	12	1			9	2		11			
7	(a)	Orient	W	1-0	Summerfield.	3,106			3	4		6	12	8	10		5		1			9*	2		11	7		
14	(h)	Exeter City	W	4-1	Brown, Brazier, O'Kelly, Shakespeare.	5,028			3	4		6	12	8	10	11	5		1			9*	2			7		
22	(a)	Newport C.	L	1-3	Rees.	4,374			3	4		6	7	8		10*	5		1			9	2		11	12		
28	(h)	Bolton W.	W	1-0	Shakespeare.	7,812	1		3	4		6	7	8	11	10*	5						2		12	9		
Feb 4	(a)	Port Vale	W	2-0	Handysides, Preece.	6,966			3	4		6		8	12	10	5		1			9	2		11*	7		
11	(h)	Southend U.	W	4-0	Hart, Handysides, Preece, Brown (pen).	8,156			3	4		6	7*	8	11	10	5		1			9			12	2		
18	(a)	Bristol Rov.	L	2-4	Childs, Buckley.	5,643			3	4		6	7*	8			5	12	1			9	2		11	10		
25	(h)	Bradford C.	L	1-2	Handysides.	6,013			3	4		6	12	8		10	5		1			9	2*		11	7		
Mar 3	(a)	Bournemouth	L	0-3		3,913	1		3	4		6	7	8	12	10	5					9*			11	2		
6	(h)	Scunthorpe U.	D	1-1	Handysides.	4,735	1		3	4*		6		8	9	10	5					12	2		11	7		
10	(a)	Gillingham	W	3-1	Summerfield (2), Shakespeare.	4,544	1		3	4		6			9	10	5					8	2		11	7		
17	(h)	Rotherham U.	D	2-2	Shakespeare, Buckley.	4,915			3	4		6	7		8		5	12				9	2*	1	11	10		
24	(a)	Wimbledon	L	0-2		4,057			3	4		6			8	10	5	12				2		1	11*	7	9	
27	(h)	Hull City	W	2-1	Bamber (2).	6,851			3	4		6		8		10	5					2		1	11	7	9	
31	(a)	Sheffield U.	L	0-2		13,227			3	4		6		8*	12	10	5					11	2	1		7	9	
Apr 7	(h)	Oxford U.	L	0-1		10,163			3	4		6		8	12	10	5					11	2*	1		7	9	
14	(a)	Millwall	L	0-2		3,458				4		6		8		10	5					11	2	1	3	7	9*	12
21	(h)	Lincoln C.	L	0-1		3,660			3	4		6*		12		10	5					8	2	1	11	7	9	
23	(a)	Burnley	W	2-0	Brown, Kelly.	3,953		6	3	4				8		10	5				7	11	2	1				9
28	(h)	Wigan Ath.	W	3-0	Mower, Kelly, O'Kelly.	3,286		6	3	4		2		8		10	5				7*	11		1			12	9
May 5	(a)	Plymouth A.	L	1-3	Kelly.	5,144		6	3	4		2	7		12	10	5					11		1			8*	9
7	(h)	Preston N.E.	W	2-1	Brazier, O'Kelly.	3,273		6	3	4		2	7			10	5					11		1			8	9
12	(a)	Brentford	D	1-1	Bamber.	5,281			3	4*		6	7			10	5					11	2	1	12		8	9
						Apps	10	11	44	46	4	45	29	37	21	41	45	4	17	2	2	39	32	19	27	17	9	5
						Subs							4	1	12			9			2	1			3	1	1	1
League position: 6th						Goals			1	6		3	6	13	8	3	2	2				12			2	4	3	3

F.A. Cup

Date		Opponents	Rd	Score	Scorers	Att	Kearns	Hawker	Mower	Shakespeare	Sinnott	Hart	Rees	Brown	Summerfield	Preece	Brazier	Buckley	Green	Bates	Jones	O'Kelly	Caswell	Godden	Childs	Handysides	Bamber	Kelly
Nov 19	(a)	Bournemouth	1	0-4		4,298	1		3	4*		6	7	8	9	10	5					12	2		11			
						Apps	1		1	1		1	1	1	1	1	1						1		1			
						Subs																1						

Milk Cup

Date		Opponents	Rd	Score	Scorers	Att	Kearns	Hawker	Mower	Shakespeare	Sinnott	Hart	Rees	Brown	Summerfield	Preece	Brazier	Buckley	Green	Bates	Jones	O'Kelly	Caswell	Godden	Childs	Handysides	Bamber	Kelly
Aug 30	(a)	Blackpool	1/1	1-2	Buckley.	3,353	1	2	3	4*	4	5	6	7	8	10	11	12										
Sept 13	(h)	Blackpool	1/2	3-1	Summerfield, Preece, O'Kelly.	2,879		5	3	4		2	12	8	9	7	6	10	1			11*						
Oct 4	(h)	Barnsley	2/1	1-0	Rees.	3,681	1		3	4		6	7	8	9		5	11				10	2					
25	(a)	Barnsley	2/2	2-0	Preece, Rees.	7,844	1		3	4		6	7		9	10	5				8		2		11			
Nov 8	(h)	Shrewsbury T.	3	2-1	Preece, Childs.	7,952	1		3	4*		6	7	8	12	10	5					9	2		11			
30	(a)	Arsenal	4	2-1	Rees, Brown.	22,406	1		3	4		6	7	8		10	5					9	2		11			
Jan 18	(a)	Rotherham U.	5	4-2	Rees 2, O'Kelly, Brown.	14,487			3	4		6	7	8		11	5		1			9	2		10			
Feb 7	(a)	Liverpool	SF1	2-2	Neal (og), Summerfield.	31,073			3	4		6	7	8	12	10	5		1			9	2		11*			
14	(h)	Liverpool	SF2	0-2		19,591			3	4		6	7	8	11	10	5		1			9	2					
						Apps	5	2	9	9	1	9	8	8	5	8	9	2	4		1	7	7		5			
						Subs							1		2			1										
						Goals							5	2	2	3		1				2			1			

Own Goal: 1.

Associate Members Cup

Date		Opponents	Rd	Score	Scorers	Att	Kearns	Hawker	Mower	Shakespeare	Sinnott	Hart	Rees	Brown	Summerfield	Preece	Brazier	Buckley	Green	Bates	Jones	O'Kelly	Caswell	Godden	Childs	Handysides	Bamber	Kelly
Feb 21	(h)	Northampton T.	1	3-1	Childs, Handysides, O'Kelly.	3,190			3	4		6					5	10*	1		8	9	2		11	7		12
Mar 13	(a)	Swindon T.	2	0-3		2,705			3	4*		6				10	5	12	1	2	9	8			11	7		
						Apps			2	2		2				1	2	1	2	1	2	2	1		2	2		
						Subs												1										1
						Goals																1			1	1		

SEASON 1984-85

Division 3

Date	Opponents	Res	Score	Scorers	Att	Cherry	Caswell	Mower	Shakespeare	Hawker	Hart	Handysides	Eastoe	O'Kelly	Preece	Childs	Brazier	Rees	Kelly	Bamber	Jones	Buckley	Elliott, S.	Obi	Taylor	Palgrave	Naughton	Kearns
Aug 25	(a) York City	D	1-1	O'Kelly.	4,364	1	2	3*	4	5	6	7	8	9	10	11	12											
Sept 1	(h) Brentford	L	0-1		4,747	1	2	3	4	5	6	7	8	9	10*	11		12										
8	(a) Bradford C.	D	1-1	O'Kelly (pen).	3,945	1	12	3	4	6*	2	10	8	9		11	5	7										
15	(h) Millwall	D	3-3	O'Kelly (2), Shakespeare.	4,382	1	2	3	4		6	10	8	9		11*	5	7	12									
18	(h) Reading	W	3-1	Eastoe, Handysides, O'Kelly (pen).	4,467	1	2	3	4		6	7	8	9	10	11	5											
22	(a) Gillingham	L	0-3		4,102	1	2	3	4*		6	7	8	9	10	11	5			12								
29	(h) Bristol C.	W	4-1	Bamber, Kelly (2), O'Kelly (pen).	4,754	1		3	4	6*	2	7		8		11	5		10	9	12							
Oct 2	(a) Bolton W.	L	1-3	Bamber.	4,445	1	2	3	4		6	7		8		11	5		10*	9	12							
6	(a) Cambridge U.	W	1-0	Shakespeare.	1,907	1		3	2		6	7		8		11	5		10	9	4							
13	(h) Wigan Ath.	D	0-0		5,361	1		3	4		6	7		9*	10	11	5		8	12	2							
20	(a) Swansea C.	W	2-1	Rees (2).	4,124	1		3	4		6	11			10		5	7	8	9	2							
23	(h) Derby County	D	0-0		9,733	1		3	2		6	11			10		5	7	8	9	4							
27	(h) Newport C.	D	1-1	Kelly.	4,694	1	2	3	4		6	12			10	11	5	7*	8	9								
Nov 3	(a) Orient	W	3-0	Bamber (2), Rees.	2,182	1	2	3	4		6	12			10	11	5	7	8*	9								
10	(h) Bournemouth	D	0-0		4,519	1	2	3	4		6	12			10	11*	5	7	8	9								
24	(a) Plymouth A.	W	3-1	Childs, Handysides, Shakespeare.	4,907	1	2	3	4		6	7			9	12	5		8		11	10*						
Dec 1	(h) Rotherham U.	L	0-2		4,538	1	2*	3	4		6	7			10	11	5	12	8		9							
15	(a) Hull City	L	0-1		6,075	1	2	3	4	5	6	7*		10		11			8				9		12			
22	(a) Burnley	W	2-1	Kelly, Mower.	3,264	1	2	3	4	10	6					11	5	7	8				9					
26	(h) Preston N.E.	W	2-1	Kelly, Shakespeare.	5,856	1	2	3	4	5	6			10*		11		7	8			12	9					
29	(h) Lincoln C.	D	0-0		4,613	1	2	3	4	5	6	11*				10			8				9	7	12			
Jan 1	(a) Doncaster R.	L	1-4	Handysides.	3,485	1	2	3	4*	5	6	7		10		11			8				9	12				
26	(a) Millwall	D	0-0		4,745	1	2		4	3	6	7		10		11	5		8				9					
Feb 2	(a) Bristol C.	W	2-1	Kelly, Shakespeare.	7,240	1	2		4	3	6	7		10		11	5		8				9					
23	(h) Orient	W	4-2	Elliott, S, O'Kelly (2 pens) , Shakespeare.	4,490	1	2	3	4		6	11		8			5	7			10*		9		12			
26	(h) York City	W	3-0	O'Kelly, Rees (2).	5,031	1	2	3	4		6	11*		8			5	7	12		10		9					
Mar 2	(a) Newport C.	W	2-1	Rees, Shakespeare.	2,698	1	2	3	4		6	11		8			5	7	12		10*		9					
6	(a) Derby County	L	0-2		9,157	1	2	3			6	11		8		4*	5	7	10				9		12			
9	(h) Swansea C.	W	3-0	Elliott, S (2), O'Kelly.	4,756	1	2	3*			6	10		8		11	5	7	12		4		9					
17	(a) Wigan Ath.	W	2-1	O'Kelly (pen), Rees.	2,221	1	2	3*			6	11		8		10	5	7	12		4		9					
19	(h) Bolton W.	W	1-0	O'Kelly.	4,941	1	2*	3			6	11		8		10	5	7	12		4		9					
23	(h) Cambridge U.	W	5-0	Kelly, O'Kelly (2, 1 pen), Rees, Shakespeare.	4,425	1		3	4		6	10		8		9	5	7	11*		2					12		
27	(a) Brentford	L	1-3	Rees (pen).	3,021	1	2	3	4		6	12				10*	5	7	8				9				11	
30	(h) Bristol Rov.	L	1-2	Elliott, S.	4,829	1	2	3	4		6			8		10	5	7	12				9				11*	
Apr 2	(h) Bradford C.	D	0-0		6,160	1	2	3	4		6					10	5	7	12		8*		9				11	
6	(a) Preston N.E.	L	0-1		3,776	1	2	3	4		6	7		8		10	5				12		9				11*	
8	(h) Doncaster R.	W	1-0	Childs.	3,706	1	2	3		4	6	11		8		10	5				7*		9				12	
13	(a) Bournemouth	L	1-4	Handysides.	2,954	1	2	3	4	11	6	7		8		10*	5	12					9					
16	(h) Gillingham	L	0-1		3,585	1			4	3	6	7*		8		11	5	12			2		9				10	
20	(h) Plymouth A.	L	0-3		2,775	1		3	4		6	7		8		11*	5		2		12		9				10	
23	(a) Bristol Rov.	D	0-0		4,040	1		3	4	6	2			8			5	7			12		9			11	10*	
27	(h) Rotherham U.	W	1-0	Elliott, S.	2,293			3	4	6	2			8		12	5	7					9			11	10*	1
May 1	(a) Reading	D	1-1	O'Kelly.	1,739			3	4	6	2			8		7	5		12				9			11*	10	1
4	(h) Hull City	L	0-1		4,809		3		4	6	2			8		11	5		12		7*		9				10	1
6	(a) Lincoln C.	D	0-0		1,473		3		4	6	2	12		8		11	5	7					9				10*	1
11	(h) Burnley	L	2-3	O'Kelly (pen), Shakespeare.	3,396		2	3	4	10	6	7		8		11*	5						9				12	1
					Apps	41	34	41	41	20	46	33	6	35	12	38	40	23	22	8	17	1	28	1		3	11	5
					Subs		1					5				2	1	4	10	2	5	1		1	4	1	2	
League position: 11th					Goals			1	9			4	1	16		2		9	7	4			5					

F.A. Cup

Date	Opponents	Rd	Score	Scorers	Att	Cherry	Caswell	Mower	Shakespeare	Hawker	Hart	Handysides	Eastoe	O'Kelly	Preece	Childs	Brazier	Rees	Kelly	Bamber	Jones	Buckley	Elliott, S.	Obi	Taylor	Palgrave	Naughton	Kearns
Nov 17	(a) Stockport C.	1	2-1	Shakespeare, Kelly.	2,781	1	2	3	4		6	7			9		5		8		11	10						
Dec 8	(h) Chesterfield	2	1-0	Mower.	5,519	1	2	3	4	5	6	7		10		9		11	8									
Jan 5	(a) York City	3	0-3		5,493	1	2	3	4	5	6	7				11			8		10*		9		12			
					Apps	3	3	3	3	2	3	3		1	1	2	1	1	3		2	1	1					
					Subs																				1			
					Goals			1	1										1									

Milk Cup

Date	Opponents	Rd	Score	Scorers	Att	Cherry	Caswell	Mower	Shakespeare	Hawker	Hart	Handysides	Eastoe	O'Kelly	Preece	Childs	Brazier	Rees	Kelly	Bamber	Jones	Buckley	Elliott, S.	Obi	Taylor	Palgrave	Naughton	Kearns
Aug 28	(a) Swansea C.	1/1	2-0	Childs, O'Kelly.	3,633	1	2	3	4	5	6	7	8	9	10	11												
Sept 4	(h) Swansea C.	1/2	3-1	Shakespeare, Eastoe, Hawker.	4,305	1		3	4	6	2	7	8	9	10*	11	5	12										
25	(h) Coventry C.	2/1	1-2	Shakespeare.	8,399	1	2	3	4		6	7		9	10*	11	5			8		12						
Oct 9	(a) Coventry C.	2/2	3-0	Kelly (2), O'Kelly.	9,214	1		3	4		6	7		9	10	11	5		8		2							
30	(h) Chelsea	3	2-2	Preece, Shakespeare.	11,102	1	2*	3	4		6	12			10	11	5	7	8	9								
Nov 6	(a) Chelsea	3R	0-3		19,502	1	2	3	4		6	12			10	11	5	7	8	9*								
					Apps	6	4	6	6	2	6	4	2	4	6	6	5	2	3	3	1							
					Subs							2						1				1						
					Goals				3	1			1	2	1	1			2									

Freight Rover Trophy

Date	Opponents	Rd	Score	Scorers	Att	Cherry	Caswell	Mower	Shakespeare	Hawker	Hart	Handysides	Eastoe	O'Kelly	Preece	Childs	Brazier	Rees	Kelly	Bamber	Jones	Buckley	Elliott, S.	Obi	Taylor	Palgrave	Naughton	Kearns
Feb 6	(a) Derby County	1/1	0-1		3,950	1	2	12	4	3	6	7		10		11*	5		8				9					
19	(h) Derby County	1/2	5-3	Rees (3), Elliott (2).	3,663	1		3	4	2	6	11		8			5	7			10		9					
Mar 12	(h) Colchester U.	2	1-0	Childs	4,106	1	2	3			6	11		8		10	5	7*	12		4		9					
Apr 18	(a) Bournemouth	3	1-2	Kelly	2,567	1	2*		4		6	11†		8		10	5	7	3		12	14	9					
					Apps	4	3	2	3	2	4	4		4		3	4	3	2		2		4					
					Subs			1											1		1	1						
					Goals											1		3	1				2					

SEASON 1985-86

Division 3

Date	Opponent	Res	Score	Scorers	Att	Cherry	Hart	Mower	Shakespeare	Brazier	Hawker	Handysides	Cross	O'Kelly	Elliott	Daley	Childs	Jones	Kelly	Naughton	Taylor	Rees	Gunn	Prudhoe	Palgrave
Aug 17	(a) Bristol C	W	3-2	Cross, Daley, O'Kelly (pen).	7,196	1	2	3	4	5	6	7	8	9	10	11*	12								
24	(h) Swansea C.	W	3-1	Elliott (2), Handysides.	3,772	1	2	3		5	6	7	8		10	11	9	4							
26	(a) Lincoln C.	L	2-3	Elliott, Kelly.	2,282	1	2	3		5	6	7	8		10	11*	9	4	12						
31	(h) Chesterfield	W	3-0	Kelly, Cross, Handysides.	4,528	1	2	3		5	6	7	8	9	10	11			12	4*					
Sept 7	(a) Reading	L	1-2	Hawker.	3,573	1	2	3	4*	5	6	7	8		10	11			12		9				
14	(h) Bolton W.	W	2-0	O'Kelly (pen), Cross.	4,532	1	2	3	4	5	6*		8	9	10	11	7		12						
17	(h) Rotherham U.	W	3-1	Elliott (2), O'Kelly (pen).	4,861	1	2	3	4	5	6		8	9	10	11*	7		12						
21	(a) Bristol Rov.	W	1-0	Brazier.	3,787	1	2	3	4	5	6		8		10	11	7			9					
28	(h) Newport C.	W	2-0	Mower, Kelly.	4,586	1	5	3	4		6		8		10	11	7*	2	12	9					
Oct 1	(a) Wigan A.	L	0-2		4,818	1	5	3	4		6	12			10	11*	7	2	8	9					
5	(a) Doncaster R.	L	0-1		2,901	1	5	3	4		6			9	10	11	7*	12	8	2					
12	(h) Plymouth A.	D	2-2	Rees (2).	4,253	1	5	3*	4		6		8	9	10			2	12	11		7			
19	(a) Wolves	D	0-0		7,522	1		3	4	5			8*	12	10	9	6	2		11		7			
22	(h) Brentford	L	1-2	Elliott.	4,318	1		3	4	5			8	12	10	9	6	2		11		7*			
27	(a) Darlington	W	3-0	Cross, Evans (og), Naughton.	3,879	1	5	3	4				8	12	10	9	6	2		11		7*			
Nov 2	(h) Notts County	D	0-0		4,967	1	6	3	12		5		8	9	10		4	2		11		7*			
5	(h) Cardiff City	W	6-3	Shakespeare (2), Elliott (3), Cross.	3,282	1	6	3	4		5		8	9*	10		7	2		11		12			
9	(a) Gillingham	L	2-5	Shakespeare, O'Kelly (pen).	3,339	1	6	3	4				8	9	10		5	2*		11	12	7			
23	(h) Blackpool	D	1-1	O'Kelly.	5,161	1	6	3	4		5	12	8	9	10*		7	2		11					
30	(a) Bury	L	1-2	Cross.	2,559	1	6	3	4		5		8	9	10		7	2*		11		12			
Dec 14	(h) Bournemouth	W	4-2	Childs, Cross (2), Brazier.	4,460	1	2	3	4	5	6		8		10	9*	7		12	11					
28	(h) Lincoln C.	W	2-1	Childs, Kelly.	4,493	1	2	3	4*	5	6		8		10	9	7		12	11					
Jan 1	(h) York City	W	3-1	Cross (2, 1 pen), Elliott.	5,643	1	2	3	4	5	6		8		10	9	7		12	11*					
7	(a) Swansea C.	L	1-2	Kelly.	4,250	1	2	3	4	5	6		8	10		9*	7		12	11					
18	(h) Bristol C.	W	2-1	Cross (pen), Elliott.	4,952	1	6		4	5	3		8		10	9*	7		12	11			2		
25	(a) Bolton W.	L	1-3	Hart.	4,088	1	6		4	5	3		8		10		7*	9		11		12	2		
Feb 1	(h) Reading	W	6-0	Naughton, Taylor, O'Kelly, Cross (2), Elliott.	5,113	1	6	3	4	5			8	9	10					11	7		2		
4	(a) Brentford	W	3-1	Cross, Hart, Shakespeare.	3,015	1	6	3	4	5			8	9	10*					11	7	12	2		
9	(h) Wolves	D	1-1	Naughton.	10,480	1	6	3	4	5			8	9	10*					11	7	12	2		
15	(a) Rotherham u.	L	0-3		3,516	1	6	3	4	5			8		10		12		9	11	7*		2		
28	(a) Newport C.	W	5-1	Kelly, Jones, Cross (pen), Childs (2).	1,530		6	3			5		8			9	7	4	10	11	2			1	
Mar 8	(h) Doncaster R.	W	1-0	Stead (og).	4,810		6	3			5		8		12	9	7	4	10	11*	2			1	
12	(a) Derby County	L	1-3	Naughton.	13,434		6	3			5		8		10	9*	7	4	12	11	2			1	
15	(a) Plymouth A.	L	0-2		6,079		6	3			5		8		10	9	7	4		11*	2	12		1	
18	(h) Bristol Rov.	W	6-0	Elliott (2), Cross, Hawker (2), Kelly.	3,734		6	3			5	7	8		10	9	4*		12	11	2			1	
22	(h) Darlington	D	0-0		4,618		6	3			5	7	8		10*	9	4		12	11	2			1	
25	(a) Chesterfield	W	3-2	Handysides, Cross (2).	2,177		6	3	4	5		11	8	9			12		10		2	7*		1	
29	(a) York City	L	0-1		3,695		6	3	4	5			8	9		10		12		11	2*	7		1	
31	(h) Derby County	D	1-1	Cross (pen).	8,294		6	3		5			8	10		9	7	4		11	2			1	
Apr 5	(a) Cardiff City	D	1-1	Brignull (og).	1,777		6	3		5			8	9	10	4*		2	12	11		7		1	
8	(a) Notts County	L	1-3	Cross.	2,490		6	3		5			8	9	10			2	4	11*		7		1	12
12	(h) Gillingham	W	4-1	O'Kelly, Hawker, Cross, Elliott.	3,889		2	3		5	6		8	9	10			4	12	11		7*		1	
15	(h) Wigan A.	D	3-3	Elliott, Palgrave, Kelly.	4,293		2	3		5	6		8	9	10			4	12	11				1	7*
19	(a) Blackpool	L	1-2	Kelly.	2,964		5		3		6		8	9	10			4*	12	11	2	7		1	
26	(h) Bury	W	3-2	Naughton, Childs, Kelly.	3,454		5	3	4		6		8*	9	10		7		12	11	2			1	
May 3	(a) Bournemouth	W	1-0	Taylor.	3,047		5	3	4		6		8*	9	10				12	11	2	7		1	
					Apps	30	44	43	31	27	33	8	44	25	40	28	30	24	7	39	17	13	6	16	1
					Subs				1			2		3	1		3	2	21		1	6			1
League position: 6th					Goals		2	1	4	2	4	3	21	7	16	1	5	1	10	5	2	2			1

Own Goals : 3.

F.A. Cup

Date	Opponent	Rd	Score	Scorers	Att	Cherry	Hart	Mower	Shakespeare	Brazier	Hawker	Handysides	Cross	O'Kelly	Elliott	Daley	Childs	Jones	Kelly	Naughton
Nov 16	(h) Preston N.E.	1	7-1	Naughton (3), Elliott, Childs (2), O'Kelly.	4,035	1	6	3	4		5		8	9	10		7	2		11
Dec 8	(a) Port Vale	2	0-0		11,736	1	2	3	4	5	6		8	12	10	9	7			11*
10	(h) Port Vale	2R	2-1	Cross, Hawker.	5,671	1	2	3	4	5	6		8		10	9	7		12	11*
Jan 4	(h) Manchester C.	3	1-3	O'Kelly (pen).	10,836	1	2	3	4	5	6		8	10		9*	7		12	11
					Apps	4	4	4	4	3	4		4	2	3	3	4	1		4
					Subs									1					2	
					Goals						1		1	2	1		2			3

Milk Cup

Date	Opponent	Rd	Score	Scorers	Att	Cherry	Hart	Mower	Shakespeare	Brazier	Hawker	Handysides	Cross	O'Kelly	Elliott	Daley	Childs	Jones	Kelly	Naughton
Aug 20	(h) Wolves	1/1	1-1	Cross.	11,330	1	2		4	5	6	7	8	9*	10	11	3			12
Sept 3	(a) Wolves	1/2	1-0	Cross.	11,310	1	2	3	4	5	6	7	8	9	10	11				
25	(a) Leeds Utd	2/1	0-0		8,869	1		3	4	5	6		8		10	11	7	2		9
Oct 8	(h) Leeds Utd	2/2	0-3		7,085	1		3		5	6		8	9	10	11*	7	2	12	4
					Apps	4	2	3	3	4	4	2	4	3	4	4	3	2		2
					Subs														1	1
					Goals								2							

Freight Rover Trophy

Date	Opponent	Rd	Score	Scorers	Att	Cherry	Hart	Mower	Shakespeare	Brazier	Hawker	Handysides	Cross	O'Kelly	Elliott	Daley	Childs	Jones	Kelly	Naughton	Taylor	Rees	Gunn
Jan 21	(a) Plymouth A.	Grp	1-0	O'Kelly.	3,198	1	6		4		5			9		11		8	10		3	7	2
28	(h) Bristol City	Grp	1-2	Shakespeare.	2,625	1	6		4	5	3†		8		10	9*	7		12	11		14	2
					Apps	2	2		2	1	2		1	1	1	2	1	1	1	1	1	1	2
					Subs														1			1	
					Goals				1					1									

SEASON 1986-87

Division 3

Date	Opponent	Res	Score	Scorers	Att	Prudhoe	Dornan	Mower	Shakespeare	Hawker	Hart	Taylor	Cross	Kelly	Jones, P.	Naughton	Jones, R.	Dolan	Rees	Forbes	Brazier	Childs	Palgrave	Train	Christie	Barber	Hutchinson	Jones M.
Aug 23	(h) Bristol Rov.	L	0-3		6,269	1	2	3	4	5	6	7*	8	9	10	11	12											
30	(a) Chesterfield	L	2-3	Cross (2).	2,603	1	2	3	4		6		8	9	10	11	12	5	7*									
Sept 5	(h) Doncaster R.	L	1-3	Cross.	4,939	1	2	3	4		6		8	9	10	11	12		7*	5								
13	(a) Carlisle Utd	W	3-0	Cross, Kelly, Shakespeare.	3,281	1	2	3	4		6		8	9	10	11			7		5							
16	(a) Wigan Ath.	L	1-5	Kelly.	2,185	1	2*	3			6		8	9	10	11	12			5	4	7						
27	(a) Port Vale	L	1-4	Kelly.	4,482	1	2	3	4		6			9	10	11			12	5		7	8*					
30	(h) Fulham	D	1-1	Kelly.	4,110	1	2	3	4		6			9	10	11*			7	5		12		8				
Oct 4	(a) Blackpool	D	1-1	Kelly.	5,554	1	2	3	4		6			9	10	11			7	5				8				
11	(h) Bolton W.	D	3-3	Mower, Shakespeare, Kelly (pen).	4,677	1	2	3*	4		6			9	10	11	7			5		12		8				
18	(a) Middlesbro.	L	1-3	Christie.	8,511	1	2	3	4		6			9		11			7	5				8	10			
21	(h) Rotherham U.	W	4-1	Kelly, Christie, Childs (2).	3,663		2	3	4		6			9		11				5		7		8	10	1		
25	(h) Brentford	W	5-2	Shakespeare (2, 1 pen), Kelly (2), Christie.	4,495		2	3	4		6			9		11				5		7		8	10	1		
Nov 1	(a) Chester C.	D	0-0		2,872		2	3	4		6		12	9		11*				5		7		8	10	1		
4	(h) Bournemouth	W	2-0	Childs, Cross.	5,056		2	3	4		6		8	9						5		7		11	10	1		
8	(a) Notts County	L	1-2	Kelly.	5,266		2	3*	4		6		8	9		12				5		7		11	10	1		
22	(a) York City	W	5-1	Shakespeare, Childs, Kelly (2), Cross.	3,149		2*	3	4	12	6		8	9						5		7		11	10	1		
25	(h) Swindon T.	W	1-0	Kelly	5,807		2	3	4		6		8	9						5		7		11	10	1		
29	(h) Mansfield T.	W	2-0	Forbes, Shakespeare (pen).	5,702		2	3*	4		6		8		12	11				5		7		9	10	1		
Dec 13	(h) Darlington	W	4-2	Jones, Childs (2), Cross.	5,004		2		4	3	6		8	9	11					5		7			10	1		
20	(a) Bury	L	0-4		2,311		2	3	4	12	6		8	9						5		7*		11	10	1		
25	(h) Newport C.	W	2-0	Christie, Naughton.	6,855		2	3	4		6		8	9		11				5				7	10	1		
27	(a) Bristol C.	L	1-2	Kelly.	10,193		2	3	4	12	6		8	9		11				5				7*	10	1		
Jan 1	(a) Gillingham	L	0-4		6,036		2	3	4	5	6*		8	9	11	10			12					7		1		
24	(a) Doncaster R.	D	1-1	Christie.	2,613		2		4	3	6		8	9	11				7	5					10	1		
Feb 7	(h) Wigan Ath.	L	2-3	Cross, Hawker.	6,959		2	3	4	7	6		8	9	11					5					10*	1	12	
28	(a) Fulham	D	2-2	Christie (pen), Cross.	5,994		2		4	5	6	3	8	9					7						10	1	11	
Mar 7	(a) Brentford	W	1-0	Cross.	3,442		2		4		6	3	8		11				7	5					10	1	9	
11	(a) Bristol Rov.	W	3-0	Christie, Kelly, Cross.	2,282		2			3	6		8	9	11				7	5					10	1	4	
14	(h) Middlesbro.	W	1-0	Cross.	7,332		2		4	3	6		8		11	9			7*	5					10	1	12	
17	(a) Rotherham U.	L	0-1		2,140		2		4	3	6		8		11	9*				5		12			10	1	7	
21	(a) Bolton W.	L	0-1		4,308		2		4	5*	6	3	8	9	11							7			10	1	12	
24	(h) York City	W	3-2	Shakespeare, Childs, Forbes.	3,811		2		4		6	3	8	9	11*					5		7			10	1	12	
28	(h) Blackpool	W	2-1	Christie, Childs.	5,061		2		4	3	6		8	9						5		7			10	1	11	
Apr 4	(h) Notts County	D	1-1	Kelly.	5,206		2	3*	4		6		8	9	12					5		7			10	1	11	
7	(h) Carlisle U.	W	3-0	Shakespeare, Jones, P, Kelly.	4,102		2		4		6	3	8	9	7					5					10	1	11	
11	(a) Bournemouth	L	0-1		8,626		2		4	12	6	3	8	9	7					5					10	1	11*	
12	(h) Chesterfield	W	2-1	Kelly, Christie.	4,391		2		4	11*	6	3	8	9						5		7			10	1	12	
18	(h) Gillingham	W	1-0	Cross.	5,109		2		4	11	6	3	8	9						5		7			10	1		
21	(a) Newport C.	W	4-2	Shakespeare, Christie (2, 1 pen), Cross.	2,003		2		4	11	6	3	8	9						5		7			10	1		
22	(h) Chester C.	W	1-0	Kelly.	5,117		2		4	11	6	3	8	9						5		7			10*	1	12	
25	(h) Bury	W	3-1	Shakespeare, Cross (2).	5,146		2		4	11*	6	3	8	9	12					5		7			10	1		
28	(h) Port Vale	W	5-2	Kelly, Christie (2), Jones, P, Forbes.	5,696		2		4		6	3	8	9*	11	12				5		7			10	1		
May 2	(a) Mansfield T	L	0-2		3,389		2	12	4		6	3	8	9	11*					5		7			10	1		
4	(h) Bristol C.	D	1-1	Kelly.	7,684			3	4	11	6	2	8	9						5		7			10	1		
8	(a) Swindon T.	D	0-0		7,911			3	4	11	6	2	8	9		12				5		7			10*	1		
9	(a) Darlington	W	3-1	Kelly (2), Shakespeare.	1,114			3	4	11	6	2	8	9	7	10				5						1		
					Apps	10	43	27	44	19	46	17	38	42	24	20	1	1	11	40	2	25	1	16	35	36	8	
					Subs			1		4			1		3	3	4		2			3					6	
League position: 8th					Goals			1	11	1			16	23	3	1				3		8			13			

F.A. Cup

Date	Opponent	Rd	Score	Scorers	Att	Prudhoe	Dornan	Mower	Shakespeare	Hawker	Hart	Taylor	Cross	Kelly	Jones, P.	Naughton	Jones, R.	Dolan	Rees	Forbes	Brazier	Childs	Palgrave	Train	Christie	Barber	Hutchinson	Jones M.
Nov 15	(h) Chesterfield	1	2-0	Shakespeare, Mower.	5,417	1	2	3	4	14	6		8	9	11	12				5†		7			10*			
Dec 6	(h) Port Vale	2	5-0	Naughton, Cross, Shakespeare (2 pens), Christie	7,033		2		4	3	6		8		12	11	14			5†		7*		9	10	1		
Jan 10	(a) Charlton	3	2-1	Kelly, Shakespeare.	4,541		2*	3	4	5	6		8	9	11				7					12	10	1		
31	(h) Birmingham C.	4	1-0	Cross.	14,824		2	3	4	7	6		8	9	11					5					10	1		
Feb 21	(h) Watford	5	1-1	Christe (pen).	15,621		2	3	4	7	6		8	9	11					5					10	1		
24	(a) Watford	5R	4-4	(a.e.t.) Cross, Christie (2), Hawker.	20,350		2		4	3	6		8	9	11				7*	5†		14		12	10	1		
Mar 2	(h) Watford	52R	0-1		15,897		2	3*	4	7	6†	12	8	9	11				14	5					10	1		
					Apps	1	7	5	7	6	7		7	6	6	1			2	6		2		1	7	6		
					Subs					1		1			1	1	1		1			1		2				
					Goals			1	4	1			3	1		1									4			

Littlewoods Cup

Date	Opponent	Rd	Score	Scorers	Att	Prudhoe	Dornan	Mower	Shakespeare	Hawker	Hart	Taylor	Cross	Kelly	Jones, P.	Naughton	Jones, R.	Dolan	Rees	Forbes	Brazier	Childs	Palgrave	Train	Christie	Barber	Hutchinson	Jones M.
Aug 26	(h) Mansfield T.	1/1	1-0	Shakespeare.	3,942	1	2	3	4		6		8	9	10	11	7*	5	12									
Sep 2	(a) Mansfield T.	1/2	4-2	Naughton (2), Jones. P., Kelly.	3,069	1	2	3	4		6		8	9	10	11			7									5
Oct 7	(h) Millwall	2/1	0-1		3,475	1	2	3	4		6			9	10	11*	14		7†	5		12		8				
14	(a) Millwall	2/2	2-3	Kelly, Shakespeare (pen).	2,207	1	2	3	4		6			9	10	11	7*		14	5		12		8†				
					Apps	4	4	4	4		4		2	4	4	4	2	1	2	2				2				1
					Subs												1		2			2						
					Goals				2					2	1	2												

Freight Rover Trophy

Date	Opponent	Rd	Score	Scorers	Att	Prudhoe	Dornan	Mower	Shakespeare	Hawker	Hart	Taylor	Cross	Kelly	Jones, P.	Naughton	Jones, R.	Dolan	Rees	Forbes	Brazier	Childs	Palgrave	Train	Christie	Barber	Hutchinson	Jones M.
Dec 9	(a) Swansea City	1	0-3		2,909		2		4	3	6		8	9	7	11		5†						14	10	1		
16	(h) Torquay Utd.	2	1-0	Forbes.	3,107		2		4	3	6		8	9		14				5		7†		11	10	1		
Jan 26	(a) Brentford	3	2-4	Christie (2).	1,774		2	3	4†		6		8	9	11	14				5				7	10	1		
					Apps		3	1	3	2	3		3	3	2	1		1		2		1		2	3	3		
					Subs											2								1				
					Goals															1					2			

SEASON 1987-88

Division 3

Date	Opponent	Res	Score	Scorers	Att	Barber	Dornan	Mower	Shakespeare	Forbes	Hart	Goodwin	Cross	Kelly	Jones, P.	Naughton	Palgrave	Jones, M	Taylor	Rees	Hutchinson	Christie	Hawker	Marsh	O'Kelly	Sanderson
Aug 15	(h) Fulham	L	0-1		4,691	1	2	3	4*	5	6	7	8	9	10	11	12									
22	(a) Blackpool	W	2-1	Cross (2).	4,614	1	2	3*		5	6	7	8	9	10	11		12	4							
29	(h) Northampton T	W	1-0	Jones P.	5,993	1	2		4	5	6	7	8	9*	10	11			3	12						
31	(a) York City	W	3-1	Naughton, Cross, Forbes.	2,661	1	2		4	5	6	7	8		10	11			3	9*	12					
Sept 5	(h) Sunderland	D	2-2	Kelly, Shakespeare.	6,909	1	2		4	5	6	7	8	9	10	11*			3			12				
12	(a) Rotherham U.	W	1-0	Shakespeare.	3,325	1	2		4	5	6	7	8	9	11				3		12	10*				
15	(h) Bristol C.	D	1-1	Kelly.	6,425	1	2		4	5	6	7	8	9	11				3			10				
19	(h) Wigan Ath.	L	1-2	Kelly.	5,353	1	2		4	5	6	7*	8	9	11				3			10	12			
26	(a) Grimsby T.	W	2-0	Naughton, Taylor.	3,314	1	2	9	4	5	6	7	8		11	10			3							
29	(a) Bury	D	2-2	Forbes, Jones.	2,449	1	2	3	4	5	6	7	8		11	9						10				
Oct 3	(h) Preston N.E.	W	1-0	Christie.	5,467	1	2	3	4	5*	6	7	8		11	10			12			9				
10	(h) Brighton & H.A.	D	1-1	Bremner (og).	5,020	1	2		4	5	6		8	9	11	7			3			10				
17	(a) Brentford	D	0-0		5,056	1	2	3	4	5	6	7	8	9	11*				12				10			
20	(a) Doncaster R.	W	4-0	Kelly, Goodwin, Christie, Shakespeare.	1,387	1	2	3	4	5	6*	12	8	9		14			7†			10	11			
24	(h) Port Vale	W	2-1	Kelly (2).	6,083	1	2	3	4	5		6	8*	9	12	14			7†			10	11			
30	(a) Southend U.	D	1-1	Shakespeare.	2,692	1	2	3	4	5	6	7	8†	9	11*	14			12			10				
Nov 3	(h) Aldershot	W	2-0	Kelly (2).	4,816	1	2	3	4	5	6			9	8	11			7			10				
7	(a) Chester C.	D	1-1	Jones (pen).	3,269	1	2	3	4	5	6		12	9	8	11			7			10*				
21	(a) Notts County	L	1-3	Hart.	7,211	1	2		4	5*	6	12	8	9	7				3			10	11			
28	(h) Mansfield T.	W	2-1	Shakespeare (2).	4,227	1		3	4	5	6	12		9	7	8			2			10	11*			
Dec 12	(h) Bristol Rov.	D	0-0		4,234	1	2	3	4	5	6		8*	9	7	11			14			12	10†			
18	(a) Gillingham	W	1-0	Jones (pen)	4,020	1	2	3	4	5	6		8	9	7	11							10			
26	(h) Grimsby T.	W	3-2	Kelly (2), Cross.	6,272	1	2		4	5†	6	14	8	9*	7	11			3			12	10			
28	(a) Chesterfield	L	1-2	Jones (pen).	3,916	1	2		4	5	6		8		7	11			3			9	10			
Jan 1	(a) Northampton T.	D	2-2	Jones, Cross.	5,832	1	2		4	5	6	10	8*	9	7	11†			3			12	14			
2	(h) Rotherham U.	W	5-2	Cross (3), Kelly, Shakespeare.	5,051	1			4	5	6	10	8*	9	7†	11			2			12	3	14		
9	(a) Aldershot	W	1-0	Hawker.	3,270	1			4	5	6	10	8	9	7	11			2				3			
16	(a) Wigan Ath.	L	1-3	Kelly.	5,063	1			4	5	6	10	8	9	7*	11†			2			12	3	14		
30	(h) York City.	W	2-1	Kelly, Christie.	4,371	1			4	5	6	8*		11	7	10			2			9	3	12		
Feb 6	(a) Sunderland	D	1-1	Goodwin.	18,311	1		3	4	5	6	8		10	12	11			2*			9	7†		14	
9	(a) Bristol C.	D	0-0		8,454	1		3	4	5	6	8		10	7	11		2				9*			12	
13	(h) Chesterfield	D	0-0		4,162	1		3	4	5	6	8*		10	7	11		2					12		9	
20	(a) Fulham	L	0-2		3,718	1	12	3	4	5*		8		10	6	11		2	7			9				
23	(h) Blackpool	W	3-2	Christie, Jones P. (2 pens).	4,252	1	2	3	4			8		10	6	11		7				9			5	
27	(a) Preston N.E.	L	0-1		6,479	1	2		4			8		10	6	11†		7*	3	14		9	5		12	
Mar 1	(h) Bury	W	2-1	Jones P, Shakespeare.	3,920	1	2		4	5		8			6	11			3			9	7		10	
5	(h) Brentford	W	4-2	Christie, O'Kelly, Jones P (pen), Forbes.	4,494	1	2*		4	5				8	6	11		12	3			9	7		10	
12	(a) Brighton & H.A.	L	1-2	Christie.	8,345	1	2		4	5				8	6	11			3			9	7		10	
19	(h) Southend U.	W	2-1	Kelly (2).	4,479	1	2		4	5		12		8	6	11			3			9*	7		10	
26	(a) Port Vale	L	1-2	Jones P.	6,347	1		2	4	5		8			6	11*		9	3				7		10	12
Apr 2	(h) Chester C.	W	1-0	Hawker	4,978	1		2	4	5	8			10	6	11			3			9	7			
5	(a) Mansfield T.	W	3-1	Kelly (3).	4,900	1		2	4	5	8			10	6	11			3			9	7			
9	(h) Doncaster R.	W	2-1	Christie, Kelly.	6,631	1		2	4	5†	8	14		10	6*	11			3			9	7		12	
30	(h) Notts County	W	2-1	Kelly, Naughton (pen).	11,913	1		2	4	5	8	12		10	6*	11			3			9	7			
May 2	(a) Bristol Rov.	L	0-3		6,328	1		2	4	5	8	6†		10		11			3			9*	7		12	14
7	(h) Gillingham	D	0-0		8,850	1		2	4	5	8	6		10		11*			3			9	7			12
					Apps	46	30	26	45	44	37	29	25	39	41	38		6	36	1		30	26		7	
					Subs		1					7	1		2	3	1	2	4	2	2	6	3	3	5	3
League position: 3rd					Goals				8	3	1	2	8	20	11	3			1			7	2		1	

Own Goal 1.

Play-offs

Date	Opponent	Rd	Score	Scorers	Att	Barber	Dornan	Mower	Shakespeare	Forbes	Hart	Goodwin	Cross	Kelly	Jones, P.	Naughton	Palgrave	Jones, M	Taylor	Rees	Hutchinson	Christie	Hawker	Marsh	O'Kelly	Sanderson
May 15	(a) Notts County	SF1	3-1	Kelly (2), Shakespeare	11,522	1			4	5	8	6		10		11			2			9	7		3	
18	(h) Notts County	SF2	1-1	Christie.	8,901	1	12		4	5	8*	6		10		11			2			9	7		3	
25	(a) Bristol City	F1	3-1	Christie, Kelly (2).	25,128	1			4	5	8	6		10		11			2			9	7		3	
28	(h) Bristol City	F2	0-2		13,941	1	3		4	5	8	6		10		11			2			9	7			
30	(h) Bristol City	FR	4-0	Kelly (3), Hawker.	13,007	1	3*		4	5	8	6†		10		11		14	2			9	7			12
					Apps	5	2		5	5	5	5		5		5			5			5	5		3	
					Subs		1											1								1
Walsall promoted to Division Two .					Goals				1					7								2	1			

F.A. Cup

Date	Opponent	Rd	Score	Scorers	Att	Barber	Dornan	Mower	Shakespeare	Forbes	Hart	Goodwin	Cross	Kelly	Jones, P.	Naughton	Palgrave	Jones, M	Taylor	Rees	Hutchinson	Christie	Hawker	Marsh	O'Kelly	Sanderson
Nov 14	(a) Southend U.	1	0-0		3,035	1	2		4	5	6			9	8	11			7			10	3			
17	(h) Southend U.	1R	2-1	Jones (2 pens).	5,162	1	2		4	5	6		8	9	7	11			3			10				
Dec 5	(a) Gillingham	2	1-2	Kelly.	4,916	1		3	4	5	6		12	9	7	11*			2			10	8			
					Apps	3	2	1	3	3	3		1	3	3	3			3			3	2			
					Subs								1													
					Goals									1	2											

Littlewoods Cup

Date	Opponent	Rd	Score	Scorers	Att	Barber	Dornan	Mower	Shakespeare	Forbes	Hart	Goodwin	Cross	Kelly	Jones, P.	Naughton	Palgrave	Jones, M	Taylor	Rees	Hutchinson	Christie	Hawker	Marsh	O'Kelly	Sanderson
Aug 19	(a) W.B.A.	1/1	3-2	Shakespeare, Jones P., Forbes.	9,605	1	2	3*	4†	5	6	7	8	9	10	11		12	14							
25	(h) W.B.A.	1/2	0-0		8,965	1	2		4	5	6	7	8	9	10	11			3							
Sep 23	(a) Charlton A.	2/1	0-3		2,948	1	2		4	5	6	7	8	9	11				3			10				
Oct 6	(h) Charlton A.	2/2	2-0	Christie, Forbes	4,099	1	2		4	5	6	12	8	9*	11	7			3			10				
					Apps	4	4	1	4	4	4	3	4	4	4	3			3			2				
					Subs							1						1	1							
					Goals				1	2					1							1				

Sherpa Van Trophy

Date	Opponent	Rd	Score	Scorers	Att	Barber	Dornan	Mower	Shakespeare	Forbes	Hart	Goodwin	Cross	Kelly	Jones, P.	Naughton	Palgrave	Jones, M	Taylor	Rees	Hutchinson	Christie	Hawker	Marsh	O'Kelly	Sanderson
Oct 27	(a) Wrexham	Prel.	2-2	Kelly, Hart.	1,039	1	2		4	5	6	8	14	9	12	11			3	7*		10†				
Nov 24	(h) Cardiff City	Prel.	3-1	Kelly, Cross, Hawker.	2,420	1		3	4	5	6		8	9	7				2			10	11			
Jan 19	(h) Peterborough	1	1-2	Christie.	2,894	1			4	5	6	10	8	9		11			2			7	3			
					Apps	3	1	1	3	3	3	2	2	3	1	2			3	1		3	2			
					Subs								1		1											
					Goals						1		1	2								1	1			

SEASON 1988-89

Division 2

Date		Opponent	Res	Score	Scorers	Att	Barber	Dorman	Taylor, M.	Shakespeare	Forbes	Hart	Pritchard	Goodwin	Taylor, A.	Christie	Naughton	Hawker	Marsh	Mower	Callaghan	Rees	Bertschin	Jones, P.	Banton	Goldsmith	Rimmer	Smith	Saville	Green
Aug 27	(h)	Plymouth A.	D	2-2	Taylor A (2).	6,178	1	2	3	4*	5	6	7	8	9	10	11	12												
Sept 3	(a)	Manchester C.	D	2-2	Naughton (2).	17,104	1	2	3	4	5	6	7*	8	9	10	11	12												
10	(h)	Crystal P.	D	0-0		6,525	1	2	3	4	5	6		8*	9	10	11	7	12											
17	(a)	W.B.A.	D	0-0		13,977	1	2	3	4	5	6		8	9	10	11		7											
20	(h)	Birmingham C.	W	5-0	Forbes, Shakespeare, Taylor A, Naughton, Rees.	8,780	1	2	3	4	5	6		8	9		11			7	10*	12								
24	(h)	Stoke City	L	1-2	Callaghan.	7,795	1	2	3	4*	5	6	14	8†	9		11			7	10	12								
Oct 1	(a)	Hull City	D	0-0		4,845	1	2	3	4	5	6	10*		9		11	7	12				8							
4	(a)	Chelsea	L	0-2		6,747	1		2	4	5	6	11		9†	10	14	7		3			8*	12						
8	(h)	Sunderland	W	2-0	Christie, Pritchard.	6,150	1		2	4	5	6	14		9	10†	11	7		3			12	8*						
15	(a)	Shrewsbury T.	D	0-0		5,026	1		2	4	5	6	8*		9	10	12	7		3			11							
22	(h)	Portsmouth	D	1-1	Hawker.	5,626	1		2	4	5	6	14		8	9	11†	7		3			10*	12						
26	(a)	Brighton & HA	D	2-2	Pritchard, Naughton.	8,311	1		2	4	5	6	8*		9	10	11	7	12	3										
29	(h)	Watford	L	0-1		6,682	1		2	4	5	6			9	8	11*	7	12	3					10					
Nov 5	(a)	Oldham A.	L	0-3		5,760	1		2	4	5	6	7			8	11*		12	3				9	10					
8	(a)	Ipswich T.	L	1-3	Christie (pen).	9,067	1		2	4	5	6	12			9	11†		7*	3			14	8	10					
12	(h)	Leicester C.	L	0-1		6,895	1		2	4	5	6	11†			9		7	12	3			14	8	10*					
19	(h)	Blackburn R.	L	1-2	Sellars (og).	5,848	1	7	2	4	5	6	11			9				3*		12	14	8	10†					
26	(a)	Swindon T.	L	0-1		5,328	1	2	3	4	5	6	11*							7		12	9	8	10					
Dec 3	(h)	Leeds United	L	0-3		6,885	1	2	3	4	5	14	12	8		10		6†		7*			9	11						
10	(a)	Barnsley	L	0-1		5,173	1	2	3	4	5	6	7	8†		10	14					12	9*	11						
17	(a)	Bournemouth	L	1-2	Shakespeare.	6,985	1	2	3	4	5	6	7	8		10			12				9*	11						
26	(h)	Oxford Utd.	L	1-5	Naughton (pen).	6,332	1	2	3	4	5	6	7	8		10	11							9						
31	(h)	Bradford C.	L	0-1		5,366	1	2	3	4	5	6	7†	8		10*	11		14					9	12					
Jan 2	(a)	Crystal P.	L	0-4		9,352	1	2	3	4	5	6	7	8			11		12	9					10*					
14	(h)	Ipswich T.	L	2-4	Taylor M, Pritchard.	4,623	1	2	4		5	6	7	8		10*			11†	3		12	9			14				
21	(a)	Plymouth A.	L	0-2		11,505	1	2		4	5	6		8†		12		11		3		7	10	14	9*					
Feb 4	(h)	Chelsea	L	0-7		6,860	1	2		4	5	6*	7	14		9		11†		3		12		10			8			
11	(a)	Sunderland	W	3-0	Rimmer (3).	14,203	1	2		4	5		7	8		12				3		11	10*				9	6		
18	(a)	Portsmouth	D	1-1	Rimmer.	7,310	1	2	12	4	5		7	8						3*		11			10†	14	9	6		
25	(h)	Shrewsbury T.	D	1-1	Pritchard.	5,871	1	2		4	5		7	10		9				3		11					8	6		
28	(h)	Brighton & H.A.	W	1-0	Naughton (pen).	4,613	1	2		4	5		7	10		9	11			3							8	6		
Mar 4	(a)	Leicester C.	L	0-1		9,375	1	2		4	5		7	10		9	12	14		3†		11*					8	6		
11	(h)	Oldham A.	D	2-2	Milligan (og), Hawker.	5,576	1	2		4	5		7	10		9	11	3									8	6		
18	(a)	Birmingham C.	L	0-1		6,558	1	2		4	5		7*	10		9	11	3				12					8	6		
25	(h)	Manchester C.	D	3-3	Saville (2), Rimmer.	7,562	1	2		4	5		7*	10			11	3				12					8	6	9	
27	(a)	Oxford Utd.	L	0-1		5,101	1		12	4	5		7	10			11*	3		6		2					8		9	
Apr 1	(h)	W.B.A.	D	0-0		9,520	1		3	4			7	10			11	6				2					8	5	9	
4	(h)	Bournemouth	D	1-1	Shakespeare.	3,619	1		3	4	5		7	10			11	6				2					8		9	
8	(a)	Bradford C.	L	1-3	Naughton (pen).	8,763	1		3	4	5		7	10			11	6				2					8		9	
15	(h)	Hull City	D	1-1	Rimmer.	3,935	1		3	4	5		7	10*			11	6				2	12				8		9	
18	(a)	Watford	L	0-5		9,777	1			4	5		7	10*			11	3		12		2					8	6	9	
22	(a)	Stoke City	W	3-0	Rimmer, Saville (2).	8,132	1			4	5		7				11	10		3		2	12				8*	6	9	
29	(h)	Swindon T.	D	2-2	Rimmer, Pritchard.	5,288	1			4	5		7	12			11	10*		3		2					8	6	9	
May 1	(a)	Leeds Utd.	L	0-1		13,280	1		12	4	5		7	10			11*			3		2	14				8	6	9†	
6	(a)	Blackburn R.	L	0-3		8,236			12	4	5		7	10			11†			3*		2	14				8	6	9	1
13	(h)	Barnsley	L	1-3	Pritchard.	3,966			3	4	5		7				11*		14			2	12	10			8†	6	9	1
						Apps	44	26	30	45	45	26	36	30	13	26	31	23	3	28	2	16	11	13	9		20	15	12	2
						Subs			4			1	5	2		2	4	3	10	1		9	9	3	1	2				
League position: 24th						Goals			1	3	1		6		3	2	7	2			1	1					8		4	

Own Goals: 2.

F.A. Cup

Date		Opponent	Rd	Score	Scorers	Att	Barber	Dorman	Taylor, M.	Shakespeare	Forbes	Hart	Pritchard	Goodwin	Taylor, A.	Christie	Naughton	Hawker	Marsh	Mower	Callaghan	Rees	Bertschin	Jones, P.	Banton
Jan 7	(h)	Brentford	3	1-1	Pritchard.	5,375	1	2†	12	4	5	6	7	8		10			11	3			14		9*
10	(a)	Brentford	3R	0-1		8,163	1	2	12	4	5	6	7	8		10			11*	3†		14			9
						Apps	2	2		2	2	2	2	2		2			2	2					2
						Subs			2													1	1		
						Goals							1												

Littlewoods Cup

Date		Opponent	Rd	Score	Scorers	Att	Barber	Dorman	Taylor, M.	Shakespeare	Forbes	Hart	Pritchard	Goodwin	Taylor, A.	Christie	Naughton	Hawker	Marsh	Mower	Callaghan	Rees	Bertschin	Jones, P.
Aug 30	(a)	Shrewsbury T.	1/1	2-2	Naughton, Shakespeare.	4,579	1	2	3	4	5	6	7	8	9	10	11							
Sep 6	(h)	Shrewsbury T.	1/2	3-0	Goodwin, Hawker, Taylor A.	5,552	1	2	3	4	5	6	7*	8	9	10	11	12						
28	(a)	Liverpool	2/1	0-1		18,084	1		2	4	5	6	10		9		11	7		3			8	
Oct 12	(h)	Liverpool	2/2	1-3	Shakespeare	12,015	1		2	4	5	6	8		9*	10	11†	7		3			12	14
						Apps	4	2	4	4	4	4	4	2	4	3	4	2		2			1	
						Subs												1					1	1
						Goals				2				1	1		1	1						

Simod Cup

Date		Opponent	Rd	Score	Scorers	Att	Barber	Dorman	Taylor, M.	Shakespeare	Forbes	Hart	Pritchard	Goodwin	Taylor, A.	Christie	Naughton	Hawker	Marsh	Mower	Callaghan	Rees	Bertschin	Jones, P.	Banton
Nov 22	(a)	Crystal Palace	1	2-4	Pritchard, Bertschin.	2,893	1	2	3	4	5	6	11†			9*	7					14	12	8	10
						Apps	1	1	1	1	1	1	1			1	1							1	1
						Subs																1	1		
						Goals							1										1		

SEASON 1989-90

Division 3

Date	Opponent	Res	Score	Scorers	Att	Barber	Gritt	Mower	Kelly	Forbes	Skipper	Pritchard	Rimmer	Saville	Goodwin	Thorpe	Hawker	Bertschin	Green	Smith	Rees	Jones	Taylor	O'Hara	Marsh	Wilder	Lemon	Dornan	Littlejohn	Whitehouse	Hart	Ford	Lyne	Bremner	Shaw	Goldsmith
Aug 19 (h)	Northampton T.	W	1-0	Rimmer (pen).	5,020	1	2	3	4	5*	6	7	8	9	10	11	12																		
26 (h)	Huddersfield T.	L	2-3	Rimmer, Pritchard.	4,173	1	2	3	4*	5	6	7	8†	9	10	11	12	14																	
Sept 2 (a)	Rotherham U.	D	2-2	Hawker, Thorpe.	5,926		2	3*	12	5	6	7†	8	9	4	11	10	14	1																
9 (h)	Leyton Orient	L	1-3	Rimmer.	3,894		2	3	10	5	6	7*	8	9	4	11	12		1																
16 (a)	Reading	W	1-0	Gritt	3,819		2	3	4		6		8*	9		11		12	1	5	7	10													
23 (h)	Fulham	D	0-0		3,969		2	3	4		6		8	9		11	12		1	5	7	10*													
26 (a)	Birmingham C.	L	0-2		10,834		2		4	5	6		8*	9		11	3	12	1		7	10													
30 (h)	Preston N.E.	W	1-0	Saville (pen).	4,045		2	3	12	5	6			9		11	10	8	1		7*		4												
Oct 7 (h)	Notts County	D	2-2	Kelly, Rimmer.	4,592		2	3	7	5	6		12	9	10	11*		8	1				4												
14 (a)	Mansfield T.	W	2-0	Taylor, Bertschin.	3,229		2*		7	5	6			9	10	11		8	1				4	12	3										
17 (h)	Shrewsbury T.	L	0-2		4,266		2		7	5	6		12	9	10*	11		8	1				4	3											
21 (a)	Wigan Ath.	L	0-3		2,229		2†		7	5	6		12	9	10	11		8	1				4*	3	14										
28 (h)	Swansea C.	L	0-1		3,469		2		7	5	6		8	9*		11	10	12	1				4	3											
31 (a)	Bolton W.	D	1-1	Bertschin.	7,363		2		7	5	6		8	12	14	11	10†	9	1					3	4*										
Nov 4 (h)	Bristol C.	L	0-2		5,286				7	5	6		8	12	10*	11		9	1					3		2	4								
10 (a)	Tranmere R.	L	1-2	Rimmer (pen).	6,281				7	5	6		8	12		11		9	1					3*	10	2	4								
24 (a)	Chester C.	D	1-1	Rimmer.	2,507		4	3	7	5	6		8	12		11		9	1						10*	2									
Dec 2 (h)	Bristol Rov.	L	1-2	Bertschin.	4,038			3	7	5	6		8		4	11		9	1						10	2									
16 (a)	Bury	W	2-0	Bertschin (2).	2,797		2	3	7	5	6		8*	12	4		11	9	1						10										
26 (h)	Crewe Alex.	D	1-1	Walters (og).	5,693		2	3	7†	5	6		8	12	4		11	9	1				14		10*										
30 (h)	Cardiff C.	L	0-2		4,256	1	2	3		5			8	12	4	11	10	9		6					7*										
Jan 1 (a)	Brentford	L	0-4		5,259	1	2		7*	5				8	4	11	10	9		6			12					3							
13 (a)	Huddersfield T.	L	0-1		5,856	1	3		7	5	6		8	14	10		12	9†					4					2	11*						
27 (a)	Leyton Orient	D	1-1	Rimmer.	3,565	1				5	6		8		7		10	9					4					2	11	3					
Feb 10 (h)	Reading	D	1-1	Forbes.	3,506	1				5	6		8		7	14	10†	9					4	12				2	11†	3					
18 (a)	Bristol Rov.	L	0-2		6,223	1			10	5	6		8	12	7	11		9*					4					2		3					
20 (a)	Northampton T	D	1-1	Taylor.	2,617	1		12	7	5	6		8	11		14*		9					4					2		3	10†				
24 (h)	Chester C.	D	1-1	Rimmer.	3,315	1			7*	5	6		8			12		9					10					2	11	3	4				
Mar 3 (a)	Blackpool	L	3-4	Rimmer (2), Morgan (og).	3,174	1				5	6		8	12	10	7		9					4					2	11*	3					
6 (a)	Preston N.E.	L	0-2		5,210	1		3		5	6		8	11	10	7		9					4							2					
10 (h)	Birmingham C.	L	0-1		6,036	1		3		5	6		8		7	10	12	9			2		4	11*												
17 (a)	Notts County	L	0-2		5,207	1		3	11	5	6		8		7		10	9			2		4													
20 (h)	Mansfield T.	W	1-0	Rees.	3,017	1		3		5	6		8				10	9			7*		4	12					11		2				
24 (a)	Shrewsbury T.	L	0-2		3,225	1		3		5	6		8				10*	14					4						11†		2	7	9	12		
27 (h)	Blackpool	D	1-1	Skipper.	3,134	1		3		5	6		8				10*						4						11		2	7†	9	12	14	
31 (h)	Wigan Ath.	L	1-2	Ford.	3,182	1		3		5	6		8				10*						4						11†		2	7	9	12	14	
Apr 4 (a)	Fulham	D	0-0		2,652	1		3		5	6		8										4					2	11			7	9	10		
7 (a)	Swansea C.	L	0-2		2,474	1		3		5	6		8				12						4					2	11*			7	9†	10	14	
10 (h)	Bolton W.	W	2-1	Bertschin (2).	3,376	1		3		5	6*		8		12		10	9					4	11				2				7				
14 (h)	Brentford	W	2-1	Bertschin (2).	2,903	1		3		5			8				10	9					4	11				2			6	7				
16 (a)	Crewe Alex.	L	1-3	Shaw.	4,289	1		3		5			8				10	9					4	11				2			6	7*			12	
21 (h)	Bury	D	2-2	Ford, Shaw (pen).	3,621	1		3		5			8				10	9					4	11*				2			6	7			12	
24 (a)	Cardiff C.	L	1-3	Shaw.	2,509	1		3		5			8				10						4	11*				2			6	7	12		9	
28 (h)	Tranmere R.	W	2-1	Forbes, Taylor.	3,287			3		5	7								1	6			4	12				2		11		8	10*		9	
May 1 (h)	Rotherham U.	D	1-1	Dornan.	5,697			3		5	6						12		1	4			10	8*				2		11		7			9	
5 (a)	Bristol C.	L	0-4		17,859					5	6		8†				3		1	4*			10	11				2				7		12	9	14
					Apps	25	20	29	24	44	40	4	38	16	22	24	22	29	21	7	7	3	30	14	8	4	2	18	11	9	10	13	6	2	4	
					Subs			1	2				3	10	2	3	8	6						2	4	1										1	4	5	1
League position: 24th					Goals		1		1	2	1	1	10	1		1	1	9			1		3					1				2			3	

Own Goals: 2.

F.A. Cup

Date	Opponent	Rd	Score	Scorers	Att	Barber	Gritt	Mower	Kelly	Forbes	Skipper	Pritchard	Rimmer	Saville	Goodwin	Thorpe	Hawker	Bertschin	Green	Smith	Rees	Jones	Taylor	O'Hara	Marsh	Wilder	Lemon	Dornan	Littlejohn	Whitehouse	Hart	Ford	Lyne	Bremner	Shaw	Goldsmith
Nov 18 (a)	Telford U.	1	3-0	Rimmer, Bertschin, Forbes.	2,832		4	3	7	5	6		8			11		9	1						10	2									
Dec 9 (h)	Rotherham U.	2	1-0	Rimmer.	4,240		2	3	7		6		8		4	11		9	1	5					10										
Jan 6 (a)	Hereford U.	3	1-2	Bertschin.	5,569	1	2*	3		5	6		8		7		10	9					4		12					11						
					Apps	1	3	3	2	2	3		3		2	2	1	3	2	1			1		2	1			1							
					Subs																			1										
					Goals					1			2					2																	

Littlewoods Cup

Date	Opponent	Rd	Score	Scorers	Att	Barber	Gritt	Mower	Kelly	Forbes	Skipper	Pritchard	Rimmer	Saville	Goodwin	Thorpe	Hawker	Bertschin	Green	Smith	Rees	Jones	Taylor	O'Hara	Marsh	Wilder	Lemon	Dornan	Littlejohn	Whitehouse	Hart	Ford	Lyne	Bremner	Shaw	Goldsmith
Aug 22 (h)	Port Vale	1/1	1-2	Pritchard	4,774	1	2	3	4*	5	6	7	8	9	12	11	10																		
28 (a)	Port Vale	1/2	0-1		4,441		2	3	12	5	6	7†	8	9	4	11*	10	14	1																
					Apps	1	2	2	1	2	2	2	2	2	1	2	2		1																
					Subs				1						1			1																	
					Goals							1																							

Leyland DAF Trophy

Date	Opponent	Rd	Score	Scorers	Att	Barber	Gritt	Mower	Kelly	Forbes	Skipper	Pritchard	Rimmer	Saville	Goodwin	Thorpe	Hawker	Bertschin	Green	Smith	Rees	Jones	Taylor	O'Hara	Marsh	Wilder	Lemon	Dornan	Littlejohn	Whitehouse	Hart	Ford	Lyne	Bremner	Shaw	Goldsmith
Nov 7 (a)	Cardiff City.	Prel.	5-3	Skipper, Bertschin (2), Rimmer, Kelly.	1,487				7	5	6		8			11		9	1					3	10	2	4								
28 (h)	Shrewsbury T.	Prel.	0-1		2,120		4	3	7	5	6		8	10		11		9	1							2									
Jan 9 (a)	Aldershot	1	4-1	Rimmer (2), Forbes, Kelly.	1,214	1	3		7	5	6		8	12	10			9					4					2	11*						
30 (h)	Southend U.	2	4-1	Rimmer 3, Bertschin.	2,255	1				5	6		8		7		10	9					4					2	11	3					
Mar 14 (a)	Bristol Rov.	3	0-0	(lost 2-3 on pens.)	4,740	1		3		5	6		8		7		10	9*			2		4						11		12				
					Apps	3	2	2	3	5	5		5	1	3	2	2	5	2		1		3	1	1	2	1	2	3	1						
					Subs									1																	1				
					Goals				2	1	1		6					3																	

SEASON 1990-91

Division 4

Date	Opponent	Res	Scorers	Att	Green	Hutchings	Mower	Grealish	Bryant	Skipper	Ntamark	Kelly	Rimmer	Cecere	Marsh	Barnett	Goldsmith	Whitehouse	Smith	Littlejohn	O'Hara	Bodak	Lowery	Singleton	McDonald	Methven	Gordon	Naughton	McParland	Thompson	Barber	Jackson	Bertschin
Aug 25	(h) Torquay U.	D 2-2	Rimmer, Goldsmith.	5,219	1	2	3	4†	5	6	7	8*	9	10	11	12	14																
Sept 1	(a) Stockport C.	L 0-3		2,668	1	2		12	5	6			9	10	11	8†	7*	3	4	14													
8	(h) Darlington	D 2-2	Rimmer, Littlejohn.	4,348	1	2	3	7	5	6			9	10		8			4	11													
15	(a) Peterboro. U.	D 0-0		4,099	1	2	3	7	5	6			9	10		8				11	4												
18	(a) Doncaster R.	L 0-2		3,925	1	2	3	7*	5	6	12		9	10		8†	14			11	4												
22	(h) Hereford U.	D 0-0		4,558	1	2	3	7	5	6*	8		9	10						11	4	12											
29	(a) Rochdale	L 2-3	Cecere, Rimmer (pen).	1,933	1	2	3		5	6	8		9	10						11		7	4										
Oct 2	(h) Scunthorpe U.	W 3-0	Cecere, Bodak, Rimmer.	3,676	1	2			5	6	8		9	10						11	12	7†	4*	3	14								
6	(h) Carlisle U.	D 1-1	Rimmer (pen).	4,284	1	2			5	6	8		9	10						11		7*	4	3	12								
13	(a) Maidstone U.	W 3-1	Singleton, McDonald, Cecere.	2,329	1	2	12	7	5		8		9	10							6		4*	3	11								
19	(a) Northampton T	L 0-5		4,055	1	2		7†	5		8*	12	9	10						14	6		4	3	11								
23	(h) York City	D 1-1	Rimmer	3,761	1	2		7*	5		8		9	10						12	6		4	3	11								
27	(h) Aldershot	D 2-2	Rimmer (pen), Cecere.	3,567	1	2	3		5	6	7	4	9	10*						12				8	11								
Nov 3	(a) Blackpool	W 2-1	Rimmer (2).	3,233	1	2				6	11	4	9	10					5	7				3	8								
10	(h) Burnley	W 1-0	Rimmer.	5,710	1	2				6	11	7	9	10					5					3	8	4							
25	(a) Chesterfield	D 2-2	Brien (og), Methven.	3,687	1	2				6	8	7	9	10*					5	12				3	11	4							
Dec 1	(h) Halifax T.	W 3-1	McDonald, Rimmer (2).	4,153	1	2				6	8	7	9	10					5	12				3	11*	4							
15	(a) Cardiff C	W 2-0	Goldsmith, Rimmer (pen).	2,017	1	2				6	8	7	9				10		5	11				3		4							
21	(h) Wrexham	W 1-0	Gordon.	4,420	1	2		12		6	8	7	9						5	14				3†	11*	4	10						
26	(a) Gillingham	L 0-1		3,695	1	2		7*		6	8		9					12	5†	14				3	11	4	10						
Jan 1	(h) Scarborough	D 0-0		4,914	1	2				6	8	7	9						5	12				3	11	4	10*						
5	(a) Lincoln C.	L 1-2	McDonald.	2,500	1	2				6	8	7	9						5*	12				3	11	4	10						
12	(h) Stockport C.	L 0-2		4,364	1	2				6	8	7	9					12	5	14				3*	11	4	10†						
19	(a) Torquay U.	D 0-0		3,191	1	2		7		6	8		9						5					3	11	4	10						
26	(h) Peterboro. U.	L 0-1		4,438	1	2		7		6	8	11†	9		12				5*	14				3		4		10					
Feb 2	(h) Doncaster R.	W 1-0	Marsh.	3,805	1	2	10	7		6	8				9				5						11	4		3					
6	(a) Hereford U.	D 0-0		1,947	1	2	10	7		6	8				9				5						11	4		3					
16	(h) Chesterfield	W 3-0	McDonald, Skipper, Ntamark.	3,995	1	2	3	7†		6	8			12	9*				5					14	10	4		11					
19	(h) Lincoln	D 0-0		3,582	1	2*	3			6	8		9		12				5					7	10	4		11					
23	(a) Burnley	L 0-2		7,783	1	2†	3	7		6	8		9	12	14				5						10	4		11*					
Mar 2	(a) Halifax T.	L 2-5	Naughton (pen), Marsh.	1,464	1	2	3†	7		6	8			12	9				5	14					10	4		11*					
5	(a) Darlington	L 0-1		3,971	1	2	3	7†		6	8			12	9				5					14	10	4		11*					
9	(h) Cardiff C.	D 0-0		3,950	1		3	7		6	8			9	2				5	12					10	4		11*					
12	(a) Scunthorpe U.	L 0-1		3,352	1		3*	7		6	8			9	2				5†	11	12			14	10	4							
16	(h) Rochdale	L 0-1		2,890	1	2		7		6	8			12	9				5*	14	3				10	4		11†					
20	(h) Maidstone U.	D 0-0		2,475	1	2		7		6	8			9†	12				5	14	3*				11	4			10				
23	(a) Carlisle U.	W 3-0	Cerere (2), McParland (pen).	2,433	1	2*		7		6	8			9	12				5		3				14	4		11*	10				
26	(a) Hartlepool U.	L 1-2	McDonald.	2,556	1			7*		6	8			9	2				5†	14	3			12	11	4			10				
30	(h) Gillingham	D 0-0		3,074	1			7*		6	8†			9	2				5	14	3			12	11	4			10				
Apr 1	(a) Wrexham	D 1-1	McParland.	1,588	1					6				9	2				5	11*	3			7		4		12	10	8			
6	(h) Hartlepool U.	L 0-1		2,758	1					6	8			9*	2						3			12	11	4		5	10	7			
13	(a) Scarborough	L 0-1		1,538	1	2		7		6	12								5		3			14	11	4		9†	10	8*			
20	(h) Northampton T.	D 3-3	Grealish, Ntamark, McParland.	3,345	1	2		7		6	8				9					11	3				12	4		5*	10				
26	(a) York City	L 0-1		1,717	1	2		7		6†	8				9				14	11	3				12	4		5*	10				
May 4	(a) Aldershot	W 4-0	Jackson (2), McParland, Ntamark.	1,826		2		7*			8			14	12				6	11†	3				5	4			10		1	9	
11	(h) Blackpool	W 2-0	McParland (2).	8,051		2		7†			8			9	12				6	11*	3			14	5	4			10		1		
				Apps	44	40	16	29	13	41	40	12	27	26	16	4	2	1	32	15	18	3	6	20	31	32	6	15	11	3	2	1	
				Subs			1	2			2	1		6	7	1	2	2	1	18	2	1		8	5			1					
League position: 16th				Goals				1		1	3		13	6	2		2			1		1		1	5	1	1	1	6			2	

Own Goal: 1.

F.A. Cup

Date	Opponent	Rd	Res	Scorers	Att	Green	Hutchings	Mower	Grealish	Bryant	Skipper	Ntamark	Kelly	Rimmer	Cecere	Marsh	Barnett	Goldsmith	Whitehouse	Smith	Littlejohn	O'Hara	Bodak	Lowery	Singleton	McDonald	Methven	Gordon	Naughton	McParland	Thompson	Barber	Jackson	Bertschin
Nov 17	(a) Aylesbury	1	1-0	McDonald.	3,366	1	2				6	8	7	9	10					5					3	11	4							
Dec 8	(a) Swansea C.	2	1-2	Hutchings	3,744	1	2		12		6	8	7*	9	10	5†					14				3	11	4							
					Apps	2	2				2	2	2	2	2	1				1					2	2	2							
					Subs				1												1													
					Goals		1																			1								

Rumbelows Cup

Date	Opponent	Rd	Res	Scorers	Att	Green	Hutchings	Mower	Grealish	Bryant	Skipper	Ntamark	Kelly	Rimmer	Cecere	Marsh	Barnett	Goldsmith	Whitehouse	Smith	Littlejohn	O'Hara	Bodak	Lowery	Singleton	McDonald	Methven	Gordon	Naughton	McParland	Thompson	Barber	Jackson	Bertschin
Aug 28	(h) Cambridge U.	1/1	4-2	Goldsmith, Rimmer (2), Hutchings.	4,085	1	2	3*		5	6			9	10	11	8	7	12	4														
Sep 4	(a) Cambridge U.	1/2	1-2	Rimmer (pen).	3,517	1	2	3	7	5	6			9	10	11	8			4														
26	(h) Chelsea	2/1	0-5		5,666	1	2	3	12	5	6	8		9	10			14			11	4†	7*											
Oct 10	(a) Chelsea	2/2	1-4	Rimmer	10,037	1	2	14	7*	5†		8		9	10						12	6		4	3	11								
					Apps	4	4	3	2	4	3	2		4	4	2	2	1		2	1	2	1	1	1	1								
					Subs			1	1									1	1		1													
					Goals		1							4				1																

Leyland DAF Trophy

Date	Opponent	Rd	Res	Scorers	Att	Green	Hutchings	Mower	Grealish	Bryant	Skipper	Ntamark	Kelly	Rimmer	Cecere	Marsh	Barnett	Goldsmith	Whitehouse	Smith	Littlejohn	O'Hara	Bodak	Lowery	Singleton	McDonald	Methven	Gordon	Naughton	McParland	Thompson	Barber	Jackson	Bertschin
Nov 6	(h) Birmingham C.	Prel.	0-1		5,053	1	2				6	11	4	9	10					5	7				3	8*								12
Dec 12	(a) Lincoln City	Prel.	1-1	Rimmer.	868	1	2		11		6	8	7	9	10*					5	12				3		4							
Jan 29	(a) Cambridge U.	1	0-1		2,140	1	2	10	7		6	8	12			9				5					3*	11	4							
					Apps	3	3	1	2		3	3	2	2	2	1				3	1				3	2	2							
					Subs								1								1													1
					Goals									1																				

SEASON 1991-92

Division 4

Date	Venue	Opponent	Res	Score	Scorers	Att	Gayle M.	Williams W.	Statham D.	Methven C.	Musker R.	Smith D.	MacDonald K	Ntamark C.	Jackson R.	Cecere M.	McDonald R.	Marsh C.	Lane M.	Anderson C.	Grealish A.	Sinclair R.	Hobson	McLoughlin P	O'Hara S.	Walsh	Essers	McKnight A.	Tolson	Edwards D.	Winter	Brown R.	Robinson	May	Chine
Aug 17	(a)	Blackpool	L	0-3		4,141	1	2	3	4	5	6	7	8	9*	10†	11	12	14																
24	(h)	Wrexham	D	0-0		3,307	1	2	3	4	5†	6	7	8	12	10	11	14		9*															
31	(a)	Scarborough	W	3-2	McDonald (2), Cecere	2,002	1	2		4		6	7	8		10	11		5	3	9														
Sep 3	(h)	Rochdale	L	1-3	McDonald	3,111	1	2	3	4	5	6	7	8		10	11			9															
7	(h)	Hailfax Town	W	3-0	MacDonald, McLoughlin, McDonald	2,981		2	3	4		6	7	8			11	10				1	5	9											
14	(a)	Maidstone Utd	L	1-2	Methven	1,139		2	3	4			7	8			11	14			10†	1	5	9	6										
17	(a)	Chesterfield	W	1-0	McLoughlin	2,690		2	3	4			7	8			11	9		12		1	5	10	6										
21	(h)	Hereford Utd	W	3-0	Anderson, McLoughlin, Marsh	4,509		2	3	4			7	8			11	10		5		1		9	6										
28	(a)	Carlisle Utd	D	3-3	McLoughlin, Anderson, McDonald	2,148		2	3*	4			7	8		12	11	10		5		1		9	6										
Oct 5	(h)	Barnet	W	2-0	Methven, McDonald	4,981		2	3	4				8		12	11	10		5		1		9*	6	7									
11	(a)	Crewe Alexandra	W	1-0	McDonald	4,749		2	3	4				8			11	10		5		1		9	6	7									
19	(a)	Burnley	L	0-2		7,289		2	3	4				8			11	10		5		1		9	6	7									
26	(h)	Aldershot	W	3-1	Anderson, McLoughlin, McDonald	3,025		2	3*	4			7	8			11	10	12	5†		1		9	6	14									
Nov 2	(a)	York City	L	0-2		1,605		2	3	4			7			12	11	10	14		8†	1		9	6	5*									
5	(h)	Lincoln City	D	0-0		2,555		2	3	4			7	8		12	11	10		5		1			6		9*								
22	(a)	Rotherham Utd	L	1-2	McDonald	4,192		2		4			7	8		9*	11	10	3	5	14				6†			1	12						
30	(a)	Mansfield Town	L	1-3	McDonald	3,398		2		4			7	8	9*	12	11	10	3	5					6			1							
Dec 20	(a)	Wrexham	L	1-2	Cecere	2,571		2		4			7	8	9†	10	11	3		5					6			1			14				
26	(h)	Blackpool	W	4-2	McDonald (3), MacDonald	4,675		2		4			7†	8	9*	10	11	3	12	5					6			1			14				
28	(h)	Scarborough	D	0-0		3,488		2		4				8	9			3	10	5†					6			1		7	11	14			
Jan 1	(a)	Rochdale	D	1-1	McDonald	3,001		2		4				8	9		11	10	3	5					6			1		7					
4	(h)	Doncaster Rovers	L	1-3	O'Hara	3,444		2		4				8	9*	10	11†		3	5					6			1		7	12	14			
11	(a)	Gillingham	L	0-4		2,715		2	3†	4				8		10	11			5					6			1	12	7*	9	14			
18	(h)	Cardiff City	D	0-0		3,654	1	2		4				8		10	11	9		5					6					7*	14	3†	12		
25	(a)	Scunthorpe Utd	D	1-1	Ntamark	3,165	1	2		4				8		10	11	9		5†					6					14	7	3			
28	(h)	Northampton Tn	L	1-2	Cecere	2,399	1	2*		4				8		10	11	9		5					6				12	14	7†	3			
Feb 1	(h)	Burnley	D	2-2	O'Hara, Cecere	5,287	1	2		4†				8		10	11	9		5					6				12	14	7*	3			
8	(a)	Aldershot	D	1-1	Ntamark	2,078	1	2						8	12	10	11	9	4		5*				6					7†	14	3			
11	(h)	Mansfield Tn	D	3-3	Cecere (2), Ntamark	2,963	1	2		4				8		10	11	9		5					6						7	3			
15	(a)	Northampton Tn	W	1-0	McDonald	2,480	1	2	3	4				8		10	11	9		5					6						7				
22	(h)	Gillingham	L	0-1		2,987	1	2	3	4				8		10	11*	9		5					6				12		7				
29	(a)	Doncaster Rovers	W	1-0	Cecere	1,919	1	2	3	4				8		10		9		5					6				11*	12	7				
Mar 3	(a)	Cardiff City	L	1-2	Perry (og)	7,517	1	2	3	4				8		10		9	12						6				11†	5	7*			14	
7	(h)	Scunthorpe Utd	W	2-1	Edwards, Cecere	2,722	1	2	3	4				8		10	11	9							6					5	7†			14	
11	(a)	Lincoln City	L	0-1		2,021	1	2	3	4				8		10	11	9							6				14	5	7				
14	(h)	York City	D	1-1	Tolson	2,541	1	2	3	4				7		9	10†	8							6				11	5	14				
28	(h)	Rotherham Utd	L	0-2		3,524	1	2	3	4				8	12	10	11								6					5	7*				9
31	(h)	Maidstone Utd	D	1-1	Ntamark	3,045	1	2	3	4		6*		8		10	11†	9							12					5				14	7
Apr 3	(a)	Halifax Town	L	0-1		1.006	1	2	3	4				8		10*	12	9							6					5				11	7
11	(h)	Chesterfield	D	2-2	McDonald (2)	2,472	1	2	3	4			5*	8		10	11	9							6					12					7
18	(a)	Hereford Utd	W	2-1	Cecere, McDonald	2,291	1	2	3	4		6	5	8		10	11	9							7										
21	(h)	Carlisle Utd	D	0-0		2,406	1	2	3	4		6	5	8		10†	11	9							7*					14					12
25	(a)	Barnet	W	1-0	MacDonald	3,207	1	2	3	4		6	5	8		10	11	9												7					
May 2	(h)	Crewe Alexandra	L	2-3	McDonald, O'Hara	4,995	1	2	3	4			5	8		10	11	9							7							6			
						Apps	24	42	29	42	3	9	20	41	7	29	38	34	6	25	3	10	3	9	35	4	1	8	3	13	13	6		1	4
						Subs									2	5	1	3	3	1	1				1				6	6	6	3	1	3	1
League position: 15th						Goals				2			4	3		9	17	1		2				4	3				1	1					

* Games vs Aldershot declared null and void

own goal: 1

F.A.Cup

Date	Venue	Opponent	Rd	Score	Scorers	Att	Gayle M.	Williams W.	Statham D.	Methven C.	Musker R.	Smith D.	MacDonald K	Ntamark C.	Jackson R.	Cecere M.	McDonald R.	Marsh C.	Lane M.	Anderson C.	Grealish A.	Sinclair R.	Hobson	McLoughlin P	O'Hara S.	Walsh	Essers	McKnight A.	Tolson	Edwards D.	Winter	Brown R.	Robinson	May	Chine
Nov 16	(a)	Yeovil Town	1	1-1	Tolson	4,635		2		4	12		7	8	9*	11†		10	3	5					6			1	14						
27	(h)	Yeovil Town	R	0-1	(aet)	3,869		2		4			7	8	9*	12	11	10	3	5					6			1							
						Apps		2		2			2	2	2	1	1	2	2	2					2			2							
						Subs					1					1													1						
						Goals																							1						

Rumbelows Cup

Date	Venue	Opponent	Rd	Score	Scorers	Att	Gayle M.	Williams W.	Statham D.	Methven C.	Musker R.	Smith D.	MacDonald K	Ntamark C.	Jackson R.	Cecere M.	McDonald R.	Marsh C.	Lane M.	Anderson C.	Grealish A.	Sinclair R.	Hobson	McLoughlin P	O'Hara S.	Walsh	Essers	McKnight A.	Tolson	Edwards D.	Winter	Brown R.	Robinson	May	Chine
Aug 21	(a)	Swansea City	1/1	2-2	MacDonald (pen), Ntamark	2,029	1	2	3	4	5	6	7	8		10*	11	12	9																
28	(h)	Swansea City	1/2	0-1		2,812	1	2	3	4		6	7	8	9	10	11	14	5†																
						Apps	2	2	2	2	1	2	2	2	1	2	2		2																
						Subs												2																	
						Goals							1	1																					

Autoglass Trophy

Date	Venue	Opponent	Rd	Score	Scorers	Att	Gayle M.	Williams W.	Statham D.	Methven C.	Musker R.	Smith D.	MacDonald K	Ntamark C.	Jackson R.	Cecere M.	McDonald R.	Marsh C.	Lane M.	Anderson C.	Grealish A.	Sinclair R.	Hobson	McLoughlin P	O'Hara S.	Walsh	Essers	McKnight A.	Tolson	Edwards D.	Winter	Brown R.	Robinson	May	Chine
Oct 22	(h)	Stoke City	PR	0-2		3,578		2	3	4				8	14	9	11	10		5†		1			6	7									
Jan 7	(a)	Birmingham	PR	1-0	Ntamark	5,239		2	3	4†				8		10				5	12				6			1	9*	7	11	14			
21	(a)	Hereford Utd	1	1-0	(aet) Marsh	1,503	1	2		4				8		10	11	9		5†					6					14	7	3			
Feb 5	(a)	Stoke City	2	1-3	Marsh	7,381	1	2						8		10	11	9	4	5*					6				12	14	7†	3			
						Apps	2	4	2	3				4		4	3	3	1	4		1			4	1		1	1	1	3	2			
						Subs									1						1								1	2		1			
						Goals								1				2																	

SEASON 1992-93

Division 3

Date	Opponent	Res	Scorers	Att	Gayle, M.	Williams, W.	Statham, D.	MacDonald, K.	O'Hara, S.	Smith, D.	Ntamark, C.	Clarke, W.	Marsh, C.	Cecere, M.	McDonald, R.	Ollerenshaw, S.	Methven, C.	Demetrios, C.	West, G.	Edwards, D.	Winter, S.	Knight, R.	Parker, R.	Ryder, S.	Reece, A.	Fearon, R.	McManus, S.	O'Connor, M.	Kelly, J.
Aug 15	(a) Carlisle Utd	W 4-3	Oghani (og), Clarke, Marsh, McDonald	4,199	1	2	3	4	5	6	7	8	9	10	11*	12	14												
22	(h) Cardiff City	L 2-3	Ntamark, O'Hara	4,611	1	2	3	4	5	6	7	8	9	12	11	10*	14												
29	(a) Hereford Utd	W 3-1	McDonald, Clarke (2, 1 pen)	2,895	1	2	3	4	5	6	7	8	9	12	11*	10†		14											
Sep 1	(a) Scunthorpe Utd	L 0-2		2,828	1	2	3	4	5	6†	7	8	9	12	11	10*		14											
5	(h) York City	W 3-1	Ollerenshaw, Clarke, Marsh	3,574	1	2	3	4*	12	6	7	8	9		11	10†			5	14									
12	(a) Colchester Utd	L 1-3	Ntamark	3,218	1	2	3	4		6	7	8	9		11	10†			5	14									
15	(h) Bury	W 4-3	Clarke (3), West	3,097	1	2	3*		4	6	7	8	9	12	11	10			5										
26	(a) Gillingham	W 1-0	Ollerenshaw	2,821	1	2	3		4	6	7	8	9		11	12			5	10*									
Oct 10	(a) Lincoln City	W 2-0	Cecere (2)	3,095	1	2	3	14	4	6	7†	8*	9	5	11	12				10									
17	(h) Halifax Town	L 1-2	Clarke (pen)	3,867	1	2	3		4*	6	14	8	9	5	11†	12			7	10									
24	(a) Rochdale	L 3-4	McDonald, Whitehall (og), Cecere	1,836	1	2*	3†	10	4	6	7	9	8	11	12			5		14									
31	(h) Doncaster R	W 3-1	McDonald, Clarke, Cecere	3,525	1		3†	10	4	6	7	8	9	2	11*	12			5			14							
Nov 3	(a) Barnet	L 0-3		2,632	1	2		10	4	6	7		9	8†	11*			3	5				12	14					
7	(h) Scarborough	W 3-2	MacDonald, Demetrios, Cecere	3,001	1			10	4	14	7	8†	9	2	11		6	3	5										
21	(a) Shrewsbury Tn	W 3-0	MacDonald, Clarke (pen), Cecere	4,353	1			10		6	7	8	9	2	11		4					5			3				
28	(h) Wrexham	D 1-1	Cecere	3,519	1			10		6	7	8	9	2	11*	12	4					5			3				
Dec 12	(h) Darlington	D 2-2	MacDonald, Clarke	3,002	1			10		6	7	8	9	2	11		4					5			3				
26	(a) Torquay Utd	W 1-0	Smith	3,010	1			10		6	7	8	9	2	11		4					5			3				
28	(h) Northampton Tn	W 2-0	Reece, Clarke (pen)	5,080	1		14	10†		6	7	8	9	2	11*		4					5		12	3				
Jan 2	(h) Colchester Utd	L 1-3	Clarke	3,669	1		14	10		6	7†	8	9	2	11		4					5			3				
9	(a) Bury	L 1-2	Clarke	2,421	1		10	11		6	7	8	9	2			4					5			3				
16	(h) Gillingham	D 1-1	Ollerenshaw	3,253	1		10	11		6	7	8†	9	2		14	4					5			3				
23	(a) Wrexham	L 1-3	Ollerenshaw	5,324	1		3†	10		12		8	9	14	11	7	4					2*		6	5				
26	(h) Hereford Utd	D 1-1	Ntamark	2,719	1		3†	10		12	5	8	9	14		7	4*				11	2		6					
30	(a) Cardiff City	L 1-2	McDonald	9,012	1			10*	7	4	5	8	9	3	11	14		12				2†		6					
Feb 6	(h) Carlisle Utd	W 2-1	Clarke, Cecere	2,817					7	4	5	8	9	10	11			3				2		6		1			
13	(a) York City	W 1-0	Williams	3,467	1	2			7	4	5	8	9	10	11		3							6					
20	(h) Scunthorpe Utd	W 3-2	Clarke (2), McDonald	2,935	1	2			7	4	5	8†	9	10	11	14	3							6					
27	(h) Lincoln City	L 1-2	Cecere	3,345	1			12	10	4	5	8	9*	7	11	14	3†					2		6					
Mar 9	(h) Chesterfield	W 3-2	Clarke, McDonald, Knight	2,884	1		3	9	10	4	5	8		7	11							2		6					
13	(a) Scarborough	L 1-4	MacDonald	1,681	1		3*	9	7	4	5	8		10†	11	14		12				2		6					
20	(h) Barnet	W 2-0	McDonald (2)	3,418	1			9	7	4	5	8		10	11		3					2*		6			12		
27	(h) Shrewsbury Tn	D 1-1	Clarke	5,573	1				7	4*	5	8		9	11		3					2		6				10	12
Apr 3	(a) Chesterfield	L 1-2	Cecere	3,278	1					4	5	8		9	11		3					2		6				10	7
6	(a) Darlington	W 2-1	Kelly, O'Connor	1,739	1					4	5	8		9	11		3					2		6				10	7
10	(h) Torquay Utd	D 2-2	McDonald, Clarke	3,541	1			14		4	5	8		9	11		3					2†		6				10	7
12	(a) Northampton Tn	D 0-0		4,177	1			14	12	4	5	8		9*	11		3					2		6				10	7†
17	(h) Crewe Alexandra	W 1-0	Cecere	4,643	1			14	12	4	5	8		9	11		3					2		6				10*	7†
24	(a) Halifax Town	W 4-0	Cecere (3), McDonald	2,829	1			7*		4	5	8	14	9	11†		3					2		6				10	12
27	(a) Crewe Alexandra	W 1-0	Ntamark	4,549	1			7†	12	4	5		14	9	11		3*					2		6				10	7
May 1	(h) Rochdale	W 3-1	Clarke, McDonald, Marsh	4,118	1			7*	3	4	5	8	14	9	11†							2		6				10	12
8	(a) Doncaster Rovers	W 3-0	Cecere (2), Kelly	2,900	1		12	7		4	5	8†	14	9	11							2*		6				10	3
				Apps	41	14	18	28	22	39	40	39	29	33	39	8	23	3	9	3	1	26		20	9	1		10	7
				Subs			3	5	4	3	1		4	6		12		4		2	1	1	1	2			1		3
League position: 5th				Goals		1		4		1	4	21	3	16	12	4		1	1			1			1			1	2

Own Goals 2

Play-offs

Date	Opponent	Rd	Res	Scorers	Att	Gayle, M.	Williams, W.	Statham, D.	MacDonald, K.	O'Hara, S.	Smith, D.	Ntamark, C.	Clarke, W.	Marsh, C.	Cecere, M.	McDonald, R.	Ollerenshaw, S.	Methven, C.	Demetrios, C.	West, G.	Edwards, D.	Winter, S.	Knight, R.	Parker, R.	Ryder, S.	Reece, A.	Fearon, R.	McManus, S.	O'Connor, M.	Kelly, J.
May 16	(a) Crewe Alexandra	SF1	1-5	Cecere	6,198	1			7		4	5	12	14	9	11		8*					2†		6				10	3
19	(h) Crewe Alexandra	SF2	2-4	Clarke, O'Connor	7,398	1		12	7*		4	5	8	2	9	11†	14								6				10	3
					Apps	2			2		2	2	1	1	2	2		1					1		2				2	2
					Subs			1					1	1			1													
					Goals								1		1														1	

F A Cup

Date	Opponent	Rd	Res	Scorers	Att	Gayle, M.	Williams, W.	Statham, D.	MacDonald, K.	O'Hara, S.	Smith, D.	Ntamark, C.	Clarke, W.	Marsh, C.	Cecere, M.	McDonald, R.	Ollerenshaw, S.	Methven, C.	Demetrios, C.	West, G.
Nov 14	(a) Rotherham Utd	1	0-4		4,201	1	6		10	14		7	8*	9	2	11	12	4	3†	5
					Apps	1	1		1			1	1	1	1	1		1	1	1
					Subs					1							1			
					Goals															

Coca-Cola Cup

Date	Opponent	Rd	Res	Scorers	Att	Gayle, M.	Williams, W.	Statham, D.	MacDonald, K.	O'Hara, S.	Smith, D.	Ntamark, C.	Clarke, W.	Marsh, C.	Cecere, M.	McDonald, R.	Ollerenshaw, S.	Methven, C.	Demetrios, C.	West, G.	Edwards, D.
Aug 19	(h) Bournemouth	1/1	1-1	Clarke	3,001	1	2	3	4†	5	6	7	8	9	10	11*	12	14			
25	(a) Bournemouth	1/2	1-0	McDonald	3,567	1	2	3	14	5	6*	7	8	9	12	11	10	4†			
Sep 23	(h) Chelsea	2/1	0-3		5,510	1	2	3		4	6	7	8	9		11	10†			5	14
7	(a) Chelsea	2/2	0-1		7,646	1	2		14	4	6	7	8*	9	3	11	12			5	10
					Apps	4	4	3	1	4	4	4	4	4	2	4	2	1		2	1
					Subs				1						1		2	1			1
					Goals								1			1					

Autoglass Trophy

Date	Opponent	Rd	Res	Scorers	Att	Gayle, M.	Williams, W.	Statham, D.	MacDonald, K.	O'Hara, S.	Smith, D.	Ntamark, C.	Clarke, W.	Marsh, C.	Cecere, M.	McDonald, R.	Ollerenshaw, S.	Methven, C.	Demetrios, C.	West, G.	Edwards, D.	Winter, S.	Knight, R.	Parker, R.	Ryder, S.	Reece, A.
Dec 8	(h) Mansfield Town	PR	2-0	McDonald, Clarke	1,837	1			10	14	6	7	8†	9	2	11		4					5			3
Jan 5	(a) West Bromwich A	PR	0-4		6,702	1		10			6	7	8	9	2	11		4					5			3
18	(a) Brighton	1	2-4	Ollerenshaw, Cecere	1,577	1	5	3	11		6*			9	10		7†	4					2	14	12	8
					Apps	3	1	2	2		3	2	2	3	3	2	1	3					3			3
					Subs					1														1	1	
					Goals								1		1	1	1									

SEASON 1993-94

Division 3

Date		Opponent		Score	Scorers	Att	Gayle, M.	Evans, W.	Marsh, C.	Watkiss, S.	Ryder, S.	Smith, D.	Ntamark, C.	Tinkler, J.	Cecere, M.	Reece, A.	McDonald, R.	Knight, R.	O'Hara, S.	Walker, J.	Gayle, J.	Wright, E.	Peer, D.	Keister, J.	Lightbourne, K.	Butler, M.	Lillis, J.	Byrne, D.	Saunders, C.	O'Connor, M.	Livingstone, G.
Aug 14	(h)	Torquay Utd	L	1-2	McDonald	3,324	1	2	3	4†	5	6	7	8	9	10	11		14												
21	(a)	Shrewsbury Tn	W	2-1	Gayle J, Cecere	3,681	1	2*	3	4	5	6	7	9	12	10	11†		14		8										
28	(h)	Doncaster R	L	1-2	McDonald	2,965	1	2	3†	4*	5	6	7	9	14	10	11				8	12									
31	(h)	Scunthorpe Utd	D	0-0		2,519	1	2		4*	5	6	7	9		10	11		3		8	12									
Sep 4	(a)	Northampton Tn	W	1-0	McDonald	3,266	1	2	3*	4	5	6	7	9		10	11				8	12									
11	(h)	Crewe Alexandra	D	2-2	Cecere, Wright	4,404	1	2*		4	5	6	3	8	9	10	11	12				7									
18	(h)	Chesterfield	W	1-0	Wright	2,846	1		3	4	5	6	7		9		11	2*				8	10	12							
25	(a)	Darlington	D	0-0		1,613	1	2*	3	4	5	6	7		9†		11					8	10	12	14						
Oct 2	(h)	Hereford Utd	D	3-3	Lightbourne, Wright (2)	3,725	1	2	3	4		6	7				11		5			9	10		8						
9	(h)	Gillingham	W	1-0	Peer	4,639	15	2	3	4		6	7				11		5	1#			10	9†	8	14					
16	(a)	Rochdale	D	0-0		2,923		2	3	4		6	7				11		5	1		9	10		8						
23	(h)	Scarborough	W	1-0	Wright	3,941		2	3	4		6	7				11		5	1		8	10		9†		14				
30	(a)	Carlisle United	L	1-2	Lightbourne	4,216		2	3	4	12	6*	7				11†		5	1		8	10		9		14				
Nov 2	(h)	Preston North E	W	2-0	Lillis (2)	4,446		2	3	4	6		7				11			1			10	5	9		8				
6	(a)	Colchester Utd	W	1-0	Peer	2,736		2	3	4	6		7				11†			1		14	10	5	9		8				
20	(h)	Lincoln City	W	5-2	Peer (3), Lightbourne (2)	4,580		2	3	4	6		7				11†			1		8	10	5	9		14				
27	(a)	Mansfield Town	W	2-1	Peer, Marsh	2,875		2	3	4	6		7				11			1		8	10	5	9†		14				
Dec 11	(h)	Shrewsbury Tn	L	0-1		4,979		2	3	4	6	12	7				11†			1		8	10	5	9*		14				
18	(a)	Torquay Utd	W	1-0	Keister	2,754		2	3		4	6	7							1		8	10	5	9		11				
27	(h)	Bury	L	0-1		6,248		2	3	12	4*	6	7				11			1		14	10	5	9†		8				
Jan 1	(h)	Wycombe W	W	4-2	McDonald, Marsh. Lightbourne, Lillis	6,473		2	3	4		6	7				11			1		14	10	5	9†		8				
3	(a)	Scunthorpe Utd	L	0-5		3,417		2	3	4		6	7				11†			1		14	10	5	9		8				
11	(a)	Wigan Athletic	D	2-2	Lillis (2)	1,561		2	3	4	12	6	7						14	1		11	10	5†	9		8*				
15	(h)	Rochdale	W	1-0	Lillis	4,437		2	3	4	12	6	7†						14	1		11	10*	5	9		8				
22	(a)	Gillingham	D	1-1	Smith	3,211		2	3	4		6	7						14	1		11†	10	5	9*	12	8				
29	(h)	Carlisle Utd	L	0-1		4,833		2	3	4	14	6	7				11			1		12	10	5	9		8*				
Feb 5	(a)	Scarborough	L	0-1		1,851		2	3	4	7	6					11		5	1			10		9†	14	8				
12	(h)	Chester City	D	1-1	Watkiss	4,602		2	3	4	14	6					11†			1			10	5	9		8*	7	12		
19	(a)	Doncaster R	L	0-4		2,029		2*		4	14	6							3	1			10	12	9†		8	7	11	5	
26	(h)	Northampton Tn	L	1-3	Lightbourne	4,533		2	3	4		6	7							1		14		5	9	12	8†	11*		10	
Mar 5	(a)	Crewe Alexandra	W	2-1	Peer, Lightbourne	4,358		2	3		4	6	7						14	1		8	5†		9	12		11*		10	
12	(h)	Chesterfield	L	0-1		4,157		2	3	6	4		7				14		5	1		8†			9		12	11*		10	
15	(a)	Chester City	L	1-2	O'Connor (pen)	3,324		2	3	4	6		7				11		5	1					8	9				10	
19	(h)	Darlington	W	3-0	Butler, O'Connor (pen), McDonald	2,983		2	3		4	6	12				11†		5	1		14	10		8	9				7*	
26	(a)	Hereford Utd	W	1-0	McDonald	2,744		2	3	4		6	12				11†		5	1			10		8	9*	14			7	
Apr 2	(a)	Bury	W	2-1	Peer, Butler	2,263		2	3	4		6					11*		5	1		12	10		8	9				7	
5	(h)	Wigan Athletic	D	1-1	Marsh	3,815		2	3	4		6					11		5*	1		12	10		8	9				7	
9	(a)	Wycombe W	L	0-3		5,512		2	3	4		6	5				11			1		12	10		8	9*				7	
16	(a)	Preston North E	L	0-2		7,020		2	3	4		6	5†				11			1			10	9*	8	14	12			7	
23	(h)	Colchester Utd	L	1-2	Watkiss	2,980		2	3	4		6	14				11		5†	1#			10		7	9				8	15
30	(a)	Lincoln City	W	2-1	Marsh, Butler	2,665		2	3	4		6	5				11						10†	12	7	9*	14			8	1
May 7	(h)	Mansfield Tn	L	0-2		4,304		2	3	4		6	5				11†						10	12	7	9*	14			8	1
						Apps	9	41	39	38	20	35	34	6	4	6	34	1	15	31	4	16	33	17	34	9	14	5	1	14	2
						Subs	1			1	6	1	3		2		1	1	6			13		5	1	6	10		1		1
League position: 10th						Goals			4	2		1			2		6				1	5	8	1	7	3	6			2	

F A Cup

Date		Opponent	Rd	Score	Scorers	Att	Gayle, M.	Evans, W.	Marsh, C.	Watkiss, S.	Ryder, S.	Smith, D.	Ntamark, C.	Tinkler, J.	Cecere, M.	Reece, A.	McDonald, R.	Knight, R.	O'Hara, S.	Walker, J.	Gayle, J.	Wright, E.	Peer, D.	Keister, J.	Lightbourne, K.
Nov 13	(a)	Wrexham	1	1-1	Lightbourne	5,151		2	3	4	6		7				11			1		8	10	5	9
23	(h)	Wrexham	R	2-0	Lightbourne, McDonald	3,971		2	3	4	6		7				11			1		8	10	5	9
Dec 4	(h)	Scunthorpe Utd	2	1-1	Wright	4,962		2	3	4	6		7				11†		14	1		8	10	5	9
14	(a)	Scunthorpe Utd	R	0-0	Lost 6-7 on penalties	3,300		2	3		4	6	7		14		11†		12	1		8	10	5*	9
					Penalty scorers:	Apps		4	4	3	4	1	4				4			4		4	4	4	4
					Smith, Cecere, Marsh, Lightbourne,	Subs									1				2						
					Peer, Evans	Goals											1					1			2

Coca-Cola Cup

Date		Opponent	Rd	Score	Scorers	Att	Gayle, M.	Evans, W.	Marsh, C.	Watkiss, S.	Ryder, S.	Smith, D.	Ntamark, C.	Tinkler, J.	Cecere, M.	Reece, A.	McDonald, R.	Knight, R.	O'Hara, S.	Walker, J.	Gayle, J.	Wright, E.
Aug 17	(h)	Exeter City	1/1	0-0		2,024	1	2*	3	4†	5	6	7	8	9†	10	11	12	14			
25	(a)	Exeter City	1/2	1-2	McDonald	2,037	1	2	3	4	4	6	7	8*	9*	10	11					12
						Apps	2	2	2	2	2	2	2	2	2	2	2					
						Subs												1	1			1
						Goals											1					

Autoglass Trophy

Date		Opponent	Rd	Score	Scorers	Att	Gayle, M.	Evans, W.	Marsh, C.	Watkiss, S.	Ryder, S.	Smith, D.	Ntamark, C.	Tinkler, J.	Cecere, M.	Reece, A.	McDonald, R.	Knight, R.	O'Hara, S.	Walker, J.	Gayle, J.	Wright, E.	Peer, D.	Keister, J.	Lightbourne, K.	Butler, M.	Lillis, J.
Sep 28	(a)	Hereford Utd	PR	0-1		1,044	1	2	3	4	5†	6	7		9		11		14				10		8		
Oct 19	(h	Northampton Tn	PR	0-0		1,897		2	3†	4		6	7				11		5	1		9	10		8		14
						Apps	1	2	2	2	1	2	2		1		2		1	1		1	2		2		
						Subs													1								1
						Goals																					

SEASON 1994-95

Division 3

Date	Opponents	Res	Score	Scorers	Att	Wood, T.	Evans, W.	Rogers, D.	Watkiss, S.	Marsh, C.	Palmer, C.	O'Connor, M.	Ntamark, C.	Lightbourne, K.	Wilson, K.	Mehew, D.	Lillis, J.	Keister, J.	Butler, M.	Peer, D.	Ryder, S.	Embleton, D.	Houghton, S.	Gibson, C.	Walker, J.
Aug 13	(a) Fulham	D	1-1	Lightbourne	5,308	1	2	3	4	5	6	7	8	9	10	11†		14							
20	(h) Lincoln City	W	2-1	O'Connor (pen), Marsh	3,813	1	2	3	4	5	6	7†	8	9	10	11*	12	14							
27	(a) Hereford United	D	0-0		3,004	1	2	3		5	6	7	8	9	10	11#			4*	12		15			
30	(h) Carlisle United	L	1-2	Marsh	3,610	1	2	3	4	5	6	7	8	9	10	11†			14						
Sep 3	(h) Northampton Town	D	1-1	Lightbourne	4,249	1	2	3	4	5	6	7	8	9	10								11		
10	(a) Chesterfield	D	0-0		3,027		2†	3		5	6	7	8	9	10						14		11	4	1
13	(a) Colchester United	L	2-3	Lightbourne, Houghton	2,239			3		5	6		8	9	10					7	2		11	4	1
17	(h) Fulham	W	5-1	Marsh (2), Lightbourne (3)	3,378	1	2	3		5	6	7	12	9	10*					8			11	4	
24	(h) Gillingham	W	2-1	Wilson, Ryder	3,654	1	2	3	4†	5		7		9	10					8	14		11	6	
Oct 1	(a) Preston North End	W	2-1	O'Connor, Marsh	7,852	1		3	4	5		7		9	10					8	2		11	6	
8	(h) Scarborough	W	4-1	O'Connor (2 pens), Ryder, Houghton	3,601	1	5†	12	4*		6	7		9	10	8			14		2		11	3	
15	(a) Scunthorpe United	W	1-0	Wilson	3,609	1		4			6	7†	5	9	10	8				14	2		11	3	
22	(a) Hartlepool United	D	1-1	Lightbourne	1,704	1		4		5	6	7	8	9*	10				12		2		11	3	
29	(h) Bury	L	0-1		5,255	1		4		5	6	7	8	9	10	14					2		11†	3	
Nov 5	(a) Darlington	D	2-2	Gregan (og), Marsh	2,186	1		4		5	6	7	8	9	10						2		11	3	
19	(h) Exeter City	W	1-0	O'Connor	3,629	1	2			5	6	7	8	9	10				14		4		11†	3	
26	(a) Mansfield Town	W	3-1	Wilson, O'Connor, Ntamark	2,733	1	2			5	6	7*	8	9	10	14				12	4		11†	3	
Dec 10	(a) Lincoln City	D	1-1	Wilson	2,717	1	2			5	6	7	8†	9	10				14		4		11	3	
17	(h) Hereford United	W	4-3	Houghton, Lightbourne (2), Ryder	3,652	1	2			5	6	7	8	9	10†				14		4		11	3	
26	(h) Barnet	W	4-0	Palmer, Wilson, Lightbourne (2)	5,392	1	2	12		5	6	7*	8	9	10†	14					4		11	3	
27	(a) Rochdale	W	2-0	Wilson (pen), Lightbourne	2,438	1	2	12		5	6		8	9	10			7		14	4		11†	3*	
31	(h) Doncaster Rovers	W	1-0	Marsh	4,561	1	2			5	6	7	8	9	10						4		11	3	
Jan 14	(a) Torquay United	L	2-3	Houghton, Marsh	2,976	1	2			5	6	7	8	9	10						4		11	3	
Feb 4	(h) Mansfield Town	W	1-0	Wilson	4,369	1	2	3		5	6	7	8	9	10						4		11		
18	(h) Torquay United	W	1-0	Ryder	3,708	1	2	3		5	6	7	8	9	10						4		11		
28	(h) Preston North End	D	2-2	Marsh, Wilson	4,429	1	2			5	6	7	8	9	10						4		11	3	
Mar 4	(a) Gillingham	W	3-1	Lightbourne (2), Houghton	3,669	1	2			5	6	7	8	9	10						4		11	3	
7	(h) Hartlepool United	W	4-1	O'Connor, Houghton (2), Wilson	3,314	1	2			5	6	7	8	9†	10	14					4		11	3	
11	(h) Chesterfield	L	1-3	Lightbourne	6,219	1	2			5	6	7	8	9	10						4		11	3	
14	(h) Darlington	W	2-0	Lightbourne, Wilson	3,154	1	2	12		5	6		8	9	10†	14		7			4		11	3*	
18	(a) Carlisle United	L	1-2	Wilson	7,769	1	2	3		5	6	7		9	10			8			4		11		
25	(h) Northampton Town	D	2-2	Lightbourne, Wilson	6,282	1	2		6	5		7		9†	10	14		8			4		11	3	
Apr 1	(h) Colchester United	W	2-0	Lightbourne, O'Connor (pen)	3,622	1	2			5	6	7	14	9	10			8			4		11	3	
4	(a) Exeter City	W	3-1	O'Connor, Lightbourne (2)	1,551	1	2			5	6	7		9	10†	14		8			4		11	3	
8	(a) Doncaster Rovers	W	2-0	Wilson (2)	2,368	1	2	14		5	6	7		9	10			8			4		11	3†	
11	(a) Wigan Athletic	L	0-1		2,176	1	2			5*	6	7	12	9	10			8			4		11	3	
15	(h) Rochdale	D	0-0		3,766	1	2			5	6	7	12	9	10			8*			4		11	3	
17	(a) Barnet	W	3-1	Ryder, Wilson, Lightbourne	2,078	1	2	12			6	7	8	9	10†				14	5	4		11*	3	
22	(h) Wigan Athletic	W	2-0	O'Connor, Lightbourne	3,508	1	2	12			6	7	8	9	10					5	4		11	3*	
29	(h) Scunthorpe United	W	2-1	Palmer, Lighbourne	4,539	1	2	3		14	6	7†	8	9	10					5	4		11		
May 2	(a) Scarborough	W	2-1	Houghton, Wilson	2,841	1#	2	3		14	6	7	8	9	10					5†	4		11*	12	15
4	(a) Bury	D	0-0		6,790		2	3		5	6	7*	8	9	10						4		11	12	1
					Apps	39	36	20	8	36	39	39	31	42	42	6		9	1	8	34		38	31	3
					Subs			7		2			4			7	1	2	7	4	2	1		2	1
League position: 2nd					Goals					9	2	10	1	23	16						5		8		

Own goals 1

F A Cup

Date	Opponents	Rd	Score	Scorers	Att	Wood, T.	Evans, W.	Rogers, D.	Watkiss, S.	Marsh, C.	Palmer, C.	O'Connor, M.	Ntamark, C.	Lightbourne, K.	Wilson, K.	Mehew, D.	Lillis, J.	Keister, J.	Butler, M.	Peer, D.	Ryder, S.	Embleton, D.	Houghton, S.	Gibson, C.	Walker, J.
Nov 12	(h) Rochdale	1	3-0	Lightbourne, Butler (2)	3,619	1	2	4		5	6	7	8	10†		14			9*	12			11	3	
Dec 3	(a) Preston North E	2	1-1	Wilson	9,767	1	2			5	6	7	8	9	10				14		4		11†	3	
13	(h) Preston North E	R	4-0	Houghton, Wilson, Lightbourne (2)	6,468	1	2			5	6	7*	8	9	10†				14	12	4		11	3	
Dec 4	(h) Leeds United	3	1-1	Marsh	8,619	1	2			5	6	7	8	9	10	14					4		11	3†	
14	(a) Leeds United	R	2-5	O'Connor (pen), Wilson	17,881	1		12	2	5	6	7*	8	9	10†	14					4		11	3	
					Apps	5	4	1	1	5	5	5	5	5	4				1		4		5	5	
					Subs											3			2	2					
					Goals					1		1		3	3				2				1		

Coca-Cola Cup

Date	Opponents	Rd	Score	Scorers	Att	Wood, T.	Evans, W.	Rogers, D.	Watkiss, S.	Marsh, C.	Palmer, C.	O'Connor, M.	Ntamark, C.	Lightbourne, K.	Wilson, K.	Mehew, D.	Lillis, J.	Keister, J.	Butler, M.	Peer, D.	Ryder, S.	Embleton, D.	Houghton, S.	Gibson, C.	Walker, J.
Aug 16	(h) Plymouth Argyle	1/1	4-0	Wilson (2), Lightbourne, O'Connor	2,810	1	2*	3	4	5	6	7	8	9	10	11	12								
30	(a) Plymouth Argyle	1/2	1-2	Wilson	2,801	1	2	3	4	5	6	7	8	9*	10	11			12						
Sep 20	(h) West Ham Utd	2/1	2-1	Watkiss, Potts (og)	5,994	1	2	3	4	5	6†	7	11*	9	10	12				8	14				
Oct 5	(a) West Ham Utd	2/2	0-2		13,553	1	12	3	4	5†	6	7*	14	9	10	11				8	2				
					Apps	4	3	4	4	4	4	4	3	4	4	3				2	1				
					Subs		1						1			1	1		1		1				
					Goals				1			1		1	3										

Own goals 1

Auto Windscreen Shield

Date	Opponents	Rd	Score	Scorers	Att	Wood, T.	Evans, W.	Rogers, D.	Watkiss, S.	Marsh, C.	Palmer, C.	O'Connor, M.	Ntamark, C.	Lightbourne, K.	Wilson, K.	Mehew, D.	Lillis, J.	Keister, J.	Butler, M.	Peer, D.	Ryder, S.	Embleton, D.	Houghton, S.	Gibson, C.	Walker, J.
Oct 18	(a) Birmingham City	PR	0-3		1,044	1		4			6		5	9	10	8†		14		7	2		11	3	
Nov 8	(h Peterborough Utd	PR	2-3	Gibson, Marsh	1,897	1	2	4		5	6	7	8		10				9				11	3	
					Apps	2	1	2		1	2	1	2	1	2	1			1	1	1		2	2	
					Subs													1							
					Goals					1														1	

SEASON 1995-96

Division 2

Date		Opponent	Res	Score	Scorers	Att	Walker, J.	Evans, W.	Daniel, R.	Ryder, S.	Marsh, C.	Watkiss, S.	O'Connor, M.	Ntamark, C.	Lightbourne, K.	Wilson, K.	Bradley, D.	Butler, M.	Rogers, D.	Wood, T.	Keister, J.	Palmer, C.	Houghton, S.	Roper, I.	Viveash, A.	Rollo, J.	Smith, C.	Mountfield, D.	Richards, D.	Kerr, J.	Platt, C.	Ricketts, M.
Aug 12	(h)	Stockport County	L	0-2		4,884	1	2	3	4	5	6	7	8	9	10	11															
19	(a)	Shrewsbury Town	W	2-0	Lightbourne, Stewart (og)	4,019	1	2	3		5*	4	7	8	9	10	11					6	12									
26	(h)	Bristol Rovers	D	1-1	Wright (og)	4,851	1	2	3		5	4	7		9	10	8				6	11										
29	(a)	Crewe Alexandra	L	0-1		4,377	1	2	3		5	4			9	10	8				7	6	11									
Sep 6	(a)	Burnley	D	1-1	Lightbourne	8,778	1	2	3	13	5	4		12	9#	10†	8	14			7	6	11*									
9	(h)	Swansea City	W	4-1	Houghton, O'Connor, Edwards (og), Wilson	3,728	1	2	3		5	4†	7	12	9	10#	8	14	13			6	11*									
12	(h)	Oxford United	D	2-2	O'Connor, Wilson	3,905	1	2	3		5	4	7	12	9	10	8					6	11*									
16	(a)	Brentford	L	0-1		4,717	1	2†	3	13	5*	4	7	12	9#	10	8	14				6	11									
23	(a)	York City	L	0-1		3,541	1	2	3†		5*	4	7	12	9	10	8		13			6	11									
30	(h)	Carlisle United	W	2-1	O'Connor (pen), Wilson	4,214		2	3		5	4	7	11	14	10#	8	9†		1		6	13									
Oct 7	(h)	Peterborough Utd	D	1-1	Lightbourne	3,768		2	3		5#	4	7	11	14	10	8†	9		1	13	6										
14	(a)	Wycombe W	L	0-1		4,724		2			5*	4	7	12	11	10	8	9	3	1		6										
21	(h)	Wrexham	L	1-2	Wilson	4,020		2			5		7	14	11	10	8	9#	3	1		6			4							
28	(a)	Bristol City	W	2-0	Houghton, Wilson	6,475	1	2#			5	12	7	14	9	10	8†	13	3			6*	11		4							
31	(a)	Bradford City	L	0-1		4,310	1				5	6	7	2	9	10	8		3				11		4							
Nov 4	(h)	Bournemouth	D	0-0		3,626	1				5	6	7	2	12	10	8#	9*	3		14		11	4								
18	(a)	Brighton & HA	W	3-0	Wilson, Houghton (2)	4,976	1				5		7	2	9	10	8#	12	3		14		11*		4			6				
25	(h)	Blackpool	D	1-1	Wilson	4,459	1				5		7	2	9*	10	8#	12	3		14		11		4			6				
Dec 9	(h)	York City	W	2-0	Mountfield, Marsh	3,193	1				5		7#	2	14	10†	8	13	3		9		11		4			6				
16	(a)	Carlisle United	D	1-1	Wilson	5,308	1				5		7	2	9	10	8	13	3				11		4			6				
23	(h)	Swindon Town	D	0-0		5,624	1				5		7	2	9	10	8		3				11		4			6				
26	(a)	Rotherham Utd	W	1-0	Wilson	3,694					5		7	2	9	10	8	13	3	1			11†		4			6				
Jan 13	(h)	Shrewsbury Town	W	3-0	Wilson, O'Connor (pen), Lightbourne	5,008			14		5*		7	2	9†	10	8	13	3#	1	12		11		4			6				
20	(a)	Stockport County	W	1-0	Houghton	5,870					5†		7	2		10	8	9	3	1		4	11	13				6				
Feb 3	(a)	Bristol Rovers	L	0-2		4,948			14		5†		7	2	9†	10	8		3	1	12	4#	11					6		13		
10	(h)	Notts County	D	0-0		4,378			3		5		7	2	9	10	8			1			11	14	4			6#				
17	(a)	Oxford United	L	2-3	Butler(2)	4,329		2	3		5		7			10	8	9		1			11	6	4							
24	(h)	Brentford	L	0-1		3,506		2	3†		5				13	10	8	9#		1	7		11	6	4		14					
27	(a)	Swansea City	L	1-2	Lightbourne	3,546					5†		7#	2	13	10	8	9	3	1	14		11		4			6				
Mar 2	(h)	Rotherham Utd	W	3-1	Lightbourne (2), Wilson	3,001					5		7	2	9	10	8#	12	3	1	14		11*		4			6				
6	(h)	Notts County	L	1-2	Lightbourne	4,050					5		7	2	9	10	8		3	1			11		4			6				
9	(a)	Swindon Town	D	1-1	Houghton	9,559					5		7	2	9	10	8	13	3†	1			11		4			6				
12	(h)	Crewe Alexandra	W	3-2	Wilson, Marsh, Lightbourne	3,171			3		5		7	2	9	10	8			1			11		4			6				
16	(h)	Chesterfield	W	3-0	Lightbourne, O'Connor (2, 1 pen)	4,127			3		5		7	2	9	10	8			1			11		4			6				
23	(a)	Hull City	L	0-1		3,060			3				7	2	9	10	8	5		1			11		4			6				
30	(a)	Peterborough Utd	W	3-2	O'Connor (2), Wilson	4,954		5	3				7	2	9	10	8#			1	14		11		4			6				
Apr 2	(h)	Wycombe W	L	0-1		3,252		5	3				7#	2†	9	10	8	13		1	14		11		4			6				
6	(h)	Bristol City	W	2-1	Nugent (og), Bradley	4,141	1	5	3		14			2#	9	10	8				7		11		4			6				
8	(a)	Wrexham	L	0-3		3,309	1	5#	3		14			2	9	10	8				7		11		4			6				
13	(h)	Bradford City	W	2-1	Lightbourne (2)	3,679	1		3		5		7	2	9	10		13			8		11†		4			6				
16	(a)	Chesterfield	D	1-1	Lightbourne	4,508	1		3		5		7	2	9	10	8						11		4			6				
20	(a)	Bournemouth	D	0-0		4,380	1	14			5		7*	2		10#	8	13	3		9		11†		4			6			12	
23	(h)	Hull City	W	3-0	Butler, Lightbourne, Platt	2,752	1	14			5		7	2	9#	10*	8†	11	3		13				4			6			12	
27	(a)	Blackpool	W	2-1	Butler, O'Connor	9,148	1				5		7	2	9	10	8	11	3						4			6				
30	(h)	Burnley	W	3-1	Wilson, Platt, Lightbourne	3,411	1	14					7†	2	9	10	8#	11	3		13		5*		4			6			12	
May 4	(h)	Brighton & HA	W	2-1	Wilson, Ricketts	4,840	1	14					7#	2†	9	10*	8		3		5		11		4			6			12	13
						Apps	26	20	23	1	39	14	41	34	37	46	45	13	23	20	9	15	38	3	31			28				
						Subs		4	2	2	2	1		8	6			15	2				2	2			1			1	4	1
League position: 11th						Goals					2		9		15	15	1	4					6					1			2	1

Own goals 4

F A Cup

Date		Opponent	Rd	Score	Scorers	Att	Walker, J.	Evans, W.	Daniel, R.	Ryder, S.	Marsh, C.	Watkiss, S.	O'Connor, M.	Ntamark, C.	Lightbourne, K.	Wilson, K.	Bradley, D.	Butler, M.	Rogers, D.	Wood, T.	Keister, J.	Palmer, C.	Houghton, S.	Roper, I.	Viveash, A.	Rollo, J.	Smith, C.	Mountfield, D.	Richards, D.	Kerr, J.	Platt, C.	Ricketts, M.
Nov 10	(a)	Burnley	1	3-1	Bradley, Wilson, Houghton	6,525	1				5	6	7	2	9#	10	8†	12	3		14		11*	13	4							
Dec 2	(a)	Torquay United	2	1-1	Lightbourne	3,552	1				5		7	2	13	10	8	9†	3				11		4			6				
12	(h)	Torquay United	R	8-4	Marsh (2), Wilson, Bradley, Lightbourne (2), O'Connor, Houghton	3,230	1				5	12	7	2	13	10	8		3		9†		11		4			6*				
Jan 6	(h)	Wigan Athletic	3	1-0	Pender (og)	5,672					5*		7	2	9†	10	8	13	3	1	12		11		4			6				
Feb 13	(a)	Ipswich Town	4	0-1		18,489		14	3		5		7	2*	9*	10	8	13		1			11†	6	4					12		
						Apps	3		1		5	1	5	5	3	5	5	1	4	2	1		5	1	5			3				
						Subs		1				1			2			3			2			1						1		
						Goals					2		1		3	2	2						2									

Own goals 1

Coca-Cola Cup

Date		Opponent	Rd	Score	Scorers	Att	Walker, J.	Evans, W.	Daniel, R.	Ryder, S.	Marsh, C.	Watkiss, S.	O'Connor, M.	Ntamark, C.	Lightbourne, K.	Wilson, K.	Bradley, D.	Butler, M.	Rogers, D.	Wood, T.	Keister, J.	Palmer, C.	Houghton, S.	Roper, I.	Viveash, A.	Rollo, J.	Smith, C.	Mountfield, D.	Richards, D.	Kerr, J.	Platt, C.	Ricketts, M.
Aug 15	(h)	Brentford	1/1	2-2	Wilson, O'Connor	2,405	1	2	3	4	5	6	7	8	9	10	11															
22	(a)	Brentford	1/2	2-3	Evans, Houghton	3,149	1	2	3		5	4	7	8	9*	10	11					6	12									
						Apps	2	2	2	1	2	2	2	2	2	2	2					1										
						Subs																	1									
						Goals		1					1			1							1									

Auto Windscreen Shield

Date		Opponent	Rd	Score	Scorers	Att	Walker, J.	Evans, W.	Daniel, R.	Ryder, S.	Marsh, C.	Watkiss, S.	O'Connor, M.	Ntamark, C.	Lightbourne, K.	Wilson, K.	Bradley, D.	Butler, M.	Rogers, D.	Wood, T.	Keister, J.	Palmer, C.	Houghton, S.	Roper, I.	Viveash, A.	Rollo, J.	Smith, C.	Mountfield, D.	Richards, D.	Kerr, J.	Platt, C.	Ricketts, M.
Oct 17	(a)	Fulham	PR	5-2	Butler (2), Wilson, Lightbourne, O'Connor	1,315		2†			5		7#	14	11	10		9	3	1	4	12		8*	6	13						
Nov 7	(h)	Wycombe W	PR	5-0	Lightbourne (4), Viveash	2,592	1				5			2	9*	10†	8#	12	3		7		11		4		13	6	14			
28	(h	Brighton & HA	1	1-2	Lightbourne	3,454	1				5		7	2#	9*	10	8†	12	3		14		11		4			6		13		
						Apps	2	1			3		2	2	3	3	2	1	3	1	2		2	1	3			2				
						Subs								1				2			1	1				1	1		1	1		
						Goals							1		6	1		2							1							

SEASON 1996-97

Division 2

Date	Opponent	Result	Scorers	Att	Walker, J.	Evans, W.	Daniel, R.	Viveash, A.	Marsh, C.	Mountfield, D.	Ntamark, C.	Bradley, D.	Lightbourne, K.	Wilson, K.	Butler, M.	Rogers, D.	Riketts, M.	Keister, J.	Platt, C.	Blake, M.	Roper, I.	Watson, A.	Wood, T.	Hodge, J.	Thomas, W.	Keates, D.	Donowa, L.	Beckford, D.	Ryder, S.
Aug 17	(h) Rotherham Utd	D 1-1	Butler	4,040	1	2	3*	4	5#	6	7†	8	9	10	11	12	13	14											
24	(a) Burnley	L 1-2	Wilson	10,322	1	2	3	4	5*	6	7#	8	9	10†	11		13	14		12									
27	(a) Chesterfield	L 0-1		3,561	1	2†	3	4	5	6		8#	9	10	11			14	13	7									
Sep 7	(a) Blackpool	L 1-2	Blake	5,176	1			4		6	2	8*	9	10	11		12	3		7		5							
10	(h) Wycombe W	D 2-2	Wilson, Watson	2,659			3	4	14	6	2	8	9	10	12			5		7*		11#	1						
14	(h) Gillingham	W 1-0	Viveash	3,419	1			4	3	6	2	8	9	10	5					7		11							
21	(a) Bristol City	L 1-4	Lightbourne	7,412	1			4	3	6	2	8	9	10	5					7		11							
24	(h) Wrexham	L 0-1		2,832				4	3	6	2	12	9	10	5#			8		7*		14	1	11					
28	(h) Bury	W 3-1	Viveash, Lightbourne, Blake	3,254				4	3	6	2	12	9	10	5			8		7			1	11*					
Oct 1	(a) Bournemouth	W 1-0	Hodge	2,747				4	3	6	2		9	10	5			8		7			1	11					
5	(a) Luton Town	L 1-3	Lightbourne	5,002			13*	4	3	6	2	12	9	10	5#			8		7		14	1	11†					
12	(h) Plymouth Argyle	L 0-1		3,720				4	3	6	2	8*	9	10			11#			7		14	1		5	12			
15	(h) Preston North E	W 1-0	Wilson	3,224				4	3	6	2		9	10						7		14	1	11	5		8#		
19	(h) Brentford	D 1-1	Lightbourne	5,419				4	3	6	2		9	10						7			1	11	5		8		
26	(h) Stockport County	D 1-1	Wilson (pen)	3,767				4	3	6	2		9	10						7			1	11	5		8		
29	(a) Notts County	L 0-2		3,127			12	4	3	6	2*		9	10						7		14	1	11	5		8#		
Nov 2	(a) Millwall	L 0-1		9,176	1			4	3	6	2		9	10				13		7		14		11#	5†		8		
9	(h) Peterborough Utd	W 4-0	Lightbourne (2), Wilson (pen), Donowa	3,921	1		3	4	11	6	2		9	10#				13		7		14			5†		8		
23	(h) Crewe Alexandra	W 1-0	Wilson	3,653	1		3	4	5*	6	2		9	10				8		12				11	7				
30	(a) Stockport County	L 0-2		5,333	1		3	4	5	6	2	12	9	10#				8				14		11	7*				
Dec 3	(h) Bristol Rovers	W 1-0	Viveash	4,084	1	3		4	5		2	7*	9	10#	12			8			6	14		11					
14	(h) Watford	D 1-1	Keister	3,674	1	3		4	5#	6	2	7	9	10				8				14		11					
20	(a) Shrewsbury Town	D 2-2	Viveash, Wilson	3,007	1	3		4	5#	6	2	7	9	10				8*		12		14		11					
26	(a) Wycombe W	W 2-0	Blake, Lightbourne	5,075	1	3		4	5	6	2		9	12				8		7		10		11#	14				
Jan 18	(h) Bournemouth	W 2-1	Viveash, Lightbourne	3,037	1	12	3	4	5*	6	2	7	9	10						8		11#		14					
25	(h) Notts County	W 3-1	Viveash, Ntamark, Hodge	3,261	1	5		4		6	2	7†	9	10#						8		11		14	13	3			
Feb 1	(a) Peterborough Utd	W 1-0	Watson	4,940	1	5		4		6*	2	7	9					3†		8	12	10		11	13				
8	(h) Millwall	W 2-1	Watson, Viveash	3,833	1	5		4		6	2	7	9				13	3		8*	12	10		11†					
11	(a) York City	W 2-0	Lightbourne, Viveash	2,136	1	5		4		6*	2	7†	9	10#				3		8	12	11		14	13				
15	(a) Crewe Alexandra	L 0-1		4,648	1	5		4		6	2	7†	9	10				3		8*	12	11#		14	13				
22	(h) York City	D 1-1	Lightbourne	3,664	1	5		4		6	2	7	9	10#				3		8*	12	11		14					
Mar 1	(a) Bristol Rovers	W 1-0	Watson	5,891	1	3		4	5	6	2	7†	9				13	8				10		11					
4	(h) Bristol City	W 2-0	Lightbourne (2)	4,322	1	3		4	5	6	2		9				13	8				10†		11	7				
8	(h) Shrewsbury Town	D 2-2	Lightbourne, Ricketts	4,819	1	3		4	5	6	2		9				13	8				10†		11	7				
15	(a) Watford	L 0-1		7,818	1	3		4	5†	6			9	14	13		10#	8		2				11	7				
18	(h) Blackpool	D 1-1	Hodge	3,459	1	3		4	5†	6				10	9		13	8		2				11	7				
22	(h) Burnley	L 1-3	Lightbourne	6,306	1	3		4	13	6			9	10†	5#			8		2		14		11	7				
29	(a) Rotherham Utd	W 2-1	Lightbourne, Viveash	2,428	1	3		4		6*			9	10#	5			8		2	12	7		11				14	
Apr 1	(h) Chesterfield	D 1-1	Blake	3,784	1	3#		4					9	10	5			8		2	6	7		11				14	
5	(a) Wrexham	W 2-1	Lightbourne, Watson	3,266	1	3		4					9	10#	5			8		2	6	7		11				14	
8	(a) Bury	L 1-2	Lightbourne	4,082	1			4		6			9	10	5			8		2	3	7		11					
12	(h) Luton Town	W 3-2	Lightbourne (2), Hodge	5,415	1	3		4		6	13		9	10#	5			8		2		7		11†				14	
19	(a) Plymouth Argyle	L 0-2		5,535	1	3		4		6	2	12	9	10#	5			8				7*		11				14	
26	(h) Brentford	W 1-0	Lightbourne	5,359	1	3		4		6	2	8#	9		5					7		14		11				10	
29	(a) Gillingham	L 0-2		4,095	1	3		4		6*	2	8	9		5			13		7		14		11				10#	12
May 3	(a) Preston North E	L 0-2		10,800	1	3		4			12		9			5	14	8*		2	6	7†		11#	13			10	
				Apps	36	27	8	46	28	42	36	21	45	36	20	1	2	30		35	5	22	10	32	14	1	6	3	
				Subs		1	2		2		2	5		1	3	1	9	6	1	3	6	14		5	6	1		5	1
League position: 12th				Goals				9			1		20	7	1		1	1		4		5		4			1		

F A Cup

Date	Opponent	Rd	Result	Scorers	Att	Walker, J.	Evans, W.	Daniel, R.	Viveash, A.	Marsh, C.	Mountfield, D.	Ntamark, C.	Bradley, D.	Lightbourne, K.	Wilson, K.	Butler, M.	Rogers, D.	Riketts, M.	Keister, J.	Platt, C.	Blake, M.	Roper, I.	Watson, A.	Wood, T.	Hodge, J.	Thomas, W.	Keates, D.	Donowa, L.	Beckford, D.	Ryder, S.
Nov 16	(a) Northwich V	1	2-2	Wilson, Lightbourne	3,142	1		3	4	5	6	2		9	10				8							11	7			
26	(h) Northwich V	R	3-1	Lightbourne (2), Wilson (pen)	3,491	1		3	4	5	6	2		9#	10				8				14			11	7			
Dec 7	(h) Burnley	2	1-1	Lightbourne	5,031	1	3		4	5	6	2	7	9	10				8*		12		14			11#				
17	(a) Burnley	R	1-0	Lightbourne (Abandoned at half-time)	5,955	1	3		4	5	6	2	7	9	10				8							11				
23	(a) Burnley	R	1-1	Viveash (Lost 2-4 on penalties)	5,799	1	3		4	5	6	2	7*	9	10#				8		12		14			11				
				Penalty scorers:	Apps	4	2	2	4	4	4	4	2	4	4				4							4	2			
				Lightbourne, Watson	Subs																2		3							
					Goals				1					4	2															

Coca-Cola Cup

Date	Opponent	Rd	Result	Scorers	Att	Walker, J.	Evans, W.	Daniel, R.	Viveash, A.	Marsh, C.	Mountfield, D.	Ntamark, C.	Bradley, D.	Lightbourne, K.	Wilson, K.	Butler, M.	Rogers, D.	Riketts, M.	Keister, J.	Platt, C.	Blake, M.	Roper, I.	Watson, A.	Wood, T.	Hodge, J.	Thomas, W.	Keates, D.	Donowa, L.	Beckford, D.	Ryder, S.
Aug 20	(h) Watford	1/1	1-0	Lightbourne	2,659	1	2	3	4	5	6	7	8	9	10†	11*		13		12										
Sep 3	(a) Watford	1/2	0-2		5,325	1		3	4	5	6	2	8	9	10	11					7									
					Apps	2	1	2	2	2	2	2	2	2	2	2					1									
					Subs													1		1										
					Goals									1																

Auto Windscreen Shield

Date	Opponent	Rd	Result	Scorers	Att	Walker, J.	Evans, W.	Daniel, R.	Viveash, A.	Marsh, C.	Mountfield, D.	Ntamark, C.	Bradley, D.	Lightbourne, K.	Wilson, K.	Butler, M.	Rogers, D.	Riketts, M.	Keister, J.	Platt, C.	Blake, M.	Roper, I.	Watson, A.	Wood, T.	Hodge, J.	Thomas, W.	Keates, D.	Donowa, L.	Beckford, D.	Ryder, S.
Jan 21	(a) Peterborough Utd	2	0-2		2,274	1	5	3	4		6	2	7	9	10						8		11#			14				
					Apps	1	1	1	1		1	1	1	1	1						1		1							
					Subs																					1				
					Goals																									

SEASON 1997-98

Division 2

Match	Res	Scorers	Att	Walker, J.	Evans, W.	Rogers, D.	Viveash, A.	Ryder, S.	Donowa, L.	Boli, R.	Keister, J.	Platt, C.	Porter, G.	Hodge, J.	Mountfield, D.	Keates, D.	Williams, J.	Blake, M.	Watson, A.	Peron, J-F.	Roper, I.	Ricketts, M.	Skinner, J.	Thomas, W.	Marsh, C.	Tholot, D.	Eydelie, J-J.	Gadsby, M
Aug 9 (a) Chesterfield	L 1-3	Platt	5,193	1	2	3	4	5	6#	7	8	9	10	11			14											
16 (h) Fulham	D 1-1	Mountfield	4,418	1	2		4		6	7	8	9	10*	11	5	3			12									
23 (a) Gillingham	L 1-2	Boli	5,083	1	2		4		12	7	8	9	10†	11	5	3*			13	6								
30 (h) Southend United	W 3-1	Boli (3)	3,304	1	2		4	3		7	8	12	10					11	9*	6	5							
Sep 2 (h) Northampton Tn	L 0-2		4,435	1	2		4	3*	8	7		12	10#	14				11†	9	6	5	13						
9 (a) Bristol Rovers	L 0-2		6,225	1	2		4		8*	7		9		11	5	13		10†	12	6	3							
13 (a) Preston North E	D 0-0		9,092	1	2	3	4			7		9*		11	5	10				6		12	8					
20 (h) York City	W 2-0	Boli, Hodge	2,972	1	2	3	4			7		14		11		9			10#	6	5		8					
27 (a) Plymouth Argyle	L 1-2	Boli	6,207	1	2	3#	4			7		14	12	11	5	9*			10	6			8					
Oct 4 (h) Carlisle United	W 3-1	Boli (2), Watson	3,957	1	2		4			7			12	11*	5	9			10	6			8		3			
11 (h) Wrexham	W 3-0	Boli, Hodge (pen), Watson	4,042	1	2		4			7				11	5	9			10	6			8		3			
18 (a) Brentford	L 0-3		4,874	1	2		4			7		14	9*	11#	5			12	10	6			8		3			
21 (a) Wycombe W	L 2-4	Viveash, Watson	3,884	1	2		4			7		14		12	5†	9		11*	10	6	13		8		3#			
25 (h) Bristol City	D 0-0		4,618	1	2		4					7#		11	5	9			10	6		14	8		3			
Nov 1 (a) Burnley	L 1-2	Viveash	9,293	1	2		4			7				11#	5	9			10	6		14	8		3			
4 (h) Grimsby Town	D 0-0		2,599	1	2		4			7				11†		9		12	10	6	5	13	8*		3			
8 (h) Watford	D 0-0		5,077	1	2		4		11	7	8					9			13	6	5	10†			3			
22 (a) Luton Town	W 1-0	Hodge	4,726	1	2		4			7†			8	11	5	9			10	6		13			3			
29 (h) Blackpool	W 2-1	Watson, Boli	3,933	1	2		4			7			8	11	5	9†			10	6		13			3			
Dec 3 (a) Millwall	W 1-0	Keates	4,647	1	2		4			7			8	11*	5	9		12	10	6					3			
14 (h) Bournemouth	W 2-1	Boli, Hodge	3,548	1			4			7	8			11	5	9*		2	10	6		12			3			
19 (a) Oldham Athletic	D 0-0		4,677	1				4		7	8			11	5	9		2	10	6					3			
26 (h) Bristol Rovers	L 0-1		6,634	1				4		7	8*		12	11	5	9		2	10	6					3			
28 (a) Northampton Tn	L 2-3	Porter, Hodge	7,094	1*	2		4	5		7			8	11		9		12	10	6					3			
Jan 10 (h) Chesterfield	W 3-2	Reeves (og), Watson (2)	4,042	1	2		4			7			8	11	5†	9			10	6	13				3			
17 (a) Southend United	W 1-0	Watson	3,310	1	2		4			7			8	11	5†	9		6	10	13				3				
31 (h) Preston North E	D 1-1	Hodge (pen)	5,377	1	2		4	13		7			8*	11	5†	9		12	10	6					3			
Feb 7 (a) York City	L 0-1		2,959	1	2		4	5		7				11†		9*		8	10	6		13		12	3			
14 (a) Carlisle United	D 1-1	Hodge	4,530	1	2		4			7#				11		9		8	10	6	5	14			3			
21 (h) Plymouth Argyle	L 0-1		4,612	1	2		4			7		14		11		9		8#		6	5	10			3			
24 (h) Brentford	D 0-0		3,166	1	2		4			7		10		11		9		8		6	5				3			
28 (a) Wrexham	L 1-2	Ricketts	3,622	1	2		4			7	11	10				9		8		6#	5	14			3			
Mar 3 (a) Watford	W 2-1	Tholot, Blake	8,096	1	2		4			7†	13					9		8			5	11			3	10	6	
7 (h) Burnley	D 0-0		5,212	1	2		4			7			13	11				8†			5	9			3	10	6	
14 (a) Grimsby Town	L 0-3		4,916	1	2		4*					9	8	11	12	3		7			5	14		13		10#	6†	
21 (h) Wigan Athletic	W 1-0	Peron	3,169	1	2		4			7		9#	8			10				6	5	11			3	14		
28 (h) Luton Town	L 2-3	Viveash, Tholot	3,922	1	2		4			7		9#	10			8†				6	5	14			3	11	13	
31 (h) Gillingham	W 1-0	Evans	3,117	1	2			4					10	11†	5	9		13		6					3	8	7	
Apr 4 (a) Blackpool	L 0-1		4,451	1	2			4#		7	12		10	11	5					6		14			3	9	8*	
7 (a) Fulham	D 1-1	Boli	6,733	1	2		4	8		7#			10	12	5					6		14			3	9*	11	
11 (h) Millwall	W 2-0	Tholot, Hodge (pen)	3,307	1	2		4			7			10	11	5					6					3	9	8	
14 (a) Bournemouth	L 0-1		3,404	1	2		4			7			10	11	5#					6		14			3	9	8	
18 (h) Oldham Athletic	D 0-0		3,562	1	2		4	12		7			10	11	5*					6#		14			3	9	8	
25 (a) Wigan Athletic	L 0-2		2,725	1	2		4	6#		7			10	12							5	14		11*	3	9	8	
May (a) Bristol City	L 1-2	Tholot	15,059	1	2		4				8	13	10	11							5	7		6†	3	9		
2 (h) Wycombe W	L 0-1		4,412	1	2		4†				8	7	10					12		6	5			11*	3	9		13
			Apps	46	43	4	42	11	5	41	11	12	25	35	26	32		16	23	38	18	6	10	3	36	13	10	
			Subs					2	1		2	8	4	4	1	1	1	7	4		3	18		2		1	1	1
League position: 12th			Goals		1		3			12		1	1	8	1	1		1	7	1		1				4		

Own goals 1

F A Cup

Match	Rd	Res	Scorers	Att	Walker, J.	Evans, W.	Rogers, D.	Viveash, A.	Ryder, S.	Donowa, L.	Boli, R.	Keister, J.	Platt, C.	Porter, G.	Hodge, J.	Mountfield, D.	Keates, D.	Williams, J.	Blake, M.	Watson, A.	Peron, J-F.	Roper, I.	Ricketts, M.	Skinner, J.	Thomas, W.	Marsh, C.	Tholot, D.	Eydelie, J-J.	Gadsby, M
Nov 15 (h) Lincoln United	1	2-0	Watson, Boli	3,279	1	2		4			7	8			15	14	9			10x		6	5#	11			3		
Dec 6 (a) Macclesfield Tn	2	7-0	Boli (2, 1 pen), Hodge (2, 1 pen), Viveash, Porter (2)	3,566	1	2		4	5		7x		16	8	11		9			10~		6		15			3		
Jan 13 (a) Peterborough Utd	3	2-0	Watson (2)	12,809	1	2		4			7			8	11	5	9		12	10		6*					3		
24 (a) Manchester Utd	4	1-5	Boli	54,669	1	2		4			7			8	11	5	9			10		6					3		
				Apps	4	4		4	1		4	1		3	3	2	4			4		4	1	1			4		
				Subs									1		1	1			1					1					
				Goals				1			4			2	2					3									

Coca-Cola Cup

Match	Rd	Res	Scorers	Att	Walker, J.	Evans, W.	Rogers, D.	Viveash, A.	Ryder, S.	Donowa, L.	Boli, R.	Keister, J.	Platt, C.	Porter, G.	Hodge, J.	Mountfield, D.	Keates, D.	Williams, J.	Blake, M.	Watson, A.	Peron, J-F.	Roper, I.	Ricketts, M.	Skinner, J.	Thomas, W.	Marsh, C.	Tholot, D.	Eydelie, J-J.	Gadsby, M
Aug 12 (h) Exeter City	1/1	2-0	Platt, Boli	2,321	1	2		4		6	7	8	9	10	11	5	3												
26 (a) Exeter City	1/2	1-0	Boli	2,467	1	2		4	3		7	8		10		5†	13		11	9		6							
Sep 17 (a) Nottingham F	2/1	1-0	Skinner	7,841	1	2	3	4			7				11	5*	9†			10		6	12		8	13			
24 (h) Nottingham F	2/2	2-2	Watson (2)	6,037	1	2	3#	4			7		14	12	11	5†	9			10		6	13		8*				
Oct 14 (h) Sheffield United	3	2-1	Watson, Tiler (og)	8,239	1	2		4			7				11	5	9			10		6			8		3		
Nov 19 (a) West Ham United	4	1-4	Watson	17,463	1	2		4			7	8*		12	11	5	9			10		6		13			3†		
				Apps	6	6	2	6	1	1	6	3	1	2	5	6	5		1	5		5			3		2		
				Subs									1	2			1						2	1		1			
				Goals							2		1							4					1				

Own goals 1

Auto Windscreen Shield

Match	Rd	Res	Scorers	Att	Walker, J.	Evans, W.	Rogers, D.	Viveash, A.	Ryder, S.	Donowa, L.	Boli, R.	Keister, J.	Platt, C.	Porter, G.	Hodge, J.	Mountfield, D.	Keates, D.	Williams, J.	Blake, M.	Watson, A.	Peron, J-F.	Roper, I.	Ricketts, M.	Skinner, J.	Thomas, W.	Marsh, C.	Tholot, D.	Eydelie, J-J.	Gadsby, M	
Dec 9 (a) Barnet	1	2-1	Blake, Boli	754	1	2#		4	5		7		14	8*	11		9		12			6		10			3			
Jan 6 (h Brighton & HA	2	5-0	Watson, Boli (2), Keates, Allan (og)	2,562	1	2		4			7		14	8	11	5†	9*		12	10#		6	13				3			
28 (a) Bristol Rovers	3	1-0	Boli	4,165	1	2			4		7			8	11		9			10		6	5				3			
Feb 17 (a) Peterborough Utd	SSF	2-1	Boli, Ricketts	4,199	1	2		4			7				11#		9		8	10		6	5	14			3			
Mar 10 (h) Bournemouth	SF1	0-2		6,017	1	2			4		7		14	8	11								5	9			3#		10	6
17 (a) Bournemouth	SF2	3-2	Thomas, Boli, Tholot	8,972	1	2		4			7		9	8	12		3					6*	5	10#		11			14	
				Apps	6	6		4	3		6		1	5	5	1	5		1	3		5	4	3		1	5		1	1
				Subs									3		1				2				1	1					1	
				Goals							6						1		1	1				1		1			1	

Own goals 1

SEASON 1998-99

Division 2

Date	Opponent	Res	Scorers	Att	Walker, J.	Marsh, C.	Pointon, N.	Keister, J.	Roper, I.	Viveash, A.	Wrack, D.	Brissett, J.	Rammell, A.	Porter, G.	Keates, D.	Watson, A.	Ricketts, M.	Davis, N.	Green, R.	Platt, C.	Gadsby, M.	Dyer, W.	Evans, W.	Thomas, W.	Simpson, P.	Larusson, B.	Lambert, J.	Otta, W.	Mavrak, D.	Cramb, C.	Eyjolfsson, Z.	Henry, N.	Steiner, R.	Carter, A.	Garrault, R.
Aug 8	(a) Gillingham	W 1-0	Carr (og)	5,712	1	2	3	4	5	6	7*	8#	9	10	11†	12	13	14																	
15	(h) Northampton Tn	D 0-0		4,360	1	2	3	4#		6	7	11	9	10*	12	8†	14		5	13															
22	(a) Wycombe W	W 2-1	McCarthy (og), Rammell	4,102	1	2*	3			6	7	11	9	10	4†	8#	14		5		12	13													
29	(h) Burnley	W 3-1	Brissett, Wrack (2, 1 pen)	4,599	1	2	3			6	7	8	9	10	4		11		5																
Sep 2	(a) Manchester City	L 1-3	Rammell	24,021	1	2*	3			6	7	8	9	10	4	12	11†		5				13												
8	(h) York City	L 2-3	Rammell, Wrack (pen)	3,098	1	2	3			6	7	8	9	10	4†		11		5					13											
12	(a) Chesterfield	W 1-0	Rammell	4,169	1	11†	3			6	7	8	9	10	4				5				2	13											
18	(h) Notts County	W 3-2	Simpson, Rammell, Brissett	3,991	1		3			6	7	8	9	10†	4				5				2	13	11										
26	(a) Luton Town	W 1-0	Rammell	5,530	1	2	3			6	7	8*	9		4	12			5						11	10									
30	(h) Reading	L 0-2		3,729	1	2				6	7	8	9		4				5		3				11	10									
Oct 3	(h) Preston N. E.	W 1-0	Rammell	5,802	1	2†	3			6	7	8	9*		4	12*			5		13				11	10									
10	(a) Wrexham	L 1-2	Watson	3,842	1	2	3		13	6	7	8			4	9			5	11†						10									
17	(h) Blackpool	W 1-0	Wrack	4,728	1	2	3		13	6	7			8	4	9*			5†	11						10	12								
20	(h) Colchester United	D 1-1	Platt	3,319	1	2	3			6	7	11		8*	4				5	9						10	12								
24	(a) Fulham	L 1-4	Morgan (og)	8,452	1	2	3		5	6	7	8			4	12				9						10	11*								
31	(a) Bristol Rovers	W 4-3	Larusson (2), Smith (og), Rammell	5,753	1	2	3			6	7	8	9		4				5							10	11								
Nov 7	(h) Millwall	W 3-0	Green, Wrack, Rammell	4,237	1	2	3		6		7†	8*	9	10	4	12			5		13						11#	14							
10	(h) Lincoln City	W 2-1	Wrack, Otta	3,698	1	2	3		13	6†	7	8	9		4				5							10	11*	12							
21	(a) Macclesfield Town	D 1-1	Otta	3,183	1	2	3		6		7	11*	9		4	12			5							10		8							
28	(h) Bournemouth	W 1-0	Wrack	3,895	1	2	3		6		7				4	11†	13		5	9						10		8							
Dec 12	(a) Oldham Athletic	W 2-0	Otta, Rammell	4,195	1	2†	3		6		7		9	14	4#	12					5		13		11	10		8*							
19	(h) Stoke City	W 1-0	Rammell	9,056	1	2	3		6		7	12	9		4				5						11	10		8*							
26	(h) Wycombe W	D 2-2	Rammell (2)	6,258	1	2	3			6	7		9	4					5						11	10		8							
28	(a) Wigan Athletic	L 0-2		4,579	1	2	3			6	7	12	9	4	14				5						11	10#		8*							
Jan 2	(a) Burnley	D 0-0		10,892	1	2	3		6		7		9	4		8			5						11	10									
9	(h) Gillingham	W 2-1	Wrack, Rammell	5,495	1	3			6	5	7		9		4	8†							2	13	11	10									
23	(h) Manchester City	D 1-1	Watson	9,517	1	2	3		6	5	7	11			4	8	14			9*				12		10									
30	(h) Wigan Athletic	L 1-2	Keates	5,473	1	2	3		6	5	7	11	9		4	8										10									
Feb 6	(a) Reading	W 1-0	Keates	9,481	1	2	3		6	5	7	13	9		4	8							14	12		10			11						
13	(a) York City	W 2-1	Wrack, Watson	2,969	1	2	3		6	5	7	12	9		4	8								13		10			11						
20	(h) Chesterfield	D 1-1	Rammell	5,268	1	2	3		6	5	7	12	9		4	8										10			11						
23	(a) Northampton T	W 1-0	Mavrak	5,631	1	2	3		6	5	7	8*	9		4									13		10			11		12				
27	(a) Notts County	L 1-2	Rammell	6,172	1	2	3		6	5	7		9		4								12	13		10†			11*	8#	14				
Mar 6	(h) Luton Town	W 1-0	Wrack	4,508	1	2	3#		6	5	7	12	9		4								14	13		10†			11*	8					
13	(a) Millwall	W 2-1	Cramb (2, 1 pen)	6,248	1	2			6	5	7	9			4*				13				3	12		10			11†	8					
20	(h) Bristol Rovers	D 3-3	Rammell, Cramb (2, 1 pen)	4,967	1		3		6	5*	7	11	9						12				2	4		10				8					
Apr 3	(a) Blackpool	W 2-0	Larusson, Mavrak	5,432	1	2	3		6	5	7†		9		13				12							10			11#		14	4	8*		
6	(h) Wrexham	W 1-0	Steiner	5,763	1	2*	3		6	5	7	12	9		13											10†			11		14	4	8#		
10	(a) Colchester United	L 0-1		4,082	1	2	3*		6	5	7	14	9		13				12							10†			11#			4	8		
13	(a) Bournemouth	W 1-0	Wrack	8,390	1	2	3		6	5	7	11	9		10																	4	8		
17	(h) Macclesfield Town	W 2-0	Steiner, Rammell	6,256	1	2	3		6	5	7	11	9#		10											13					14	4	8†		
20	(a) Preston N. E.	L 0-1		13,337	1	2†	3		6	5	7	11	9		10											13					14	4	8#		
24	(a) Lincoln City	W 1-0	Wrack	4,588	1		3		6*	5	7		9		10				12		2					11†			13		14	4	8#		
May 1	(h) Oldham Athletic	W 3-1	Wrack, Marsh, Eyjoffsson	9,184	1	2	3		6	5	7	11	9*		10†				12							13					14	4	8#		
4	(h) Fulham	D 2-2	Steiner, Roper	8,326	1	2	3		6	5	7†		9		10				12							4			11*		14		8#	13	
8	(a) Stoke City	L 0-2		12,091	1	2*	3		6	5	7		9#		10		13		12							4†			11		14		8		
				Apps	46	43	43	2	29	40	46	27	39	14	38	12	3		22	6	3		5	1	10	33	4	6	12	4		8	10		
				Subs					3			8		1	5	8	6	1	8	1	3	1	5	11		3	2	2	1		10			1	
League position: 2nd				Goals		1			1		13	2	18		2	3			1	1					1	3		3	2	4	1		3		

Own goals 4

F. A. Cup

Date	Opponent	Rd	Res	Scorers	Att	Walker, J.	Marsh, C.	Pointon, N.	Keister, J.	Roper, I.	Viveash, A.	Wrack, D.	Brissett, J.	Rammell, A.	Porter, G.	Keates, D.	Watson, A.	Ricketts, M.	Davis, N.	Green, R.	Platt, C.	Gadsby, M.	Dyer, W.	Evans, W.	Thomas, W.	Simpson, P.	Larusson, B.	Lambert, J.	Otta, W.	Mavrak, D.	Cramb, C.	Eyjolfsson, Z.	Henry, N.	Steiner, R.	Carter, A.	Garrault, R.
Nov 14	(h) Gresley Rovers	1	1-0	Roper	4,274	1	2	3		6		7	11*	9	14	4	12			5					16		10#		8~							
Dec 5	(a) Preston N. E.	2	0-2		8,488	1	11	3		6		7		9		4	12			5				2~			10		8*							16
					Apps	2	2	2		2		2	1	2		2				2				1			2		2							
					Subs										1		2								1											1
					Goals					1																										

Worthington Cup

Date	Opponent	Rd	Res	Scorers	Att	Walker, J.	Marsh, C.	Pointon, N.	Keister, J.	Roper, I.	Viveash, A.	Wrack, D.	Brissett, J.	Rammell, A.	Porter, G.	Keates, D.	Watson, A.	Ricketts, M.	Davis, N.	Green, R.	Platt, C.	Gadsby, M.	Dyer, W.	Evans, W.	Thomas, W.	Simpson, P.	Larusson, B.	Lambert, J.	Otta, W.	Mavrak, D.	Cramb, C.	Eyjolfsson, Z.	Henry, N.	Steiner, R.	Carter, A.	Garrault, R.
Aug 11	(h) Queens Park R	1/1	0-0		3,691	1	2	3	4		6	7	8	9	10	11*	12			5																
	(a) Queens Park R	1/2	1-3	Rammell	5,052	1	2	3*		12	6	7	11	9	10	4+	8#	14		5			13													
					Apps	2	2	2	1		2	2	2	2	2	2	1			2																
					Subs					1							1	1					1													
					Goals									1																						

Auto Windscreen Shield

Date	Opponent	Rd	Res	Scorers	Att	Walker, J.	Marsh, C.	Pointon, N.	Keister, J.	Roper, I.	Viveash, A.	Wrack, D.	Brissett, J.	Rammell, A.	Porter, G.	Keates, D.	Watson, A.	Ricketts, M.	Davis, N.	Green, R.	Platt, C.	Gadsby, M.	Dyer, W.	Evans, W.	Thomas, W.	Simpson, P.	Larusson, B.	Lambert, J.	Otta, W.	Mavrak, D.	Cramb, C.	Eyjolfsson, Z.	Henry, N.	Steiner, R.	Carter, A.	Garrault, R.
Dec 8	(h) Bristol Rovers	1	2-2	Larusson (pen), Otta (Won 5-4 on pens)*	2,210	1	2	3#		6		7		9	14	4				5+	12	13					10		8							11*
Jan 5	(a) Luton Town	2	3-0	Watson, Wrack, Keates	1,890	1		3		6#	5	7		9*		4	8				12	14		2	13	11	10+									
20	(a) Brentford	3	0-0	(Won 4-3 on pens)**	2,040	1	2	3		5	6	7	11	9		4	8				14			13	12		10									
Feb 16	(h) Cambridge United	4	1-1	Rammell (Won 4-3 on pens)†	5,087	1	2	3		5	6	7	13	9		4	8							12	14		10			11						
Mar 9	(a) Millwall	AF/1	0-1		11,626	1	2	3		5	6	7	12	9*		4											10			8	11					
16	(h) Millwall	AF/2	1-1	Eyjoffsson (lost 1-2 on aggregate)	9,128	1	2	3		5	6	7	9			4								14	13		10			8	11	12				
					Apps	6	5	6		6	5	6	2	5		6	3			1				1	4	1	6		1	3	2					1
					Subs								2		1						3	2		3	4							1				
					Goals							1		1		1	1										1		1			1				

Penalty scorers: *Keates, Porter, Larusson, Marsh, Rammell. † v. Cambridge Thomas, Brissett, Watson, Keates. ** v. Brentford Pointon, Thomas, Watson, Brissett.

Town & Swifts in FA Cup

Walsall Town

1882-83
Round 1
Oct 21 v Staveley (a) 4-1
Arblaster, Harrison, Hill, Tonks
Team: W.Keay; T.Reynolds, E.J.Newman, E.Collington, H.Taylor, J.Tonks, W.Bird, H.Harrison, C.Hill, S.Arblaster, W.Dodsworth.
Att: 1,500
Round 2
Dec 2 v Stafford Road (h) 4-1
Bird 2, Bradbury 2
Team: W.Keay; T.Reynolds, E.J.Newman, H.Taylor, W.Cox, W.Dodsworth, S.Arblaster, C.Hill, S.Bradbury, H.Harrison, W.Bird.
Att: 2,000
Round 3
Jan 27 v Aston Villa (a) 1-2
Hill
Team: W.Keay, T.Reynolds, E.J.Newman, C.Collington, H.Taylor, W.Dodsworth, S.Arblaster, C.Hill, S.Bradbury, W.Bird, H.Harrison.
Att: 5,000

1883-84
Round 1
Nov 10 v Calthorpe (a) 9-0
Collington 2, Bird 4, Brettle, Harrison, Ashe
Team: J.Icke, G.Cox, T.Reynolds, E.J.Newman, J.Brettle, H.Taylor, S.Arblaster, H.Harrison, G.Collington, T.Ashe, W.Bird.
Att: 800
Round 2
Dec 1 v Wednesbury T (h) 2-2
Arblaster 2
Team: J.Icke, G.Cox, T.Reynolds, G.Collington, J.Brettle, H.Taylor, S.Arblaster, H.Harrison, W.Dodsworth, T.Ashe, W.Bird.
Att: 2,000
Replay
Dec 6 v Wednesbury T (a) 0-6
Team: W.Keay, G.Cox, T.Reynolds, G.Collington, H.Taylor, J.Brettle, H.Harrison, E.J. Newman, W.Dodsworth, T.Ashe, J.Beech.
Att: 1,200

1884-85
Round 1
Nov 8 v Derby County (a) 7-0
Cope 2, Shaw, Hunter, Bird 2, Ashe
Team: J.Icke, G.Cox, E.J.Newman, J.Brettle, W.Dodsworth, G.Collington, G.Hunter, C.Shaw, W.Bird, T.Ashe, B.Cope.
Att: 3,000
Round 2
Dec 6 v Aston Villa (h) 0-2
Team: J.Icke, T.Reynolds, G.Cox, J.Brettle, G.Collington, J.Beech, C.Shaw, G.Hunter, B.Bradbury, T. Ashe, W.Dodsworth.
Att: 5,000

1885-86
Round 1
Oct 10 v Aston Villa (h) 0-5
Team: R.Beech, G.Cox, T.Reynolds, G.Collington, J.Brettle, R.Heys, G.Hunter, C.Shaw, B.Bradbury, T.Wilson, B.Cope.
Att: 7,000

1886-87
Round 1
Oct 30 v Derby St Luke's (a) 3-3
Bradbury 2, Davis
Team: J.Osborne, A.Jones, T.Reynolds, G.Collington, J.Beech, R.Heys, G.Cox, T.Wilson, C.Shaw, B.Bradbury, R.Davis.
Att: 2,000
Replay
Nov 13 v Derby St Luke's (h) 6-1
Bradbury 2, Davis 2, Cox, Wilson
Team: J.Osborne, A.Jones, T.Reynolds, S.Lee, J.Beech, R.Heys, G.Cox, T.Wilson, B.Bradbury, B.Cope, R.Davis.
Att: 1,500
Round 2
Town received a bye
Round 3
Dec 11 v B'ham St George's (h) 2-7
Bradbury, Wilson
Team: J.Osborne, A.Jones, T.Reynolds, S.Lee, J.Beech, R.Heys, G.Cox, T.Wilson, B.Bradbury, B.Cope, R.Davis.
Att: 2,000

1887-88
Round 1
Dec 8 v B'ham St George's (h) 1-2
Webster
Team: J.Osborne, A.Jones, J.Brettle, W.Pearson, E.Bennett, C.Lea, D.Webster, R.Eveson, C. Shaw, B.Cope, J.Summerfield.
Att: 1,500

Walsall Swifts

1882-83
Round 1
Oct 21 v Aston Villa (a) 1-4
Farmer
Team: C.H.Hobson, A.Aldridge, J.Sheldon, J.Baker, W.Yates, E.Dyson, R.Davis, T.Farmer, J.Hayes, J.Higgins, D.Lunn.
Att: 5,000

1883-84
Round 1
Nov 10 v Aston Villa (h) 1-5
Farmer
Team: W.Phillips, A.Aldridge, A.Jones, W.Brandrick, R.Morris, R.Davis, J.Farmer, T.Farmer, S.Mills, J.Higgins, H.Dyoss.
Att: 3,000

1884-85
Round 1
Nov 8 v Stafford Road (h) 0-0
Team: J.Tracey, A.Jones, A.Aldridge, H.Allen, J.Morely, G.Morris, R.Davis, J.Higgins, R.Jefferies, A.Horton, J.Farmer.
Att: 2,000
Replay
Nov 11 v Stafford Road (a) 2-1
Jefferies 2
Team: W.Phillips, A.Aldridge, G.Morris, H.Pearce, J.Morely, H.Allen, R.Davis, R.Jefferies, J.Garbett, J.Farmer, J.Higgins.
Att: 2,000
Round 2
Dec 6 v Derby St Luke's (a) 1-0
Davis
Team: J.Tracey, A.Jones, A.Aldridge, J.Morely, G.Morris, H.Allen, J.Farmer, J.Higgins, J.Garbett, R.Davis, R.Jefferies.
Att: 1,500
Round 3
Jan 10 v B'ham St George's (a) 3-2
Aldridge, Morely, Richards og
Team: J.Tracey, A.Aldridge, G.Morris, H.Allen, J.Morely, R.Pearce, R.Davis, J.Farmer, J.Garbett, R.Jefferies, J.Higgins.
Att: 1,500
Round 4
Jan 24 v Notts County (a) 0-4
Team: J.Tracey, A.Aldridge, G.Morris, J.Morely, H.Allen, R.Pearce, R.Davis, T.Farmer, J.Garbett, J.Higgins, J.Farmer.
Att: 3,500

1885-86
Round 2
Nov 14 v Derby Midland (a) 3-1
Higgins, Webster 2
Team: G.Wood, A.Aldridge, G.Morris, J.Morely, H.Allen, R.Pearce, J.Farmer, J.Higgins, T.Farmer, R.Webster, D.Clarkson.
Att: 1,200
Round 3
Dec 12 v Wolverhampton W (a) 1-2
T.Farmer
Team: G.Wood, A.Aldridge, G.Morris, J.Morely, H.Allen, R.Pearce, J.Farmer, J.Higgins, T. Farmer, R.Webster, D.Clarkson.
Att: 2,500

1886-87
Swifts did not enter the competition.

1887-88
Round 1
Oct 15 v Wolverhampton W (a) 1-2
Higgins
Team: J.Tracey, W.Prophitt, T.Reynolds, J.Morely, C.A.L.Jenkyns, G.Morris, J.Jones, R.Colley, T.Athersmith, J.Higgins, J.Fallon.
Att: 2,000

Walsall in the FA Cup

Walsall have registered five wins over First Division opposition in the FA Cup. In 1932-33 they clipped mighty Arsenal 2-0 at Fellows Park; in 1965-66 they won 2-0 at Stoke City in front of a near 33,000 crowd; beat Newcastle United at home by 1-0 in 1974-75; knocked out Leicester City, also by 1-0, in 1977-78 and accounted for Charlton Athletic at The Valley in 1986-87 (2-1).

In contrast, as a Football League club themselves, the Saddlers have suffered knockouts at the hands of the following non-League opponents: Brierley Hill Alliance 1893-94, Druids 1898-99, Peterborough United 1959-60 and Yeovil Town (twice) in 1960-61 and 1991-92. Against the latter, Walsall in fact went out each time by losing at home 1-0, the second time after a replay.

As a non-League club, Walsall beat Second Division Burnley 1-0 in a first round FA Cup-tie in 1901-02.

The farthest Walsall have gone in the competition was to a second replay in round 5 in season 1986-87. They eventually fell to Watford, Andy Dornam giving away an own-goal to decide the contest at Fellows Park.

12-0 v Warmley (away) in season 1890-91 is Walsall's best-ever FA Cup victory. In 1896-97 they beat Dresden United 11-0 at home.

Close on 45,500 fans saw Everton beat Walsall 2-1 at Goodison Park in the 1971-72 FA Cup competition.

Walsall's heaviest defeat in the FA Cup came in October 1913 when they lost a first qualifying round tie 7-0 to Worcester City. The previous season the Saddlers had crashed out in the first round proper to Aston Villa by 6-1. Earlier, in 1899-1900 they had lost 6-1 to West Bromwich Albion in a replay.

The longest Cup-tie Walsall have been involved in to date was that against Brighton & Hove Albion in season 1969-70 which went to four games spanning 320 plus minutes. The Saddlers eventually won through 2-1 at neutral Fulham following 1-1 draws at home and away and a goalless contest at Coventry.

Walsall lost 5-2 at Anfield against Liverpool in the 1946-47 competition; 21 years later the same scoreline was recorded after the sides had drawn 0-0 at Fellows Park.

In 1945-46 Walsall almost achieved the impossible by coming back from a massive five-goal deficit. In the two-legged tie against Shrewsbury Town they lost the opening fixture at Gay Meadow by 5-0 but in the return game at Fellows Park, Walsall won 4-1 to go out 6-4 on aggregate.

In 1938-39 Huddersfield Town, Wembley runners-up from the previous season, beat Walsall 3-0 at Leeds Road in the fifth round; and Arsenal, en route to the Final in 1978, defeated the Saddlers 4-1 at Highbury in this same round.

Walsall were involved in three epic FA Cup games with mighty Manchester United in the mid-1970s. In 1974-75 the Saddlers won 3-2 after a replay at Fellows Park having forced a superb 0-0 draw at Old Trafford, and in 1976-77 a crowd of almost 49,000 saw United gain revenge with a 1-0 home win on their way to the Final.

Walsall in the League Cup

Walsall's first-ever League Cup-tie was against Everton at Goodison Park in October 1960. A crowd of 14,137 saw the Saddlers lose 3-1, John Davies scoring the visitor's only goal.

Walsall reached the semi-final of the competition in 1983-84 – the best they have ever done in the League Cup. Their victims were, in turn, Blackpool (4-3 on aggregate), Barnsley (3-0 on aggregate), Shrewsbury Town (the team Walsall have played against most times in this competition), Arsenal and Rotherham United (4-2). After drawing 2-2 at Anfield before a 31,073 crowd in the semi-final, Walsall were then knocked out 2-0 by Liverpool in the return leg when the attendance was almost 19,600, the best crowd for a Walsall home League Cup-tie.

In September 1967 Walsall crashed 5-1 at home to West Ham United in a second-round tie – their heaviest defeat in the competition. In October 1961 Walsall lost 5-2 at Sunderland, also in a second-round match.

Walsall have beaten four First Division clubs in the League Cup – Arsenal 2-1 in 1983-84, Charlton Athletic 2-0 at home in 1987-88 (although the Londoners went through 3-2 on aggregate), Ipswich Town 1-0 at home in a second-round replay in 1963-64 and Coventry City 3-0 at Highfield Road in 1984-85 (after Walsall had lost the first leg 2-1 at Fellows Park).

Walsall played Shrewsbury Town three seasons running in the League Cup: 1967-68, 1968-69 and 1969-70, winning twice. Then later, the Saddlers and the Shrews met each other three times in four seasons in the mid-1970s, again Walsall were victors twice.

The Saddlers were involved in three exciting games with Manchester City in 1973-74. Two ended 0-0 but the third clash at Maine Road went in City's favour 4-0.

A crowd of 41,188 saw West Bromwich Albion beat Walsall 3-1 in a second-round League Cup game at The Hawthorns in September 1965 – a record attendance for the competition at that time.

Staffordshire Cup Finals

A team from Walsall (the Swifts, the Town, the Town Swifts and then as Walsall FC) first entered the prestigious Staffordshire Cup competition in season 1880-81, and for a number of years afterwards, certainly up to the 1950s, invariably the first XI was fielded. But around 1953-54 Football League clubs still entering the competition, usually put out their reserve team, Walsall being among them.

Here are details of all the Staffordshire Cup Finals a Walsall team has played in:

16 April 1881
Walsall Swifts 1 Aston Villa 5 (at Stoke)
Farmer
Att: 6,000
Swifts: Davies; Sheldon, Jones, Dyoss, Baker, Ashwell, Tapper, Lunn, Yates, Farmer, Meek.

25 March 1882
Walsall Swifts 1 Walsall Town 1 (at Wood Green Oval)
Lunn (Swifts) and Bradbury (Town)
Att: 3,000
Swifts: Hobson; Jones, Sheldon, Dyoss, Yates, Harrison, Brandrick, Dyoss, Farmer, Lunn, Higgins.
Town: Keay; Newman, Tonks, Collington, Taylor, Evans, Bird, Dodsworth, Bradbury, Hill, Arblaster.

Replay: 1 April 1882
Walsall Swifts 1 Walsall Town 4 (at Stoke)
Lunn (Swifts) and Bird 2, Bradbury, Hill (Town)
Att: 2,000
Town: Keay; Newman, Tonks, Collington, Taylor, Evans, Bird, Dodsworth, Bradbury, Hill, Arblaster.
Swifts: Hobson; Jones, Sheldon, Dyoss, Yates, Tappin, Brandrick, Dyoss, Farmer, Lunn, Higgins.

4 April 1885
Walsall Town 2 Wolverhampton Wanderers 1 (at Stoke)
Bradbury, Hunter
Att: 5,100
Walsall Town: Beach; Cox, Reynolds, Collinton, Brettle, Heyes, Hunter, Bradbury, Cope, Shaw, Bangor.

9 April 1887
Walsall Swifts 0 West Bromwich Albion 5 (at Stoke)
Att: 3,950
Swifts: Wood; Profitt, Morris, Morely, Jenkins, Peace, Wood, Jones, Athersmith, Evanson, Somerfield.

26 April 1890
Walsall 3 Birmingham St George's 5 (at Wood Green Oval)
Tipper, S. Holmes 2
Att: 4,000
Walsall: Edge; Jones, Reynolds, Tonks, C. Holmes, Stokes, Shaw, S. Holmes, Tipper, Tapper, Cope.
*This match also counted as a Football Alliance fixture.

17 April 1893
Walsall 0 Aston Villa 3 (at Wood Green Oval)
Att: 300
Walsall: Hawkins; Woodward, Pinches, Withington, Shaw, Forsyth, Robinson, Davis, Holmes, Allcock, Marlow.

20 February 1899
Walsall 0 Aston Villa 2 (at Villa Park)
Att: 6,694
Walsall: Tennant; Peers, Davies, S. Holmes, Jenkyns, Taggart, Dean, Aston, Vail, Martin, Griffiths.

8 April 1911
Walsall 0 Aston Villa 3 Walsall (at Wednesbury)
Att: 4,054
Walsall: Moult; Cook, Chance, Richards, Bird, Mansell, Davies, Rodgers, Parsonage, Caddick, Rampton.

25 April 1921
Walsall 0 Stoke 2 (at Molineux)
Att: 4,534
Walsall: Houghton; Mackenzie, Timmins, Allan, Groves, Mann, Bowyer, Lane, Edwards, Leedham, Rogers.

3 May 1922
Walsall 1 Wolverhampton Wanderers 2 (at Molineux)
Scorer: Bowen
Att: 5,723
Walsall; Houghton; Webster, Timmins, Wilson, Groves, Leedham, Bowyer, Bowen, Reid, Butler, Spence.

12 May 1949
Walsall 0 Port Vale 1 (at Stoke)
Att: 5,375
Walsall: Lewis; Jones, Skidmore, Methley, Foulkes, Russon, Mullard, Hazeldine, Chapman, Devlin, Lawley.

8 May 1950
Walsall 1 Wolves 3 (a.e.t) (at Fellows Park)
Scorer: Corbett
Att; 5,929
Walsall: Lewis; Jones, Skidmore, Walters, Russon, Devlin, Whitehouse, Dearson, Foulkes, Corbett, Green.

7 May 1953
Walsall 1 Port Vale 2 (at Fellows Park)
Scorer: Green (pen)
Att: 2,440
Walsall: Chilvers; Rowe, Green, Dean, Home, Hodges, Bowen, Morgan, Morris, Scarlett, Giles.

29 March 1966 (1st leg)
Walsall 1 Tamworth 1 (at Fellows Park)
Scorer: Morris
Att: 2,521
Walsall: Ball; Ford, Evans; R. Smith, Cross, Meath, Foster, Hodgkisson, Holbutt, McMorran, Morris.

7 May 1966 (2nd leg)
Walsall 0 Tamworth 2 (at The Lamb, Tamworth)
Att: 1,598
Walsall: Ball; Coton, Evans, Smith, Cross, Gough, Foster, Meath, Jones, Ford, Morris.

24 April 1968 (1st leg)
Walsall 0 Kidderminster Harriers 0 (at Aggborough)
Att: 1,772
Walsall: Parkes; Coton, Sissons, Simpson, Cross, Mighalls, Jackson, Middleton, Harris, Baker, Allner.

4 May 1968 (2nd leg)
Walsall 6 Kidderminster Harriers 0 (at Fellows Park)
Murray (2), Simpson, Gough (2), Allner
Att: 1,875
Walsall: Ball; Coton, Sissons, Simpson, Cross, Mighalls, Jackson, Middleton, Murray, Gough, Allner.

Walsall Town reached the semi-final stage of the Staffordshire Cup in season 1885-86 only to be beaten 3-1 by Stoke. But it might well have been a completely different story because the Saddlers had two men carried off injured inside the first hour and finished the game with only seven fit players on the pitch.

The Swifts' best win in the Staffordshire Cup came in 1880-81 (round three) when they beat Leek 12-0 at home.

The Town team defeated Stone 13-0 at home in a second-round tie in 1883-84 ('Shiner' Shaw scored 5 that day); Burton Strollers 10-1 (also at home, and a hat-trick for Hunter) in the opening round of the 1884-85 competition and Aston Villa 9-0 in the first round in 1885-86 when both George Cope and Sammy Holmes registered hat-tricks.

On their way to the 1885 Final the Town scored a total of 25 goals in four games, including an 8-0 win over Burton Rangers and a 2-0 triumph over West Bromwich Albion in the semi-final.

Birmingham Senior Cup

Before the amalgamation of Walsall Swifts and Walsall Town in 1888, both clubs played in the very prestigious and highly competitive Birmingham Senior Cup and hereunder are the respective results of both teams from 1876 to 1888 inclusive:

Walsall Swifts

1876-77
First round v Wednesbury Town (a) 1-2

1877-78
First round v West Bromwich (a) 0-2

1878-79
First round v West Bromwich (a) 2-2
Replay v West Bromwich (h) 4-1
Second round v St Thomas's (h) 5-1
Third round v St George's (a) 3-0
Semi-final v Stafford Road (n) 1-1

(This game was abandoned after 55 minutes, crowd encroachment)
Replay v Stafford Road (n) 2-7

1879-80
First round v Perry Athletic (h) 14-0
(Stokes scored five in this tie)
Second round v Fenton Sutherland (h) 5-0
Third round v Elwells (h) 3-1
Fourth round v Wednesbury Strollers (n) 2-1
Semi-final v Aston Villa (n) 1-2

1880-81
First round v Harborne (h) 16-0
(Nine different players scored in this tie, with Tapper hitting four)
Second round v Wednesbury Strollers (a) 5-1
Third round v Walsall Town (h) 3-0
Fourth round v Small Heath Alliance (n) 2-2
Replay v Small Heath Alliance (n) 4-0
Semi-final – Swifts received a bye
Final v Aston Villa (n) 1-0
Team: Hobson; Sheldon, Jones, Dyoss, Baker, Ashwell, Tapper, Lunn, Yates, Stokes, Meek.
Scorer: Meek
Att: 1,500

1881-82
First round v Aston Unity (h) 2-0
Second round v Notts Wanderers (h) 6-0
Third round v Walsall Town (a) 2-1
Fourth round v Derby Midland (n) 4-2
Semi-final v Aston Villa (n) 0-1

1882-83
First round v Calthorpe (h) 8-0
Second round v Aston Clifton (h) 15-1
(Higgins scored 6 and Davis 4)
Third round v Saltley College (h) 9-0
(Three goals here for Farmer)
Fourth round v Wednesbury Strollers (n) 7-1
(Another hat-trick for Davis)
Semi-final v Wednesbury Old Athletic (n) 1-2

1883-84
First round v Birmingham Standard (h) 12-0
(4 goals for Higgins in this game)
Second round – Swifts received a bye
Third round v Small Heath Alliance (a) 2-2
Replay v Small Heath Alliance (h) 2-0
Fourth round v Nottingham Rangers (h) 2-1
Semi-final v West Bromwich Albion (n) 1-0
Final v Aston Villa (n) 0-4
Team: Sheldon; Aldridge, Jones, Allen, Morris, Brandrick, Mills, Horton, Higgins, Farmer, Davis.
Att: 2,500

1884-85
First round v Nettlefolds (h) 19-0
(Eight goals in this tie for Garbett)
Second round v Trafalgar (h) 3-0
Third round v Burton Wanderers (h) 61
Fourth round – Swifts received a bye
Semi-final v Walsall Town (n) 1-0
Final v Aston Villa (n) 0-2
Team: Tracey; Aldridge, Jones, Morley, Peace, Allen, Davis, Garbett, T. Farmer, Higgins, J. Farmer.
Att: 2,000

1885-86
First round v Bournville (h) 18-1
(5 goals for Jones, 4 for Clarkson and 3 for Webster)
Second round v Wellington Town (a) 2-2
Replay v Wellington Town (h) 7-0
Third round v Walsall Town (h) 2-2
Replay v Walsall Town (a) 0-0
Second Replay v Walsall Town (h) 2-1
Fourth round – Swifts received a bye
Semi-final v Wolverhampton Wand's (n) 3-1
Final v West Bromwich Albion (n) 1-1
Replay v West Bromwich Albion (n) 0-1
Team (for both games): Wood; Aldridge, Profitt, Morley, Allen, Morris; Webster, Jenkyns, Jones, Higgins, Clarkson.
Scorer (first game): Jones.
Att: 4,250 (1st game); 10,500 (replay)
Note – All three games v Walsall Town played at The Chuckery

1886-87
First round v Great Bridge Unity (h) 3-0
Second round v Aston Unity (h) 5-4
Replay v Aston Unity (a) 0-1
(Replay ordered as original game finished in darkness!)

1887-88
First round v Wolverhampton Wand's (a) 1-1
Replay v Wolverhampton Wanderers (h) 0-1

Walsall Town

1880-81
First round v Aston Clifton (h) 6-0
Second round v Walsall White Star (h) 2-2
Replay v Walsall White Star (h) 4-1
Third round v Walsall Swifts (a) 0-3
(Both games v White Star played at Chuckery).

1881-82
First round v Wednesfield Rovers (h) 4-2
Second round v Walsall Alma Athletic (a) 6-1
Third round v Walsall Swifts (h) 1-2

1882-83
First round v Small Heath Alliance (h) 1-0
Second round v St George's (a) 2-6

1883-84
First round v West Bromwich All Saints (h) 5-1
Second round v Derby St Luke's (h) 4-1
Third round v Excelsior (a) 3-1
Fourth round v Stafford Road (n) 8-0
(4 goals for 'Shiner' Shaw in this tie)
Semi-final v Aston Villa (n) 1-2

1884-85
First round v Stourbridge Standard (a) 11-0
(4 goals in the game for Bradbury and there were also three own-goals.)
Second round v Aston Shakespeare (a) 9-1
(Hat-tricks for both Shaw and Hunter)
Third round v Excelsior (h) 10-0
(Another treble for 'Shiner' Shaw)
Fourth round v St George's (n) 4-1
Semi-final v Walsall Swifts (n) 0-1

1885-86
First round v Milton (a) walk over
Second round v Bloxwich (h) 17-0
(5 goals for Shaw and 4 for Cope)
Third round v Walsall Swifts (a) 2-2
Replay v Walsall Swifts (h) 0-0
Second Replay v Walsall Swifts (a) 1-2
** See note re Walsall Swifts*

1886-87
First round v Kidderminster Harriers (h) (walk over)
Second round v Nottingham Rangers (h) 4-2
Third round v Stoke (h) 2-2
Replay v Stoke (a) 0-2

1887-88
First round v Worcester Rovers (h) 7-2
Second round v Mitchell St George's (a) 0-5

Walsall Town Swifts

1888-89
First round v Notts Olympic (a) 6-4
Second round v Aston Villa (h) 1-2

1889-90
First round v Nottingham Forest (a) 1-0
Second round v Kidderminster Olympic (h) 4-0
Semi-final v West Bromwich Albion (n) 1-2

1890-91
First round v Warwick County (h) 2-2
Replay v Warwick County (h) 6-5 (a.e.t.)
Second Replay v Warwick County (a) 0-4
Second replay ordered after protest that extra-time took place in darkness. W T S fielded their reserve team for the second replay.

1891-92
First round v Stoke (h) 1-3
Both teams fielded their reserve sides for this tie.

1892-93
First round v Wolverhampton Wand's (h) 1-1
Replay v Wolverhampton Wanderers (a) 0-3

Walsall

1893-94
First round v West Bromwich Albion (h) 0-1

1894-95
First round v West Bromwich Albion (a) 2-6

1895-96
First round v Singers (Coventry) (h) 3-2
Second round v Sheffield United (h) 2-5

1896-97
First round v Leicester Fosse (h) 8-3
Second round v Brierley Hill Alliance (a) 3-3]
Replay v Brierley Hill Alliance (a) 4-1*
Semi-final v Derby County (n) 3-1
Final v Wolverhampton Wanderers (n) 2-1
Team: Bunyan; Peers, C. L. Aston; Holmes, Wilkes, Taggart, Horobin, J. Aston, Griffin, Copeland, Johnson.
Griffin, Horobin.
Att: 3,500
** Replay staged at Brierley Hill as Walsall refused to play extra-time in first game.*

1897-98
First round v Wrockwardine Wood (h) 11-0
(Hat-trick in this tie for Alf Griffin)
Second round v Small Heath (h) 2-1
Semi-final v Burton Wanderers (n) 4-0
Final v Wolverhampton Wanderers (n) 3-0
Team: Hawkins; Peers, C. L. Aston, Wilkes, Jenkyns, Taggart, Holmes, J. Aston, Griffin, Johnson, Devey.
J. Aston, Griffin, Johnson.
Att: 3,122.

1898-99
First round v Burton Swifts (a) 3-2
Second round – Walsall received a bye
Third round v Burslem Port Vale (n) 1-1
Replay v Burslem Port Vale (n) 0-2
Replay was abandoned after 65 minutes when Walsall refused to return to the field after a snowstorm. They were subsequently disqualified from the competition.

1899-1900
First round – Walsall received a bye
Second round v Wolverhampton Wanderers (a) 1-3

1900-01
First round v Burton Swifts (h) 5-1
Semi-final v Aston Villa (a) 2-6

1901-02
First round v Burton United (h) 2-3

1902-03
First round v Burton United (a) 3-1
Semi-final v West Bromwich Albion (h) 1-7

1903-04
Walsall did not enter the competition this season.

1904-05
Preliminary Round v Stourbridge (a) 0-5
Note: From 1905, Football League clubs were allowed to enter their reserve side in the competition and invariably fielded either a complete second XI or a mixed team, made up of mainly reserve-team players.

Walsall did, however, progress to the semi-final stage on the following occasions:

1921-22
Fifth round v Nuneaton (h) 3-3
Reid, Franklin 2
Att: 2,082
Replay v Nuneaton (a) 4-0
Reid 3, Butler
Att: 3,960
Semi-final v Birmingham Reserves (a) 1-2
Reid
Att: 3,135

1923-24
(Walsall received a bye in first round)
Semi-final v Aston Villa Reserves (h) 0-1
Att: 1,822

Attendance Facts & Figures

The record crowd for a Walsall home game is that of 25,453 for the visit of Newcastle United to Fellows Park for a Second Division fixture on 29 August 1961.

This is how the Saddlers record home attendance (in League and Cup competition) has been broken down the years (over 10,000):

10,627	v Lincoln City	Division Three N	3 September 1921
15,340	v Bradford City	FA Cup Round 1	7 January 1922
16,607	v Corinthians	FA Cup Round 3	8 January 1927
19,982	v Newcastle Utd	FA Cup Round 3	11 January 1936
20,383	v Notts County	Division Three S	31 January 1948
21,811	v Port Vale	FA Cup Round 3	7 January 1956
25,453	v Newcastle Utd	Division Two	29 August 1961

The best Fourth Division crowd at Fellows Park was 15,403 v Carlisle United, 10 September 1959.

The top League/Littlewoods/Milk/Rumbelows Cup gate was 19,591 v Liverpool, Semi-final, 2nd leg, 14 February 1984.

The highest crowd for an Associate Members/Freight Rover/Sherpa Van/Leyland DAF Cup game was 4,106 v Colchester United (FRT) 12 March 1985.

The lowest home League gate Walsall have played in front of over the years, is 500 v Darwen (Division Two), 2 September 1893 at The Chuckery.

The lowest League crowd at Fellows Park was 1,047 v Halifax Town (Division Three North) on 25 January 1926.

And the lowest at Bescot Stadium has been that of just 2,045 v Maidstone United (Division Four), on 30 March 1992.

Only 200 supporters saw Walsall's home Third Division South Cup-tie v Aldershot in October 1937.

On a bitterly cold, snowy day in January 1895, just 23 paying spectators witnessed a Staffordshire Cup-tie between the Saddlers and Burton – the lowest-ever turnout for a home first-team game in the history of the club.

Just 70 fans paid to watch Walsall's home Southern League game against Pontypridd on 30 April 1912 – the last in this competition for the Saddlers.

The best two League crowds Walsall have ever played in front of were at Ninian Park, Cardiff, in April 1947, when 45,234 fans saw the Welsh side win 3-0 in Division Three South and then at Villa Park in March 1972 when 45,953 spectators saw a Third Division match end goalless.

The top crowd in all games to see the Saddlers was that of 74,626 at Villa Park for that FA Cup-tie of January 1930 when Aston Villa won 3-1. A crowd of 48,870 witnessed the Manchester United-Walsall FA Cup clash at Old Trafford in January 1977; 45,462 saw the Everton-Walsall FA Cup-tie at Goodison Park in February 1972 and the top League Cup gate was at The Hawthorns in September 1965 when 41,188 fans saw the Albion win 3-1.

Apart from those attendances listed previously, here are the other instances where Walsall's home crowd has exceeded 18,000:

24,045	v Fulham	FA Cup Round 4 R	30 January 1962
21,066	v Liverpool	League Cup Rd 4	17 February 1968
20,585	v Peterborough	FA Cup Round 2	5 December 1959
19,998	v Newcastle Utd	FA Cup Rd 4	24 January 1975
19,591	v Liverpool	Milk Cup SF 2L	14 February 1984
19,589	v Notts County	Division Three S	18 March 1950
19,203	v Aston Villa	Division Three	2 January 1971
18,786	v Leyton Orient	Division Three S	20 August 1955
18,799	v Tottenham H	FA Cup Round 3	4 January 1969
18,689	v Southampton	Division Two	19 September 1961
18,420	v Sunderland	Division Two	19 August 1961
18,394	v Ipswich Town	Division Three S	4 October 1947

18,370	v Liverpool	FA Cup Round 3	11 January 1947
18,311	v Shrewsbury T	FA Cup Round 1	20 November 1954
18,213	v Southend Utd	Division Three S	6 September 1947
18,153	v Bournemouth	Division Three S	14 February 1948
18,105	v Manchester U	FA Cup Rd 3R	7 January 1975
18,026	v Torquay Utd	Division Three S	28 August 1948
18,004	v Watford	Division Three S	8 November 1947

Walsall's best seasonal average home attendances came during the period 1959 to 1962 when they won promotion from the Fourth to the Second Division in successive campaigns. In 1959-60 the average crowd at Fellows Park (for a League game) was 12,045; in 1960-61 it was 10,670, and in 1961-62 the average was 12,711.

In contrast Walsall's average home crowds in their two Southern League seasons of 1910-11 and 1911-12 were 741 and 288 respectively – the latter the lowest in the club's history (for first-team football).

In the early to middle 1950s Walsall averaged around 11,000 at home games – exceptionally good considering they had three First Division teams – Aston Villa, West Brom and Wolves – on their doorstep and all doing very well.

This is a breakdown of Walsall's records in all the competitions they have played in at first-team level

Competition	*P*	*W*	*D*	*L*	*F*	*A*
Football League	3,386	1,215	809	1,362	4,965	5,214
Play-offs	7	3	1	3	14	14
FA Cup	290	139	52	99	477	385
Football League Cup	113	42	22	49	144	168
Division Three N Cup	2	1	0	1	1	2
Division Three S Cup	5	1	1	3	6	13
Associate Members Cup	2	1	0	1	3	4
Freight Rover Trophy	9	4	0	5	12	15
Sherpa Van Trophy	3	1	1	1	6	5
Leyland DAF Cup	8	3	2	3	14	9
Simod Cup	1	0	0	1	2	4
Autoglass Trophy	9	3	1	5	7	14
Auto Windscreen Shield	18	8	4	6	33	23
Midland Association	14	8	2	4	28	30
Southern League	48	21	5	22	81	82
Birmingham League	476	201	84	191	779	827
Midland League	88	43	20	25	195	131
Football Alliance	66	23	9	34	111	179
Walsall District League	18	8	4	6	45	29
Wartime (1939-46)	261	90	55	116	494	545
Totals	4,824	1,815	1,072	1,937	7417	7,693

Not included are the many local competitions the Saddlers played in during the club's early years (i.e. the Staffordshire, Birmingham Senior, Wednesbury Charity, Lord Mayor of Birmingham and Walsall & District Cup tournaments).

The FA Cup-ties played in 1945-46 have not been included in wartime statistics. The Football League Cup competition has been played for under the following guises: Milk Cup from 1982, Littlewoods Cup from 1986 and the Rumbelows Cup from 1990. In 1992 it became the Coca-Cola Cup, followed by the Worthington Cup in 1998.

Walsall's seasonal records in the Football Alliance, Birmingham League, Midland League, Southern League and Walsall & District League

Midland Association

Season	*P*	*W*	*D*	*L*	*F*	*A*	*Pts*	*Pos*
1888-89	14	8	2	4	28	30	18	4th

Football Alliance

Season	*P*	*W*	*D*	*L*	*F*	*A*	*Pts*	*Pos*
1889-90	22	8	3	11	44	59	19	9th
1890-91	22	9	3	10	34	61	21	7th
1891-92	22	6	3	13	33	59	15	11th
Totals	66	23	9	34	111	179	55	

Midland League

Season	*P*	*W*	*D*	*L*	*F*	*A*	*Pts*	*Pos*
1895-96	28	17	6	5	92	48	40	3rd
1901-02	28	14	7	7	51	35	35	5th
1902-03	32	12	7	13	52	48	31	8th
Totals	88	43	20	25	195	131	106	

Birmingham League

Season	*P*	*W*	*D*	*L*	*F*	*A*	*Pts*	*Pos*
1903-04	34	11	7	16	45	65	29	13th
1904-05	34	11	6	17	44	77	28	14th
1905-06	34	7	6	21	41	90	20	16th
1906-07	34	14	4	16	58	78	32	13th
1907-08	34	15	3	16	67	72	33	10th
1908-09	34	10	8	16	47	56	28	15th
1909-10	34	18	7	9	66	44	43	5th
1910-11	34	20	6	8	60	44	46	3rd
1911-12	34	17	7	10	56	34	41	4th
1912-13	34	15	5	14	60	54	35	7th
1913-14	34	13	8	13	48	61	34	10th
1914-15	34	21	5	8	66	44	47	3rd
1919-20	34	11	6	17	53	62	28	16th
1920-21	34	18	6	10	68	46	42	5th
Totals	476	201	84	191	779	827	486	

Southern League

Season	*P*	*W*	*D*	*L*	*F*	*A*	*Pts*	*Pos*
1910-11	22	7	4	11	37	41	18	9th
1911-12	26	14	1	13	44	41	29	6th
Totals	48	21	5	22	81	82	47	

Walsall & District League

Season	*P*	*W*	*D*	*L*	*F*	*A*	*Pts*	*Pos*
1915-16	18	8	4	6	45	29	20	5th

Walsall in Wartime

1915-19 & 1939-46

Though hostilities had broken out in August 1914, the 1914-15 season was completed more or less as normal as far as Walsall were concerned, and the Saddlers in fact finished third in the Birmingham League behind the reserve teams of both Birmingham and West Bromwich Albion, so that they actually won the Keys Cup which was awarded to the non-League side finishing highest in the competition. The fact that many men had joined the forces and others had been engaged on military work on Saturday afternoons had an adverse effect on attendances, however, and a loss of £240 on the season was sustained with gate receipts down from £1,800 to just over £1,000. The situation would have been worse financially but for the players taking a wage cut!

The following close season was a bad one for Walsall with the club being fined five guineas for playing David Williams, a registered player of Stourbridge, under the name of E. G. Williams against West Bromwich Albion. There was also the announcement that the Birmingham League would not operate in 1915-16. A Walsall and District Combination was formed, however, and the Saddlers joined it together with some pretty useful teams, such as Walsall Wood, Darlaston, Bloxwich and Willenhall Pickwick.

Walsall did reasonably well and finished in fifth place with eight wins and four draws from their 18 matches, scoring 45 goals and conceding 29 for a points total of 20.

Cannock were beaten twice by the same score, 7-1, and Wednesbury Old Park were defeated 61 at home and 5-1 away.

Sid Perry top scored with 11 goals, followed by three players all with five: Clark, Ted Collins and Crossley. Collins was the Wolves full-back who guested for the Saddlers and in the final game of the season v Cannock at home he performed at centre-forward and scored five times, three coming from powerhouse headers from set pieces.

Welsh international goalkeeper Teddy Peers also guested for the Saddlers (from Wolves) in 1915-16 as did Jim Hill, who had been at Molineux a few years earlier.

There is no record anywhere of Walsall playing any further competitive matches after May 1916 until July 1919 when on the 12 of that month, they entertained Willenhall Pickwick in a friendly match at Hillary Street. The game ended 1-1 and during the course of events directors of the club, including Mr Alf Medlam, asked the supporters to take up shares so that the club could be put on a more solid foundation for the future. The club managed to purchase the Hillary Street ground in time for the start of the 1919-20 season, which kicked-off on 30 August with the visit of Shrewsbury Town in a Birmingham League fixture.

For this game just one player was in the Saddlers line-up who had actually appeared in the club's last pre-war game v Shrewsbury Town in April 1915, before the Birmingham League programme was suspended. He was outside-right Harry Bates.

Some 20 years later it was a much more difficult time for clubs up and down the country as World War Two began.

In early August 1939, when the players dutifully reported back to their respective clubs for pre-season training, the atmosphere was one of apprehension and uncertainty.

Banner headlines in all the newspapers clearly predicted 'Football to go if war comes'.

War was imminent, and subsequently, on 21 August, the FA decided to forego Rule 33 which stated that 'no player serving in His Majesty's Forces could be registered as a professional footballer' thus anticipating quite clearly that the game would suffer in due course.

However, when the League programme for that ill-fated 1939-40 season commenced five days later over 600,000 supporters attended the 44 matches with Walsall drawing a 6,000 crowd away to Southend United (lost 3-2).

Following the normal series of midweek games when Walsall drew 0-0 at Torquay, Friday, 1 September saw the start of the evacuation of children from London, but it was agreed that the scheduled Saturday afternoon fixtures should go ahead as planned – and they did with the Saddlers winning 1-0 at home to Queen's Park Rangers, Charlie Bulger scoring the match-winner in front of a 5,000 crowd.

On the same day the Germans invaded Poland and consequently on the Sunday morning (3 September) it was universally declared that Britain was at War and competitive football up and down the country came to a halt... for the time being.

There was an immediate ban on the assembly of crowds until further notice, yet within 48 hours, the Football League president, Mr W. C. Cuff, announced publicly that all clubs should retain their players under contract to stand by as a result of the Government's order to close all places of entertainment (i.e. soccer grounds).

The three League games played at the start of the season were declared null and void. Thus, the general flow of League and Cup football in Britain was seriously disrupted by the hostilities and in consequence several players had their respective careers virtually ruined by the war in Europe.

Surprisingly though, after a relatively short interval, competitive games recommenced as all the League clubs were divided systematically into Regional Leagues.

Walsall in 1939-40 were placed in the Midland Regional League with the likes of West Brom, Wolves, Birmingham and Leicester City. And indeed their first match in this section was at Leicester on 21 October. But it was one to forget as Walsall crashed 6-1 in front of a 1,600 crowd.

It had been anticipated that war should have broken out a good twelve months earlier and a lot of footballers had, in fact, joined the Territorial Army or other National Service organisations during 1938-39 and in April 1939 the FA issued a circular encouraging players to display a patriotic example to the youth of the nation and 'sign up'. Several opted for the Terriers and Militia while others preferred to wear totally different uniforms.

As the days ticked by more reservists were called up, and it was duly recorded at the Football League Management Committee meeting in July 1939 that 'there is no onus on clubs to pay players called up for Military Service during the period of Military Training. If, however, arrangements can be made with the Military Authorities for the players' services on match days, their liability would arise during such week (or weeks) as the players are available for the club.'

During this same AGM Walsall were re-elected to the Football League (South) receiving a total of 35 votes.

The watering of pitches (Fellows Park included) was officially banned before November and after February and it was also made law for players to wear numbered shirts for the very first time.

Going back to Regional League Football in season 1939-40, in the interests of public safety there was a limit put on attendances. This was initially set at 8,000, or half of the capacity of the ground, which ever was the less.

The League also sanctioned a payment of 30 shillings (£1.50) per match to each player for seasons 1939-40 to 1942-43 inclusive. In 1943-44 the amount was increased to £2.00 per man and by 1945-46 players were receiving £4.00 each time they took the field.

Competition throughout the 1939-46

period was excellent – and to a certain extent very well supported.

Several players guested for various clubs as most of them were based at camps well away from their own clubs and wanted to play as much football as they possibly could.

Walsall participated in each of the seven seasons of World War Two.

They fulfilled a total of 245 matches and were undefeated in 134 of them, scoring over 450 goals.

Unfortunately the Saddlers finished bottom of the Midlands Regional League in 1939-40 with just 19 points out of a total of 56. Their best win of the season came in the League Cup: 6-0 v Port Vale at home – but they crashed 8-1 and 7-2 to Birmingham and WBA respectively in the Regional League competition. Gilbert Alsop top-scored this term with 28 goals.

In 1940-41 they ended up in a higher League position than neighbours West Bromwich Albion and Birmingham, and also finished above Leicester City, Northampton Town, Nottingham Forest, Notts County and Stoke City in the League South, and only Coventry City did better in the table overall, although the Highfield Road club played only 10 games!

Walsall's best win was a thrilling 11-4 victory over Notts County at Fellows Park in November when both Jack Rowley and Ted Vinall hit 4 goals apiece. They also beat neighbours West Brom 10-3 on the last day of the season with Rowley again cracking in a four-timer. Rowley netted 23 goals this term including four 4's.

Walsall, in fact, scored over 100 goals during this campaign and were beaten by Leicester City (2-0) in the Midland Cup Final when they fielded this team: Biddlestone; Shelton, Male, Wood, Morgan, Godfrey, Hancocks, Brown, Thayne, Starling, Beesley. The attendance at Filbert Street was 6,562.

Nothing outstanding was achieved in 1941-42, Walsall's best wins coming at home to Nottingham Forest in mid-October (8-2) and at Swansea in mid-September (7-4). They lost 60 at Leicester and 8-0 at Stoke.

In 1942-43, the Saddlers struggled in the second phase of the Football League North competition, eventually finishing third from bottom with a mere 8 points out of 32. A 6-0 win over Northampton Town (home) was their best result, while their heaviest defeat came at Stoke, a week before Christmas when they crashed 7-1.

In 1943-44 the Saddlers fared no better, dropping down a place in the final table of the League North Championship, recording the same number of points (12) as the bottom club, Tranmere Rovers, and also Wolves, who finished a place above them. Two heavy defeats this term were suffered at West Bromwich Albion (7-1) and Birmingham (5-0).

There came another frustrating season in 1944-45, Walsall gaining nothing out of either the League or Cup competitions. They had to settle for a place third from bottom of the final League table (Second Championship).

Perhaps the best game of this campaign was against Coventry City at Fellows Park in January when the Saddlers won 6-5.

In the transitional season of 1945-46, the Saddlers at last gave their diehard supporters something to cheer about when they reached the Final of the League South Cup, only to lose 1-0 to Bournemouth at Stamford Bridge where the gate topped 19,700.

Walsall put out this team against the Cherries: Lewis; Methley, Shelton, Crutchley, Foulkes, Newman, Hancocks, Talbot, Mullard, Wilshaw, Alsop.

They also put on some exciting home performances in the Third Division South (North) beating Southend United 6-0 (when Fred Kelly scored 4) and Clapton Orient 5-3 (a hat-trick here for Doug Darby).

Shrewsbury Town knocked the Saddlers out of the FA Cup, winning a first round tie 6-4 on aggregate.

The up-and-coming Johnny Hancocks top-scored this season with 14 goals.

Among the guest players who turned out for the Saddlers during the hostilities were internationals 'Sandy' McNab (Scotland and WBA), Ivor Powell (Aston Villa and Wales) and the England duo of W. G. Richardson (WBA) and Ronnie Starling (ex-Sheffield Wednesday, then Aston Villa).

Also lining up for Walsall were Scottish inside-forward Jack Beattie (ex-Birmingham and Wolves, then of Grimsby), former Walsall goalkeeper Fred Biddlestone with his Aston Villa co-star George Edwards, full-back George Male of Arsenal, Manchester United's ace marksman Jack Rowley, another goal man Jack Vinall (ex-Norwich City and Luton), Ike Clarke, George Dudley, Charlie Evans, Sammy Heaselgrave, Harry Lowery, Bobby Newsome and Jack Sankey (all from West Bromwich Albion) and Dennis Wilshaw (Wolves), later to become an England star who was taken on loan by the Saddlers in 1945-46.

Summary of Walsall's Wartime matches

Season 1915-16							
Competition	*Pos*	*P*	*W*	*D*	*L*	*F*	*A*
Walsall/District League	5th	18	8	4	6	45	29
Season 1939-40							
Competition	*Pos*	*P*	*W*	*D*	*L*	*F*	*A*
Division Three South	-	3	1	1	1	3	3
Regional League	8th	28	7	5	16	51	83
League Cup	-	4	2	1	1	10	5
Totals	-	35	10	7	18	64	91
Season 1940-41							
Competition	*Pos*	*P*	*W*	*D*	*L*	*F*	*A*
Regional League	12th	24	9	6	9	78	62
Midland Cup	-	8	5	1	2	22	18
League Cup	-	2	1	0	1	4	10
Totals	-	34	15	7	12	104	90
Season 1941-42							
Competition	*Pos*	*P*	*W*	*D*	*L*	*F*	*A*
League (South)	7th	21	11	1	9	54	50
League Cup	-	10	2	0	8	9	30
Totals	-	31	13	1	17	63	80
Season 1942-43							
Competition	*Pos*	*P*	*W*	*D*	*L*	*F*	*A*
League (North) 1st	24th	24	7	5	12	42	48
League (North) 2nd	52nd	10	2	2	6	13	18
Totals	-	34	9	7	18	55	66
Season 1943-44							
Competition	*Pos*	*P*	*W*	*D*	*L*	*F*	*A*
League (North)	25th	25	6	10	9	33	44
League (North) Cup	-	10	2	3	5	11	22
Totals	-	35	8	13	14	44	66
Season 1944-45							
Competition	*Pos*	*P*	*W*	*D*	*L*	*F*	*A*
League (North)	32nd	25	7	7	11	37	39
League (North) Cup	-	11	3	2	6	14	22
Totals	-	36	10	9	17	51	61
Season 1945-46							
Competition	*Pos*	*P*	*W*	*D*	*L*	*F*	*A*
FA Cup	-	2	1	0	1	4	6
League (South)	9th	20	6	3	11	31	42
Division Three S Cup	-	18	11	4	3	37	20
Totals	-	40	18	7	15	72	68

Overall Totals: 1915-16 & 1939-46

P	*W*	*D*	*L*	*F*	*A*
263	91	55	117	498	551

International Saddlers

Ten players have been capped at full international level by their country whilst they were associated with Walsall (Town and Swifts included).

England

Aldridge, Albert James (full-back) (1) v Ireland 1888-89.
Jones, Alfred (full-back) (3) v Scotland, Wales 1881-82, v Scotland 1882-83.

Ireland

Taggart, John (Jack) (wing-half) (1) v Wales 1898-99.

Republic of Ireland

Dennehy, Jeremiah (forward) (2) v Poland (sub) 1975-76, Poland (sub) 1976-77.
Griffith, Robert (winger) (1) 1934-35 v Hungary.
Kearns, Michael (goalkeeper) (15) v Poland (sub), Uruguay, Chile 1973-74, v Norway, Poland 1975-76, v England, Turkey, France (2), Spain, Bulgaria 1976-77, v Norway, Denmark 1977-78, v Northern Ireland, England 1978-79.
Kelly, David T. (striker) (3) v Italy, Romania, Yugoslavia 1987-88.
O'Brien, Michael (defender) (1) v Belgium 1928-29.

Wales

Jenkyns, Caesar, Augustus, Llewellyn (centre-half) (2) v Scotland, England 1897-98.
John, W. Roy (goalkeeper) (1) v Northern Ireland 1930-31.

Sierra Leone

Keister, John (midfield) (3)

Bermuda

Lightbourne, Kyle (striker)

Other Representative Honours

(gained whilst with Walsall)

England Youth

Allner, Graham 1967-68, **Giles, Philip** 1947-48, **Sinnott, Lee** 1982-83.

Football League XI

Morgan, Llewellyn 1941-42.

FA XI

Williams, Bert F. 1944-45.

RAF

Williams, Bert F. (5) 1941-42, 1944-45, **Strong, James** 1943-44.

Western Command

Hancocks, Johnny 1944-45.

Birmingham Association

Aldridge, A. J., Morely, J., Morris, G., Shaw, C. S., 1888-89.

Staffordshire County FA

Aldridge, A. J., Morely, J., Shaw, C. S., 1888-89.

Players who gained full international caps either before or after playing for Walsall

England

Aldridge, A. J. (West Bromwich Albion) (1) 1887-88.
Baugh, R. (Stafford Rd & Wolverton W) (2) 1885-86/1889-90.
Bowser, S. (West Bromwich Albion) (1) 1919-20.
Carter, J. H. (West Bromwich Albion) (3) 1925-26/1928-29.
Clarke, A. J. (Leeds United) (19) 1969-70/1975-76.
Crowe, C. (Wolverhampton Wanderers) (1) 1962-63.
Fairhurst, D. L. (Newcastle United) (1) 1933-34.
Hancocks, J. (Wolverhampton Wanderers) (3) 1948-49/1950-51.
Jones, A. (Great Lever) (1) 1882-83.
Lofthouse, J. M. (Blackburn Rovers & Accrington Stanley) **(7)** 1884-85/1888-89.
Olney, B. A. (Aston Villa) (2) 1927-28.
Parkes, P. B. (QPR) (1) 1973-74.
Rawlings, A. (Preston North End) (1) 1920-21.
Smith, T. (Birmingham City) (2) 1959-60.
Statham, D. J. (West Bromwich Albion) (3) 1982-83.
Thomson, R. A. (Wolverhampton Wanderers) (8) 1964-65.
Wilkes, A. (Aston Villa) (5) 1901-02.
Williams, B. F. (Wolverhampton Wanderers) (24) 1948-49/1955-56.
Wilshaw, D. J. (Wolverhampton Wanderers) (12) 1953-54/1956-57.
Wood, H. (Wolverhampton Wanderers) (3) 1889-90/1895-96.

Scotland

Bremner, D. G. (Hibernian) (1) 1975-76.
Fraser, D. M. (West Bromwich Albion) (2) 1967-68/1968-69.
Robertson, J. G. (Tottenham Hotspur) (1) 1964-65.

Northern Ireland

Bambrick, J. (Linfield and Chelsea) (11) 1928-29/1937-38.
Connor, M. J. J. (Woolwich Arsenal, Brentford, Fulham) (3) 1902-03/1903-04.
McKnight, A. (Celtic and West Ham United) (10) 1987-88/1989-90.
O'Brien, M. T. (QPR, Leicester, Hull and Derby County) (10) 1920-21/1926-27.
Reid, G. H. (Cardiff City) (1) 1922-23.
Renneville, W. T. (Leyton and Aston Villa) (4) 1910-11/1911-12.
Sloan, D. (Oxford United) (2) 1968-69/1970-71.
Walsh, D. J. (West Bromwich Albion) (9) 1946-47/1949-50.
Wilson, K. (Ipswich Town, Chelsea, Notts County) (40) 1987-88/1993-94.

Republic of Ireland

Dennehy, J. (Cork Hibs and Nottingham Forest) (11) 1971-72/1974-75.
Grealish, A. (Leyton Orient, Luton Town, Brighton & Hove Albion, West Bromwich Albion) (44) 1975-76/1985-86.
Kearns, M. (Oxford Utd and Wolverhampton Wanderers) (3) 1969-70/1979-80.
Kelly, D. T. (West Ham, Leicester and Newcastle United) (10) 1988-89/1992-93.
Macken, A. (Derby County) (1) 1976-77.
Muldoon, T. (Aston Villa) (1) 1926-27.
O'Brien, M. T. (Derby County, Norwich City and Watford) (4) 1926-27/1931-32.

Walsh, D. J. (West Bromwich Albion and Aston Villa) (20) 1945-46/1953-54.

Wales

Dearson, D. J. (Birmingham) (3) 1938-39.
Green, A. W. (Aston Villa, Notts County and Nottingham Forest) (8) 1900-01/1907-08.
Hewitt, R. (Cardiff City) (5) 1957-58.
Jenkyns, C. A. L. (Small Heath, Arsenal, Newton Heath) (6) 1891-92/1896-97.
John, W. R. (Stoke, Preston North End, Sheffield United and Swansea) (13) 1932-33/1938-39.
Mays, A. W. (Wrexham) (1) 1928-29.
Parry, E. (Liverpool) (5) 1921-22/1925-26.
Price, I. H. (Aston Villa, Burton United and Wrexham) (5) 1906-07/1908-09.
Pritchard, H. K. (Bristol City) (1) 1984-85.
Richards, D. T. (Wolverhampton Wanderers, Brentford and Birmingham) (21) 1930-31/1938-39.
Williams, G. O. (Wrexham) (1) 1906-07.

Australia

Ollerenshaw, S. (2) 1991-92.

Cameroon

Ntamark, C. (Borehamwood) (6) 1989-90/1990-91.

Irish Free State
(amateur)

Leckie, J. T. (Raith Rovers, Port Vale and Cardiff City) (4) 1931-33/1935-36.

International Managers

Nine managers gained full international recognition before taking charge of Walsall

England

Allen, R. 1951-52/1954-55.
Buckley, Major F. C. 1913-14.
Hibbs, H. E. 1929-30/1935-36.

Denmark

Sorensen, J. 1973-74/1977-78.

Northern Ireland

Nicholl, C. 1975-76/1984-85.

Scotland

Fraser, D. M. 1967-68/1968-69.
Mackay, D. M. 1956-57/1965-66.
Martin, N. 1964-65/1965-66.
Wilson, A. N. 1919-20/1922-23.

Under-21 International at Bescot Stadium

Monday, 20 May 1991
England 2 Switzerland 1

This was the first senior representative match played on a Walsall ground, and a crowd of 10,628 saw the action.

The game itself was not a classic, but both teams played some inventive football, with England just about deserving their success.

The Swiss took the lead on nine minutes when Frederic Chassot headed home from six yards after England's defence had failed to clear Ciriaco Storza's corner. But inspired from midfield by West Ham's Ian Bishop and Carlton Palmer of Sheffield Wednesday, England gradually got back into the game and they duly equalised on 28 minutes when Palmer's team-mate at Hillsborough, David Hirst, drove home from close range after a free-kick from King's (another Wednesday player) had been nodded on by Palmer.

Soon afterwards Hirst was there again to make it 2-1, his bullet header from Dale Gordon's cross giving 'keeper Walker no chance.

Graham Le Saux went close to increasing that lead before half-time and although there was very little goalmouth action after the break, it was England who came closest to scoring again when Hirst (twice) and Deane had shots saved by the Swiss 'keeper.

England: Martyn (Crystal Palace); Joseph (Wimbledon), King (Sheffield Wednesday), Bishop (West Ham United), Elliott (Celtic), Barrett (Oldham), Gordon (Norwich), Hirst (Sheffield Wednesday), Deane (Sheffield United), Palmer (Sheffield Wednesday), Le Saux (Chelsea). Subs: Curle (Wimbledon, for Joseph), Ebbrell (Everton, for Bishop), Slater (West Ham United, for Gordon).

Switzerland: Walker; Gamperle, Heldman, Gambino, Fischer, Sylvestre, Storza, Penzavalli, Douglas, Nadig, Chassot. Subs: Corminboeuf (for Walker), Studer (for Gambino), Isabella (for Penzavalli), Gion (for Nadig), Studer (for Chassot).

Hat-trick Heroes

Here is a detailed list of all the hat-tricks scored by Walsall players at competitive level down the years:

1883-84
W. Bird (4) v Calthorpe (a) FA Cup

1888-89
S. Holmes (4) v Derby St Lukes (h) Midland Association
S. Holmes (3) v Derby Junction (h) Midland Association

1889-90
G. Tapper (3) v Darwen (h) Football Alliance

1890-91
F. Whittick (4) v Warmley (a) FA Cup

1891-92
S. Holmes (3) v Wednesbury Old Athletic (h) FA Cup

1893-94
S. Holmes (3) v Stourbridge (a) FA Cup
W. McWhinnie (3) v Ardwick (h) League Division Two

1895-96
W. Taylor (3) v Matlock (h) Midland League
S. Holmes (3) v Newark (h) Midland League
J. Aston (3) v Doncaster Rovers (h) Midland League
A. Brocksopp (3) v Kettering (h) Midland League

1896-97
A. Wilkes (3) v Arsenal (h) League Division Two
T. Johnson (4) v Dresden United (h) FA Cup
G. Johnson (3) v Dresden United (h) FA Cup
A. Griffin (3) v Dresden United (h) FA Cup

1897-98
S. Holmes (3) v Blackpool (h) League Division Two

1898-99
A. Dean (3) v Gainsborough Town (h) League Division Two
T. Vail (3) v Blackpool (h) League Division Two
J. Aston (4) v Darwen (h) League Division Two
A. Dean (3) v Darwen (h) League Division Two
A. Griffith (3) v Burton Swifts (h) League Division Two

1899-1900
J. Moftart (3) v Luton Town (h) League Division Two
W. McAuley (3) v Luton Town (h) League Division Two

1900-01
A. Dean (5) v Wellington Town (h) FA Cup

1901-02
A. Green (3) v Coalville Town (h) Midland League

1904-05
J. Ellard (3) v Small Heath Res (h) Birmingham League

1908-09
E. Newman (3) v Dudley Town (a) Birmingham League

1909-10
J. Crump (3) v Stourbridge (a) Birmingham League
J. Lyon (3) v Shrewsbury Town (h) Birmingham League

1910-11
W. Robinson (3) v Wellington Town (h) Birmingham League

1911-12
W. Izon (3) v Stourbridge (h) Birmingham League
J. Bird (3) v Ton Pentre (h) Southern League
W. Freeman (4) v Treharris (h) Southern League
J. Stanton (4) v Chesham (h) Southern League

1912-13
J. Davies (4) v Stoke reserves (h) Birmingham League
A. Baddeley (3) v Worcester City (h) Birmingham League

1913-14
A. Green (3) v Birmingham res (h) Birmingham League
C. Crossley (3) v Darlaston (a) Birmingham League
M. Lane (3) v Wolverhampton res (h) Birmingham League

1914-15
A. Campey (3) v Coventry City res (h) Birmingham League
A. Campey (3) v Wellington Town (h) Birmingham League
A. Campey (3) v Willenhall S (h) Birmingham League
A. Campey (3) v Hednesford Town (h) FA Cup
A. Campey (5) v Cradley St Lukes (h) FA Cup

1915-16
S. Perry (3) v Wednesbury OP (h)Walsall & District League
T. Clark (3) v Cannock (a) Walsall & District League
E. Collins (5) v Cannock (h) Walsall & District League

1919-20
G. Benton (3) v Worcester City (h) FA Cup

1920-21
E. Edwards (3) v Darlaston (h) Birmingham League
H. Leedham (3) v Brierley Hill All (h) Birmingham League

1921-22
J. Franklin (4) v Ashington (h) League Division Three North
G. Reid (3) v Accrington Stanley (h) League Division Three North

1922-23
G. Reid (3) v Wellington St George's (a) FA Cup

1926-27
H. White (3) v Rochdale (a) League Division Three North
H. White (3) v Accrington Stanley (a) League Division Three North

1927-28
M. Lane (4) v Gillingham (h) League Division Three South
M. Lane (3) v Brentford (h) League Division Three South
M. Lane (3) v Luton Town (h) League Division Three South
J. Walker (3) v Exeter City (h) League Division Three South

1928-29
M. Lane (3) v Crystal Palace (h) League Division Three South
N. Thompson (3) v Exeter City (h) League Division Three South

1929-30
A. Walters (3) v Merthyr Town (h) League Division Three South
J. Eyres (3) v Torquay United (h) League Division Three South
A Walters (3) v Newport County (a) FA Cup

1930-31
J. Cooper (3) v Clapton Orient (h) League Division Three South
J. Cooper (3) v Norwich City (h) League Division Three South
J. Barnes (3) v Norwich City (h) League Division Three South
J. Eyres (3) v Thames (h) League Division Three South
A. Mays (3) v Exeter City (a) League Division Three South
J. Eyres (3) v Brighton & HA (a) League Division Three South
J. Cooper (3) v Newport County (h) FA Cup

1931-32
G. Alsop (3) v Halifax Town (h) League Division Three North
G. Alsop (3) v Accrington Stanley (h) League Division Three North

1932-33
G. Alsop (4) v Mansfield Town (h) League Division Three North
W. Coward (3) v Southport (h) League Division Three North

1933-34
G. Alsop (4) v Chester (h) League Division Three North
G. Alsop (3) v Accrington Stanley (h) League Division Three North
F. Lee (3) v Barrow (a) League Division Three North
G. Alsop (4) v Hartlepool United (h) League Division Three North

1934-35
G. Alsop (3) v Accrington Stanley (h) League Division Three North
G. Alsop (4) v Barrow (h) League Division Three North
G. Alsop (4) v Carlisle United (a) League Division Three North
G. Alsop (3) v New Brighton (h) League Division Three North
G. Alsop (3) v Accrington Stanley (a) League Division Three North
G. Alsop (3) v Lincoln City (a) League Division Three North Cup

1935-36
G. Alsop (3) v Darlington (h) League Division Three North
W. Evans (5) v Mansfield Town (h) League Division Three North
J. Collins (4) v York City (h) League Division Three North
W. Evans (3) v Hartlepool United (h) League Division Three North
W. Evans (3) v Barrow (h) League Division Three North

1936-37
W. Dunderdale (3) v Watford (h) League Division Three South
T. Bate (3) v Swindon Town (h) League Division Three South
W. Evans (3) v Scunthorpe United (h) FA Cup

1938-39
G. Alsop (4) v Torquay United (h) League Division Three South
G. Alsop (3) v Swindon Town (a) League Division Three South
G. Alsop (3) v Bristol City (h) League Division Three South
G. Alsop (4) v Swindon Town (h) League Division Three South
J. Bambrick (3) v Carlisle United (h) FA Cup
G. Alsop (4) v Notts County (h) FA Cup

1939-40
W. Brown (3) v Luton Town (h) Midland Regional League
G. Alsop (3) v Luton Town (h) Midland Regional League
G. Alsop (3) v Wolverampton Wanderers (a) Midland Regional League
G. Alsop (3) v Mansfield Town (h) Football League Jubilee

1940-41
J. Rowley (4) v Notts County (h) Regional League South
E. J. Vinall (4) v Notts County (h) Regional League South
J. Rowley (4) v Birmingham (h) Regional League South
E. J. Vinall (3) v Stoke City (h) Regional League South
J. Rowley (4) v Nottingham Forest (h) Regional League South
J. Rowley (4) v West Bromwich A (h) Regional League South

1941-42
E. J. Vinall (3) v Bristol City (h) Football League South

1942-43
H. Nicholls (3) v Stoke City (h) League North 2nd Comp.

1943-44
G. Hinsley (3) v West Bromwich A (a) Football League North
G. Dudley (3) v Coventry City (h) Football League Cup

1944-45
G. Alsop (4) v Mansfield Town (h) Football League North

1945-46
D. Darby (3) v Clapton Orient (h) League Division Three (S/N)
F. Kelly (4) v Southend United (h) League Division Three (S/N)
A. Mullard (3) v Northampton Town (h) League Division Three (S/N) Cup

1946-47
D. Wilshaw (3) v Northampton Town (a) League Division Three South
A. Mullard (3) v Northampton Town (a) League Division Three South

1947-48
D. Massart (3) v Exeter City (h) League Division Three South
D. Massart (3) v Leyton Orient (h) League Division Three South
D. Massart (3) v Southend United (h) League Division Three South
D. Massart (4) v Brighton & H.A. (a) League Division Three South

1948-49
J. Devlin (3) v Notts County (h) League Division Three South
P. Chapman (3) v Crystal Palace (h) League Division Three South
P. Chapman (3) v Exeter City (h) League Division Three South

1949-50
J. Devlin (5) v Torquay United (h) League Division Three South

1950-51
J. Winter (3) v Colchester United (h) League Division Three South

1951-52
H. Evans (3) v Norwich City (h) League Division Three South

1953-54
E. Holding (3) v Brighton & HA (h) League Division Three South
F. Morris (3) v Brighton & HA (a) League Division Three South

1954-55
A. Richards (3) v Reading (h) League Division Three South
D. Dorman (3) v Northampton Town (h) League Division Three South
A. Richards (3) v QPR (h) League Division Three South

1955-56
D. Walsh (3) v Margate (h) FA Cup

1956-57
D. Dorman (3) v Millwall (h) League Division Three South
S. Moore (3) v Brentford (h) League Division Three South
A. Richards (3) v Brentford (h) League Division Three South)

1957-58
A Richards (3) v Coventry City (h) League Division Three South

1958-58
A. Richards (3) v York City (h) League Division Four

1959-60
C. Taylor (3) v Southport (h) League Division Four

1960-61
C. Taylor (3) v Tranmere Rovers (h) League Division Three

A. Richards (3) v QPR (h) League Division Three
A. Richards (4) v Port Vale (h) League Division Three
C. Taylor (3) v Bournemouth (a) League Division Three

1961-62
A. Richards (3) v Sunderland (h) League Division Two

1963-64
B. Llewellyn (3) v Barnsley (a) League Division Three

1964-65
A. Clarke (3) v Reading (h) League Division Three
C. Taylor (3) v Brentford (h) League Division Three

1965-66
H. Middleton (4) v Gillingham (h) League Division Three

1967-68
C. Taylor (3) v Scunthorpe United (a) League Division Three

1973-74
R. Shinton (3) v Huddersfleld Town (h) League Division Three
A. Buckley (3) v Shrewsbury Town (h) League Cup

1975-76
A. Buckley (4) v Rotherham United (h) League Division Three
A. Buckley (3) v Gillingham (h) League Division Three
A. Buckley (3) v Aldershot (h) League Division Three

1976-77
L. Dennehy (3) v Reading (h) League Division Three
A. Birch (3) v Peterborough United (a) League Division Three

1977-78
A. Buckley (3) v Swansea City (h) FA Cup

1981-82
R. O'Kelly (3) v Newport County (h) League Division Three

1984-85
M. Rees (3) v Derby County (h) Freight Rover Trophy

1985-86
S. Elliott (3) v Cardiff City (h) League Division Three
W. Naughton (3) v Preston North End (h) FA Cup

1987-88
N. Cross (3) v Rotherham United (h) League Division Three
D. Kelly (3) v Mansfield Town (a) League Division Three
D. Kelly (3) v Bristol City (h) Promotion Play-offs

1988-89
S. Rimmer (3) v Sunderland (a) League Division Two

1989-90
S. Rimmer (3) v Southend United (h) Leyland DAF Cup

1991-92
R. McDonald (3) v Blackpool (h) League Division Four

1992-93
W. Clarke (3) v Bury (h) League Division Four
M. Cecere (3) v Halifax Town (h) League Division Three

1993-94
D. Peer (3) v Lincoln City (h) League Division Three

1994-95
K. Lightbourne (3) v Fulham (h) League Division Three

1995-96
K. Lightbourne (4) v Wycombe Wanderers (h) Auto Windscreen Shield

1997-98
R. Boli (3) v Southend United (h) League Division Two

Note: In 1883-84 (before the amalgamation) William Bird scored 4 goals in an away FA Cup-tie v Calthorpe.

Hat-trick Pot Pourri

Gilbert Alsop scored a record 22 hat-tricks for the Saddlers including six in season 1934-35 and five in 1938-39. Out of that total, 16 came in the Football League, including four in April 1939 when, in fact, he netted 16 goals in a spell of just five matches. Gilbert actually scored hat-tricks in both games against Swindon Town in 1938-39.

Tony Richards notched eight trebles, two against QPR.

Sammy Holmes hit six hat-tricks in the late 1800s.

Arthur Campey grabbed five – all in 1914-15, this after he had been converted into a centre-forward from the right-back position.

Dave Massart scored a hat-trick in each of his first three home League Division Three South games for Walsall at the start of the 1947-48 season.

Alan Buckley netted hat-tricks in League, FA Cup and Football League Cup competitions.

During World War Two **Jack Rowley** (from Manchester United) guested for the Saddlers and in 1940-41 he grabbed four four-timers, with both Notts County and Nottingham Forest being on the receiving end.

Colin Taylor has been the most prolific goalscoring winger Walsall have ever had and he netted five hat-tricks from the left-flank during his three spells at Fellows Park. Inside-forward **Alan Buckley** also scored five trebles during his association with the Saddlers.

Walsall's first League hat-trick was registered in the Second Division by **Bill McWhinnie** against Ardwick at home in season 1893-94; Ted Whittick hit the first FA Cup hat-trick (after the amalgamation) versus Warmley (away) in 1890-91 when the Saddlers won 12-0, and the first League Cup treble was claimed by **Alan Buckley** v Shrewsbury Town in season 1973-74.

Albert Wlkes, normally a defender, was moved up to centre-forward for one game in season 1896-97 and he promptly scored a hat-trick as Walsall whipped Woolwich Arsenal 5-3 at home in a Second Division match.

Jack Bird was also a recognised centre-half, and in 1911-12 he ventured up field and scored a hat-trick against Ton Pentre in a Southern League game.

Ted Collins, a prominent and highly efficient full-back with Wolves before World War One, guested for the Saddlers in season 1915-16 and he played centre-forward against Cannock in the final Walsall & District League fixture of that campaign and hit five goals in a 7-1 win.

Five players have each scored five goals in a game for Walsall: **Alf Dean** v Wellington in the FA Cup in 1900-01; **Arthur Campey** v Cradley St Luke's also in the FA Cup in 1914-15; **Collins** in that Walsall & District fixture v Cannock in 1916 (see above); **Billy Evans** v Mansfield Town, League Division Three South in 1935-36 and **Johnny Devlin** v Torquay United, League Division Three South in 1949-50.

Those who have recorded four-timers for the Saddlers are: **Sammy Holmes** (1888-89), **Ted Whittick** (1890-91), **Tom Johnson** (1896-97), **Jack Aston** (1898-99), **Wally Freeman** and **Jack Stanton** (both in 1911-12), **Jack Davies** (1912-13), big **Jack Franklin** (1921-22), **Moses Lane** (1927-28), **Gilbert Alsop** (in 1932-33, twice in 1933-34, twice more in 1934-35, three times in 1938-39 and once in 1944-45), **Jack Rowley** (four times in 1940-41), **Dave Massart** (1947-48), **Tony Richards** (season 1960-61), **Harry Middleton** (1965-66), **Alan Buckley** (season 1975-76), and **Kyle Lightbourne** (1995-96).

Three players – **Tom Johnson, Alf Griffin** and **George Johnson** – all scored hat-tricks in Walsall's 11-0 FA Cup win over Dresden United in 1896-97.

Willie Naughton fired in a hat-trick for the Saddlers against his former club, Preston North End, in an FA Cup-tie in 1985-86, and **Tony Richards** cracked in a treble against his future club (Port Vale) in 1960-61.
Perhaps the most important hat-trick ever scored by a Walsall player was that netted by **David Kelly** in the vital promotion Play-off Final replay against Bristol City in front of 13,000 fans at Fellows Park in May, 1988. Walsall won that game 4-0 and so clinched a place in Division Two.

The first hat-trick scored by a Walsall player at the Bescot Stadium came from **Rod McDonald** v Blackpool in the Fourth Division game in 1991-92, while **Roger Boli** (v Southend United in 1997-98) was the first foreign player to score a League treble at the Bescot Stadium.

Stuart Rimmer (v Southend United in 1989-90) secured the last hat-trick at Fellows Park.

Ever-Presents

Here are details of all the players who were ever-present during a League season for Walsall – 1892 to 1992 inclusive:

Midland Association

Season	*Player*	*Games*
1888-89	Jones, A.	14

Football Alliance

Season	*Player*	*Games*
1889-90	Edge, G.	22
	Jones, A.	22
1890-91	Holmes, S.	22

Football League

Season	*Player*	*Games*
1892-93	Forsyth, N.	22
	Hawkins, T.	22
	Pinches,A.	22
1894-95	Forsyth, N.	30
	Holmes, S.	30
1897-98	Taggart, J.	30
1898-99	Tennent, W.	34
1899-00	Tennent, W.	34
1900-01	Holmes, S.	34

Midland League

Season	*Player*	*Games*
1902-03	Pee, R.	32
1903-04	Law, W.	34
	Waters, J.	34

Birmingham League

Season	*Player*	*Games*
1904-05	Pickering, T.	34
1905-06	Adams, W.	34
1907-08	Bird, J.	34
	Bytheway, G.	34
1908-09	Richards, T.	34
1909-10	Dilly, T.	34
1910-11	Bird, J.	34
	Moult, J.	34
1911-12	Bird, J.	34
	Richards, T.	34
1914-15	Richards, T.	34
	Rushton, J.	34
1919-20	Rogers, T.	34

Football League

Season	*Player*	*Games*
1922-23	Webster, W. G.	38
1924-25	Wait, H.	42
1925-26	Wait, H.	42
	Smith, G. H.	42
1926-27	Wait, H.	42
1927-28	Wait, H.	42
1928-29	Wait, H.	42
	Lochhead, D.	42
1929-30	Bradford, W.	42
	Eyres, J.	42
1932-33	Cunningham, J.	42
	Bird, S.	42
1933-34	Woolhouse, R.	42
1934-35	Alsop, G. A.	42
1937-38	Shelton, J. G. T.	42
1970-71	Wesson, R.	46
	Jones, S. G.	46
1971-72	Harrison, C.	46
1972-73	Harrison, C.	46
1973-74	Buckley, A.	46
1974-75	Andrews, G.	46
	Buckley, A.	46
	Kearns, M.	46
1975-76	Kearns, M.	46
	Buckley, A.	46
1976-77	Kearns, M.	46
1977-78	Buckley, A.	46
1981-82	Green, R.	46
	Serella, D.	46
1982-83	Buckley, A.	44+2
1983-84	Shakespeare, C.	46
1984-85	Hart, P.	46
1986-87	Hart, P.	46
1987-88	Barber, F.	46
1994-95	Lightbourne, K.	42
	Wilson, K.	42
1995-96	Wilson, K.	46
1996-97	Viveash, A.	46
1997-98	Walker, J.	46
1998-99	Walker, J.	46
	Wrack, D.	46

Walsall's Leading Appearance-Makers & Goalscorers

Football League Appearances
(Qualification: 200)
473* C. Harrison
457* C. Taylor
439* N. Atthey
419* A. Buckley
415* K. Mower
400* B. Caswell
393* F. Gregg
390* P. Hart
386* S. Bennett
345* C. Marsh
338 A.Richards
336* K. Hodgkisson
284* C. Shakespeare
275 M. Kearns
267* D. Serella
264 H. Wait
254 H. Walters
243 E. Groves
237* M. Rees
235* S. Jones
230 R. Green
226 H. Haddington
224* M. Evans
219* J. Walker
216* B. Taylor
216* R. O'Kelly
214 S. Holmes
213 F. Morris
200 S. Rawlings
*Includes appearances as sub.

FA Cup Appeaaances
43 S. Holmes
42 N. Atthey
38* C. Harrison
33 S. Bennett
33* C. Marsh
31* A. Buckley
31 K. Mower
31 C. Taylor
30 F. Gregg
28 P. Hart
25 B. Caswell
24 J. W. Bradford
24 M. Kearns
22 R. Wesson
21 G. Alsop
21 S. Jones
21 L. D. Morgan
21 C. Shakespeare
20* M. Evans
20 T. Richards
20 D. Serella
19 B. Taylor
19 B. Wright
* Includes appearances as sub.

League Cup Appearances
(Top ten listed)
38* K. Mower
35 P. Hart
31 C. Shakespeare
30* A. Buckley
29 B. Caswell
23 M. Kearns
22* C. Marsh
21 N. Atthey
21* F. Gregg
19 S. Bennett
19 C. Harrison
* Includes appearances as sub.

Overall Appearances
(Qualification: 250)
530* C. Harrison
502* N. Atthey
502* C. Taylor
494* K. Mower
483* A. Buckley
474* P. Hart
458* B. Caswell
444* F. Gregg
438* S. Bennett
426* C. Marsh
381 S. Holmes
367 A. McPherson
358 A. Richards
355* C. Shakespeare
352* K. Hodgkisson
322 M. Kearns
304* D. Serella
286 J. Lewis
275 H. Wait
274* M. Rees
274 T. Richards
266 H. Walters
265 R. Green
264* S. Jones
264* J. Walker
263* M. Evans
257 J. Bird
256 E. Groves
254* R. O'Kelly
* Includes appearances as sub.

Top Goalscorers in all Competitions
(Qualiftcation 40 or more)
202 A. Buckley
198 A. Richards
189 C. Taylor
169 G. Alsop
108 S. Holmes
83 K. Lightbourne
80 D. Kelly
66 C. Shakespeare
65 R. O'Kelly
60 K. Hodgkisson
58 D. Penn
57 W. Robinson
55 M. Lane
50 J. Devlin
50 K. Wilson
49 F. Morris
48 B. Wright
46 R. McDonald
46 B. Woolhouse
44 S. Rimmer
42 M. Rees
41 G. Morris
*58 of Holmes' goals came in the period when Walsall not in the Football League.

Top League Goalscorers
(Qualification 50 goals)
185 A. Richards
174 A. Buckley
170 C. Taylor
151 G. Alsop
63 D. Kelly
59 K. Hodgkisson
57 R. O'Kelly
54 D. Penn
51 M. Lane
51 C. Shakespeare

FA Cup Goalscorers
(Top ten players)
22 S. Holmes
14 A. Buckley
13 G. Alsop
12 A. Richards
11 A. Campey
11 C. Taylor
8 C. Shaw
7 A. Dean
7 W. Evans
7 B. Wright

League Cup Goalscorers
(top ten players)
14 A. Buckley
9 C. Taylor
8 C. Shakespeare
S D. Preece
4 G. Andrews
4 A. Biggs
4 D. Kelly
4 R. O'Kelly
4 M. Rees
4 S. Rimmer

Player	Seasons	League		FAC		FLC		Others		Totals	
		A	G	A	G	A	G	A	G	A	G
Abrahams E	1926-27	13								13	
Adams WE	1925-28	45	1	2						47	1
Adams WG	1905-15			3				133	2	136	2
Alcock HS	1925-27	45	13	1						46	13
Alcock JT	1892-94	10	4	1						11	4
Aldred A	1948-49	11	1	4	1					15	2
Aldridge AA	1888-89			2				13		15	
Allan R	1919-21			2	.			22	1	24	1
Allen G	1953-54	2	1							2	1
Allison J	1950-52	47	1	1						48	1
Allsop N	1953-54	9		2	1					11	1
Alsop GA	1931-47	195	151	21	13			6	5	222	169
Anderson C	1991-92	25 /1	2	2				1		28 /1	2
Andrews G	1972-77	156 /3	38	13 /1	2	4				173 /4	40
Anson E	1902-04			1				32	6	33	6
Archer FJ	1920-25	29	1							29	1
Archer JW	1929-31	26		2						28	
Arthur D	1981-82	8 /1			1					9 /1	
Askew W	1937-39	26	2	2				2		30	2
Askey C	1958-62	83	12	3		2				88	12
Aston C L	1895-98	52	1	4				14		70	1
Aston J	1895-99	88	38	5	2			15	12	108	52
Aston J	1903-06			2	2			11	1	13	3
Aston P	1951-52	10								10	
Atkinson P	1949-52	2								2	
Atthey N	1963-77	429 /10	17	42	1	21				492 /10	18
Attwood AA	1928-29	14	13	4						18	13
Austin TW	1977-79	44 /3	19	1		3				48 /3	19
Baddeley A	1911-14			3				24	16	27	16
Bailey A	1953-54	1								1	
Bailey T	1908-11			3				29	7	32	7
Bailey TT	1893-94	23		3				1		27	
Baines S	1980-82	47 /1	5			2				49 /1	5
Baker A	1966-71	128 /9	31	17	3	10	2			155 /9	36
Baker G	1900-02	6	1	7	1			26	6	39	8
Baldwin H	1953-55	37		3						40	
Ball CG	1931-35	112	20	9	3			2		123	23
Ball E	1890-91			4	2			14		18	2
Ball K	1958-73	48		1		2				51	
Bamber D	1983-85	17 /3	7			3				20 /3	7
Bambrick J	1938-39	35	15	6	5					41	20
Bancroft JG	1923-27	18	1							18	1
Banton D	1988-89	9 /1		2				1		12 /1	
Barber F	1986-91	153		12		9		15		189	
Barker J	1951-52	6								6	
Barnes J B	1929-31	68	18	7						75	18
Barrett D	1990-91	4 /1			2					6 /1	
Bartley JE	1930-31	5		1	1					6	1
Bastock R	1901-04			1				32	10	33	10
Bate TE	1934-39	78	24	5	1			8		91	25
Bates F	1919-20			1						1	
Bates HJ	1912-15			7	2			46	8	53	10
Bates M	1982-84	6		1				1		8	
Bates MJ	1976-78	84 /1	4	12	1	8	1			104 /1	6
Baugh R	1896-97	6								6	
Beale G	1903-04			3	2			17	4	20	6
Beaman RW	1961-62	1								1	
Beck HA	1921-28	42		4						46	
Beckford D	1996-97	3 /5								3 /5	
Beddow R	1954-55	1								1	
Bedford L	1922-30	142	13	5						147	13
Beech K	1982-84	78 /1	5	6		4				88 /1	5
Beeson GW	1938-39	34	1	4				1		39	1
Bell J	1936-37	6						1		7	
Bell JG	1930-33	8								8	
Bell R	1928-29	1								1	
Bennett JB	1932-38	182		19				9		210	
Bennett S	1945-46			1	1					1	1
Bennett S	1961-75	378 /8	12	33	1	19				430 /8	13
Benton G	1919-20			2	3			29	8	31	11
Benwell LA	1894-95	15		1						16	
Bertschin K	1988-91	40 /15	9	4	2	1 /2		5 /2	4	50 /19	15
Betts E	1949-50	30	3	1						31	3
Bewick J	1936-37	3								3	
Bicknell J	1953-54	3								3	
Biddlestone F	1929-30	21		3						24	
Biddulph EZ	1890-91			3				1		4	
Bidmead C	1901-02			2				13	6	15	6
Biggs A	1967-69	23 /1	9			3	4			26 /1	13
Billingham P	1955-60	99	9	3	1					102	10
Binks GF	1922-27	107	1	3						110	1
Birch A	1972-79	158 /13	23	9 /2		9	1			176 /15	24
Birch F	1923-25	35	1	1						36	1
Bird J	1906-13			13				244	23	257	23
Bird S	1932-35	90	2	7						97	2
Bird W	1919-20			2				25	7	27	7
Blackburn R	1935-36	10	4	2						12	4
Blake M	1996-98	51 /10	5	0 /3		2		2 /2		55 /15	5
Blincow E	1946-47	1								1	
Boli R	1997-98	41	12	4	4	6	2	6	6	57	24
Boswell A	1961-63	66		5		1				72	
Boswell W	1924-25	8	1							8	1
Bourne RA	1908-11			2				14		16	
Bowdak P	1990-91	3 /1	1			1				4 /1	1
Bowen D	1925-26	2								2	
Bowen T	1950-53	94	7	3						97	7
Bowen TG	1921-25	74	14	7	3					81	17
Bowers R	1914-15			1				2		3	
Bowser S	1924-25	27		1						28	
Bowyer T	1919-22	34	5	8	1			32	13	74	19
Boyden J	1952-53	4								4	
Bradburn E	1913-15			5	1			31	1	36	2
Bradburn G	1922-23	12								12	
Bradford B	1930-31	11								11	
Bradford JW	1926-38	318	21	24				9	1	351	22
Bradley D	1995-97	66 /5	1	7	2	4		3		80 /5	3
Bratt HJ	1923-24	2		1						3	
Brawn W	1909-10			1				13	2	14	2
Brazier C	1983-87	114 /1	4	5		18		7		144 /1	4
Bremner DG	1989-90	2 /4							2	/4	
Brettle J	1888-89			2				12	1	14	1
Brettle N	1893-96	31	2	4				9	1	44	3
Bridgett J	1950-55	106	18	10						116	18
Brissett J	1998-99	27 /8	3	1		2		2		32 /8	3
Broadhurst K	1979-80	3								3	
Brocksop A	1895-97	2		3				22	13	27	13
Bromley T	1953-54	13	1							13	1
Brookes WN	1930-32	16	2							16	2
Brown A	1983-84	37 /1	13	1		8	2			46 /1	15
Brown K	1973-75	8 /2								8 /2	
Brown R	1930-31	1								1	
Brown R	1991-92	6 /3						2 /1		8 /4	
Brown T	1956-58	38	9							38	9
Brown WS	1938-47	20	4	1				1		22	4
Bryan W	1935-36	9								9	
Bryant M	1990-91	13				4				17	
Buckley AP	1973-85	402 /17	177	30 /1	14	28 /2	14	1 /2		461 /22	205
Bulger CG	1936-46	78	11	12	2			4	1	94	14
Bullock PL	1968-69	7								7	
Bunch W	1899-1901	61		11						72	
Bunyon C	1896-98	44		3						47	
Bunyon G	1896-97	1								1	
Burden F	1903-08			6				122	3	128	3
Burgess R	1953-54	2	1							2	1

Player	Seasons	League		FAC		FLC		Others		Totals	
		A	G	A	G	A	G	A	G	A	G
Burrill F	1924-25	39	14	1						40	14
Burton EC	1904-05			2				25	4	27	4
Bushell W	1931-32	30	4	1						31	4
Butler M	1993-96	43 /31	8	2/5	2	2/1		2 /2	2	49/39	12
Butler T	1921-22	28	12	6	3					34	15
Buttery A	1938-39	15	4					1		16	4
Buttery H	1915-20			2				16	2	18	2
Byrne D	1993-94	5								5	
Bytheway G	1907-08			1	1			34	16	35	17
Bytheway GD	1919-20	1								1	
Caddick WA	1908-12			1				74	35	75	35
Caesar WC	1927-28	8								8	
Callaghan W	1988-89	2	1							2	1
Cameron E	1922-24	63	4	4	2					67	6
Campbell J	1946-48	14	1	1						15	1
Campey A	1913-16			6	11					6	11
Capewell LK	1929-30	7								7	
Carlin T	1964-67	101		5		9				115	
Carter A	1998-99	0 /1								0/1	
Carter JH	1936-37	19	4	5						24	4
Carver T	1900-01	2								2	
Caswell B	1972-85	388 /12	17	25	2	29		4		446/12	19
Cecere M	1990-92	55 /11	15	3/1		6		6		70/12	15
Cecere M	1990-94	92 /20	32	4/2		10/1		12	2	118/23	34
Ceney J	1922-24	7	1							7	1
Chadwick G	1964-65	9				1				10	
Chance B	1909-14			11				173	5	184	5
Chapman P	1948-51	63	38	5						68	38
Chappell I	1914-15			1						1	
Cherry J	1935-36	1						1		2	
Cherry SR	1984-86	71		7		10		6		94	
Childs G	1983-87	120 /11	17	9/21	2	14/2	2	7	2	150/34	23
Chilvers GS	1951-58	123		7						130	
Chine WR	1991-92	4 /1								4/1	
Christie A	1921-22	30	1	6	1					36	2
Christie J	1959-63	102		3		2				107	
Christie T	1986-89	91 /8	22	12	4	5	1	12	5	120/8	32
Clark E	1902-03			1				4	2	5	2
Clark H	1891-93	3						17	4	20	4
Clark J	1925-26	26	5							26	5
Clark T	1948-49	9	2							9	2
Clarke AJ	1963-66	72	14	5	4	5	1			82	19
Clarke D	1967-68	6	2	4						10	2
Clarke KL	1974-78	4 /5				0/1				4/6	
Clarke W	1992-93	39	21	1		4	1	3 /1	2	47/1	24
Clarkson D	1888-89			1						1	
Clarkson O	1902-07			2	1			41	4	43	5
Cochrane J	1958-59	6	1							6	1
Colley R	1901-02			7	1			17	5	24	6
Collins J	1935-36	22	14	4	1					26	15
Colombo D	1953-54	20	1	3						23	1
Condie J	1947-50	49	2	4	1					53	3
Conneally MP	1980-81	3								3	
Connolly J	1893-94	4								4	
Connor MJ	1899-1901	48	14	5	2					53	16
Cooch H	1909-10			1				32		33	
Cook R	1892-95	32	1	3	1					35	2
Cook WJ	1909-16			8				99		107	
Cooper J	1930-31	14	15	3	3					17	18
Cooper L	1955-56	5	2							5	2
Cooper TA	1929-32	6								6	
Cope GB	1888-92			5	3			21	9	26	12
Copeland D	1892-1903	76	19	7				30	21	113	40
Corbett AD	1949-50	25	5	1	2					26	7
Corbett WS	1913-22			7				62	1	69	1
Corrigan FJ	1973-74	1								1	
Corwe C	1969-70	10 /3	1							10/3	1
Coton PS	1966-67	1								1	
Cousans WE	1954-55	4	1							4	1
Coward WC	1932-33	35	8	4						39	8
Cox G	1913-15			2				2		4	
Cox S	1893-95	4	1	2						6	1
Cramb C	1998-99	4	4					2		6	4
Crockford H	1925-26	24	17	1						25	17
Crook W	1954-56	45	2	6						51	2
Cross NJ	1985-88	107 /2	45	12/1	4	10	2	6 /1	1	135/4	52
Cross R	1966-70	11 /1				0/1				11/2	
Crossley CG	1913-16			2				32	21	34	21
Crump J	1908-11			1	1			32	16	33	17
Crutchley R	1945-50	62	4	9						71	4
Culdicott TW	1933-34	1	1							1	1
Cullum CH	1922-23	22	9							22	9
Cunningham G	1935-37	10	2	3						13	2
Cunningham J	1932-34	49		4						53	
Dailly H	1899-00	28	5	6	2					34	7
Dainty J	1971-73	4 /1								4/1	
Daley S	1985-86	2	1	3		4		2		11	1
Daniel R	1996-97	31 /4		3		4		1		39/4	
Darby D	1946-47	15	4	1	1					16	5
Davidson J	1955-56	5								5	
Davie W	1957-58	7								7	
Davies E	1938-39	12	1							12	1
Davies G	1896-97	2								2	
Davies HS	1909-16			4				107	12	111	12
Davies J	1911-14			1				9	8	10	8
Davies J	1958-61	65	17	1	2	1	1			67	20
Davies JW	1893-94	6		3						9	
Davies K	1947-48	28	5	3	2					31	7
Davies R	1955-57	53		5						58	
Davies T	1938-39	1								1	
Davis C	1948-49	1								1	
Davis H	1898-1900	60		7						67	
Davis L	1953-55	25	5							25	5
Davis N	1998-99	0 /1								0/1	
Davis R	1898-00			7	3			15	4	22	7
Davis WR	1892-94	17	5	1						18	5
Davis WW	1908-09			1						1	
Day H	1923-24	1								1	
Deakin A	1969-72	46 /4		2/1						48/5	
Dean A	1898-01	65	29	7	7			3		75	36
Dean G	1909-10			1				3		4	
Dean G	1950-54	73	13	4	1					77	14
Dearson DJ	1949-51	51	13	1						52	13
Demetrias C	1992-93	3 /4	1	1						4/4	1
Dennehy J	1975-78	123 /5	22	12/1		10				145/6	22
Devey W	1894-98	38	13	2						40	13
Devlin D	1972-73	15 /3		2		0/1				17/4	
Devlin J	1947-52	159	49	7	1					166	50
Devlin TS	1932-33	4								4	
Dews G	1955-56	9	1							9	1
Dilly T	1909-10			1				34	7	35	7
Dodd RI	1937-38	18	9	2	2	2				22	11
Dolan P	1986-87	1				1		1		3	
Dolphin A	1923-24	13	1	2						15	1
Donowa L	1996-97	11 /1	1			1				12/1	1
Dorman D	1954-57	114	34	8	1					122	35
Dornan A	1986-89	117 /1	1	11		10		9 /1		147/2	1
Dover H	1935-37	5								5	
Driver A	1952-53	26	2							26	2
Dudley JD	1959-64	167	3	6		3				176	3
Duggins AE	1924-25	12		1						13	
Duggins J	1952-53	16	3							16	3
Dunderdale W	1935-38	32	19							32	19
Dunn W	1893-94	2								2	

Player	Seasons	League		FAC		FLC		Others		Totals	
		A	G	A	G	A	G	A	G	A	G
Dyas G	1955-56	12								12	
Dyer W	1998-99	0 /1						0 /1		0 /2	
Dyke GR	1889-90			2	1			2	1	4	2
Ealing WH	1952-53	1								1	
Earl A	1902-03			1				13	5	14	5
Eastoe P	1984-85	6	1			2	1			8	2
Eden A	1960-63	14		1						15	
Eden E	1921-22	9								9	
Edgar DJ	1930-31	9								9	
Edge G	1888-92			11				47		58	
Edwards D	1991-92	13 /6	1					1 /2		14 /8	1
Edwards EJ	1919-21			2				42	24	44	24
Edwards HP	1925-26	3								3	
Edwards RT	1933-34	1								1	
Edwards S	1991-93	15 /11	1			1 /1		1 /2		17 /14	1
Edwards WJ	1952-53	12								12	
Edwards WJT	1926-28	34	5	2						36	5
Ellard J	1904-06			2				37	9	39	9
Elliott S	1984-86	68 /1	21	4	1	4		65	2	141 /1	24
Ellis P	1921-22	1		3						4	
Embelem D	1994-95	0 /1								0 /1	
Essers P	1991-92	1								1	
Evans A	1975-78	78 /9	7	10	1	3 /1				91 /10	8
Evans H	1951-52	36	12	1						37	12
Evans KP	1957-58	2								2	
Evans M	1965-73	229 /2	7	19 /1	1	12				260 /3	8
Evans W	1921-22	1						1		2	
Evans W	1934-39	115	54	9	7			8	3	132	64
Evans W	1993-99	172 /10	1	15 /1		14 /1	1	12 /3		213 /15	2
Eydelie JJ	1997-98	10 /1						1		11 /1	
Eyjoffsson Z	1998-99	0 /10	1					0 /1	1	0 /11	2
Eyres J	1929-31	81	34	8	3					89	37
Fairhurst DL	1927-29	56		3						59	
Faulkner R	1957-61	100	45	4		1				105	45
Fearon R	1992-93	1								1	
Felix E J	1925-26	25	3							25	3
Fell J	1963-64	21	4	1		3				25	4
Fellows G	1919-21			1				7	3	8	3
Fereday DT	1927-28	10								10	
Ferriday L	1954-55	32	1	1						33	1
Finlay J	1953-54	11		3	2					14	2
Flack D	1953-54	11								11	
Flavell J	1953-54	22		5						27	
Flavell JF	1903-07			4	1			65	8	69	9
Flynn H	1900-01	31	6	5	1					36	7
Flynn J	1898-99	7								7	
Forbes G	1986-90	173	9	13	1	12	2	16	2	214	14
Ford C	1964-67	11 /3		1						12 /3	
Ford G	1989-90	13	2							13	2
Forsyth N	1892-96	78	9	10	2			38	6	126	17
Fort SM	1953-55	28								28	
Foster L	1921-22	4								4	
Foster T	1960-65	63	12							63	12
Foulkes RE	1945-50	160	6	15						175	6
Francis S	1908-09			2	3			33	12	35	15
Franklin J	1921-22	6	4							6	4
Franks A	1903-07			3				59	4	62	4
Fraser DM	1973-74	26 /1			4					30 /1	
Freeman HG	1952-53	20	1	1						21	1
Freeman N	1980-81	8								8	
Freeman W	1910-12			2	2			54	21	56	23
Fry RN	1973-77	120	1	6	1	10				136	2
Gadsby M	1997-99	3 /4						0 /2		3 /6	
Gallier W	1955-56	10		2						12	
Gayle J	1993-94	4	1							4	1
Gayle M	1991-94	74 /1		1		8		6		89 /1	
Gayle N	1991-92	24				2		2		28	

Player	Seasons	League		FAC		FLC		Others		Totals	
		A	G	A	G	A	G	A	G	A	G
Gee JH	1893-95	10	6	1						11	6
Genever ED	1898-99	4	1							4	1
Gerrault R	1998-99			0 /1				1		1 /1	
Gibbons W	1925-26	4								4	
Gibson C	1994-95	31 /2		5				2	1	38 /2	1
Giles P	1948-53	68	14	2	1					70	15
Godden AL	1983-84	19								19	
Godderidge AE	1952-53	3								3	
Godfrey C	1938-39	27	1			1				28	1
Godfrey T	1930-31	38	2	4						42	2
Goffin WC	1954-55	8	1							8	1
Goldie S	1913-15			1				2		3	
Goldsmith M	1988-91	2 /5	2			1 /1	1			3 /6	3
Goodwin M	1987-90	81 /11	2	4		6 /2	1	10		101 /13	3
Gordon C	1990-91	6	1							6	1
Gough AV	1928-29	16	4	3	3					19	7
Gough K	1969-72	11 /4								11 /4	
Gough RG	1966-68	1								1	
Gray FJS	1888-93	7	1	6	5			33	8	46	14
Grealish AP	1990-92	32 /4	1	0 /1		2 /1		2 /1		36 /7	1
Greatwich FE	1898-99	4	1							4	1
Green A	1901-02			7				20	12	27	12
Green A	1912-14			2	1			5	4	7	5
Green J	1912-15			1				5	1	6	1
Green J	1936-37	5								5	
Green R	1998-99	22 /8	1	2		2		1		27 /8	1
Green RR	1977-91	230		15		13		7		265	
Green W	1948-54	180	8	8						188	8
Gregg F	1960-73	389 /4	3	30		20 /1				439 /5	3
Gretton T	1930-31	3								3	
Grice TW	1934-35	5								5	
Griffin A	1896-00	82	30	6	4					88	34
Griffith R	1934-35	8	1							8	1
Griffiths W	1901-05			2				35	4	37	4
Gritt S	1989-90	20	1	3		2		2		27	1
Grosvenor S	1907-08			1						1	
Groves A	1919-24	79	15	12	2			33	7	124	24
Groves E	1921-30	243	25	13	2					256	27
Grubb AJ	1953-54	15		5						20	
Guest WE	1947-48	5								5	
Gunn B	1985-86	6						2		8	
Guttridge W	1954-62	198		10		2				210	
Haddington H	1955-61	226		9						235	
Haddington J	1953-54	1								1	
Haddleton GA	1934-35	15	4			3				18	4
Hadlington JE	1926-27	1								1	
Hague EM	1928-30	8	1							8	1
Hall R	1954-56	2								2	
Hancocks J	1938-46	30	9	8	1	1				39	10
Handysides I	1983-86	58 /8	11	3		6		6		73 /8	11
Hargreaves G	1902-03			1				28	8	29	8
Harker G	1926-27	1								1	
Harley CE	1893-94	3	2							3	2
Harper CH	1921-24	40	9	2	2					42	11
Harper K	1937-39	22	2	4						26	2
Harris G	1965-68	13 /2	1	4		1				18 /2	1
Harris J	1964-69	74	2	7		4				85	2
Harris S	1902-03			1				6		7	
Harris WN	1929-30	6	1							6	1
Harrison C	1964-82	453 /20	33	35 /2		19	1			507 /22	34
Hart PO	1980-90	389 /1	12	28		35		20 /1	1	472 /2	13
Hartley CJ	1894-95	7	1	1						8	1
Harwood I	1936-37	28	6	2	1	1				31	7
Hawker P	1982-90	159 /18	10	15 /1	2	12 /1	2	15	2	201 /20	16
Hawkins T	1892-96	67		4				28		99	
Haynes AA	1892-96	3						1	1	4	1
Haynes AE	1948-49	2								2	

Player	Seasons	League A	League G	FAC A	FAC G	FLC A	FLC G	Others A	Others G	Totals A	Totals G
Haywood H	1900-02	1								1	
Haywood W	1921-26	3								3	
Heath S	1889-90			3				5	1	8	1
Helliwell S	1929-32	98	8	6						104	8
Henry CE	1931-32	18		1						19	
Henry N	1998-99	8								8	
Hestletine GV	1948-50	8								8	
Hewitt R	1949-50	8	2	1						9	2
Hickinbothom W	1898-1900	7								7	
Higgs F	1934-35	2								2	
Higgs S	1924-25	13	2							13	2
Higham F	1924-25	2								2	
Hill J	1938-39	8	2							8	2
Hill K	1958-67	130	1	7		4				141	1
Hill T	1924-25	15								15	
Hill WT	1927-28	1								1	
Hirons JW	1902-09			2				58	11	60	11
Hitch A	1897-98	2								2	
Hobson G	1991-92	3								3	
Hodge J	1996-98	67 /9	12	7/1	2	5		5 /2		84/12	14
Hodgkisson KW	1955-56	335 /1	55	11	1	5				351/1	56
Hodson AS	1893-94	3								3	
Hodson F	1897-98	1								1	
Hodson TJ	1892-93	2								2	
Holdin E	1950-52	39	6	2	2					41	8
Holmes C	1888-90			5				21	2	26	2
Holmes S	1888-92	214	28	43	22			124	58	381	108
Holt G	1905-06			2				28	13	30	13
Holt T	1920-27	84		5						89	
Horn JR	1979-82	10 /6	1							10/6	1
Horn L	1952-54	52	1	4						56	1
Horrabin D	1895-98	23	3	2	1			22	7	47	11
Horton L	1946-47	1								1	
Houghton JC	1920-23	15						27		42	
Houghton S	1994-96	76 /2	14	10	3	0/1	1	4		90/3	18
Houldey CA	1928-31	100		12						112	
Howarth S	1952-53	6								6	
Howells R	1963-64	13		1		3				17	
Hughes H	1927-28	16	5	1						17	5
Hughes J	1950-52	44	10							44	10
Hulbert B	1965-66	0 /1								0/1	
Humphries CW	1947-48	6								6	
Humphries E	1910-15			9				108	1	117	1
Hunt A	1906-09			1				58	26	59	26
Hunt H	1936-37	6								6	
Hunter AE	1931-32	35		1						36	
Hunter W	1928-29	10		3						13	
Hurst GM	1930-31	11	2	2						13	2
Husler WT	1909-12			2				12		14	
Hutchings C	1990-91	40		2	1	4	1	3		49	2
Hutchinson R	1986-88	8 /8								8/8	
Hynd RS	1975-78	89	1	9		8				106	1
Inger J	1972-73	2								2	
Ingram S	1919-21			2				37	3	39	3
Izon CJ	1897-98	7								7	
Izon WJ	1911-12			1				30	11	31	11
Jackson A	1966-68	36 /2	7	4	1	0/1	1			40/3	9
Jackson AR	1921-22	18		6						24	
Jackson R	1990-92	8 /2	2	2		1		0 /1		11/3	2
Jarman J	1956-58	37	2	2						39	2
Jarvis J	1945-46			1						1	
Jeffries R	1953-54	3		1						4	
Jenkins L	1974-75	3								3	
Jenkyns CAL	1897-1901	80	2	8						88	2
John WR	1928-32	88		5						93	
Johnes M	1986-88	6 /2				1/1		0 /1		7/4	
Johnson C	1956-57	7	1							7	1
Johnson G	1895-98	55	23	4	3					59	26
Johnson GW	1972-73	3								3	
Johnson JJ	1929-30			1	1					1	1
Johnson JW	1911-14			3				15	2	18	2
Johnson TW	1895-97	17	4	3	5					20	9
Johnston G	1970-71	5	1							5	1
Johnston J	1897-98	2	1							2	1
Johnstone JW	1928-29	3								3	
Jones A	1888-92			7				36	1	43	1
Jones B	1953-54	2								2	
Jones C	1971-73	54 /5	14	3	1	1				58/5	15
Jones G	1953-54	10		4	1					14	1
Jones H	1903-04			3				28		31	
Jones JH	1908-09			2				32	1	34	1
Jones PA	1982-90	125 /18	15	12/1	2	12/3	2	9 /2		158/24	19
Jones R	1986-87	1 /4		0/1		2/1				3/6	
Jones S	1948-52	146	1	6						152	1
Jones S	1978-79	15								15	
Jones SG	1957-73	234 /2	7	21		8				263/2	7
Jones T	1934-37	6								6	
Jones WG	1912-13			1				23	7	24	7
Kearns M	1973-83	275		24		23				322	
Kearns O	1982-83	31 /7	11	2	1	2				35/7	12
Keates D	1996-99	71 /7	3	6		3		11	2	91/7	5
Keister J	1994-99	78 /27	2	10/2		4		2 /2		94/31	2
Kelly D T	1983-88	115 /32	63	12/3	3	11/1	4	14 /3	10	152/39	80
Kelly F C	1945-48	16	6	3						19	6
Kelly J	1958-59	8	1							8	1
Kelly J	1978-80	19 /7	3	1		5				25/7	3
Kelly J	1989-91	36 /3	1	4		1/1		5 /1	2	46/5	3
Kelly J	1992-93	7 /3	2					2		9/3	2
Kelly N	1925-27	2								2	
Kerr J	1995-96	0 /1		0/1				0 /1		0/3	
Kimberley K	1946-47	1								1	
King HW	1930-31	11	4							11	4
King J	1977-79	50 /1	4	5	2	3				58/1	6
Kinsella J	1919-21			2				20		22	
Kirby G	1965-67	74 /1	25	7	3	5	2			86/1	30
Kletzenbauer F	1963-65	12								12	
Knight G	1907-09			1				35		36	
Knight JW	1952-53	4								4	
Knight R	1992-94	27 /2	1			0/1		4		31/3	1
Knott H	1937-38	9	2			2				11	2
Knott W	1954-55	1								1	
Knowles H	1950-51	9	1							9	1
Lake WH	1927-29	25	8							25	8
Lambert J	1998-99	4 /2								4/2	
Landells J	1936-37	19	1					1		20	1
Landsale A	1927-28	8	1							8	1
Lane M	1991-92	6 /3		2		2		1		11/3	
Lane MA	1920-29	57	51					10	4	67	55
Langelove E	1922-23	2								2	
Langford A	1932-33	24	1	2						26	1
Lanyon WJ	1929-31	20	3	2						22	3
Larusson B	1998-99	33 /3	3	2				6	1	41/3	4
Law W	1903-04			3				34	7	37	7
Lawley G	1925-26	26	3	1						27	3
Leadbetter T	1903-04			2				9	1	11	1
Leatherbarrow C	1893-95	24	12							24	12
Leckie J	1936-37	26		5		1				32	
Ledbrook L	1893-94	6	2							6	2
Lee F	1932-35	85	24	6	3	2	1			93	28
Leedham H	1920-24	63	2	2				8	5	73	7
Leedham JR	1964-65	13				2				15	
Lemon P	1989-90	2						1		3	
Leslie GW	1932-36	88	2	7		2				97	2
Lester F	1901-05			11	1			77	2	88	3

Player	Seasons	League A	League G	FAC A	FAC G	FLC A	FLC G	Others A	Others G	Totals A	Totals G
Leverton R	1956-57	17	2	1						18	2
Lewis AE	1901-02			7				24		31	
Lewis G	1894-97	32	1	6				26	1	64	2
Lewis J	1945-53	271		15						286	
Lewis K	1953-54	19	1							19	1
Lewis W	1929-30	2								2	
Lightbourne K	1993-97	158 /7	65	16/2	11	8	1	7	6	189/9	83
Lillis J	1993-95	14 /11	6			0/1		0 /1		14/13	6
Lishman D	1946-48	59	25	6	4					65	29
Littlejohn A	1989-91	26 /18	1	1/1		1/1		4 /1		32/21	1
Livingstone A	1931-32	1								1	
Livingstone G	1993-94	2 /1								2/1	
Llewellyn B	1963-65	17	6			2	1			19	7
Lloyd P	1953-54	5								5	
Lloyd T	1902-04			1	1			37	5	38	6
Lloyd TW	1923-24	5								5	
Lochhead D	1928-29	42		4						46	
Lofthouse JM	1893-95	33	4	1						34	4
Long WK	1931-32	3								3	
Love J	1954-56	40	11	1						41	11
Loveridge J	1981-82	23 /3	2	2						25/3	2
Lowery A	1981-91	10 /2	1			1				11/2	1
Lowery S	1970-71	0 /2		1						1/2	
Loynes J	1897-98	8	1							8	1
Loynes W	1891-92			1				4		5	
Lyne N	1989-90	6 /1								6/1	
Lynex J	1900-03	17	2	4	1			1		22	3
Lyons AT	1922-23	1								1	
Lyons JW	1898-1901	44	1	6						50	1
McAuley W	1899-00	24	7	4						28	7
McBride V	1954-55	11								11	
McClure A	1927-28	11								11	
McCreadie E	1953-54	4								4	
MacDonald K	1991-93	68 /5	10	5		5/1	1	4		82/6	11
McDonald R	1990-92	69 /6	22	3	1	3		5		80/6	23
McDonald R	1990-94	142 /7	41	8	2	9	2	12	1	171/7	46
McDonald W	1893-94	2								2	
McDonough R	1978-81	76 /6	15	7	1	4	1			87/6	17
MacEwan J	1966-67	10	1	1		1				12	1
McGairy T	1954-55	7	1							7	1
McGowan K	1947-49	11	4	2	1					13	5
McIntosh WD	1952-53	22	9	1						23	9
McIntyre G	1901-02			4	3			19	8	23	11
Macken A	1977-82	190	1	15	1	9				214	2
MacKenzie J	1919-22	4		2				32		38	
McKnight A	1991-92	8		2				1		11	
McLanesclan A	1893-94	2								2	
McLaren H	1955-56	31	8	2	2					33	10
McLean JC	1899-1901	59	5	10	2					69	7
McLean WG	1953-54	2								2	
McLoughlin J	1948-50	14								14	
McLoughlin P	1991-92	9	4							9	4
McManus S	1992-93	0 /1								0/1	
McMorran J	1964-69	102 /2	10	9		7				118/2	10
McMorran R	1949-50	8	1							8	1
McParland I	1990-91	11	6							11	6
McPherson A	1954-64	351	8	12		4				367	8
McSevich P	1933-36	102		11		8				121	
McWhinnie W	1893-95	29	11	3						32	11
Mahon J	1954-55	1								1	
Male NA	1938-49	70	2	10	1	1				81	3
Maloney R	1925-26	3								3	
Mann J	1919-21			2				29	6	31	6
Mann RJ	1922-23	33		2						35	
Manning J	1971-72	13 /1	6	2		1				16/1	6
Marlow T	1892-94	19	3	4	3					23	6
Marsh C	1987-92	61 /24	3	7/1		2/2		5	2	75/27	5
Marsh C	1987-99	311 /34	22	32/1	3	20/2		25 /1	3	388/38	28
Marshall FA	1892-93	6	2	2						8	2
Marshall GH	1923-24	11								11	
Marshall JP	1982-83	10				1				11	
Martin HH	1925-26	2								2	
Martin J	1898-1901	93	28	10	5					103	33
Martin JR	1894-96			6						6	
Mason M	1963-64	4								4	
Mason S	1929-30	3	1	2						5	1
Massart D	1947-48	27	23	2						29	23
Matthews G	1963-65	67	21	1		5	1			73	22
Maund JH	1946-48	32	7	6	2					38	9
Mavrak D	1998-99	12 /1	2				3			15/1	2
May L	1991-92	1 /3								1/3	
Maybury AE	1905-06			2				24		26	
Mayo J	1972-73	2 /5	1							2/5	1
Mays AW	1930-31	17	11							17	11
Meath T	1964-70	59 /8	11	2/2	1	3/2	1			64/12	13
Medd GE	1949-50	22	2	1						23	2
Meek G	1953-65	172	28	10	1	5				187	29
Mehew D	1994-95	6 /7		0/3		3/1		1		10/11	
Merrick J	1920-22	28		6						34	
Merrick R	1919-20			1						1	
Metcalfe J	1958-59	2								2	
Methley I	1945-50	113		8						121	
Methven C	1990-92	74	3	4		2	5			85	3
Methven C	1990-93	97	3	5		5/1		9		116/1	3
Middleton H	1965-68	56 /3	27	1		6	3			63/3	30
Millard R	1950-51	10	1							10	1
Milligan D	1948-49	5	1							5	1
Millington E	1898-99	1								1	
Millington J	1951-53	23								23	
Milner JA	1895-96			2	1			4		6	1
Moffat H	1928-29	41	5	4	1					45	6
Moffat J	1899-1900	27	13	5						32	13
Montgomery AW	1951-53	29		1						30	
Moore F	1896-97	2								2	
Moore S	1955-58	64	10	5	1					69	11
Morely J	1888-92			11	2			46	2	57	4
Morgan AS	1948-49	10	1							10	1
Morgan G	1973-74	1								1	
Morgan J	1933-34	19		3						22	
Morgan LD	1934-39	192	1	21		11				224	1
Morris F	1950-57	213	44	17	5					230	49
Morris G	1888-89			2				21	1	23	1
Morris G	1965-73	172 /5	35	15/1	6	8				195/6	41
Morris GJ	1949-50	6	2							6	2
Morton JW	1893-94	1								1	
Moseley G	1977-78	3								3	
Moss D	1912-16			2				26	2	28	2
Moult J	1909-15			10				125		135	
Mountfield D	1995-98	94 /1	2	9/1		8		4		115/2	2
Mower K	1978-91	410 /5	8	31	2	37/1	10			478/6	20
Mtamark C	1990-97	256 /20	12	23		17/1	1	18 /1	1	314/22	14
Muldoon T	1929-31	52		8						60	
Mullard A	1945-49	61	13	6	1					67	14
Murphy V	1928-31	30	4							30	4
Murray J	1966-69	53 /4	13	2		5	2			60/4	15
Murray JW	1957-59	14	2							14	2
Musker R	1991-92	3		0/1		1				4/1	
Mutch A	1925-26	4								4	
Myerscough W	1954-55	26	6	3						29	6
Narrowmore W	1928-29	3								3	
Naughton W	1984-91	154 /13	17	8/1	4	13/1	3	10 /2		185/17	24
Newman E	1907-09			2				35	10	37	10
Newman N	1945-50	135	2	14						149	2
Newton G	1962-64	30	10	1	1	3	1			34	12

Player	Seasons	League		FAC		FLC		Others		Totals	
		A	G	A	G	A	G	A	G	A	G
Newton H	1977-78	16				5				21	
Nicholls R	1953-54	2								2	
Nicholls W	1902-06			5	1			60	2	65	3
Nix AJ	1906-07			1				13		14	
Noakes GW	1924-25	12	1							12	1
Ntamark C	1990-97	256 /20	12	23		17 /1	1	18 /1	1	314 /22	14
Obi AL	1984-85	1 /1								1 /1	
O'Brien J	1893-95	34	9	2						36	9
O'Brien MT	1928-29	34		3						37	
O'Connor M	1993-96	104	12	10	2	6	2	5	2	125	18
O'Doherty EF	1923-24	18	2	2	1					20	3
O'Hara S	1989-92	67 /7	3	2		2		5		76 /7	3
O'Hara S	1989-94	104 /18	3	2 /3		6 /1		6 /2		118 /24	3
O'Kelly R	1980-88	197 /20	57	9 /2	2	15 /1	4	10	2	231 /23	65
Ollerenshaw	1992-93	8 /12	4	0 /1		2 /2		1 /1	1	11 /16	5
Olney BA	1931-32	3								3	
O'Neill J	1962-65	38	12	1		1				40	12
O'Neill WA	1950-52	51	16	1						52	16
Osborne J	1972-73	3								3	
O'Shaughnessy B	1953-54	1								1	
Otta W	1998-99	6 /2	3	2				1		9 /2	3
Owen AG	1904-06			2				33	9	35	9
Pace DJ	1966-67	4 /1	1			1				5 /1	1
Paddock J	1896-97	3						8	2	11	2
Palgrave EU	1984-88	5 /3	1							5 /3	1
Palin G	1960-64	129	10	3		7				139	10
Palmer C	1994-96	90 /2	3	9		5		2 /1		106 /3	3
Pangbourne T	1891-93	5	1	3	2			19	4	27	7
Parker R	1992-93	0 /1						0 /1		0 /2	
Parkes P	1968-70	52		7		1				60	
Parle JJ	1930-31	24	1	3						27	1
Parridge ME	1961-63	3								3	
Parry E	1926-27	27		3						30	
Parsonage H	1909-20			2	1			51	18	53	19
Paul I	1977-81	68 /2	9	7	1	6	1			81 /2	11
Payne J	1955-56	1								1	
Payne L	1937-39	27		6						33	
Peacock D	1972-73	10								10	
Pearson C	1935-36	9								9	
Pearson G	1904-07			2				33	3	35	3
Pearson GW	1934-35	12		3		1				16	
Pearson M	1962-63	3	1			1				4	1
Pee R	1900-05	2		4				61	1	67	1
Peer D	1993-95	41 /4	6	4 /2		2		3		50 /6	6
Peers E	1896-99	73	2	2						75	2
Peers H	1898-99	10	4							10	4
Pember L	1903-04			3	1			33	10	36	11
Pendleton JJ	1924-25	39		1	1					40	1
Pendrey GS	1982-83	8	1							8	1
Penman WT	1970-73	118 /5	6	9		3				130 /5	6
Penn D	1977-83	132 /9	54	10 /2	2	6	2			148 /11	58
Penton R	1912-16			2				38	7	40	7
Perkins E	1956-59	67	1	10						77	1
Peron J	1997-98	38	1	4		5		5		52	1
Perry L	1953-54	3								3	
Phillips LA	1925-26	1	1							1	1
Phillipson TW	1931-32	7	3							7	3
Philpott W	1898-1904	7						1		8	
Pickering G	1902-09			9				143	18	152	18
Piddock F	1953-54	1								1	
Pinches A	1892-97	72		6				45		123	
Pitt J E	1925-26	4	2							4	2
Platt C	1995-99	18 /14	3	0 /1		1 /2	1	1 /6		20 /23	4
Plimmer GR	1895-96			1				13	5	14	5
Plunkett A	1927-28	25								25	
Pointon J	1931-32	17	4							17	4
Pointon N	1998-99	43		2		2		6		53	

Player	Seasons	League		FAC		FLC		Others		Totals	
		A	G	A	G	A	G	A	G	A	G
Pollock MA	1973-74	1 /1								1 /1	
Poole WA	1931-32	2								2	
Pope F	1907-08			1				1		2	
Porter G	1998-99	39 /5	1	3 /1	2	4 /2		5 /1		51 /9	3
Potter JJ	1925-26	16	1	1						17	1
Potts AA	1922-23	1								1	
Pountney R	1972-73	1								1	
Poxton JH	1935-36	25	5	4						29	5
Pratt J	1898-99	1	1							1	1
Preece D	1980-85	107 /4	5	6	1	17	5	1		131 /4	11
Prentice V	1931-32	23	4	1						24	4
Prew JH	1937-38	4								4	
Price H	1910-14			7				67	12	74	12
Price T	1908-09			1				24		25	
Prichard H	1988-90	40 /5	7	2	1	6	1	1	1	49 /5	10
Prince A	1929-30	1								1	
Pritchett D	1954-55	1								1	
Proffitt T	1891-92			1				8		9	
Proffitt W	1925-26	21	2							21	2
Prudhoe M	1985-87	26		1		4				31	
Pumford GL	1926-27	6	2							6	2
Purcell G	1901-02			7				20		27	
Radford JW	1916-20			2	1			40	16	42	17
Rammell A	1998-99	39	18	2		2	1	5	1	48	20
Rampton G	1909-12			2	1			30	10	32	11
Ramsay S	1921-22	2								2	
Rawlings A	1926-27	23		3						26	
Rawlings CJ	1956-63	200	5	6		1				207	5
Raynes CB	1925-27	5	1							5	1
Readman J	1934-35	1								1	
Redwood DJ	1937-39	27	6	2		3	2			32	8
Reece A	1992-94	15	1			2		3		20	1
Reed J	1931-37	124	6	10		7				141	6
Rees M	1978-90	188 /49	37	7 /5		14 /3	2	7 /1	3	216 /58	42
Reeve F	1927-28	1								1	
Reid GH	1921-24	47	31	8	6					55	37
Reynolds G	1888-89			1				2		3	
Reynolds T	1888-92			7				33		40	
Richards AW	1954-63	338	185	17	12	3	1			358	198
Richards D	1995-96							0 /1		0 /1	
Richards T	1908-16			20				254	6	274	6
Richmond WC	1935-38	89		6		5				100	
Ricketts M	1996-99	11 /34	3	1 /1		0 /3		3 /1		15 /39	3
Riley H	1965-66	24	3	2	1					26	4
Rimmer S	1988-91	85 /3	31	5	2	6	4	7	7	103 /3	44
Roberts A	1894-95	5								5	
Roberts DA	1922-23	3								3	
Roberts W	1894-95	16	6					1		17	6
Robertson HR	1894-95	12								12	
Robertson J	1977-78	16		2		2				20	
Robinson D	1972-77	164 /1	3	11		4 /1				179 /2	3
Robinson H	1892-94	27	1	4						31	1
Robinson J	1946-48	5		1	1					6	1
Robinson RT	1923-24	4	1							4	1
Robinson S	1991-92	0 /1								0 /1	
Robinson TE	1937-38	15	1							15	1
Robinson W	1907-13			9	5			137	52	146	57
Robson G	1926-30	80	27	3						83	27
Roe TW	1929-30	41	8	4						45	8
Rogers D	1994-98	57 /10		5		6		5		73 /10	
Rogers J	1911-12			3	1			14	1	17	2
Rogers JR	1902-03			1				25	3	26	3
Rogers T	1920-22	1		3	1			34	3	38	4
Rollo J	1995-96							0 /1		0 /1	
Roper AJ	1962-65	53	2	2		5				60	2
Roper I	1995-99	55 /14	1	4 /1	1	0 /3		11 /1		70 /19	2
Ross LA	1948-49	8								8	

Player	Seasons	League		FAC		FLC		Others		Totals	
		A	G	A	G	A	G	A	G	A	G
Rotton WH	1931-32	7	3							7	3
Round S	1981-83	5 /19	3	1	1	0 /3				6 /22	4
Rowe N	1959-62	6		2						8	
Rowe VN	1952-53	25								25	
Rushton G	1913-16			7				31		38	
Russell JH	1892-93	2								2	
Russon R	1948-55	145	1	3						148	1
Ryder S	1992-98	86 /15	5	9		5 /1		7 /1		107 /17	5
Sadler JZ	1892-93	1						1		2	
Salt H	1932-33	10		2						12	
Salt HR	1894-96	11		2				6		19	
Sanders G	1913-15			1				20	2	21	2
Sanderson PD	1987-88	0 /3						0 /1		0 /4	
Sarvis WJ	1926-27	9	2	3	1					12	3
Satchwell K	1964-67	54 /3	7	3	1	3				60 /3	8
Saunders C	1993-94	1 /1								1 /1	
Saunders JT	1972-76	94 /5	2	6 /1		2				102 /6	2
Savage J	1957-59	51		1						52	
Saville A	1988-90	28 /10	5			2		1 /1		31 /11	5
Sawyer T	1904-05			2	2			12	2	14	4
Sbragia R	1978-80	77	4	5		2				84	4
Scarlet JE	1952-54	10	2							10	2
Scholes R	1926-27	4								4	
Scott J	1931-33	45	2	1						46	2
Seal J	1969-71	41	14							41	14
Selby TO	1888-89			1				4		5	
Serella D	1974-82	265 /2	12	20		17	1			302 /2	13
Shakespeare D	1982-89	276 /8	45	21	5	31	8	19	2	347 /8	60
Sharples J	1959-64	125	1	4		3				132	1
Shaw CJ	1888-92			14	8			72	22	86	30
Shaw G	1989-90	4 /5	3							4 /5	3
Shaw GA	1930-31	10	1							10	1
Shaw GT	1894-95	1								1	
Shaw T	1892-94	22	1							22	1
Sheldon D	1908-09			2				12	1	14	1
Shelton G	1975-78	12 /12		2 /2	1	0 /1				14 /15	1
Shelton JBT	1935-47	103	5	8	1	7	1			118	7
Sheppard W	1932-35	71	27	9	2	2				82	29
Shingler S	1913-15			2	1			5		7	1
Shinton R	1971-74	78 /1	20	2		5	3			85 /1	23
Sibbold J	1924-25	39	12	1						40	12
Siddons WR	1892-93	4		2						6	
Simmons DJ	1970-71	5	2							5	2
Simpson P	1998-99	10	1					1		11	1
Simpson T	1966-68	50 /1	4	6	2	2				58 /1	6
Simpson WS	1937-39	77	4	8	2	4				89	6
Sinclair R	1991-92	10						1		11	
Singleton M	1990-91	20 /8	1	2		1		3		26 /8	1
Sinnott L	1981-84	40	2	4		2				46	2
Sissons G	1964-68	93 /5	1	5 /1		7				105 /6	1
Skidmore W	1945-51	99	10	8	1					107	11
Skinner J	1997-98	10				3	1			13	1
Skipper P	1989-91	81	2	5		5		8	1	99	3
Sloan D	1973-75	44 /5	3	2		0 /1				46 /6	3
Slynn F	1953-54	10								10	
Smellie R	1893-94	14		3						17	
Smith A	1953-54	1								1	
Smith C	1995-96	0 /1						0 /1		0 /2	
Smith CS	1980-82	17 /2	3							17 /2	3
Smith D	1988-92	63 /1		2		4		3		72 /1	
Smith D	1988-94	137 /5	2	3		10		10		160 /5	2
Smith F	1919-20			2				26		28	
Smith G	1898-99	10		2						12	
Smith G	1905-08			1				37	3	38	3
Smith G	1953-54	1								1	
Smith GH	1924-27	92	2	2						94	2
Smith H	1925-26	8								8	
Smith HJ	1928-29	16	4	1						17	4
Smith HR	1907-09			2				30		32	
Smith J	1948-49	2								2	
Smith J	1971-72	13	1			1				14	1
Smith JJ	1935-36	14	4	1						15	4
Smith N	1938-39	1								1	
Smith R	1910-11			1				1		2	
Smith R	1962-65	51 /1	2	1 /2		7				59 /3	2
Smith T	1964-66	12		1						13	
Smith TJ	1971-73	15 /1	1			1				16 /1	1
Smith TJ	1972-73	2								2	
Southall R W	1901-02			7	1			26		33	1
Spence D	1921-23	44	4	5						49	4
Spencer HJ	1924-25	2								2	
Spier R	1910-11			2	2			2	1	4	3
Spinner TJ	1974-76	10 /6	5			1 /1				11 /7	5
Springell GW	1927-28	33	1	1						34	1
Statham D	1991-93	47 /3				5		4 /1		56 /4	
Statham DJ	1991-92	29				2		2		33	
Stayle H	1927-28	25		1						26	
Steel A	1948-50	2								2	
Steiner R	1998-99	10	3							10	3
Stephens K	1969-71	6 /1								6 /1	
Stevenson J	1935-36	3								3	
Steventon E	1910-20			1				31		32	
Stewart J	1957-58	28	4							28	4
Stockin R	1951-52	6	3							6	3
Stokes AW	1890-94	2		3				48	1	53	1
Strong GJ	1945-46			2						2	
Summerfield K	1982-84	42 /12	17	1		5 /2	2			48 /14	19
Summers GJ	1965-67	41 /3	1	5	1	2				48 /3	2
Sutcliffe FW	1950-51	4								4	
Syertt DK	1978-80	11	3			0 /1				11 /1	3
Taggart J	1896-1901	113	1	10						123	1
Talbot FL	1945-47	18	4	5	1					23	5
Tapper G	1889-90			5	2			25	5	30	7
Tarrant EJ	1953-58	102	12	7	1					109	13
Taylor A	1893-94	1								1	
Taylor A	1988-90	43 /2	6	1		4	1	3		51 /2	7
Taylor B	1971-78	204 /12	25	19	4	11 /1				234 /13	29
Taylor BJ	1954-58	77	17	2						79	17
Taylor C	1958-73	446 /11	169	31	11	14	9			491 /11	189
Taylor D	1955-57	36	8	3						39	8
Taylor M	1984-89	100 /13	4	3 /4		7 /1		10		120 /18	4
Taylor S	1932-33	20	4	2	1					22	5
Taylor W	1894-97	26	6	6				24	7	56	13
Teasdale J	1981-83	13	3			1				14	3
Tennent D	1963-65	19								19	
Tennent W	1898-1901	100		12						112	
Tetlow A	1924-25	18	7							18	7
Tewkesbury KC	1936-39	75		7				2		84	
Tholot D	1997-98	13 /1	4					1 /1	1	14 /2	5
Thomas AC	1924-25	25		1						26	
Thomas W	1996-99	18 /13	6	2 /1		0 /1		1 /4	1	21 /19	7
Thompson C	1990-91	3								3	
Thompson D	1928-29	2								2	
Thompson GW	1925-26	1								1	
Thompson N	1928-29	35	13	4	2					39	15
Thompson S	1904-06			2				10	1	12	1
Thomson R	1971-72	9	1							9	1
Thorpe A	1989-90	24 /3	1	2		2		2		30 /3	1
Thorpe WT	1900-05	2		2				47		51	
Tilford A	1934-35	25		4		3				32	
Timmins B	1921-24	104		10				12		126	
Timmins S	1899-1901	30		5						35	
Timms GH	1925-26	1								1	
Tindall M	1968-69	7				1				8	

Player	Seasons	League		FAC		FLC		Others		Totals	
		A	G	A	G	A	G	A	G	A	G
Tinkler J	1993-94	6				2				8	
Tinkler L	1948-49	18								18	
Tolson N	1991-92	3 /6	1	0/1	1			1 /1		4 /8	2
Tonks J	1901-02			3				17	4	20	4
Tonks JR	1890-92			6				33	1	39	1
Torrants J	1925-27	38		3						41	
Towe J	1896-97	3		3				17		23	
Tracey D	1893-94	3	1							3	1
Train R	1968-87	83 /8	11	6 /2	1	2		2 /1		93 /11	12
Trevis D	1968-70	63 /2	6	11	1					74 /2	7
Tuft W	1900-01	33		5						38	
Turner A	1931-33	21	1							21	1
Turner I	1972-81	42				4				46	
Turner J	1892-93	14	7	2	1					16	8
Vail T	1898-99	30	16	1						31	16
Vaughan GW	1931-32	2								2	
Vinall A	1954-56	78		5						83	
Vinall EJ	1945-47	2								2	
Viveash A	1995-99	159	12	13	2	10		13	1	195	15
Waddington P	1978-82	14 /5								14 /5	
Waddington S	1978-82	122 /8	13	7	1	4 /1				133 /9	14
Wainwright B	1923-24	1								1	
Wait H	1923-36	264		11						275	
Walker A	1905-07			1				5	2	6	2
Walker A	1958-60	7								7	
Walker CW	1932-33	2								2	
Walker D	1913-15			6	1			50	14	56	15
Walker D	1926-27	12								12	
Walker DJ	1927-29	20	7							20	7
Walker F	1936-37	3								3	
Walker J	1993-99	218 /1		17		12		16		263 /1	
Walker W	1914-15			7				33	4	40	4
Wall L	1921-22	3								3	
Wallington M	1971-72	11		1						12	
Walsh A	1991-92	4						1		5	
Walsh DJ	1954-55	20	6	3	3					23	9
Walsh W	1946-48	33	4	1	1					34	5
Walters AV	1929-31	50	30	5	4					55	34
Walters F	1924-32	133	14	6						139	14
Walters H	1946-53	254	2	12						266	2
Walton G	1945-46			1						1	
Walton J	1922-24	69	1	4						73	1
Warner S	1993-94	12		3						15	
Waters J	1900-04			11				90	11	101	11
Watkiss S	1993-95	60 /2	2	5 /1		8	1	2		75 /3	3
Watson A	1997-99	57 /26	15	4 /5	3	6 /1	4	6 /1	2	73 /33	24
Watson EA	1904-05			2				5		7	
Watson J	1955-56	1								1	
Watson T	1967-70	84 /2	17	15 /1	5	4				103 /3	22
Watson W	1931-32	35		1						36	
Webb R	1954-55	9	3							9	3
Webster WG	1921-25	132	3	5						137	3
Wedge A	1897-99	6	1							6	1
Wedge JH	1910-11			1				4		5	
Wesson R	1966-73	191		22		7				220	
West G	1992-93	9	1	1		2				12	1
West T	1964-65	12				1				13	
Wharton TJ	1973-74	1								1	
Wheeler AJ	1931-32	11	3							11	3
White HA	1925-28	44	29	4	3					48	32
White M	1963-64	28		1		3				32	
Whitehouse AF	1992-93	6		3						9	
Whitehouse F	1933-35	4								4	
Whitehouse JE	1949-50	20	8	1						21	8
Whitehouse P	1989-91	10 /2				0 /1		1		11 /3	
Whitehouse S	1912-13			1				6		7	
Whitehouse T	1904-07			2				7		9	
Whitehouse W	1933-34	3	1							3	1
Whittaker G	1919-20			2				17	4	19	4
Whittick EA	1889-93	1		6	2			15	3	22	5
Wickham T	1914-15			2				1		3	
Wiggin R	1962-64	19	6							19	6
Wilcox J	1910-15			7				89		96	
Wilder C	1989-90	4		1				2		7	
Wiles GH	1932-38	167	2	11		7				185	2
Wiles HS	1933-35	11	5							11	5
Wilkes A	1895-98	45	6	3				15	2	63	8
Wilkes S	1914-16			4				30		34	
Wilkins E	1919-20			2				43	4	45	4
Williams BF	1937-39	25		1		2				28	
Williams G	1924-25	7	1							7	1
Williams G	1979-80	9								9	
Williams J	1997-98	0 /1								0 /1	
Williams JL	1978-80	29 /9	2	1 /2						30 /11	2
Williams R	1907-09			3				62	1	65	1
Williams W	1991-92	42		2		2		4		50	
Williams W	1991-93	56	1	3		6		9		74	1
Wills G	1962-64	35	2	1		4				40	2
Wilmot K	1935-36	3								3	
Wilshaw DJ	1946-49	74	17	8	4					82	21
Wilson D	1968-70	33 /2	10	4	1					37 /2	11
Wilson J	1890-92				3			28	8	28	11
Wilson J	1930-31	9								9	
Wilson K	1994-97	124 /1	38	13	7	8	4	6	1	151 /1	50
Wilson T	1960-62	53	19	2		2	1			57	20
Wilson W	1921-22	19		3	1					22	1
Winter J	1950-52	41	12							41	12
Winter S	1991-92	13 /6						3		16 /6	
Winter S	1991-93	14 /4						3		17 /4	
Withington SH	1889-93	20		9				38		67	
Wood AE	1977-78	26 /3	2	6	2	1 /1	1			33 /4	5
Wood H	1891-92			2	1			9	2	11	3
Wood S	1935-36	4	1							4	1
Wood T	1994-97	69		7		4		3		83	
Woodward HJ	1953-54	5								5	
Woodward J	1889-93	9						3		12	
Woodward J	1969-73	116 /9	23	16	5	4	1			136 /9	29
Woodward L	1938-39	29		6						35	
Woodward P	1958-59	13								13	
Woolhouse R	1933-38	181	43	14	3	8				203	46
Wootton CG	1902-16			5				68	17	73	17
Wrack D	1998-99	46	13	2		2		6	1	56	14
Wragge F	1928-29	2								2	
Wright A	1958-59	1	1							1	1
Wright B	1971-77	160 /7	40	17 /2	7	10	1			187 /9	48
Wright DW	1920-21			2						2	
Wright E	1993-94	16 /13	5	4	1	0 /1		1		21 /14	6
Wright EW	1906-07			1				25	2	26	2
Wright GD	1952-53	16	1	1						17	1
Yates HR	1898-03	4		8				36	1	48	1
Young ER	1973-74	8				2				10	
Younger W	1961-62	8	5							8	5

List of other players who did not appear in Football League matches for the Saddlers but played in other competitive matches at first team level.

Player	Seasons	Apps	Goals
Adams G	1909-11	11	
Ager A	1904-05	3	
Allcock R	1919-20	1	
Allsop R	1913-14	1	
Anson J	1910-11	1	
Archer W	1904-05	13	2
Arrowsmith G	1919-20	2	
Atkins G	1908-09	1	
Austin W	1913-14	1	
Bailey AH	1911-12	7	1
Barnard G	1906-07	3	
Barnes JR	1912-13	4	
Beebee R	1915-16	5	
Bentley S	1919-20	1	
Benton WA	1904-05	1	
Bishop AG	1913-14	1	
Boardman T	1906-07	2	
Bollington R	1906-12	21	1
Bolton SD	1905-06	2	
Bott A	1902-05	2	
Bourne H	1904-05	2	
Bower AL	1919-20	2	
Bowser W	1910-11	1	
Boycott S	1913-14	2	
Brannan J	1906-07	2	
Bridge JW	1913-14	8	
Bromage T	1902-03	25	
Brookes D	1903-04	11	2
Brown WW	1911-12	1	
Bryant R	1905-06	3	
Burnett G	1913-14	9	
Burton GH	1919-20	1	
Bywater S	1903-06	2	
Cameron A	1905-06	2	1
Cartlidge W	1906-07	2	2
Chambers S	1915-16	5	
Clark G	1915-20	18	5
Clewes G	1901-02	1	
Colclough S	1905-06	2	
Cole A	1903-05	9	
Colby T	1902-03	1	
Collins E	1915-16	10	5
Cooper S	1910-11	1	
Copeland DF	1910-11	3	
Corbett WD	1907-08	18	
Corfield S	1904-05	1	
Coffey W	1909-10	2	
Coyle S	1909-10	1	
Cresser W	1902-03	7	
Crowe G	1912-13	1	
Crutchley A	1907-08	2	1
Davenport F	1910-11	5	1
Davies SJ	1913-14	3	
Daw RS	1911-12	1	
Dawson JW	1909-10	1	
Dennis G	1919-20	1	
Dickinson E	1904-05	2	
Dolman G	1908-09	7	
Doggett R	1905-06	2	
Duggan R	1920-21	1	
Dunn J	1919-20	1	
Dyall D	1915-16	3	
Dyer G	1904-05	1	
Edwards B	1907-08	1	
Evans F	1912-13	1	
Farnell J	1905-06	2	

Player	Seasons	Apps	Goals
Fessey M	1920-21	1	
Fieldson J	1913-14	1	
Fletcher J	1902-03	1	
Fletcher S	1919-20	2	
Fletcher N	1908-09	1	
Foster RE	1901-02	3	
Fox H	1907-08	2	
Frost D	1910-11	1	
Gaffney R	1906-07	1	
Gardner P	1910-11	1	
Garrattly G	1907-08	14	
Garrattly J	1915-16	2	1
Garrattly W	1915-16	13	
Green EH	1905-06	3	2
Haddon G	1913-14	2	
Hadley BR	1915-16	8	
Handley A	1906-07	6	
Hanley G	1904-05	2	
Harper SL	1913-14	1	
Harrison A	1906-07	2	1
Harrison J	1913-20	2	
Hartland WH	1906-07	18	9
Hayes E	1910-11	1	
Hayes G	1901-02	1	
Hayes DG	1919-20	3	
Hayward HC	1910-12	21	2
Haywood M	1912-13	2	
Henshall G	1919-20	1	
Hewitt G	1905-06	4	
Hill J	1915-16	8	
Hogg WE	1902-03	3	
Hollins G	1910-11	1	1
Hollinshead T	1912-13	1	
Hopkins L	1910-11	1	
Horton G	1913-14	5	
Houlston C	1910-11	22	7
Hughes R	1920-21	4	1
Hulse R	1910-11	6	
Hurst C	1909-14	27	6
Ireland R	1920-21	2	
James R	1912-13	4	2
Jeavons S	1906-07	2	
Jenkins F	1910-12	21	5
Johnson C	1901-02	3	
Johnson H	1919-21	25	
Jones R	1902-04	2	
Kelly G	1905-06	5	
Kimberley W	1913-14	11	
Labeta A	1913-14	4	
Lamb R	1911-12	1	
Lane E	1913-14	8	4
Lazenby T	1919-20	1	
Lester G	1912-13	1	
Lewis B	1911-13	5	
Lewis S	1908-09	7	3
Lindop FW	1909-11	4	4
Lloyd E	1902-03	1	
Lord W	1902-03	1	
Lote G	1919-21	2	
Lynch W	1904-05	1	
Lyon W	1909-10	33	16
McAllister D	1905-06	1	
Managhan S	1905-07	27	7
Mansell G	1905-06	1	
Mansell RG	1910-12	64	3
Mason T	1910-11	1	

Player	*Seasons*	*Apps*	*Goals*
Massey C	1907-09	24	7
Maybury J	1905-06	5	1
Middleton G	1904-05	1	
Millington C	1915-16	1	
Moore N	1913-14	7	1
Morris A	1906-07	2	
Morris T	1910-11	2	2
Morton TG	1907-08	26	1
Moule R	1915-16	1	
Needham J	1915-16	6	2
Newbrooke S	1911-12	2	1
Newbrooke WJ	1911-12	4	1
Newman R	1901-02	5	2
Newton CJ	1907-08	4	
Nichols J	1910-11	2	
Nicholls A	1911-12	1	
Nickless D	1910-12	9	
Noble S	1901-02	3	
Nightingale T	1905-06	6	1
O'Connor R	1919-20	2	
Ogden S	1913-14	6	1
Ore J	1903-04	10	
Palmer G	1919-20	1	
Parker G	1906-07	2	
Parkes H	1919-20	1	
Peers E	1915-16	2	
Pemberton JG	1905-06	2	1
Perry J	1915-16	17	11
Perry SH	1910-12	9	4
Peters JG	1910-11	1	
Pointon RS	1913-14	39	11
Powner T	1919-20	1	
Powell R	1913-14	1	
Preedy S	1902-03	1	
Pykitt P	1912-13	1	1
Randall W	1919-20	3	
Rankle W	1906-07	14	6
Ravenscroft D	1904-05	1	
Reddall J	1905-06	2	
Reece A	1901-02	4	2
Renneville W	1919-20	3	1
Richardson A	1912-13	5	
Roberts GF	1906-07	3	
Rochelle W	1908-09	1	
Rochetti L	1910-11	3	
Rodgers A	1910-11	2	
Rogers T	1910-14	72	11

Player	*Seasons*	*Apps*	*Goals*
Salt T	1913-14	1	
Shufflebotham G	1909-10	1	
Shelton D	1904-05	2	
Simcox T	1905-06	10	
Sivorns R	1912-13	5	
Smith EF	1902-06	4	
Smith J	1920-21	1	
Snout S	1904-05	1	
Stanton WJ	1911-13	19	14
Steventon J	1911-12	4	
Stokes H	1911-12	1	
Stych E	1910-11	1	
Swaby AB	1911-12	2	
Swann R	1920-21	3	
Taylor R	1904-05	1	
Thomas R	1904-05	1	
Thompson S	1904-06	12	1
Tolley S	1901-02	1	
Tough G	1919-20	1	
Trinder W	1908-09	1	
Truelove T	1919-20	1	
Turnbull R	1902-03	5	1
Tustin R	1913-14	1	
Upton WG	1919-20	2	
Urmson S	1906-10	25	
Vernon RF	1902-03	1	
Wainwright G	1919-20	7	
Walters W	1920-21	2	1
Walton R	1910-11	3	
Watterson RV	1904-05	1	
Watson V	1901-02	1	
Weate S	1919-20	1	1
Weaver J	1906-07	3	
Webb B	1902-03	1	
Webster H	1905-06	10	3
West F	1906-07	3	
Weston FW	1910-11	1	
White A	1913-14	11	3
Whitehouse W	1912-13	4	1
Wilkinson T	1913-14	2	
Williams E	1913-14	1	1
Williams S	1913-14	1	
Williams T	1919-20	5	
Woodward R	1910-11	6	
Wright R	1904-05	10	
Wyke C	1920-21	9	

Subscribers

Bryn Adams
Glynn Adams
Steve Adams
Thomas Adams
Nicholas Adshead
Brian Allen
Dean Allen
Nick Allen
Geoff Allman
John and William Anderson
Les Andrews
Sally and Terry Andrews
Dennis A Anson
Andrew Kenneth Aplin
Kenneth Charles Aplin
Charles Archer
F A Archer
D Arrowsmith
Mr S Arrowsmith
Neil Ash
Clifford Ashwin
Esther Asprey
Lee Paul Asson
Keith Attwood
S H Bailey
Stuart Andrew Bailey (Bilbrook)
Mark Badger
Kieron Baker
Peter Baker
Peter David Baldwin
David Ball
Kerry Banks
Melvyn Victor Banks
Brian Barker
Alan Barnard
Lee Barnard
Mr D Barnes
Jon Barwood
P Bayliss
Alan Beavis
Colin Beard
Jason Beech
Robert Beech
Ronald Bennett
Keith Billingham
Raymond Birch
Michael Bird
Michael Blackmoore
Steve Blake
Stan Blandford
Roy Bottomer
Joe Boyden
Ian and James Bradin
Patricia Bradley
Paul Bridge
Charlotte Brindley
Roger Brindley
Gary Brisbourne
P Bromley
Daniel Brookes
Paul Brookes
Joanne Brough
Mike Brough
Nicholas Brown
Jan Burbridge
Jennifer Burton
Paul and Noel Burton
Arthur Campbell
Michael John Carless
John Carlyle
John Carter
S M Cartwright
Darren Andrew Cattell
Thomas and Elliott Causer
D J Chapman
Michael Cheadle
James F Clements
Trevor Cockayne
William S Cockbill
Kevin Cooksey
Gerald Cooper
Nigel Corbett
Andrew J Cotterill
Melvyn Cotterill
Paul Cotterill
Victor John Cotterill
Gary Cowley
Carl Cresswell
David Crichton
Norman Crutchley
Neil Curl
Adrian Cuthbert
Kevin Danks
Harry Davenhill

Matthew Davies
Paul Dean
Jim Deare
Beverley Ann Derry
Kathryn Dicken
Karen A Dickens
Stephen H Dickens
Richard John Dobson
Tom Dobson
Matt Dodd
Philip Dodd
M J Done
Alison Dowding
Chris Downs
Michael Doyle
James Dutton
Lee Dyke
David J Edge
Raymond A Edge
Kevin Edmonds
Tony Edmonds
Bob Edwards
Keith Edwards
James Thomas Edwards
Sue Edwards
Mike, Mark and Philip Egan
Simon Ellson
Tom Elmer
David P Evans
Michael Evans
Rick Evans
Dave Evenson
M J Eyre
Andy Fallon
Neil Farden
David Farmer
Paul Fasey
John Faulkner
Daren Fellows
John Fellows
Keith Fisher
Michael Flood
Pat Foley
Jason Ford
Mark Foster
Royston Foster
Kevin Foulkes
Mr William Fox
M C Garratt
Paul Giess
Peter Gittings
F M Godridge
Margaret Godwin
Paul Goldby
David Gough
Paul J Griffiths
Brian Guttridge
Winnie Hackett
Geoff Hadley
Dennis Hallsworth
Clive Hamblett Jnr
Mark Hamer
Peter Hamer
Keith Handley
Dave Hanson
Robert M Harding
Neil Harris
Steven Harris
Terry Harrison
Stanley Hasketh
Andy Hawes
Mark Hawkins
Keith Hawley
Philip Hawley
Mr H N Hazlewood
Richard Heap
Andy Heaton
Leslie Heighway
Robert Heighway
G R Hickinbottom
N G Hickinbottom
Jason Hicklin
Malcolm George Higgins
Richard Thomas Higgs
Alan William Highway
Wendy Hill
Robert Ian Hipkiss
Lee Hodgkins
Kevin Hogan: 'Season 98/99 promoted to Division One Dedicated to his memory'
Philip J Holland
Ben Hope
Tom Hopton
David Howdle
John Hughes
Paul A Humphreys
Joe Humphries
Michael Humphries
Kenneth Irons
Brian H Ison
Geoff Jackson
Jeff Jackson
Lloyd James
Neville James

Steve Jenkins
Terry Jenkinson
Carl Johnson
Richard and Steven Johnson
Bernard Johnston
Patrick Johnston
Barrie Jones
Chris Jones
David Jones
Mike Jones
Robert Jones
Robert S Jones
John Jukes
Mark Keats
Dave Keeling
Craig Keenan
Mike Kelly
Paul Kelly
Larry Kemp
Mike Kennerley
Ben Kilhams
Neville King
Ivan Kitic
Robert R Langley
D M Larcombe
Chris Larkin
B Lawrence
Andrew Lee
Pete Lee
Brian Lester
Jean Lever
Steve Lever
Adam J R Lewis
Peter Littler
Claire Livesey
Stephen Llewellyn
Phil Lloyd
Paul Lockley
Ian G Lowndes
J W Lyons
Iain McCallum
Mark Mackay
Peter Maddox
David and Susan Marsh
Keith Marsh
Phil Marsh
J 'Ernie' Marshall
Donald Martin
John Mason
John Phillip Mason
Freda Matthews
Trevor Matthews
Daniel Mayne
Michael James Mayo
Albert Meredith
Peter Meredith
Chris, David and Thomas Miller
Roger Miller
Roger Millerchip
Iain Milne
Thomas Mitchell
Paul Mold
Jon Mole
Anthony B Morgan
Brin Morgan
Jack Morgan
Philip Morris
Simon Morris
Stephen Morris
Thomas Mortimer
Andrew Moseley
David John Moseley
Derek Moseley
Graham Thomas Moseley
Howard Moseley
John Murkett
Robert Mustard
Michael Nardone
Andrew Nash
Alec Neville
A J Newman
Mark Nicholls
Paul and Ben Nicholson
Stan Noble
Robert Nock
William Nock
Jeffrey J Norman
Kate Oakley
Daniel O'Connor
D A Onions (Epi)
Gemma Orchard
Douglas Owen
Stephen Paddock
Edward John Padmore
Colin Parker
Martin Parker
Calvin Parker-Evans
The A B Parsons Family
Alan Paterson
Ian Peace
Chris Peake
Christopher Pearce
Andy Pearsall
Jim Pearson

Gordon Perkins
Neil Perks
Ronald Perrin
Maurice Perry
Adam James Phillips
Matt Pitt
Mark Poole
Pete Poole/Andrew Poole (Walsall FC Programme Editor)
Colin Porter
Darren Powell
Ian Powell
Len Powell
P A Powell
Fred Powick
David Preece
Alan Preston
Stuart Preston
Alan H Price
Royston Randle
John Ranford
Geoff Ratcliffe
David Ravenhill
Ian Ray
David Raybould
Kevin Raybould
Kevin Renshaw
Mr A J Reynolds
Dennis J Reynolds
Tony Richards
John Richardson
Pete Richardson
C M Rigby
Graham Rigby
B T Riley
Jonathan Roberts
Malcolm Roberts
Richard Roberts
John Robotham
Gillian Ann Robottom
David Timothy Rogers
Dennis Rolls
Alan John Roper
Denis Round
Jack Round
Paul Rowley
Sean Russell
R E Sadler
Keith Sargent
Paul Scully
Stephen Seaborne
Robert Selmes
S B Sheldon
David Sheldrick
Ross Shelton
D A Shorters
E Siddons
Andrew Smith
Mark Smith
Michael Sorrell
D J Speke
David Spiers
Tim Spiers
Sharon Southam
Russell Stanley
Sam Stanton
Gary , Michelle and Nicole Staples
Mick Starkey
Peter Starkey
S Starkey
Danielle Steed
Charles A Steinmetz
Alan and Keith Stephenson
Alan Stray
G Stuart
Stuart Summers
Mr Howard Sutton
David Talbot
Arthur Tapper
Bob Taylor
Brian Taylor
Mrs N G Taylor
Peter Taylor
Norman E Teppin
Adrian Thomas
R M Thomas
Mr Ronald Thomas
P Thornhill
Michael H Till
W Timmington
Ian J Turner
Peter Turton
Lisa Underwood
Ian Vaughan and Hannah Staples
Malcolm Vincent
Terry Wakelam
John Walerzak
Bernard Walker
Dave Walker
Roger Walker
Christopher Ward
Geoff Ward
Peter Wardle
Tim and Louise Warner